PRINCIPLES OF PROPERTY LAW

Second Edition

Cavendish Publishing Pty Limited

Sydney • London

PRINCIPLES OF PROPERTY LAW

Second Edition

Samantha J Hepburn, BA, LLB (Mon), LLM (Melb)
Senior Lecturer in Law, Deakin University

SERIES EDITOR
Professor Philip H Clarke
Professor of Law,
Dean of the Faculty of Business and Law,
Deakin University

Cavendish
Publishing
(Australia)
Pty Limited

Sydney • London

Second edition first published in 2001 by Cavendish Publishing (Australia) Pty Limited, 3/303 Barrenjoey Road, Newport, New South Wales 2106
Telephone: (02) 9999 2777 Facsimile: (02) 9999 3688
Email: info@cavendishpublishing.com.au

Cavendish Publishing Limited, The Glass House, Wharton Street, London WC1X 9PX, United Kingdom
Telephone: +44 (0)20 7278 8000 Facsimile: +44 (0)20 7278 8080

First edition 1998
Second edition 2001

National Library of Australia Cataloguing in Publication Data

Hepburn, Samantha
Principles of property law
2nd ed
Includes index
1 Property – Australia
I. Title (Series: Principles of law series)
346.9404

ISBN 1 876905 08 5

Printed and bound in Great Britain

This book is dedicated to my family – especially my children who are a constant source of delight and inspiration to me.

ACKNOWLEDGMENTS

I would like to thank my family in particular for their patience and understanding during the preparation of this second edition. Without their support and enthusiasm, especially the support of my wonderful mother, it would have been very difficult for me to have completed this new edition. I would also like to extend my thanks to the editorial team at Cavendish Publishing who have been particularly helpful in the preparation of this edition. Gratitude must also be extended to colleagues at Deakin University, who made suggestions and constructive comments, as well as administrative staff and the staff at the Deakin University Law Library. The law is as stated at June 2001.

CONTENTS

TABLE OF CASES

TABLE OF STATUTES

New South Wales

South Australia

Tasmania

Victoria

Western Australia

United Kingdom

CHAPTER 1

WHAT IS PROPERTY?

1.1 Understanding the concept of property

The common understanding of property within Western societies is the right to exclusive ownership and control of a specified object. In a legal sense, property is defined not as the object itself but, rather, the relationship which an individual or a corporation has with the object and with the rest of the world in relation to that object. The character of the relationship may vary according to a range of factors which include: the nature of the object (the object may be tangible or intangible, land or chattels), the duration of time for which the relationship is expressed to exist, the jurisdiction in which the relationship is legally enforceable and, more fundamentally, the political, legal and economic structure of the society in which it is enforced.

Private property has become the dominant form of property relationship in the modern capitalist world. Private property is one of the fundamental tenets of a capitalist system as it promotes a liberalist, *laissez faire* society whereby individuals have the right to accumulate property and wealth for their own exclusive means. Inevitably, however, capitalist systems produce disparities in property and wealth distribution, and the evolution of private property has helped to perpetuate social inequality and oppression.

Socialist, communist regimes espouse communal, collective ownership in preference to private property. Karl Marx considered private property to be not only a source of social oppression but also alienation; he felt private property and the fundamental desire to 'have' eventually overwhelms other natural physical and intellectual senses in man and in this way alienates man from his true being. Marx notes:

> Private property has made us so stupid and narrow minded that an object is only ours when we have it, when it exists as capital for us or when we directly possess, eat, drink, wear, inhabit it, etc, in short, when we use it. Yet private property itself in its turn conceives of all these direct realisations of property merely as means of life, and the life which they serve is that of private property, labour, and capitalisation. Thus all physical and intellectual senses have been replaced by the simple alienation of all these senses, the sense of having. [*Economic and Philosophical Manuscripts: Private Property and Communism*. Taken from Marx, K, *Early Writings*, Colletti, L (ed), 1975, London.]

The sense of 'having' and the desire to acquire property exclusively continues to dominate many modern cultures. Monopolisation of the world's resources and the desire to own and control is the backbone of the current social and economic ideology. The expansion of private property has produced social divisions resulting in a separation between those who have the power to control resources and those who do not. Proudhon has claimed that private property is tantamount to theft, because the acquisition of property in modern capitalist societies increasingly confers power and authority. This 'theft' has become so much a part of the modern world that it is now an accepted practice. Exclusive ownership and the further acquisition of property rights now identifies most of modern capitalist existence.

In its essence then, property is a social dynamic; mutable, mercurial and value laden, it forms the primal core of most social activity in the modern world. It is, as one commentator has noted, 'an emotive phrase in search of a meaning'. (Gray, K, 'Property in thin air' [1991] CLJ 252.)

In a legal context, property is used to describe a range of interests. The diversity and erudition of the property concept was appraised by the High Court in *Yanner v Eaton* (1999) 166 ALR 258:

> Property is used in the law in various senses to describe a range of legal and equitable estates and interests, corporeal and incorporeal. Distinct corporeal and incorporeal property rights in relation to the one object may exist concurrently and be held by different parties. Ownership may be divorced from possession. At common law, wrongful possession of land might give rise to an estate in fee simple with the rightful owner having but a right of re-entry. Property need not necessarily be susceptible of transfer. A common law debt, albeit not assignable, was nonetheless property. Equity brings particular sophistications to the subject ... Sometimes it is employed to indicate the physical object to which various legal rights, privileges, etc, relate; then again – with far greater discrimination and accuracy – the word is used to denote the legal interest (or aggregate of legal relations) appertaining to such physical objects. Frequently there is a rapid and fallacious shift from the one meaning to the other. At times, also, the term is used in such a 'blended' sense as to convey no definite meaning whatever.[1]

1.2 Characteristics of the property relationship

1.2.1 Property is a right and not a thing

Property describes the relationship between an individual and an object or resource; it does not refer to the object itself. The property relationship confers a legally enforceable right or, more accurately, a bundle of rights entitling the holder to control an object or resource. Once it is understood that property describes the relational interplay between individual and object rather than the object itself, the breadth, diversity and potential for expansion that is

1 For further reading, see Hohfeld, WN, 'Some fundamental legal conceptions as applied in judicial reasoning' (1913) 23 Yale LJ 16, esp at p 21; Gray, KJ and Gray, SF, 'The idea of property in land', in Bright, S and Dewar, J (eds), *Land Law: Themes and Perspectives*, 1998, OUP, p 15 at pp 27–30.

characteristic of property rights is easier to appreciate. Almost any usable object, corporeal or incorporeal, is capable of being owned, although restrictions upon what is capable of being owned may be legally introduced by common law development or express statutory provisions, or through changing social mores, where ownership is considered to offend the prevailing moral milieu. For example, most modern societies refuse to recognise the ability of one person to own another as it contravenes basic human rights of freedom and liberty.

Ownership rights focus upon rights of use, control and possession over an object and include:

- the right to exclusive physical control of the property;
- the right to possess the property;
- the right to use and enjoy the property; and
- the right to alienate (that is, transmit, devise or bequeath) the property.

The definitive right in private property relationships is the right of the owner to the use, possession and enjoyment of the object to the exclusion of the rest of the world. Legally, this right is known as an *'in rem'* right because it is enforceable against the rest of the world. Other rights which generally characterise the private property relationship, although are not definitive in nature, include the right to possess and enjoy the object and the right to get rid of or 'alienate' the object. In combination, these rights entitle an owner of property to deal with that property in whatever manner the owner chooses, provided it is lawful and proper.

1.2.2 *Property is only enforceable by law*

Private property rights can only truly exist where the prevailing legal system protects and enforces such rights. Without legal recognition, private property rights would be unenforceable. As noted by Felix Cohen, in his 'Dialogue on private property' (quoting Jeremy Bentham), 'Property and Law are born together, and die together. Before laws were made there was no property; take away the laws, and property ceases'.[2] Most mature societies have a legal system which recognises and enforces a variety of different types of property rights. Nevertheless, despite being legally enforceable, the rights of property owners are not absolute; both the courts and Parliament may impose restrictions. Restrictions may be placed upon both the type of rights associated with ownership and/or the manner in which those rights may be performed. The right to impose such restrictions stems from the fact that property owners are bound to comply with the legal system which regulates them. This is not to suggest that property rights may be arbitrarily taken away from the holder.

2 Cohen, FS, 'Dialogue on private property' (1954) 9 Rutgers LR 357, p 372.

For example, the owner of a piece of land does not have the right to refuse its compulsory acquisition by the government but does have the right to seek just compensation for such an acquisition.[3]

1.2.3 *Several property interests may exist in a single object*

As property is a relationship, it is possible for a range of differing forms of property interests to arise in a single object. Property interests may be fragmented according to time or according to the jurisdiction in which they are enforced. This means that a single object may be the subject matter of a variety of different property relationships – whether they be common law, equitable or statutory in nature and whether they be for an indefinite or precisely defined period.

Where a property right is expressly limited to a particular period of time, the limitation will create a surplus and this surplus will constitute a different type of property right. For example, a piece of land may be owned by A for the duration of her life and, once she dies, be owned absolutely by B. In such a case, both A and B acquire an interest in the property, with A's interest being limited by her life and B's being unlimited but only coming into possession upon the death of A. In such a case, it can be said that both A and B hold a property interest in the land, although each interest is of a different character because of the fact that the right to possession vests at different times. (See, further, Chapter 3: The doctrine of tenure and estates.)

1.2.4 *Not everything is capable of being owned*

With our rapidly developing technology, the range of objects capable of being owned is constantly expanding; nevertheless, in all societies there are some things which are not capable of being owned. For example, most societies either do not recognise or expressly prohibit ownership over such things as air or water because of their fundamental significance to human existence. If, as noted above, private property results in the accumulation of wealth and resources into the hands of a few, it would be detrimental to a large proportion of society to allow fundamental necessities such as air and water to be owned. Sometimes, to ensure a fairer distribution and equal access, property which is considered to be beneficial to society as a whole is owned by the state. The state then regulates this property in accordance with the needs of the community overall. For example, in Australia, everyone has a right of access to beaches and national parks, and the government owns these areas in order to ensure their protection and upkeep for the community as a whole.

Ownership may also be restricted where it offends prevailing moral attitudes. Parents are not regarded as capable of owning their children and a

3 See s 51, para xxxi of the Federal Constitution.

husband does not own his wife. Society deems such ownership as morally reprehensible even though, in some situations, the effective control that one person may have over another is tantamount to ownership. Some rights are incapable of being owned because ownership would interfere with the proper cultural and intellectual development of society as a whole; for example, there is no property in such rights as the right to produce children, to watch a particular film or to read a particular book.

Some rights are incapable of being owned because there is no clear method by which such rights could be properly enforced or because enforcement would unduly interfere with the rights of others. If a resource is incapable of excluding others, it may not be capable of becoming property; this may occur where it is impossible to prevent third parties from using or accessing the resource. For example, there is, as yet, no property in the right to a view or the right to light, primarily because there is no way of effectively regulating its access.[4]

1.3 The philosophical evolution of private property

The centrality of private property in the evolution of social and political institutions has, inevitably, encouraged a wide variety of philosophical discourse. Most of these discussions reflect the prevailing social or political structure in existence at the time that they were written. An examination of the broad elements of some of these theories is an integral part of the appreciation of the overall dynamic of property law.

Perhaps one of the first and most fundamental theories justifying the existence of private property is the natural rights theory, the earliest advocate of which was John Locke. According to Locke, property was originally owned in common by all men; however, men had a natural right to appropriate this common property for their own private use where they themselves had laboured to create it. Locke conceptualised what became known as the 'social contract', whereby individuals agreed to hand over particular powers to the government to control in exchange for a guarantee of protection of fundamental natural rights of life, liberty and property.[5]

The evolution of 'money' and the establishment of structured communities assisted in the regulation of the agreements which, according to Locke, labour and industry had begun. The Lockean philosophy formed an essential part of the social ethic during the period of the American and French revolutions and the rise of the middle class liberalists. Locke's natural right theory became the classic liberalist theory and functioned as a benchmark for middle class

4 See *op cit*, Cohen, fn 2, p 373, for a discussion of the importance of the right to exclude.

5 'The second treatise of government' (1698) taken from *The Second Treatise of Government: An Essay Concerning the True Original Extent and End of Civil Government*, Gough, JW (ed), 3rd edn, 1976, Blackwells.

revolutionaries, in particular the large group of independent workers in the 18th century who produced their own goods and lived by their own trade. For such people, natural rights symbolised a perfect sense of equity and justice because they ensured that each individual enjoyed the profits of his own labour. Such an approach was deemed much fairer than the blatant inequality apparent in the old feudal customs and royal privileges.

By the start of the 19th century, however, with the rise of a more structured, omniscient government and a more established social structure, the classical approach to natural rights began to diminish. The emergence of a powerful parliament and the increasing regulation of society meant that individuals were subjected to greater control. In a social climate where most private property was rapidly being acquired by the government, and very little was being acquired by the peasants who worked the land, a natural rights theory based upon individual labour had very little relevance.

In such an environment, property discourse increasingly examined governmental rights and the notion of 'royal dominion'. Royal dominion assumed that all land ownership was ultimately vested in the Crown. Nevertheless, the natural rights philosophy did not disappear altogether. Private ownership was still assumed to be a natural right, but only where it was granted in accordance with the legitimate governmental process. Gradually, parliamentary authority began to subjugate the autonomy of individual property rights.

In his famous *Commentaries on the Laws of England*, William Blackstone pointed out that natural rights, as willed by God and discoverable by reason, would only be protected where the individual agreed to comply with the rules and regulations of society, and that these rules were capable of limiting or altering the ambit of natural rights. He noted:

> All property is derived from society, being one of those civil rights which are conferred upon individuals, in exchange for that degree of natural freedom which every (person) must sacrifice when entering into social communities. If a member of any national community violates the fundamental contract of association, by transgressing the municipal law ... the State may very justly resume that portion or property, or any portion of it, which the laws have before assigned.[6]

Given the significance of societal regulation, it was important, as John Rawls has noted, for individuals to choose a society which would best enable them to select and properly enjoy their natural rights. If individuals wished to maximise their right to life, liberty and property, they needed to enter into a society, the rules of which were consistent with 'the most extensive, total

6 *Blackstone's Commentaries*, Vol 2, 'Of the rights of things', p 11, taken from *Commentaries on the Laws of England*, reprint of the 1st edn, 1765, Clarendon. Reprint 1992, Buffalo, NY: William S Hein. See, also, Morrison, W (ed), *Blackstone's Commentaries on the Laws of England*, 2001, Cavendish Publishing.

system of equal basic liberties compatible with a similar system of liberty for all'.[7]

In the late 19th century, discussion and thought on private property began to take a slightly different course. This new direction stemmed from the increasing belief that governments were set up for the common good of all members of society and that private property rights were consistent with public utility. This new approach was encapsulated in the emerging philosophy, referred to generally as utilitarianism.

Utilitarianism became a major political philosophy in the late 19th century. Its original concept was espoused by Jeremy Bentham, who saw the aim of government as being the promotion of the greatest happiness in the greatest number of people.[8] Providing a structure for the accumulation of private property was one way in which government could promote public happiness. In this sense, utilitarians believed that private property was not a natural right but rather a societal creation.

David Hume was one of the early proponents of utilitarianism; he rejected the natural rights approach, believing that reason alone was incapable of determining social and political obligations. Private property existed because it had become a social convention that individuals obeyed, it being in their mutual interests and the general public utility to do so. Hume believed that common good led an individual to concur with a system of rules implementing private property but that, ultimately, all property was subordinate to the authority of civil laws.[9] Private property, and the creation of wealth that it stimulated, were considered by the utilitarians to enhance the general welfare of the community, and this advantage was felt to outweigh the inequality and oppression it inevitably created.

Other philosophers in the 19th century rationalised property on a more metaphysical level. Kant and Hegel felt that private property only existed where an individual exerted his or her will upon it, and they rejected the Lockean theory of natural rights. These philosophies became known as 'idealist philosophy'. According to Kant, a person acquires property, not by the mechanical operation of mixing labour with external objects, but through the transcendental operation of directing will upon a given object; where a person has possession of an object and believes he owns that object to the exclusion of all others, private property may exist, provided it is in accordance with what Kant refers to as the 'general will'. Under Kant's theory, there must be a union of wills or a recognition of a general will which can convert the individual's possession into a right:

7 Rawls, J, *A Theory of Justice*, 1972, Clarendon, pp 11–15.

8 See *Collected Works of Jeremy Bentham: Principles of Legislation*, Burns, JH (ed), 1996, Clarendon.

9 Schlatter, RB, *Private Property: The History of an Idea*, 1951, Clarendon.

> In a word, the mode in which anything external may be held as one's own in the state of nature, is just physical possession with a presumption of right thus far in its favour, that by union of the Wills of all in a public Legislature, it will be made juridical.[10]

The 'general will' refers to a legal system which approves of an individual's assertion of right where it was perceived to be for the benefit of the community as a whole. Like Kant, Hegel felt that a person had the right to direct will upon any object in order to make that object his own. It was individual will which, according to Hegel, gave an object a true meaning and existence. He noted, 'A person has the right to direct his will upon any object as his real and positive end. The object thus becomes his. As it has no end in itself, it receives its meaning and soul from his will'.[11]

Hegel therefore felt that an object only truly exists when an individual directs his attention to it and claims it as his own. This direction of will is important for an individual's realisation of freedom; appropriating property for private use is one of the primary ways in which an individual may objectify himself as he has the freedom to use his property in any manner in which he may see fit. The more communal the ownership, the more that this freedom is restricted. Hence, according to Hegel, ownership of property by an individual is essential for the realisation of liberty.

Like Kant again, Hegel believed that consent for this appropriation of property came from the commands of the general will as expressed in the state. Hegel felt, however, that the state embodied the general will of all its members and its claim to property would always be superior to those of the individual; hence, the rights of property owners are always subject to the higher spheres of state rights. The state cannot, however, capriciously interfere with an individual's rights and cannot redefine those rights to favour communal rather than private ownership. The state can only interfere with private property rights where it can be established that those rights are no longer achieving the desired goals. Hegel justified the inequality associated with private property by noting that the human spirit is itself unequal: different people need different levels of property to achieve self-fulfilment. Inequality is an intrinsic part of the human condition, hence, an unequal division of property is an appropriate reflection of human individuality.

The Lockean notion of private property as a natural right was critically reassessed with the rise, in the late 19th century, of what became known as the 'philosophy of history'. The emergence of the philosophy of history encouraged a reappraisal of existing beliefs and perceptions concerning property rights; it claimed that property may have been a product of a number of rights, and the significance of any one right depended upon the traditional cultures and customs adopted by individual societies. It was found that

10 Kant, *Philosophy of Law*, Albrecht, A (trans), Kocourek, A (ed), 1969, AM Kelley, Modern Legal Philosophy Series, p 79.

11 Taken from *op cit*, Schlatter, fn 9, pp 256–58.

common ownership of property was preferred by primitive societies to private, exclusive ownership, and this historical reconstruction was used as a basis for the rejection of the natural rights analysis and the construction of a communal property philosophy.

In the Communist Manifesto of 1848, Marx suggested that the time was ripe for the transformation of private capital into common property. Proudhon, in 1840, had previously reached the conclusion that land, because it is not created by labour, ought to remain common property, but that capital should belong to the workers. This approach was broadly consistent with natural rights theories although it combined a labour justification with a communal property theory. Marx followed a similar approach; in the Communist Manifesto he advocated the transfer of private property from the capitalist class (the 'bourgeoisie') to the class whose labour had created that property (the 'proletariat'). Marx stated that, 'Communism deprives no man of the power to appropriate the products of society; all that it does is to deprive him of the power to subjugate the labour of others by means of such appropriation'.[12]

The ultimate ambition of communism as advocated by Marx was a more equal distribution of property so that it could be distributed 'from each according to his ability, to each according to his needs'.

The socialist reassessment of property rights revealed very clearly the fact that private property relations are simply a societal construct. Once the fundamental customs and values of society change or are reinterpreted, the right to exclude may not be the defining feature of the property relationship. Private property, whilst pervasive in the modern world, does only represent one form of ownership, and there is always the potential for different forms of ownership to emerge. Whether private property exists as a natural right, a social construct or the metaphysical application of individual will, it can only exist to the extent that it emulates the needs and demands of society. This is something that most modern socialists recognise. Engels, like most socialists of the 20th century, expressed the view that in an ideal society, the natural right theory may simply be an historical formula and that 'need' will eventually form the primary right to property, replacing 'labour'. If this approach were adopted, it would represent the ultimate destruction of the natural right philosophy.

In recent times, economic arguments have emerged in defence of private property structures, although such theories do not focus upon the humanist concerns about the inequality and oppression that the expansion of private property has engendered.[13] It has been suggested that communal property

12 *Communist Manifesto*, 1848, taken from *Karl Marx Selected Writings*, McLellan, D (ed), 1977, OUP, p 232.

13 See, generally, Ackerman, B, *Social Justice in the Liberal State*,1980, Yale UP; and Posner, R, *Economic Analysis of Law*, 1972, Little, Brown.

encourages waste and an inefficient use of resources. Where property is owned communally, each owner has an incentive to make sure that he or she gains the most out of the property without necessarily taking into account the overall benefit of the property; this invariably leads to a more immediate destruction in the resources of the property due to overuse. Where property is owned privately, those resources may be utilised more efficiently. Individuals are not competing against each other for use, and may therefore spend more time and effort planning the most resource effective activities.[14] These arguments are particularly potent in a society increasingly concerned with resource efficiency and environmental protection.[15]

This economic rationalisation of private property is a persuasive one except when we recall some of the consequences of private property in a capitalist system in human terms. Those who own large amounts of property in a free enterprise, capitalist society, of which there are very few, tend also to control the capital, and this gives them the power to affect directly the lives of individuals who depend upon the proper management of capital. Whilst there may be some limitations upon this power, usually in the form of basic standards of wage and minimal legislative safeguards for working environments, those who control the capital generally have the institutional power to sustain the repression of those who do not. Inevitably this perpetuates the division between the 'haves' and the 'have nots' and results in the segregation of production from need. The rich may lavish money upon extravagant lifestyles when the poor barely have enough to survive. The rich have the power to exploit, whether this be of production, industry, natural resources or poorer nations, thereby entrenching inequality and oppression. In human terms, the injustice of such a system is overwhelming.[16]

Contemporary society is, however, unlikely to move towards a socialist, communal system of property distribution. Private property has become such an entrenched part of the social and economic milieu of modern society that major structural change is unlikely to be accepted, and those in control are unlikely to allow such change to occur anyway. All that can be realistically expected is that the power and control of those in charge of existing property resources be effectively restrained for the interests of the community as a whole.

The increasing public face of private property resources, particularly those having a direct impact upon the needs of the public at large, such as oil companies, and private institutions catering for health and education, has meant that those in charge must exercise a greater degree of public obligation and accountability. Nevertheless, such obligations do not represent a sufficient

14 See Rose, CM, 'The comedy of the commons: custom, commerce and inherently public property' (1986) 53 University of Chicago Law Review 711.

15 See, Prosser, T, 'Towards a critical public law' (1982) 9 J Law & Soc 1.

16 See, also, Morawetz, AJ, 'Efficiency, morality and rights: the significance of cleaning up' (1987) 10 Harvard Journal of Law and Public Policy 433.

check on the way in which power and control are exercised in these areas and, with the increasing trend towards the privatisation of fundamental social services, greater legislative protection may be necessary. Future discussions concerning the type of resources capable of forming the subject matter of property and the social obligations that holders of such property rights should face are likely to become more relevant than discussions critically analysing the existence of private property, because these discussions have already been well aired.[17] As Lawrence Becker notes:

> The main lines of argument for the general justification of property have long since been laid down; the vulnerable areas in those justifications have been identified; alternatives to private ownership have been proposed; weaknesses in those proposals have been explored. It seems unlikely that any new discussion could make a significant contribution to theory.[18]

1.4 The justification of private property

All private property philosophies espouse a particular rationale for the continued existence of private ownership. These defences vary according to the period in which they were discussed and the perspective of the individual philosopher. They have been broadly grouped into three categories which are critically examined below.

1.4.1 Occupational rights

One of the most historically prominent justifications for private property lies in the notion that an occupant or possessor of property who acquires property by discovering and occupying it should be entitled to exert proprietary rights. This principle focuses upon the primacy of possession. A person in possession of property should have the right to retain that possession until a better claim is proven. There are a number of reasons why such a claim may be made: the occupant or possessor of property may have expended money on the property, established a secure place of residence or exercised general management and control over the property, and such actions should not be interfered with unless the interference can be properly justified. Possession and occupation should be protected in order to encourage security and certainty and to reduce the inevitable conflict that would ensue from an unjustified interference with a secure occupation.

Despite the apparent value in these views, they contain flaws and may be criticised. In a modern world, it is relatively rare for a person simply to discover and occupy property for the first time: most property is obtained through the accumulation of wealth and labour. In such an environment,

17 See Tay, AE and Kamenka, E, 'Introduction, some theses on property' (1988) 11 UNSWLJ 1.

18 See Becker, L, *Property Rights: Philosophic Foundations*, 1977, Routledge and Kegan Paul, p 3.

occupational justifications for property rights are somewhat outdated. Furthermore, why should such significance be given to occupation? The mere fact that a person may discover or occupy property does not necessarily mean that he has earned the right to own it. Focusing upon occupation or possession results in an ad hoc, fortuitous approach to the recognition of property rights and fails to encourage or reward productivity and labour. In truth, what is really being rewarded is not the actual fact of occupation but rather the labour process involved in attaining it.[19]

1.4.2 The labour reward

A fundamental premise of most Western societies, founded by the natural rights theorists, is that individuals are entitled to the profits of their own labour. This defence of private property is powerful as it is centred upon the premise of just exchange: if an individual has worked to produce something, ownership of the product should be the reward for the labour. In fairness, every individual should be entitled to the full produce of his or her own labour, otherwise there would be no incentive to perform, and it is important to encourage production.

The difficulty with this reasoning is that the causal relationship between product and labour no longer truly exists in a capitalist system. As Marx notes, the separation of labour, capital and landed property, and the inception of the monetary system, have alienated the worker from the product and externalised the labour process. According to Marx, the externalisation of labour means that the product no longer reflects the essence of the worker; this shows itself in the fact that the product is not his own but someone else's, that it does not belong to him, and that he does not belong to himself in his labour but to someone else.[20]

Further, even where an individual does labour to produce his or her own property, the production is rarely the work of a single individual. It is difficult to delineate the individual labour value of a product where ten different persons have contributed to its overall creation. This is a particular issue in modern industries where the basic tools, information and materials for creation have already been established, making production simpler and more efficient: in such a situation, it is not easy to determine the extent of the labour value (if any) of those who have provided the raw materials.

Whilst the labour reward theory is persuasive, it cannot operate as a complete defence. There are many situations where property is either conferred upon those who are non-productive or not conferred upon those who are. The labour theory is an important social justification because it

19 See, further, Rose, CM, 'Possession as the origin of property' (1985–86) 52 University of Chicago Law Review 73.

20 'Economic and philosophical manuscripts; alienated labour', taken from Marx, *op cit*, fn 12, p 80.

encourages enterprise. However, just like the occupation theory, it is ultimately incapable of providing a comprehensive justification for the accumulation of private property.

1.4.3 *Economic justifications*

The economic rationale of private property lies essentially in the fact that it provides an efficient infrastructure and incentive for the proper management and use of resources. If an individual owns property, the individual is more likely to take greater care of that property and to maximise its resources, thereby encouraging a more productive industry and greater economic development. The economic implications of a society in which private property rights have been eradicated have been well illustrated by Posner in the following example:

> A farmer plants corn, fertilises it and erects scarecrows, but when the corn is ripe his neighbour reaps it and takes it away for his own use. The farmer has no legal remedy against his neighbour's conduct since he owns neither the land that he sowed nor the crop ... after a few such incidents, the cultivation of land will be abandoned and society will shift to methods of subsistence that involve less preparatory investment.[21]

Economic justifications do, nevertheless, tend to overlook the social and environmental cost of greater productivity. The accumulation of private property has stimulated monopolisation, economic restriction and price distortions. It has also inhibited an egalitarian approach to the distribution of property and perpetuates inequalities of wealth and opportunity. Private businesses tend to waste a great deal of natural resources and use them to maximise immediate profit without considering long term environmental and social repercussions. Indeed, private ownership does not encourage industries to have consideration for the interests of future societies, because its primary incentive is present gain.

1.4.4 *Conclusions*

Of all the justifications raised in favour of the entrenchment of private property rights, perhaps the most persuasive, which has not yet been discussed, is that private property confers a level of dignity and self-respect upon individuals because of the liberty and freedom associated with ownership. Ownership is a method by which, in the words of Kant, 'individuals can objectify their true meaning and spirit'. In modern society, people develop certain aspirations and expectations which are often expressed through the accumulation of particular objects; it is important that the law acknowledges these expectations in order to regulate social behaviour and to

21 See *op cit*, Posner, fn 13, p 32.

reinforce human expression. Private property can confer freedom and self-sufficiency and stimulate a sense of personal dignity.

It is impossible to develop a perfect unimpeachable defence of private property. Combined, the arguments focus upon the importance of private ownership for productivity and economic development, the importance of private property as a means of stimulating labour and human expression, and as a way of protecting individual privacy and possession. In a modern world, despite the centrality of private ownership, the pervasive desire to 'have' is increasingly being challenged by rights associated with personal and social well being. This shift has encouraged a broader, more interpretative private property discourse which corresponds with the beginning of post-modernity. As Brendan Edgeworth has stated:

> ... the valorisation of democratic and personal rights as against the prerogatives of property resonate with a politics of *becoming* rather than a politics of *getting*. Theirs is part of the radical democratic tradition for which personal, moral and cultural aims are at least as important as distributional ones, where sexual and racial equality, the right to control one's body, the right to a safe and clean environment rank alongside the question of who owns what.[22]

Post-modern property critiques are not interested in reconstructing the traditional, polarised rationales and justifications for private ownership within an existing social and economic order. Rather, focus is given to the examination of new methodologies, a broader, more contextual and pluralised range of individual and social rights and the deconstruction of established property discourses.[23]

A good example of this new 'property methodology' lies in the recognition and acceptance of native title as a valid form of property interest under common law despite its fundamental difference from traditional common law estates (native title is discussed in detail in Chapter 6). The evolution of native title reflects the increasing awareness of the significance of property and property related rights to continuing social cohesion. As noted by the High Court in *Fejo v Northern Territory* (1998) 195 CLR 96:

> ... in every society, rights in land which afford an enforceable entitlement to exclusive possession are basic to social peace and the order as well as to economic investment and prosperity. Any significant disturbance of such established rights is therefore, ordinarily, a matter for the legislature not the courts.

22 See 'Post-property? A post-modern conception of private property' (1988) 11 UNSWLJ 87, taken from Bradbrook, AJ, MacCallum, JS and Moore, A, *Australian Property Law: Cases and Materials*, 1996, LBC, p 147.

23 See Harris, JW, 'Private and non-private property: what is the difference?' (1995) 111 LQR 42. See, also, *op cit*, Becker, fn 18, p 69; Borzel, Y, *Economic Analysis of Property Rights*, 1989, CUP.

1.5 Classifications of property interests

Property, being legally defined as a relationship which an individual has with an object rather than the object itself, may arise in a variety of different ways. In order to fully appreciate the differences between proprietary interests, consideration must be given to the categories pursuant to which property interests have been traditionally classified. There are two fundamental categories, the first being the nature of the object, the second being the source of law enforcing the interest.

An individual may hold an interest in land or over movable chattels and the interest may be tangible or intangible in nature. Tangible real property is land. Intangible real property refers to easements. Tangible chattels are personal property and intangible chattels are choses in action.

Furthermore, property interests will vary according to the source of law enforcing it. Common law interests in land vary in form and principle from equitable interests, and statutory interests are entirely regulated by the statutory provisions that create them. It is important to appreciate the jurisdictional distinctions between property interests as this is extremely relevant to the principles concerning the creation and enforcement of such rights.

1.5.1 *Real and personal property*

One of the most fundamental distinctions made in property law lies in the separation between land and chattels. In a legal sense, land refers to a particular portion of the earth's surface and includes the space above and below the earth. Land is permanent, indestructible and immovable. As Peter Butt has noted:

> Ultimately, as a juristic concept, 'land' is an area of three dimensional space, its position identified by natural or imaginary points located by reference to the earth's surface. This space may be on the earth's surface, or above it or below it, or it may be on the surface, but extend also from below the surface to above it. It may be a void, for any three dimensional quantum of the airspace can be 'land', or it may have contents. If it has contents that are fixed in position, those fixed contents are part of the 'land'. But the 'land' is more than those fixed contents. The contents of the space may be physically severed, destroyed or consumed, but the space itself – and so the 'land' – remains. In this sense, land is indestructible. It is also immovable.[24]

Land, in a legal sense, is also referred to as 'real' property, the description connoting its permanent, solid and identifiable character. Chattels, on the

24 Butt, P, *Land Law*, 3rd edn, 1996, LBC, p 10; Gray, K, 'Property in thin air' [1991] CLJ 252.

other hand, are movable, destructible items, the categories of which include such objects as furniture, jewellery, vehicles, clothing, and books. Chattels may also be described as 'personal property', a description referring to the individual character of such objects; they are not permanent, they are not indestructible and can vary markedly in shape and form.

The distinction between land and chattels, or real and personal property, is crucial to property law. Land interests have historically been categorised and enforced in a completely different way from personal property. This is particularly manifest in the type of remedies which may be applied. Real property is enforceable by what is traditionally referred to as a 'real action'. A real action entitles an applicant to recover the actual subject matter of the action, namely the land. Personal property rights, on the other hand, are only enforceable pursuant to a personal order, directing a defendant to pay damages. Hence, an owner of a piece of land who has been dispossessed may bring an action to gain repossession of the land, whereas an owner of personal property has to rely upon a personal award of damages for interference with the chattel.

The right of owners of real property to recover possession of the land evolved from a number of different forms of writ. One of the original writs was the *praecipe in capite*, which required a court to command the defendant to convey possession of land which was the 'right and inheritance' of the applicant. This writ was one of the oldest forms of legal relief and could only be brought in a royal court by an applicant known in the feudal system as a 'tenant in chief'.

The writs of entry were a subsequent development, allowing an applicant to bring an action which alleged that a current possessor's title was flawed and that the applicant had a better title which entitled him to repossession of the land. Even if an applicant was not the true owner, he could be repossessed of the land provided he was able to prove that his title was better than the flawed title of the possessor. In this sense, the writ of entry was based upon proof of a superior right rather than proof of actual ownership.[25] These writs were eventually replaced by the writ of ejectment which evolved in the 16th and 17th centuries. Originally, the writ of ejectment was a remedy which was only available to a wrongfully dispossessed leaseholder. However, it was extended to actions for the recovery of real property by means of a legal fiction whereby an applicant claiming the property alleged that he had entered a 'fictitious lease' and had been improperly ejected from the land and, in the course of substantiating the lease, was able to prove his better title to the land. The writ of ejectment was, however, abolished in England pursuant to the Common Law Procedure Act 1852 (Imp). The writ of ejectment has now been abolished in New South Wales. The Supreme Court Act 1970 (NSW) now

25 See Hazard, H, 'The early evolution of the common law writs: a sketch' (1962) 6 American Journal of Legal History 114.

includes a specific action for the recovery of possession of land which is set out in s 79. Most other states have equivalent provisions, although, in some instances, the action is still founded upon provisions set out in the Common Law Procedure Act 1852 (Imp).

Personal property is only enforceable by way of a personal action for damages. Under common law, there are three main torts which may be used to protect or recover chattels: trespass to goods, conversion and detinue. Where one of these torts is established, an action for damages may be raised, although where an action in detinue is established, the court has a statutory discretion pursuant to s 78 of the Common Law Procedure Act 1852 (Imp) to order the return of the chattel in cases where the chattel is recoverable and the court sees fit to do so.[26]

1.5.2 *Tangible and intangible property*

Property interests are also categorised according to whether the object is tangible or intangible in nature. Tangible property rights exist where the object is actually visible and in existence. Land and personal property are tangible interests. Intangible property rights exist where the object has no concrete, corporeal existence and may be created over both real and personal property. Intangible property rights over land include easements and *profits à prendre*, each giving the holder particular enforceable rights over burdened land. For example, an easement conferring a right of way over burdened land gives the holder the right to enter and cross over a defined area in order to access the 'benefited' land. A *profit à prendre* confers permission upon the holder to enter the land for the purpose of taking away the soil or the natural produce of the soil.

Easements are also referred to as 'incorporeal hereditaments', hereditaments being an old term of reference for real property which was capable of being devolved to an heir upon an intestacy. Incorporeal hereditaments are enforceable in the same way as tangible land interests. Nevertheless, because incorporeal hereditaments are intangible, they cannot be physically possessed in the same way as land, and therefore owners are not able to be dispossessed, but may seek injunctive relief or damages if their reasonable enjoyment of the right is substantially interfered with.

Intangible rights may also exist over personal property. These rights are known as 'choses in action'. A chose in action is a legally enforceable right to procure the payment of a sum of money due under a contract or to recover pecuniary relief for a legal wrong. As with incorporeal hereditaments, the rights conferred under a chose in action are proprietary because they confer a right to the enjoyment of the property rather than the actual possession of the

26 In Victoria, this is set out in the Common Law Procedure Act 1854, 17 & 18 Vict c 125 (Imp), Ord 48 r 1.

property. In this regard, choses in action should be distinguished from 'choses in possession'.

A chose in possession is simply another way of describing personal property or tangible chattels which a person actually has in his or her possession. A chose in action refers to enforceable rights to personal property not in the possession of an owner. For example, the contractual right of a person to recover personal property which he has hired out for a specified period is a chose in action, provided the contract is enforceable. The owner holds a contractual right to receive rents for the property for the hire period, but does not enjoy current possession of the goods.

Choses in action may be 'pure' or 'documentary'. Pure choses are those rights which are enforceable but are not identifiable by way of any documentary evidence. Documentary choses are enforceable rights expressly set out in specific documents.

The traditional meaning of choses in action is well summarised in *Blackstone's Commentaries* which states:

> Property, in chattels personal, may be either *in possession*; which is where a man hath not only the right to enjoy, but hath the actual enjoyment of the thing; or else it is *in action*; where a man hath only a bare right, without any occupation or enjoyment ... the possession whereof may however be recovered by a suit or action at law; from whence the thing so recoverable is called a thing or *chose in action*.[27]

1.5.3 *Leasehold interests*

Leasehold interests have been categorised into a specific group because of their ambiguous character. A leasehold interest is primarily a personal contract between an owner of land and a tenant, conferring upon the tenant the right to exclusive occupation for a specified period of time in return for the tenant paying an agreed rental to the owner. Being personal and contractual in nature, the leasehold interest did not traditionally come within the ambit of 'real property' interests. Nevertheless, the lease was a contract conferring an exclusive right to possession of land, and with the evolution of the writ of ejectment allowing a dispossessed lessee to recover possession, the enforceability of the leasehold interest was akin to real property.

To accommodate the changing character of the leasehold interest, personal property was further subdivided into two categories, 'chattels real' and 'chattels personal'. Chattels real are leasehold interests, the title identifying the mixed character of the leasehold estate through the reference to 'chattel' and the reference to 'real'. Chattels personal, on the other hand, are all forms of personal property other than leasehold interests.

---

27 See *op cit*, Blackstone, fn 6, Vol 2, pp 389 and 396.

1.5.4 Distinction between common law and equitable interests

The distinction between common law and equitable proprietary interests is based upon jurisdiction rather than the nature or classification of the object. Once the category of the interest is clear, the sphere of enforceability should also be examined. For example, if the interest is an easement over land it will be classified as intangible real property; it must then be determined whether the easement is legal or equitable in nature, as easements are enforceable in both jurisdictions.

If the interest is properly created and recognised by the common law, it will be considered as 'legal' in nature; legal proprietary interests may arise over real, personal, tangible or intangible property. An interest cannot be legal unless it fits within one of the recognised categories of existing common law estates and interests. Furthermore, an interest may only be legal where it is created in accordance with the relevant statutory rules and formalities. Legal interests may be enforced by common law damages, by equitable relief where damages are inadequate or, in some instances, by specific statutory forms of relief.

An interest will be equitable in nature where it is recognised and enforced by the equity jurisdiction. Equity will enforce proprietary interests which have been expressly created or imposed by a court where fairness requires it. The categories of equitable interests are more amenable to development and expansion because they are founded on principles of fairness. Equitable proprietary interests may arise in a variety of different situations, including the interest of a purchaser who has entered into an enforceable contract of sale and acquires beneficial title under a constructive trust, the interest of a tenant under an enforceable equitable lease, the interest of a purchaser as a beneficiary under a 'purchase money resulting trust' and the interest of a beneficiary under a trust expressly created.[28]

1.5.5 Statutory proprietary interests

Not all proprietary interests are recognised and enforceable under common law or equity. Some proprietary interests are created and regulated by statute alone. Statutory interests are generally created in circumstances where proprietary protection is needed and, due to the complex and detailed nature of the area, the precision and clarity of statutory provisions is to be preferred to the ad hoc, piecemeal approach of court made law. Statutory proprietary interests tend to cover new areas of proprietary development, the most obvious being intellectual property but also, more recently, the regulation of native title interests. Statutory interests are generally regulated completely by

28 These categories are outlined in more detail in Chapter 5. See, also, Parkinson, P, *The Principles of Equity*, 1996, LBC, Chapter 3, and Hepburn, S, *Principles of Equity and Trusts*, 2nd edn, 2001, Cavendish Publishing, Chapter 4.

the terms of the statute. In most cases, this means that the jurisdictional limitations applicable to legal and equitable interests do not apply to statutory proprietary interests and, consequently, all the remedies specifically noted in the particular statute, whether legal or equitable in nature, are applicable.

1.5.6 *Conclusions*

The classification of property interests according to the nature of the object is based upon traditional distinctions between the form of remedies available for real and personal rights. Whilst such classification assists in the co-ordination and categorisation of proprietary interests, it tends to focus unduly upon the nature of the object and this often obscures the fact that, legally, property is defined as the relationship that an individual has with the object. In determining whether a particular relationship is proprietary in nature, the character of the object is irrelevant. The traditional classification does nothing to emphasise this point and often encourages misconceptions. Hence, even if it is possible to identify a particular piece of land or a chattel, or an enforceable right relating to either of these objects, it will not necessarily mean that the rights that an individual has over these things are proprietary in nature. In order to constitute property, it is not necessary to prove some form of spatial or physical reality; all that must be established is that the right is enforceable against the rest of the world and is therefore *'in rem'* in nature. As noted by Felix Cohen in his famous 'Dialogue on private property': '... the institution of property that we are trying to understand may or may not involve external physical objects, but always does involve relations between people.'[29] Once a proprietary right is established, it will confer the same type of rights as any other proprietary right. The rights held by the holders of private property are identical – whatever the character of the object. Hence, the owner of land has a right to exclude unauthorised persons from using it in just the same way as the owner of a car does.[30]

It is also important to distinguish between the classification of a property interest based upon the character of the object and the classification of property interests based upon its sphere of enforceability. All property interests, whether they relate to land or personal property and whether they are tangible or intangible in nature, can only exist where they are recognised and enforced by a particular source of law, whether that source be common law, equity or statute. This latter form of classification provides a greater insight into the nature of the interest because it indicates the legal status of the interest, its method of creation and the type of remedies available for its enforcement.

29 *Op cit*, Cohen, fn 2, p 362.

30 The 'private' property analysis should, however, be distinguished from native title claims. See, generally, Chapter 6.

1.6 Distinction between proprietary and contractual rights

In order to establish a proprietary interest it must be proven that the holder has an enforceable, *in rem* right to exclude the rest of the world; it is this right alone which distinguishes *in rem* rights from other enforceable legal rights. Contractual rights are not enforceable against the rest of the world; they are only enforceable against the parties to the contract and are therefore *in personam* in nature. Contracts which deal with land or personal property may confer similar rights of use and enjoyment; however, without the right to exclude, such rights will only be *in personam*.

It is not always easy to distinguish between *in rem* and contractual rights. Some contracts may become proprietary in nature and others may co-exist with proprietary rights. A contract which is expressed to exist for the benefit of a third party may be subsequently interpreted by a court as creating a trust for the benefit of the third party and thereby confer an equitable proprietary interest upon the third party. (See *Trident General Insurance v McNeice* (1988) 165 CLR 107, especially Mason CJ and Wilson J, and *Bahr v Nicolay (No 2)* (1988) 164 CLR 604.) Furthermore, where a commercial loan contract is given for a specific purpose, equity has been prepared to impose a resulting trust in order to protect the specified purpose (*Barclays Bank Ltd v Quistclose Investments Ltd* [1970] AC 567). Obviously, however, there are significant policy factors which should be borne in mind by courts when elevating a contractual right into a trust relationship and conferring an *in rem* right upon a third party to the contract. Such factors include:

(a) the nature of the contract and the intention of the parties (particularly where it results in the conferral of priority upon one creditor against other 'unsecured creditors');

(b) the impact that the proprietary interest will have upon third parties;

(c) the hardship (if any) caused to the contracting parties; and

(d) the suitability of other, available remedies.

Recent cases have warned against the arbitrary creation of trusts out of unenforceable loan contracts, particularly where the parties have become insolvent, because of the unfair priority conferred upon the beneficiaries of the trust as against other unsecured creditors (*Westdeutsche Landesbank Girozentrale v Council of the London Borough of Islington* [1996] 2 WLR 802; [1996] 2 All ER 961).

It is important to distinguish between contracts which are purely contractual and those which confer both contractual and *in rem* rights. For example, a lease contract holds a unique position in that it has historically been regarded as purely contractual in nature although today it is classified as chattels real. The leasehold interest creates a contractual relationship between the lessor and the lessee and confers a proprietary interest upon the lessee existing for the duration of the lease.

Similarly, a mortgage creates both contractual and proprietary rights. A loan contract is entered into between the mortgagor and mortgagee and a security interest in the mortgaged property is conferred upon the mortgagee for the duration of the mortgage. Consequently, the mortgagee holds a proprietary right securing compliance with the terms and conditions of the loan contract. If the mortgagor breaches the loan contract, the security interest may be enforced and the mortgagee may exercise his proprietary rights.

1.6.1 *Distinction between leases and licences*

A licence does not, in itself, constitute a proprietary right; it merely amounts to permission to enter or occupy premises: a licensee does not have the right to exclude the rest of the world from the premises. It is not always easy to determine whether a particular right amounts to a licence or a lease. The established test for determining whether a contract creates a lease or a licence in Australia is whether, by its terms, the contract confers exclusive possession of premises upon an individual for a specified period of time; if so, it constitutes a lease rather than a licence (*Radaich v Smith* (1959) 101 CLR 209).

A lease may be construed in circumstances where exclusive possession is expressly conferred or where the substance of the agreement makes it very clear that exclusive possession was intended. This test has now been adopted by English courts in *Street v Mountford* [1985] AC 809. On the facts of that case, the occupant of certain rooms entered the premises pursuant to an agreement which specified the arrangement to constitute a licence. The agreement was described in this way specifically to avoid any protection which may be granted to the occupant pursuant to the provisions of the English rental legislation. Despite the specific description of the agreement as a licence, the House of Lords held that the circumstances of the arrangement clearly indicated an intention to confer exclusive possession of the rooms upon the occupant for a prescribed rent and that, as a result, the right was, in substance, a lease rather than a licence.

1.6.2 *Distinction between irrevocable contractual licences and proprietary interests*

A bare licence is a right to enter or occupy land with no further legal rights. Such a licence may be revoked at any time where permission is withdrawn by the licensor. A contractual licence confers additional contractual protection upon a licensee. Where a contract specifically sets out that the licence is irrevocable, a licensee may sue the licensor for damages for breach of contract where permission is revoked. It has been argued that an irrevocable contractual licence confers a right which is akin to a proprietary interest upon the licensee: *Hurst v Picture Theatres Ltd* [1915] 1 KB 1. This decision was rejected by the High Court in *Cowell v Rosehill Racecourse Co Ltd* (1937) 56 CLR

605, which held that the existence of a contractual term prohibiting the licensor's right to revoke did not transform the relationship into a proprietary one.

On the facts of this case, the plaintiff was a racegoer who sued the defendant for damages for assault when he was forcibly removed from the defendant's racetrack. The plaintiff argued that he had paid his four shillings to enter the racetrack and view the races, and that this conferred a contractual licence upon him and that the defendant had agreed not to revoke the licence. The full court of the Supreme Court of New South Wales found in favour of the defendant. The plaintiff appealed to the High Court.

The court considered the distinction between a contractual licence and a proprietary right. Latham CJ stated:

> I cannot regard the transaction of buying a ticket for an entertainment as creating anything more than a contractual right in the buyer against the seller – a right to have the contract performed. For the breach of such a right there is a remedy in damages, but the remedies applicable to the protection of proprietary rights are not legally (or equitably) appropriate in such a case. There is, strictly, no grant of any interest. What is created is something quite different, namely, contractual rights ... [p 609].

A further argument which was raised in the *Cowell* decision was that the right to view the races conferred an incorporeal hereditament upon the licensee which was akin to an easement. The difficulty with such an argument was, however, that this right was too broad and indefinite and it would be very difficult to determine its boundaries, and consequently difficult to prove an infringement. Furthermore, there were important policy reasons for refusing to recognise and uphold this argument. If a contractual licence was regarded as proprietary, it would prevent the racetrack owners from being able to remove racegoers, even in circumstances where their own safety required it, and, in the circumstances, this was unreasonable and irresponsible.

In some circumstances, equity may issue a decree of specific performance to prevent a licensor from revoking a contractual licence. Specific performance is an equitable remedy, available at the discretion of the court. It is unlikely, however, that such a decree would have been granted on the facts of the *Cowell* case because of the hostility between the two parties to the contract.

1.6.3 Distinction between a mortgage and a loan contract

A mortgage confers a proprietary interest upon the mortgagee for the duration of the loan in order to secure its repayment. The interest which the mortgagee has is a security interest rather than absolute ownership, and may be redeemed by the mortgagor once the loan is completely repaid. Where a loan contract creates a mortgage, a security interest in the nature of a charge will automatically arise in favour of the mortgagee; where it does not, and in the absence of any other conferral of property as security, the agreement will be purely contractual in nature. In determining whether a loan contract creates a mortgage, a court will look to the substance of the agreement. If it can be shown that the purpose of the transaction was to provide security to the lender for the duration of the loan, then a court will usually hold in favour of a mortgage despite its form: *Gurfinkel v Bentley Pty Ltd* (1966) 116 CLR 98. Generally, this intention is evidenced through express words, but in the absence of this, the intentions of the parties, the nature of the loan and the overall circumstances may be examined.

Where the term of a loan contract indicates that the loan is to be repaid over a significant period of time and is to be used to purchase a specific piece of property, such as land, a court may be more prepared to find in favour of a mortgage. Where the property which is purchased with moneys obtained from the loan contract is transferred to the lender, it may also provide evidence of an intention to create a mortgage. In such circumstances, proof of a mortgage will ensure that the lender retains only a security interest in the property rather than absolute ownership.

It is important to distinguish between a mortgage contract resulting in the transfer of property to the mortgagee and a bare contract of sale. A contract of sale is a straightforward transfer of property from one person to another, whereas a mortgage involves the transfer of property as security for the repayment of a loan. Under a contract of sale, once the transfer is legally executed, the purchaser acquires absolute ownership. Under a mortgage, the mortgagee acquires a limited security interest and the purchaser holds a property interest which is subject to the mortgage encumbrance. If the contract of sale stipulates that the vendor is to retain a right to repurchase, it does not necessarily mean that a mortgage was intended. As noted by Lord Cranworth in *Alderson v White* (1958) 2 De G & J 97, p 105; 44 ER 924, p 928:

> The rule of law on this subject is one dictated by common sense; that *prima facie* an absolute conveyance, containing nothing to show that the relation of debtor and creditor is to exist between the parties, does not cease to be an absolute conveyance and become a mortgage merely because the vendor stipulates that he shall have a right to repurchase.

A mortgage can only be truly inferred by courts where the following points can be proven:

(a) a clear intention to confer an interest as security for the repayment of the loan;

(b) property which is the subject of the loan can be properly identified; and

(c) the transaction, in substance, resembles a mortgage.

Courts are reluctant to impose mortgages without clear evidence because of the remedial consequences associated with the conferral of a proprietary right.

1.7 New forms of proprietary interests

New forms of proprietary interests have emerged as society recognises new types of objects which may be owned and new forms of relationships which are proprietary in nature. The existing proprietary infrastructure is not static and developments are continually occurring. For example, courts are often considering whether new forms of intangible rights over land can constitute valid and enforceable easements. A good example of this lies in the High Court decision of *Victoria Park Racing and Recreation Grounds Co Ltd v Taylor* (1937) 58 CLR 479. On the facts of that case, the plaintiff conducted races at Victoria Park and wanted to stop the defendant, Taylor, from broadcasting details of the race meetings from a platform he had constructed on his own residence, near the racecourse. Victoria Park argued that that the broadcasts from that platform stopped people from paying to enter and watch the races directly. One of the arguments raised by Victoria Park was that, as owners of the park, they acquired an intangible right to any spectacle they created on that property.

The court ultimately held that it was impossible to own a spectacle because it could only be described as property in a metaphysical sense. The exclusive right to view a spectacle on land and exclude that view from occupying neighbours was not a natural right of an occupier and could not legitimately form a foundation for an easement, under either common law or equity. New forms of intangible rights associated with land can only be properly established where the boundaries of such rights are identifiable and their creation does not unduly interfere with the fundamental proprietary rights of others. It would be extremely difficult to establish the boundaries of a 'spectacle', and preventing its infringement may effectively deprive the right of neighbouring land owners to use and enjoy their own property. It would, as noted by Latham CJ in his judgment, be more appropriate to require the occupier of the racetrack to erect fences and other physical structures to prevent persons who have not paid for admission viewing the races rather than requiring the court to erect those fences by way of an injunction. His Honour made the following comments:

> I find difficulty in attaching any precise meaning to the phrase 'property in a spectacle'. A 'spectacle' cannot be 'owned' in any ordinary sense of that word. Even if there were any legal principle which prevented one person from gaining an advantage for himself or causing damage to another by describing a spectacle produced by that other person, the rights of the latter person could be described as property only in a metaphysical sense.

In some cases, despite difficulty or obscurity associated with the nature of the object, the law is prepared to recognise new forms of proprietary interests for the purposes of social or technological advancement. Intellectual property provides an excellent example. Intellectual property rights confer ownership over indistinct objects which include original ideas, inventions and designs. The rapid expansion of intellectual processes in a developing, technological society has made the protection of intellectual property rights imperative. The limited and piecemeal approach of court made law to the creation of new forms of proprietary interests made statutory protection a more sensible alternative in this area. Comprehensive regulatory legislation has now been introduced to enforce intellectual property rights in Australia. See the Copyright Act 1968 (Cth); the Patents Act 1990 (Cth); the Trade Marks Act 1955 (Cth); and the Designs Act 1906 (Cth).

Each of these statutes comprehensively deals with the particular category of intellectual property involved setting out the requirements for establishing a valid interest, the rights associated with such an interest, and all of the remedies available for the protection of such interests. Unlike common law or equitable proprietary interests, intellectual proprietary interests are regulated exclusively by the terms of the statute so that the usual jurisdictional or judicial constraints associated with common law or equity are inapplicable.

Statute is an appropriate method of introducing new proprietary interests that are associated with a difficult subject matter because it ensures the introduction of detailed provisions to regulate unclear or ambiguous areas. Statutory proprietary interests can only arise where the requirements expressly set out in the statute are proven. The statute will also specifically set out the rights attached to the interest.

Within a rapidly changing and technological world, statute has become one of the primary methods of ensuring that property law keeps in touch with societal demands. Nevertheless, some areas of potential ownership are fraught with controversy and public policy issues, making the likelihood of statutory intervention more difficult. A particularly good example of this lies in the vexed question of property rights in the human body.

The question of who actually owns the cells, organs and parts of the human body is a debatable point. On the one hand, many individuals feel that, as they have control of their body, they also have ownership in it. Naturally, this raises difficulties in cases where emergency operations are required to be conducted without the consent of the person involved, where medical research on a particular disease or virus associated with particular human cells needs to be carried out, and where issues concerning ownership of a human foetus are raised. Whilst it has been recognised that property ownership is a societal construct and, as noted by Murphy J in *Dorman v Rodger* (1982) 148 CLR 365, p 372, 'The limits of property are the interfaces between accepted and unaccepted social claims', establishing an 'acceptable' social claim for ownership in this area is difficult and a range of competing policy questions need to be taken into account.

In the United States decision, *Moore v Regents of the University of California* 793 P 2d 479 (1990), the court dismissed an action in conversion where the plaintiff claimed that the defendant's acts of taking his body cells – including blood samples, cells, skin and semen samples – during the course of treatment for leukaemia, and using those samples to establish and patent a new cell line for the treatment of leukaemia, constituted an interference with his actual ownership of those cells. The court ultimately held that, whilst protection may be conferred on the grounds of fiduciary duty or a failure to obtain informed consent, the proprietary arguments must fail. Despite the important policy arguments raised by the plaintiff, relating to the need to protect the privacy and dignity of an individual where his or her body is being submitted to external treatments, the court felt that the societal policy arguments ultimately outweighed such individual considerations. In particular, the court emphasised the importance of encouraging socially useful medical research to help in the prevention, treatment and cure of diseases. According to the court, the extension of personal property rights to interfere with the proper and effective development of medical research would be socially unacceptable and unjustified. Whilst concerns over individual rights and privacy may be pertinent, adequate areas of legal redress currently exist for dealing with such complaints without needing to artificially extend the proprietary analysis.[31] The *Moore* case provides an excellent example of the impact that social policy issues can have upon the development of proprietary claims.

Another interesting and related area to this decision lies in the determination of ownership in cases of organ transplants. For example, if a person dies and does not set out what she wishes to do with her organs, the question may arise as to whether or not her organs may be used for the benefit of other sick persons. If the body remains the property of the estate, the decision may depend upon the consent of the relatives who, in a sense, assume control over the deceased body. In many cases, however, conferring such control to the relatives may be inappropriate because their refusal, for whatever reasons, may effectively prevent life saving operations from being carried out. Hence, just as societal policy arguments overwhelmed the individual rights analysis in the *Moore* decision, it may well be that societal well being, advanced through the development of organ transplant operations, should defeat the claims of relatives. Furthermore, the adoption of a strict proprietary assessment to organ transplants may threaten the integrity of the human body and increase the potential for an exploitation of fundamental human rights. For example, the proprietary analysis of human organs has helped encourage an already flourishing market in the third world for the purchase of vital organs from impoverished persons. This has, to a large degree, resulted in the objectification of the body as something owned

31 See, generally, Magnusson, R, 'The recognition of proprietary rights in human tissue in common law jurisdictions' (1992) 18 Mon ULR 601 and the excellent discussion of this whole topic in Neave, MA, Rossiter, CJ and Stone, MA, *Sackville and Neave's Property Law Cases and Materials*, 5th edn, 1994, Butterworths, pp 57–69.

by, but separate from, the human spirit. The problem of objectifying the body into the proprietary analysis is well summarised by R Scott:

> If the body is studied as an object in which rights may be claimed or acquired by others, links can be discerned between events which otherwise have no apparent connection. The vulnerability of the body to treatment as property can readily be seen by using this classification and temporarily ignoring non-corporeal attributes such as spirit, soul and personality ... Present and future threats to the integrity of the human body and to individual liberty can be illustrated by the treatment of the body as a kind of property with the support of the legal system.[32]

A final issue of concern in this area relates to the ownership and control of human embryos. Can an embryo be owned and, if nobody has the right to claim ownership, who has the power to make decisions on its behalf? This problem has become more obvious with the emergence of advances in fertility research and, in particular, in vitro technology. In the case of artificial insemination under the new in vitro fertilisation (IVF) technology, where the ovum is fertilised outside the womb, control and ownership of the fertilised embryo becomes a significant legal and social issue. Whilst legislation may regulate the area, the ethical debate surrounding the ownership and control of life remains controversial. Australian legislation regulating the control of embryos does not comment directly on the issue of ownership. Legislation has been introduced in Victoria, Western Australia and South Australia regulating the IVF programme and other related reproductive procedures.[33] Under the Victorian legislation, fertilisation of an ovum is prohibited unless it is implanted in a woman's body or fits within experimental procedures approved by the Standing Review and Advisory Committee. Prior to implantation, control of the embryo is shared between the man and the woman, giving them the right to determine how it is to be dealt with and/or disposed of.[34]

The legislation in each of these states does not expressly deal with some of the ethical disputes associated with artificial insemination. For example, if the parties cannot agree how to use fertilised embryos, there may be some difficulty in determining who has the final word. Furthermore, the rights of the embryo, as a life in itself, need to be considered. A particularly difficult and controversial question in this regard is that of abortion. The heart of the abortion debate lies in the issue of personal autonomy: who has the power to control a pregnant woman's body? If a woman owns the embryo in her body then, provided abortion is permitted by law, the woman will have the power

32 Taken from Scott, R, *The Body as Property*, 1981, A Lane, p 253. See, also, Matthews, P, 'Whose body? People as property' (1983) 36 CLP 193.

33 Infertility (Medical Procedures) Act 1984 (Vic), s 5; Reproductive Technology Act 1988 (SA); Human Reproductive Technology Act 1991 (WA). See, also, the excellent article by Magnusson, RS, 'The recognition of proprietary rights in human tissue in common law jurisdictions' (1992) 18 Melbourne University Law Review 601.

34 See ss 9A(3), 11(5), 12(5), 13(5)–(6), 13A(5) and 15.

to determine what will happen to her body and the embryo in it. Yet if we say, as do the anti-abortion activists, that life commences as soon as fertilisation occurs, should we permit a woman to have the right to terminate that life? – and would this not interfere with the unborn child's rights? The question raises many theological and medical debates concerning the rights of the woman, the rights of the child and the difficulty of applying a proprietary analysis to the creation of human life. There is no easy solution and the issues become more difficult as technology progresses. Ultimately, however, if human life is considered too important and too unique both individually and socially to be subject to basic property law principles, consideration must be given to the availability and adequacy of other forms of legal protection.

CHAPTER 2

POSSESSION, SEISIN AND OWNERSHIP IN REAL AND PERSONAL PROPERTY

2.1 The distinction between proprietary and possessory title

Possession is a usual incident of property ownership. Many individuals who hold a proprietary interest in an object also possess that object, and in many cases this is because the proprietary interest was acquired for the purpose of using, occupying or controlling the object to which it relates. Nevertheless, possession is not a definitive characteristic of a proprietary interest, and a person might have possession of an object without actually owning it. For example, if Ben purchases an investment property and leases it out to Ralph, Ralph acquires a leasehold interest in, and possession of, the property, and Ben retains ownership without possession of the property. Hence possession does not identify ownership and, indeed, may exist without it.

Possession itself is a physical rather than a legal notion. Possession exists where it can factually be proven that an individual is in occupation or control of an object. On the other hand, a proprietary interest can only be established where it can be proven that an individual has a legally enforceable right to exclude the rest of the world.

2.1.1 Possession: forms of control

Whether an individual has possession of property will depend upon the character of that property. Where the property is land, possession will generally exist where it can be established that the individual is in full occupation of that land. Where the property is personal, a person may take control by the act of finding and retaining the property in a private capacity. Hence, in *Hannah v Peel* [1945] 1 KB 509, the finder of an old, valuable brooch was held to be in possession of it, despite the fact that the house in which it was found did not belong to the finder. The court held that the act of finding and retaining the brooch constituted the physical act of possession and thereby conferred a possessory title upon the finder. An individual will retain control of personal property where they place that property in an area which is controlled by them privately. For example, where an individual takes a car and places it in a locked garage at their home, they have taken control and will therefore be regarded as having possession over that car.

In some situations, a person may take control of personal property which is discovered in an area open to public access. The general principle here is that personal property which is found upon land rather than attached to it, where the land is open to public access, may be controlled by the finder –

unless the owner of the land indicates a clear intention to control all objects existing on that land. In *Waverley BC v Fletcher* [1995] 4 All ER 756, the English Court of Appeal held that the local council could claim a brooch discovered by a person using a metal detector in the park because the lawful owner or possessor of land owned all that was attached to it and that included things found in the ground of that land. Furthermore, metal detecting was not permitted under the terms of public entry to the park and, therefore, using a metal detector and digging up the land constituted acts of trespass. Auld LJ noted that possession of land generally carries with it possession of everything which is attached to or under that land – including the right to possess in the absence of a better title; it makes no difference that the possessor of the land is not aware of the thing's existence. Auld LJ went on to adopt two general principles: (1) where an article is found in or attached to land, as between the owner or lawful possessor of the land and the finder of the article, the owner or lawful possessor of the land has the better title; and (2) where an article is found unattached on land, as between the two, the owner or lawful possessor of the land has a better title only if he exercised such manifest control over the land as to indicate an intention to control the land and anything that might be found on it.[1]

2.1.2 *Consensual possession*

Where the holder of property has acquired possession with the consent of the owner, the possessor will hold a legally enforceable right – existing for the duration of the possession. Hence, where an owner of land confers exclusive possession of that land on another for a limited duration of time, that other will hold a lease existing for the duration of the possession. (Leases are discussed in detail in Chapter 15.) Where the owner of personal property delivers that property to another for a limited duration of time, that other will have bailment in the property. Bailment will arise where possession of goods is conferred on another. Bailment only applies to personal property and gives the bailee (transferee) a legally enforceable right to retain the goods and the bailor (transferor) a legally enforceable right to regain possession. Bailment can arise where the owner of goods delivers possession to a third party, or where the possessor of goods delivers them to a third party.

Significantly, bailment differs from a sale or transfer because the bailor retains a right to regain possession. This right is not retained in an ordinary sale or transfer, unless it is conditional. A hire purchase contract is a good example of a bailment. Usually, a hire purchase company retains ownership of the hired goods for the duration of the contract and gives the hirer possession of the hired goods – with an option to purchase at the expiration of the contract. During the term of the hire purchase contract, the hirer is the bailee

1 See, also, *Parker v British Airways Board* [1982] 1 QB 1004.

and the bailor retains the right to regain possession in the event that the terms of the hire purchase contract are breached.

2.1.3 Non-consensual possession

Where a person acquires possession of real property without the consent of the true owner, this possession is protected under the law until the true owner enforces his rights. Where the true owner exercises his or her proprietary rights and reclaims possession of the property, a non-consensual possessory title will be defeated. If the true owner does not exercise these rights within an appropriate time frame, the possession may amount to an adverse possession in which case the true owner will be prevented from enforcing his or her rights. Adverse possession is discussed in detail in Chapter 4.

Where a person acquires possession of personal property without the consent of the true owner, the possession will also be protected until the true owner enforces his rights. Non-consensual acquisition of personal property may occur in a number of ways: (1) a person may find goods which have been misplaced by the true owner; (2) a person may find goods which were never previously possessed; and (3) a person may steal goods from the true owner.

Where possession can be proven, the possessor will acquire what is referred to as a 'possessory title'. A person holding physical possession of an object is in a fairly strong position – a position which has been consistently protected by English law. The only title that can defeat a possessory title is a proprietary title, hence giving credence to the old adage, 'possession is nine-tenths of the law'. The strength of possessory title was clearly enunciated in the classic case *Armory v Delamirie* (1722) 1 Str 505. On the facts of that case, the plaintiff, a chimney sweep, discovered a valuable jewel and took it to a goldsmith for it to be valued. The attendant to the goldsmith pretended to weigh the jewel but in fact took out the valuable stones without the knowledge of the plaintiff and offered him a small sum in return. The plaintiff demanded the jewel be returned and the attendant returned it without the valuable stones. The plaintiff then brought an action in trover. The court held that the 'finder of a jewel, though he does not by such finding acquire an absolute property or ownership, yet he has such property as will enable him to keep it against all but the rightful owner, and consequently may maintain trover'. This principle forms the backbone of what has come to be known as the relativity of title principle; each title that an individual holds in an object carries with it a relative strength which is measured according to its level of enforceability. The holder of a possessory title holds a good title against all but the true owner who holds absolute title and, until 'absolute title' or a 'full and better' ownership is proven, the courts will protect the rights of an actual possessor. This has been reiterated in the classic statement by Bracton:

'Everyone who is in possession, though he has no right, has a greater right than one who is out of possession and has no right.'[2]

The primary justification underlying the courts' persistent protection of possessory title is twofold: to protect the established occupation of a possessor against unjustified intervention and, as noted by Maitland, 'to uphold the public peace against violent assertions of proprietary right'.[3] The legally enforceable rights of a possessory title holder are of a similar kind to those conferred under proprietary title, although a possessory title holder does not have the right to exclude the rest of the world because the true owner may assert title. Nevertheless, every possessor has the right to use, enjoy, sell or devise his title. This principle was clearly established in *Asher v Whitlock* (1865) LR 1 QB 1. On the facts of that case, Whitlock took possession of some land in 1842 and eventually built a cottage upon it. He died in 1860 and devised it to his wife, provided she remained unmarried, and when she died, to his daughter. Both the widow and the daughter continued to live in the cottage, and in 1861, Asher married the widow. In 1863, both the mother and daughter died. Asher continued to occupy the property until the daughter's heir-at-law brought an action to eject him.[4]

Cockburn CJ held that the holder of a possessory title is entitled to bequeath it and the law will protect and enforce those rights against subsequent possessors. The court held that if the daughter had survived, she could have brought an action for ejectment against Asher, and therefore there was no reason why the heir to the daughter should not acquire this right.

In *Perry v Clissold* [1907] AC 73, the court expressly approved of *Asher v Whitlock* and, on the facts, held that the holder of a possessory title over land was entitled to just compensation for the acquisition of that land by the Crown. During the course of his judgment, Lord MacNaghten noted that the act which requisitioned the land contemplated the payment of compensation for all persons having a secure title in the land, and it did not matter whether that title was proprietary or possessory.

2.1.4 The distinction between proprietary and possessory title.

Possessory title is comprised of two aspects: actual possession and the right to possession; the law protects both aspects. Hence, where a possessor is dispossessed of that property, he or she acquires what is known as a 'prior possessory title'. Prior possessory title will, as a general rule, defeat actual

2 Taken from the 13th century writings of Bracton, extracted in *Bracton on the Laws and Customs of England*, Vol III, 1977, OUP, p 134. See, also, Tay, AE, 'The concept of possession in the common law: foundations for a new approach' (1964) 4 Melbourne University Law Review 476.

3 See Maitland, FW, 'The mystery of seisin' (1886) 8 LQR 481.

4 It should be borne in mind that adverse possession could not be established on the facts because at the time the limitation period was 20 years.

possession under the general principle that the earlier right is generally the better right. This principle is qualified by the *jus tertii* defence in the context of disputes between possessory title holders of personal property. (See below, 2.3.)

2.2 The meaning of seisin

Seisin is an historical concept, associated with the possession and ownership of land. It is, as noted by Maitland, difficult to define because it represents a combination of concepts, a 'primeval confusion between possession and ownership'.[5] Nevertheless, it is a concept which is commonly referred to by the old courts and its presence highlights the deeply embedded significance of possession in the evolution of proprietary title. Originally and fundamentally, seisin simply referred to possession of land. Nevertheless, because of the form that the old real actions assumed, seisin came to be directly associated with ownership of land.

The first point to make is that seisin is a concept which is only associated with real property; it is not used with respect to any proprietary interest which may exist in movable personal chattels. Secondly, seisin can only exist where an individual holding a proprietary interest in land also holds actual possession. Without possession, a proprietary interest holder would be 'disseised' of the land and left with a right of action against the disseisor. Hence, in order to have seisin, it had to be proven that an individual had possession of the land. To fully appreciate the meaning and effect of seisin, an examination of the old forms of real action is necessary.

Historically, seisin was an important part of ownership because of the fact that proof of ownership of land was based upon actual physical possession of that land rather that the proof of a title to the land. An individual in possession of land has always been accorded a certain degree of protection, and this is evidenced through the form and approach of the old real actions. In the early feudal times, the feudal courts administered relief according to what became known as 'trial by battle', whereby the two claimants to the land, the person with 'seisin' and the 'disseised' party, would fight to the death and the victor would retain ownership. With the evolution of the King's courts and the introduction of the writ system, more civilised methods of resolving land disputes began to emerge. The real actions which were introduced by the King's courts were divided into two basic groups: the early writs of right and the subsequent writs of entry.

The primary writ of right was known as the *praecipe in capite*,[6] whereby a dispossessed or 'disseised' land owner claimed ownership of the land held by the defendant as his fundamental 'right and inheritance'. The tenant then had the choice of selecting either trial by battle in the feudal court or the

5 See *op cit*, Maitland, fn 3.

6 See, generally, Holdsworth, W, *History of English Law*, 1936, OUP, Vol 11.

determination of a body of knights, known as a 'grand assize', who were selected from the neighbouring vicinity of the land.[7] Both of these writs were primarily focused upon the issue of proprietary right, that is, who had the better right to the land? Gradually, however, such enquiries began to be replaced with a simpler, easier and more direct query: had the person in occupation unfairly and unjustly disseised the plaintiff? This enquiry was often much easier to resolve and was consequently determined by a smaller body of neighbours who formed what came to be known as a 'petty assize'. The emergence of this type of action had a great significance upon the evolution of proprietary disputes; for the first time, attention was focused upon the nature of possession rather than the nature of the title claimed. This action formed the basis for the emergence of what came to be known as the writs of entry.

Under these writs, the important question was not 'who had the better right?' but rather, 'who had the better possession?' It was these writs which truly introduced the relativity of title principle into the English property system, because they required the courts to examine the quality and nature of each party's possessory title and determine which was the superior. It was these writs which introduced the established notion that seisin – that is, a possessory title – is the root of all title: it was only where seisin could be proven that a right of entry could be conferred. A plaintiff who lost seisin acquired a right of entry which amounted to a right to regain possession against the disseisor where it could be proven that the plaintiff had a better right to seisin. The person who could prove the oldest seisin would generally be entitled to recover possession against all subsequent claimants.

For example, if George owned a large block of land in rural England and was disseised by his brother, Jim, who, after working the land as a profitable farm for a couple of years, was wrongfully disseised by Robert, a determination as to who was entitled to possession would depend upon who brought the action. If George sought a writ of entry, he would succeed not because he could prove a better ownership, right and inheritance, but rather because he held the earliest seisin and thereby acquired the best right of entry. If Jim sought a right of entry against Robert he would succeed because he held an earlier seisin to that of Robert.

The old writs of entry were eventually replaced by the writ of ejectment. The writ of ejectment was a writ which was originally introduced to allow leaseholders to recover possession of the land where they had been dispossessed by ejecting a person in possession without a valid title. As discussed in Chapter 1, leasehold interests were traditionally classified as personal property, hence the real actions discussed above were not available. The writ of ejectment eventually became a popular writ for the holders of real

7 See the excellent discussion of this in Butt, P, *Land Law*, 3rd edn, 1996, LBC, pp 74–83.

property where they had been disseised of their land, replacing the old writs of entry. Where a holder of real property was dispossessed, he was able to raise the writ of ejectment by claiming a fictitious lease. The primary reason for the increased popularity of the writ of ejectment amongst holders of real property was that the old writs of right and entry were complex and time consuming compared to the relatively expeditious operation of the writ of ejectment. The writ of ejectment was abolished in England by the Common Law Procedure Act 1852, and the old technical forms have now been replaced by a simple action for recovery of land which sets out the relevant facts and demands possession.

This historical background reveals the intricate relationship between ownership, possession and seisin. It is clear that, whilst possession does not equate with ownership, it forms the basis of a proprietary claim in land. Where both proprietary title and possession are held, the individual is said to have 'seisin' of the land. Where an individual disseises the holder and takes possession, the occupier retains possessory title and acquires a limited seisin. Possessory title will be protected unless and until an applicant can prove a better title. A mere possessory title may be defeated by proof of ownership or by proof of a prior, and therefore superior, possessory title.

The old writ of right was brought where an owner and possessor was disseised of the land and sought to reclaim possession by proving a better 'right' to the land. Alternatively, the old writs of entry and ejectment were brought where a disseised applicant sought to prove a better 'possession' of the land; the question for the court to determine was not 'who is the true owner', but rather 'who has the better seisin'.

In modern times, the concept of seisin is not as significant. Courts have gradually accepted the fact that a person can own land without necessarily having possession of it, and it is now possible to prove a proprietary title to the land without needing to establish possession. The only practical significance of seisin today lies in the fact that it distinguishes freehold and non-freehold title. Nevertheless, the concept of seisin has had a lasting effect upon our entire property system, which defies the established liberalist conception of property interests as solid, secure and inviolable. No interest in property is indestructible and all title to property is relative. An owner of land may be dispossessed and the strength and validity of the new possessory title will be protected by the law until a better claim can be established. As recently summarised by Toohey J in *Mabo v State of Queensland* (1992) 175 CLR 1, 'In sum, English land law, in 1879 and now, conferred an estate in fee simple on a person in possession of land enforceable against all the world except a person with a better claim'.

2.3 The *jus tertii* defence

An important consideration, when examining the strength and validity of possessory title, is whether or not a defendant in possession is entitled to raise the *jus tertii* defence. The *jus tertii* defence states that even though the plaintiff may have a better possessory title to the land than the defendant, a superior title to both claims lies with a third person who is not a party to the case. There is some debate as to whether or not the *jus tertii* defence may be raised by possessory title holders in land. Following the determination of the Privy Council in *Perry v Clissold* [1907] AC 73, the general consensus seems to be that the defence is not available for interests in land as it would contradict the established principle that proof of a prior possessory title may defeat the claim of a subsequent possessor. If a defendant in possession of land were able to defend any prior possessory claim by noting the existence of superior rights in a third party, the position of a party in possession would be significantly strengthened. Not only would this go against established precedent, it would have a deleterious effect upon the peaceable occupation of possessory titleholders.

In *Asher v Whitlock* (1865) LR 1 QB 1, the court held that a prior possessory title which was devised to the plaintiffs could defeat the defendant who was in actual possession. The success of the plaintiff's claim, despite the fact that a third party was the true owner, was considered to constitute sufficient evidence that the *jus tertii* defence was not available to land claims. Whilst the *jus tertii* plea appears to have been successfully raised in *Doe d Carter v Barnard* (1849) 13 QB 945; 116 ER 1524, which, on the facts, held that the existence of an adverse possession claim in a third party prevented a prior possessor from defeating the claim of a person in actual possession, the case has been the subject of some debate.[8] If the *jus tertii* defence could be raised by any defendant in possession, it would effectively mean that the plaintiff would not simply have to prove a better title than that held by the defendant, but rather a better title than the rest of the world. In effect, such an approach undermines the relativity of title principle and, as mentioned above, is contrary to well established and firmly entrenched principle.[9]

Slightly different arguments may be raised where a defendant attempts to raise the *jus tertii* over personal property. The issue is well explored in *Jeffries v The Great Western Railway Co* (1856) 5 E & B 802; 119 ER 680. On the facts of that case, the plaintiff brought a tortious action in trover, an action for the

---

8 See Hargreaves, AD, 'Terminology and title in ejectment' (1940) 56 LQR 376, p 396, where, in discussing the case, the author notes that, 'There is no reference in the judgment to any authorities, nor is there that attempt at justification which one would expect from a court accepting for the first time an entirely novel plea in an action which had been in constant use for over 250 years'.

9 See the excellent discussion in Neave, MA, Rossiter, CJ and Stone, MA, *Sackville and Neave's Property Law Cases and Materials*, 5th edn, 1994, Butterworths, pp 144–46.

recovery of the value of goods against a person who had wrongfully converted them to his own use, against the defendants with respect to a number of trucks. The plaintiff established that the trucks were his according to an assignment from a third party. However, the defendant proved that, prior to the assignment, the third party had become bankrupt and the trucks were the subject of a bankruptcy order. The court held that the *jus tertii* defence could be raised in personal property disputes but not be applied to assist wrongdoers. As noted by Lord Campbell LC:

> I am of opinion that the law is that a person possessed of goods as his property has a good title as against every stranger, and that one who takes them from him, having no title in himself, is a wrongdoer, and cannot defend himself by shewing that there was title in some third person; for against a wrongdoer possession is a title.

Whilst, *prima facie*, it would seem that the *jus tertii* is a defence which may be raised by a defendant in possession of personal property, it cannot be used to assist a wrongful possession, as is clearly enunciated in the *Jeffries* case. Hence a defendant who wrongfully interferes with a plaintiff's possessory title over personal property will be *prima facie* liable to pay damages to the plaintiff amounting to the full market value of the property, and such damages will not be reduced on the basis that the true owner of the property may seek its recovery; a defendant who has had to pay out such damages to a plaintiff may also be subjected to an action for recovery of the goods or payment of their equivalent value by the true owner.

Following this decision, the *jus tertii* defence may only be effectively raised in a limited number of situations: where the defendant defends the action on behalf of the true owner; where the wrongful acts of the defendant were committed with the authority of the true owner; and where the plaintiff was never in actual possession. In the latter case, the plaintiff must rely upon the strength of his proprietary title rather than any prior possession, and in such a case, proof by the defendant of the *jus tertii* will inevitably defeat the plaintiff's claim.[10] It should also be remembered that a plaintiff may prove prior possession where he or she has actual possession, constructive possession or the right to immediate possession.

2.4 Remedies applicable to personal property

As personal property interests are enforceable by personal actions, it is important to understand the nature and scope of these actions. Unlike real actions, personal actions are actions which are directed against the person rather than the property in issue. The most common personal action which may be instigated by the aggrieved owner of a chattel is one which is based in

10 See the discussion in *Salmond on Tort*, 13th edn, OUP, p 280.

tort. The owner of a chattel which has been interfered with may raise the tort of conversion, trespass or detinue.

The tort of conversion may be raised where it can be proven that chattels have been dealt with in a manner which is inconsistent with that of the true owner. For example, where a person wrongfully takes possession of chattels and then delivers them into the hands of a third party, an action of conversion may be made out. Conversion may be raised by a person in possession or a person with a right to possession.

Trespass to goods may be made out where it can be established that the possession of the plaintiff has been wrongfully interfered with. For example, where a person wrongfully uses a chattel without permission, thereby interrupting the possessory title of the plaintiff, trespass to goods may be made out. Trespass to goods may be raised by a person in possession or a person with a right to possession.

Detinue is a tort which may be raised where it can be established that a defendant has wrongfully retained chattels belonging to the plaintiff after a lawful demand for their safe return has been made. Detinue and conversion may overlap because most actions for detinue will also constitute the tort of conversion. Generally, where trespass, conversion or detinue can be proven, the relief awarded will be damages. Nevertheless, where a plaintiff can establish detinue and prove that the defendant is refusing to return goods despite a lawful order, a court has a discretion to issue an award of specific restitution of the chattel, particularly where it has a special or unique value or interest.[11] Various forms of goods legislation have also been introduced to protect and uphold the interests of personal property holders, and in Victoria these include the Goods Act 1958 (Vic), the Hire Purchase Act 1958 (Vic), the Chattel Securities Act 1987 (Vic) and the Credit Act 1984 (Vic). A comprehensive examination of the scope and contents of such legislation is beyond the scope of this book.

11 Common Law Procedure Act 1854 (Imp), s 78; Ord 20 (NSW); Ord 52 r 1 (Qld); Ord 48 r 1 (SA); Ord 53 r 1 (Tas); Ord 48 r 1 (Vic). These are orders of the Privy Council.

CHAPTER 3

THE DOCTRINE OF TENURE AND ESTATES

3.1 The history of feudalism

The doctrine of tenure has its origins in the feudal system of land ownership which emerged during the middle ages in England. Two important points can be gleaned from this fact alone: first, the doctrine of tenure is only relevant to interests relating to real property, and secondly, the social developments of modern society have meant that the incidents of the doctrine are no longer of great relevance, particularly in Australia. Feudalism has never existed in Australia and, as the doctrine of tenure is an emanation of this system, its continuing importance is negligible, particularly in light of the High Court determinations on native title in *Mabo v Queensland (No 2)* (1992) 175 CLR 1. As noted by Toohey J in *Wik Peoples v The State of Queensland* (1996) 141 ALR 129:

> The decision of the court in [*Mabo (No 2)*] introduced a new and radical notion. It disturbed the previous attempts of the Australian legal system to explain all estates and interests in land in this country by reference to the English legal doctrine of tenure derived ultimately from the sovereign as Paramount Lord of the Colonies as he or she had been in England after the Conquest.

Nevertheless, as Australia has inherited the English system of land law, remnants of the doctrine remain. In order to appreciate fully these principles, an examination of the feudal origins of the doctrine is necessary.[1]

Simply defined, a feudal system represents a type of society in which the primary social force is the relationship between the lord and his tenant. Historically, this relationship was established for the mutual benefit of the tenant and the lord; the lord promised protection and defence of the tenant and the land occupied by the tenant in return for the loyalty and service of that tenant. The tenant held occupational rights upon the land, including the right to subsist on any produce grown on the land, and the lord protected that right, but the lord retained ultimate ownership of the land. This type of early tenure was known as 'knight service'. The ultimate 'lord' of all lands in early English history was the king. The king granted land to his knights and protection over that land in return for their military loyalty and other personal services. However, the king retained absolute authority over that land which included the right to extract feudal dues.

1 See, also, Devereux, J and Dorsett, S, 'Towards a reconsideration of the doctrines of estates and tenure, (1996) 4 Australian Property Law Journal 30.

The feudal system was operational during the 12th and 13th century in England and quickly became a founding social dynamic. It was successful because it operated on the basis of a fundamental exchange: personal services in return for land occupation and protection. Other forms of tenure which existed included: 'frankalmoin', where land was conferred in exchange for religious services; 'serjeanty', whereby land was conferred in exchange for a variety of different forms of personal services; and 'socage', which was a residual category that included agricultural services and the payment of monetary amounts.

Prior to the emergence of the feudal system, there was very little an individual could do to protect both himself and the land on which he subsisted from external invasion. The feudal system provided a much needed security net for individuals and assisted in the creation of a social hierarchy. Without a system of protectionism, chaos would have reigned. The transferral of ownership to a higher lord was considered a small price to pay for the assurance of a peaceful habitat. Naturally, the feudal system resulted in the centralisation of power and authority in the king which was mutually beneficial: the king acquired an army whilst still retaining ultimate control over the land.

In England, with the reign of William the Conqueror, all land came under the feudal system and was therefore protected; none remained 'allodial' (that is, without the protection of a lord). Furthermore, the land was divided into large tracts, and each tenant in chief retained control over these areas. The lords of each area governed the villagers (known as 'villeins') who worked the land to create subsistence and profit for these lords. The king did not interfere with the relationship between the lord and the villeins, and the rules governing their relationship were developed and administered separately from those regulating the king and the lord.[2]

3.2 Statute of *Quia Emptores*

The grants which were made directly to the knights were able to be sublet to further tenants. This meant that the person holding the land directly from the king no longer retained occupation of the land but passed this on to another person. The primary lord, known as the 'tenant in chief', passed on the right to use the land to a person who became known as a 'mesne lord'. There was no limit to the number of mesne lords that could exist over a single piece of land. The process of subletting the grant of land in this way became known as 'subinfeudation'. Inevitably, subinfeudation resulted in the creation of extremely complex and difficult land relationships.

2 See the excellent discussion of the history of feudalism in Butt, P, *Land Law*, 3rd edn, 1996, LBC. See, also, Holdsworth, W, *History of English Law*, 4th edn, 1936, OUP, Vol II, pp 56–78.

Eventually, the Statute of *Quia Emptores* was introduced in 1290. The primary purpose of this statute was to prevent complicated subinfeudation from continuing. The concept underlying the legislation was that new tenants taking occupation of land from prior grantors would not create another link in the chain, but rather, would be substituted into the position of the previous grantor. Effectively, this meant that the grantor acquired the right to alienate the land to a new tenant; the new tenant took complete control over the land and the grantor stepped out of the picture completely.

For example, if the king granted rights over a particular area of land to A (the tenant in chief), who then, under the feudal system, conferred the right of occupation over to B (the mesne lord), then A would retain rights over B, with the ultimate lord being the king. After the Statute of *Quia Emptores*, if B wanted to grant his rights of occupation over to C, B could alienate those rights to C, who would then take the place of B in the chain of tenure. B would drop out of the chain completely. The statute did not, however, affect the ultimate ownership of the king.

The statute effectively prohibited the complex progression of subinfeudation by prohibiting all future forms and conferring the power upon all free tenants to alienate the whole or any part of their land to new tenants who would be substituted into the position of the grantor and hold the same services as the old. There was, however, a significant qualification to the operation of the statute: it only prohibited the future subinfeudation of fee simple grants and did not apply to other freehold estates such as the life estate or the fee tail. (For a discussion on the nature of freehold estates, see, further, in this chapter under 3.5, 'The doctrine of estates'.)

Eventually, the statute helped to simplify the complexity of the tenurial relations under the feudal system. By prohibiting the future expansion of subinfeudation, the long chain of tenure was eventually reduced so that many pieces of land were held directly to the king. Furthermore, with the passage of time, the old form of services was replaced by a pecuniary equivalent. Instead of the tenant in chief conferring military services as a 'knight' or other personal or religious services, the king and eventually Parliament began to demand a monetary payment for all grants. By the time the Tenures Abolition Act 1660 was introduced, abolishing most of the remaining features of the feudal system, the traditional incidents of tenure had already been greatly reduced.

Upon annexation, it was assumed that the Australian colonies also adopted the doctrine of tenure as it operated under the *quia emptores* system, retaining all the fundamental principles of the English feudal system. According to British imperial law, colonisation of an uninhabited land automatically results in an assumption of sovereignty by the Crown. The concept of sovereignty in this respect is broken down into two primary components: sovereignty of power and sovereignty of title. Sovereignty of power gave the Crown full power to control and legislate over the land, whilst sovereignty of title conferred radical title upon the Crown, thereby enabling it to issue tenurial grants to grantees in a similar manner to that which had existed under the feudal system in England. The form of tenure which Australia adopted was referred to as 'free and common socage' and had existed in England since the introduction of the Tenures Abolition Act 1660. The relevant legislative provisions in Australia are s 5 of the Imperial Acts Application Act 1980 (Vic) and s 37 of the Imperial Acts Application Act 1969 (NSW).

One of the most important incidents of the doctrine of tenure which the Australian colonies inherited from the English system was the concept of escheat. Escheat essentially gave the Crown the right to the property of a deceased, intestate person without any heirs (*proper defectum sanguinis*) or in circumstances where the tenant had committed a crime. Today, the concept of escheat has been abolished and replaced by the notion of *bona vacantia* (Lang's Act 1863 (26 Vic c 20)).[3] *Bona vacantia* means that property may pass on to the Crown as 'property without an owner' rather than reverting to the Crown as ultimate owner. The eradication of escheat and its replacement with *bona vacantia* can be seen as an important watershed for the operation of tenure in Australia, indicating the altered character of the Crown's right to title. Under escheat, the Crown resumed control over land in which it always had ultimate ownership, and therefore the title was reverted; under *bona vacantia*, the Crown acquires subsequent rights to the land because the deceased has left no heirs, and therefore the title is successive. *Bona vacantia* effectively means that the Crown acquires a new title rather than resuming control over property it had always owned.[4]

3.3 The meaning of radical title

An important aspect of the doctrine of tenure in Australia is sovereignty of title. In order to appreciate the operation of Australian tenure, the meaning and scope of sovereign or 'radical' title needs to be explored. In England, radical title refers to the title automatically assumed by the Crown once lands were either acquired or conquered. As the historical background to the

3 The modern legislative provisions are set out in the Administration and Probate Act 1958 (Vic), ss 20(3), 20(9) and 55; the Wills, Probate and Administration Act 1898 (NSW), s 61B(7–8); the Trustee Act 1925 (NSW), s 100; the Administration and Probate Act 1929 (ACT), s 49 and Sched 6; the Administration Act 1903 (WA), s 13(3); the Escheat (Procedure) Act 1940 (WA); the Administration and Probate Act 1935 (Tas), s 45; the Administration and Probate Act 1919 (SA), s 72g; the Succession Act 1867 (Qld), Pt 4.

4 See Edgeworth, B, 'Tenure, allodialism and indigenous rights at common law: England, United States and Australian land law compared after *Mabo v Queensland*' (1994) 23 Anglo-American Bar Review 397, pp 405–06. See, generally, Campbell, E, 'Escheat and *bona vacantia* in New South Wales' (1965) 38 ALJ 303.

settlement of Australia was never classified in terms of a 'conquering' of the lands, the application of radical title in Australia is quite different. According the traditional construction of Australian history, upon the annexation of what were classified as 'uninhabited' colonies, the Crown acquired sovereignty of power and radical title over all lands. The radical title held by the Crown is based upon the premise that the sovereign, supreme lord is the ultimate possessor of all lands. Once radical title is assumed, it confers upon the Crown the right to issue tenurial grants and to remain absolute owner of all unalienated lands.[5]

It is important, however, to distinguish between radical title and full beneficial title. The radical title that the Crown acquires as a 'concomitant' of tenure exists merely to enable the Crown to become 'paramount lord', through the exercise of sovereign power, over all who hold a tenure granted by the Crown. It is not a corollary of this to assume that the title acquired by the Crown was absolute beneficial title which would effectively exclude all other claims. It is not necessary for the doctrine of tenure that Crown title be absolute and exclusive of all other interests. Absolute beneficial title to the land can only exist where the land is truly *terra nullius* and the myths of extended *terra nullius* have now been exploded by the *Mabo* decision. This is well summarised in the leading judgment of Brennan J:

> The notion of radical title enabled the Crown to become paramount lord of all who hold a tenure granted by the Crown and to become absolute beneficial owner of unalienated land required for the Crown's purposes. But it is not a corollary of the Crown's acquisition of a radical title to land in an occupied territory that the Crown acquired absolute beneficial ownership of that land to the exclusion of the indigenous inhabitants. If the land were desert and uninhabited, truly a *terra nullius*, the Crown would take an absolute beneficial title (an allodial title) to the land ... there would be no other proprietor. But if the land were occupied by the indigenous inhabitants and their rights and interests in the land are recognised by the common law, the radical title which is acquired with the acquisition of sovereignty cannot itself be taken to confer an absolute beneficial title to the occupied land. Nor is it necessary to the structure of our legal system to refuse recognition to the rights and interests in land of the indigenous inhabitants. The doctrine of tenure applies to every Crown grant of an interest in land, but not to rights and interests which do not owe their existence to a Crown grant. The English legal system accommodated the recognition of rights and interests derived from occupation of land ...

Following the *Mabo* decision and in order to ensure recognition of native title rights, radical title will vest a bare legal right in all lands in the Crown and operate as a 'postulate of the doctrine of tenure'; the historical reassessment by the High Court in *Mabo* means that full beneficial title cannot be conferred upon the Crown because the land was not 'truly *terra nullius*'. Hence, the

5 See Wright, W (Sir), *Introduction to the Law of Tenures*, 4th edn, 1792, p 5.

radical title that is assumed is bare, and the usual beneficial rights associated with full title do not attach. Despite its description as a 'pure legal estate', radical title will, nevertheless, entitle the Crown to issue full beneficial estates to grantees pursuant to the doctrine of tenure and to acquire 'plenary title' in circumstances where the Crown has expressly appropriated land for its own use. Furthermore, following the *Mabo* decision, radical title is capable of being burdened by native title rights which may be raised by indigenous persons. The nature of radical title in this context is properly described by Viscount Haldane in *Amodu Tijani v Secretary, Southern Nigeria* [1921] 2 AC 399, p 403:

> As a rule, in the various systems of native jurisprudence throughout the Empire, there is no such full division between property and possession as English lawyers are familiar with. A very usual form of native title is that of a usufructuary right, which is a mere qualification of or burden on the radical or final title of the sovereign where that exists. In such cases the title of the sovereign is a pure legal estate, to which beneficial rights may or may not be attached.

Native title may burden radical title unless the radical title has been transformed, through the conferral of an estate or express appropriation, into a full beneficial title. The *Mabo* decision makes it clear that, in the absence of such acts having occurred, native title may be recognised consistently with radical title and will not be extinguished by the mere assumption of sovereign power.

As noted by Brennan CJ in *Mabo (No 2)*, 'It is only the fallacy of equating sovereignty and beneficial ownership of land that gives rise to the notion that native title is extinguished by the acquisition of sovereignty'.[6]

The question of when radical title may be transformed into an absolute beneficial title, or *plenum dominium*, so as to extinguish native title, was directly raised in the important High Court decision of *Wik Peoples v The State of Queensland* (1996) 141 ALR 129, in which Brennan CJ (in dissent) concluded that the radical title retained by the Crown upon the granting of a pastoral lease would expand into a *plenum dominium* in the form of a reversionary interest which was capable of extinguishing native title. His Honour noted that this was a natural consequence of the interplay between the doctrine of tenure and the doctrine of estates, both of which continue to function as founding principles in our system of land interests, and it is too late to contemplate constructing a different system:

> It is only by treating the Crown, on exercise of the power of alienation of an estate, as having the full legal reversionary interest that the fundamental doctrines of tenure and estates can operate. On those doctrines the land law of this country is largely constructed. It is too late now to develop a new theory of

6 See *Mabo v The State of Queensland (No 2)* (1992) 175 CLR 1, p 39.

> land law that would throw the whole structure of land titles based on Crown grants into confusion.[7]

Significantly, however, this conclusion was not accepted by Toohey J (in the majority), who felt that the doctrine of estates should be regarded separately to radical title and that the two should not interact where the effect would be to extinguish native title over large tracts of land. His Honour noted that the doctrine of estates is essentially 'a feudal concept' used to 'explain the interests of those who held from the Crown, but not the title of the Crown itself'. His Honour said, 'to contend that there is a beneficial reversionary interest in the Crown which ensures that there is no room for the recognition of native title rights is, in my view, to read too much into the Crown's title'.[8]

3.4 The doctrine of tenure and the *Mabo* decision

The exact scope of the doctrine of tenure in Australian colonies has been reassessed in the controversial aboriginal land rights case, *Mabo v The State of Queensland* (1992) 175 CLR 1. In this decision, the High Court re-examined the underlying foundation of the doctrine of tenure, and in so doing, limited its application with respect to indigenous inhabitants of the Australian colonies. The court held that upon annexation of the Australian colonies, the Crown retained radical title over all of the land; however, absolute beneficial title could not be assumed in areas already occupied by indigenous inhabitants, because this could not truly be regarded as 'uninhabited land'. To this extent, the doctrines of *terra nullius* and extended *terra nullius* were abolished. In the leading judgment, Brennan J made the following comments:

> ... it is not a corollary of the Crown's acquisition of a radical title to land in an occupied territory that the Crown acquired absolute beneficial ownership of that land to the exclusion of the indigenous inhabitants. If the land were desert and uninhabited, truly a *terra nullius*, the Crown would take an absolute beneficial title (an allodial title) to the land ... But if the land were occupied by the indigenous inhabitants, and their rights and interests in the land are recognised by the common law, the radical title which is acquired with the acquisition of sovereignty cannot itself be taken to confer an absolute beneficial title to the occupied land. Nor is it necessary to the structure of our legal system to refuse recognition to the rights and interests in land of the indigenous inhabitants. The doctrine of tenure applies to every Crown grant of an interest in land, but not to rights and interests which do not owe their existence to a Crown grant.

7 See *Wik Peoples v The State of Queensland* (1996) 141 ALR 129, p 158.

8 *Ibid*, p 187.

Uninhabited land has traditionally been defined according to the principle known as *terra nullius* (literally meaning 'land of no one'). Where the land was *terra nullius*, the sovereign acquired full and absolute beneficial title. 'Uninhabited' was not only defined as unoccupied; it also included circumstances where the land was, in fact, physically occupied. However, this occupation was considered so different from the forms and customs of British society that it did not fit within the established British concept of 'occupied land'. Consequently, according to British imperial law, the land was treated as 'uninhabited'. This extended notion of uninhabited and *terra nullius* was applied to the indigenous inhabitants of Australia to justify an assumption by the Crown of absolute beneficial ownership over all lands to the exclusion of indigenous occupants. This notion of extended *terra nullius* has, however, now been rejected by the High Court in the *Mabo* decision.

Brennan J concluded that the extended theory of *terra nullius*, establishing that indigenous inhabitants of a 'settled' colony had no proprietary interest in their ancestral land, depended upon a discriminatory denigration of indigenous inhabitants and their social organisation and customs, and it ignored and devalued their whole way of life. His Honour felt that the common law should not be, or be seen to be, frozen in an age of racial discrimination, and the fiction by which the rights and interests of indigenous inhabitants in land were treated as non-existent was justified by a policy which has no place in the contemporary law of this country. Hence, the doctrine of tenure was read down so that the Crown only acquired sovereignty of power and radical title over land which was capable of being burdened by native title rights.

Significantly, the High Court did not abolish the doctrine of tenure altogether. The 'skeletal' principles of the doctrine were retained. As Brennan CJ noted:

> It is not surprising that the fiction that land granted by the Crown had been beneficially owned by the Crown was translated to the colonies and that Crown grants should be seen as the foundation of the doctrine of tenure which is an essential principle of our land law. It is far too late in the day to contemplate an allodial or other system of land ownership. Land in Australia which has been granted by the Crown is held on a tenure of some kind, and the titles acquired under the accepted land law cannot be disturbed.

Nevertheless, even though native title could be recognised, it could still be extinguished through either the grant of an estate over the land which was inconsistent with the rights of native title holders or the introduction of legislation which either acquired the land for Crown purposes or had the effect of extinguishing, modifying or altering native title in some way: see Chapter 6 for more detail on the nature of native title and how it may be extinguished.

Inevitably, the *Mabo* decision has substantially altered the operation of the doctrine of tenure in Australia. Whilst recognising the 'fiction' that tenure represents, and accepting its basic vestiges, the decision severely limits its application to land which can be proven to be subject to traditional native title. The abolition of extended *terra nullius* has paved the way for an acceptance of the existence and validity of indigenous land rights which operate independently of the tenure system. The relationship which the holders of native title rights have with the Crown is not tenurial: native title has not been expressly conferred by the Crown and there are no tenurial rights and incidents associated with native title. In this respect, native title exists outside the doctrine of tenure, because it does not owe its existence to a Crown grant.[9]

The aftermath of the *Mabo* decision upon the doctrine of tenure is discussed by Edgeworth, who states:

> Predictably, the significance of these various differences led the majority of the court to query whether the doctrine of tenure was to a meaningful degree appropriate to Australian land law at any stage from the time of settlement onwards. After all, once these differences are catalogued, the local animal begins to look very unlike its imperial progenitor. Yet despite overruling the cluster of cases which extended the *terra nullius* doctrine to the Australian colonies, their Honours refused to go one step further and unequivocally reject the doctrine of tenure ... The implicit conclusion of Brennan J's argument is that the doctrine of tenure denotes little more than the legal capacity of the Crown to confer valid title to land on citizens, or, more simply, radical title – a public rather than a private law concept.[10]

The subsequent decision by the High Court in *Wik Peoples v The State of Queensland* (1996) 141 ALR 129 represents a further endorsement of this new approach to tenure, and the High Court displays a clear desire to protect the 'new and radical notion' of tenure which the *Mabo* decision outlined. In line with the *Mabo* decision, in *Wik,* Toohey J concluded that radical title was 'not a real title for property purposes', but more 'in the nature of a political notion and, in that sense, a legal fiction'.[11] As such, his Honour concluded that radical title could not be transformed into absolute title so as to extinguish native title rights without proving the clear exercise of sovereign power and proof that the legal rights associated with such an exercise were directly inconsistent with those existing under native title.

In commenting upon the continuing function of the doctrine of tenure following the *Mabo* decision, Kirby J stated that: 'A new ingredient has been injected into the previously settled land law of Australia by the decision in *Mabo (No 2)*. Settled principles and assumptions must be re-examined to accord with the decision of the court in that case.'[12]

---

9 See, also, *Re Wadi Wadi Peoples* (1995) 124 FLR 110.

10 *Op cit,* Edgeworth, fn 4, pp 421–22.

11 *Wik Peoples v The State of Queensland* (1996) 141 ALR 129.

12 *Ibid*, p 260.

In advocating the importance of developing and expanding fundamental principles relating to the doctrine of tenure, Gummow J made the following comments:

> ... the further elucidation of common law principles of native title, by extrapolation to an assumed generality of Australian conditions and history ... is pregnant with the possibility of injustice to the many, varied and complex interests involved across Australia as a whole. The better guide must be 'the time honoured methodology of the common law' whereby principle is developed from the issues in one case to those which arise in the next.[13]

In *Fejo v Northern Territory* (1998) 195 CLR 96, the High Court noted the difficulty of reconciling the doctrine tenure and native title, and the problems in extracting a common approach:

> The ways in which each of the former colonies and territories of the Crown addressed the reconciliation between native title and the legal doctrine of tenure sustaining estates in land varied so markedly from one former territory to the other and were affected so profoundly by local considerations (legal and otherwise), that it is virtually impossible to derive applicable common themes of legal principle. Still less can a common principle be detected which affords guidance for the law of this country. Australia is a late entrant to the field following the change of understanding in the common law as it was previously conceived, evidenced in this Court's decision in *Mabo (No 2)* and cases since.

In *Anderson v Wilson* [2000] 97 FCR 453, the Federal Court concluded that contemporary courts should focus upon legislative provisions rather than the feudal doctrine of tenure in order to properly identify the place that any such incidents of tenure have within the statutory scheme.[14] In *State of Western Australia v Ward* (2000) 170 ALR 159, the High Court noted that native title is not an institution of the common law and therefore not a common law tenure, and the interface between native title and the doctrine of tenure is, necessarily, artificial:

> Native title rights and interests thus give rise to jural rights which are 'artificially defined' under the common law because they arise from the acknowledgment and observance of traditional laws and customs under a different legal system. The common law accords a status to, and permits enforcement of, those rights according to common law principles. The artificiality is a consequence of the intersection of the common law system of law with traditional laws and customs of the indigenous people.

In *Yanner v Eaton* (1999) 166 ALR 258, the High Court, in considering the nature, content and scope of native title, clearly noted that whilst native title as a proprietary right is recognised and validated by the common law, its form and content arises independently to the common law tenurial system. In

13 See *Wik Peoples v The State of Queensland* (1996) 141 ALR 129, p 232.

14 See p 464.

Lansen v Olney [1999] 169 ALR 49, the Federal Court noted that the practical effect of tenure and the vesting of 'radical title' in the Crown was 'merely to enable the English system of private ownership of estates held of the Crown to be observed in the colony' and that in the end, 'the concept of radical title has little if any relevance to the grant of interests in land in post-federation Australia as it was invoked to support native title. The court further noted that 'territorial sovereignty may not equate, even under the common law doctrine of tenure, to absolute beneficial ownership, the latter being arguably alien to the medieval case of mind'. Under this approach, tenure and radical title are presented as artificial constructs with little practical relevance, utilised purely in order to achieve a desired result.[15]

Following these decisions, the distinction between traditional English tenure and its Australian counterpart has become more pronounced; it is now clear that the medieval notions of tenure are inappropriate for Australian conditions. Whilst free, socage tenure remains, its application has withered extensively. It is no longer appropriate to talk of tenure conferring an absolute and ultimate ownership of all Australian land upon the Crown. In Australia, such ownership is qualified by the existence and enforceability of native title rights. Cases like *Mabo, Wik* and *Fejo* indicate the extent to which traditional assumptions of tenure have had to be adapted to suit a changing societal perspective in order to promote and uphold a fairer and more just system for all members of the Australian public.[16] (See a more detailed discussion on native title and the *Mabo* and *Wik* decisions in Chapter 6.)

3.5 The doctrine of estates

One of the consequences of the feudal system of land ownership was that land interests were classified according to the terms of the relationship under which they were granted. The ability to fragment proprietary rights eventually encouraged the creation of a range of different types of common law interests over a single piece of land. This fragmentation is embodied in the doctrine of estates, which focuses upon the segregation of individual interests in land according to the length of time they are to exist for.

As land is a permanent object, it is possible to create interests or impose restrictions according to the duration of time that an individual spends on the land. In this respect, land differs from chattels, which are more temporal. The durability and permanence of land allowed successive interests to be created, each being based upon a particular period of time. The doctrine of estates is not concerned with absolute beneficial ownership (this is technically vested in

15 See, also, Simpson, AWB, *A History of the Land Law*, 2nd edn, 1986, OUP, esp p 47.

16 See *op cit*, Edgeworth, fn 4, and *op cit*, Devereux and Dorsett, fn 1. See, also, Love, P, 'Native title – the end of property as we know it?' (1998) 8 Australian Property Law Journal 19.

the Crown under the doctrine of tenure anyway) but, rather, the individual character of the interests granted to each person taking under a Crown grant. Hence, an estate held by a tenant is not the land itself, or the *dominium*, but a conceptual, abstract portion of ownership, the scope of which depends upon the particular form it assumes and the length of time for which it is to exist. In effect, the estate operates as a surrogate form of ownership over land which has a present existence (in a relational sense) with rights that do not necessarily include actual possession.

3.5.1 Freehold estates

A freehold estate historically means that a person holds the estate in a free status. Freehold estates were the first form of estates recognised by the courts and their primary characteristic is that they exist for an indefinite period of time. The holder of such an estate also carried the right to seisin, allowing that holder to seek a real action for recovery of possession where dispossessed: see Chapter 2.

There are three primary forms of freehold estates: fee simple, fee tail (no longer valid) and the life estate.

3.5.1.1 Fee simple

The fee simple is the highest form of ownership that an individual can have, bearing in mind the fact that the Crown retains ultimate ownership. Historically, the holder of a fee simple held the land absolutely for as long as that holder had heirs apparent. Today, a fee simple will exist absolutely and indefinitely, even if heirs cannot be proven, and the holder has the power to deal with the estate as he or she thinks fit. The word 'fee' describes the status of the estate as freehold and capable of being inherited. The word 'simple' indicates that there is no restriction as to whom the estate may be passed on to.

Under common law, in order to create a fee simple, it was necessary to refer to the heirs so that the character of the estate as a 'fee' could be determined: *Sexton v Horton* (1926) 38 CLR 240. Hence A could transfer land he held to B in fee simple by setting out that the land was to go to 'B and his heirs'. The words 'and his heirs' were called 'words of limitation', because they defined the limits of the estate and revealed that the estate could be passed on to successive generations for as long as heirs existed. The words which indicated an intention to confer an estate upon a particular person were known as 'words of purchase'. Once created, the fee simple estate only passed to B; the heirs did not take any estate until B died. This principle stemmed from what was known as the rule in *Shelley's Case* (1581) 1 Co Rep 93b; 76 ER 206. This case set out the rule that any words of limitation in an estate of freehold will constitute words of limitation to the person receiving the estate, and not words of purchase in favour of the heir. For example, if X gave 'Y and Y's heirs' an interest in land, Y's heirs took nothing and Y received a fee simple estate.

The common law rules have now been modified by statute. In Victoria, according to s 130 of the Property Law Act 1958 (Vic), words which were formerly, *per* the rule in *Shelley's Case*, read as words of limitation, now operate as words of purchase. Furthermore, the use of the word 'heir' is no longer necessary to pass a fee simple estate. All deeds executed after 1905 simply using the word 'fee' or the words 'fee simple' will be sufficient to pass a fee simple estate. This provision was further modified some years later, so that after 31 December 1918, a disposition of freehold land, in the absence of any words of limitation or expressions of contrary intention, is presumed to pass a fee simple: s 60 of the Property Law Act 1958 (Vic).

3.5.1.2 Fee tail

Unlike the fee simple, where the heirs who could inherit the estate were unrestricted, a fee tail was a freehold estate where the heirs were restricted to a particular lineage. The origin of this type of estate lay in family planning: when conferring this type of estate, the grantor intended to benefit the grantee and any heirs 'of his body'. The fee tail could only exist for as long as lineal descendants could be established, and once they all died, the estate would be extinguished. The general principles of inheritance still applied to fee tails. Hence, if a piece of land was restricted to the 'heirs of the body' of a particular person, the first to take would be the eldest son. If there were no sons, the daughters could take in equal shares as co-parceners.[17]

Under common law, the words of limitation necessary to create a fee tail included the word 'heirs' and what were called 'words of procreation'. Words of procreation referred to words indicating that the heirs were to be restricted to those of the grantee's own body. Any words indicating this limitation could be classified as words of procreation sufficient to create a fee tail including 'to A and the heirs proceeding from him' or 'to A and the heirs apparent from his body'. It was also possible to restrict the lineage even further, so that, for example, it was restricted to male heirs. The 'male tail' was a common form of estate in early English history, and was often the subject of much social commentary. As evidenced through the lament of Mrs Bennet in Jane Austen's classic novel, *Pride and Prejudice*, 'There is no knowing how estates will go when once they come to be entailed!'.

---

17 See the excellent chapter, 'The fee tail', in *op cit*, Butt, fn 2, pp 124–32, for a more detailed discussion of this.

Since 1 January 1886, the creation of fee tail estates in Victoria has been prohibited. Any limitation which, prior to this date, would have created a fee tail is, in instruments coming into effect after 1 January 1886, deemed to create an estate in fee simple: s 249 of the Property Law Act 1958 (Vic). Furthermore, a person holding a fee tail who is of full age is entitled, since 31 December 1918, to dispose of that estate as if it had been a fee simple: s 251 of the Property Law Act 1958 (Vic).[18]

3.5.1.3 Life estate

The life estate is the final form of freehold estate in existence. Unlike the fee simple and the fee tail, the life estate is not a 'fee' estate and therefore, under common law, is not capable of being inherited by an heir upon intestacy. Nevertheless, the life estate still constitutes a freehold estate, because it is considered to exist indefinitely: it can never be certain when a person's life will cease, and it confers seisin upon the holder. The life estate will exist for the duration of a life. The appropriate words of limitation will be words specifically confining the estate to a particular life.

As there is no limitation upon whose life by which the estate may be defined, there are two primary forms of life estate: a life estate which exists for the duration of the grantee's life, a 'life estate *sa vie*'; and a life estate which exists for the duration of a third person's life, which is known as a 'life estate *pur autre vie*'. Historically, the life estate was a popular method of establishing family settlements, and was often created *inter vivos*. In modern times, the life estate is rarely seen, because the large estates of previous times no longer exist, and there is little reason to limit the creation of an estate to a single life. Nevertheless, unlike the fee tail, the creation of a life estate has not been prohibited, and, when it does arise, it is most commonly seen in wills and testamentary dispositions.

To create a life estate which exists for the duration of the grantee's life, actual words proving an intention to limit the estate to the grantee's life must exist. For example, if X transfers land to Y for life, Y will receive an estate which exists for the duration of his or her own life. There is no precise form which the words of intention must assume; any words indicating a general intention to limit the estate to the duration of Y's life will suffice.

In order to create an express life estate *pur autre vie*, actual words proving an intention to limit the estate to the life of a third party other than the grantee must be proven. For example, if X transfers land to Y for the duration of Z's life, Y will hold a life estate *pur autre vie* which will exist for the duration of Z's

18 The equivalent legislation in other states is set out in the Conveyancing and Law of Property Act 1898 (NSW), s 3; the Conveyancing Act 1951 (ACT), s 3; the Real Property Acts Amendment Act 1952 (Qld), s 5; the Land Titles Act 1980 (Tas), s 113; the Property Law Act 1969 (WA), s 23(1).

life. An estate *pur autre vie* may also arise impliedly where the holder of a life estate which exists for the duration of that holder's life transfers it to a third party. For example, if X transfers land to Y for the duration of Y's life, and Y then transfers this estate to Z, Z will impliedly receive a life estate *pur autre vie*, which will extinguish upon the death of Y.

Where an estate *pur autre vie* is created, the person receiving the estate is the person to whom it is transferred. The person upon whose life the interest is dependent does not receive any interest in the property and is relevant only because the estate will exist for the duration of that person's life. An interesting issue arises where the person holding a life estate *pur autre vie* dies before the third person upon whose life the estate is measured. In such a circumstance, the question arises as to whether the life estate can be passed on to another person. The problem with this is that as the life estate is not a fee; it was never considered to constitute an estate of inheritance. If, however, an heir to the life estate grantee cannot inherit a continuing *pur autre vie* estate, where does it go?

Courts eventually developed the notion of general occupancy to resolve this difficulty. Under general occupancy, the life estate *pur autre vie* would pass to the first person to obtain possession of the property. If the estate happened to be granted to the holder and his heirs, the heir did not acquire title to the estate but did gain the right to enter the property under what was referred to as a 'special occupancy'. Eventually, statutory provisions were enacted to the effect that the holder of a life estate *pur autre vie* could dispose of his or her estate by will: see s 26 of the Wills Act 1958 (Vic). This legislation has effectively granted the life estate *pur autre vie*, to a limited extent, similar rights as those applicable to an estate of inheritance.

The grantee of a life estate holds the land for the duration of a life, after which it will generally pass on to another person. The successive nature of the life estate has meant that the 'life tenant' acquires certain rights and obligations with respect to the land. During the term of the estate, the life tenant holds the usual proprietary rights, including the right to possession of the property, the right to use and enjoy the property, the right to receive any income from the property and the right to deal with the property.

The life tenant is also, however, under certain restrictions as to how he or she may treat the land. Under what is known as the 'doctrine of waste', the life tenant is prohibited from exploiting the land to the extent that it results in a deterioration in the overall value of the land. It will not only be conduct which results in actual damage or lack of repair which offends the doctrine, but also conduct which alters the character of the land. If, however, the conduct results in an overall appreciation in the value of the land, damages will generally be unavailable (*Doherty v Allman* (1878) 3 App Cas 709). The categories of waste are generally divided into four:

(1) permissive waste, where the life tenant under an express obligation to maintain good repair and upkeep of the property fails to do so;

(2) voluntary waste, where the life tenant carries out an intentional act of injury or destruction to the property;

(c) equitable waste, where a life tenant, not liable under voluntary waste, is prohibited from committing grievous acts of damage to a property; and

(d) ameliorating waste, where the life tenant commits an alteration to the property which improves the value of the land but changes its character.[19]

3.5.2 *Future estates*

The term 'future' is a general term and is used to cover a variety of different forms of estates, both vested and contingent, which arise where successive interests in land are created. Indeed, a more definitive description of such estates is 'estates not involving a right of present possession'.[20] All vested future estates confer present proprietary title in their holders. However, this title does not include the right to possession. The fundamental characteristic of a future estate lies in the fact that possession is deferred until a future date. Future estates exist because of the desire, particularly of medieval estate holders, to ensure that the land was held in the family by successive generations. One method of achieving this was through the creation of the fee tail, which is discussed above. Another method was through the creation of successive interests, whereby a life estate was conferred to one person and, upon the expiration of this interest, the land passed on to another person (usually a member of the next generation of the family).

For example, if Grandfather X holds a large estate and grants a life estate to his son, Y, for the duration of Y's life and then to his grandson, Z, in fee simple, two successive interests are created. Y holds a life estate, which will expire upon his death, and Z holds a fee simple 'in remainder'. The interest which Z holds is proprietary; however, it assumes differing forms. During the life of Y, Z's interest constitutes a 'future remainder interest', which gives him proprietary title but no present right to possession. When Y dies, Z's interest will 'vest in possession', and he will acquire a full fee simple estate.

It was quite common for a grantee to make the vesting of a future estate conditional upon the happening of a certain event, often the requirement of reaching a certain age. Until the future estate holder fulfilled this condition, providing it was valid and enforceable, the estate was 'contingent', and no proprietary title was conferred.

For Example, if Grandfather X holds a large estate and grants a life estate 'to his son, Y, for the duration of Y's life and then to his grandson, Z, in fee

19 See, also, the Settled Land Act 1928 (Vic) for a discussion on the rights of life tenants to enter into transactions without the consent of persons holding remainder intereests in the property.

20 This phrase was used by Tiffany, HT, in his excellent article, 'Future estates' (1913) 65 LQR 290.

simple ... when Z turns 21', one vested estate is created and one contingent future estate is created. Y holds a life estate which vests immediately and will expire upon his death. Z holds a contingent future interest, the title of which will vest when he turns 21. Possession of the fee simple estate will vest in Z once Y's life estate expires *and* he turns 21.

The different forms of future estates are categorised and discussed below:

3.5.2.1 *Vested remainder estates*

A vested remainder interest will exist where expressly created by the grantor to vest upon the expiration of the life estate. A remainder interest, as defined by Coke, represents 'a residue of an estate in land depending upon a particular estate, and created together with the same'.[21] Essentially, the term refers to that which is left over after the granting of a first estate and which, unlike the reversionary estate, is expressly conferred to a third party. A vested remainder estate will naturally take effect upon the expiration of the previous estate without the need to satisfy any further contingency. As the remainder estate is expressly created by the grantor, it is possible for a number of successive remainder estates to be created. The number of remainder interests which may be created is qualified only by the legal remainder rules and the rule against perpetuity.

A remainder interest must be created by express words proving an intention to confer successive interests. For example, Grandfather X confers a life estate to his son, Y, for the duration of Y's life and then to grandson, Z, in fee simple. In this case, Y acquires a life estate which is vested in possession and Z acquires a fee simple remainder which is vested in title, possession being deferred until the death of Y.

3.5.2.2 *Contingent remainder estates*

A contingent remainder estate will arise where the vesting of a remainder estate is made contingent upon the happening of a particular event. All interests which are expressly created are capable of being contingent. However, contingencies are most commonly attached to remainder interests, because they are successive interests and the grantor will often want to ensure that future generations comply with particular requests concerning the land. A grantor may wish to make sure that the future estate holder is old enough and sufficiently capable and responsible of managing the property, and may impose conditions to this effect.

For example, if X Grandfather wishes to transfer land to son Y for life and then to grandson Z, provided Z has reached 21 years of age and has worked

21 Co Litt 49a.

on the land for a period of two years, the fee simple in remainder held by Z will not vest until these conditions are complied with.

Until the conditions set out in the contingent remainder interest are complied with, the future estate holder will have no vested title to the property but merely the *possibility* of an estate. Once the conditions are complied with, title will vest. As with all future estates, however, possession will only vest when the previous estate expires. In order to be valid, a contingency must be an event which is certain to happen; there should be no doubt. A remainder will be contingent only when the estate is limited to commence upon a future event which is bound to occur.

3.5.2.3 *Legal remainder rules*

The common law developed certain strict rules concerning the creation of legal remainder rules. These rules were developed in order to protect the purity of existing freehold estates by ensuring that successive interests were only created over interests which could be properly limited and to prevent the creation of complicated successive interests which interrupted seisin and engendered doubt and uncertainty. The rules can be summarised as follows:

(a) *No future estate can exist after the creation of a fee simple.* This rule is absolute and was introduced to prevent any interference or erosion in the strength of the fee simple. The fee simple estate is the highest possible form of ownership and, once created, no future estate can be created because the land has been completely divested. Hence, if X conveyed land to Y in fee simple, remainder to Z, only one estate will be created. Y will hold the fee simple estate and Z will hold no interest, because the whole estate has passed over to Y so that X has nothing left to pass on to Z. Even where the fee simple is contingent, no future remainder estate may pass. Hence, if a fee simple is made conditional upon the occurrence of a particular event which does not occur, the holder may be divested and the estate will pass back to the grantor or the estate of the grantor. For example, X conveys a fee simple to Y provided Y continues to use part of the land as a natural history museum, and if Y does not, the remainder is to go to Z absolutely. In this example, Y receives a conditional fee simple and Z receives nothing, because a remainder estate cannot be created after the conferral of a fee simple. If Y does not comply with the condition, the land will revert to X or the estate of X.

(b) *A remainder interest can only exist where it is supported by an existing freehold estate.* A remainder interest cannot be created unless it operates successively with an existing freehold estate. A remainder interest cannot be created in itself to operate at some date in the future, because the essence of a future estate is the limitation of a previous estate. The previous freehold estate must be some form of life estate. If X, the holder of a fee simple, conferred a leasehold interest (non-freehold estate) to Y with remainder to Z, the remainder interest would be invalid. Similarly, if X attempted to confer a fee simple to Y but, for whatever reason, the fee simple was invalid, any remainder interest to Z would also be invalid (*Goodright v Cornish* (1694) 1 Salk 226; 91 ER 200).

(c) *A remainder interest could not take effect prior to the natural determination of the prior freehold estate.* A remainder interest is a successive rather than a primary interest. It can only take effect in the future when the prior limited estate has been extinguished naturally. The justification for this is that a remainder interest can not interfere with or interrupt the ownership of the prior estate. This rule was often offended where the grantor imposed conditions which had the effect of cutting down the freehold estate. For example, Grandfather X grants a life estate to Y, but if Y has three children, the estate is to go to daughter Z absolutely. In this example, Z will not acquire a remainder interest because it can only take effect where the previous life estate is cut short. Under the terms of the grant, the life estate is not allowed to extinguish naturally hence the remainder interest is automatically invalid.

(d) *A contingent remainder interest is invalid if it does not vest either before or at the moment of the natural expiration of the prior freehold estate.* A contingent remainder interest confers merely the possibility of an estate upon a holder. If the prior freehold estate upon which it is based expires before the contingency has been complied with, the remainder interest will be invalid because the common law required seisin to be vested in somebody, and such an event would result in an cessation of seisin. As a consequence, many contingent remainders interests were struck down as invalid. If the contingency is not capable of being carried out during the term of the freehold estate upon which it is dependent or at the very moment that it is determined, the remainder interest will be void. For example, Grandfather X confers a life estate to son Y for the duration of Y's life and then to Z absolutely provided Z has a child exactly 21 years after the death of Y. In this example, the remainder interest to Z will be invalid from the outset because the condition is only capable of being complied with *after* the death of Y and the determination of Y's life estate.

If the contingency is ostensibly capable of being carried out during the term of the freehold estate or upon its determination, the remainder interest will be valid from the outset but may become invalid if the contingency is not complied with in time. For example, Grandfather X confers a life estate to son Y for the duration of Y's life and then to Z absolutely provided Z has two children. In this example, Z will hold a remainder interest for the duration of Y's life. However, if, upon Y's death, Z has not had two children, the remainder interest will be void. Hence, a validly created contingent remainder interest may subsequently become invalid if the contingency is not complied with in time.

3.5.2.4 *Reversion*

A reversion is an interest which a grantor retains after conveying to a grantee an estate which is less than the whole interest held by the grantor. Hence, the reversion is not expressly conveyed but, rather, retained by the grantor, and possession is deferred until the expiration of the estate held by the grantee.

For example, Grandfather X conveys a life estate to son Y for the duration of Y's life but does not specify where the remainder of the estate is to be held. In this example, Y holds the life estate and, while they are both alive, X retains a fee simple *reversion* in the property. Whilst Y is alive, Y will have possession of the property, and if Y dies before X, the fee simple reversion will vest in possession to X.

A reversion is a presently existing estate meaning that a holder has title immediately vested in him and that title is not contingent upon the performance of any particular act. Title to a reversion interest must necessarily be vested in the holder because it operates automatically and is not expressly created. The mere fact that possession is deferred until the expiration of the estate held by the grantee does not, as discussed above, preclude the reversion from being vested in title. All future estates will be vested in title unless they are dependent upon the performance of certain conditions, as is the case with contingent remainders.

In some cases, however, the conferral of a contingent fee simple will create what has been described as a 'possibility of reverter'. What this means is that the condition attached to a fee simple has failed so that the fee simple cannot vest and the estate reverts to the original grantor. In such a case, until it is clear that the condition has failed, all that the grantor has is the *prospect* of a reversion. The title to such an estate cannot vest until the condition is actually proven to have failed. The 'possibility of reverter' is the only form of reversion interest that can truly be described as contingent and, like other contingent interests, really only constitutes a *potential* estate.

For example, Grandfather X conveys a fee simple estate to Y absolutely 'provided Y retains the period buildings on the property'. Y maintains these buildings for 10 years and then demolishes them. For the 10 years that Y has kept the buildings, Y holds a vested fee simple estate and X holds the possibility of a reverter. Once Y demolishes the buildings, his fee simple may be divested and, where this occurs, X acquires the fee simple as the estate reverts, in both title and possession, to X.

All reversion interests, whilst constituting future estates, must nevertheless be identical in status to the original estate held by the grantor. This is a consequence of the fact that, unlike the remainder estate, the reversion is an estate in abeyance, retained by the grantor until the expiration of the grantee's estate. Therefore, what reverts to the grantor must necessarily be identical in status to the estate which the grantor held in the first place: it cannot be a greater or lesser estate. By contrast, as the remainder interest is expressly created, it may consist of any type of estate provided it does not actually exceed the estate held by the original grantor.

For example, Grandfather X owns a fee simple and confers a life estate in land to Y which is to exist for the duration of X's life. Y transfers this life estate to son Z, who acquires a life estate *pur autre vie*, because it exists for the duration of X's life. When Z dies, if X is still alive, the life estate may pass to the estate of of Y under relevant 'wills' legislation. When X dies, however, the estate will revert in possession to the estate of X. The reversion interest must be a fee simple estate because that is what X originally held. This example should be distinguished from the following example: Grandfather X holds a life estate and confers it over to son Y for the duration of X's life. In this situation, X will retain no reversionary interest because the estate is to exist for the duration of X's life. If Y dies before X, the principles relating to the passing of life estates *pur autre vie* will apply. If X dies before Y, the estate will be completely determined because the original estate held by X was a life estate *sa vie*.

It is possible for a reversion interest to exist simultaneously with a remainder interest. This will arise where the grantor does not completely extinguish the estate. For example, Grandfather X owns the fee simple in land and conveys a life estate to son Y for the duration of Y's life, remainder to grandson Z for life. In this example, Y holds a life estate in possession; Z holds a life interest in remainder; and during the life of Y and Z, X holds a fee simple reversion which will vest in possession upon the death of Y and Z.

In the context of native title, the granting of a statutory lease by the Crown will not, according to the High Court in *Wik Peoples v Queensland*[22] result in the creation of a beneficial reversionary interest in the Crown. The mere exercise of sovereignty over the land by the Crown could not expand radical title into absolute beneficial title – hence, a reversionary estate cannot arise in the absence of a full and beneficial estate.[23]

3.5.2.5 *Determinable and condition subsequent estates*

All estates which are expressly created may be qualified by a condition, although reversionary interests occupy a special position ,which is discussed above. It is important to understand the nature of the condition, because there are different forms, and differing consequences will follow depending upon the form and nature of the condition imposed. Where a condition precedent exits, the interest cannot vest until the condition is satisfied. Where the condition attaches to but does not qualify the estate, it is important to

22 See *Wik Peoples v The State of Queensland* (1996) 141 ALR 129, *per* Toohey J, p 129; Gummow J, p 189; Gaudron J, p 155 and Kirby, pp 234–35.

23 See, also, *Lansen v Olney* (1999) 169 ALR 49.

determine the nature of the condition, because this will have an impact upon the consequences of non-compliance.

There are two primary forms of limitations which may be attached to an estate: determinable limitations and conditions subsequent. A determinable limitation defines the nature and boundaries of the estate itself. Where a determinable limitation applies to an estate and is not complied with, the estate of the grantee will automatically be divested and revert to the grantor. Until the point of non-compliance, the grantor merely holds a possibility of a reverter, and the grantee a potential estate.

Alternatively, a condition subsequent does not define the limits of the estate but is simply a supplementary qualification which, if not complied with, may, at the option of the grantor, result in the estate being divested. The estate is not, however, automatically divested; the grantor simply acquires the right to divest the estate.

For example, if Grandfather X grants a fee simple to son Y, provided Y 'uses the land for agricultural purposes', the qualification to the fee simple estate is likely to be conditional rather than determinable. The word 'provided' indicates that the estate is to be transferred to Y, and that condition is an additional limitation. This means that Y will hold a vested estate, capable of being divested if subsequently proven not to have been complied with. Alternatively, if Grandfather X grants a fee simple to Y 'for as long as Y continues to use the land for agricultural purposes', the qualification to the fee simple estate is likely to be determinable rather than conditional, because the words 'for as long as' indicate that the qualification marks the boundaries of the actual estate. If the land is not used for agricultural purposes, it is clear in the second example that X does not intend to vest the estate in Y, and it automatically reverts to X.

The distinction between determinable limitations and conditions subsequent is often very fine and can be based upon marginal semantic differences. Use of the words 'provided' or 'on condition that' rather than 'for as long as' or 'whilst the land is' are often the only grounds for distinguishing between each form of qualification, and yet this determination can have a dramatic impact upon the estate of the grantee. This was clearly highlighted in the decision of *Zapletal v Wright* [1957] Tas SR 211.

On the facts of that case, the plaintiff and the defendant lived together for about 15 years until 1955, when the plaintiff went off and married someone else. During the course of the 15 years, two children were born and the defendant purchased some land. The plaintiff did not actually contribute to the purchase, but the property was put in the names of both the purchaser and the defendant. It was determined that the defendant intended to make a gift of a joint interest in the property provided the plaintiff agreed to remain with him and that, if she ceased to live with him, her interest in the property should cease.

The issues for the court to determine were, first, what type of qualification this amounted to, and secondly, whether it was valid on grounds of public policy. The court referred to the distinction between a determinable limitation and a condition subsequent and noted its particular importance because:

> ... a condition subsequent void on a ground of illegality or because it is *contra bonos mores* [contrary to the accepted canons of decent behaviour] may be ignored leaving the primary gift good but a determinable limitation void for the same reason fails entirely.

On the facts, it was held that the condition was void on the grounds that it promoted immoral behaviour by encouraging the continuance of unmarried cohabitation. The court held, however, that, as the condition was a condition subsequent rather than a determinable limitation, the primary gift to the plaintiff remained intact. The court found the condition to constitute a condition subsequent, because the form of the condition was such that it did not denote the extent of the estate but, rather, listed the event whereby the estate which was conferred could be cut short.

3.5.3 Non-freehold estates: leasehold interest

Freehold estates are defined by the fact that they exist for an indefinite duration and confer the right to seisin upon the estate holder. The common law does, however, also recognise a further category of proprietary interests known as 'non-freehold' interests, which are solely comprised of 'leasehold interests'. Unlike freehold estates, leasehold interests are defined by the fact that they exist for a specified duration and will cease once that duration has expired. It does not matter how long the duration is; provided it is definite in time, a leasehold interest may be created. Hence a leasehold interest may exist for 99 years or it may exist for one month. As the leasehold exists for a specified period of time, upon its expiration, unless the original owner has granted the property to another party, the title will revert to the original owner. Hence, if the owner of the land, known as the 'lessor' or the 'landlord', grants a lease for five years and confers no other estate, the person holding the leasehold interest, known as the 'lessee' or 'tenant', will acquire a leasehold interest which exists for five years, and during this time, the landlord will retain a fee simple reversion. At the expiration of five years, the fee simple will automatically vest in the lessor.

Leasehold interests were traditionally classified as personal rather than real property. As a result, leasehold interests were never included within the category of estates and therefore were not subject to the categorisation of estates according to rights of inheritance, or the creation of successive estates through the limitation of an estate to a life and the conferral of future estates in remainder or reversion. The primary reason the treatment of leasehold interests as personal property lay in the fact that the lease was regarded as a contractual arrangement between the owner of the land and the tenant. Under this contract, the owner agreed to allow the tenant to use and occupy the land for a specified period in return for a periodic payment. There was no actual transfer of ownership, merely the conferral of a right to possession for a specified duration in accordance with mutually agreed contractual provisions. It was felt that this type of arrangement conferred personal rights between the parties rather than a freehold estate in land.

As a result, the lessee acquired a contractual right to possession of the land and the right to enforce the terms of the lease contract, but seisin remained with the landlord. The possession which the lessee held under the lease did not constitute seisin. Seisin could only exist where a person was in possession of a freehold estate in land or in receipt of rent from a lessee occupying the land. Consequently, a tenant who held under a leasehold interest did not have the right to bring a real action to recover possession of the land where dispossessed. Where wrongfully dispossessed, a tenant was left with a personal action for damages.

Eventually, however, as discussed in Chapter 1, courts began to recognise new forms of remedies allowing dispossessed tenants to recover possession. By about the end of the 15th century, the writ of ejectment was established, whereby a dispossessed tenant could recover possession of the land over which he held a lease by issuing ejectment against the wrongful occupant on the grounds of trespass.[24] Eventually, as discussed in Chapter 2, the writ of ejectment was also used to protect holders of freehold estates, in place of the old, complex and cumbersome real actions.

The evolution of the writ of ejectment effectively conferred real property characteristics upon personal, non-freehold leasehold interests. To accommodate this change, courts divided the category of chattels into two sub-categories: chattels personal and chattels real. The leasehold interest was subsequently referred to and categorised as chattels real, emphasising both its contractual and proprietary characteristics. (See, also, the discussion in Chapter 1.)

In modern society, the distinction between freehold and non-freehold estates has diminished and has little practical value. The most obvious effect of the historical demarcation today lies in the fact that the creation of leasehold interests involves contractual negotiations as to the terms and conditions of the lease and confers continuing contractual relations. All leasehold interests are governed by contractual provisions which regulate the rights and obligations of the landlord and tenant during the period of the lease, making careful negotiation, particularly for large commercial leases, an

24 For a general discussion of the writ of trespass and ejectment, see, generally, Plucknett, TFT, *A Concise History of the Common Law*, 5th edn, 1956, OUP, pp 562–74.

important requirement. By comparison, freehold estates are generally created through the execution of appropriate transfer documents, with full payment for the estate being issued upon the proper execution of the transfer, with contractual relations ceasing after execution and payment. (See *Chan v Cresdon* (1989) 64 ALJR 111.)

As the creation of the leasehold interest is based upon contractual negotiation, the lessor has the power to determine the terms and conditions upon which the transfer of possession is leased. The scope and nature of the lease will depend upon the mutual agreement between the lessor and lessee, and there is no need for specific words of limitation, although a clear intention to confer exclusive possession upon the tenant for a specified duration of time must be apparent (*Radaich v Smith* (1959) 101 CLR 209). A further consequence of the personal, contractual nature of the lease is that the obligations under the lease contract will only bind the lessor and lessee, and not third parties who are not privy to the contract (unless they constitute 'restrictive' land covenants: see Chapter 12). Hence, if a lessor or lessee wishes to assign the lease to a third party, it is advisable to draw up a new lease contract to ensure that the rights and obligations of the lease agreement are enforceable against the third party assignee. (For a more detailed discussion on leases, see Chapter 15.)

CHAPTER 4

ADVERSE POSSESSION

4.1 The nature of adverse possession

Possessory title confers a good title upon the holder and is enforceable against the entire world except for the true owner. In some cases, however, possessory title over land can be held for such a long period of time that the true owner is precluded under the limitations of actions legislation from bringing an action to recover possession of that land. Such a prohibition effectively results in the possessor acquiring what is called an 'adverse possession' of the land. There are a number of justifications for imposing a limit upon the length of time that land owners may take in exercising their proprietary rights when dispossessed, the first and most important being that it is in the public interest to encourage certainty and predictability in land ownership. Where a person has taken possession of land to the exclusion of the real owner, and made that land his home for a significant period of time without interruption, the possessors should be entitled to a certain peace of mind. If the owner has failed to enforce proprietary title against such possessors, whether it be due to negligence or mere tardiness, public interest requirements favour the possessor against the owner so that the owner loses the right to regain possession. This reasoning is well highlighted in the classic words of Sir Thomas Plumer MR in *Marquis Cholmondeley v Lord Clinton* (1820) 2 Jac & W 1; 37 ER 527, p 577: 'It is better that the negligent owner who has omitted to assert his right within the prescribed period should lose his right than that an opening should be given to interminable litigation.'

The second justification underlies the whole premise of imposing limitations upon legal actions: it is desirable that the possibility of litigation should not loom indefinitely. There should be a period when the right to bring an action ceases. Such time restrictions are beneficial in two significant ways: they tend to encourage prompt action, so reducing the possibility of evidential uncertainties, and they prevent the courts from being clogged up with outdated suits.

Finally, and perhaps most importantly, the law should not be seen to thwart the legitimate expectations of occupants. To allow a possessory title holder to be defeated by a true owner after years of occupying and developing the land as his home, paying rates and looking after or improving the land, would be patently unfair and would undoubtedly cause significant hardship.

In balancing the competing considerations, the policy has always been to protect the interests of a patient possessor against those of a tardy owner.[1]

Where the limitation period has expired and the possessor acquires adverse possession of the land, the title of the true owner is effectively extinguished and the rights usually associated with ownership are no longer enforceable. The possessor attains a form of ownership, not through the positive conferral of proprietary title, but rather through the extinguishment of the true owner's right to claim repossession of the land.

4.2 Statutory provisions

The limitation period which applies to the enforcement of rights over land varies amongst the states. In Victoria and South Australia, the period is 15 years.[2] In New South Wales, Western Australia, Tasmania and Queensland, the limitation period for land is 12 years.[3] The limitation periods in each of these states remain current.

Where adverse possession is sought to be enforced against Crown land, there are different provisions in each state. It is only in Tasmania and New South Wales that adverse possession can actually be claimed against the Crown, and in these states the limitation period is 30 years.[4] In Tasmania, however, adverse possession may not be claimed against the Crown in particular circumstances, including cases where land has been compulsorily acquired for council purposes. In Victoria, Western Australia and Queensland, adverse possession cannot be raised against the Crown at all.[5] Where the Crown transfers land to an individual, the limitation period may commence, and in Victoria, the period will be 15 years from the date of the transfer.[6] Where there are no specific provisions dealing with Crown lands, it would seem that the Crown Suits Act 1769 (Imp) will apply, and this states that the Crown may be barred by adverse possession after a period of 60 years.

The reason for conferring special provisions for adverse possession against Crown land lies in the fact that the Crown owns large amounts of land, and it is difficult and time consuming to keep up to date with the state of these lands. In order to prevent large pieces of land being claimed by adverse

1 See Irving, DK, 'Should the law recognise the acquisition of title by adverse possession?' (1994) 2 Australian Property Law Journal 112.

2 Limitation of Actions Act 1958 (Vic), ss 8, 15, 18 and 20; Limitations of Actions Act 1936 (SA), s 4.

3 Limitation of Actions Act 1969 (NSW), s 27(2); Limitation of Actions Act 1935 (WA), s 4; Limitation of Actions Act 1974 (Tas), s 10(2); Limitation of Actions Act 1974 (Qld), s 13.

4 Limitation of Actions Act 1969 (NSW), s 27(1); Limitation of Actions Act 1974 (Tas), s 10(4)–(6).

5 Limitation of Actions Act 1958 (Vic), s 7; Limitation of Actions Act 1935 (WA), s 36; Limitation of Actions Act 1974 (Qld), s 6(4).

6 Limitation of Actions Act 1958 (Vic), s 8.

possession, statute either prohibits its application or greatly extends the limitation period.

4.3 When the limitation period commences

Most legislative provisions set out that the limitation period will commence at the point when the owner has been either dispossessed or has discontinued possession and a third person has taken up actual possession. Dispossession is used to imply a physical ejection from the land by the possessor, whereas discontinuance suggests that an owner has discontinued possession and a third party has subsequently assumed possession. If an owner holds a future right over land, the limitation period can only begin to commence against that person once the right to possession has vested.

For example, if X passes on all of her estate and property to Y in her will, the limitation period will commence against Y as soon as X dies and probate is administered. In Victoria, if an occupier remains on the estate for a period of 15 years from the date of X's death, the occupier may claim adverse possession.

Dispossession implies an act of force. Generally, owners who have been dispossessed have not done so of their own accord but, rather, have been forcibly removed. It is quite rare to raise adverse possession on the basis of a dispossession, because, in such a case, the owners are usually well aware of the fact that a third party has taken possession of their property and act promptly to enforce their rights. More commonly, adverse possession will arise where the true owner has discontinued his possession leaving the land vacant and thereby making it possible for a third person to take possession: *Rains v Buxton* (1880) 14 Ch D 537.

For example, X holds a fee simple over rural land in Victoria and decides to move out of the property, leaving it vacant, in 1980. Y discovers the land and subsequently moves in, taking control of the property, in 1982. In 1997, X brings an action for recovery of the land against Y. However, Y claims adverse possession. In this example, the limitation period will commence in 1982, because this is the year when Y assumed possession of vacant land. Provided it can be proven that Y's possession is adverse, by 1997 Y will acquire a possessory title which cannot be defeated by X.

If an owner of land, who has been dispossessed, or who has discontinued possession, passes the land on to a third party assignee, the third party will be in the same position as the previous owner. Hence, the third party assignee will take the land subject to the accrued possessory rights of the adverse possessor.[7]

7 Limitation of Actions Act 1958 (Vic), s 10(3); Limitation of Actions Act 1935 (WA), s 7; Limitation of Actions Act 1974 (Qld), s 15(3); Limitation of Actions Act 1974 (Tas), s 12(5).

The courts have not focused upon a strict determination of the meaning of dispossession or discontinuance in the legislative provisions, as the primary consideration has been the determination of whether the possession is 'adverse' in the circumstances. Nevertheless, it is important to establish the starting date in order to ensure that the appropriate time period has expired. The limitation period commences not just from the date of discontinuance or dispossession, but from the date when, as a result of either of these states, a third party 'adversely' possesses the land.

4.3.1 *The meaning of adverse possession*

Adverse possession refers to a particular form of land possession which must be distinguished from mere occupation. In order to establish adverse possession, it must first be established that the individual has, in fact, taken possession of the land and that this possession demonstrates a degree of physical control that is open rather than secret, peaceful rather than forceful, and without the actual consent of the true owner (*Mulcahy v Curramore Pty Ltd* [1974] 2 NSWLR 464, particularly p 475). Furthermore, it must be established that the person in occupation actually intended to possess the land adversely (*Riley v Pentilla* [1974] VR 547). It is important to establish the requisite intention or *animus possidendi*, because an accidental or unintentional possession will not constitute an *adverse* possession. The determination of these factors forms the foundation of an adverse possession claim. The mere fact that an individual has occupied land for the specified limitation period is not enough to permanently preclude the rights of the true owner. The significant consequences of an adverse possession claim upon the true owner, make it vital that the possession in issue be proven to be 'adverse' rather than merely fortuitous.

The acquisition of title by way of adverse possession must be distinguished from the acquisition of title through long standing use. This corresponds with the distinction between prescription and limitation. Title by prescription confers the right to possession where the possessor has used the land continually for a period of at least 20 years, whereas title by limitation may be described as a wrongful possession which, due to its character and length, precludes the true owner from enforcing his or her rights (*Buckinghamshire CC v Moran* [1989] 2 All ER 225). Unlike prescriptive rights, where a person acquires an actual right to possession, and the focus is upon the acts and intention of the true owner, under limitation, the conduct and intention of the possessor is the decisive factor in the determination. For a further discussion on prescriptive rights, see Chapter 13, at para 13.4.5.

4.3.2 *Factual possession*

A possessor must prove that he or she has satisfied the requisite degree of physical possession over the land. It must be proven that the possessor has actually taken control over the entirety of the land and that this control is apparent and contrary to the consent of the true owner. As noted by Slade LJ in *Powell v McFarlane* (1977) 38 P & CR 452, pp 470–71:

> Factual possession signifies an appropriate degree of physical control. It must be a single and exclusive possession ... an owner of land and a person intruding on that land without his consent cannot both be in possession of the land at the same time. The question what acts constitute a sufficient degree of exclusive physical control must depend on the circumstances, in particular the nature of the land and the manner in which land of that nature is commonly used or enjoyed.

Clearly, if the true owner has given permission in the form of a licence or a lease for a person to be in possession of the land, the possession cannot constitute adverse possession (*Hughes v Griffin* [1969] 1 WLR 23). The limitation period for adverse possession may only commence where the permission has either ceased or has been withdrawn and the person remains in possession without consent.

Furthermore, the possession must amount to more than a mere occupation of the property. The possessor must prove that he or she has possessed the property in a manner which is directly inconsistent with the rights of the true owner. The occasional use of land, for example, as a convenient short cut or for other recreational purposes will not constitute adverse possession where it is not inconsistent with and does not interfere with the purpose for which the true owner intended to use the land (*Leigh v Jack* (1879) 5 Ex D 264). The question of the requisite degree of physical control was raised in *George Wimpey and Co Ltd v Sohn* [1967] Ch 487. On the facts of that case, the issue was whether or not the applicant had adversely possessed a hotel garden. The applicant was the purchaser of the hotel adjacent to the garden and, along with neighbouring lots, acquired an easement over the hotel garden when the hotel was initially purchased. The garden was subsequently fenced completely in order to protect it from the public, but not to exclude the rights of the easement holders. The Court of Appeal held that the fencing was insufficient to constitute adverse possession because it was erected as a safeguard from the public and, as the easement holders retained access, was not inconsistent with their rights.

In some instances, however, the fencing of land may be sufficient to constitute adverse possession. For example, in *Buckinghamshire CC v Moran* [1989] 2 All ER 225, the defendant owned a block of land and the plaintiff council owned the adjacent block. The defendant had used the council land by enclosing it with a fence and a locked gate over the only access to the land and parking a horse float on the land. The defendant effectively used the land as an extension of his own land. The court held that the defendant, by fencing off the land, had gained full physical control over the land to the exclusion of the true owner. Consequently, at the expiration of the limitation period, the defendant was able to claim adverse possession over the land.

Factual possession may not be raised in circumstances where, despite a clear possession of the land in issue, it is not directly inconsistent with the purposes for which the owner uses the land. For example, where land is used to graze livestock and a neighbouring person's livestock roams onto the land to feed, the intrusion will only interfere with the owner's purposes where the amount of livestock is so great that it effectively displaces the existing livestock (*Powell v McFarlane* (1977) 38 P & CR 452, especially p 478). If the owner of land is not using it for any present purpose but has future plans, a person may take full possession of the land during this period, and it will not constitute adverse possession until the future date is reached. For example, in *Leigh v Jack* (1879) 5 Ex D 264, the defendant's acts of placing garbage onto the plaintiff's land, which was intended to be developed in the future as a roadway, did not constitute a factual possession of the land. In the words of Cockburn CJ in that case:

> I do not think that any of the defendant's acts were done with the view of defeating the purpose of the parties to the conveyances; his acts were those of a man who did not intend to be a trespasser, or to infringe upon another's right. The defendant simply used the land until the time should come for carrying out the object originally contemplated.

Of course, what this meant was that where an owner of land has no present purpose for the land – only future plans – the land cannot be adversely possessed prior to these plans being instigated. Older English decisions concluded that this was a desirable result because, in such circumstances, the owner had effectively conferred implied permission to the possessor and, consequently, the possession was not adverse (*Wallis's Cayton Bay Holiday Camp Ltd v Shell-Mex and BP Ltd* [1975] QB 94). Subsequent legislation abrogates the 'implied permission' line of authority (Sched 1, para 8(4) of the Limitation Act 1980 (UK)) and the tenor of recent cases has also moved away from it (*Powell v McFarlane* (1977) 38 P & CR 452). Exactly what constitutes an act of adverse possession will depend upon the individual circumstances. The type of acts, the extent of the occupation and the degree of inconsistency necessary to constitute adverse possession will vary in each case. Despite earlier authority, recent cases are no longer stringently adhering to the rule that acts of possession must be directly inconsistent with the purpose for which the owner intends to use the land. In *Quach v Marrickville Municipal Council (Nos 1 and 2)* (1991) 22 NSWLR 55, the plaintiffs owned land over which the local council had acquired a small reserve for the purposes of drainage pursuant to s 398 of the Local Government Act 1919 (NSW). Neither the council nor the plaintiffs were aware of the effect of this legislation. The plaintiffs were in occupation of the land since 1956 and claimed adverse possession of the drainage reserve. During the course of his judgment, Young J emphasised the importance of determining each form of possession according to the individual circumstances, and, in this regard, referred to the decision of *Lord Advocate v Lord Lovat* (1880) 5 App Cas 272, where it was noted that the question of what constitutes a sufficient possession to establish adverse possession:

> ... must be considered in every case with reference to the peculiar circumstances ... the acts implying possession in one case may be wholly inadequate to prove it in another. The character and value of the property, the suitable and natural mode of using it, the course of conduct which the proprietor might reasonably be expected to follow with regard to his own interests – all these things, greatly varying as they must, under various conditions, are to be taken into account in determining the sufficiency of a possession.

On the facts of *Quach*, his Honour held that there was no need to prove categorically that the acts of the possessor are directly inconsistent with those of the true owner. A possessor may carry out acts over a certain part of the land which are adverse in nature without those acts directly conflicting with the owner's rights. In this case, it seemed that the very fact that the land had been fully occupied for 34 years without the council having made a claim to the drainage reserve was sufficient to establish the adverse possession claims.

4.3.3 *Intention to possess: animus possidendi*

Apart from proving the relevant degree of factual possession, in order to establish adverse possession it is also necessary to prove that the possessor intends to possess the land to the exclusion of the rest of the world (*Powell v McFarlane* (1977) 38 P & CR 452). The intention which a possessor must prove focuses upon exclusion of the rest of the world and it is not necessary to prove that the possessor intended actually to own the land. As noted by Slade LJ in *Powell v McFarlane*:

> ... the *animus possidendi* involves the intention, in one's own name and on one's own behalf, to exclude the world at large, including the owner with the paper title if he be not himself the possessor, so far as is reasonably practicable and so far as the processes of the law will allow.

Intention is an extremely important element of the adverse possession claim. If a person takes possession of land, without intending to exclude the rest of the world, and allows third parties to roam freely over the property without incurring any recourse, it cannot be said that the possession was intended to be adverse. For example, in *Riley v Pentilla* [1974] VR 547, the defendants claimed adverse possession over land in a communal park which they had enclosed for the purposes of constructing a tennis court and garden. The defendant had built the tennis court with wire netting, fencing and gates at each end, which were not locked. The court held that enclosing the tennis court and garden did not evince an intention to exclude the rest of the world and therefore the possession did not constitute adverse possession. The erection of high fences around the tennis court was necessary for the purposes of the game itself, and the fences were not built to preclude other people from using the courts and the gardens. Furthermore, the surrounding owners had been expressly invited to make use of the recreational facilities constructed.

Acts of possession which do point towards adverse possession include the complete and secure enclosure of the land, the construction of a sign declaring the property to be 'private', or the construction of a security device around the property to ward off third parties and the payment of rates and taxes owing on the land (*George Wimpey & Co Ltd v Sohn* [1966] 1 All ER 232). It is not necessary to prove that the possessor is in sole occupation to establish the requisite intention. However, if others are shown to be using the land, they must prove either an express or an implied licence or authorised permission from the adverse possessor (*Petkov v Lucerne Nominees Pty Ltd* (1992) 7 WAR 163).

It has been generally accepted that the intention to exclude must be apparent to the world at large. Whilst there is no need to directly communicate such intention, the acts of possession should make this intention obvious to the rest of the world (*Powell v McFarlane* (1977) 38 P & CR 452). Where a possessor has securely enclosed the property and erected signs warning trespassers and informing the world that the land is private, the intention will be publicly apparent. Other acts of possession which are not patently obvious but which, when investigated, clearly reveal such intention, will generally be acceptable. For example, in some cases, the payment of rates and taxes is sufficient to establish adverse possession (*Kirby v Cowderoy* [1912] AC 599).

A more debatable issue is whether or not the intention to exclude must include an express intention to exclude the true owner. Older cases have suggested that the possessor must intend to exclude the whole world, including the documentary owner: (*Clement v Jones* (1909) 8 CLR 133; *Powell v McFarlane* (1977) 38 P & CR 452). It has, however, been argued that this requirement is inconsistent with the underlying rationale of the intention test.[8] The intention test considers the objective of the possessor when taking possession of the land. In cases where the true owner has discontinued possession, the possessor may either have not thought about the true owner or, eventually, believed himself to have become the true owner. This point was raised by Murray J in *Petkov v Lucerne Nominees Pty Ltd* (1992) 7 WAR 163:

> The mental element in the requisite intention to possess will also be of great importance, but must be understood. When the law speaks of an intention to exclude the world at large, including the true owner, it does not mean that there must be a conscious intention to exclude the true owner. What is required is an intention to exercise exclusive control.

8 See, generally, Dockray, MS, 'Adverse possession and intention – I' [1982] Conv 256.

To satisfy the *animus possidendi* test, a clear and unequivocal intention to exercise exclusive control over the whole of the land in issue must be established; however, additional proof that the possessor intended specifically to exclude the true owner is extraneous and rarely raised as a separate requirement by the courts.

4.4 Adverse possession against different forms of ownership

Where an applicant claims adverse possession against the true owner of land, it is important to consider how the land is owned and, if the ownership is fragmented and there are a number of different types of interests over the land, which interest holders will be affected by such a claim. Adverse possession will not debar all interest holders from seeking to enforce their proprietary rights. The case is straightforward where the land is owned absolutely by a single individual who holds a fee simple. In such a case, adverse possession will result in the owner being completely prohibited from enforcing his or her proprietary rights. The position will vary, however, against other, less absolute, forms of ownership.

4.4.1 Future interests

Future interests, as discussed in Chapter 3, are interests in land which confer a present title but do not vest in possession until a future date. As the nature of adverse possession is based upon possession which is *adverse* to the true owner, it cannot operate against the holder of a future interest until that interest vests in possession. Effectively, then, adverse possession can only be enforced against or interest where the right to possession has vested; it cannot be raised against future interests.

For example, if X holds a life estate in land for the duration of X's life and Y holds a fee simple remainder, a possessor may adversely possess the life estate of X. After the required limitation period, X will be prohibited from enforcing his or her proprietary rights. Once X dies, however, Y's estate will vest and Y may recover the land against the possessor. The limitation period will commence against Y as soon as X dies and Y is vested in possession.

In some Australian states, the limitation period which may apply against a future interest which has vested in possession has been reduced. Section 10(2) of the Limitation of Actions Act 1958 (Vic) sets out that a future interest holder has either 15 years from the date on which the right of action accrued to the holder of the preceding estate (that is, 15 years from when the previous owner was ousted) or six years from the date when the future interest vests in possession, whichever is the longer. Equivalent provisions are also apparent in other states.[9]

9 Limitation of Actions Act 1974 (Tas), s 12(2); Limitation of Actions Act 1935 (WA), s 7; Limitation of Actions Act 1974 (Qld), s 15(2).

Where a person holds both a present estate and a future interest, it will only be necessary for an adverse possessor to dispossess the person of the present estate. In such a case, the future interest may not vest in possession unless the possessor has, in the interim, been dispossessed of the land.

4.4.2 *Leasehold interests*

A leasehold interest is a non-freehold interest conferring the right to exclusive possession of the land for a limited period of time. Where a lessee is dispossessed of land which he or she holds under a current lease, the lessee will acquire a right to recover the land and, if the land is not recovered within the limitation period, adverse possession may be claimed. Adverse possession against a tenant is, however, a rare occurrence because of the fact that the lease will usually have expired within the limitation period.

Of greater interest is the issue of adverse possession against a landlord. A stranger may dispossess a tenant and, upon the expiration of the lease, the limitation period may commence against the landlord. As the landlord holds a reversion interest in the land for the duration of the lease, the limitation period for adverse possession cannot commence until the lease expires and the landlord is vested in possession. Furthermore, in Victoria and Tasmania, the reduced statutory limitation period applicable to future interests does not apply.[10] Where a lessee claims adverse possession against a landlord, the limitation period cannot commence until the lease expires and the lessee is no longer paying rent. A tenancy at will shall be deemed to have expired one year from its creation, and a periodic tenancy shall expire at the end of the particular period.[11]

4.4.3 *Trusts*

A trust, as is discussed in Chapter 5, is defined as the separation of legal and equitable estate. The trustee holds the legal estate over the property for the benefit of the beneficiary who holds an equitable interest in the property. The equitable interest represents an enforceable *in rem* right over the trust property; the beneficiary may enforce his proprietary rights in certain circumstances. However, generally, until the trust vests, actual possession of the trust property will remain with the trustee.

---

10 Limitation of Actions Act 1958 (Vic), s 10(1); Limitation of Actions Act 1935 (WA), s 7; Limitation of Actions Act 1974 (Qld), s 15(1); Limitation of Actions Act 1974 (Tas), s 12(1); Limitation of Actions Act 1969 (NSW), s 31; Limitations of Actions Act 1936 (SA), s 9.

11 Limitation of Actions Act 1958 (Vic), s 13(1); Limitation of Actions Act 1935 (WA), s 9; Limitation of Actions Act 1974 (Qld), s 18; Limitation of Actions Act 1974 (Tas), s 15; Limitation of Actions Act 1969 (NSW), s 34; Limitations of Actions Act 1936 (SA), s 15.

A trustee of land cannot adversely possess the land. The trustee holds the property for the benefit of the beneficiary and the equitable duty of the trustee prevents the possession from becoming adverse in nature. Furthermore, a beneficiary seeking to enforce his or her rights against the land will not generally be bound by limitation periods where the trustee has committed a fraudulent breach or trust property is retained or converted by the trustee.[12] The fraud does not have to be intentionally dishonest, although it must be proven that the trustee has, in some way, been privy to it. For other breaches of trust, including innocent breaches of trust, a beneficiary has six years to bring an action against the trustee. Alternatively, the beneficiary must prove that the trustee has retained possession of the trust property, having converted such property to his or her own use. Where this can be proven, the limitation period will not apply. The position is slightly different in New South Wales where, pursuant to s 47 of the Limitation of Actions Act 1969, a limitation period of 12 years applies from the date when the beneficiary either does establish a cause of action or could have discovered such a cause if he or she had acted with reasonable diligence.

Where no statutory limitation period applies, it is still possible for the general equitable discretion to preclude a right of action from being enforced. Where a plaintiff has taken too long to enforce his or her rights (the doctrine of laches) or acquiesced to a violation of his or her rights, equity may effectively impose its own limitation period and preclude the equitable interest holder from enforcing his or her rights.

A third party stranger may make an adverse possession claim against a trust and the usual limitation periods will apply. The legal title of a trustee may be statute barred where all of the beneficial interests have been barred.[13] Where a beneficial title has not been barred, the legal title of the trustee will be preserved for as long as the beneficiary retains the right to recover the land.

4.5 Interference with the limitation period

Particular conduct carried out by a possessor may result in a temporary or permanent interference with the limitation period. Obviously, where the possessor confirms that the true owner holds the best title, the possession will cease to be adverse. Similarly, where the true owner discovers the possessor and an agreement is made whereby the possessor remains with the permission of the true owner, the possession will cease to be adverse. Where possession has been abandoned, the limitation period will stop running

12 Limitation of Actions Act 1958 (Vic), s 21(1); Limitation of Actions Act 1935 (WA), s 47(1); Limitation of Actions Act 1974 (Qld), s 27(1); Limitation of Actions Act 1974 (Tas), s 24(1); Limitations of Actions Act 1936 (SA), s 32(1).

13 Limitation of Actions Act 1958 (Vic), s 11(2); Limitation of Actions Act 1974 (Qld), s 16(2); Limitation of Actions Act 1974 (Tas), s 13(3); Limitation of Actions Act 1969 (NSW), s 37.

altogether. Where the possessor has been involved in some fraud, or the true owner has a disability precluding enforcement of his or her rights, the limitation period will be suspended. Each of these circumstances is considered below.

4.5.1 *Abandonment*

Where a possessor abandons possession of the land prior to the expiration of the limitation period, the possessor will automatically lose all accrued time, and the true owner will revert to the position he or she was in prior to the possession. Once an abandonment has occurred, a possessor cannot reclaim possession for the remainder of the limitation period (*Mulcahy v Curramore Pty Ltd* [1974] 2 NSWLR 464).

In order to prove abandonment, it must be established that the possessor has completely vacated the land. The fact that the possessor is temporarily away, or has a short absence from the land, will not necessarily mean that he or she has abandoned the land. What needs to be proven is that the possessor has actually deserted any claim he or she may have had to the property and can no longer be described as an 'adverse possessor'.

4.5.2 *Disability and fraud*

Where the true owner is under a disability so that, in effect, he may be unaware of the adverse possession of his land, the limitation period will be suspended in order to give him adequate time to assert his legal rights. Disability is defined in the legislation to include a person under 18 years old; a person impaired by reason of a disabilitating medical or physical disease; or, in some states, a person who has been imprisoned.[14] Where a disability is established, there are differing provisions according to each state. In Victoria, Tasmania, Western Australia and Queensland, a person who has a proven disability at the date when possession is assumed will have the limitation period, if accrued, suspended from taking effect until the disability expires. Once the disability expires, that person will have six years in which to enforce his or her rights before adverse possession may be claimed.[15]

This should be distinguished from the position in New South Wales and South Australia, where the disability may be proven to exist at the date when possession is assumed and the true owner acquires a cause of action, or the

14 Limitation of Actions Act 1958 (Vic), s 3(2); Limitation of Actions Act 1935 (WA), s 16; Limitation of Actions Act 1974 (Qld), s 5(2); Limitation of Actions Act 1974 (Tas), s 2(2); Limitation of Actions Act 1969 (NSW), s 11(3)(a); Limitations of Actions Act 1936 (SA), s 45(2).

15 Limitation of Actions Act 1958 (Vic), s 23(1); Limitation of Actions Act 1935 (WA), s 16; Limitation of Actions Act 1974 (Qld), s 29(1); Limitation of Actions Act 1974 (Tas), s 26(1).

disability may arise during the limitation period. In either case, the limitation period will be suspended until the disability ceases and, whilst there is no express limitation of six years for the true owner to enforce his or her rights, no limitation period may, in any circumstances, be extended to more than 30 years from the date when the cause of action arose.[16]

Where fraud or a fraudulent concealment as to either the nature of the cause of action or the existence of such a cause can be proven, the limitation period will be suspended until the true owner either discovers this fraud, or should, with reasonable diligence, have discovered it.[17] Whilst fraud, for the purposes of this section, is not expressly defined, it would seem that some form of dishonesty must be established. It is not necessary to prove actual deceit; if it can be proven that giving effect to the limitation period is inequitable or unconscionable, this will probably suffice (*Tito v Waddell (No 2)* [1977] Ch 106).

4.6 Consequences of adverse possession

Before the expiration of the limitation period, a person in possession holds a mere possessory title. Such title, whilst not proprietary in nature, is enforceable against the rest of the world except for the true owner, and may be transferred or devised. At the expiration of the limitation period, the title of the adverse possessor, whilst still possessory, is far stronger. It is a title founded upon possession which, due to the expiration of the limitation period, acquires proprietary characteristics; it is enforceable against the whole world, including the true owner, who is prohibited from claiming repossession of the land under the terms of the limitations legislation. An adverse possessor's title arises negatively rather than positively because the possessor does not have the title transferred to her directly but, rather, acquires a right through the extinguishment of the true owner's title.

The adverse possessor's title, whilst extinguishing that of the true owner, will not affect rights acquired by third parties over the land. In particular, intangible rights, such as easements, will not be extinguished through adverse possession. This is expressly provided for in the legislation, because the definition of land to which the legislation applies does not include incorporeal hereditaments.[18]

Following the expiration of the limitation period and proof that the possession is adverse, the title of the true owner is extinguished. This is clearly

16 Limitation of Actions Act 1969 (NSW), ss 51 and 52; Limitations of Actions Act 1936 (SA), s 45(1) and (3).

17 Limitation of Actions Act 1958 (Vic), s 27; Limitation of Actions Act 1974 (Qld), s 38; Limitation of Actions Act 1974 (Tas), s 32; Limitation of Actions Act 1969 (NSW), s 55.

18 Limitation of Actions Act 1958 (Vic), s 3(1); Limitation of Actions Act 1935 (WA), s 3; Limitation of Actions Act 1974 (Qld), s 5(1); Limitation of Actions Act 1974 (Tas), s 2(1); Limitation of Actions Act 1969 (NSW), s 11(1); Limitations of Actions Act 1936 (SA), s 3(1).

set out in the legislation.[19] As the limitation defence is a personal defence, it must be emphasised that it will only be the true owner who holds an immediate right to possession who will have his title barred. The title may still be enforceable against other third parties. For example, where an adverse possessor dispossesses a person holding a fee simple with a mortgage over the land, the owner cannot enforce his rights against the adverse possessor, but he may still enforce his proprietary rights under the mortgage contract.

4.6.1 Right to alienate

An adverse possessor will acquire a title capable of being devised, bequeathed, transferred or sold. As discussed in Chapter 2, possessory title is capable of being passed on or otherwise alienated (*Asher v Whitlock* (1865) LR 1 QB 1; *Perry v Clissold* [1907] AC 73). Prior to the expiration of the limitation period, the title of an adverse possessor is merely possessory, hence, if the possessor abandons, surrenders or loses possession, the title will be extinguished and cannot be alienated. After the expiration of the limitation period, the title of an adverse possessor cannot be extinguished against the true owner, and even if the possessor abandons, surrenders or loses possession, the true owner will be unable to enforce his or her proprietary rights over the land. The scope of the rights and title of an adverse possessor were discussed by Lord Radcliffe in *Fairweather v St Marylebone Property Co Ltd* [1963] AC 510, where his Lordship stated that an adverse possessor:

> ... is in possession by his own right, so far as it is a right: and it is a right so far as the statutes of limitation which govern the matter prescribe, both when the rights to dispossess him are to be treated as accruing and when, having accrued, they are thereafter to be treated as barred. In other words a squatter has as much protection as, but no more protection than, the statutes allow: but he has not the title or estate of the owner or owners whom he has dispossessed, nor has he, in any relevant sense, an estate 'commensurate' with the estate of the dispossessed. All that this misleading phrase can mean is that, since his possession only defeats the rights of those to whom it has been adverse, there may be rights not prescribed against, such, for instance, as equitable easements, which are no less enforceable against him in respect of the land than they would have been against the owners he has dispossessed.

In *Markfield Investments Ltd v Evans* (2000) Court of Appeal (Civil Division) November 9, the court considered the question whether the mere fact of issuing and serving proceedings for the recovery of land stops time running in favour of the adverse possessor. Simon Brown LJ noted that if proceedings to recover land are begun before the expiration of the requisite adverse possession period, it could not be a correct reading of the legislation to hold

19 Limitation of Actions Act 1958 (Vic), s 11(1); Limitation of Actions Act 1935 (WA), s 24; Limitation of Actions Act 1974 (Qld), s 16; Limitation of Actions Act 1974 (Tas), s 13(1); Limitation of Actions Act 1969 (NSW), s 36; Limitations of Actions Act 1936 (SA), ss 31–32.

that the title of the owner of the land is extinguished while an action for the recovery of the land is still pending. His Honour felt that, consistent with the approach of Lord Radcliffe in *Fairweather v St Marylebone Property Co Ltd*, if the action is commenced prior to the expiration of the adverse possession period and the action is unsuccessful, it will not extinguish the adverse possession claim and the time will continue on rather than starting afresh (*Mount Carmel Ltd v Peter Thurlow Ltd* [1988] 3 All ER 129), whereas if the action is successful, adverse possession will be immediately extinguished. The mere bringing of an action for the recovery in itself will not automatically stop time running for the adverse possessor – were it otherwise, all the true owner would have to do to avoid adverse possession claims is issue and serve a writ every 12 years without more.

4.6.2 *Multiple possessors*

Where successive adverse possessors occupy property continuously, without losing possession, the limitation period of each possessor may be added together, so that the person in possession at the expiration of the limitation period will acquire adverse possession over the land. It does not matter that each possessor is unrelated, nor that a great number of possessors have occupied the land over the limitation period. If the possession in each case is adverse, and is proven to be continuous and uninterrupted, adverse possession may be raised (*Mulcahy v Curramore Pty Ltd* [1974] 2 NSWLR 464). The reason that the person in possession at the expiration of the limitation period acquires adverse possession, rather than the previous possessors, is because the title held by each of the previous possessors is purely possessory and will not become adverse until the accumulated period of time satisfies the limitation period. It is not necessary for an individual possessor expressly to pass on his possessory title to a successive possessor. If the possession is proven to be continuous, the transferral of possessory title is automatically assumed (*Mulcahy v Curramore Pty Ltd* [1974] 2 NSWLR 464).

Continuous and uninterrupted possession will be assumed where it can be established that each possessor has remained in occupation of the property, and there has been no interim period where the property was abandoned or possession was discontinued prior to a third party resuming possession. Where each possessor is dispossessed by a successive possessor, continuous and uninterrupted possession may be established. Similarly, where a possessor abandons or forfeits the land to a successor, provided the resumption of possession is immediate, continuous and uninterrupted possession may also be established.

In *London Borough of Lambeth v Bigden and Others* (2000) Court of Appeal (Civil Division), 1 December, Mummery LJ concluded that a multiple, continuous and uninterrupted possession cannot exist where a property is occupied via a series of disjointed, ad hoc possessions with no consensual arrangement regulating subsequent possession and no clearly established joint or communal control over the possession. In Australia, the emphasis is upon continuous possession – there is no requirement for consensual regulation of that possession and indeed, the nature and purpose of the possession has been found to be irrelevant. Hence, in *Shaw v Garbutt* [1997] NSW Conv R 56-277, Young J in the New South Wales Supreme Court held that it is possible to combine the period of occupation of a series of trespassers who do not derive title from each other – provided the possession is continuous and adverse.

4.7 Adverse possession and the Torrens system

The Torrens system, as discussed in Chapter 11, is a system for the registration of interests in land. Upon registration, the title holder acquires what is described as an 'indefeasible title' and gains priority over any preceding interests not already noted on the register or coming within the statutory or non-statutory exceptions to indefeasibility. The philosophy of the Torrens system is to protect a *bona fide* purchaser of land and to guarantee security of title. For a more detailed discussion on the Torrens system, see Chapter 11.

In Victoria, adverse possession is not affected by the operation of the Torrens system because it stands outside registration principles. The Torrens legislation sets out that the rights acquired by an adverse possessor amount to what is known as a 'paramount interest' which cannot be defeated by the subsequent registration of an interest in land. Hence, an adverse possessor may enforce 'any rights subsisting under any adverse possession of the land' against a registered proprietor.[20] It would seem that the reference in the Torrens legislation to the 'rights of an adverse possessor' may include those existing prior to the expiration of the limitation period as well as those existing afterwards. Hence, recognition is given to mere possessory title holders. In *Rose v Curtis* (1995) 7 BPR 14-430, Young J noted that the person who had registered title over land, and who was in possession of a disputed strip of land adjacent to the registered land, had a better title to the land than a mere trespasser. Similar provisions exist in other states with some variations.[21] In Tasmania, the provisions require adverse possession under the Torrens system to be treated in the same way as adverse possession under general law. In New South Wales, the enforceability of adverse possession in the Torrens system was only introduced as recently as 1979, and under Pt V1A of the

20 Transfer of Land Act 1958 (Vic), s 42(2)(b). See, also, similar provisions in the Western Australian legislation: Transfer of Land Act 1893 (WA), s 68.

21 See the Land Titles Act 1980 (Tas), ss 40(3)(h) and 117; Real Property (Possessory Titles) Amendment Act 1979 (NSW), ss 45B–45K; Land Titles Act 1994 (Qld), s 170(1)(d); and Real Property Act 1886 (SA), s 69VI.

legislation, an adverse possessor may make an application to have themselves registered as proprietor over a particular parcel of land in the register where adverse possession can be established. Section 45E of the Real Property Act 1900 (NSW) permits the Registrar General to make such alterations to the register as might be appropriate to give effect to a proper claim for possessory title. In *McGuiness v Registrar General* (1998) 44 NSWLR 61, Hodson CJ held that purchasers of two Torrens title lots who had, in fact, through mistake, become registered title holders over the other, could apply under s 45E to have the lot numbers transposed because their 'mistaken' ownership of the titles for over 50 years amounted to a sufficient possessory title under s 45D(1)(b) of the new legislation.

CHAPTER 5

EQUITABLE INTERESTS

5.1 Introduction

This chapter considers the rules governing the creation and enforcement of equitable interests in property. Property law draws a fundamental distinction between legal and equitable interests. The distinction is a product of the organisation of the courts prior to the judicature legislation of the 19th century. Originating from the jurisdiction of medieval chancellors, the equity jurisdiction has survived the introduction of the Torrens system of establishing title to land by registration, which recognises established legal and equitable interests in real property while radically reforming the methods by which they can be transferred and enforced. (See further discussion on the Torrens system, Chapter 11.)

The most significant creation of the chancellors and courts of equity is the trust. This is a device enabling real or personal property to be held by the legal owner for the benefit of some other person. For example, A, a landowner, might want to leave all her property to her children, who are minors. A may decide to leave the property by will to a friend or relative, B, to be held on trust for the children. Upon A's death, B will hold legal title to the property (historically a title enforceable in common law courts). However, a court administering an equity jurisdiction will compel B to administer the property solely for the benefit of the children. The children themselves are entitled to an equitable interest in the property, enforceable in a court of equity not only against B, but also against most persons who acquired the legal title to the property from B. The trust can therefore be used as a method of making provision for the children. Historically, the trust was often used as a means for providing for members of a family at a time when the common law rules of inheritance to real property on death permitted land to pass only to the eldest son.

The express trust is, according to a perceptive epigram, 'a gift projected on the plane of time and subjected to a management regime'.[1]

A trust can be expressly created by a property owner. It is a flexible device, responsive to social change over the centuries, and has been adapted to promote a wide range of family, commercial and public purposes. The ability to fragment, or divide up, interests in property is often important to landowners, and the trust remains the primary mechanism for implementing

1 Bernard Rudden, review of John P Dawson, 'Gifts and promises' (1981) 44 MLR 610.

such a fragmentation. Some reasons for fragmenting property interests are contrary to public policy, and the efficacy of the trust in these areas has largely been neutralised by legislation: they include the use of trusts to evade tax or the claims of creditors or family court orders. But trusts are created for many more worthwhile purposes, including provision for physically or intellectually disadvantaged members of a family, and the promotion of charitable purposes. Contemporary applications of the trust include the trading trust (an Australian mutation evolved from the system of taxing business activity) and the superannuation trust, where legislation has adapted the trust as the model for regulating the provision of superannuation.[2]

A trust is not always the deliberate act of creation of a property owner. A resulting trust is a transfer of property in circumstances in which the law compels the transferee to hold the property on trust for the transferor.[3] For example, if A buys property and places it in the name of B, B will generally be presumed to hold the property on resulting trust for A. The resulting trust in this case is an evidentiary presumption and not a rule of law: it can be rebutted by B showing that A intended to make a gift of the property to her.

A constructive trust is a trust imposed by operation of law, irrespective of the intention of the legal owner of the property affected by the imposition of the trust. Australian law now recognises the principle that a constructive trust will be imposed upon a legal owner of property whenever it would be unconscionable for him to deny the plaintiff an equitable interest in property.[4] This type of constructive trust has been applied in recent years to resolve property disputes between former *de facto* partners as well as other family property disputes, such as those arising between parent and child.

Disputes between spouses upon divorce are now determined under the Family Law Act 1975 (Cth), and state legislation is increasingly superseding constructive trust principles in providing a regime for the distribution of property upon the breakdown of a *de facto* marriage relationship. Nevertheless, it is important to bear in mind that the imposition of this form of trust is not confined to family property litigation: it is a formula for equitable relief applied to a wide array of commercial and family disputes.

As well as the trust, courts of equity have fashioned other interests in property which were not recognised at common law. They include:

(a) the estate contract. This is a specifically enforceable contract for the sale or lease of property. The purchaser under such a contract is not only entitled to obtain an order of specific performance of the contract; she also has an equitable interest in the property which is enforceable against anyone to

2 Superannuation Industry (Supervision) Act (Cth), s 19.

3 Chambers, R, *Resulting Trusts*, 1997, Clarendon.

4 *Baumgartner v Baumgartner* (1987) 164 CLR 137.

whom the property is later conveyed by the vendor who has notice of the contract;

(b) the restrictive covenant.[5] A landowner selling a plot of land may wish to restrict its use if she retains any adjoining land. A term, or covenant, may be inserted into the contract of sale prohibiting some use of the land (for example, not to build on the land). If the covenant is restrictive – in other words, if it is negative in substance – a court of equity will enforce the covenant not only against the purchaser but also against anyone who buys the land with notice of the covenant;

(c) the mortgagor's equity of redemption. At common law, a mortgage took the form of a conveyance of property by the borrower (mortgagor) to the lender (mortgagee), with a proviso that the property had to be reconveyed if the money lent, and interest, were paid by the stipulated date. A court of equity would allow the borrower to recover her property after the date for repayment was passed upon payment of the money due, and interest and legal costs. This is known as the equitable right to redeem the mortgage. The recognition of the equitable right to redeem a mortgage generated a proprietary interest, the equity of redemption, which arises as soon as the contract is made. The equity of redemption entitles the mortgagor to recover the land not only from the mortgagee, but from anyone to whom the mortgagee has conveyed the land, provided he takes with notice of the mortgage.

The equity of redemption will arise in equity whenever a secured loan contract amounts, in substance, to a mortgage. Unlike any right to redeem contained within the actual mortgage contract, the equitable right is proprietary. A mortgagor may resort to the equitable proprietary right where the date for repayment under the loan contract has passed, so that the contractual right is unenforceable. The equity of redemption was justified in equity on the basis that it was against good conscience to permit the mortgagee to retain both the property and the loan repayments simply because the legal date for repayment of the loan had passed. Equity gives effect to the substance of a mortgage as a security device and will not allow the form of an absolute conveyance to prevail. Where a mortgagor seeks to enforce the common law right of redemption, the appropriate relief will be specific performance in aid of a contractual right; where, on the other hand, a mortgagor seeks to enforce the equity of redemption, she will be enforcing an equitable proprietary right. Six months' notice of an intention to redeem must be given to the mortgagee. The rationale for this under the equitable jurisdiction is that the six month period gives the mortgagee a chance to replace the investment. If, however, the mortgagee expressly agrees to accept

5 See further discussion in Chapter 12.

the repayment over a shorter period, the six month period will not apply. (See further discussion on this in Chapter 14.)

Equitable proprietary interests are distinguishable from legal interests in two primary respects:

(a) *The application of the doctrine of notice*

The holder of a legal interest in property is entitled to enforce it against anyone into whose hands the property comes; it is no defence to an action for interference with a legal property right that the interferer was unaware of the legal owner's title.

Equitable property interests, on the other hand, confer a more fragile protection on the interest holder. Whereas legal rights are said to be 'good against all the world', equitable rights are enforceable against all persons except a good faith purchaser of the legal estate in the property for value and without notice of the equitable interest. 'Value' does not, for this purpose, mean 'full value': it refers to any consideration, not being nominal consideration, in money or money's worth.

There are three kinds of notice:

- actual notice: a person has actual notice of all facts of which he or she has actual knowledge;
- constructive notice: a person has constructive notice of all facts which he would have discovered if he had made reasonable inquiries. Where the property is land, a purchaser of the land will be expected to inspect the land and the title to the land. The Torrens system of title registration has today superseded most of the inquiries formerly carried out by inspection of the title deeds (see, further, Chapter 11 and Chapter 9, para 9.4.3, for an examination of the operation of the doctrine of notice under old title land);
- imputed notice: if a purchaser employs an agent, such as a solicitor, any actual or constructive notice which the agent receives will be imputed to the purchaser.

For example, V, who holds the fee simple of land, creates a restrictive covenant in favour of X. V later sells the fee simple to P. P will be bound by the restrictive covenant if she has actual, constructive or imputed notice of its existence.

(b) *The availability of equitable remedies*

If a legal right is infringed, the person injured is entitled as of right to common law damages. Legal rights may be enforced by an equitable remedy if the damages are an inadequate or inappropriate remedy. The infringement of an equitable right, on the other hand, entitles the injured party to an equitable remedy. Equitable remedies include specific performance (an order that a contract, or a term of a contract, be performed); an injunction (an order compelling the wrongdoer to carry out some act or, more commonly, to refrain from carrying out an act); or equitable rescission (an order setting aside a contract or other transaction and substantially restoring both parties to their original position before the contract was entered into).

For example, if V enters into a valid contract to sell land to P, P has an estate contract, an equitable interest affecting the land. P can obtain the equitable remedy of specific performance of the interest. P can additionally obtain an injunction to prevent an improper disposition of the property to a third party.

Whereas a legal remedy is available as of right to an injured party, the award of equitable remedies is discretionary. This does not mean that a court enjoys an unfettered discretion to award or withhold relief. The circumstances in which specific performance, for example, will be awarded are governed by a reasonably clear body of judicial precedent, and the grounds for refusing a remedy, such as the plaintiff's delay in applying for the remedy or the hardship the award would cause the defendant, are also regulated by judicial decision.

5.2 A brief history of equity

English common law, by the 13th century, had developed into a formulary legal system: a plaintiff was entitled to a remedy in the royal courts if the facts of the claim could be adapted to the formula of an established writ. Naturally, litigants alleged wrongs from time to time which did not fit the formula of a writ. The problem was aggravated by Chapter 24 of the Statute of Westminster II 1288, which provided that new writs could only be issued if they were substantially similar to established writs. Litigants left without a remedy petitioned the King for a remedy, and the King developed the practice of referring the petitions to his chief minister, the Chancellor. In this way, the Chancellor gradually developed a jurisdiction, later exercised by a Court of Chancery, to remedy wrongs for which no remedy could be obtained in the common law courts. The early chancellors were usually ecclesiastics, administering a court of conscience, but by the 17th century only lawyers were appointed to the office.

This was also the period in which the system of equity began to be systematised by precedent, very much as the common law already was, although individual chancellors, such as Lord Nottingham and Lord Hardwicke, still exercised their right to innovate from time to time.

The decrees of the chancellor would sometimes conflict with the judgments of the common law courts. For example, an injunction might be obtained forbidding a party from enforcing a common law judgment. The chancellor's power to issue such injunctions was confirmed in the *Earl of Oxford's Case* (1615) 1 Ch Rep 1, which thereby established the principle, later confirmed by 19th century Judicature Acts, that, in the event of a conflict between law and equity, the latter was to prevail.

The chancellor began to enforce the trust, then known as the 'use', from the 15th century. Under this device, if land was conveyed by A to B to the use of C, the common law courts refused to compel B (known as the 'feoffee to uses') to hold the land for C (known as the *cestui que use*). The chancellor, however, enforced B's promise to hold land for the benefit of C, since uses were pre eminently matters of good faith and trust, and therefore appropriate subject matter of a court of conscience.

The use of land was popular with medieval landowners for a number of reasons: they enabled the common law rules of succession to land to be avoided in favour of flexible settlements, and they were also the means whereby the payment of feudal dues, for incidents of tenure, could be avoided. Many of the principles of modern trust law, including the doctrine of notice, were elaborated as part of the law of uses in the 15th and 16th centuries.

Although legislation, such as the Statute of Uses 1535, attempted to minimise the tax avoidance aspects of the use, the use itself, and later the trust, remained a pervasive feature of the legal system, and the ingenuity of conveyances ensured that it was adapted to meet the need of the property owning classes in later centuries. The use was a central feature of the 'strict settlement of land', whereby land was retained in aristocratic families for a number of generations, while at the same time income from the land was applied by the trustees to maintain the landowner's children and other members of the family.

By the 19th century, the increasing inconvenience of administering the common law and equity in separate courts, combined with some inefficiency in the administration of equity itself, led to the enactment in England of the Judicature Act 1873. Henceforward, common law and equity were to be administered in one court; it was no longer necessary to prove the existence of a contract in a common law court and then to obtain an order of specific performance of the contract in a court of equity. Section 25(11) of the Act confirmed the superiority of equity in the event of a conflict between the common law and equitable rules. In practice, cases of conflict rarely arise, since the circumstances in which a conflict might occur have by now mostly been identified and the equitable rule is routinely applied.

The judicature legislation was received by the Australian states. This occurred in most states in the later years of the 19th century,[6] although in New South Wales a separate Court of Equity existed, and maintained the old equity

6 See Meagher, RP, Crummow, WMC and Lehane, JRF, *Equity, Doctrines and Remedies*, 3rd edn, 1992, Butterworths, Chapter 2.

learning until 1972.[7] The Supreme Court of each state and territory is empowered to apply both common law and equitable doctrine and remedies. Similar powers have also been conferred upon lower courts.[8]

It is important to appreciate that the judicature legislation did not achieve a 'fusion' of law and equity, in the sense of amalgamating legal and equitable doctrine. Law and equity remain distinct. A legal interest remains enforceable against any purchaser of the property, whereas an equitable interest continues to be unenforceable against a good faith purchaser for value without notice of the equitable interest in the property. The administration of common law and equity has been fused, but the actual law itself has not. Inevitably, however, the nature process of doctrinal evolution has brought the common law and equity closer together, and Sir Anthony Mason has suggested that, in a number of areas, a convergence of doctrine and remedies can be identified.[9] Any convergence is not, however, a consequence of the judicature legislation, but, rather, of the tendency of the courts, particularly the High Court over the last 15 years, to reorganise and restate doctrine in a manner that emphasises the common features of law and equity and not their differences.[10]

5.3 The express trust

Real and personal property can both be held on trust. There are two basic types of trust. Under a 'fixed' trust, each beneficiary is entitled to a predetermined share of the trust property. For example, a settlor might settle $100,000 on trust, the fund to be invested and divided equally between each of the settlor's children at a specified date, or upon the occurrence of an event, such as each child attaining 18. Under a 'discretionary' trust, the identity of the beneficiaries is determined by the instrument setting up the trust, but the share of the property, if any, that each beneficiary is to receive will be determined by the trustees. For example, a settlor might settle $100,000 on trust to be divided among such of the settler's children as the trustees shall determine.

A beneficiary under a fixed trust enjoys an equitable interest which can be disposed of by gift, sale or bequest just like any other property interest. A beneficiary under a discretionary trust, in contrast, has no equitable interest in the trust property. She has a 'mere hope' or 'expectation' that the trustee's discretion will be exercised in her favour. She is, however, entitled to secure the proper administration of the trust and can sue the trustee if the latter has

7 Supreme Court Act 1972 (NSW) 1972, coming into force 1 January 1972.

8 See *op cit*, Meagher, Crummow and Lehane, fn 6, paras [146]–[252].

9 Mason, A (Sir), 'The place of equity and equitable remedies in the common law world' (1994) 110 LQR 238.

10 Eg, the restatement of the principles of estoppel in *Walton Stores (Interstate) Ltd v Maher* (1988) 164 CLR 387.

committed a breach of trust. The equitable proprietary interest under a discretionary trust is actually vested in the entire class of beneficiaries. The right held by each 'potential' beneficiary under that class is simply a personal right against those to whom the obligations are owed. The position has been well summarised by Viscount Radcliffe in *Commissioner of Stamp Duties (Qld) v Livingston* [1965] AC 694, p 712 (discussing the legal relationship of an executor and beneficiary in an unadministered estate, which is similar in many respects to that of trustee and beneficiary under a discretionary trust):

> When the whole right of property is in a person, as it is in an executor, there is no need to distinguish between the legal and equitable interest in that property, any more than there is for the property of a full beneficial owner. What matters is that the court will control the executor in the use of his rights over assets that come to him in that capacity, but it will do it by the enforcement of remedies which do not involve the admission or recognition of equitable rights of property in those assets. Equity in fact calls into existence and protects equitable rights and interests in property only where their recognition has been found to be required in order to give effect to its doctrines.

An express trust can be created by one of two methods:

(a) A transfer of property by a settlor to trustees on trust

S (Settlor) – **T** (Trustee) – **B** (Beneficiary)

Where a trust by transfer is created, the property must be transferred by S to T in accordance with the statutory formalities, if any, applicable to the property in question. For example, old title land must be transferred by way of a properly executed deed, and Torrens title land must be transferred by way of a registered instrument of transfer. In addition, the settlor must declare a trust in favour of the beneficiary.

(b) Self-declaration of trust by a settlor

S/T – B

The settlor must declare that he holds identified property on trust for the beneficiary. No formalities are required to declare a trust, except in the case of a trust of land, where legislation in all states and territories, based on the Statute of Frauds 1677, provides that a declaration of trust of land, or any interest in land, must be manifested and proved by some writing, signed by some person able to declare such trust or by will.[11]

Trustees must administer the trust exclusively in the interests of the beneficiaries. A trust is a device for separating the management and enjoyment of property and the managerial responsibilities imposed upon the trust include the duty to observe strictly the terms of the trust, to safeguard trust property, and to promote the financial well being of beneficiaries by prudently investing trust assets. A trustee can be sued personally by the

11 Conveyancing Act 1919 (NSW), s 23C; Property Law Act 1958 (Vic), s 53(1)(b).

beneficiaries for acting in breach of obligation. The beneficiaries are also entitled to proprietary remedies allowing them to recover misappropriated trust property from transferees from the trustee.

5.4 Resulting trusts

A resulting trust arises where property is transferred in circumstances in which the transferee is not entitled to a beneficial interest in the property. The creation of such a trust is exempt from statutory writing requirements.[12] A division sometimes drawn in this type of trust lies between 'presumed' resulting trusts, where the resulting trust is simply a rebuttable evidential presumption, and 'automatic' resulting trusts which arise by operation of law.[13]

A presumed resulting trust will be recognised where:

(a) X voluntarily (that is, without consideration) transfers property to Y. In the absence of rebutting evidence, Y will be presumed, again rebuttably, to hold the property on resulting trust for X. The presumption, which certainly seems counter intuitive, arose from the medieval conveyancing practice of landowners voluntarily conveying land to trustees while leaving the precise terms of the trust to be declared at a later date. Until such time as the express trust should be fully declared and the identity of the beneficiaries made fully known, the trustees held the land on trust for the settlor. Today, the presumption readily yields to countervailing evidence that a gift to the transferee was intended.[14]

    The presumption of resulting trust does not apply to a voluntary transfer made by a parent to a child, or to transfers between spouses. The presumption of advancement, or gift, applies to these transfers.[15] As with the presumption of a resulting trust, the presumption of advancement is also rebuttable. Traditionally, the presumption of advancement has only applied in transfers from a father to his children or a husband to his wife and not vice versa: *Moore v Whyte (No 2)* (1922) 22 NSW StR 570.

(b) X purchases property in the name of Y. Y will be presumed – but this presumption is capable of being rebutted – to hold the property on trust for X. A 'purchase money' resulting trust will most often be presumed where joint owners provide the purchase money for the acquisition of a property in unequal shares. In such a case, they will be presumed to hold the property on resulting trust for themselves as tenants in common in the proportions to which they contributed to the purchase. If they contributed

12 Conveyancing Act 1919 (NSW), s 23C(2); Property Law Act 1958 (Vic), s 53(2).

13 *Re Vandervell's Trusts (No 2)* [1974] Ch 269, p 290, Megarry VC.

14 *Napier v Public Trustee (Western Australia)* (1980) 32 ALR 153.

15 *Nelson v Nelson* (1995) 184 CLR 538.

equally to buying the property, it will be held as joint tenants for them both.[16]

In Australia, the purchase money resulting trust is restricted to moneys paid over at the time of entering into the contract, because the evidentiary materials used to assess the existence of a purchase money resulting trust is restricted to that which has occurred before or at the time of the purchase or so immediately after it as to constitute a part of the overall transaction. This means that subsequent contributions to a mortgage will not be considered for the purposes of determining the amount held under the purchase money resulting trust (*Calverley v Green* (1984) 155 CLR 242). The position is somewhat different in England. In *Midland Bank v Cooke* [1995] 4 All ER 562, Waite LJ felt that such a restriction was inappropriate and that, in assessing such trusts, the 'duty of the judge is to undertake a survey of the whole course of dealing between the parties relevant to their ownership and occupation of the property and their sharing of its burdens and advantages'. His Honour went on to note that a restrictive approach does not correspond with the realities of cohabitation:

> When people, especially young people, agree to share their lives in joint homes, they do so on a basis of mutual trust and in the expectation that their relationship will endure. Despite the efforts that have been made by many responsible bodies to counsel prospective cohabitants as to the risks of taking shared interests in property without legal advice, it is unrealistic to expect that advice to be followed on a universal scale. For a couple embarking on a serious relationship, discussion of the terms to apply at parting is almost a contradiction of the shared hopes that have brought them together. There will inevitably be numerous couples, married or unmarried, who have no discussion about ownership and who, perhaps advisedly, make no agreement about it. It would be anomalous, against that background, to create a range of home buyers who were beyond the pale of equity's assistance in formulating a fair presumed basis for the sharing of beneficial title, simply because they had been honest enough to admit that they never gave ownership a thought or reached any agreement about it. (p 569.)

The comments by Wait LJ in *Midland Bank* do not, however, draw a clear distinction between the approach to be taken in purchase money resulting trusts and that assumed in common intention constructive trust cases. This distinction was, however, raised in *Drake v Whipp* [1996] 1 FLR 826; 28 HLR 53, where the English Court of Appeal noted that the assessment of a purchase money resulting trust was quite different to that of a constructive trust where a 'broad brush' examination could be carried out.

The leading authority on the purchase money resulting trust is the High Court decision of *Calverley v Green*.[17] The parties, while living together as *de*

16 *Calverley v Green* (1984) 155 CLR 242.

17 *Ibid*.

facto partners, bought a house in joint names for $27,000. The defendant paid $9,000 as a deposit. The balance of $18,000 was borrowed on mortgage, both parties assuming liability under the mortgage. The defendant paid the mortgage instalments. The High Court held that the house was held on resulting trust for both partners in the proportions in which they had contributed to the purchase. The shares under the resulting trust were calculated as follows:

(a) the defendant was entitled to a one-third share in the house by reason of his payment of the deposit, which amounted to one-third of the purchase price;

(b) the parties were entitled to an equal share of the remaining equitable interest in the house by reason of their joint liability to repay the mortgage. Liability to repay the mortgage, and not the actual repayments, provides the basis for quantifying equitable interests under a resulting trust;

(c) the plaintiff was required to account personally to the defendant in respect of the share of the share of the mortgage for which she was legally liable but which he had paid. This, however, in no way affected the assessment of beneficial interests under the resulting trust.

Property purchased by a parent in the name of a child, or by one spouse which is placed in the name of the other, is presumed, rebuttably, to have been advanced to the transferee.[18] In *Calverley v Green*, Gibbs CJ was of the opinion that transfers between *de facto* partners should also attract the operation of the presumption of advancement.[19] This view did not, however, attract support in the other judgments.[20]

Finally, Murphy J in *Commissioner of Stamp Duties (Qld) v Livingston* [1965] AC 694 argued that the presumptions of resulting trust and advancement should be discarded. Equitable title should follow legal title to property, unless circumstances could be shown which would displace this principle. The High Court in the later decision of *Nelson v Nelson*,[21] while conceding its logic, rejected this argument on the ground that the presumptions are established benchmarks in property law which are still relied upon in conveyancing practice.[22]

The court did, however, conclude that the presumption of advancement should be reformed, in particular, that it should be given a more expansive operation and not limited in scope purely on the grounds of gender. Dawson J

18 *Nelson v Nelson* (1995) 184 CLR 538.

19 (1984) 155 CLR 242, pp 250–51.

20 For further authority on this point, see *Jenkins v Wynen* (1992) 1 QdR 40, pp 46–47, and cf *Kais v Turvey* (1994) 17 Fam LR 498, pp 499–500.

21 (1995) 184 CLR 538.

22 *Ibid*, pp 548–49, *per* Deane and Cummar JJ.

noted that 'in modern society, there is no reason to suppose that the probability of a parent intending to transfer a beneficial interest in property to a child is any the more or less in the case of a mother than in the case of a father'. This extension is desirable as it overrules gendered, anachronistic stereotypes concerning the role of fathers and husbands which do not accord with the range and diversity of parenting roles in modern society.[23]

The overall significance of presumptions of advancement and presumptions of resulting trust are, however, diminished in the context of matrimonial property in Australia as s 79 of the Family Law Act 1975 (Cth) gives the Family Court a broad discretionary power to alter property interests on the dissolution of marriage, despite the existence of any presumption of a resulting trust or presumption of advancement. Section 285 of the Property Law Act 1958 (Vic) gives courts a similar discretionary power to that held by the Family Court to alter property rights of parties within a *de facto* relationship. Similar powers exist in most other states.[24]

A resulting trust will arise automatically, in other words, as a rule of law, and not as a presumption, where property is settled on express trust and the express trust fails on the ground of uncertainty, voidness, illegality, or because property remains after the fulfilment of the trust purpose. The practical outcome of applying resulting trust principles to cases of failure of an express trust will be to restore the property to the settlor of the express trust. In *Re Gillingham Bus Disaster Fund*,[25] an appeal fund was set up after a road accident in which 24 cadets were killed. The money collected was devoted to defraying funeral expenses, caring for injured cadets, and to purposes which were later held not to be valid charitable purposes. Harman J declared that a surplus remaining after the trust purposes had been fulfilled was to be held on resulting trust for the benefit of the subscribers to the fund. The application of resulting trust principles to cases of failure of appeals and subscription funds can, however, be practically inconvenient, since the donors will generally be very numerous and often anonymous or unascertainable.[26]

5.5 Constructive trusts

A constructive trust is imposed by operation of law, irrespective of the intention of the party holding legal title to the property. Constructive trusts are imposed for a variety of reasons to fulfil expectations, to perfect informal legal

23 See, also, McInnes, M, 'Advancement, illegality and restitution' (1997) 5 Australian Property Law Journal 3; Sarmas, L, 'A step in the wrong direction: the emergence of gender "neutrality" in the equitable presumption of advancement' (1994) 19 Melbourne UL Rev 758.

24 De Facto Relationships Act 1996 (SA), ss 9–11; De Facto Relationships Act 1991 (NT), s 18; De Facto Relationships Act 1994 (ACT); Property (Relationships) Act 1984 (NSW), s 20.

25 [1958] Ch 300.

26 Legislation has displaced the application of resulting trust in some cases.

arrangements, and to reverse unjust enrichment. Being imposed trusts, they are naturally exempt from statutory writing requirements which apply to express trusts. Constructive trusts, like purchase money resulting trusts, are often applied to resolve family property disputes, although in many states and Territories, discretionary legislation is superseding equity in this area.[27]

Different types of constructive trust have been developed in recent years in response to the growing number of such disputes coming before the courts. Although there is some variation in the criteria for the award of these types of trusts, they share the overriding objective of fulfilling the reasonable expectations of the claimant.

One such trust is the 'common intention' constructive trust. It will be imposed if two conditions are satisfied:

(a) the claimant must show that there is an agreement or common intention between the legal owner and the claimant that the latter shall have a beneficial interest in the property; and

(b) the claimant must have acted to her detriment in reliance on the agreement or common intention.

It is unclear whether this trust is, strictly speaking, a constructive trust or an express trust not required to satisfy the statutory writing requirements for such a trust, on the principle that equity will not allow a statute to be used as an instrument of fraud.[28] The agreement or common intention can be express or inferred from the acts or words of the parties. Intentions should not, however, be imputed to the parties where no factual basis for imputation exists.[29] In spite of repeated judicial warnings against 'inventing intention', however, courts have, on occasions, exercised considerable ingenuity in construing an intention to confer an interest on a claimant from very slight evidence, where to do so would achieve substantial justice.[30]

The principal objection to the common intention constructive trust is that the 'intention' of the parties is often a fiction, judicial assertions to the contrary notwithstanding. The problem of ascertaining the 'fugitive common intention'[31] has been a significant factor in the development of alternative models of constructive trust. Nevertheless, the 'common intention' constructive trust has not been superseded by these models, and examples of its application can be found in recent cases.[32]

27 De Facto Relationship Act 1984 (NSW); Property Law Act 1958 (Vic), Pt IX; De Facto Relationship Act 1996 (SA); De Facto Relationship Act 1991 (NT); De Facto Relationship Act 1994 (ACT).

28 *Allen v Snyder* [1977] 2 NSWLR 658.

29 *Ibid*, p 690, *per* Glass JA.

30 *Green v Green* (1989) 17 NSWLR 343.

31 *Pettrus v Becker* (1980) 117 DLR (3rd) 257, p 269, *per* Dickson J; *Drake v Whipp* (1996) 1 FLR 826; 28 HLR 53.

32 *Harmer v Pearson* (1993) 16 Fam LR 596; *Rasmussen v Rasmussen* [1995] 1 VR 613; *W v G* [1998] Fam LR 49.

A trend of recent High Court decisions has been to reassert equity's historic concern with matters of conscience, and to impose a constructive trust where it would be unconscionable for a legal owner of property to deny the claimant a beneficial interest. In *Muschinski v Dodds*,[33] a *de facto* couple purchased a dilapidated cottage for $20,000. They intended to restore it as an arts and crafts centre to be run by the plaintiff, and to erect a prefabricated house elsewhere on the land. The plaintiff paid the purchase price, while the defendant agreed to renovate the cottage and pay for the prefabricated house. The land was transferred to them as tenants in common in equal shares. The couple were unable to obtain council approval for the renovation, and the money the defendant had available for the venture proved to be less than expected. The plaintiff incurred the greater costs in the venture. When they separated, the plaintiff sought a declaration that she was beneficial owner of the whole property. The High Court, Brennan and Dawson JJ dissenting, held that the respective legal interests of the parties as tenants in common were subject to a constructive trust, after repayment of any joint debts incurred in the improvement of the property, to repay to each their contributions and then to hold the residue for them both in equal shares.[34] Deane J, with whom Mason J agreed, expounded the principles applicable to the award of a constructive trust. He identified three features which would justify an award:

(a) failure of a joint relationship or endeavour, similar to the winding up of a commercial partnership, frustrated contract or the failure of a contractual joint venture;

(b) absence of blame attributable to the claimant;

(c) money or other property contributed for the purposes of the venture.

It is uncertain how close the analogy to the failed joint venture has to be. It was particularly apt on the facts of *Muschinski v Dodds*, where the personal relationship and business enterprise had simultaneously failed, but it may be less appropriate where the facts disclose no commercial element. Similarly, it is unclear whether the second requirement necessitates a judicial inquiry into the causes of the relationship breakdown, which would appear inconsistent with the 'no fault' basis of the Family Law Act 1975 (Cth) and other family legislation.

In the later decision of *Baumgartner v Baumgartner*,[35] the High Court incorporated the criteria laid down by Deane J in *Muschinski v Dodds* into a broader assessment of the unconscionability of the defendant's denial of a beneficial interest to the plaintiff. The defendant in *Baumgartner* had brought

33 (1986) 160 CLR 583.

34 Gibbs CJ agreed with the order proposed, but based his judgment on the principles of equitable contribution, rather than constructive trusts: *ibid*, pp 596–98.

35 (1987) 164 CLR 137.

some land in his own name, applying the proceeds of a previous sale for this purpose. He and his partner, the plaintiff, pooled their earnings, out of which they paid all their living expenses and commitments, including the mortgage instalments. Throughout the time they were living together, except for three months after the birth of their son, the plaintiff worked full time outside the home and handed the defendant her pay packet as a part of the pooling arrangement. Because of her contributions, the defendant was able to make 'double repayments' off the mortgage loan on four occasions. After separation, the defendant asserted that the land was his sole property.

The High Court held that the plaintiff was entitled to an interest in the property to the extent of her contribution to the pool, which was calculated as a 45% share in the property. The judgment of Mason CJ and Wilson and Deane JJ concluded that:

> ... the appellant's assertion, after the relationship had failed, that the [matrimonial] property, which was financed in part through pooled funds, is his sole property, is his property to the exclusion of any interest at all on the part of the respondent, amounts to unconscionable conduct which attracts the intervention of equity and the imposition of a constructive trust at the suit of the respondent.[36]

The plaintiff was awarded an interest primarily on the basis of her financial contributions to the pooling arrangements, but the High Court also credited the plaintiff with a hypothetical income she would have been able to earn if she had not had to take time off work when her son was born. In the opinion of Gaudron J:

> ... in the context of domestic relationships, it is relevant to inquire whether the asset was acquired for the purpose of the relationship, and whether non-financial contributions should be taken into account.[37]

In spite of this *dictum* and the High Court's willingness to credit contributions to reflect domestic responsibilities, some inconsistency is apparent in the recognition by lower courts of non-financial contributions to relationships. A commercial ethos pervades equity decisions on constructive trusts.[38] In *Bryson v Bryant*,[39] for example, a wife was held not to be entitled to an equitable interest in a home purchased by her husband 50 years previously, the marriage itself having lasted 60 years. A majority of the New South Wales Court of Appeal rejected the view that a 'wife would become entitled to any property acquired by the husband merely because she had carried out her role as the homemaker'.[40]

36 *Baumgartner v Baumgartner* (1987) 164 CLR 137, p 149.

37 *Ibid*, p 156.

38 *Bryson v Bryant* (1992) 29 NSWLR 188, pp 200–05, *per* Kirby P (dissenting).

39 *Ibid*.

40 *Ibid*, p 231, *per* Samuels AJA.

The relationship of the resulting trust to the *Baumgartner* constructive trust has been little explored in the cases. Indeed, the facts of the *Baumgartner* constructive trust itself closely resemble those of a purchase money resulting trust. The pooling arrangement was really nothing more than a form of indirect purchase in the name of the defendant. In general terms, however, the principles relating to voluntary transfers and purchase money resulting trusts will determine beneficial title to property. They can later be modified by the application of *Baumgartner* constructive trust principles to reflect direct and indirect contributions to the enhancement of the value of the property.

Although the *Baumgartner* constructive trust is arguably the most significant model of constructive trust in Australian law today, it is not the only model, and not all constructive trusts are imposed with the objective of preventing unconscionable conduct. Another important category of constructive trust is that imposed upon property wrongly acquired by fiduciaries, such as trustees and solicitors, acting in breach of obligation. Recipients of property from the fiduciary may also be held accountable as constructive trustees, as are those who assist in a breach of fiduciary obligation. Yet another category of constructive trust is imposed upon a vendor of property under a specifically enforceable contract of sale; the purchaser will be entitled to the benefit of the constructive trust until the transfer has been completed. Except at an unhelpfully high level of generality, not all constructive trusts can be said to have as their object the avoidance of unconscionable conduct. Their aims are various: deterrent, restitutionary, compensatory, and to perfect legally imperfect transactions. As elsewhere in equity, some discrimination needs to be shown in applying notions of conscience to the various manifestations of the constructive trust.

In *Giumelli v Giumelli* (1999) 73 ALJR 547; 161 ALR 473, the Australian High Court considered whether a 'proprietary' constructive trust could apply in an estoppel scenario where the plaintiff had detrimentally relied upon various representations concerning his future ownership of property he worked upon. On the facts, a son brought proceedings against his parents over property owned by the parents. The son had worked on the property for no wages and the parents promised that the property would be subdivided to establish a lot in his favour. The Full Court of the Supreme Court of Western Australia declared that the parents held the property under a constructive trust and that the parents were obliged to do all things reasonably necessary to subdivide the property. On appeal, the High Court concluded that the award of a constructive trust went beyond what was required for conscientious conduct by the parents and that relief should be expressed not in terms of acquisition of title to land, but in a money sum. The court clearly noted that the remedial constructive trust should only be imposed in circumstances where other forms of relief do not adequately address the particular inequity involved. In *Cierpiatka v Cierpiatka* [1999] FLC 86-206 the court reiterated the approach of *Giumelli* noting that the classic estoppel scenario (acting to one's detriment in reliance upon an expectation) does not necessarily require the making good of a representation and even where it does, the court should first consider whether there is an appropriate equitable remedy falling short of a constructive trust.

5.6 Equitable interests and equities

A beneficiary's interest under a trust, restrictive covenants, estate contracts and equitable mortgages are all examples of equitable interests in property. Such interests are distinguishable from a 'mere equity' or 'personal equity'. The 'mere equity' is an ambiguous concept. It sometimes connotes the right to bring an action to obtain equitable remedies against a defendant. But it can also mean the right to set aside a transaction on the ground of fraud, misrepresentation, unconscientious dealing or undue influence. Rights arising under estoppel actions have been referred to as 'mere equities' but, where a constructive trust is imposed, may actually constitute full equitable interests.[41] The right will be enforceable not only against the wrongdoer, but also against third parties who have received the subject matter of the impugned transaction. In such cases, the equity assumes a limited proprietary character.[42]

The 'proprietary' character is attached to the mere equity because of the proprietary consequences it has when enforced: the correction of the error or the setting aside of the transaction on the grounds of undue influence, for example, result in the re-acquisition of a proprietary interest. It has been argued that one of the most convincing reasons for utilising the proprietary analysis in this context is to ensure that such rights are protected as holders are often unable to do so because they are unaware of the existence of the defect.[43] The 'mere equity' should be distinguished from mere personal rights which simply confer on the holder a right to seek equitable relief. The nature and enforceability of personal rights was discussed in *National Provincial Bank Ltd v Ainsworth* [1965] AC 1175; [1965] 2 All ER 472, where the House of Lords considered the enforceability of an equitable personal right, known as the 'deserted wife's equity' and concluded that this right, despite being directed at the marital home, could not be enforceable against the holder of a full proprietary interest in the home – on the facts, a mortgagee bank – even if the bank took its proprietary interest knowing of the existence of the personal right held by the wife. The reason for this, in the words of Lord Upjohn, was because an 'equity naked and alone is ... incapable of binding successors in

41 See *Giumelli v Giumelli* (1999) 73 ALJR 547 and *Re Jonton Pty Ltd* (1992) 2 QdR 105.

42 See generally, Neave, M and Weinberg, M, 'The nature and function of equities' (1978) U Tas LR (Pt 1) 24.

43 See the excellent discussion on this in Chambers, R, *An Introduction to Property Law in Australia*, 2001 , LBC, pp 422–23.

title even with notice; it is personal to the parties'. By contrast, a mere equity, because of its limited proprietary status, can only be defeated by a successor in title who is a *bona fide* purchaser for value. This makes the distinction between personal equity and mere equity an important one. Just as important, however, is the distinction between mere equity and full equitable interest.

No legal test exists for distinguishing mere equities from equitable interests; indeed, the context in which the matter arises for decision may determine how an interest will be classified. The mere equity often exists as an ancillary right to a full equitable interest: a 'mere equity' can only arise if its enforcement has direct proprietary consequences. Hence, a right to rectify a document or an agreement by correcting an error in it, resulting in the subsequent recovery of an asset is a good example of a personal right with proprietary results. A mere equity arising out of a right to rectify may be defeated by a full proprietary interest, acquired *bona fide* and for value without notice. The nature and enforceability of mere equities and full equitable interests was considered by the High Court in *Latec Investments Ltd v Hotel Terrigal Pty Ltd* (1965) 113 CLR 265. In that case, Latec was the registered mortgagee of land owned by Terrigal. When Terrigal fell into arrears with its repayments, Latec exercised its power of sale and sold the property to Southern, a wholly owned subsidiary of Latec. The sale was liable to be set aside for the fraud of Latec, to which Southern was party: a high reserve had been set, the advertising period for the auction was short, and the sale to Southern was at well below reserve price. Before Terrigal could set the sale aside for fraud, however, Southern had contracted to sell the property to MLC Nominees, who were innocent of the fraud and who acquired an equitable interest, namely an estate contract, as purchasers under a specifically enforceable contract.

An important issue for the High Court was to classify Terrigal's right to set aside the sale by Latec to Southern; whether Latec were entitled to an equitable interest or an equity would determine whether Terrigal's claim to the land prevailed over that of MLC as an honest purchaser. Menzies J identified two lines of authority. One held that the right to set aside a sale for fraud constituted a full equitable interest; it focused on the result of setting aside the transaction, which was to compel the purchaser to hold the property on trust for the defrauded party.[44] The other, focusing on the nature of the right to set aside the sale before it had been exercised, characterised it as a mere equity.[45] Menzies J held that the classification of Terrigal's right depended on the circumstances in which it arose. The second line of authority was directly applicable to a priority dispute, the effect of which was that Terrigal's right was a mere equity.

44 *Bryson v Bryant* (1992) 29 NSWLR 188, pp 289–90, based on *Stump v Gaby* (1852) 24 ER 1015.

45 *Ibid*, pp 288–89, based on *Phillips v Phillips* (1861) 45 ER 1164.

Kitto J also held that Terrigal's right was a mere equity. However, if Terrigal had succeeded in obtaining a court order setting aside the sale, it would then have been entitled to a full equitable interest. The third judge, Taylor J, dissented on this issue, holding that Terrigal was entitled to a full equitable interest, albeit one that would take subject to a later equitable interest if it required the 'assistance of a court of equity to remove an impediment to title as a preliminary'.

Even though a majority of the High Court decided that the right to set aside a sale for fraud was an equity, the court's classification of the right cannot be said to be definitive. Menzies J stressed the importance of paying due regard to the context in which the question has to be decided before characterising such a right as an equity or an equitable interest. The indeterminacy of legal classification was demonstrated by the later High Court decision of *Breskvar v Wall*[46] where, without undertaking a full review of the authorities, it was held that the right to have a sale set aside for fraud was a full equitable interest, rather than a mere equity. On this basis, the High Court assumed that the holders of the right were entitled to all of the rights generally associated with full proprietary interests, including, in the context of Torrens title land, the ability to protect the interest through the lodgement of a caveat.[47]

46 (1971) 126 CLR 376.

47 This approach should be distinguished from *Swanston Mortgage Pty Ltd v Trepan Investments Pty Ltd* [1994] 1 VR 672, where the Supreme Court of Victoria concluded that mere equities were not capable of being registered. See discussion below, para 9.5.2.1.

CHAPTER 6

NATIVE TITLE

6.1 Introduction

From very early history, the Australian colonies continued to grant land to settlers despite the fact that, when they arrived, the land was inhabited by indigenous Aboriginal people. It was always simply assumed that the British Crown had a right to claim sovereignty over the land; no compensation was ever paid to the Aboriginal people, and there was no specific legal formalisation of this assumed right in the form of a treaty. The only real recognition given to the Aboriginal people was the conferral of specific reserves for the creation and development of Aboriginal communities.

During early settlement, land became an important commodity for the settlers, as it represented a means by which income could be produced. By cultivating and growing productive crops and using the land as a means of feeding and raising working and productive agricultural animals, the early settlers were able to establish rudimentary communities. Furthermore, when gold was discovered in the 1850s, the ensuing gold rush confirmed the value and importance of land ownership. At no point during these early days was the right of the British Crown to issue grants of land to settlers questioned, despite the fact that all of these activities resulted in the widespread alienation, estrangement and destruction of the indigenous communities which had existed on these lands for many thousands of years beforehand. The attitude of the courts during these times was well summarised in the decision of *Attorney General v Brown* [1847] 1 Legge 312; 2 SCR (NSW) App 30, where the full court of the New South Wales Supreme Court noted that Australian lands 'are, and ever have been, from the time of its first settlement in 1788, in the Crown'.

The perceived view, which remained an entrenched part of the common law until the momentous decision of *Mabo* in 1992, was that the British Crown could assume sovereignty over the lands because the Aboriginal communities in existence were devoid of any form of settled inhabitants and settled law at the time when the British Crown decided to annex the lands to its dominions. Consequently, it was believed to be unnecessary to acquire sovereignty from the Aboriginals by way of conquest or cession. This attitude is entrenched in the concept, referred to in *Mabo* as 'extended *terra nullius*'. Lord Watson aptly summarised the belief in the decision of *Cooper v Stuart* (1889) 14 App Cas 286, p 291:

> There is a great difference between the case of a Colony acquired by conquest or cession, in which there is an established system of land, and that of a Colony

> which consisted of a tract of territory practically unoccupied, without settled inhabitants or settled law, at the time when it was peacefully annexed to the British dominions. The Colony of New South Wales belongs to the latter class.

The fact that the Aboriginal people lived in their own well constructed societies, according to their own customs and cultures, was pretty much ignored by the courts and the legislature until the *Mabo* decision. This is itself a consequence of the entrenched parochialism apparent in the underlying foundation of colonialism; it was unable to recognise not only the validity but also the independence and value of separate, self structured, self-governing societies. These communities were either marginalised or ignored completely. The problem, as noted by Kent McNeil, lay in the fact that colonialist perceptions were (and, in many cases, still are) firmly ingrained in the Western European psyche:

> Yet Aboriginal people were there at the time, living in stable societies governed by elaborate systems of rules and customs which were highly adapted to the country in which they led their lives ... Though Western European concepts of sovereignty were no doubt unknown to them, they lived in factually self-governing communities which were independent of any foreign power. The assumption of the Crown and courts of English law that the Aboriginals were devoid of sovereignty is rooted in a European view of the world, which probably would have been incomprehensible to the Aboriginals. It involves a denial of a valid Aboriginal perspective, and is thus characteristic of the self-serving ethnocentricity upon which colonialism is based.[1]

The question of whether the Aboriginal people retained any land rights since the annexation of the territories to the British Crown has, until the *Mabo* decision, been a vexed one. Until this point, the courts had generally denied the existence of any form of ownership, interest or land right in indigenous communities, because of the belief that, upon annexation, the British Crown assumed sovereignty and, under the doctrine of tenure, acquired full beneficial title over all land. As discussed in Chapter 3, the basis of the doctrine of tenure is that title to all land vests in the Crown. This gives the Crown the right to issue subsequent grants to individuals, thereby creating a tenurial relationship between the Crown and the grantee. The presumption of most courts until the *Mabo* decision was that, upon annexation, the doctrine of tenure gave the Crown title to all lands, irrespective of the presence of Aboriginal peoples. This was clearly confirmed by Blackburn J in *Milirrpum v Nabalco Pty Ltd* (1971) 17 FLR 141, in which he stated:

> On the foundation of New South Wales, therefore, and of South Australia, every square inch of territory in the Colony became the property of the Crown. All titles, rights and interests whatever in land which existed thereafter in subjects of the Crown were the direct consequence of some grant from the Crown.

---

1 See McNeil, K, 'A question of title: has the common law been misapplied to dispossess the Aboriginals?' (1990) 16 Mon ULR 91.

6.2 Pre-*Mabo* approach

Prior to the *Mabo* decision, the Aboriginal people tried, on numerous occasions, to have their claims to the land upheld. A number of different approaches were adopted, each one being ultimately unsuccessful. One method was the attempt to reclassify the so-called 'annexation' of Australian territories to the British Crown as a 'conquering' of Australian territories. From the perspective of the Aboriginal community, such a reclassification has the advantage that, unlike annexation, it is not dependent upon a determination that Aboriginal communities did not have a societal structure and that the land was *terra nullius*. Furthermore, if the colonisation of Australia were to be reclassified as a 'conquering' of the Aboriginal community, it would at least provide recognition that the Aboriginal people did, in fact, exist. The distinction between an 'annexation' of land and a 'conquering' of the land appears, however, to be somewhat obscure: whether the colonisation of Australia can be formally classified as an act of conquest or annexation would ostensibly depend upon the enactment of a formal battle. Whilst a 'particular' battle cannot be historically detected, the ultimate annihilation of the indigenous communities upon annexation through weapons, disease, abuse and exploitation has practically the same effect.

Despite the obscurity between the two terms, it is argued that a reclassification of 'annexation' as a 'conquering' of indigenous communities would provide a better springboard for land right claims. This is founded upon the basic tenet of British colonial law that, where a land has been conquered, the existing societal structure and laws will remain in place until they are either expressly repealed or replaced. By contrast, under annexation, British law is applicable from the outset.[2] If the laws of indigenous communities remained intact, their proprietary claims over the land might never have been extinguished.

This argument was raised in *Milirrpum v Nabalco Pty Ltd* (1971) 17 FLR 141 as well as in *Coe v Commonwealth of Australia* (1979) 53 ALJR 403. However, in both instances, it provided no greater judicial inspiration for the acceptance of indigenous land claims. Indeed, in the *Milirrpum* decision, Blackburn J concluded that indigenous land rights could only be enforceable where expressly recognised by legislation, even if such a reclassification of history could be accepted. Where no such legislative recognition could be established, it was to be assumed that the Crown acquired immediate title to all lands whether the title was annexed or whether it was achieved by conquering the indigenous inhabitants.

2 See *op cit*, McNeil, fn 1; Bartlett, R, 'Aboriginal land claims at common law' (1983) 15 University of Western Australia Law Review 293.

What Blackburn J said in *Milirrpum v Nabalco* was similar to what had already been said by Stephen CJ in *Attorney General v Brown* [1847] 1 Legge 312 and in a long line of authority prior to the *Milirrpum* decision – that is, that the Crown acquired absolute title to all lands in the Australian colonies at the time they were settled. This principle was held to be unimpeachable and not alterable by historical reinterpretation.

In *Attorney General v Brown* [1847] 1 Legge 312, the existence of Crown title over coal mines was challenged. The defendant argued that the Crown had neither title nor possession to the mines and, consequently, without further documentary record, could not claim title. The court held that all lands are automatically vested in the Crown from the date of its first settlement. Stephen CJ set out two broad justifications for this. First, the Crown has taken occupancy of these lands as the representative and executive authority of the nation, and secondly, 'by the adaptation of the feudal fiction' the Crown's title could be justified on the basis of the doctrine of tenures. The doctrine of tenures postulated that the Crown, as ultimate conqueror, owned all lands, which it then granted to its subjects.

This English doctrine was applied in substance to the Australian context. The obvious difficulty with this decision was that the complicated system of tenures, as had evolved in England, had no history in or relevance to the Australian colonies. The application of the doctrine of tenure within Australia was, nevertheless, confirmed by the Privy Council in *Cooper v Stuart* (1889) 14 App Cas 286.

The continued refusal of the courts to reject the doctrine of tenure and reassess its claims to sovereignty over the lands meant that Aboriginal land right claims, whatever form they took, were consistently rejected. On the facts of *Milirrpum v Nabalco Pty Ltd* (1971) 17 FLR 141; [1972–73] ALR 65, Aboriginal clans claimed to hold a customary land title to land in the Gove Peninsula area on the basis of their continuing traditional and cultural association with the land which predated the Crown's acquisition of sovereignty. They proceeded to challenge the validity of mineral licences granted by the Crown in this area.

Blackburn J, in the Northern Territory Supreme Court, rejected the validity of these customary land claims. His Honour held that such title did not, and never had, formed the basis of fundamental principles of land law as they exist in Australia, stating that 'communal title ... does not form and has never formed, part of the law of any part of Australia' (p 245). His Honour went on to hold that the mining leases were valid exercises of the sovereign power of the Crown, and that, as the Aboriginal peoples did not hold any title over the land, they could not challenge these licences. In making this determination, Blackburn J, unlike the earlier authority of *Cooper v Stuart* (1889) 14 App Cas 286, at least recognised the existence of indigenous communities at the time of settlement. Nevertheless, his Honour concluded that 'as a matter of law' the principles of *terra nullius* were still applicable. Furthermore, Blackburn J held that the relationship that the indigenous people had with the land involved rights which were 'non-proprietary' in nature. One of the reasons given by Blackburn J in this regard was that the Aboriginal clans accepted communal rather than private notions of property and therefore, as they did not recognise the right to exclude, the relationship could not properly be regarded as proprietary. This argument is quite circular because indigenous land claims, by their very nature, will be different to the proprietary rights existing in Western societies.

After continued judicial rejection, statutory measures dealing with Aboriginal land rights were eventually introduced. In 1976, the Commonwealth government introduced the Aboriginal Land Rights (Northern Territory) Act, which provided for the establishment of Land Councils which were to represent the Aboriginal peoples in various negotiations and dealings with the government concerning land rights. In particular, the Land Councils sought to enforce customary land claims over areas of land which had traditional cultural significance. Following the introduction of these councils, a variety of states introduced legislation dealing with the regulation of successful land claims over specific areas of traditional significance. These acts include: Pitjantjatjara Land Rights Act 1981 (SA); Maralinga Tjarutja Land Rights Act 1984; and Aborigines and Torres Strait Islanders (Land Holding) Act 1985 (Qld). Unfortunately, however, the statutory measures were not consistent throughout the states and often failed to provide basic protective measures to Aboriginal claimants. Consequently, it was deemed necessary to resort again to the courts for further legal support.

6.3 The *Mabo* decision

The *Mabo* decision is important for its re-assessment of property rights in terms of traditional Aboriginal culture and society, and for its recognition and substantiation of customary, native title in the land. The judgment shows a new awareness of the difficulties of trying to fit fundamental English property law principles into a totally different social structure, and it attempts to identify Aboriginal property rights in terms of their own social rules and regulations rather than classifying them according to English principles. The case is extremely significant, not only for its advancement of Aboriginal land rights, but also, more generally, for its recognition and explication of the inherently discriminatory and unjust history of the Crown's assumption of ownership over the Australian colonies. The recognition of native title in the *Mabo* case provides explicit recognition of a long standing tenet of common law which has finally obtained authoritative judicial support. As noted by Richard Bartlett:

> The decision in *Mabo* is of benefit to resource development in Australia. The decision gave explicit recognition to the concept of native title at common law.

> The common law has, over two centuries, established the concept. It is a pragmatic compromise derived from experience and disputes over that time between settlers, resource developers and Aboriginal peoples. It provides a long term regime that enables the interests of all parties to be substantially met. The concept enables resource development to proceed with the support of the Aboriginal people. The decision in *Mabo* is also of significance in the establishment of human rights in Australia. The common law has long set the minimum standard of human rights. The *Mabo* decision gives explicit recognition to native title as part of that threshold standard.[3]

6.3.1 The determination

The plaintiffs[4] were Murray Islanders who initiated proceedings in the High Court in 1982 in response to the Queensland (Aboriginal and Islander Grants) Amendment Act 1982, which established a system for issuing land grants on trust for Aboriginals and Torres Strait Islanders. The Murray Islanders refused to accept the system introduced under this legislation. The action was brought as a test case to determine the rights of the Meriam people to land on the islands of Mer, Dauar and Waier in the Torres Strait, which were annexed by the State of Queensland in 1879. The Meriam people had been in occupation of the islands for generations prior to the colonisation and have continued to live in the villages. The plaintiffs sought declarations *inter alia* that the Meriam people were entitled to the Murray Islands as owners, as possessors, as occupiers or as persons entitled to use and enjoy the said islands.

In 1985, the Queensland government attempted to terminate the proceedings by enacting the Queensland Coast Islands Declaratory Act, which declared that, on annexation of the islands in 1879, they vested in the State of Queensland and were 'freed from all other rights, interests and claims whatsoever'. No provision was made in the legislation to compensate the Meriam people. In the first *Mabo* case (*Mabo v Queensland* (1988) 166 CLR 70 (*Mabo (No 1)*), the High Court held that this legislation was invalid as it was contrary to the Racial Discrimination Act 1975 (Cth).

In the second *Mabo* case (*Mabo v The State of Queensland* (1992) 175 CLR 1 (*Mabo (No 2)*), the High Court case based its findings of fact on the determinations of Moynihan J of the Supreme Court of Queensland in November 1990. Moynihan J determined that, prior to colonisation, the Meriam people had lived on the islands in a subsistence economy based on gardening and fishing. Gardening was a central part of the social organisation of the Meriam people, and the village land itself was divided into plots owned

3 Bartlett, R, '*Mabo*: another triumph for the common law', in *Essays on the Mabo Decision*, 1993, Sydney: LBC, Chapter 5, p 66.

4 There were initially five plaintiffs but, by the time the case was decided, only two were still alive.

by individuals or family groups. Land was regarded by the Meriam people as belonging to either individuals or groups, and not to the general community. The Meriam people currently occupying the land were held to be direct descendants of the original population, as there was little permanent immigration. Furthermore, the present Meriam people have retained a strong affiliation with their traditional customs and cultures. In May 1991, the court heard arguments on questions of law concerning rights to land existing under common law. The final decision of the High Court was handed down on 3 June 1992. Unfortunately, Eddie Mabo's individual claim was unsuccessful, and he and two of the other five applicants died before the final determination was handed down.

In a six to one majority (Mason CJ, McHugh, Gaudron, Brennan, Deane and Toohey JJ, with Dawson J in dissent), the High Court held that the people of the Murray Islands retained native title to their lands which was not extinguished by the annexation of the islands to Queensland in 1879 or by legislation subsequently enacted. Three of the judges went further to hold that native title holders could claim compensation for wrongful extinguishment of their title through an inconsistent Crown grant. Mason CJ, Brennan, McHugh and Dawson JJ concluded that no compensation was payable.

The judgment of Brennan J

In his leading judgment, Brennan J (accepted by Mason CJ and McHugh J) illustrates the general approach taken by the majority and provides an excellent summary of the fundamental common law principles in issue. His Honour critically examined the proposition of the defendant that when the Crown assumed sovereignty over an Australian colony it became the universal and absolute beneficial owner of the land. If this principle is accepted, as soon as the land was colonised, the interests of the indigenous inhabitants in colonial land were extinguished in favour of the Crown. His Honour notes:

> The proposition that, when the Crown assumed sovereignty over an Australian colony, it became the universal and absolute beneficial owner of all the land therein, invites critical examination. If the conclusion at which Stephen CJ arrived in *Attorney General v Brown* be right, the interests of indigenous inhabitants in colonial land were extinguished as soon as British subjects settled in a colony, though the indigenous inhabitants had neither ceded their lands to the Crown nor suffered them to be taken as the spoils of conquest. According to the cases, the common law itself took from indigenous inhabitants any right to occupy their traditional land, exposed them to deprivation of the religious, cultural and economic sustenance which the land provides, vested the land effectively in the control of the imperial authorities without any rights to compensation, and made the indigenous inhabitants intruders in their own homes and mendicants for a place to live. Judged by any

> civilised standard, such a law is unjust, and its claim to be part of the common law to be applied in contemporary Australia must be questioned.[5]

His Honour felt that, in declaring the common law of Australia, the court was not free to adopt rules, even where they accord with contemporary notions of human rights and justice, if those rules damage or interfere with the 'skeleton of principle which gives the body of our law its shape and internal consistency'. Brennan J concluded that, since the Australia Act 1986 (Cth) came into operation, the law of this country has been entirely free of imperial control; the ultimate responsibility of declaring the law lies with the High Court of Australia; the law that should govern Australia is 'Australian law'. His Honour noted that the task of the court was to consider whether or not the principles relied upon by the defendants, which offended contemporary fairness notions, were nevertheless an inextricable part of the common law.

The proposition that the sovereign acquired absolute beneficial ownership of all land rested, according to Brennan J, upon a number of grounds. First, the sovereign acquired absolute beneficial ownership because there is no other proprietor. Clearly, this ground completely denies the existence of any proprietary interest in the indigenous inhabitants. This proposition is reinforced by the belief that when English law was brought to Australia, the common law which was to be applied to the colonies included the feudal doctrine of tenure. On this basis, just as the Crown acquired all land in England, so too, when the Australian colonies were settled, the Crown acquired universal ownership of Australian land. Universal title, under the feudal doctrine of tenure, could be acquired by conquest, cession and occupation of territory that was *terra nullius*. The foundation for the application of Crown sovereignty and ownership in Australia was that the land was *terra nullius*, and therefore absolute ownership could be properly assumed.

6.3.2 Terra nullius *and extended* terra nullius

Brennan J examined the principles relating to *terra nullius*. Literally, *terra nullius* means land which is vacant, empty, null and void. With respect to land, it traditionally meant that the conquering lords found the land uninhabited. Under the feudal system of tenure, the Crown was able to acquire any land which was considered to 'belong to no one'. The concept of *terra nullius* was extended when new inhabited lands were being discovered. Sovereignty over these lands was able to be recognised where the territory was inhabited by 'backward people'. The theory here was that, because there was no local law already in existence, the law of England became the law of the territory. Upon annexation, the assumption was that the indigenous people were 'backward

5 *Mabo v The State of Queensland (No 2)* (1992) 175 CLR 1, p 18.

people' and therefore that the land was effectively *terra nullius*. The indigenous people of a settled colony were thus taken to be without laws, without a sovereign, and primitive in their social organisation. This conclusion was established despite the fact that, in 1879, the Meriam people were settled on their land, the gardens were being tilled and the 'Mamoose' and the 'London Missionary Society' were keeping the peace with a form of justice being administered.

Brennan J concluded that the extended theory of *terra nullius*, establishing that indigenous inhabitants of a 'settled' colony had no proprietary interest in their ancestral land, depended upon a discriminatory denigration of indigenous inhabitants, their social organisation and their customs, and it ignored and devalued their whole way of life. His Honour felt that the common law should not be or be seen to be frozen in an age of racial discrimination. The fiction by which the rights and interests of indigenous inhabitants in land were treated as non-existent is justified by a policy which has no place in the contemporary law of this country. His Honour stated:

> The facts as we know them today do not fit the 'absence of law' or 'barbarian' theory underpinning the colonial reception of the common law of England. That being so, there is no warrant for applying in these times rules of the English common law which were the product of that theory. It would be a curious doctrine to propound today that, when the benefit of the common law was first extended to Her Majesty's indigenous subjects in the Antipodes, its first fruits were to strip them of their right to occupy their ancestral lands. Yet the supposedly barbarian nature of indigenous people provided the common law of England with the justification for denying them their traditional rights and interests in land ... The theory that the indigenous inhabitants of a 'settled' colony had no proprietary interest in the land thus depended on a discriminatory denigration of indigenous inhabitants, their social organisation and customs.[6]

Brennan J felt that it would be contrary to international standards and to the fundamental values of our common law to entrench a discriminatory rule; he therefore concluded that the principle of 'extended *terra nullius*' should not longer be recognised and accepted by contemporary common law.

6.3.3 *Radical title*

Brennan J then went on to consider the proposition that colonial land became a 'royal demesne' upon occupation. In this respect, it is important to distinguish between the two forms of sovereignty that the Crown could assume. The first relates to the power of government; the second relates to title and ownership of the land. Sovereignty of power can only belong to the Crown, whereas title to land is not so restricted. His Honour noted that it was

6 *Mabo v The State of Queensland (No 2)* (1992) 175 CLR 1, p 27.

only by accepting the notion of extended *terra nullius* that sovereignty of title could be asserted. This did not, however, mean that the fundamental principles of common law ownership were now overruled:

> It was only on the hypothesis that there was nobody in occupation that it could be said that the Crown was the owner because there was no other. If that hypothesis be rejected, the notion that sovereignty carried ownership in its wake must be rejected too. Though the rejection of the notion of *terra nullius* clears away the fictional impediment to the recognition of indigenous rights and interests in colonial land, it would be impossible for the common law to recognise such rights and interests if the basic doctrines of the common law are inconsistent with their recognition.[7]

6.3.4 *The doctrine of tenure*

Feudal tenure is the English legal theory whereby every parcel of land in England is held either mediately or immediately of the King, who is the 'Lord Paramount'. (See the discussion in Chapter 3.) The term 'tenure' signifies the relationship which exists between the tenant and the lord rather than the tenant and the land. When the Crown acquired land outside England, it was naturally assumed that the doctrine of tenure would apply. It is possible, as noted by Brennan CJ, that the assumption need not have been made ,because the doctrine of tenure may, in fact, be a purely English phenomenon which is only applicable where the land is conquered. In this sense, it is clearly arguable that the universality of tenure is not reasonably applicable to the Australian colonies. Nevertheless, the doctrine of tenure is an integral component of the Crown's claim to title over land in Australia; the radical title assumed by the Crown is a direct result of the feudal system. As pointed out by Brennan J:

> The radical title is a postulate of the doctrine of tenure and a concomitant of sovereignty ... The notion of radical title enabled the Crown to become Paramount Lord of all who hold a tenure granted by the Crown and to become absolute beneficial owner of unalienated land required for the Crown's purposes.[8]

His Honour held, however, that it was not a corollary of the Crown's acquisition of a radical title to land in an occupied territory that the Crown acquired absolute beneficial ownership of that land to the exclusion of all indigenous inhabitants. If the land was truly *terra nullius,* then the doctrine of tenure and radical title would enable the Crown to acquire absolute beneficial title to the land because there would, in fact, be no other proprietor. As 'extended *terra nullius*' was rejected, the inevitable conclusion was that radical title 'cannot itself be taken to confer an absolute beneficial title to the occupied land'.

---

7 *Mabo v The State of Queensland (No 2)* (1992) 175 CLR 1, p 34.

8 *Ibid*, p 37.

Hence, whilst the doctrine of tenure was perceived as a skeleton principle firmly entrenched in the common law, to refuse recognition of the rights and interests in land of the indigenous inhabitants was not an essential feature of the Australian form of tenure. Brennan J noted: 'The doctrine of tenure applies to every Crown grant of an interest in land, but not to rights and interests which do not owe their existence to a Crown grant.'[9]

Ultimately, then, Brennan J felt that both radical and native title could exist jointly because the doctrine of tenure never applied to native title interests. Radical title could therefore be burdened by native title. It was only if sovereignty of power was automatically equated with sovereignty of title that native title would have been extinguished upon colonisation and, as his Honour points out, these two concepts are quite distinct: 'It is only the fallacy of equating sovereignty and beneficial ownership of land that gives rise to the notion that native title is extinguished by the acquisition of sovereignty.'[10]

6.3.5 Recognition of native title

The ownership of land within a territory in the exclusive occupancy of a people should be vested in that people: land is susceptible to ownership and, where there are no other owners, it is only fair and just that the 'occupiers' of that land be recognised as having 'good' title. This does not necessarily mean that the 'good title' be equivalent to a common law estate. Land which is in the possession of indigenous people is not alienable, for the laws and customs of an indigenous people do not generally contemplate alienation of traditional land, nor is it 'exclusive' or 'private' in nature; however, this does not prevent the interests from being recognised as proprietary. Indeed, the very fact that the Crown retains sovereignty of power over the land supports this. For if it is contemplated that the Crown could extinguish indigenous people's interests in the land and create proprietary rights in their place, it would be 'curious if, in place of interests that were classified as non-proprietary, proprietary rights could be created'. As explained by Brennan J:

> The fact that individual members of the community, like the individual plaintiff in *Milirrpum*, enjoy only usufructuary rights that are not proprietary in nature is no impediment to the recognition of a proprietary community title. Indeed, it is not possible to admit traditional usufructuary rights without admitting a traditional proprietary community title.[11]

Hence, the fact that the Meriam people simply used and cultivated the land does not mean that their interest and relationship with the land cannot be regarded as proprietary. They hold a 'native', communal title which is usufructuary in nature.

9 *Mabo v The State of Queensland (No 2)* (1992) 175 CLR 1, p 37.

10 *Ibid*, p 39.

11 *Ibid*, p 40.

Native title, in this context, refers to the interests and rights of indigenous inhabitants in land, whether communal, group or individual, possessed under the traditional laws acknowledged by, and the traditional customs observed by, the indigenous inhabitants. Native title can only be assumed by the indigenous inhabitants of a territory and their descendants; it is recognised by the common law; however, it is not an institution of the common law and therefore not alienable by the common law. Alienability depends upon the laws or customs of the indigenous community. Native title will cease with the abandoning of traditional laws and customs which cannot be revived for contemporary recognition. As Brennan CJ expressly notes:

> It follows that a right or interest possessed as a native title cannot be acquired from an indigenous people by one who, not being a member of the indigenous people, does not acknowledge their laws and observe their customs; nor can such a right or interest be acquired by a clan, group or member of the indigenous people unless the acquisition is consistent with the laws and customs of that people.[12]

Both legal and equitable remedies will be available to enforce and protect native title rights, and the form of remedy which is appropriate will depend upon the form of rights asserted. The rights acquired under native title will vary according to the particular laws and customs recognised by the indigenous clan in occupation. As long as those individual laws do not offend natural justice and good conscience, they will be protected.

Brennan J felt that the Meriam people had proven a sufficient connection with traditional customs and culture to establish native title rights; they had maintained their identity as a people and they continued to observe and uphold long standing traditional customs.

6.3.6 *Extinguishment of native title*

Native title may cease to exist in a number of circumstances. First, where the traditional title holders lose their connection with the land, any title that may have existed will automatically cease. Native title will not, however, cease merely through proof of a modified lifestyle or minor changes in customs, but only where it can be established that a complete cessation of traditional customs and a fundamental change of lifestyle have occurred.

Secondly, native title may be extinguished by an act of Parliament or the granting of a freehold or non-freehold estate which is inconsistent with the legal rights conferred under native title. Once established, native title can only be extinguished by a clear and plain intention to do so by the legislature or the executive. The statutory intention must be explicit because of the seriousness of the consequences upon indigenous inhabitants. Where a common law

12 *Mabo v The State of Queensland (No 2)* (1992) 175 CLR 1, p 49.

estate has been granted by the Crown, Brennan J noted that native title would only be extinguished to the extent of the inconsistency:

> A Crown grant which vests in the grantee an interest in land which is inconsistent with the continued right to enjoy a native title in respect of the same land necessarily extinguishes the native title. The extinguishing of native title does not depend on the actual intention of the Governor in Council (who may not have adverted to the rights and interests of the indigenous inhabitants or their descendants), but on the effect which the grant has on the right to enjoy the native title.[13]

Brennan J felt that the grant of lease would extinguish native title because it confers the right to exclusive possession upon the lessee for the duration of the lease, with the Crown retaining the reversion expectant. Where the Crown grants land in trust or on reserve, or dedicates land for a public purpose, native title may be extinguished if it can be proven that the rights conferred under such a grant are inconsistent with native title rights. His Honour felt that this will sometimes be a question of fact, sometimes of law, and sometimes of mixed fact and law. Where, however, the Crown has not granted estates or interests, or has reserved the land inconsistently with the rights of native title holders, native title must survive and will be legally enforceable.[14] Where native title is extinguished, the Crown will become the absolute beneficial owner of the land.

Applying this to the Meriam people, Brennan J concluded that the Meriam people were entitled to possession, occupation and the use and enjoyment of the whole island of Mer except for that parcel of land which had been validly leased out. The lease granted to the London Missionary Society, which was later transferred to the Australian Board of Missions, and the sardine factory lease had the effect of extinguishing native title claims in that area because the rights conferred under the lease were inconsistent with the native title claims. The fact that the leases contained express conditions ensuring that the lessees would not interfere with native use of gardens or plantations on the land or with native fishing on the reefs did not, according to his Honour, preserve native title from extinguishment because the very effect of granting a lease was inconsistent with native title rights.

Joint judgment of Deane and Gaudron JJ

Deane and Gaudron JJ both issued a judgment similar in substance to that of Brennan J. One of the primary differences lay in the fact that their Honours went on to deal with the issue of compensation for the extinguishment of native title. Whilst their Honours both recognised that native title could be

13 *Mabo v The State of Queensland (No 2)* (1992) 175 CLR 1, p 57.

14 See the discussion of the majority and Brennan CJ in dissent over the issue of extinguishment of leases in more detail in the *Wik* decision – for a detailed discussion of which, see below, para 6.5.

extinguished through clear legislative action, they felt that compensation would be payable in this instance unless clearly exempted within the express terms of the legislation. Significantly, their Honours felt that, as the Crown had the right to extinguish native title and exclude the right to compensation, native title rights should truly be classified as personal rather than proprietary rights.

Further, their Honours felt that, where extinguishment results as a consequence of a grant of an inconsistent estate or interest in the land, the extinguishment may be classified as wrongful and, in such a situation, the Crown will also be liable to pay compensation. Their Honours felt that the obligation to pay compensation was supported by s 51(xxxi) of the Commonwealth Constitution, which confers on the Commonwealth the power to acquire property on just terms provided just compensation is granted. Deane and Gaudron JJ further note that any state legislation which attempts to override this would be ineffective under the inconsistency provision in s 109 of the Commonwealth Constitution:

> ... the power of the Crown wrongfully to extinguish the native title by inconsistent grant will remain, but any liability of the Crown to pay compensatory damages for such wrongful extinguishment will be unaffected.[15]

Unlike Brennan J, their Honours held that the leases which had been granted over the lands claimed by the Meriam people were not inconsistent with native title claims. In discussing the 'sardine factory' lease, their Honours stated: 'It would seem likely that, if it was valid, it neither extinguished nor had any continuing adverse effect upon any rights of Murray Islanders under common law native title.'[16]

No firm conclusion on this issue of inconsistency between leases and native title rights was established, although the matter has now been directly raised in the *Wik* decision: see below, 6.5.

The judgment of Toohey J

Toohey J agreed in substance with Brennan, Deane and Gaudron JJ that the doctrine of *terra nullius* should be rejected and that traditional native title continued after annexation of the Murray Islands. Like Brennan J, Toohey J concluded that an inquiry into the kind of society from which rights and duties emanate is ultimately irrelevant to the existence of title, because it is inconceivable that indigenous inhabitants in occupation of land did not have a system by which land was utilised in a way determined by that society. Hence, extended *terra nullius* was both discriminatory and ineffective as a

15 *Mabo v The State of Queensland (No 2)* (1992) 175 CLR 1, p 102.

16 *Ibid*, p 108.

means of conferring absolute title upon the Crown. According to Toohey J, the important issue was that native title claims may be established through proof of continuous occupation of and association with the land. For this purpose, a nomadic lifestyle could amount to occupancy and, furthermore, title will not be precluded merely on the basis that more than one group utilises the land.

6.3.7 *Fiduciary duties of the Crown*

Toohey J also went on to consider in some detail whether any equitable, fiduciary duties should be imposed on the Crown. The majority of the court did not come to any firm conclusion on this issue. Brennan J simply noted that: '... there may be a fiduciary duty on the Crown to exercise its discretionary power to grant a tenure in land so as to satisfy the expectation, but it is unnecessary to consider the existence or extent of such a fiduciary duty in this case.'[17] Dawson J expressly rejected the application of fiduciary obligations in such circumstances. His Honour distinguished the United States authorities in this regard by concluding that the cases relied upon the specific 'history of protection' of Indian tribes which had been assumed by the United States. He also distinguished the Canadian authorities on the basis that the fiduciary relations in those cases were dependent upon the finding of Aboriginal title to the land, and, as he had rejected this conclusion, the Canadian authorities were inapplicable. As a majority of the High Court has now accepted the validity of native title, the rejection of such authorities would now seem to have little foundation. Furthermore, unlike Toohey J, Dawson J did not examine the question of whether a fiduciary relationship could be raised as a consequence of the power and discretion vested in the Crown.

Toohey J undertook a more detailed and expansive analysis of fiduciary obligations. His Honour noted that the foundation of a fiduciary relationship is the ability of one party to exercise a discretion which is capable of affecting the legal position of the other. Where a relationship confers this type of discretion, conferring a special opportunity on one party to abuse the interests of the other, or involving an undertaking to act on behalf of another with the potential to detrimentally affect the interests of that other, a fiduciary relationship may arise. His Honour considered the applicability of such a relationship between the Queensland government and Aboriginal peoples and noted that, given the objective of protecting the rights and interests of indigenous persons which can be detected from the legislature, equitable obligations were not expressly excluded.

Furthermore, Toohey J felt that fiduciary obligations were not excluded on the grounds that they would interfere with the proper exercise of 'governmental discretion'. In particular, his Honour referred to the Canadian

---

17 *Mabo v The State of Queensland (No 2)* (1992) 175 CLR 1, pp 43–44.

authority of *Guerin v R* (1984) 13 DLR (4th) 321, where the Supreme Court of Canada held that the Crown owed a fiduciary duty towards the Indians. As Dickson J (Beetz, Chouinard and Lamer JJ concurring) stated:

> The fact that Indian Bands have a certain interest in lands does not, however, in itself give rise to a fiduciary relationship between the Indians and the Crown. The conclusion that the Crown is a fiduciary depends upon the further proposition that the Indian interest in the land is inalienable except upon surrender to the Crown.[18]

By direct analogy, Toohey J felt that if native title rights were, similarly, inalienable, except by surrender to the Crown, and the Crown has the power to extinguish such rights, a fiduciary relationship between the Crown and Aboriginal peoples should exist. The basis for this relationship lies in the need to protect indigenous persons against the prospect of governmental destruction or damage to their native title rights. His Honour stated:

> The power to destroy or impair a people's interests in this way is extraordinary and is sufficient to attract regulation by equity to ensure that the position is not abused. The fiduciary relationship arises, therefore, out of the power of the Crown to extinguish traditional title by alienating the land or otherwise; it does not depend on an exercise of that power.[19]

Apart from the Canadian authority, Toohey J felt that a fiduciary relationship was justified on the particular facts, given the nature of the dealings entered into by the Queensland government. The statutory creation of reserves over the land held by the Meriam people, and the continuing exercise of control and regulation through such initiatives as welfare legislation, was, according to Toohey J, sufficient in itself to warrant the imposition of fiduciary obligations.

His Honour concluded that the Queensland government should be regarded as a constructive trustee of the interests of indigenous persons, and the usual fiduciary duties applicable to this position existed. The exact content of the fiduciary obligations owed would vary according to the individual circumstances involved. One fundamental duty of the government which did arise was the obligation to act in the best interests of all of the beneficiaries when exercising discretionary powers which may adversely affect their interests. On the facts, this meant that, if the government impaired or destroyed the interests of the titleholders without their prior consent, it would be in breach of its equitable obligations. As Toohey J noted:

> A fiduciary obligation on the Crown does not limit the legislative power of the Queensland Parliament, but legislation will be a breach of that obligation if its effect is adverse to the interests of the titleholders, or if the process it establishes does not take account of those interests.[20]

18 *Guerin v R* (1984) 13 DLR (4th) 321, p 376. Quoted by Toohey J in his judgment, *Mabo v The State of Queensland (No 2)* (1992) 175 CLR 1, p 202.

19 *Mabo v The State of Queensland (No 2)* (1992) 175 CLR 1, p 203.

20 *Ibid*, p 205.

The application of fiduciary obligations to governments may, potentially, have broad effects. In the first place, any governmental action which has an impact upon native title rights would, under Toohey J's analysis, have the potential to constitute a breach of fiduciary duty if implemented without the consent of indigenous persons. Hence, it is possible that any governmental dealings with native title, including general policy statements and initiatives, may be questionable. Furthermore, the fiduciary status may impact upon the processes of governmental decision making in the future. Fiduciary duties may ensure that decisions respecting the rights of indigenous persons are not made without making sure that the titleholders affected have access to independent legal advice and that any consent to dealings, if obtained, is full, proper and informed.

The exact status of the Crown as a constructive trustee under Toohey J's analysis remains unclear, because the nature and scope of the corresponding beneficial interest is not properly explored. It is not clear if, by raising the constructive trust relationship, his Honour believed indigenous peoples held a beneficial interest in the land or (as seems more probable) his Honour was simply intending to impose the trust as a protective relationship without further exploring its proprietary consequences.

Furthermore, it remains unclear from the judgment whether the usual array of equitable remedies, including equitable compensation, would be available for a breach of fiduciary duty in these circumstances. Given that the majority of the High Court determined that lawful extinguishment of native title will not in itself give rise to a claim for compensation, the question of whether a breach of fiduciary duty could independently give rise to such a claim in the equitable jurisdiction remains doubtful. The need to resolve the fiduciary issues raised in *Mabo* has, for the most part, been overtaken by the introduction of the native title legislation, which specifically prescribes the procedures for creation and extinguishment of native title and, in particular, the circumstances in which compensation is payable.

6.4 Native title legislation

Following the *Mabo* decision, the federal government passed the Native Title Act 1993 (Cth) in order to provide some structure and regulation to the native title rights introduced by the High Court. The primary purpose of the legislation was to set up a special Native Title Tribunal, where native title claims could be assessed, and to examine the validity of past actions of the government. The specific objects of the Act are listed in s 3 and may be summarised as follows:

(a) to recognise and protect the validity of native title;

(b) to provide for the validation of past acts which may be invalid due to the existence of native title;

(c) to provide for a future regime in which native title rights are protected and specific conditions imposed upon acts affecting native title land and waters;

(d) to provide a tribunal process by which native title claims can be properly considered, compensation issues examined, and to determine the permissibility and validity of future grants or acts done over native title land and waters; and

(e) to provide for a range of other miscellaneous matters, including the establishment of a National Aboriginal and Torres Strait Islander Land Fund.

6.4.1 *Legislative definition of native title*

One of the primary purposes of the Commonwealth, in enacting this legislation, was to recognise and protect native title interests. In pursuing these objectives, the legislation seeks to adopt the common law definition of native title as set out by the majority of the High Court in the *Mabo* decision. Section 223(1) defines native title to mean the communal, group or individual rights and interests of Aboriginal peoples or Torres Strait Islanders in relation to land or waters, where:

(a) the rights and interests are possessed under the traditional laws acknowledged, and the traditional customs observed, by the Aboriginal peoples or Torres Strait Islanders; and

(b) the Aboriginal peoples or Torres Strait Islanders, by those laws and customs, have a connection with the land or waters; and

(c) the rights and interests are recognised by the common law of Australia.

Section 223(2) adds to the legislative definition of native title by setting out that the reference to 'rights and interests' includes hunting, gathering or fishing rights and interests.

The focus of the section lies upon rights which relate to the actual use and cultivation of the land. Section 223(3) sets out that native title rights will still cover rights over land or water which may have been replaced or compulsorily converted into statutory rights.

The Act protects and entrenches native title and, pursuant to s 10, native title as defined by the Act will be recognised and protected in accordance with the provisions of the Act. Furthermore, according to s 11(1), native title as defined by the Act is not able to be extinguished in a manner which is contrary to the Act. The combined effect of these provisions is to immunise native title from destruction by acts which would ordinarily destroy or impair common law and equitable estates and interests.

An application may be made under the Act for a determination as to whether or not native title exists over a claimed area. The National Native

Title Tribunal (NNTT) will consider the application.[21] The actual application may be instigated by the persons claiming a right to native title or by the Commonwealth or State minister – depending upon the jurisdictional requirements of the area in issue.

Once the application requirements are met, the Registrar of the Tribunal must then make a determination on the native title issue. Native title rights must be accepted by the Tribunal where the application contains the necessary requirements. An application may be refused where the Registrar considers that the application has not been made out or that the application is either vexatious or frivolous.[22] Once the native title claim has been accepted, the Registrar must give notice of the accepted application to all persons whose interest may be affected, and such persons are entitled to oppose the application. The NNTT will then make a final determination as to the existence, nature and rights associated with the native title claim. This determination will be made whether the application is opposed or not. However, where it is opposed, a mediation conference should be held to try and reach an agreement between all parties involved. Where the NNTT cannot reach a final agreement, the Federal Court has jurisdiction to make a final determination.[23] In making its determination, the Federal Court has a degree of flexibility: it will not be bound by rules of evidence or legal form and may make a determination on the facts, with the assistance of outside experts and commentators.[24]

6.4.2 Validation of past, intermediate and future acts

6.4.2.1 Past acts

The native title legislation provides for the validation of past grants of land or acts to third parties which have been carried out in respect of land or waters over which native title claims have been made. Validation in this context refers to the substantiation of actions or transactions, retrospectively, over previous actions. Past acts will include any government action taken prior to 1 January 1994 and legislation enacted prior to 1 July 1993 that may have been invalid to any extent due to the recognition and enforcement of native title: s 228. The legislation indicates that compensation is payable if native title is extinguished after 1975; that is, after the introduction of the Racial Discrimination Act 1975 (Cth). The Native Title Act (Cth) expressly provides that the Racial Discrimination Act 1975 (Cth) will not affect the validation of past acts – however, its existence since 1975 prevents the Commonwealth from excluding

21 Native Title Act 1993 (Cth), s 161.

22 *Ibid*, s 63.

23 *Ibid*, ss 69–74.

24 *Ibid*, ss 169–70.

native title holders from the right to seek compensation where ordinary title holders would, in the same circumstances, have been compensated: ss 17(2), 240 of the Native Title Act (Cth). The aim of the legislation in this regard is to remove any lingering doubts there may be concerning the status of such actions. Sections 14–18 of the legislation provide for the validation of past acts attributable to the Commonwealth, whilst ss 19–20 provide for the validation of past acts attributable to a state or territory. Examples of past acts which may be validated include the making of legislation, the grant of a licence or permit, the creation of any interest in land or waters, and the exercise of executive power.

There are four categories of Commonwealth past acts which are described in the legislation alphabetically as A, B, C and D. Category A acts are acts involving the grant of a freehold estate or of a commercial, agricultural, pastoral or residential lease. Category B acts are grants of leasehold estates other than those set out in category A and excluding mining leases. Category C acts are grants of mining leases. Category D is a miscellaneous, umbrella category which includes any other acts.

Under the terms of ss 14 and 19, category A acts will extinguish native title absolutely. Category B acts will extinguish native title to the extent that the acts are inconsistent with the existence or exercise of native title.[25] Category C and D acts are effectively subject to the 'non-extinguishment principle' whereby native title is not extinguished but it is invalid to the extent of the inconsistency.[26] Category C attracts mining leases which have been granted and are in force from 1 January 1994. Validating a past act effectively confers priority on that act as against native title rights. This priority is manifested through complete extinguishment for category A acts, partial extinguishment, to the extent of the inconsistency, for category B acts, and priority rather than extinguishment for categories C and D.

The legislation provides that native title holders will be entitled to compensation on 'just terms', payable by the Commonwealth, where the effect of a validation of past acts is to extinguish or impair native title rights.

Compensation will be available for the validation of a category A or B past act. The validation of a category C or D act will only entitle a native title holder to compensation if the conditions specified in s 17(2) are satisfied. This provision requires compensation to be paid where it would have been payable had the acts been carried out over ordinary title. Section 51 specifies that compensation must be determined on 'just terms', taking into account any loss, diminution or impairment of the rights of native title holders.

25 Native Title Act 1993 (Cth), s 15(1)(c).

26 *Ibid*, s 238.

The legislation allows for the payment of compensation by the Commonwealth even in situations where the validation is over a state or territory act. Section 20 of the Act expressly sets out that native title holders will be entitled to compensation for validation of past acts by states or territories in the same manner as they would be for the validation of past acts by the Commonwealth. Despite this entitlement, s 20(3) sets out that native title holders may also recover compensation from the state or territory.

6.4.2.2 *Intermediate period acts*

The legislation also deals with what it describes as 'intermediate period acts'. These acts must have taken place between 1 January 1994 and 23 December 1996 and, as a result of the decision in *Wik Peoples v State of Queensland and Others* (1996) 141 ALR 129, have been presumed to be invalid as a consequence of the recognition and enforcement of native title. In *Wik*, the court held that that the conferral of statutory pastoral leases did not, in the circumstances, extinguish native title. This conclusion left the status of pastoral leases executed within this time frame uncertain. Hence, the Native Title Act was amended to ensure that such acts were validated. Consequently, where an act comes within this category, it will be validated by the legislation entitling the holder of native title to seek compensation. Section 22A validates Commonwealth intermediate period acts and s 22F allows states and territories to validate their intermediate period acts.

The validation of intermediate period acts is almost the same as the validation process for past acts discussed above. The only difference is that category A acts, resulting in a complete extinguishment of native title are not freehold estates but rather, agricultural and pastoral leases which confer upon the tenant, exclusive possession: s 23B. Where the agricultural or pastoral lease does not confer exclusive possession of the land upon the holder it will constitute a category B rather than a category A act, which only entitles the holder to extinguish native title to the extent of the inconsistency: s 22B.

Where an intermediate period act is validated, holders of native title affected by the validation are entitled to compensation: s 22A.

6.4.2.3 *Future acts*

The legislation also validates what are described as 'future acts'. A future act is any legislation enacted after the 30 June 1993 or any other act which has taken place after 31 December 1993, but does not include acts coming within the definition of past acts or intermediate period acts: s 233. Future acts must comply with the requirements set out under the legislation in order to be valid. A proposed act or dealing will constitute a future act and be required to comply with the procedures in the Native Title Act if the land, which is the subject of the dealing, is affected by native title. If the land used to be affected by native title, however the native title has been extinguished prior to 31 October 1975 or, if no native title is proven to exist at all, then the native title legislation will not regulate the future act and it will not be obliged to comply with its procedural requirements: s 24AA(1).

Where the future act is regulated by the native title legislation, the act will be invalid unless it complies with the requirements of notification, negotiation and arbitration: s 24AA(2). The procedural requirements are extensively outlined in the native title legislation. For example, notification must be given to any aboriginal representative or registered native title claimants in relation to land covered under a non-exclusive lease, dealing with a primary production activity in the area of forest operations, horticultural activity or acquacultural activity: s 24GB(9). The right to negotiate is a special procedural right given only to registered native title bodies corporate and claimants with respect to particular types of acts covered under s 24IC. For example, prior to granting any mining lease over native title land, any renewal of a lease that creates or varies a right to mine or grants involving the compulsory acquisition of native title land, negotiation between the parties must occur with a view to reaching an agreement: s 26(1)(A); s 26(1)(c)(iii). The right to negotiate does not apply to all mining grants or compulsory acquisitions (for example, the right to negotiate does not apply to grants created for the sole purpose of constructing infrastructure associated with mining: s 26(1)(c)(i)). If no agreement is reached, an arbitral body may make a determination about the renewal, grant or extension: s 25(3). If the right to negotiate is not complied with, the future act will be invalid to the extent that it affects native title: s 28. The 'arbitral body' will oversee the right to negotiate.

Generally, a valid future act will only extinguish or impair native title rights to the extent of their inconsistency: s 44H; s 24GC and in such a situation, the responsible government may be liable to pay compensation: see, for example, ss 24FA(1)(b), 24GB(7) and 24GD(4).

6.4.3 Protection of reservations

Section 16 of the legislation sets out that a validation exercise will not affect any reservations or conditions currently existing for the benefit of Aboriginal peoples or Torres Strait Islanders which have been created by a past grant or statute. The section reads as follows:

> If:
>
> (a) the act attributable to the Commonwealth contains a reservation or condition for the benefit of Aboriginal peoples or Torres Strait Islanders; or
>
> (b) the doing of the act would affect rights or interests (other than native title rights and interests) of Aboriginal peoples or Torres Strait Islanders (whether arising under legislation, at common law or in equity and whether or not rights of usage),
>
> nothing in s 15 [the validation section] affects the reservation or condition or those rights or interests.

This provision operates to protect existing rights which Aboriginal peoples or Torres Strait Islanders may have acquired by setting out that validation of past acts will only have the effect of extinguishing native title rights – not other statutory rights which may be held by indigenous groups.

6.4.4 *State native title legislation*

Legislation has also been introduced in some states emulating the Commonwealth structure, although implementing the determination of native title rights through specialist courts. Legislation to this effect has been introduced in South Australia, New South Wales and Queensland.[27] The primary difference between the state and Commonwealth legislation lies in the fact that the system is court based and relies upon the specific expertise of courts holding jurisdiction over land matters. The actual procedure is, however, not as formal as usual court matters: the courts have been directed to proceed with minimum formality and without reference to the rules of evidence and procedures, although proceedings must comply with the principles relating to natural justice.

Most states have also passed specific legislation to validate past acts of their governments, thereby supplementing the validation procedure existing under the Commonwealth legislation.[28] The legislation in these states confirms the existence of native title, and they operate in conformity with the Commonwealth Act. Western Australia, however, introduced the Land (Title and Traditional Usage) Act 1993 (WA), which purported to extinguish native title rights and replace it with statutory rights of traditional usage. In *Western Australia v The Commonwealth* (1995) 128 ALR 1, the State of Western Australia challenged the validity of the Commonwealth native title legislation in the High Court. The challenge was based upon the argument that the Commonwealth legislation was contrary to the Racial Discrimination Act 1975 (Cth) and that it interfered with the ability of the Western Australian government to legislate properly in the area of native title.

The West Australian government alleged that the Commonwealth legislation was discriminatory because the provisions of the Act effectively constituted a distinction, exclusion, restriction or preference on the basis of race which resulted in a nullification or impairment of basic human rights according to s 9(1) of the Racial Discrimination Act 1975 (Cth). Whilst the racial discrimination legislation allows for some exceptions, particularly where the acts constitute 'special measures for the sole purpose of securing adequate advancement of certain racial or ethnic groups', the West Australian government argued that the Commonwealth native title legislation did not fit

27 See Native Title Act 1994 (SA); Native Title Act 1994 (NSW); Native Title Act 1993 (Qld).

28 See Native Title Act 1994 (SA); Native Title Act 1994 (NSW); Native Title Act 1993 (Qld); Land Titles Validation Act 1994 (Vic); Native Title Act 1995 (Tas); Native Title Act 1994 (Cth); Validation of Titles and Actions Act (NT) 1994.

within those exceptions because the legislation was not for the 'sole' purpose of securing adequate advancement of the Aboriginal peoples; it was not necessary to secure the advancement of aboriginal rights because common law already recognised these rights prior to the introduction of the Act, and the legislation led to the maintenance of separate rights for different racial groups because persons other than Aboriginal peoples or Torres Strait Islanders could not hold title.

The High Court rejected these arguments and made the following comments (p 62):

> ... it is not easy to detect any inconsistency between the Native Title Act and the Racial Discrimination Act. The Native Title Act provides the mechanism for regulating the competing rights and obligations of those who are concerned to exercise, resist, extinguish or impair the rights and interests of the holders of native title. In regulating those competing rights and obligations, the Native Title Act adopts the legal rights and interests of persons holding other forms of title as the benchmarks for the treatment of the holders of native title. But if there were any discrepancy in the operation of the two Acts, the Native Title Act can be regarded either as a special measure under s 8 of the Racial Discrimination Act or as a law which, though it makes racial distinctions, is not racially discriminatory so as to offend the Racial Discrimination Act.

The second argument raised by the West Australian government was that the Commonwealth native title legislation interfered with the ability of the state government to legislate properly in this area because it interfered with the capacity of the government to regulate, obtain revenue from and otherwise deal with land and other resources. The West Australian government argued that administration of land and mineral resources was a vitally significant function in that state because of the concentration of mineral resources in the area and the fact that a greater proportion of the land was capable of being subjected to native title claims. The High Court rejected this argument, noting that the Commonwealth legislation did not serve to impede the essential functions of the West Australian government except for the fact that it regulated the payment of compensation.

Finally, the validity of the new West Australian legislation, the Land (Titles and Traditional Usage) Act 1993 (WA), which purported to extinguish native title claims which were made in that state, was considered. The court unanimously concluded that the legislation was contrary to the Racial Discrimination Act 1975 (Cth) and, or alternatively, inconsistent with the Native Title Act 1993 (Cth), and therefore invalid according to s 109 of the Commonwealth Constitution. The court felt that there was no reason why West Australia should be singled out and native title rights extinguished in that state alone. The history of the West Australian colonisation was not so peculiar that sovereignty principles in that state alone extinguished native title rights.

The decision of the High Court in the West Australian challenge is significant because it emphasises the preparedness of the courts to accept and uphold the validity and enforceability of the Commonwealth native title legislation despite state objections. Another extremely important decision in the evolution of native title has been the *Wik* decision. This case was commenced prior to the introduction of the native title legislation but handed down after its commencement.

6.5 The *Wik* decision

The decision of *Wik Peoples v State of Queensland and Others/Thayorre People v State of Queensland and Others* (1996) 141 ALR 129 is a significant one for the survival of native title. The case concerned the issue of whether or not the granting of two pastoral leases over vast areas of land, to which the Wik and Thayorre peoples claimed native title, resulted in the subsequent extinguishment of that title. The significance of the determination was well summarised by Kirby J in his judgment:

> The issues at stake in these proceedings are therefore important. If the primary argument of the contesting respondents is accepted, this court's holding in *Mabo (No 2)*, that native title survived the annexation of Australia to the Crown and the acquisition of the Crown's radical title, is revealed as having little practical significance for Australia's indigenous people over much of the land surface of the nation ... This is all the more significant to indigenous peoples as the parts of Australia where their laws and traditions (important to sustain native title) are most likely to have survived include those where pastoral leases are likely to exist. On the other hand, the issues are equally important for lessees under pastoral leases, those taking under them, potentially those holding other title to land, governments, mining interests and the population generally.

The case has its origin in proceedings brought by the Wik peoples in the Federal Court of Australia. Those proceedings were initiated prior to the operation of the Native Title Act 1993 (Cth). The action in the Federal Court was brought by the Wik peoples, who were an Aboriginal clan, for a declaration that they retained native title rights over a large area of land in north Queensland. The Thayorre people, another Aboriginal clan, cross claimed for a similar declaration in respect of lands which partly overlapped with the lands claimed by the Wik people.

The land claimed by the Wik and Thayorre peoples included land over which pastoral leases had been granted by the Crown. One of these pastoral leases was known as the Holroyd River Holding Lease (the 'Holroyd Lease'), and the others were known as the Mitchellton pastoral leases (the 'Mitchellton leases'). The central issue in the case was whether or not the native title rights claimed had survived the granting of these pastoral leases. The Wik and Thayorre peoples argued that native title was not extinguished and that it was happily 'co-existing' with the interests of the lessees.

Drummond J, in the Federal Court, held that, as each of the pastoral leases conferred on the lessee rights of exclusive possession, the granting of such estates 'necessarily extinguished all incidents of Aboriginal title ... with respect to the land demised under the pastoral leases'. A consequence of this conclusion was that his Honour did not decide on the issue of whether or not the Wik and Thayorre peoples actually held native title rights over the land. The decision of Drummond J was, however, interlocutory, and did not fully and finally dispose of the proceedings. Leave was therefore granted to appeal to the full court of the Federal Court although, subsequently, an amended notice of appeal was filed in the High Court. The appellants challenged the conclusion of Drummond J that the pastoral leases resulted in the extinguishment of native title rights.

A number of arguments were raised by the appellants, which may be broadly summarised as follows:

(a) first, that exclusive possession was not actually conferred by the terms of the pastoral leases. The statutory procedure for removing persons in unlawful occupation of the Mitchellton pastoral leases pursuant to s 204 of the Land Act 1910 (Qld) proved that the person entitled to possession of the land which was the subject of the lease was not the lessee, but rather, the Crown, and consequently the lease was effectively no more than a licence. Secondly, that the express reservation in the pastoral lease, of a right in the Crown to nominate any person to enter upon the land for any purpose and at any time, proved that the lessees did not acquire a right of exclusive possession. This reservation, in combination with the above mentioned restrictions, were argued to negate any statutory intention to confer exclusive possession upon pastoral lessees and thereby to extinguish native title. Finally, the Wik and Thayorre peoples argued that Parliament could not have intended exclusive possession to be conferred upon the lessees because the land areas covered were of such magnitude that it would effectively result in the Aboriginal inhabitants becoming trespassers on their traditional land, and such an Act would have been 'truly barbarian';

(b) that native title could only be extinguished where a practical inconsistency arose between the exercise of native title rights and the exercise of rights under the pastoral leases, and on the facts, no such practical inconsistency existed; and

(c) alternatively, that the pastoral leases only suspended native title rights during the term of the lease, and once the leases were determined, the Crown would regain radical title to the land, burdened by native title rights. The argument was that, as the lessees did not go into possession, no reversionary estate could be held by the Crown. As noted in *Coke on Littleton*,[29] 'before possession there is no reversion'.

29 2 Co Litt 270a.

The High Court held by a majority (Toohey, Gaudron, Gummow and Kirby JJ; Brennan CJ, McHugh and Dawson JJ dissenting) that the pastoral leases in question did not confer on the lessees rights to exclusive possession and, particularly, possession which was exclusive of all rights and interests held by the indigenous inhabitants. Consequently, the court further held that the granting of the pastoral leases did not automatically result in the extinguishment of native title and that native title rights remained and co-existed with rights flowing from pastoral leases. This conclusion prevented the need to consider further the alternative argument of whether or not native title rights are suspended during the existence of the pastoral leases.

In dissent, Brennan CJ, McHugh and Dawson JJ held that the Wik and Thayorre peoples' claim should fail because native title was extinguished by the pastoral leases. Their Honours felt that the leases conferred the right to exclusive possession and this right was inconsistent with native title.

The individual judgments of Toohey and Kirby JJ, in the majority, and of Brennan CJ, in dissent, are examined below.

6.5.1 The judgment of Toohey J

Toohey J noted that pastoral leases were creatures of statute rather than common law, and consequently, the rights and obligations conferred must be determined by reference to the applicable statutory provisions. In considering the intention of Parliament when enacting legislation for pastoral leases, his Honour noted the historical context and, in particular, the desire of the state to achieve a peaceful co-existence between the pastoralists, who wanted to obtain pasturage for the cattle and stock, and the indigenous peoples, who subsisted on the land. His Honour concluded that the relevant legislation granted the lessees possession of the land for pastoral purposes. However, there was nothing in the legislation which conferred a right to exclusive possession:

> A pastoral lease under the relevant legislation granted to the lessee possession of the land for pastoral purposes. And the grant necessarily gave to the lessee such possession as was required for the occupation of the land for those purposes. As has been seen, each lease contained a number of reservations of rights of entry, both specific and general. The lessee's right to possession must yield to those reservations. There is nothing in the statute which authorised the lease, or in the lease itself, which conferred on the grantee rights to exclusive possession, in particular, possession exclusive of all rights and interests of the indigenous inhabitants whose occupation derived from their traditional title. In so far as those rights and interests involved going on to or remaining on the land, it cannot be said that the lease conferred on the grantee rights to exclusive possession. That is not to say the legislature gave conscious recognition to native title in the sense reflected in *Mabo (No 2)*. It is simply that there is nothing in the statute or grant that should be taken as a total exclusion of the indigenous people from the land, thereby necessarily treating their

> presence as that of trespassers or, at best, licensees whose licence could be revoked at any time.[30]

Following this conclusion, his Honour noted that, strictly, the question of extinguishment did not arise. Nevertheless, he went on to consider when an 'inconsistency' would result in an extinguishment of native title. His Honour felt that it would be necessary to prove an inconsistency between native title rights and legislative legal rights, such that the two could not co-exist, before an extinguishment would occur. Inconsistency to such an extent could only be proven where the particular form of native title results in a 'direct interference' with the rights conferred under pastoral leases.

Finally, in considering the character of the Crown's continuing interests in the land, his Honour noted that, following the grant of pastoral leases, the Crown did not acquire a reversionary estate, and that it would be stretching the bounds of the doctrine of estates to reach such a conclusion. Attention was given to the status of the radical title held by the Crown before the leases were executed and the fact that the leases did not change that status:

> The invocation of reversion and *plenum dominium*, as those expressions are usually understood, does not lie easily with the position of the Crown under the relevant statutes ... To contend that there is a beneficial reversionary interest in the Crown which ensures that there is no room for the recognition of native title rights is, in my view, to read too much into the Crown's title. Furthermore, if it is the reversion which carries with it beneficial title, why is that title not there in the first place? And if it is the existence of that beneficial title which extinguishes native title rights, why were those rights not extinguished before the grant of a pastoral lease? There is a curious paradox involved in the proposition.[31]

In summary, his honour noted the 'undue emphasis' granted to the issue of extinguishment when the true heart of the matter was whether or not the Crown intended, by the grant of a lease, to deprive indigenous peoples of huge tracts of land:

> It is a large step to conclude that, because there has been a grant of a 'lease' of many square miles for pastoral purposes, all rights and interests of indigenous people in regard to the land were intended thereby to be brought to an end. Where is the necessary implication of a clear and plain intention?[32]

6.5.2 *The judgment of Kirby J*

Kirby J developed three 'potential' tests dealing with the issue of extinguishment. The first he called the 'exercise of sovereignty test'. According

30 *Wik Peoples v State of Queensland and Others/Thayorre People v State of Queensland and Others* (1996) 141 ALR 129, p 181.

31 *Ibid*, p 187.

32 *Ibid*, p 188.

to this test, once the Crown proceeded in any way to convert its radical title into any other estate or interest in land, it exercised its sovereignty and would thereby extinguish any native title rights in existence.

The second test, Kirby J called the 'inconsistency of incidence test'. According to this test, if the legal rights of an estate or interest are inconsistent with the continuance of native title rights, those rights will be extinguished.

The third test, Kirby J called the 'factual conflict test'. Under this test, if it can be established that the practical exercise of the interest or estate conferred conflicts with the exercise of surviving native title rights, the latter may be extinguished. If, however, they may be reconciled, no extinguishment will occur.

His Honour then considered which test was the most appropriate. The first test was not accepted by Kirby J as valid and appropriate, although he noted that it was used by Drummond J in the Federal Court. After examining the decision in *Mabo (No 2)*, Kirby J concluded that it did not provide a determinable *ratio* concerning extinguishment of native title for all leases and that, given the number and variety of Crown leasehold interests, it could not possibly have done so. Furthermore, given the extent to which *Mabo (No 2)* went in constructing native title as an interest, it would be inappropriate to allow it to be extinguished so easily:

> The first theory is not compatible with the authority of the court in *Mabo (No 2)*. The decision of the court in that case introduced a new and radical notion. It disturbed the previous attempts of the Australian legal system to explain all estates and interests in land in this country by reference to the English legal doctrine of tenure derived ultimately from the sovereign as Paramount Lord of the colonies as he or she had been in England after the Conquest. Now, a different source of title must be accommodated by the recognition of the continuance of native title as a burden on the Crown's radical title. Something more is needed to remove that burden, and to extinguish the native title, than a mere exercise by the Crown of rights of *dominium* in respect of the land. Native title might be subject to extinguishment. However, it is not as fragile as the first theory propounded.[33]

The third 'factual inconsistency' test was also rejected by Kirby J. His Honour felt that extinguishment of native title on the basis of inconsistency was not simply a question of fact and that the issue was whether the legal rights were compatible. The question, then, is not whether the Aboriginal peoples have, in fact, been expelled from their traditional lands 'but whether those making claim to such lands have the legal right to exclude them'.[34]

Hence, the most appropriate test for determining whether or not native title rights had been extinguished was the second 'inconsistency of incidence'

33 *Wik Peoples v State of Queensland and Others/Thayorre People v State of Queensland and Others* (1996) 141 ALR 129, p 273.

34 *Ibid*, p 274.

test. In examining the application of this test, Kirby J considered the character of pastoral leases and their legal status. His Honour noted that pastoral leases are creatures of statute, rather than common law, and that their character and incidence must be derived from the statute. In light of the huge areas of land covered by the pastoral leases, his Honour felt that it was extremely unlikely that the Queensland Parliament intended to confer exclusive possession to the pastoralists.

Kirby J found nothing 'expressed in the legislation' to indicate an intention to confer an inconsistent lease. His Honour felt that the mere use of the word 'lease' did not automatically mean that a common law lease had been conferred and that the correct approach was to examine the rights actually conferred on the pastoralists by the instrument rather than assuming its form. His Honour noted that, not only did the historical background and statutory purpose preclude the conclusion that the statute conferred a common law lease with exclusive possession, some of the actual terms of the statute went against this. In particular, Kirby J focused upon the terms dealing with the removal of trespassers in s 204 of the 1910 legislation and s 373(1) of the 1962 legislation. His Honour noted that these sections entitled pastoralists to remove trespassers by 'taking possession on behalf of the Crown' and, by their very terms, indicated that the pastoralists did not hold exclusive possession in the first place.

Finally, and perhaps most importantly, Kirby J noted the 'strong presumption that a statute is not intended to extinguish native title'.[35] This is a natural and just presumption and defers to the fact that Parliament would not normally take away the rights of individuals or groups without making such a purpose unequivocally clear in the statute.[36] Consequently, in applying the second 'inconsistency of incidence test', his Honour concluded that the legal interests created by the pastoral lease Acts did not extinguish native title, because there was no inconsistency:

> When, therefore, the legal interests granted by the pastoral leases here are analysed and considered with our present knowledge that native title survived annexation of the Australian lands to the Crown, the nature of such legal interests is such that they do not necessarily extinguish native title. This conclusion can more comfortably be reached with the assistance of the presumption that, without express words or necessary implication, Australian legislation will not be construed to take away proprietary rights, particularly without compensation. The holders of pastoral leases are left with precisely the legal rights which they enjoyed pursuant to the leases granted under the Land

35 *Wik Peoples v State of Queensland and Others/Thayorre People v State of Queensland and Others* (1996) 141 ALR 129, p 282. See, also, *Mabo v The State of Queensland (No 1)* (1988) 166 CLR 186, p 224 and *Mabo v The State of Queensland (No 2)* (1992) 175 CLR 1, p 111; *Western Australia v Commonwealth* (1995) 183 CLR 373, p 422.

36 In *Mabo (No 2)* above, Toohey J noted the possibility of the Parliament being under a fiduciary obligation towards its subjects. See *Mabo v The State of Queensland (No 2)* (1992) 175 CLR 1, pp 201–03.

> Acts 'for pastoral purposes only'. Those rights will prevail, to the extent of any inconsistency with native title ... It is the peculiarity of the legal rights conferred by such statutory leases, in the factual setting in which they were intended to operate, which permits the possibility of coexistence of the rights under the pastoral lease and native title.[37]

6.5.3 The judgment of Brennan CJ (in dissent)

The judgment of Brennan CJ is significant because he issued the leading judgment of the majority in *Mabo (No 2)*. In the *Wik* decision, however, Brennan CJ issued a strong dissent, Brennan CJ held that the Wik and Thayorre peoples' claim failed because native title was extinguished by the pastoral leases. His Honour concluded that exclusive possession had been conferred by the terms of the leases and, as that right was inconsistent with native title, the rights of the pastoral lessees prevailed and native title was extinguished.

In the first part of his determination, Brennan CJ examined the character of the interest conveyed and, whilst he noted that the interests were statutory creations, and that the statutory restrictions upon entry and possession qualified the common law right to exclusive possession, he ultimately concluded that they did not extinguish it. His Honour also referred to the fact that, whilst attention must be given to substance rather than form so that the references in the statute to the term 'lease' should not be regarded as the ultimate touchstone for determining the exact character of the interests, 'the ordinary rules of interpretation require that, in the absence of any contrary indication, the use in a statute of a term that has acquired a technical legal meaning is taken *prima facie* to bear that meaning'.[38]

His Honour felt that a lease rather than a licence was clearly intended to be conferred and, consequently, exclusive possession must exist, because otherwise, there would be no difference between these two rights. Furthermore, in dealing with the argument raised by the Wik and Thayorre peoples that the Queensland government had a protective motive and did not want to oust the Aboriginal peoples from their traditional lands, his Honour emphasised the point that, at the time of passing the legislation, native title rights were not recognised by the courts, hence the legislation could not have been introduced with the intention of protecting such rights. Consequently, Brennan CJ concluded that the Land Acts of 1910 and 1962 created legal leasehold estates which conferred exclusive possession upon the pastoral lessees and a reversionary expectant estate upon the Crown. It was, his

37 *Wik Peoples v State of Queensland and Others/Thayorre People v State of Queensland and Others* (1996) 141 ALR 129, p 285.

38 *Ibid*, p 145.

Honour concluded, too late to develop a new theory of land law that would throw the whole structure of land titles into confusion and undermine the doctrines of tenure and estates.

In determining the issue of extinguishment, Brennan CJ focused upon intention. Like Kirby J, his Honour felt that the intention must be manifest through the exercise of legal rights and powers, and is therefore an objective test rather than a subjective inquiry into the state of minds of the legislators. To postulate a test which focuses upon the manner in which rights are exercised rather than the creation of rights would:

> ... produce situations of uncertainty, perhaps conflict. The question of extinguishment of native title by a grant of inconsistent rights is – and must be – resolved as a matter of law, not of fact. If the rights conferred on the lessee of a pastoral lease are, at the moment when those rights are conferred, inconsistent with a continued right to enjoy native title, native title is extinguished.[39]

Where the legal effect of the interest is to create rights in third parties which are inconsistent with native title, native title will be extinguished to the extent of the inconsistency. Furthermore, where the Crown exercises its sovereign power to use unalienated land for its own purposes, native title may be partially or wholly extinguished.

On the facts, Brennan CJ concluded that there was a direct inconsistency between the right of exclusive possession acquired by the pastoral lessees and native title rights. There was no room, according to his Honour, for the alternative argument by the Wik and Thayorre peoples that, even if leasehold interests did confer exclusive possession, native title rights were merely suspended during the term of the lease. Brennan CJ felt that once a legal leasehold estate is conferred and the Crown acquires a reversionary estate, an inconsistency arises and native title is extinguished absolutely, and to argue otherwise would go against fundamental land law principles.

Whilst Brennan CJ noted the 'significant moral shortcoming' apparent in the fact that the mere grant of leases could extinguish completely the native title of the traditional Aboriginal inhabitants to possess and enjoy lands in which they are living and have lived since time immemorial, he felt that this 'shortcoming' could not, ultimately, deny the true legal effect of the pastoral leases according to fundamental and entrenched land law principles. This did not, however, mean that the Wik and Thayorre peoples became trespassers, because their presence on the land was expected, and an implied consent could be inferred.

39 *Wik Peoples v State of Queensland and Others/Thayorre People v State of Queensland and Others* (1996) 141 ALR 129, p 153.

6.5.4 *Conclusions*

The majority judgments in the *Wik* decision not only provide further strength and foundation to the native title rights first recognised and endorsed by the High Court in *Mabo (No 2)*, by adopting a firm native title stance. Toohey, Kirby, Gummow and Gaudron JJ emphasise the historical and cultural importance of native title rights and reinforce this practically through a careful assessment of what actions can constitute an extinguishment. Extinguishment should not, as each judge emphasises, be readily inferred from a statute because of the significant impact it would have upon the Aboriginal peoples. Extinguishment of native title should only validly occur where the legal rights of a subsequent estate or interest are so directly inconsistent with native title rights that the two cannot co-exist. Extinguishment should not, however, be justified by anything less than this.

The manner in which the majority judges assessed and applied the facts of the *Wik* decision highlights the strength of this conviction. The assessment of the facts involved three significant stages. First, the determination that the pastoral leases were statutory constructions and that any rights flowing from these interests should not be inferred from common law but, rather, determined according to the express terms of the statutes creating them.

Secondly, and extremely significantly for the Wik and Thayorre peoples, the conclusion that, despite an express description of the interests as leases, the statutory rights were not the same and did not confer the same entitlements as common law leasehold estates. This was justified on a number of grounds. One important ground lay in the fact that the pastoralists did not actually take the leases in possession and the Crown retained limited statutory rights to take possession for the 'purposes of removing trespassers'. A further ground lay in the analysis of the intention of the drafters at the time of introducing the legislation. All majority judges focused upon the fact that the statutes were introduced as a regulatory measure rather than an attempt to oust Aboriginal peoples from the land on which they subsisted. Given the huge tracts of land covered by the statutes, most judges felt that, if the legislators had intended to confer traditional common law leasehold rights of exclusive possession upon the pastoralists, they would have effectively intended to exile these people. There is no expression of this intention, either in the express terms of the legislation or in the historical discussions concerning the implementation of this legislation. This is well summarised by Gaudron J, who notes:

> ... the vastness of the areas which might be made the subject of pastoral leases and the fact that, inevitably, some of them would be remote from settled areas militate against any intention that they should confer a right of exclusive possession entitling pastoralists to drive native title holders from their traditional lands. Particularly is that so in a context where, in conformity with

> the prescribed form, the grants were expressed to be made 'for pastoral purposes'.[40]

The third and final stage in the fact assessment lay in the conclusion by the majority that the limited form of interest that the statutory 'pastoral leases' represented was not inconsistent with native title, and therefore did not extinguish the rights of native title holders. Most of the majority judges adopted an objective assessment of extinguishment, concluding that it was the legal interest granted, and not just the way in which that interest was enforced, that had to be considered. As the majority had already concluded that the pastoral leases did not confer exclusive possession upon the pastoralists, the natural conclusion was that there was no legal inconsistency between the rights of the pastoralists and those of the Wik and Thayorre peoples and, consequently, no extinguishment.

The *Wik* decision represents a further milestone in the evolution of native title. The *Mabo (No 2)* decision was significant for its reconstruction of historical and feudal principles in colonial Australia, its endorsement of the validity of native title rights which are recognised, although not regulated, by the common law, and the laying down of the fundamental features of native title. The *Wik* decision takes this further by setting down the boundaries of native title enforceability, and laying down the tests for determining what circumstances may extinguish native title and when those circumstances can legitimately be found to exist. It is, like *Mabo (No 2)*, a powerful and extremely important decision, not only for its confirmation of the validity and enforceability of native title, but also, more generally, in its recognition of the rights of Aboriginal peoples. Whilst, in *Mabo (No 2)*, the majority concluded that erroneous assumptions of historical fact could no longer justify a continued refusal to recognise native title rights in Aboriginal peoples, in *Wik*, the majority clearly indicated that, in enforcing native title rights, it is prepared to re-examine the character and operation of fundamental common law principles. The continuing development and adaptation of the common law to the new and expanding concept of native title will take time and must proceed slowly and cautiously. This is appropriately summarised by Gummow J:

> ... the further elucidation of common law principles of native title, by extrapolation to an assumed generality of Australian conditions and history from the particular circumstances of the instant case, is pregnant with the possibility of injustice to the many, varied and complex interests involved across Australia as a whole. The best guide must be the 'time honoured

40 *Wik Peoples v State of Queensland and Others/Thayorre People v State of Queensland and Others* (1996) 141 ALR 129, p 208.

methodology of the common law', whereby principle is developed from the issues in one case to those which arise in the next.[41]

6.6 Judicial development of native title

Some of the most important issues concerning the regulation and enforcement of native title in Australia today concern such matters as the evidence required to establish native title, the scope of native title and the circumstances under which native title may be extinguished. These issues have been raised in numerous judicial decisions. Mention will be made here of a few of the more significant decisions in the evolution of native title law.

6.6.1 Approaches to extinguishment of native title post-Wik

In *Fejo v Northern Territory* (1998) 156 ALR 721, the High Court considered whether the grant of a freehold, which had subsequently been compulsorily acquired by the Commonwealth, extinguished native title. On the facts, the applicants had made a native title application over the land, which had been accepted for mediation by the registrar of the NNTT; the applicants sought a declaration that native title subsisted over the area, and to restrain the Northern Territory government from granting development leases, containing the right, provided certain conditions were met, of converting any lease to freehold without any first giving the applicants the right to negotiate. At first instance, the judge refused relief noting that the prior grant of a freehold estate extinguished any subsisting native title and the right to native title could not be revived when the land was 're-vested' in the Crown following the compulsory acquisition.[42]

The High Court dismissed the appeal noting that a grant of an estate in fee simple is the highest estate known to the law and will necessarily extinguish any native title because of the fact that the rights held by a fee simple owner are inconsistent, 'An estate in fee simple ... simply does not permit the enjoyment by anyone else of any right or interest in respect of the land unless conferred by statute, by the owner of the fee simple, or by a predecessor in title' (p 736, *per* Gleeson CJ, Gaudron, McHugh, Gummow, Kirby, Hayne and Callinan JJ).

In *The State of Western Australia v Ben Ward* (2000) 170 ALR 159, a Full Court of the the Federal Court considered the rules of evidence and proof necessary to establish native title. The case involved a native title application over approximately 7,900 square kilometres of vacant Crown land in the East

41 *Wik Peoples v State of Queensland and Others/Thayorre People v State of Queensland and Others* (1996) 141 ALR 129, p 232.

42 This situation is now covered under s 47B of the Native Title Act which sets out that prior extinguishment of native title should be disregarded where, at the time of bringing an application for native title, the land is vacant Crown land occupied by one or more members of the claimant group.

Kimberley region on the Ord River near the Gulf and on the coast from the east side of the Gulf to the state/territory border including Crown land in or about the town of Kununurra, the Ord River irrigation area, and Lake Argyle. The basic issues in the case involved: the rules of evidence and proof necessary to establish aboriginal connection with a claim area, proof required of the maintenance of that connection, the meaning of extinguishment and the types of rights which may extinguish native title.

The trial judge, Lee J, made some important comments about the nature and scope of native title. His Honour held that native title is a common law concept which is not defined or moulded to equate with estates, rights or interests in land which form the law of real property at common law. Native title does not conform to traditional common law concepts and is to be regarded as unique. Native title is a *sui generis* interest, inalienable to third parties and not capable of being lost to the Crown by prescription. In particular, customary rights not involving a profit, exercisable in respect of land by a local community but not the public at large, analogous to the character of some of the rights that arise under native title, were recognised at common law if they were ancient, certain, reasonable and continuous.

At common law, native title in land will exist at the date of sovereignty if an indigenous community had an entitlement to use or occupy the land at that time, that entitlement arising from local recognition that the presence of the community on the land reflected a particular relationship or connection between that community and the land. There is no need to prove occupancy as long as an acknowledged connection can be established, and such occupancy need not be exclusive to one community; it may be shared between several communities.

Native title that has not been extinguished by action of the Crown, or by extinction of the society that possessed it, will continue where connection with the land is substantially maintained by a community which acknowledges and observes, as far as practicable, laws and customs based upon the traditional practices of its predecessors. The activities or practices may be a modern form of exercise of those laws and customs. It will be immaterial that those laws and customs have undergone change since sovereignty, provided that the general nature of the connection remains. Native title will be ascertained by reference to practices that are based on traditional laws and customs, not by enquiring whether the traditional practices observed today are in the same form as before as if frozen in time. Native title, as recognised by the common law, shares the capacity of the common law to evolve and mould as circumstances require. An indigenous society does not surrender native title by modifying its way of life.

Difficulty in proving the boundaries of the area in respect of which native title is claimed is not in itself sufficient to deny the existence of native title. In native title proceedings, any rules of evidence must be cognisant of the evidentiary difficulties faced by Aboriginal people in presenting such claims for adjudication. Of particular importance in that regard is the disadvantage faced by Aboriginal people as participants in a trial system structured for, and by, a literate society when they have no written records and depend upon oral histories and accounts, often localised in nature.

The Native Title Act provides assistance for the application of the common law in respect of native title by, *inter alia*, moulding a form of litigation for the determination of the existence of native title at common law and by providing that such litigation is to be an exercise of federal jurisdiction. The Act does not provide jurisdiction in respect of the enforcement or protection of native title rights. The act also deals with extinguishment. Extinguishment of native title cannot be partial; where it occurs, it is absolute. Extinguishment will occur by the grant of tenures by the Crown that confer on third parties rights to use the land in a way inconsistent with the exercise of rights that attach to native title.

The extinguishment tests adopted by Lee J were those set out in the important Canadian decision: *Delgamuukw v British Columbia* (1993) 104 DLR (4th) 470:

1 that there be a clear and plain expression of intention by Parliament to bring about extinguishment;
2 that there be an act authorised by the legislation which demonstrates the exercise of permanent adverse dominion as contemplated by the legislation; and
3 unless the legislation provides, the actual use made of the land by the holder of the tenure which is permanently inconsistent with the continued existence of aboriginal title or right and not merely a temporary suspension.

After a comprehensive examination of the facts and a review of the relevant law, Lee J concluded that native title exists in the 'determination area' and is held by the Miriuwung and Gejerrong People as they had substantially maintained their connection with the land. The only extinguishment of that native title was effected by the construction of roads, permanent public works, freehold grants and some reserves. The rights include the right to possess, occupy, use and enjoy, access, make decision, use and enjoy the resources, control the use and enjoyment of the resources, trade in the resources, maintain, protect and prevent the misuses of cultural knowledge of the common law holders associated with the determination area. These rights are to be exercised in a practical way in respect of the determination area and should be resolved by negotiation with all parties concerned. native title was proved to exist over most of the area claimed, as the Miriuwung and Gajerrong people. The State of Western Australia appealed against the 'connection' and 'extinguishment' conclusions.

On appeal, Beaumont and Van Doussa JJ and North J upheld the decision of Lee J concerning the continued existence of native title over the claimed land and dismissed this aspect of the appeal but by a majority, Beaumont and

Van Doussa JJ, North J in dissent, rejection the decision of Lee J and upheld the appeal on the question of extinguishment. With respect to the issue of connection, the court held that the existence of native title is a question of fact to be ascertained by evidence of the connection of the Aboriginal community with the land at the time of occupation and evidence that this connection has been maintained since this time. Evidence of the maintenance of that connection since that time. All members of the court upheld the finding of Lee J that the members of the Miriuwung and Gajerrong community had maintained their connection with the claimed area. The majority disagreed, however with Lee J on the issue of extinguishment. Lee J noted that for native title to be extinguished, the rights issued must actually be exercisable and should be permanently inconsistent with native title rights. In effect, Lee J had adopted the adverse dominion test which was expressly rejected by the High Court in *Wik* in favour of the 'inconsistency of incidents' test which requires a comparison between the legal nature and incidents of the statutory right which has been granted and the native title rights being asserted.

Furthermore and significantly the majority concluded that 'partial extinguishment' of some of the rights which make up the native title bundle was possible and that the grant of pastoral leases in the claim area partially extinguished native title. The majority noted that reservations of land for a public purpose do not automatically cause extinguishment however the native title areas covered by mineral and petroleum claims were extinguished. The pastoral lease granted made it clear that as a matter of law, they did not authorise the total extinguishment of native title – only the partial extinguishment of some of the native title 'bundle of rights'. North J, in dissent, felt that native title was not a bundle of rights, but rather, a fundamental right and it was not possible to 'partially extinguish' some of those rights. North J agreed with Lee J and noted that extinguishment could only occur where there is a total and permanent inconsistency between the rights granted and the native title. Where a lesser degree of inconsistency exists, native title is impaired or temporarily suspended but not extinguished.

6.6.2 Native title and evidential difficulties

In *Yorta Yorta Aboriginal Community v The State of Victoria* (1998) unreported, 18 December, Federal Court of Australia, a native title application was brought over a large area of land in Northern Victoria and Southern New South Wales. Within the claim area there were a number of substantial towns including: Shepparton, Morroopna, Echuca, Mathoura, Yarrawonga and Wangaratta. The case examined the necessary proof of traditional laws and customs for the recognition of a 'continuing relationship' with the land. Olney J referred to three important factors: first, that the members of the claimant group are descendants of the indigenous people who occupied the land; secondly, the nature and content of the traditional laws acknowledged and the traditional customs observed by the indigenous people must be established; and, thirdly, it must be demonstrated that the traditional connection with the land of the ancestors of the claimant group has been substantially maintained since the time sovereignty was asserted.

Olney J held that the native title claim could not, on the facts, be established. His Honour felt that an unfortunate aspect of the applicants' evidence was that it often involved stories handed down from generation to generation, prolonged outbursts of righteous indignation at the treatment they and their forebears have received and much of the evidence was historical but failed to properly identify a continuing connection between the claimants and the land in issue. According to his Honour, there was no clear and unambiguous evidence of a connection between the known ancestors and the original inhabitants at the time of European contact.

6.6.3 *The application of native title offshore*

In *Yarmirr v Northern Territory* (1997) 143 ALR 687 and, on appeal, (1998) 156 ALR 370, an application was made to the Federal Court for a determination of native title over the sea and sea bed, and any reefs or other land in an area surrounding Croker Island. The applicants asserted that they held exclusive rights over the areas claimed, including, *inter alia*, the rights to control the access of others to the waters, or prevent other people from hunting or gathering material from the waters; to be recognised as the exclusive owners of marine organisms within the waters, and to have the right and responsibility to care for and protect the resources of the waters. Croker Island had been granted in 1980 to the Arnhem Land Aboriginal Land Trust for the benefit of Aboriginal people under the Aboriginal Land Rights (NT) Act 1976 (Cth).

Justice Olney in the Federal Court found that there was clear evidence that the applicants had exercised traditional rights in relation to the waters, to catch fish, hunt for marine organisms and collect shellfish for sustenance and for ceremonial purposes. The Northern Territory government argued that the recognition of native title could not extend beyond the the low water mark and that the applicants did not have ownership of marine or mineral resources of the sea bed. Furthermore, any native title rights that may exist must be subject to public rights of navigation and to the powers of the Northern Territory and the Commonwealth to grant fishing and other rights in the particular waters in issue.

Justice Olney held that even though sovereignty over the seas under the Seas and Submerged Lands Act 1973 (Cth) had been established in 1990, native title could still be recognised. Section 223(1)(c), which required that the rights and interests be recognised by the common law, did not impose a territorial limit measured by reference to the area where the common law applies. On appeal, the Full Federal Court in *Yarmirr v Northern Territory* (1998) 156 ALR 370, by majority upheld this decision. Justices Beaumont and von Doussa held that s 223(1)(a) already encompassed notions of extinguishment.

Olney J further concluded that although exclusive rights may have been enjoyed, 'the very nature of the sea renders it inappropriate to attempt to strictly apply concepts such as possession and occupation which are readily capable of being understood in relation to land'. Hence, the rights asserted by the claimants in relation to controlling resources were found to be, in essence, the practical consequence of any right to control access to the area, and Olney J concluded that traditional rules about sharing catches of fish did not amount to rights in relation to lands or waters within the terms of the Act. Furthermore, Olney J felt that Australia's international obligations to permit innocent passage of ships, and the existence of public rights at common law to pass and repass over the water, and to fish, prevented the recognition of exclusive rights. Olney J further concluded that there was no rights over mineral resources as title to minerals had been vested by legislation in the Crown and this extinguished any native title rights.[43]

6.6.4 *Native title and hunting rights*

In *Yanner v Eaton* (1999) 166 ALR 258, the issue of the existence and scope of any native title right to hunt was examined. On the facts, Murrandoo Yanner was charged with taking a species of protected fauna (an estuarine crocodile) without a licence, in breach of the Fauna Conservation Act 1974 (Qld). The charge was dismissed on the ground that Mr Yanner was acting in accordance with native title rights under the Native Title Act 1993 (Cth). The Crown appealed against this arguing that any native title right which existed was extinguished by operation of s 7(1) of the Fauna Conservation Act giving the Crown property in all fauna. By majority, the Court of Appeal held that native title rights to hunt fauna were extinguished by the Fauna conservation Act and were therefore not rights capable of coming within the ambit of s 223 of the Act. Yanner appealed against this decision to the High Court.

The High Court allowed the appeal by a majority decision. The majority concluded that the use of the word 'property' in the Fauna Conservation Act did not require the vesting of full beneficial ownership in the Crown because the term property has such a broad and diverse meaning and is capable of referring to a wide variety of different types of legal relationships. As noted by the majority, Gleeson CJ, Gaudron, Kirby and Hayne JJ:

> The respondent's submission (which the Commonwealth supported) was that s 7(1) of the Fauna Act gave full beneficial, or absolute, ownership of the fauna to the Crown. In part this submission was founded on the *dictum* noted earlier,

43 See, also, *Fourmile v Selpam Pty Ltd* (1998) 152 ALR 294.

> that 'property' is 'the most comprehensive of all the terms which can be used'. But the very fact that the word is so comprehensive presents the problem, not the answer to it. 'Property' comprehends a wide variety of different forms of interests; its use in the Act does not, without more, signify what form of interest is created.

Hence, on the facts, the majority concluded that the Crown's rights over the fauna were less than beneficial. Consequently, the Fauna Conservation Act 1974 (Qld) did not extinguish native title and could not prevent Mr Yanner from exercising his native title rights. In dissent, McHugh J noted that the term 'property' was not so elusive in meaning that it ought to have a more limited or restricted meaning than absolute ownership. This decision is indicative of an increasingly flexible approach assumed by courts to the conceptualisation of the nature of property – probably resulting from the deconstruction of the doctrine of tenure and the recognition of broader notions of property emerging from the *Mabo* decision. It is clear from the *Yanner* decision that courts are increasingly moving away from automatic proprietary presumptions; this is a highly appropriate response in a society where common law feudal estates sit side by side with rights based upon fundamentally different cultural perspectives.[44]

44 See the excellent article by Patricia Lane, 'Native title: the end of property as we know it' (1999) 8 Australian Property Law Journal 19.

CHAPTER 7

FIXTURES

7.1 Introduction

The law relating to fixtures is concerned with categorisation: it examines when an independent chattel is to be regarded as having become a part of the land. Basically, a fixture refers to a personal chattel which has become so annexed to land that it loses its independent status and is subsequently regarded as constituting a part of the land itself. As noted by Sir Frederick Jordan in *Australian Provincial Assurance Co Ltd v Coroneo* (1938) 38 SR (NSW) 700:

> A fixture is a thing, once a chattel, which has become, in law, land through having been fixed to land. The question whether a chattel has become a fixture depends upon whether it has been fixed to the land and, if so, for what purpose.

Land will automatically include certain objects which are naturally affixed to it, such as trees, plants and streams, and it is not necessary to prove that these natural objects comply with the fixture tests. Where, however, a separate chattel is attached or annexed to the land in some way, it is necessary to consider whether or not the attachment is such that it changes the character of the item and effectively transforms the object into a part of the land. Where this occurs, the chattel will be categorised as a fixture. Such categorisation will depend upon proof that the established fixture tests have been satisfied. Where a chattel has become a fixture, it will constitute real property from that point onwards. Alternatively, if the fixture tests are not satisfied, the object will continue to be categorised as a chattel.

7.2 The relevance of fixtures

There are many general instances where the question of whether a chattel has become a fixture will be of significance. However, there are a number of transactions where this issue has a particular relevance. The question has notable importance in circumstances where the land is being sold, mortgaged or leased. The reason for this is that, in such cases, questions often arise concerning the exact character and content of the land. For example, where land is being sold pursuant to a contract of sale, upon settlement, the purchaser will receive not only the actual land, but also all chattels which have become fixtures. There will be no need to actually specify the fixtures within the terms of the contract because they will automatically pass with the transfer of the land. If the chattel has not become a fixture, it cannot pass to a purchaser of the land unless it has been expressly included within the contract of sale. Hence, if a purchaser wishes to acquire a chattel which is attached to the land, unless it is clear that the chattel has become a fixture, it should be listed as a part of the property being sold under the contract.

Where the land is subject to a mortgage, it will also be important to determine whether or not a chattel which is attached to the land has become a fixture. A mortgagee will only be able to enforce security rights against the land which is the subject of the mortgage: the mortgaged land will include all fixtures, but not chattels which have not satisfied the fixture tests. Hence, if a chattel is attached to the land but is proven not to have become a fixture, the security rights held by the mortgagee will be unenforceable against the chattel.

Finally, and perhaps most importantly, fixtures are important in the context of leases. Where a tenant takes out a lease, he or she will often attach chattels to the land; the annexation may be effected for a number of different domestic, commercial or industrial purposes. Once the lease expires, it will be necessary to determine whether the annexed chattels have become fixtures, so that when possession of the land revests in the landlord, the landlord acquires full title to the fixtures and the tenant retains independent ownership of the chattels. Given the propensity for tenants to attach chattels to leased land, special rules have developed under the common law and statute; these rules will be considered later in the chapter.

7.3 Current fixture tests

Traditionally, the common law approach to determining whether a chattel had been transformed into a fixture forming a part of the land was an assessment of the degree to which the chattel had been annexed to the land. As a general rule, if the chattel had been substantially affixed, courts felt that it would constitute a fixture, whereas if the affixation was very slight, and the chattel could be removed without damaging the land, it remained a chattel.[1]

This rule has, however, been modified and expanded over time. In modern times, the preferred test for determining whether a fixture has become a chattel is a determination of the intention for which the particular item has been affixed. Broadly, the test can be summarised as follows: if it can be proven that the chattel was attached to the land in order to enhance the character, quality, enjoyment or status of the land, then it is likely that a court will find that the chattel has become a fixture, whereas if the chattel was attached to the land with the intention of increasing the use or enjoyment of

1 This principle is summarised in the maxim *quicquid plantatur solo, solo cedit*, which means where a chattel is attached to the land, it will form a part of the land. See *Reid v Smith* (1905) 3 CLR 656 and *Palumberi v Palumberi* (1986) NSW Conv R 55-287, where Kearney J noted, 'a perceptible decline in the comparative importance of the degree or mode of annexation, with a tendency to greater emphasis being placed upon the purpose or object of annexation'.

the chattel as an independent object, then it is unlikely that a court would find that the chattel has become a fixture.[2]

The degree of annexation remains a relevant factor in the assessment of intention. However, it is no longer the sole criterion. Each case must be assessed according to its individual circumstances.[3] Two primary factors will generally be used to establish intention in any given circumstance:

(a) the degree of annexation; and

(b) the object of annexation.

The 'relevant intention' is the intention of the person actually attaching the chattels to the land. In assessing this intention, the court will only take into account objective evidence. Subjective factors, including any oral or written agreements or statements which may be submitted by the person who has attached the chattel to the land, will be disregarded by the court.[4] In some circumstances, however, recent cases have held that subjective intention may be taken into account by the courts; for example, a court may take subjective factors into account when determining factors relating to the nature and duration of the annexation.[5]

Apart from the above two general tests, the purpose for which a chattel has been attached to the land may be ascertained in individual cases through a consideration of such factors as the nature of the chattel involved; the method and circumstances by which it has been annexed to the land; whether or not the person who has attached the chattel to the land actually owns the land and, if not, the relationship that person has with the true owner; the way in which the annexed chattel has been used; and the consequences for both the land and the owner if the chattel were removed.[6]

Furthermore, two general presumptions have arisen with respect to the degree of annexation:

(a) where a chattel is attached to the land other than by its own weight, it is presumed to be a fixture, and the burden of proof rests with the party claiming that it is not a fixture; and

(b) where a chattel merely rests upon its own weight, it is presumed to remain a chattel and not to have become a part of the land.

---

2 See *Leigh v Taylor* [1902] AC 157.

3 See *Kay's Leasing Corp Pty Ltd v CSR Provident Fund Nominees Pty Ltd* [1962] VR 429.

4 See *Love v Bloomfield* [1906] VLR 723.

5 See *Ball-Guymer v Livantes* (1990) 102 FLR 327 and the comments in Butt, P, *Land Law*, 3rd edn, 1996, LBC, p 227.

6 See the comments of Sir Frederick Jordan in *Australian Provincial Assurance Co Ltd v Coroneo* (1938) 38 SR (NSW) 700, pp 712–13. See also, *Bank of Melbourne Ltd v CBFC Leasing Pty Ltd* (1991) ANZ Conv R 561; *Permanent Trustee Australia Ltd v Esonda* (1991) ANZ Conv R 565.

Naturally, because these principles operate as general presumptions only, it will be possible to rebut them where the individual circumstances prove that they do not sufficiently reflect the intention of the person who attached the chattels. For example, it has been held that chairs which were firmly attached to a floor in a leased premises were not fixtures because they were only affixed for a temporary purpose and secure annexation was necessary for safety reasons (*Lyon & Co v London City & Midland Bank* [1903] 2 KB 135). In such circumstances, the cogency of the presumptions are overwhelmed by the presentation of clear evidence of a contrary objective and the presumption is rebutted – further highlighting the importance of an overall assessment of intention within each particular case.

Generally, however, the greater the degree of annexation, the stronger the operation of the presumption. If a chattel has been loosely connected to the land, a court is likely to conclude that there was no real intention to bind that chattel to the land, and the presumption, where raised, will be rebutted. For example, a loosely fixed wall hanging or picture will be unlikely to be held to be a fixture. There are two reasons why this is generally so. First, courts may simply hold that the annexation is so slight or inconsequential that it does not truly amount to an attachment and there is no need to rebut the presumption. This argument is not often raised, because courts have consistently held that the presumption may operate to an attachment, even where that attachment is very slight.[7] Secondly, courts may hold that, in erecting a picture or a hanging, there was no intention to benefit the wall but, rather, to improve the use and enjoyment of the hanging by enabling it to be properly viewed. The latter argument has been raised in a number of cases and produced a diversity of results.

For example, in *Leigh v Taylor* [1902] AC 157, a life estate holder of a property attached some very valuable tapestries to the wall of the drawing room in the house. The tapestries were tacked onto pieces of canvas, wooden supports were placed on each end of the canvas, and the canvas was stretched out. The wooden supports were then nailed to the wall. In determining whether or not the tapestries were fixtures, the court held that the most important issue was to determine the intention of the life estate holder when attaching the tapestries. The Earl of Halsbury concluded that, despite annexation, albeit slight, to the walls, and the presumption that the tapestries were fixtures, it was clear on the facts that the only way in which ornamental tapestries could be properly viewed and enjoyed was through such affixation; in attaching the tapestries in such a way, the life estate holder only intended to improve the enjoyment of the tapestries and not the overall land.

The decision in *Leigh v Taylor* can be directly contrasted with the decision in *Re Whaley* [1908] 1 Ch 615. On the facts of this case, a painting of Elizabeth I,

7 *Holland v Hodgson* (1872) LR 7 CP 328.

as well as a tapestry depicting a similar portrait, were affixed by screws and nails to one of the rooms in a mansion. The room was known as the 'Elizabethan room' and the pictures and hangings were placed there specifically to enhance the feel of the room. The court concluded that the affixation, despite being slight and similar to the facts of *Leigh v Taylor*, did result in the picture and tapestry becoming a fixture, because the intention of the affixation was for the beautification of the room as a whole rather than the enjoyment of the hangings as individual portraits.

Importantly, the object of annexation will always overwhelm the degree of annexation, because the focus of the court is upon the intention of the person attaching the chattel. If it is clear from the circumstances that the purpose of annexation is only temporary, without intending the chattel to become a part of the land, the fact that the chattel has been 'affixed' will be irrelevant. Alternatively, if it can be established that the chattel has been attached to the land permanently or for an indefinite period of time, and the removal of the chattel cannot be achieved without causing substantial damage to the land, both the degree of annexation and the object of annexation tests will strongly favour a determination that the chattel has become a fixture. The position has been well summarised by Jordan CJ in *Australian Provincial Assurance Co Ltd v Coroneo* (1938) 38 SR (NSW) 700, pp 712–13:

> The test of whether a chattel which has been, to some extent, fixed to land is a fixture is whether it has been fixed with the intention that it shall remain in position permanently, or for an indefinite or substantial period, or whether it has been fixed with the intent that it shall remain in position only for some temporary purpose. In the former case, it is a fixture, whether it has been fixed for the better enjoyment of the land or building, or fixed merely to steady the thing itself, for the better use or enjoyment of the thing fixed ... If it is proved to have been fixed merely for a temporary purpose, it is not a fixture. The intention of the person fixing it must be gathered from the purpose for which, and the time during which, use in the fixed position is contemplated. If a thing has been securely fixed, and, in particular, if it has been so fixed that it cannot be detached without substantial injury to the thing itself or to that to which it is attached, this supplies strong but not necessarily conclusive evidence that a permanent fixing was intended. On the other hand, the fact that the fixing is very slight helps to support an inference that it was not intended to be permanent. But each case depends on its own facts.

In some circumstances, the fact that a chattel has not been affixed to the land does not necessarily mean that it is precluded from becoming a fixture. For example, paving bricks which may be laid on the ground to form a path in a garden are generally packed tightly together but not actually affixed to the ground. The lack of affixation will not prevent the bricks from becoming a part of the land, because, generally, the bricks are used to enhance the overall character and enjoyment of the land. Hence, if the chattel was intended to form a part of the land, it does not have to be securely annexed to the land to achieve this purpose.

7.4 The determination of intention

The traditional approach to ascertaining the intention of a person attaching a chattel to land is to take into account those factors which are objectively apparent. One important consideration in this regard will be the nature of the chattel involved. In *Belgrave Nominees Pty Ltd v Barlin-Scott Airconditioning (Aust) Pty Ltd* [1984] VR 947, the plaintiff decided to renovate two buildings which he owned. After consulting with the plaintiff, the builder carrying out the renovations subcontracted with the plaintiff for the supply and installation of an air conditioning system for each building. The air conditioners were installed, and each unit was placed on a separate platform on the roof of the building, resting upon its own weight. The pipes were connected to the water supply of the building and the electric cables were connected to the machines. Final connections making the machines operative had not been achieved when the building company which had been subcontracted went into liquidation and had not made payments to the defendant company. The plaintiff arranged for a new builder to complete the installation. However, before this could be achieved, the defendant company removed the air conditioning units without informing the plaintiff.

The plaintiff sought a mandatory injunction in the Supreme Court of Victoria compelling the defendant to re-install the air conditioners or, alternatively, damages for detention, conversion and trespass. The plaintiff argued that the partial instalment resulted in the units becoming fixtures on the land. Kaye J held that the air conditioners had become fixtures and were therefore to be regarded as a part of the land. In focusing upon the purpose of the annexation, his Honour considered in particular the very nature of the air conditioning plants. The fact that, in order to be operative, each unit had to be connected to the main reticulation system of the building meant that it was of such a character that affixation generally resulted in the transformation of the unit from chattel to fixture. Furthermore, once the unit was fitted and connected to the building, it formed an essential component of each building, necessary for their use and occupancy as modern office buildings. His Honour concluded that the fact that the installation had not been fully completed did not derogate from the clear and objective purpose and nature of the unit. Hence, partial installation resulting in a connection to the main water pipes was sufficient to establish that the units had become fixtures.

A further important consideration in the determination of intention is the status of the person affixing the item. Where the person who is affixing the chattel is the owner of the land it will generally be more likely that the chattel was intended to become a fixture than in circumstances where the person does not own the land. For example, where the person affixing the chattel is a tenant of the land, there is less likely to be an intention to attach the chattel permanently and indefinitely because this will result in the tenant losing the chattel at the expiration of the lease (see para 7.6). Nevertheless, care must be exercised when examining this issue. In some cases, the owner of land may attach a chattel to the land without intending the chattel to become a fixture, particularly where the owner intends to sell the land in the near future. The question of what chattels are fixtures and what are not in a contract of sale was dealt with by the Supreme Court of New South Wales in *Palumberi v Palumberi* (1986) NSW Conv R 55-287.

At issue in the case was whether certain chattels in a house had become fixtures and therefore passed to the purchaser upon its subsequent sale. The plaintiff and defendant were co-owners as tenants in common of a building which had been divided into two self-contained flats. The defendant subsequently entered into a contract whereby he agreed to sell his half share in the property to the plaintiff. No chattels were expressly included within the contract of sale. Upon the transfer of the property, the defendant claimed that the following chattels had become fixtures and were therefore attached to the land: venetian blinds, curtains, built-in linen cupboard, television antenna, carpets, outside spotlight and timer, light fittings, portable heater and stove.

Kearney J emphasised the increasing importance of the purpose of annexation as against the degree or mode of annexation, and concluded that this resulted in a greater reliance upon the individual circumstances surrounding each case. His Honour concluded that it was only the stove and the carpets that could truly be considered to amount to fixtures, whilst the remaining items remained chattels. Attention was given to the fact that, when installing the stove and the carpets, the defendant intended them to form a part of the premises, and that intention was supported by the fact that, as prospective owner of the residence, he would obtain indefinite enjoyment of the objects, as they enhanced the amenity of the property itself. Kearney J felt that the remaining items were either indirectly or slightly affixed, or affixed without the intention of changing their status as independent chattels.

7.5 Rights of parties under hire purchase agreements, securities and chattel leases

The fact that the person who attaches the chattel is not the actual owner, but merely holds a possessory title under a hire purchase agreement, will not prevent the chattel from becoming a fixture (*Kay's Leasing Corp Pty Ltd v CSR Provident Fund Nominees Pty Ltd* [1962] VR 429). What is important is the intention of the person attaching the chattel; the fact that the person affixing the chattel does not actually own the chattel does not negate its potential to become a fixture; although, in order to constitute a fixture in such circumstances, it must be clear that the chattel was intended to function as a part of the land and proper annexation will generally need to be proven (*Belgrave Nominees Pty Ltd v Barlin-Scott Airconditioning (Aust) Pty Ltd* [1984]

VR 947).[8] Where a person in lawful possession of chattels attaches those chattels to land in such a way that they become fixtures, the person who actually owned the chattel will lose his or her property in them (*Geelong City Building Pty Ltd v Bennett* [1928] VLR 214). The fact that the contract, pursuant to which possession of the chattels has been transferred, expressly states that the chattel is not to become a fixture, does not mean that the chattel will be prevented from becoming a fixture. Proof of an intention to annex a chattel to the land will override proprietary claims, although, in such circumstances, the proof should be very clear.

If the person who affixes the chattel owns the land but has hired the chattel pursuant to a hire purchase contract and the chattel becomes a fixture attached to the hirer's land, the true owner (the hire purchase company) will acquire an equitable interest in the land entitling the true owner to enter the land and remove the chattel (subject to the usual priority principles). This is clearly discussed in *Kay's Leasing Corp Pty Ltd v CSR Provident Fund Nominees Pty Ltd* [1962] VR 429.

On the facts of that case, the plaintiff companies hired machinery to Burgess Wood and Co Pty Ltd for use in the company's plaster factory. Under the terms of the hire purchase agreements, the goods were to remain the property of the plaintiffs and could be repossessed upon default. The machinery had been bolted to the factory floor and was therefore presumed to constitute a fixture. Prior to entering into the hire purchase agreement, Burgess Wood and Co Pty Ltd granted a second registered mortgage to the defendant, CSR Provident Fund Nominees Pty Ltd. When the plaintiffs defaulted in the payment of interest, CSR appointed a receiver and manager over Burgess Nominees and notified of its intent to exercise its power of sale over the factory premises. The plaintiffs obtained interlocutory injunctions preventing the sale. Adam J held that the machinery had become fixtures. Adam J then considered the nature of the plaintiff's interest and concluded that the contractual right of the plaintiff in the machinery – allowing them to repossess on default conferred a form of equitable interest which allowed the plaintiff to enter the premises and sever and remove the chattels – despite the fact that they have become fixtures. His Honour noted that this equitable right could be defeated by the subsequent registration of an interest or title in the land but, where the subsequent registration was a Torrens title mortgage, as held by CSR Nominees, the registered mortgagee does not acquire absolute title, but only a 'security' title. Hence, until the mortgagee actually exercised its powers in a manner inconsistent with the continued existence of the equitable interests, the equitable interest held by the plaintiff company was enforceable. The exercise of a mortgagee's power of sale would, ordinarily,

8 See the further discussion on this issue in McCormack, G, 'Hire purchase, reservation of title and fixtures' (1990) 54 Conveyancer & Property Lawyer 275. See, also, Ward, N, 'The race for possession: the rights of retention of title suppliers of fixtures' (1998) 26 ABLR 184.

constitute an 'inconsistent' exercise of power where the land and fixtures were sold together; however, s 77 of the Transfer of Land Act 1958 (Vic) did not permit the sale of the fixtures separate to that of the freehold. On the facts, the notification period had not expired prior to the granting of the interlocutory injunction, so the mortgagee did not yet have the power to exercise their rights inconsistently. Hence, at the time when the plaintiffs sought injunctive relief, they still held an enforceable equitable right. A consequence of this decision is that in order for the equitable right of the hire purchase company to be enforceable, it would need to be exercised prior to the mortgagee lawfully acquiring a right to take possession of the property or, lawfully acquiring a right to foreclose over the property, or to the expiration of the notice period lawfully required as a precondition to the exercise of a mortgagee's power of sale.

In examining the nature of the equitable right held by the plaintiff company, Adam J made the following comments (p 436):

> Where chattels are hired on terms that they may be repossessed by the owner on the hirer's default in payment of hire, it is clearly established that the owner does not lose all interest in the chattels merely by reason of the hirer attaching them to land so as to make them fixtures. In law, no doubt, fixtures become part of the freehold while they remain annexed thereto and the legal title of them belongs to the person who owns the freehold. But the contractual right, which the owner has against the hirer to repossess on default, confers on him a species of equitable interest which entitles him, as against the hirer, to enter upon the premises and sever and remove the chattels which have become fixtures.

The exact character of the equitable interest which is claimed by the lawful owner of the chattel in such circumstances is uncertain. It would seem that the owner simply acquires the right to enter the land and remove the chattel, and that the interest only relates to the area of land upon which the chattel is located (*Melluish v BMI (No 3) Ltd* [1994] 3 WLR 1032). This would seem to indicate that the equitable interest is better regarded as a right to enter and sever, akin to a *profit à prendre* rather than an equitable fee simple in the land generally.

For example, W owns factory equipment which she hires to X pursuant to a lawful hire purchase agreement. A term of the contract sets out that the owner is to reserve title to the equipment even if they should become fixtures. X becomes bankrupt and Y Bank decides to enforce its security over the property (which it had entered into with X prior to the hire purchase arrangement with W) and sell the land and factory, including the factory equipment. It is clear that the equipment has become a fixture, so Y Bank claims that it is entitled to sell the equipment. Y Bank is about to sell the property to Z pursuant to a mortgagee's sale. Just prior to the completion of the sale, W lodges a caveat over the (Torrens) land to prevent the sale from going ahead. W claims an equitable interest in the property entitling her to enter onto the land and sever the equipment. In this situation, W would be able to execute her equitable rights prior to the completion of the sale. Upon completion of the sale and the registration of Z's interest in the land, W's equitable interest will, however, be defeated under usual priority principles attaching to Torrens title registration.

In *Sanwa Australia Leasing Ltd v National Westminster Finance Australia* (1988) 4 BPR 9514, the court held that the equitable interest of a prior hire purchaser would be unaffected by the legal interest of a subsequent mortgagee. On the facts of that case, the plaintiff, Sanwa Australia Leasing Limited, sought an injunction restraining the defendant, National Westminster Finance Australia Ltd, from selling the plant and equipment affixed to property. Powell J held that the equitable right held by the plaintiff to enter and remove the fixtures would not be impaired by the execution of the subsequent mortgage unless the equitable right interfered with the right of the mortgagee to exercise its powers over the secured property. His Honour concluded that the mortgage amounted to a mere statutory charge over the property, and no actual transfer of the land would occur until the mortgagee's powers had been exercised, and as the plaintiff had sought to enforce its equitable right prior to this point, its priority was retained.[9] This leads to the interesting question: when will a mortgagee extinguish a prior equitable title – after expiration of the ratification period or after the actual exercise of the power of sale by the mortgagee? According to *Kay's Leasing*, it is expiration of the notice period, but *Sanwa* indicates that it is after the exercise of the actual sale.[10]

In most states of Australia, the difficulties in this area have now been resolved by legislation. In Victoria, the Chattel Securities Act 1987 sets out that chattels, not exceeding $20,000 in value, which are the subject of a security transaction, cannot become fixtures. Section 6 reads, in part, as follows:

> (1) If, after a security interest attaches, goods subject to the security interest are affixed to land and become fixtures, the fixtures, for the purposes of the exercise of the secured party's right to take possession of, remove or sell the goods, shall be deemed not to have become fixtures.

Section 6(3) and (5) applies the same provision to chattel leases and hire purchase agreements. The operation of the provision is, however, qualified by the application of s 6(7), which sets out that a secured party will not be entitled to take possession of goods which have become fixtures where a third party has acquired an interest in the land for value in good faith and without notice of the interest held by the security interest holder.

9 See, however, the critical discussion of this case in Cooper, 'Retaining title to fixtures' (1991) 6 Auckland UL Rev 477.

10 See, also, *Whenvapai Joinery (1988) Ltd v Trust Bank Central* (1994) 1 NZLR 406.

The legislation aims to cover situations where chattels which are the subject of a pre-existing agreement are subsequently transformed into fixtures; it does not, however, extend to circumstances where chattels have become affixed to the land *prior* to the agreement being entered into. Section 6(8) qualifies this application of the provisions by noting that, where chattels have become affixed to the land *after* the agreement has been entered into but *before* the offer was accepted, the chattels will be deemed to be affixed to the land *after* the agreement was made. Similar statutory provisions also exist in other states.[11]

7.6 Special rights of removal for tenants

The common law has developed special rules concerning chattels which a tenant may affix to leased property. The policy underlying these rules is to provide greater protection to tenants when affixing their chattels to the land. As tenants do not own the land they are leasing, in most cases, they do not intend a chattel which is annexed to the land to become a fixture. Nevertheless, in some situations, the degree and purpose of annexation make it clear that the chattel has become a fixture and is therefore no longer owned by the tenant. In light of the unfairness that such situations may cause, and the desire to encourage productive, industrious usage of leased lands, the common law has developed special rules conferring rights upon tenants to remove chattels which have become fixtures.

Chattels which are attached to the land may become fixtures under the usual tests. However, in some situations, tenants will acquire greater rights of removal. What this means is that, where the fixture fits within a particular category, the tenant will acquire a right to remove it, despite the fact that it has become a fixture. Until the tenant exercises this right, the fixture will remain in the ownership of the landlord as owner of the land. Once the right to remove is exercised, however, legal title to the chattel will revert to the tenant.[12] The right exists in the nature of a chose in action until it is actually exercised and, therefore, assignable, although assignment must be in accordance with the statutory requirements for the assignment of choses in action (*Thomas v Jennings* (1876) 66 LJQB 5). The right held by a tenant will generally only be enforceable against the landlord and not unrelated third parties in the absence of an express agreement. Where third party interests are involved, basic

11 See Hire Purchase Act 1959 (Tas), s 36; Hire Purchase Act 1959 (Qld), s 32; Hire Purchase Act 1959 (WA), s 27; Hire Purchase Act 1961 (NT), s 39; Consumer Transactions Act 1972 (SA), s 5 (which only applies to chattels valued at $20,000 or under); and Hire Purchase Act 1959 (Vic), s 27 (which only applies to fixtures where the price of the goods exceeds $20,000 unless the goods are a commercial vehicle, farm machinery or the person hiring the goods is a body corporate).

12 See *Elliott v Bishop* (1854) 10 Ex 496; 156 ER 534.

priority principles dealing with equitable interests and subsequent takers of land, as applicable under either Torrens title or general law land, will apply.

The tenant will retain the right to remove fixtures for the duration of the lease and for any further period of possession where that person is regarded as a tenant (*Leigh v Taylor* [1902] AC 157).[13] It would seem that, even where a lease expires or is surrendered, where a tenant is given a new lease over the same premises, the tenant will still retain the right to remove fixtures provided that the tenant remains in possession (*New Zealand Government Property Corp v HM & S Ltd* [1982] 1 All ER 624; QB 1145; 2 WLR 837; *Penton v Robert* (1801) 2 East 88; 102 ER 302; and see, also, *D'Arcy v Burelli Investments Pty Ltd* (1987) 8 NSWLR 317). Hence, proof of a consistently maintained right to possession is the only pre-requisite for recognising and upholding the tenants right to remove the fixtures. Where a lease does expire or is surrendered, a court will give a tenant a reasonable time to remove the fixtures. This may include a situation where the tenant regards himself as having a genuine 'colour of right': see *D'Arcy v Burelli Investments Pty Ltd* (1987) 8 NSWLR 317. However, where a tenant abandons possession, he or she will lose the right to remove fixtures (*D'Arcy v Burelli Investments*). Where leased land is the subject of a mortgage, the tenant may remove fixtures prior to the mortgagee taking possession of the land – this applies generally to both old title and Torrens title mortgages. See *City Mutual Life v Lance Creek* (1976) VR 1.

Under common law, the tenant's rights of removal only applied to trade, ornamental and domestic fixtures. Trade fixtures include all fixtures used for the purposes of the business conducted upon the leased property, such as fittings attached to a bar in a hotel[14] and plants placed in the land by a nursery business which were readily removable.[15] Ornamental and domestic fixtures refer to fixtures installed by a tenant for the purpose of decoration, design or functional use. Examples include blinds on the windows[16] and kitchen stoves.[17] Whilst ornamental fixtures remains a separate category from domestic fixtures, in many cases the two will overlap because of the close association between domestic and decorative purposes.

The common law rule in Victoria has now been replaced by a more generalised statutory provision. Section 28(2) of the Landlord and Tenant Act 1958 (Vic) provides that chattels affixed by a tenant to leased land may be removed during the tenancy or whilst he or she remains in possession. The legislation also sets out that if the tenant causes any damage to the landlord's land, the tenant will be liable to repair it. The section sets out that if any tenant of leased lands:

13 This was affirmed by the Australian High Court in *Geita Sebea v Territory of Papua* (1941) 67 CLR 549.

14 See *Elliott v Bishop* (1854) 10 Ex 496; 156 ER 534.

15 See *Wardell v Usher* (1841) 5 Jur 802.

16 See *Colegrave v Dias Santos* (1823) 2 B & C 76; 107 ER 311.

17 See *Darby v Harris* (1841) 1 QB 895; 113 ER 1374.

> ... at his own cost and expense erects any building either detached or otherwise or erects or puts in any building fence engine machinery or fixtures for any purpose whatever (which are not erected or put in pursuance of some obligation in that behalf) then, unless there is a provision to the contrary in the lease or agreement constituting the tenancy, all such buildings fences engines machinery or fixtures shall be the property of the tenant and shall be removable by him during his tenancy or during such further period of possession by him as he holds the premises but not afterwards.

It is important to remember that the legislative provisions only apply where the chattel has actually satisfied the fixture tests and is considered to be a fixture. If the chattel does not satisfy these tests in the first place, then there will be no need to go on and consider the special rights of removal conferred upon a tenant. Sometimes courts blend these two stages, thereby 'blurring the distinction between items which, although attached to the land, remain chattels and items which, although fixtures, are removable'.[18] It is suggested that the proper and logical approach is to consider each stage separately; obviously there should be no need to consider an application of the tenant's right to remove fixtures if the chattel does not constitute a fixture in the first place.[19]

Under common law, fixtures which were agricultural in nature did not come within the ambit of the special tenant rules (*Elwes v Maw* (1802) 3 East 38; 102 ER 510). Hence, if the chattels were affixed by a tenant and were considered to have become fixtures, a tenant could not remove the fixtures, even whilst in possession of the lease, because the common law did not recognise any right of removal. If a tenant attempted to remove such fixtures, he or she would be liable under the doctrine of waste. Legislative developments in most states now provide specific protection in this area.[20] In Victoria, s 28(1) of the Landlord and Tenant Act 1958 provides protection in similar terms to that given in s 28(2). The provision sets out that a tenant of farm lands shall retain title to all farm equipment installed upon the land and will be entitled to remove it whilst he or she retains possession of the premises. If the removal causes damage to the property, the tenant shall be liable for repairs to the land. The operation of this provision should be contrasted with s 14 of the New South Wales legislation, which does not expressly confer any actual title to the agricultural fixture upon the tenant but allows the tenant to remove fixtures or, if the owner of the land elects to purchase the equipment, to receive a fair compensation from the owner.

18 See Butt, P, *Land Law*, 3rd edn, 1996, LBC, p 159.

19 See the basic authority of *Hobson v Gorringe* [1897] 1 Ch 182. See, also, *Mancetter Developments Ltd v Garmanson & Anor* [1986] 1 All ER 449.

20 See Landlord and Tenant Act 1958 (Vic), s 28(1); Agricultural Tenancies Act 1990 (NSW), s 14; Landlord and Tenant Act 1935 (Tas), s 26; and Property Law Act 1974 (Qld), s 155.

CHAPTER 8

THE RULE AGAINST PERPETUITIES

8.1 Introduction

Historically, the rule against perpetuities evolved in order to protect the fundamental premise that land must be freely alienable. All freehold estates in land carry with them the basic right of inheritance, and any devise or other transaction obstructing this right must be struck down. Public policy issues concerning the need to ensure that land is freely marketable and not tied up in the same family for generations – and that the right to alienate is not unduly impeded in any way – are important justifications for the evolution of the rule against perpetuities. Keeping land freely alienable is important because it ensures that the land is accessible and commercially marketable, and it guards against a disproportionate concentration of wealth and land monopolies. Furthermore, restraints upon alienation often result in basic land development and improvements being obstructed, because people are reluctant to spend money improving land where a capital gain is unlikely to be realised.

The rule against perpetuities is simply one way in which the courts have attempted to avoid, or at least reduce, restraints against alienation. The rule codifies the ongoing struggle between landowners attempting to ensure that land is kept within the family or within a prescribed body of persons and the courts in implementing public policy considerations opposed to the interference with fundamental rights of alienation. In application, the rule renders void contingent remainder interests which do not vest within a prescribed period of time.[1] Whilst the right of a grantor to deal with his land as he likes is universally respected and upheld, the rule against perpetuities aims to prevent this right from being abused. It prevents grantors from dictating 'from the grave' how land which they once owned should be dealt with in successive generations.

In Australia, the rule against perpetuities is a combination of both common law and statutory principles.[2] The implementation of specific statutory principles has tended to eradicate some rather technical and unusual common law principles in this area, although, as the statutory provisions do not completely replace the common law, the 'hobgoblins, leprechauns, and

1 The same policy has been applied to render void postponing the right to seek partition of co-owned land under relevant legislation for an unreasonable period of time: *Nullagine Investments Pty Ltd v Western Australia Club Inc* (1993) 116 ALR 26.

2 Not that the Rule against perpetuities is inapplicable to trusts of a regulated superannuation fund: Superannuation Industry (Supervision) Act 1993 (Cth), s 343. See, also, *Attorney General (Cth) v Breckler* (1999) 163 ALR 576.

gremlins that have infested the rule in the nearly 300 years of its existence' still exist and have been the reason for its continued recognition as an outdated and, in many cases, ludicrous anachronism.[3]

8.2 The old rule against perpetuities

The older rule against perpetuities is quite different from its modern counterpart. Under the older rule, where an interest in land was conveyed to an unborn person, any remainder to the issue of that person, and any subsequent limitation, was void (*Whitby v Mitchell* (1890) 44 Ch D 85). In effect, under this rule, only those persons who were in existence at the date when the remainder interest took effect could take an interest: any children not yet born would not hold any enforceable right even if the disposition expressly referred to them.

For example, A makes a gift to X for life, remainder to X's eldest child, remainder in fee simple to the children of the eldest child. If X had a child at the time of the gift, the rule was not infringed. If, however, the eldest child had, at that time, not produced any children, the gift to the eldest child would be valid, but the remainder to the children of that eldest child would be void.

The aim of this rule was to circumvent transactions which attempted to confer a series of contingent remainder interests to successive generations – often to a particular lineage. Hence, a disposition to A for life, remainder to A's son for life, remainder to A's grandson for life, remainder to A's great grandson for life, etc, would, under the old rule against perpetuities, have been effective to transfer a life estate to A and any child or grandchild of A in existence at the date of the disposition, but it would not be effective to pass the land on to successive generations.

The old rule has now been abolished in all states except South Australia.[4]

8.3 The modern rule against perpetuities

The modern rule against perpetuities takes a different approach. The essence of the modern rule against perpetuities is the imposition of a limit on the amount of time which may elapse between the creation of a future interest and the ultimate vesting of that interest; if the interest does not vest in title within the prescribed time set out under the modern rule, the interest will be invalid. The final owner must be identified and must take title to the interest (but need not be vested in possession) within the time frame prescribed by the common law. The rule will only apply to interests which are contingent and are to vest at some future date. Most commonly, the rule applies to contingent

3 See Leach, 'Perpetuities reform: London proposes, Perth disposes' [1964] UWALR 11.

4 Conveyancing Act 1919 (NSW), s 23A; Property Law Act 1969 (WA), s 114; Perpetuities and Accumulations Act 1992 (Vic), s 12; Perpetuities and Accumulations Act 1992 (Tas), s 21; Property Law Act 1974 (Qld), s 216.

remainder interests, because the successive nature of these interests has meant that they are often the primary offenders. The modern rule against perpetuities was first considered in Australia in *Cooper v Stuart* (1889) 14 App Cas 286, where the court noted that the policy underlying this rule was appropriate for all modern and complete systems of jurisprudence.

The definition of the modern rule against perpetuities was described by Creswell J in *Dungannon (Lord) v Smith* (1845) 12 Cl & Fin 546; 8 ER 1523, p 1530:

> It is a general rule, too firmly established to be controverted, that an executory devise to be valid must be so framed that the estate devised must vest, if at all, within a life or lives in being and 21 years after; it is not sufficient that it may vest within that period; it must be good in its creation; and unless it is created in such terms that it cannot vest after the expiration of a life or lives in being, and 21 years, and the period allowed for gestation, it is not valid, and subsequent events cannot make it so.

8.3.1 Vesting

There are three essential requirements for an interest to vest within the meaning of the modern common law rule against perpetuities:

(a) the person receiving the interest must be ascertainable;

(b) any condition precedent attached to the interest must be satisfied, subject only to the termination of the estate; and

(c) where the interest is taken by a number of persons, the exact amount or fraction to be taken by each person must be properly determined.

The vesting requirement refers only to vesting of title, not vesting of possession. Hence, provided title to the interest vests during or prior to the expiration of the perpetuity period, the rule will be satisfied. There is no requirement that the interest holder also be vested in possession during the perpetuity period.

8.3.2 Twenty one years

Twenty one years is the amount of time, beyond the initial life interest, within which the contingent interest must vest. The figure is historically based upon the old age of majority, so that parents were able to leave gifts to their children which could validly take effect once they reached majority but which would be invalid beyond this date.

8.3.3 Life in being

The life in being which is relevant to the common law rule is that life upon which the vesting of the gift has been made to depend. The 'life in being' will always be the life of either the person who created the gift – provided he or she is still alive – or the first life in being either expressly or impliedly mentioned in the disposition, which is not capable of increasing in number. The life in being will be the person who created the disposition where there is an express or implied reference to that person in the instrument creating the disposition or, where there is no such reference, the first life in being set out in the instrument creating the disposition, provided it satisfies the following requirements:

(a) the life in being must be a human life – not that of an animal, plant or corporation;

(b) the life in being must be in existence at the date when the instrument creating the disposition comes into effect; and

(c) the life in being must be capable of being ascertained at the date when the instrument creating the disposition comes into effect and cannot be capable of increasing in number.

It is not necessary for a life in being to receive any property from the disposition; the life in being only serves as a measure of time in order to determine whether or not an interest has vested within the common law perpetuity period.

For example, assume that the disposition in issue is as follows: to my daughter for life and upon her death to my son on the 21st anniversary of my daughter's death. In this example, it must be established that the interest of the son vests within a life in being and 21 years. The relevant 'life in being' will be the first life impliedly referred to, and in this example it is the parent – because of the reference to a 'daughter' – provided that the parent is still alive at the date when the instrument becomes effective. If the parent was dead, the life in being would be the daughter. Whilst the parent is not dead and is still of a an age to have more children, the life in being cannot be the daughter, because this 'life in being' is still capable of increasing in number.

It is important to remember that a person cannot be a life in being if there is a possibility that his or her class may increase in number because the parent making the disposition may be deemed legally capable of having further children.

For example, assume that the disposition in issue is as follows: S devises her estate to the first grandchild of A. If A has no grandchildren at the date of S's death, and A survives S, then A is the only possible life in being. A's children – if there are any – are not capable of being lives in being because A is presumed to be capable of having further children under common law (statute now imposes sensible age limits on this principle) and, hence, the category of lives is capable of increasing.

8.3.4 *At the creation of the interest*

The common law perpetuity period will start running at the date when the disposition takes effect. Hence, if the disposition is a will, the perpetuity period will commence as soon as the testator dies; if the disposition is *inter vivos*, the perpetuity period will commence as soon as a valid instrument is executed.

8.3.5 *Must vest, if at all*

Under common law, it must be established with absolute certainty at the commencement of the perpetuity period that the interest will vest within the perpetuity period. If there is a slight possibility that the interest will not vest within a life in being and 21 years, the interest will be struck down. The strictness of this approach has often produced some absurd results because, under common law, it is assumed that anyone, regardless of age is capable of bearing a child. The strange cases, classically referred to as the 'precocious toddler', 'fertile octogenarian' and 'magic gravel pit' cases, have arisen because of the fact that the common law rule requires absolute certainty. Examples of these unusual cases are illustrated below:

(a) Assume that A executes an *inter vivos* deed to the effect that she transfers her interest to her daughter, B, for life, remainder to the first grandchild of B to reach 21 years of age. When the deed is properly executed, B is 75 years old. B has one child, X, who has two children: Y who is 20 years old and Z who is 10 years old. A dies shortly after the deed is executed. The remainder interest in this deed is void under common law because it offends the rule against perpetuities. This is because B is the life in being, the perpetuity period is her life plus 21 years, and there is a possibility, at the date the deed was executed that the remainder interest would not vest within this period. It is possible that Y and Z would die and that, even if B had another child who then bore a child or X had another child (remembering that the common law presumes anyone capable of bearing a child at any age) – such children would not be born and reach 21 years of age within the perpetuity period.

    A further extreme example of this bizarre situation is evidenced patently in one old case where it was held that a gift was outside the perpetuity period because of the 'possibility' that the testator's widow (aged 65 at his death) might remarry and bear a child, who in turn could marry and bear a child, all within five years of the testator's death.[5]

(b) The 'magic gravel pits' case arose in *Re Wood* [1894] 3 Ch 381. In that case, a testator directed the trustees of his will to continue to mine gravel pits he

5 See *Re Caite's Will Trusts* (1949) 65 TLR 194.

owned until they were empty of gravel (the pits were nearly empty) and then to sell them. The proceeds of the sale were to go to his children. At the date of the testator's death, it was virtually certain that the pits would be emptied and sold within the perpetuity period. However, the court held that the bequest was invalid because of the possibility, however remote, that this eventuality would not occur within the perpetuity period. The court seemed to believe that it was possible for the gravel pits 'magically' to refill with gravel after the death of the testator – any other rationale for this decision seems ludicrous.

8.3.6 Examples of the common law rule against perpetuities

(a) A bequest by a testator to 'such of my grandchildren who reach the age of 21'. This bequest is valid under the common law perpetuity period if, on the facts, the testator already has grandchildren. The bequest will take effect upon the death of the testator; the life in being will be the testator's children – who cannot increase in size because the testator is dead – and this leaves 21 years for the grandchildren to reach 21 and, whatever age they are, there is no possibility of this not occurring unless they die and cannot take the interest anyway.

(b) A bequest by a testator to 'such of my grandchildren who reach the age of 30 years'. The bequest will be void under the common law perpetuity period even if the testator has children and grandchildren at the date of his death. The life in being will be the testator's children, and there is a possibility, for example, that they may die prior to the oldest grandchild reaching four years of age, the grandchild will not reach 30 years of age for another 26 years – and this is clearly outside the 21 year balance of the perpetuity period.

(c) An *inter vivos* disposition to 'such of my grandchildren who reach the age of 21'. This gift will be void under the common law perpetuity period even if the grantor has grandchildren at the date the disposition was executed. The life in being is the grantor – provided he is still alive. It is not clear at the date of executing the instrument that the grandchildren of the grantor will turn 21 within 21 years of the date of the grantor's death. The existing grandchildren may die and future grandchildren who may possibly be born may reach 21 years of age outside the perpetuity period. (See the 'precocious toddler'/'fertile octogenarian' cases example on the previous page.)

8.4 Statutory rule against perpetuities

In Victoria, Western Australia, Tasmania and Queensland, the perpetuity period will either be the common law period, or a statutory period which cannot exceed 80 years.[6] In New South Wales, the legislation actually abolishes the common law perpetuity period and completely replaces it with a set 80 year period which applies to all contingent interests.[7] In South Australia, the Law of Property Act 1936 has abolished the rule of perpetuities altogether.[8] This chapter considers how the Victorian provisions operate.

The legislation in Victoria sets out two options as to how to determine the perpetuity period. The grantor or creator of the disposition can choose to select a perpetuity period in the actual terms of the disposition, thereby replacing the common law perpetuity period; in order to be valid, this period must not exceed 80 years. Alternatively, the creator of the disposition can simply adopt the common law perpetuity period, and not specify a particular perpetuity period; where this is the case, the statute modifies the old common law perpetuity period by setting out that a disposition will not be automatically invalid due to a possibility of it vesting outside a life in being and 21 years: courts will 'wait and see' whether the disposition does, in fact, vest outside of this period. This approach is effectively set out under s 6 of the Perpetuities and Accumulations Act 1992 (Vic), which reads as follows:

> Where apart from the provisions of this section, and of s 9, a disposition would be void on the ground that the interest disposed of might not become vested until too remote a time, the disposition shall be treated until such time (if any) as it becomes established that the vesting must occur, if at all, after the end of the perpetuity period as if the disposition were not subject to the rule against perpetuities.

The introduction of the 'wait and see' principle under the legislation has eradicated a lot of the old problems associated with the requirement under the common law that there be 'no possibility' that the contingent interest will not vest within a life in being and 21 years. The 'no possibility' rule resulted in some absurd assumptions about the vicissitudes of life, and it makes a lot more sense simply to wait and see what happens rather than attempt to predict future events. The operation of the statute can be illustrated in the following manner. For example, assume a bequest in the following terms: 'to A for life, remainder to the first of A's children to marry'. If A is alive at the testator's death and no child is married at that time, under the terms of the legislation, the gift to the first child to marry will be presumptively valid, and it will be necessary to wait and see whether a child married within the period

6 Property Law Act 1969 (WA), s 101; Perpetuities and Accumulations Act 1992 (Vic), s 5(1), (3); Perpetuities and Accumulations Act 1992 (Tas), s 6; Property Law Act 1974 (Qld), s 209. There is no equivalent legislation in the Northern Territory and in *Hare v Cibolurin* (1988) 82 ALR 307, Sheppard J in the Federal Court felt that the trust in issue could be invalidated on the grounds that it offended the rule against perpetuities and applied the old common law period to the facts.

7 Conveyancing Act 1919 (NSW), s 7(1).

8 Note, however, that if, 80 years after the date when the disposition took effect, interests remain unvested, the court has a discretion to vary the terms of the disposition so as to vest those interests immediately (ss 61–62).

of 80 years from the testator's death. Whilst, under the common law rule, the remainder interest would be invalid, under statute it is presumptively valid until proven to have extended beyond the 80 year time frame.

The legislation also abrogates the common law presumptions concerning fertility and child birth. Section 8(1) set out that, subject to evidence that a living person was or was not capable of having a child at the time in question, a male is incapable of having a child if he is under the age of 12, and a female is presumed capable of bearing children between the ages of 12 and 55, but not otherwise. Section 8(4) sets out that these provisions apply not only to natural birth, but also to having a child by 'adoption, legitimation or other means'.[9]

8.5 Class gifts

The common law perpetuity period applicable to class gifts is known as the 'all or nothing rule'. Under this rule, it must be established that, where a number of persons are taking under a contingent interest, the precise proportion of the gift which is to vest in each member of the class of beneficiaries must be absolutely known within the perpetuity period. The 'all or nothing rule' is assessed at the date the perpetuity period commences, and it will extinguish the interest if there is any possibility of the precise calculation not being capable of assessment within the perpetuity period. Further, if the class is capable of increasing in number, outside the perpetuity period, the interests of all members in the group will fail.

For example, where a testator sets out in his will that he is leaving all of his property to his grandchildren (of which he has three) who reach the age of 30, the bequest will fail on the common law 'all or nothing' rule because of the 'possibility' that an additional grandchild may be born who will not reach 30 years of age within a life in being and 21 years and, consequently, the precise proportion of the gift vesting in each grandchild is unclear at the date of the testator's death.

To avoid this somewhat inequitable conclusion, the common developed what it called 'class closing rules'.[10] Under these rules, the common law closes the class to future members once the first member of the class becomes entitled to his or her share of the interest. All members of the class who are alive when the first member becomes entitled to a share will be included within the class and obtain a share of the interest, but members not yet born will effectively be excluded. Hence, on the example above, as soon as a grandchild of the testator's turns 30, only those other grandchildren who are alive are capable of taking under the disposition – any grandchildren not yet

9 See perpetuities legislation: WA, s 102(1), (2) and (3); Qld, ss 212 and 214; Tas, ss 7–10.

10 Originally known as the rule in *Andrews v Partington* (1791) 3 Bro CC 401; 29 ER 610.

born at this point will be excluded. This effectively makes it more likely that the precise proportion of each grandchild may be assessed within the perpetuity period and, hence, the all or nothing rule will be satisfied.

Statute in New South Wales, Queensland, Tasmania, Victoria and Western Australia has altered the common law rules with respect to class gifts and now applies, as with individual dispositions, a more sensible 'wait and see' approach – that is, a court will wait and see whether or not the precise proportion of each member's interest is allocated within an 80 year period.[11] A further important amendment in this regard relates to the type of contingencies which can be imposed. Where the contingency attaching to a class interest concerns the reaching of a particular age and, under the 'wait and see' principle, the members fail to reach this age within the statutory period, a court may, in its discretion, reduce the specified age in order to save the gift.[12] Finally, if it is still likely that the disposition to each member of the class will fail under the rule against perpetuities, statutory provisions exist which entitle a court expressly to exclude any member from the class in order for the interest to vest, thereby saving the interests of the remaining members who have satisfied the contingency.[13]

8.6 Consequences of infringing the rule against perpetuities

Under common law, where the rule against perpetuities is infringed, the interest which is subject to the contingency will be rendered void and any prior interest upon which the interest is dependent will remain valid, as if the contingent interest had not been included in the first place.

For example, assume X makes the following disposition: 'To A for life remainder to such of my grandchildren who turn 21 years of age.' If the contingent remainder interest to the grandchildren offends the common law rule against perpetuities, the remainder interest to the grandchildren will be void, but the life estate to A will remain valid. Once A dies, the property will revert to X or the estate of X; hence, for the life of A, X holds a potential reversionary estate.

In a situation where a subsequent interest follows an interest which is void for offending the rule against perpetuities, and the subsequent interest is dependent upon the prior interest, the subsequent interest is also deemed to be invalid.[14] If the subsequent interest is independent – because it takes effect whether the prior interest is valid or not – then the invalidity of the prior estate will not invalidate the subsequent interest. In the absence of any prior

11 Perpetuities legislation: NSW, s 8; Vic, s 6; WA, s 103; Qld, s 210; Tas, s 11.

12 Perpetuities legislation: NSW, s 9(1); Vic, s 9; WA, s 105(1); Qld, s 213; Tas, s 11.

13 Perpetuities legislation: NSW, s 9(4); Vic, s 9(3), (4); WA, ss 106–07; Qld, s 213(3), (4); Tas, s 11(3), (4).

14 *Robinon v Hardcastle* (1788) 2 TR 241; 100 ER 131.

estate, the void interest will simply pass as it would under usual intestacy provisions.

In all jurisdictions apart from South Australia, legislation has altered the common law position. Whereas, under common law, a later interest which is dependent upon an earlier invalid interest would deemed to be invalid for offending the rule against perpetuities, under statute, the dependent interest is deemed to be valid.[15]

For example, assume X executes the following disposition: 'To A for life, remainder to X's grandchildren who reach 21 and, if X has no grandchildren who reach 21, to B absolutely'. If the remainder interest to the grandchildren is invalid under the rule against perpetuities, the dependent interest of B will be invalid under the common law but validated under the legislative provisions.

15 Perpetuities legislation: NSW, s 17; Vic, s 11; WA, s 109; Qld, s 215; Tas, s 12.

CHAPTER 9

GENERAL LAW LAND AND PRIORITY PRINCIPLES

9.1 Introduction

Today, proprietary estates and interests in land are divided according to whether they come under the Torrens system or not. All land estates and interests which are not covered by the Torrens system are referred to as 'old title' or 'general law' land interests. Old title land interests are governed by fundamental common law and equitable rules which have developed specifically to deal with priority disputes which may arise between these interests. These rules have been further embellished through the inception of a non-compulsory, statutory system of registration known as the Deeds Registration System. The creation and enforcement of Torrens title land interests are, unless otherwise stated, governed by express statutory provisions within the Torrens legislation (this is discussed in Chapter 11). Old title land interests are not as prevalent today due to the fact that, increasingly, titles to land are being brought under the Torrens system. Nevertheless, old system titles still exist, particularly in older, more historical areas of Australia, and for this reason it is important to understand the fundamental general law. Furthermore, even interests which come within the ambit of the Torrens system may draw upon general law principles, where such interests remain unregistered or are unregistrable.

Under common law, ownership of an estate is absolute. Only one fee simple estate may exist against any single piece of land, although, as discussed in Chapter 3, it is possible to create successive common law estates, such as a life estate and a future interest. Strictly speaking, a priority dispute over ownership of a particular estate or interest cannot arise at law because common law principles will vest title and possession absolutely: it is not possible for two common law estates, both vesting the same title and possession, to exist. Hence, if A confers a fee simple in land to B absolutely, according to the common law, B holds the only fee simple in the land. It may be possible for B to 'co-own' the fee simple with another person, but no other person can claim a separate right to the fee simple, because it is already vested in B.

Despite this rigid approach to ownership, alleged priority disputes do arise under the common law. Such disputes generally occur in circumstances where the holder of a legal estate has fraudulently attempted to transfer it to two or more persons. In such a situation, it is important to determine who has the better and prior right to the estate.

The equitable jurisdiction assumes a different perspective to land ownership. Equitable interests are either created or imposed on the basis of fairness. The evolution of equitable interests and the acceptance that, under the Chancery jurisdiction, there is no limit on the number of equitable interests which can arise or be created over a single piece of land, has meant that the incidence of priority disputes has increased.

A priority dispute is essentially an argument which arises where two or more persons hold property interests in a piece of land which are inconsistent, making it necessary to determine who has the superior right to the land. Priority disputes may arise in a number of different ways. First, a priority dispute may arise where a grantor purports to grant two interests, the second of which is either completely or partially inconsistent with the first. These interests may be legal and/or equitable in nature.

For example, A holds a fee simple interest in land. A purports to sell the fee simple to B, create a trust over the land for the benefit of C, and enters into a loan contract with D, using the land as security. Following these three transactions, B, C and D all hold interests in the land. B holds a fee simple following the conveyance of that estate. C holds a beneficial interest in the land following the valid creation of an *inter vivos* trust, and D holds a security interest in the land which may be enforced if the loan agreement is not complied with. If each of the parties is aware of the existence of the other and accepts his position, there may be no priority dispute. Where, however, one party claims absolute priority to the land to the exclusion of all others, a clear priority dispute will arise. If this is the case, then the common law priority principles would suggest that, provided B is *bona fide* and has acquired the fee simple for value, he will have first priority over the interests of C and D.

Secondly, a priority dispute may arise where, despite the grantor not expressly conferring the estate or interest to a third party, a third party nevertheless claims an interest because of an alleged defect associated with the title of the grantor.

For example, if X purports to issue a conveyance of a fee simple estate to Y and, unbeknown to X, her title (which she has received from Z) is defective, a priority dispute may arise. Y will claim a fee simple estate pursuant to the transfer from X, and Z may claim a prior fee simple estate, arguing that the transfer to X was void or ineffective because it was fraudulently acquired or forged. As such, what Z is really arguing is that X never received any valid title to the land because it always remained with Z and, therefore, Y cannot have acquired any estate. This may be a question of fact in the individual case, but if it is proven that the document has been forged or fraudulently conferred, then it may be that X has never acquired any title to pass on. Alternatively, Y may raise a defence which may assist his claim. For example, Y may claim that Z contributed to the fraud or was in some way negligent in dealing with the title throughout the transaction and, as such, Z is legally precluded from asserting his legal rights. Strictly speaking, this is probably better described as a 'validity' dispute rather than a 'priority' dispute, but it does still require a court to consider who has the better claim.

Priority disputes are primarily concerned with resolving the dispute to the extent of the inconsistency. In some cases, the priority of one party will not necessarily result in the other party losing the full proprietary interest she claimed. For example, if the interest which has gained priority is of a lesser status than the subsequent interest, the subsequent interest will not be absolutely destroyed; it will only be limited or extinguished to the extent of the prior interest. Hence, if priority is given to a leasehold interest over that of a fee simple holder, the fee simple holder will only have his interest limited for the duration of the lease; it will not be completely extinguished.

This chapter examines the creation and enforceability principles relating to old title or general law land interests. This requires an analysis of the basic nature of old title claims and the fundamental common law and equitable priority principles which have developed to assist in the resolution of disputes over land. The Deeds Registration System, the first statutory system to regulate interests and disputes relating to old title land, will be examined in some detail in Chapter 10. This provides an excellent foundation for a subsequent examination of the changes and developments introduced under the Torrens system in Chapter 11.

9.2 Investigating and conveying legal title under general law

9.2.1 Good root of title

Legal title under general law land can only be properly and absolutely proven by tracing in an unbroken chain all of the transactions issued with respect to the land back to the original Crown grant. In Australia, as colonisation is still relatively recent, it is possible to make such a search, but often extremely difficult, time consuming and cumbersome to do. In England, such an investigation is virtually impossible. Consequently, in order to deal with this problem, a number of conveyancing rules have been adopted. The first is the practice of tracing old title interests back to what is known as a 'good root of title'.

The good root of title is simply an instrument or document which, by its very terms, describes the nature of the property in issue, proves that the entire legal and equitable estate has been dealt with and includes nothing to raise any concerns about the nature of the title held by the party disposing of it. The good root of title amounts to evidence that a valid and enforceable title exists.[1] It is not, and does not purport to be, absolute evidence of title: this could only

1 See Williams, TC, *Vendor and Purchaser*, 4th edn, 1936, LBC, pp 112–13; *Re Lemon & Davies Contract* [1919] VLR 481.

be achieved through a complete tracing back to the original grant. However, it purports to provide a 'good' foundation for a subsequent disposition of the title. Examples of a good root of title would include: documents evidencing a conveyance of the whole legal and equitable estate in the land or a first mortgage over the land; such documents should expressly reveal the full character, ownership and status of the old title. If the root of title does not evidence title of the land involved, it will generally be regarded as too uncertain to constitute a good root of title (*Re Bramwell's Contract* [1969] 1 WLR 1659). Disposers of old title land, particularly vendors, are only required to provide a chain of documents dating back to the 'good root of title'; there is no further legal obligation.

Originally, the practice in England was that the good root of title had to be dated back at least 60 years from the date of the particular contract of sale. In Victoria, all vendors must provide purchasers with a good root of title which is no earlier than 30 years old.[2] A lessee or an assignee receiving the land for a specified period of years will have no entitlement to such title documentation.[3] The time frame is merely a starting point. A vendor must search back for a good root of title which is at least 30 years old, but it may be older than this, and it is unlikely that a good root of title will be discovered exactly 30 years from the date of the contract. Hence, a vendor must search back for a good root of title which is *at least* 30 years old.

The fact that a vendor has adduced documents showing a good root of title will not necessarily mean that the title is not defective. It may well be that an invalidity exists in the title which occurred before the document evidencing good root of title was executed, which is not at all apparent from this document. Absolute certainty can never be achieved under this conveyancing practice. The only way to be sure is to conduct a complete and thorough search of all transactions traced back to the Crown grant.

9.2.2 *Abstract of title*

In light of the uncertainty surrounding old title land, it has been held that a vendor selling old title land must provide the purchaser with what is described as an 'abstract of title'.[4] An abstract of title is a document prepared by the vendor which evidences all the dealings with the land back to the good

2 Property Law Act 1958 (Vic), s 44; equivalent provisions exist in all states except South Australia.

3 *Ibid*, s 44(2).

4 Condition 2 of the conditions of sale in the Sched 4 to the Property Law Act 1958 (Vic) sets out that 'the vendor or his solicitor will at the written request of the purchaser or his solicitor within seven days from the day of the sale but at the cost and expense of the purchaser furnish an abstract of title over the land.' Section 23 of the legislation further sets out that, where the title involved is a legal estate, the abstract need only include transactions, including those dealing with or proving equitable interests, which will not be overreached by the conveyance of the estate. Similar provisions exist in other states.

root of title. Usually, a vendor will provide the abstract of title to the purchaser, at his own expense, once the purchaser has entered into the contract of sale.

The abstract of title should provide full details of the nature of the title, every encumbrance to which the land is subject (and which has been revealed through searching back for the good root of title, or even if the encumbrance exists before this time, if the vendor is expressly aware of it) including restrictive covenants and implied easements which may exist. The vendor should carefully set out all of the material parts of each document so that the purchaser is properly informed as to the exact nature of the land he or she is acquiring. These days, vendors commonly offer the purchaser an abstract of title in an abbreviated form; the contract of sale will usually allow the vendor to include a chronological list of the transactions and documents which would have been set out in the abstract, and a photocopy of all relevant documents is included.

9.2.3 *Conveying a legal estate in old title land*

9.2.3.1 *A legal conveyance can only be executed by deed*

All conveyances of legal estates in land must be executed by way of a deed in order to be valid (Property Law Act 1958 (Vic), s 52(1)).[5] Exceptions to this are set out in s 52(2) and include:

(a) assents by a personal representative;

(b) disclaimers made in accordance with bankruptcy laws;

(c) surrenders by operation of law;

(d) leases or tenancies not required by law to be made in writing;

(e) receipts not required by law to be under seal;

(f) vesting orders of the court; and

(g) conveyances taking effect by operation of law.

Section 54(2) goes on to set out that parol leases taking effect in possession for a term not exceeding three years (irrespective of whether an option to renew is incorporated within the term) at a best rent which can reasonably be obtained without taking a fine do not need to be executed by way of a deed in order to be legally valid.

A deed is a formal legal document which solemnly binds the parties. As set out by Young J in *Manton v Parabolic Pty Ltd* (1985) 2 NSWLR 361 (p 363):

5 Similar provisions exist in other states. See Conveyancing Act 1919 (NSW), s 23B(1); Property Law Act 1974 (Qld), s 28(1); Conveyancing and Law of Property Act 1884 (Tas), s 60(1); and Property Law Act 1969 (WA), s 9(2)(4). Please note: these Acts are referred to from here on as the 'property law statutes'.

> ... a deed is the most solemn act that a person can perform with respect to a particular property or contract involved, and the form of that deed is as laid down by the law from time to time.

The identifying feature of a deed is writing which is: (a) on paper, vellum or parchment; (b) sealed; and (c) delivered, whereby an interest, right or property passes, or an obligation binding on some person is created, or which is in affirmance of some act whereby an interest, right or property has passed.[6]

The important common law requirement for a deed is the sealing, because this provides evidence of the solemnity of the document and the seriousness of the intention of the parties. It is not necessary under common law for the deed to be signed or witnessed. The traditional method of sealing a document is through the stamping of a blob of hot red wax with an imprint at the foot of the document. Nowadays, it is sufficient if it can be proven that the document either contains a written indication that the document is sealed or is expressed to be sealed even though no actual seal has been included.

Statutory provisions have now embellished the common law approach to deeds. Section 73(1) and (2) of the Property Law Act 1958 (Vic) requires an individual who executes deeds after the commencement of the Act either to sign or to place his mark upon the deed: sealing alone is insufficient. This no longer has to be a wax seal. An ordinary adhesive seal may be used and corporations tend to emboss the corporate seal next to the signature of the appropriate corporate 'signing' officer. Section 73A of the Victorian legislation sets out that an instrument which is expressed to be sealed without actually being sealed can still take effect as if it were sealed. Section 74(1) sets out that a corporation will be deemed to have sealed a deed if its seal is affixed in the presence of, and attested by, its clerk, secretary or other officer.[7]

A deed will not take effect until it has been delivered (*Xenos v Wickham* (1867) LR 2 HL 296).[8] Delivery does not have to be actual, in the sense of a physical handing over of the deed; it may be constructive where it can be established that the party regards the deed as binding from the date of its execution and displays an intention, through conduct or words, to be bound by it (*Xenos v Wickham* (1867) LR 2 HL 296). Where a deed has been properly executed in the presence of a witness, there will be an automatic inference that it has been delivered, but this may be rebutted where it can be proven that the parties did not intend to be immediately bound. Where the deed is executed in escrow, immediate delivery will not be presumed. A deed in escrow is a conditional deed which will not come into effect until the condition is fulfilled

6 See Norton, RF, *Deeds*, 1st edn, 1906, Sweet & Maxwell, p 3.

7 See property law statutes: NSW, s 38; WA, s 9(1)(b), (c); Tas, s 63. In NSW and WA, a deed must be attested by at least one witness not being a party to the deed. In Tas, a deed must also be sealed according to common law principles. In WA, a document need not be expressed to be sealed – it simply needs to be proven that the document was intended to operate as a deed.

8 Delivery is no longer a requirement in WA (s 9(3)).

(*Beesly v Hallwood Estates Ltd* [1961] 1 Ch 105). The condition may be express or implied, and the deed is usually held by a third party until the condition has been satisfied. The deed will not come into effect until the condition is performed and hence, if the condition is never satisfied, the deed will never be effective. Delivery is the final requirement needed for the execution of a deed. Once the deed is signed, sealed and delivered, it becomes immediately effective and cannot be withdrawn (*Beesly v Hallwood Estates Ltd*).

A deed of conveyance should clearly describe the nature of the estate being transferred, the names of the transferor and transferee and the amount for which the property is being purchased. A legal estate in general law land will pass once the deed of conveyance is properly executed. If a conveyance of land does not constitute a deed or is not properly executed, and the conveyance does not fit within one of the recognised statutory exceptions, no legal estate may pass, although the equitable jurisdiction may enforce the transfer (see Chapter 5). Upon registration under the Torrens system, most instruments are deemed to have the same effect as a deed.[9]

9.2.3.2 Terms and conditions of the contract of sale

When selling land, the first stage will be to enter into an enforceable contract of sale. This is achieved when the purchaser signs the contract and (in an ordinary sale) pays a deposit of the purchase price, the balance to be paid over upon settlement date. Settlement date is the date set out, usually about three to six months later, when the actual conveyance of the legal title to the land occurs and the balance of the purchase price is handed over. Under old title land, settlement occurs once a deed of conveyance transferring the vendor's estate to the purchaser is properly executed. All persons who hold an interest in the estate which is to be conveyed should be set out in the contract so that the purchaser is aware of any encumbrances or charges which may be attached to the property.

The contract will contain all of the conditions and terms of sale. In Victoria, the conditions of sale which are usually incorporated into a contract of sale for old title land are set out in Sched 3 to the Property Law Act 1958.[10] These conditions may be varied, amended or modified to suit the particular circumstances. The conditions contained in this schedule include, *inter alia*:

(a) requirements concerning the production of title documents and requisitions on title;

(b) a condition setting out that time is deemed to be of the essence and the consequences of a default; and

9 See, eg, Transfer of Land Act 1958 (Vic), s 40(2).

10 Under Torrens title land, the conditions of sale will be those as set out in Sched 7 (Table A) to the Transfer of Land Act 1958 (Vic).

(c) a condition requiring all rates, taxes, assessments, fire insurance premiums and other outgoings to be paid by the vendor and borne by the purchaser from the date on which the purchaser becomes entitled to possession.

Other general conditions dealing with the right to possession, finance, dividing fences, etc, may all be expressly included within the contract. A sale of old title land at an auction will usually be made subject to the conditions of sale which have been adopted by Sched 3 or expressly included in the contract. Additional conditions in a contract of sale by auction include:

(a) the purchaser will be the highest bidder;

(b) if the sale is subject to a reserve price, the property cannot be sold until the reserve has been reached;

(c) the auctioneer has the power to resolve any dispute between bidders which may arise; and

(d) a bidder may not retract a bid.

9.2.3.3 *Statutory 'cooling off' period*

The Sale of Land Act 1962 (Vic) sets out that a purchaser who enters a contract for the sale of land at a price not exceeding $250,000 may, at any time before the expiration of three clear business days after he has signed the contract, give notice to the vendor that he wishes to terminate the contract and, where he has signed that notice and given it in accordance with the provisions of this section, the contract shall be terminated (s 31(2)). The three clear business days are to run from the date on which the purchaser signs the contract, irrespective of whether the contract becomes binding and enforceable on this date (*Lebdeh v Smith* [1985] VR 807).

9.2.3.4 *Statutory requirements for the vendor's statement*

The Sale of Land Act 1962 (Vic) also requires the vendor to give to the purchaser, before the purchaser signs the contract, a statement which shall include all relevant details of any matters affecting the land (s 32(1)). This statement is generally included in the actual contract of sale. The requirements under s 32(2)(a)–(e) include:

(a) particulars of any mortgage (whether registered or unregistered) over the land which is not to be discharged before the purchaser becomes entitled to possession;

(b) particulars of any charge (whether registered or otherwise) which is attached to the land;

(c) a description of any easement, covenant or other similar restriction affecting the land (whether registered or not) and particulars of any existing failure to comply with the terms of that easement, covenant or restriction;

(d) notice of any details relating to a planning instrument which may affect the land;

(e) a notice warning purchasers properly to investigate permitted land use with relevant authorities before entering into the contract;

(f) the amount of any rates, taxes, charges or other similar outgoings affecting the land and any interest payable on any part of those rates, taxes, charges or outgoings which is unpaid, including amounts for which the purchaser may become liable and of which the vendor might reasonably be expected to have knowledge;

(g) particulars of any notice, order, declaration, report or recommendation of a public authority or government department or approved proposal affecting the land; and

(h) a list of which of the following services are connected to the land and the responsible authorities: electricity supply, gas supply, water supply, sewerage and telephone services.

If a vendor provides false information on the vendor's statement, or fails to supply all the information required, the purchaser will be entitled to rescind the contract of sale at any time before title is transferred and the purchaser becomes entitled to possession (s 32(5)).

9.2.3.5 Statutory implied covenants as to title

In all conveyances of old title land, a number of implied covenants shall be deemed which, if breached, shall entitle the purchaser to damages against the vendor. Section 76(1) of the Property Law Act 1958 (Vic) sets out that all conveyances for valuable consideration, other than mortgages, where the person who conveys is expressed to convey as beneficial owner, shall contain four implied covenants as set out in Part I of Sched 4. The schedule contains one entire covenant with four separate parts. The schedule is prefaced by words indicating that the implied covenants do not represent an absolute warranty of good title but, rather, cover acts or omissions for which the vendor may be responsible. The four implied parts of the covenant are as follows:

(a) full power to convey

The vendor impliedly covenants that she has full power to convey the property. This covenant requires the vendor to disclose any defects in title which the purchaser should be aware of. If the vendor has done anything to make his or her title defective and does not disclose such a defect to the purchaser, the covenant will be breached. This covenant does not mean that the vendor guarantees the good title of the property but, rather, that he or she has not personally done anything, or is not aware of anything, which would make their title defective.

(b) quiet enjoyment

The vendor impliedly covenants that the purchaser will be undisturbed in his or her possession of the land which has been conveyed. If the vendor, or any person claiming under her, lawfully disturbs the quiet enjoyment of the purchaser, then the vendor will be in breach. In order to breach this covenant, it must be established that the interference is substantial and can be related back to some action by the vendor (*Browne v Flower* [1911] 1 Ch 219) Importantly, there will be no breach of this covenant unless it can be proven that the disturbance is lawful; unlawful interferences with possession will generally be covered by tort remedies.

(c) freedom from encumbrances

The vendor impliedly covenants that the purchaser will acquire the property free from encumbrances, apart from those which are expressly set out in the conveyance. This covenant does not in fact require the land to be free from encumbrances but, rather, that the purchaser will not have his or her enjoyment of the land interfered with by reason of the existence of covenants not expressly noted in the contract. Furthermore, the covenant will only be breached where the encumbrance has been created or imposed as a direct result of the actions of the vendor or some person lawfully claiming under him. The covenant will not be breached where an encumbrance is established which is proven to have existed without the knowledge of the vendor.

(d) further assurance

The vendor impliedly covenants that she will do everything necessary and reasonably appropriate to make good the conveyance. Hence, for example, a vendor must ensure (unless otherwise agreed to in the contract) that all previous mortgages are discharged prior to the execution of the conveyance.

If it is agreed that the purchaser will purchase the land subject to an express defect in the title, the vendor should expressly set this out in the contract and ensure that the terms of the contract modify the application of the implied covenants (s 76(7) of the Property Law Act 1958 (Vic)).

The remedies available to a purchaser for breach of the covenants as to title will include damages for all loss flowing from the breach. If the conveyance has already been executed, damages may still be sought by the purchaser, but a breach will not entitle a purchaser to a repayment of the purchase price (*Hawkins v Gaden* (1925) 37 CLR 183).

The implied statutory covenants will only apply to a vendor who conveys as full 'beneficial owner' of the land. Furthermore, the acts and omissions covered by the implied covenants will only be those which have occurred after the last sale of the land. Hence, a previous vendor will not be liable to a subsequent purchaser. The implied covenants will, however, extend to all persons lawfully claiming from the vendor and all persons claiming in trust for the vendor (s 76(1)(a)–(f) of the Property Law Act 1958 (Vic)).

9.3 Priority disputes between legal estates: the *nemo dat* principle

A legal estate will confer upon the grantee all of the rights, title and interest associated with a full common law estate and only the grantee (whether that be one person or a number of persons in co-ownership) can hold that estate. It is not possible to confer two identical legal estates to separate persons; hence, as discussed in the introduction, technically, priority disputes between legal estate holders do not exist.

For example, say A holds a fee simple estate in old title land. A decides to transfer the fee simple to B and C as co-owners of the land and, to this effect, A executes a deed of conveyance. Subsequently, A executes another deed of conveyance purporting to convey the same fee simple to D. In this situation, provided the deed of conveyance is properly executed and complies with the requirements for a valid deed, upon the execution of the first deed of conveyance, the legal estate will pass from A to B and C. This means that A has nothing to pass over to D, and even if the deed of conveyance to D is valid, it is impossible to convey a legal estate in land when you no longer hold one.

Where a person attempts to convey a legal estate which he or she no longer has, the *nemo dat quod non habet* principle will apply. Literally translated, this means that no person can give what he or she does not possess or that a person cannot assign a greater interest than the interest which is possessed. The *nemo dat* principle prevents any priority dispute between two identical legal estates from arising, because a grantor who has already transferred his or her legal estate to a grantee cannot execute a subsequent grant of that estate; the grantee cannot give away what he or she does not possess. The inevitable consequence of this is that, once created, a legal interest will prevail against any purported creation of a subsequent legal interest, to the extent of any inconsistency. The *nemo dat* principle may arise in a number of ways.

For example:

(a) A transfers to B her entire legal interest in land by way of a validly executed deed. It subsequently turns out that A does not hold any legal interest in the land, so clearly B cannot and does not obtain any legal estate. Furthermore, if A transfers to B her entire legal interest in land and then B transfers his legal interest to C, if A did not have any interest in land, then neither B nor C can acquire a legal estate.

(b) If A does hold a fee simple in land and conveys this to B through a properly executed deed, and then subsequently attempts to convey it to C also, C will receive no interest in land because A does not have any estate to pass; it has already been properly conveyed to B.

It may be the case that where two legal estates are purportedly created, no issue of *nemo dat* arises, because they either are not, or are only partially, in conflict.

For example, if A holds a fee simple estate in land and purports to create a legal leasehold estate in favour of B for a period of five years, and subsequently purports to execute a deed of conveyance of the fee simple to C, the interests of B and C may co-exist. In this circumstance, C will hold a fee simple reversion whilst B will acquire a legal leasehold interest. The two interests are not directly inconsistent because the legal leasehold interest exists for a defined period of time rather than indefinitely and, once it expires, the fee simple held by A will vest in possession. Whilst the *nemo dat* principle would prevent C from receiving a fee simple with a current right to possession, the conveyance will be deemed to transfer the fee simple reversion, the title of which A is perfectly capable of passing to C.

The decision of *Boyce v Beckman* (1890) 11 LR (NSW) (L) 139 considered what will constitute inconsistent dealings. On the facts of that case, the Crown originally granted a parcel of land in fee simple to O'Donnell. In 1841, Sparke acquired the fee simple estate in the land from O'Donnell. In 1845, Sparke conveyed some parts of the fee simple to Boyce by way of a deed. The deed referred to 'certain lots in accordance with a map or plan attached to the deed'. The deed of conveyance to Boyce was not registered under the DRS until a later date. On 1 January 1852, Sparke conveyed similar parcels of land to Turner. The deed of conveyance set out that the land to be conveyed was 'all or any other lots forming a portion of the said grant, to William O'Donnell to which Sparke is entitled ...'.

Turner registered the conveyance with the old Deeds Registration System (DRS) on 5 January 1852. Boyce registered his conveyance with the DRS after this date. Both of the conveyances to Boyce and Turner were for valuable consideration, and Turner had received no express or constructive notice of the earlier conveyance. Beckman, Turner's successor in title, claimed priority over the later registered interest of Boyce on the basis that his registration was prior in time. Boyce argued that the DRS did not confer any greater title upon an instrument and, as the later conveyance was invalid under the *nemo dat* principle (because the legal estate in the land had already been conveyed to Boyce), the priority principles could not apply.

The court ultimately held that Turner's interest had priority over that held by Boyce. It was held that the instruments held by Boyce and Turner were conflicting, and, as such, the *nemo dat* principle did not apply. The court found that the two conveyances were inconsistent, and consequently, as the latter was registered first, it was entitled to priority. The land which was passed in the first conveyance was intended to be different from that which was passed in the second. However, due to a direct written inconsistency in the deed of conveyance, this was not achieved.

Whilst it is not possible to confer two identical legal estates in the same land upon separate grantees, it is possible for successive legal and equitable interests to exist over a single piece of land. Equitable interests are created according to justice and fairness, and may be expressly created, implied by the circumstances, or imposed by a court; their existence does not conflict with legal ownership because they are recognised and enforceable in a separate jurisdiction (see Chapter 5). Hence, priority disputes between legal and equitable interests commonly arise, making it important to appreciate the relevant priority rules.

9.4 Priorities between legal and equitable interests

Priority disputes between legal and equitable interests will arise where legal and equitable interests relate to the same piece of land and the rights conferred under these interests are inconsistent. Whether the legal interest arises prior, or is subsequent to, an equitable interest, the basic priority rule is that a *bona fide* purchaser of the legal estate for value without notice will take priority over the interest of an equitable interest holder. Where the legal interest is created prior in time to the equitable interest, the primary concern for a court in assessing the dispute will be whether the grantee is *bona fide* and has given good value for the interest. Alternatively, where the legal interest is created subsequent to an equitable interest, the court must also consider whether or not the grantee took without notice of the existence of the equitable interest. Each situation is considered below.

9.4.1 Prior legal estate and subsequent equitable interest: the fraud principle

A grantee of a prior legal estate will have his interest postponed in circumstances where the conduct of the legal estate holder cannot be described as *bona fides*. Conduct fitting into this category would include circumstances where the legal estate holder is guilty of fraud, gross negligence and, in some cases, where the conduct of the legal estate holder effectively results in him being estopped from asserting his legal priority. These categories will generally arise where it can be proven that the prior legal estate holder has contributed to the creation of the subsequent equitable interest without the subsequent interest holder being aware of the prior legal estate.

This type of situation was considered by the English Court of Appeal in *Northern Counties of England Fire Insurance Co v Whipp* (1884) 26 Ch D 482. On the facts of that case, Crabtree was the manager of the plaintiff insurance company. The company agreed to lend Crabtree money pursuant to a general law mortgage. Under this transaction, the company retained legal title to land which had been owned by Crabtree until the mortgage was discharged. After the mortgage had been executed, the deed of mortgage and the title documents were handed over to the company and placed in the company safe. Crabtree, as manager of the company, had one of the keys to the safe, and after the documents had been placed in the safe, Crabtree opened the safe and took out all of the title documents except the deed of mortgage. Crabtree then used the title documents to make out to Mrs Whipp, a third party, that he retained legal title to the land, in order to acquire a further loan from Mrs Whipp.

Mrs Whipp, being unaware of the existence of the first mortgage, approved the loan and believed that she held legal title to the land. When Crabtree subsequently became bankrupt, and the full position was disclosed, it became clear that the legal interest had been granted to the company as first mortgagee and that the transaction with Mrs Whipp was enforceable in equity. Mrs Whipp then argued that her subsequent equitable interest should defeat the prior legal title of the company because the company had acted inequitably in allowing Crabtree access to the title documents and, as such, could not be properly described as a *bona fide* purchaser.

The Court of Appeal found that the conduct of the company was insufficient to result in its priority being postponed. The court then examined the type of conduct that would constitute a postponing fraud. It held that, where a prior legal estate holder stands by and lets another lend money on the estate without giving any notice of the prior interest, the conduct will amount to a fraud sufficient to postpone the initial interest. On the facts, whilst the court found that the company had been careless in the way it had dealt with the title and security documents, mere carelessness or want of prudence on the part of the prior legal interest holder was insufficient to postpone the prior legal estate. In his judgment, Fry LJ noted that, whilst the company had displayed great carelessness in the manner in which it had dealt with the title documents, gross carelessness could not amount to postponing conduct.

Today, it is unlikely that fraud would be read so narrowly. Whilst the court in the *Whipp* decision distinguished between 'gross' negligence and mere carelessness, it is likely that modern courts would take a more flexible approach; the distinction between mere and gross negligence can be difficult to establish, particularly when assessing commercial behaviour (*Hudston v Viney* [1921] 1 Ch 98). These days, courts are more likely to consider the inequity in allowing a legal estate holder to enforce her right to priority in light of all of the circumstances, including what has been described as the 'want of prudence' on the part of the legal estate holder.

In *Walker v Linom* [1907] 2 Ch 104, Parker J made the following comments:

> In my opinion, any conduct on the part of the holder of the legal estate in relation to the deeds which would make it inequitable for him to rely on his legal estate against a prior equitable estate of which he had no notice ought

> also to be sufficient to postpone him to a subsequent equitable estate, the creation of which has only been rendered possible by the possession of deeds which but for such conduct would have passed into the possession of the owner of the legal estate.[11]

On the facts of that case, his Honour held that trustees who hold a prior legal estate in land are postponed against a subsequent equitable interest holder in circumstances where the original transferor to the trustees has, unbeknown to the trustees, retained the original deed of conveyance from the chain of title.[12] His Honour held that inequitable conduct could be sufficiently established from what he termed the 'want of prudence' on the part of the trustees in failing to acquire the title deeds in the chain of title.

A prior legal estate holder may also be precluded from enforcing his priority where a valid estoppel can be raised against him. The priority of the prior legal estate holder in this situation is defeated, not because of a lack of *bona fides*, but because the availability of the estoppel defence prevents priority rights from being asserted. The operation of the estoppel defence is well illustrated in the High Court decision of *Barry v Heider* (1914) 19 CLR 197.[13] On the facts of that case, the registered proprietor of land executed a transfer of that land to Schmidt. This transfer could not be properly effected because, at the time, the Land Titles Office was in the process of issuing a new certificate of title to incorporate all of the land included in the transfer. Barry gave Schmidt an authority which stated that when the new certificate of title was released, it should be passed on to Schmidt. Schmidt subsequently entered into a mortgage with Heider. Both the interest of Schmidt and that of Heider remained unregistered. Barry sought injunctive relief to prevent Schmidt from registering the transfer, claiming it had been executed fraudulently and that he had not received any payment for the land, and a declaration that he held the land free from the mortgage. The High Court agreed with Barry about the transfer to Schmidt and, on the basis of fraud, set it aside. The important issue in the case, however, was whether the legal title which Barry now held could be postponed to the subsequent equitable interest held by Heider pursuant to the mortgage. In particular, did the conduct of Barry mean that he was estopped from asserting his legal title?

---

11 *Walker v Linom* [1907] 2 Ch 104, p 110.

12 Note that there is some debate as to the exact nature of the equitable interest held by the subsequent purchaser, Linom. See the discussion on this in Bradbrook, AJ, MacCallum, SV and Moore, AP, *Australian Real Property Law*, 2nd edn, 1996, LBC, para 3.09. It is likely that the equitable interest was one which the court was prepared to impose in the circumstances based upon the unfairness arising from the transaction, in that Linom had entered into a contract with good faith and for value. The fact that it was not possible for Linom to acquire a legal estate should not preclude the court from imposing an interest in equity.

13 Note that the case is directly relevant although it deals with Torrens title land and not old title land.

The High Court concluded that Barry was estopped from asserting the priority of his prior legal estate; his conduct in arming Schmidt with the transfer and an authority to receive the new certificate of title, and thereby giving him the power to represent that he had a good legal title to the property, operated as a representation to the rest of the world that Barry believed that Schmidt held good legal title. Barry was estopped from denying this by enforcing his priority rights under the legal estate. Griffith CJ concluded that the transfer 'operated as a representation, addressed to any person into whose hands it might lawfully come without notice of Barry's right to have it set aside, that Schmidt had such an assignable interest'.[14]

The overlap between conduct amounting to estoppel and that constituting a fraud was expressly noted. Isaacs J discussed the concepts of fraud and estoppel and noted:

> Distinctions have been drawn as to whether such a case is to be solved by the doctrine of estoppel, or by the doctrine that, where one of two innocent persons has to suffer by the fraud of a third, he who ... has enabled the third person to commit the fraud, shall bear the loss. I see no real distinction in principle. I call them both estoppel, because the second principle simply compels the person who enabled the fraud to be committed to stand by the consequences of his own conduct and precludes him from asserting his really superior title.[15]

The focus of the court in *Barry v Heider* is upon an expansive assessment of fraudulent, postponing conduct, and the estoppel action seems actually to form a subset of this broader category. It may be argued that this tendency to merge the two categories weakens the validity of the estoppel defence in this context. The court assumed that Barry's conduct in giving Schmidt the authority constituted a representation to the world that the title was unencumbered and, furthermore, that Barry knew that Schmidt would then go out and obtain a mortgage on the strength of this. This is quite a presumption to reach, particularly if it is borne in mind that Barry had given the authority to Schmidt in accordance with the terms of the original transfer agreement, which had only been obtained due to the gross fraud perpetrated by Schmidt. Whilst Barry's conduct may be regarded as unfair from the perspective of innocent mortgagees and postponement of the legal title may be justified on this ground alone, it seems more appropriate to expand the fraud category rather than impose unsuitable restrictions upon the concept of estoppel.

A good example of a contrary approach can be found in the old decision of *Ettershank v Zeal* (1882) 8 VLR 333, where the court refused to apply estoppel

14 *Barry v Heider* (1914) 19 CLR 197, p 199.

15 *Ibid*, p 207.

principles as a ground for postponing the priority of a legal estate. On the facts of that case, William Johnston Sr allowed his son, William Johnston Jr, to possess himself of title deeds to land which belonged to his father. The son subsequently represented himself to be the owner of the property, and obtained a mortgage on the strength of the title from Zeal and Cornish. The mortgage was subsequently confirmed by William Johnston Sr so that Zeal and Cornish held the legal title. William Johnston Jr then proceeded to enter into a second mortgage with the plaintiffs, still representing himself as the owner of the redemption interest which he retained after the first mortgage. William Johnston Sr refused to confirm the second mortgage and argued, as co-defendant with Zeal, priority to the estate because of the fact that they held the legal estate. The plaintiff argued that the defendants were estopped from asserting their priority because of their conduct in allowing the son to assert himself as owner of the land to the rest of the world.

The court held that estoppel could not be made out. Whilst the court noted the 'culpable negligence' of William Johnston Sr, it felt that an action in estoppel could not be made out because the father had no actual knowledge that the plaintiff was being deceived. As noted by Holroyd J:[16] 'A man is not bound to disclose his rights to all the world, lest somebody should be injured by ignorance of them, nor liable if anybody is injured by such ignorance without his knowledge.'

9.4.2 *Prior equitable interest and subsequent legal estate:* bona fide *purchaser for value*

The general principle where a priority dispute arises with a legal estate is that the holder of the legal estate may assert priority where he can prove himself to be a *bona fide* purchaser for value without notice. Where the estate is prior in time to an equitable estate, the primary question, as discussed above, will be whether or not the legal estate holder is *bona fide* and should, in all fairness, be entitled to enforce his or her priority rights. The question of notice will not be directly relevant. Where, however, the legal estate is created subsequent to a pre-existing equitable interest, a vitally important priority issue that must be examined is whether or not the subsequent legal estate holder took with notice of the prior equitable interest. Where notice can be established, the priority of the legal estate holder will be postponed (*Pilcher v Rawlins* (1872) LR 7 Ch 259). The *bona fide* purchaser for value without notice principle evolved as one of the fundamental doctrines of the Chancery jurisdiction, justifying the defeat of a legal estate at the hands of the equitable jurisdiction. The courts of equity took the view that where a legal estate holder acquired that estate with full knowledge of the existence of a prior equitable interest, that estate holder would be acting unfairly in attempting to enforce his or her

16 *Ettershank v Zeal* (1882) 8 VLR 333, p 343.

rights; acquiescing in such an enforcement would be against the conscience of the Chancery jurisdiction. The position has been well summarised by Ashburner:[17]

> An equitable claim will be enforceable against the holder of a legal title if, in the circumstances, that claim affects the conscience of the legal owner. Consequently, generally speaking, a court of equity will give effect to the plea of a purchaser for value without notice in favour of a legal owner as against an equitable claimant ...

This type of priority dispute can often arise where a trustee, in breach of his trustee duties, transfers the legal title to a *bona fide* third party purchaser who takes without any notice of the existence of a trust. In such a case, provided the title of the third party cannot be impugned on the grounds of notice – and notice, as we shall see, is defined broadly – the legal interest of the third party will defeat that of the beneficiaries under the earlier trust. This is well summarised by Mellish LJ in *Pilcher v Rawlins* (1872) 7 Ch App 259:

> Where a trustee, in breach of trust, conveys away a legal estate which he possesses, and that legal estate comes into the possession of a purchaser for valuable consideration without notice, that purchaser can hold the property against the *cestuis qui trust* who were defrauded by the conveyance of the trustee.[18]

The facts of *Pilcher v Rawlins* firmly reinforce this principle. In that case, Pilcher held legal title to a sum of money as trustee for specified beneficiaries. Pilcher subsequently advanced this money over to Rawlins pursuant to a mortgage over property known as 'Blackacre', which was owned by Rawlins. The effect of this transaction was to transfer the legal estate in Blackacre to Pilcher for the duration of the mortgage. Rawlins, as mortgagor, held an equity of redemption allowing him to obtain a reconveyance of the estate once the advance had been repaid. The beneficiaries under the trust held an equitable beneficial title in Blackacre.

Subsequently, pursuant to a fraudulent scheme, Pilcher and Rawlins decided to borrow some money from another set of trustees, Stockwell and Lamb, and issued a second 'purported' legal mortgage over Blackacre as security for this loan. The second mortgage of the estate was fraudulently prepared by Rawlins, who succeeded in convincing the trustees who were lending the money that he held the legal estate, by preparing an abstract of title, which omitted reference to the first mortgage (even though it was held by Pilcher as mortgagee under the first mortgage).

Eventually, Rawlins paid over the money under the first mortgage and Pilcher discharged this mortgage and reconveyed the legal estate in Blackacre back to Rawlins. Rawlins then executed a 'correct' legal mortgage over Blackacre to Stockwell and Lamb. The trustees did not realise that they had

17 Browne, D (ed), *Principles of Equity*, 2nd edn, 1933, Butterworths, p 50.

18 *Pilcher v Rawlins* (1872) 7 Ch App 259, p 262.

not received the legal interest under the mortgage until after the discharge of the first mortgage. The beneficiaries did not obtain any of the money received by Pilcher when the first mortgage was paid out, and one of the issues in the case was whether the prior equitable interest to the land claimed by the beneficiaries under the Pilcher trust could prevail against the subsequent legal estate acquired by the trustees pursuant to the second mortgage. The case ultimately came down to an issue of which party, in the opinion of the court, should have to bear the loss.

Mellish LJ set out that the basis upon which the fundamental principle operated was 'if you trust your property to a man who turns out to be a rogue, it stands to reason that you may lose it'. Working from this principle, Mellish LJ held that, where a trustee in breach of trust conveys away a legal estate which he possesses, and that legal estate comes into the possession of a purchaser for valuable consideration without notice, that purchaser can hold the property against the beneficiaries who were defrauded by the trustee.

The decision in *Pilcher v Rawlins* is based upon two fundamental principles: first, that the subsequent legal mortgagees acted *bona fides* and in good faith in granting the mortgage and, secondly, that they took without any knowledge that a prior estate existed. The balancing process is clearly enunciated by Mellish LJ in the following words:

> It is surely desirable that the rules of this court should be in accordance with the ordinary feelings of justice of mankind. Now if the first set of *cestuis que trust*, those who will unfortunately have to bear the loss, were asked how it happened that they had suffered this loss, they would answer that their father [Pilcher] conveyed the estate to their uncle [Rawlins], and he turned out to be a dishonest man, and parted with the estate. It might not be satisfactory to the losers, but they must see at once how it came to happen that they lost their estate.[19]

In order for the *bona fide* purchaser for value without notice principle to be established, three primary elements must be proven. First, the legal title must have been acquired by a purchaser in good faith; secondly, it must have been acquired for value; and thirdly, it must have been acquired without notice of the existence of a prior equity. The definition of purchaser includes any person who is named by the grantee of the estate as the purchaser and who acquires a legal interest in the property. The most usual 'purchaser' will be a person who actually purchases a fee simple under a contract of sale. However, 'purchaser' has also been held to include mortgagees and lessees of the legal estate (*Goodright v Moses* (1774) 2 Wm Bl 1019; 96 ER 599).

The *bona fide* purchaser principle requires the purchaser to have given value. Value can be established where money or an equivalent worth for the

19 *Pilcher v Rawlins* (1872) 7 Ch App 259, p 264. See, also, *Koorootang Nominees Pty Ltd v ANZ Banking Group* (1998) 3 VR 16.

transaction can be proven, and will include transactions executed in consideration of marriage. The amount of value which is given need not be the full value of the property. However, it should be sufficient to constitute good consideration, although it need not be pecuniary in nature. In *R v Registrar of Titles ex p Moss* [1928] VLR 411, for example, the transfer of certain fully paid shares in a company was found to constitute 'valuable consideration'.

It must also be established that the purchaser acted in good faith. Good faith will usually overlap with the doctrine of notice. However, it is itself a separate test and a much broader concept. Where it cannot be proven that the legal estate holder took with notice of the prior equitable estate, priority may still be postponed if it is established that the subsequent estate holder acted in bad faith (*Midland Bank Trust Co Ltd v Green* [1983] AC 513). Good faith is a broad, equitable concept which is based upon the principle of fair and proper conduct; it includes an assessment of the conduct of the purchaser both prior to and upon receiving the estate. Where it can be proven that the transaction was a sham, fraudulently induced or morally reprehensible, the legal estate holder will generally be unable to establish his good faith (*Doe d Irving v Gannon (No 2)* (1847) 1 Legge 400). The fact that the grantor may have acted fraudulently or in bad faith will not necessarily impugn the title of the grantee. If it can be proven that the grantee acted without notice and performed his or her obligations under the transaction honestly and fairly, then good faith may be satisfied, whatever the legal or moral nature of the grantor's actions (*Davidson v O'Halloran* [1913] VLR 367).

The *bona fide* purchaser principle is reiterated in the property law legislation in all states. In Victoria, a 'purchaser' is defined in s 18 of the Property Law Act 1958 as:

> ... a purchaser in good faith for valuable consideration and includes a lessee, mortgagee or other person who for valuable consideration acquires an interest in property except that where so expressly provided 'purchaser' means a person only who acquires an interest in or charge on property for money or money's worth; and where the context so requires 'purchaser' includes an intending purchaser; 'purchase' has a meaning corresponding with that of 'purchaser' and 'valuable consideration' and includes marriage but does not include a nominal consideration in money.

9.4.3 *The doctrine of notice*

9.4.3.1 *Timing*

The doctrine of notice is an equitable construct which imputes 'knowledge' upon a grantee of the existence of a prior estate in certain defined circumstances. The timing of the notice is important. A subsequent estate will only be set aside where it can be proven that the estate holder took with notice either before or at the time of acquiring the estate. The fact that the purchaser may have subsequently discovered the existence of a prior estate will generally be irrelevant unless this implies a lack of good faith on the part of the purchaser. In *Blackwood v London Chartered Bank of Australia* (1871) 10 SCR (NSW) Eq 20, the court held that a person who has *bona fide* paid money without notice of any other title may afterwards, even *pendente lite*,[20] acquire a valid legal title, despite the fact that, during the interval between the payment and getting in of the legal title, he or she may have had notice of some prior dealing which is inconsistent with the good faith of the title.

For example, X decides that she wants to purchase land from Y. X enters into a contract of sale and pays the full purchase price of $200,000 to Y on 1 January 1997. Two weeks later, on 15 January, a deed of conveyance is properly executed, formally transferring the legal estate over to Y. During this period, Y receives notice of the existence of a prior interest in the land. Following the *Blackwood* decision, it would seem that X will acquire a good title on 1 January, when the consideration was given, despite the fact that, during the two week interval leading up to settlement, X was affected with notice of a prior estate.

The timing of notice is generally a relevant issue where a person acquires an equitable interest (particularly an equitable mortgagee) and, after acquiring the interest without notice, seeks to tack on the legal estate because of the subsequent discovery of a prior equitable interest (*Bailey v Barnes* [1894] 1 Ch 25).

The foundation of the 'tacking' process lies in the old doctrine of *tabulo in naufragio*.[21] Under this doctrine, the holder of an equitable interest who acquires that interest without any notice of a prior equitable interest can, by acquiring the legal estate, obtain a good title unaffected by notice. This doctrine has now been abolished with respect to mortgages of land in Victoria, Queensland and Tasmania (s 94(3) of the Property Law Act (Vic) 1958; s 82 of the Property Law Act (Qld) 1974; and s 38 of the Conveyancing and Law of Property Act (Tas) 1884). See, also, the discussion in Chapter 14 at para 14.5.

Furthermore, the general law principle will not operate where it is established that the transfer of the legal estate would constitute a breach of trust – that is, that the grantor would be committing a breach of trust by transferring the estate. Exactly when a breach of trust may arise is difficult to determine. In *Mumford v Stohwasser* (1874) LR 18 Eq 556, it was held that the grantee of a subsequent legal estate pursuant to an old title mortgage could not acquire good title because the grantor was in breach of his equitable obligations as trustee to the prior equitable lessee. Following this decision, it would seem that the grantor will become a trustee where he or she actually

20 Meaning 'while the case is pending'.

21 Literally translated, this means 'a plank in a shipwreck'.

created the prior equitable estate; any subsequent transfer of the legal estate will constitute a breach of trust (*Taylor v Russell* [1891] 1 Ch 8).

For example, X is the owner of land. X grants an equitable interest to Y and subsequently to Z. Z takes the equitable interest without notice of Y's interest. Z subsequently discovers the existence of Y's interest and seeks to have the legal estate transferred. X transfers the estate to Z, knowing that it amounts to a breach of trust to Y. In this circumstance, following the *Mumford* decision, Z could not claim priority on the basis of having 'tacked' on the legal estate because of the breach of trust committed by X.

In land transactions, the legal estate can only be transferred where special statutory formalities are complied with. In some circumstances, an attempted transfer of a legal estate will be ineffective because, for example, the conveyance does not amount to a deed. In such a case, one issue to consider is whether or not the priority of the legal estate holder will be postponed if the purchaser acquires notice of a prior equitable interest after executing the defective deed, but prior to execution of a deed in proper form.

For example, X seeks to purchase land from Y, pays over the purchase price and a defective deed of conveyance is executed on 1 January 1998. On 1 February 1998, X discovers that the deed is defective and seeks to have a new and proper deed executed. The proper deed is executed on 1 March 1998. After 1 January but prior to 1 February, X receives notice of the existence of a prior equitable estate. The questions to consider here are: can X acquire an enforceable legal estate and will the execution of the deed from Y constitute a breach of trust against the holder of the prior equitable interest so that X's priority is set aside?

It is unclear whether the breach of trust principles apply in this situation, because the purchaser intended to purchase the legal estate from the outset, rather than subsequently deciding to have it tacked on. It has been argued that such transactions should not be affected by the 'breach of trust' exemption where it can be established that, at the time of entering into the transaction to purchase the legal estate, the purchaser was unaware of the existence of any trust or any potential breach of trust. The justification for modifying the exemption in this circumstance is that the transaction is classified as 'continuous' and, therefore, once it is established that the purchaser has no notice at the time of first entering into the transaction and paying the deposit, she should not be penalised for the natural progression of the transaction (*Saunders v Dehew* (1692) 2 Vern 271; 23 ER 775; *Dodds v Hills* (1865) 2 H&M 424; 71 ER 528). The position has been well summarised by Sykes:

> It will be noticed that the situations where the *tabula in naufragio* doctrine and the exception to it have been applied are all cases where a person originally intends to acquire an equity and then, by a later, separate transaction, seeks to acquire the legal estate, the acquisition of which was originally no part of his bargain. There may be positions, however, where it is not a mere equitable

> taker who seeks to snatch the legal estate. He intends *ab initio* to acquire the legal estate but, through some reason or other (not imputable to negligence), when his money is paid over he takes no conveyance at all or takes a defective conveyance. He later secures an effective conveyance but, before doing so, acquires notice of a prior equity. Does the fact that his transferor stands in a trust relationship and that the conveyance is in breach of trust destroy the plea of *bona fide* purchaser which he could clearly advance were the prior relationship not a trust one? Statements of principle certainly seem to draw no distinction between the *tabula* situation and the situation of one continuous transaction. The situations do, however, seem somewhat distinct, and it may be that in the case where the mortgagor or purchaser in getting in the legal estate is merely completing his original bargain, he takes subject to the prior trust interest only when he knew at the time of the original bargain that a trust or breach of it is involved. The matter can only be described as uncertain.[22]

Finally, where a legal estate holder intends to purchase the legal estate and, in the course of the purchase, acquires enforceable rights against the grantor, which are superior to any rights the grantor may owe to the prior equitable interest holder, the purchaser may acquire a good title (*Wilkes v Bodington* (1707) 2 Vern 599; 23 ER 991). The justification for this rule is that, because the rights which are enforceable by the subsequent estate holder are superior, the subsequent estate holder has a better right to possession of that estate.

For example, X wants to purchase the legal estate from Y. Pursuant to a contract of sale entered into on 1 January 1998, X pays a deposit of 10% of the purchase price of the land, with the balance to be paid on 1 March 1998. After payment of the deposit, Y becomes a constructive trustee of the property for the benefit of X until legal title is transferred. X has no notice of a prior 'mere equity' prior to 1 January, but acquires notice before 1 March 1998, when legal title is transferred. The legal title which X acquires will be enforceable against the prior 'mere equity' because the rights which Y owed as constructive trustee for X were superior to those which Y owed towards the third party.

Arguably, the priority principles relating to the subsequent acquisition of legal title only apply to mortgagees, because they represent an extension of the tacking principles which are enforceable against mortgages. Nevertheless, given the statutory qualifications to tacking in mortgages, combined with the fact that there is no justifiable reason to exclude the application of the principle to purchasers under a 'continuous transaction' – especially as the definition of 'purchaser' is defined broadly by the legislation in this area – there is no clear reason why the priority tacking rules should not be extended.

---

22 See Sykes, EI and Walker, S, *The Law of Securities*, 5th edn, 1993, LBC p 393.

9.4.3.2 The nature of the notice

What constitutes notice is, in the words of Story, 'a point of some nicety'.[23] The purchaser must receive notice of the existence of a prior interest. Notice means actual notice of the existence of a prior interest (including wilful blindness or contrived ignorance), as well as constructive notice where the purchaser, while not actually aware of the existence of a prior estate, should have been aware and would have discovered it if he or she had made the proper enquiries about, and inspections over, the title. The significance of notice was reinforced in *Barclays Bank plc v O'Brien* [1993] 4 All ER 417, where Lord Browne Wilkinson noted (at p 429):

> The doctrine of notice lies at the heart of equity. Given that there are two innocent parties, each enjoying rights, the earlier right prevails against the later right if the acquirer of the later right knows of the earlier right (actual notice) or would have discovered it had he taken steps (constructive notice). In particular, if the party asserting that he takes free of the earlier rights of another knows of certain facts which put him on inquiry as to the possible existence of the rights of that other and he fails to make such inquiry or take such other steps as are reasonable to verify whether such earlier right does or does not exist, he will have constructive notice of the earlier right and take subject to it.

Whether or not a subsequent interest holder is affected by constructive notice is a question of fact on the individual circumstances. It is often suggested that constructive notice is a doctrine which is relevant only priority disputes between property interests as it is easier to apply, given the existence of clearly established conveyancing procedures. In *Garcia v NAB* (1998) 155 ALR 614, the Australian High Court noted that constructive trust was a notion more relevant to property disputes than surety transactions. Indeed, the fear of extending constructive notice to other commercial transactions has been clearly expressed.[24] Nevertheless, there is also recognition that constructive notice may be useful in circumstances where it is clear that one party ought to have been put on inquiry or to have taken further reasonable steps.[25] Kirby J in *Garcia v NAB* (1998) 155 ALR 614 adopted a different approach to the majority and noted that once the doctrine of constuctive notice is understood as a principle which is wider and more flexible than the strict conveyancing standard, there is no reason why it should not give rise to liability in surety transactions.[26]

The scope of the doctrine of notice is set out in s 199 of the Property Law Act (Vic) 1958:

---

23 Story, J, *Commentaries on Equity Jurisprudence* , 1884, Stevens & Haynes at para 399; see, also, Ormiston JA in *Moffett v Dillon* (1997) 2 VR 380.

24 *Manchester Trust v Furness* [1895] 2 QB 539, at pp 545–46, *per* Lindley LJ.

25 See *Koorootang Nominees Pty Ltd v ANZ Banking Group* (1998) 3 VR 16.

26 See, also, *MacMillan Inc v Bishopsgate Investment Trust (No 3)* [1995] 1 WLR 978, at p 1000; Fox, 'Constructive notice and knowing receipt: an economic analysis' [1998] CLJ 391.

(1) A purchaser shall not be prejudicially affected by notice of any instrument, fact or thing unless:

(a) it is within his own knowledge, or would have come to his knowledge if such inquiries and inspections had been made as ought reasonably to have been made by him; or

(b) in the same transaction, with respect to which a question of notice to the purchaser arises, it has come to the knowledge of his counsel, as such, or of his solicitor or other agent, as such, or would have come to the knowledge of his solicitor or other agent, as such, if such inquiries and inspections had been made as ought reasonably to have been made by the solicitor or other agent.[27]

Actual notice refers to the situation where a subsequent interest is directly and positively aware of the existence of a prior estate. Under constructive notice, however, a subsequent interest holder may have no actual awareness of the existence of a prior interest; however, in the circumstances, it is felt that the subsequent interest holder should have been aware of it. Constructive notice will arise where it can be established that the purchaser would have been aware of the existence of the prior interest or estate if he had carried out the usual or reasonable steps included in the investigate title. Where this can be proven, the subsequent purchaser is to be treated as if they had actual knowledge of the existence of the prior estate. The legislation refers to investigations which 'ought reasonably' to be made. The particular type of investigations which are 'reasonable' will depend upon the facts in any given circumstance. For example, in a conveyance of old title land, a failure to check the registrar will affect the purchaser with constructive notice of all interests which may have been lodged (*Mills v Renwick* (1901) 1 SR (NSW) (Eq) 173). The doctrine of notice requires a purchaser to be aware of all of the interests which they would be reasonably likely to come across in the course of conducting all of the 'usual' searches and checks on the title. This may require the purchaser to check the obligations and clauses of a particular agreement or contract of sale and to make any further investigations as may be deemed necessary in the circumstances. Once a general inquiry has been made, and the accuracy of that inquiry questioned, there is no further obligation to investigate the exact nature and circumstances of the title.

In *Smith v Jones* [1954] 1 WLR 1089, the defendant purchased a farm. At the time of purchase, the defendant had known that the farm was in the occupation of a tenant, the plaintiff. Prior to the sale, the defendant had inspected the actual tenancy agreement, which was held in the office of the auctioneers and, from reading the document, had concluded that the responsibility for repairs on the farm lay with the tenant. The plaintiff, on the other hand, had always believed that the standard form tenancy agreement

27 The property law statutes in all other states except Western Australia have equivalent provisions: Qld, s 256; Tas, s 5; SA, s 117; NSW, s 164.

resulted in the landlord being responsible for the repairs. A subsequent dispute arose between the plaintiff and the defendant as to who was responsible for repairs. Following a decision at first instance in favour of the defendant, the plaintiff claimed a right to rectify the tenancy agreement against the original landlord. The defendant claimed that, as he was a *bona fide* purchaser for value without notice, he took priority to any equity to rectify which may be held by the plaintiff. One of the issues in the case was whether or not the defendant was affected by the doctrine of notice.

Upjohn J considered what inquiries and inspections were reasonably necessary on the facts, and concluded that where the purchaser has carried out an inspection of the tenancy agreement to ensure that it corresponded with the copy he held, no further enquiries were necessary. There was no additional obligation on the defendant to investigate further and question the defendant as to whether the tenancy agreement accurately reflected his rights. This type of inquiry was beyond the scope of the doctrine of notice: the defendant was entitled to rely upon the terms of the document and not bound to interpret their effect.

In a similar decision, the court in *Hunt v Luck* [1902] 1 Ch 428 concluded that the doctrine of notice must be affected by natural and reasonable boundaries. In that case, the purchaser of land was held to owe no further duty than to investigate the tenancy agreement; in particular, the purchaser was not obliged to find out who actually received the rental payments, even though such an investigation would have revealed the fact that the landlord was not actually the vendor.

The doctrine of notice will only require a subsequent purchaser to carry out investigations which are usual or reasonable, having regard to the particular nature of the transaction. Additional inspection or investigation should only be carried out where the purchaser has had his or her suspicions raised. For example, where the property is in the possession of parties other than the vendor and the interest of those parties is not noted, or where the property may be affected by interests of partners or spouses and the existence of such interest is either directly or indirectly apparent from the transaction.[28] Furthermore, where a vendor claims to hold full interest in a property, and the property is actually occupied by the vendor's wife and children, a prospective purchaser should investigate the nature of this occupation and whether the wife holds any equity in the property (*Kingsnorth Trust Ltd v Tizard* [1986] 2 All ER 54).

Where a purchaser is purchasing old title land, the purchaser should carry out all usual investigations associated with the purchase, including searching back to a good root of title and checking the accuracy of the abstract of titles. Where a possible problem is discovered, the purchaser can only be exempted

28 See *Williams & Glyn's Bank Ltd v Boland* [1981] AC 487.

from the notification of any interest which may arise from this problem in circumstances where the vendor provides a reasonable and satisfactory explanation.

Generally, the cases indicate that courts are reluctant to extend the doctrine of notice beyond reasonable and proper investigations.[29] In *Consul Development Pty Ltd v DPC Estates Pty Ltd* (1975) 132 CLR 373, the High Court displayed a clear hesitation in expanding the application of constructive knowledge beyond situations where all usual and reasonable investigations are entered into. In that case, Stephen J drew a distinction between reasonable and unreasonable investigative obligations. His Honour noted (p 392):

> In my view, the state of the authorities ... did not go so far ... as to apply to them that species of constructive notice which serves to expose a party to liability because of negligence in failing to make inquiry. If a defendant knows of facts which themselves would, to a reasonable man, tell of fraud or breach of trust, the case may well be different, as it clearly will be if the defendant has consciously refrained from enquiry for fear lest he learn of fraud. But to go further is, I think, to disregard equity's concern for the state of conscience of the defendant.

Given the basic 'inferred' nature of constructive notice, it is understandable that courts will be reluctant to extend it too extensively beyond the usual course of proceedings. Unusual or latent difficulties, not immediately apparent from the documents or the nature of the transaction, should not be included within the ambit of constructive knowledge, because this would create a situation where a purchaser could never be truly sure whether he or she had acted properly. The dangers are well summarised by Lord Esher MR in *English and Scottish Mercantile Investment Co v Brunton* [1892] 2 QB 700:

> Of late years, after the doctrine [of constructive notice] had been invented and put into form, the Chancery judges saw that it was being carried much farther than had been intended, and they declined to carry it further ... I pointed out that the doctrine is a dangerous one. It is contrary to the truth. It is wholly founded on the assumption that a man does not know the facts; and yet it is said that constructively he does know them.

It is very clear in Australian courts that the existence of constructive notice does not necessarily infer unconscientious dealing: *Garcia v NAB* (1998) 155 ALR 614. Once a purchaser is affected by actual or constructive notice, it cannot be extinguished. Where the purchaser is a corporation, or one of several members of a board of partners, trustees, etc, it has been held that notice to a director, or one member of a board, will effectively constitute notice to all members (*Jones v Collins* (1891) 12 LR (NSW) 247). Furthermore, under the principle of 'imputed notice', the law regards a principal as having all the knowledge as that of his or her agent (*Hargreaves v Rothwell* (1936) 1 Keen 154;

29 See, also, *Milne v James* (1910) 13 CLR 168, where Griffith CJ noted that it was now settled that the doctrine ought not to be extended.

48 ER 265). Section 199 of the Property Law Act (Vic) 1958 adds to this by expressly setting out that a purchaser can only be affected by notice where an agent acquires it in the course of the same transaction to which the notice relates.[30]

Notice will bind all purchasers, even where the purchaser is mistakenly led to believe that the interest has been extinguished. The rationale for this is that, once notice is gained, a purchaser should either refuse to go ahead with the transaction or, if he does, he should take subject to the prior interest. If the purchaser goes ahead with the transaction believing the interest to have been extinguished, it is the responsibility of the purchaser to check the validity and accuracy of this belief.

This point is well evidenced in *Jared v Clements* [1902] 2 Ch 399. In that case, the subsequent legal mortgagees did have notice of the existence of a prior mortgage. However, due to a fraud perpetrated by the solicitor of the legal interest holder, they had mistakenly believed that the earlier mortgage had been discharged. It was held that the mistaken fraud was not sufficient to allow the legal interest holders to stand in the position as if they had never had notice of the previous equitable mortgage and, consequently, the legal mortgagees did not gain priority. During the course of his judgment, Byrne J made the following comments:

> I am unable to say that the fraud practised upon them by the vendor's solicitor enabled the defendant to stand in the same position as if he had never had notice of the charge ... The case is a hard one upon the defendant, and not the less so because, if less diligence had been shewn by the gentleman who actually made the search in bankruptcy, the mortgage would probably never have been disclosed, and the purchaser could then have claimed to be a purchaser for value without notice.[31]

Once a purchaser has notice of a prior interest, she will be bound by it unless the principle emanating from *Wilkes v Spooner* [1911] 2 KB 473 can be invoked. In that case, a lessee of a pork butcher shop agreed under the lease agreement not to carry on any noisy or offensive trade other than that of a pork butcher. The lessee also held rights under a lease further down the street, within which he conducted a general butcher business. The lessee sold the general butcher business and covenanted not to deal in meats other than pork in the business he retained. The lessee eventually gave up his business and his lease, and a new lease was given to his son. Under the new lease, the son covenanted not to conduct any noisy or offensive trade other than that of a butcher (not confined to 'pork butcher' as in the previous lease). The son then set up a general butcher business.

30 See, also, property law statutes: Tas, s 5(1)(b); Qld, s 256(1)(b); SA, s 117(1)(b); and NSW, s 164(1)(b). No equivalent provision exists in WA.

31 *Jared v Clements* [1902] 2 Ch 399, p 412.

Vaugham Williams LJ noted that a purchaser for valuable consideration without notice can give a good title to a purchaser from him with notice – the only exception being that a trustee who has sold property in breach of trust, or a person who has acquired property by fraud, cannot protect himself by purchasing it from a *bona fide* purchaser for value without notice.

On the facts, the court held that the landlord had no actual or constructive notice of the existence of the restrictive covenant entered into by the first lessee when selling his business, and, as such, the son received a good title under the lease and was not bound by the covenant even though he took with notice of it.[32] The rationale for this principle appears to be that a legal estate holder who takes without notice of any interest should not be restricted in his or her attempts to obtain the best possible price. Hence, a court should not impugn the title of a subsequent purchaser merely because they discover an interest which the vendor was unaware of.

9.5 Priorities between equitable interests

The equitable jurisdiction takes a much broader approach to the assessment of priority disputes between subsisting equitable interests. Unlike priority disputes with common law estates, where the priority rules focus upon the *bona fide* purchaser for value without notice, the equitable disputes undertake a comprehensive examination of all circumstances relating to the nature and context in which each equitable interest was acquired. The basic determination for the court to decide is which interest is the 'better equity' in the circumstances. This assessment process is exemplified by the general rule that the prior equity will gain priority where it can be proven that they are both equal in character. The *qui prior est tempore potior est jure* (priority in time of creation gives the better equity) will be utilised only as a last resort, in circumstances where each interest is, in all other respects, equal in nature. Equitable interests will generally be regarded as 'equal' where, upon an overall assessment of justice and fairness, both interests are held in the same capacity. Factors which are relevant in a judicial examination of the 'better equity' include:

(a) the nature and condition of the respective equitable interests;

(b) the circumstances and manner of their acquisition; and

(c) the whole conduct of each party.

This process of examination is clearly emphasised in the seminal decision, *Rice v Rice* (1853) 2 Drew 73p; 161 ER 646. In that case, Michael Rice, the defendant, purchased land from Mr and Mrs George Rice and Mr and Mrs E Moore. Upon the execution of the conveyance, the Moores received their portion of the purchase money, but no money was received by the other vendors, Mr and

32 See, also, *Re Stapleford Colliery Co (Barrow's Case)* (1880) 14 Ch D 432.

Mrs George Rice, who agreed to allow payment to stand over for a few days on the promise of the purchaser to pay. The vendors agreed to this despite the fact that the actual transfer set out that the whole of the purchase money had been paid, a receipt was issued and title deeds were delivered to the purchaser. The purchaser subsequently deposited the title deeds with 'Ede and Knight' in order to secure the payment of an advance and absconded without paying the promised balance of the purchase moneys to Mr and Mrs George Rice. The issue in the case was whether the equitable interest arising from the vendors' lien for the unpaid purchase price could defeat the equitable mortgage held by Ede and Knight.

The court ultimately held that the later interest held by the equitable mortgagee had priority over the equitable lien held by Mr and Mrs George Rice. During the course of the judgment, the court considered the most appropriate priority principles to apply to a competition between equitable interests. The court noted that the accurate rule was that if the equities are in all other respects equal, priority of time gives the better equity – or *qui prior est tempore potior est jure*. The significant issue to determine is whether the equities are equal. In considering this question, the court should direct its attention to a diverse range of interests. The primary categories set out by the court were: the nature and condition of the respective equitable interests; the circumstances and manner of their acquisition; and the whole conduct of each party. The question is an equitable one, and therefore the focus should primarily be upon a flexible analysis of the fairness of the circumstances rather than a rigid application of technical rule. In the circumstances, the court found that the equitable interests were not equal in nature, and that, ultimately, the equitable mortgagees held the better equity. Some of the facts which the court found to be relevant in this determination included:

(a) the vendors made the choice to assign over the entire estate when the whole of the purchase price had not been paid, thereby arming the purchaser with the ability to hold themselves out as full, unencumbered legal owners;

(b) the vendors decided not to hold on to the title deeds as security for the balance of the unpaid purchase price despite the fact that they were in a position to require this;

(c) the vendors voluntarily armed the purchaser with the means of dealing with the property as absolute legal owner, which thereby resulted in an innocent third party acquiring an equitable title over the property;

(d) the equitable mortgagees were not guilty of any negligence;

(e) the equitable mortgagees gave good consideration for the mortgage; and

(f) the equitable mortgagees obtained a *bona fide* possession of the title.

These facts clearly indicate that equality of interest is determined not only by the character of the interest, but also by the conduct and behaviour of each party. In particular, attention is given to the 'protective' behaviour of the first interest holder in ensuring that any future equitable interest holders take with notice of the existence of their prior interest. On the facts, the court indicated that the conduct of the first equitable interest holders in arming the purchaser who had not paid the balance of the purchase price with the power to hold himself out as a full and unencumbered legal owner of the property by issuing him the title deeds to the property was, in itself, sufficient to reduce the strength of their interest in the eyes of equity. Underlying the judgment is the perception that holders of equitable interests are subject to behavioural standards: all equitable interest holders are responsible for the protection of their interests and this is primarily achieved through notification to the rest of the world of the nature and form of their interest.

It is unfair, and therefore contrary to the fundamental basis of the equitable jurisdiction, not to penalise interest holders for failing to clearly and unequivocally announce their existence to unsuspecting third parties in whatever form is appropriate in the circumstances. On the facts, this could have been achieved by the vendors retaining possession of the title deeds: the very act of transferring the deeds constituted the disqualifying conduct.

The process of determining whether or not the merits of each equitable interest are balanced is a flexible one. Equity does not regard itself as being bound by strict rules of priority and, whilst some actions may more readily indicate a greater or lesser degree of merit, no single circumstance is regarded as definitive. As Kindersley VC noted:

> ... neither the one nor the other has necessarily and under all circumstances the better equity. Their equitable interests, abstractedly considered, are of equal value in respect of their nature and quality; but whether their equities are in other respects equal, or whether the one or the other has acquired the better equity, must depend upon all the circumstances of each particular case, and especially the conduct of the respective parties. And among the circumstances which may give to the one the better equity, the possession of the title deeds is a very material one. But if, after a close examination of all these matters, there appears nothing to give the one a better equity than the other, then, and then only, resort must be had to the maxim *qui prior est tempore potior est jure*, and priority of time then gives the better equity.[33]

An important conclusion in the *Rice v Rice* decision is that the 'priority in time' maxim is only referred to as a matter of last resort, in circumstances where the equitable interests are, in all other respects, equal in merit. Since the *Rice v Rice* decision, it has long been regarded as axiomatic that any priority determination between conflicting equitable interests will be determined by an analysis of all relevant circumstances through the application of broad equitable principles of justice and fairness. In *Mercantile Credits v Jarden*

33 *Rice v Rice* (1853) 2 Drew 73; 161 ER 646, p 655.

Morgan Australia Ltd [1990] 1 ACSR 805, Derrington J noted that a competition between equitable interests is not dependent upon the grounds that one interest is inherently 'superior in status' to the other. His Honour reiterated the principle, derived from *Rice v Rice*, that 'the relative strength of the equitable interests depended upon matters of equity and conscience which had nothing to do with the quality of the interests'.

Usually, in conducting the merit analysis, a court will start with an examination of the conduct of the earlier interest holder in terms of any specific representations, negligence or carelessness she may have committed, particularly where this has been responsible – wholly or partially – for the creation of the subsequent interest. As a general principle, the earlier interest will be postponed to the later interest (despite its priority in time) where the conduct of the earlier interest holder has been such that it has induced that subsequent interest holder to believe that no prior interest exists (*Heid v Reliance Finance Corp Pty Ltd* (1983) 154 CLR 326; *Barry v Heider* (1914) 19 CLR 197).[34]

Once the conduct of the earlier interest holder has been assessed, the *bona fides* of each party will be carefully examined. The question of whether or not the subsequent equitable interest holder takes with notice of the prior equitable interest may also be relevant to the determination of the general merits of each case. If, for example, the prior equitable estate holder has armed a third party to hold himself out as having an unencumbered title, the postponing nature of this conduct may be irrelevant in a situation where the subsequent interest holder is proven to have knowledge of the existence of the previous equity. In such a situation, it cannot be argued that the subsequent interest holder has been unfairly induced by the lack of 'protective behaviour' and cannot, on this basis, argue that their interest constitutes the 'better' equity (*IAC (Finance) Pty Ltd v Courtenay* (1963) 110 CLR 550). Where a subsequent interest holder takes with notice of the existence of a prior interest, then it is the taker himself rather than the prior interest holder who is responsible for the dispute (*Courtenay v Austin* [1962] NSWLR 296).

In order to actually deprive the first interest holder of the equitable interest, it lies upon the holder of the subsequent interest to prove that the holder of the first interest has done something, or has been guilty of some omission, which would render the subsequent interest the 'better equity' (*General Finance Agency & Guarantee Co of Australia Ltd v Perpetual Executors & Trustees Association of Australia Ltd* [1902] VLR 739). It may well be, on the facts, that the prior equitable interest holders are not actually responsible for the creation of the subsequent equity. This is particularly obvious where the prior interest holder is a beneficiary under a trust and the trustee has dealt with the title documents in a fraudulent manner – such that a subsequent equitable

34 It should be noted that both of these cases deal with a competition between equitable interests relating to Torrens title rather than old title land.

interest is created. In such a case, if the prior equitable interest holder did not actually possess the title documents and was not privy to the fraud, it would be unfair to penalise him for the conduct of his trustee by postponing his priority (*Shropshire Union Rlys & Canal Co v R* (1875) LR 7 HL 496).

The equitable analysis will take into account current conveyancing practices. In a situation where a prior equitable interest holder has carried out all of the usual practices associated with the particular transaction, his conduct should not, in fairness, be regarded as postponing, even if he or she has not done everything possible to protect against the creation of a subsequent interest. Courts will, however, be cautious not to give so called 'modern practices' too liberal a construction for fear of being seen to condone a 'sloppy informality' in commercial dealings. As noted by Tadgell J in *Avco Financial Services Ltd v Fishman* [1993] 1 VR 90:

> An increasing tendency towards sloppy informality in commercial dealings is likely to carry its own consequences. There are those who nowadays seem content to deal for commercial purposes in writing and by word of mouth with others whom they do not know and have never met or even seen, addressing and identifying them merely by a Christian name or another given name, or a pet name, a nickname or a diminutive. Whatever the perceived justification today for what would once not have been generally acceptable, or even contemplated, the tendency will sometimes be found to be inconsistent with sound and sensible business dealing, and even inimical to it.[35]

In *Person-to-Person Financial Services Pty Ltd v Sharari* [1984] 1 NSWLR 745,[36] the settled conveyancing practice of competent solicitors when acting for equitable mortgagees was discussed. McLelland J noted that the general practice was to ensure either a prompt securing of the title documents or, in the case of Torrens title land, registration of the mortgage or the lodgement of a caveat. The fact that an interest holder chose to select only one method of protecting his interest should not mean that he should be considered less meritorious. However, his Honour indicated that a failure to carry out any of the protective measures would generally result in a postponement. The level of carelessness which must be established before a prior equitable interest may be postponed will vary according to the facts, but a court is not expected to conduct an examination of the 'general naughtiness' of the parties (*per* Young J in *FAI Insurances Ltd v Pioneer Concrete Services Ltd* (1987) 15 NSWLR 552, pp 554–55). It must be established that the activity of the prior equitable interest holder could be anticipated or was reasonably foreseeable to affect the interests of a third person before such priority may be postponed. Hence, where the prior interest holder either knew or should be taken to have known

35 [1993] 1 VR 90, p 95.

36 The actual facts of this case concerned Torrens title land.

that such conduct or omission may affect the interests of third parties, priority may be postponed.

Some commentators have suggested that the foundation for setting aside the priority of a prior equitable estate is estoppel. In *Rimmer v Webster* [1902] 2 Ch 163, Farwell J said, 'If the owner of property clothes a third person with the apparent ownership ... he is estopped from asserting his title as against a person to whom such third party has disposed of the property, and who took it in good faith and for value'.[37] In many priority disputes between equitable interests, the underlying unfairness is based upon estoppel principles: the failure of the prior equitable interest holder to protect his or her interest properly constitutes a representation to the rest of the world that the title is unencumbered and, where a *bona fide* third party for value does acquire an interest, it would be unfair to allow an interest holder to enforce his priority in time. For example, in *Abigail v Lapin* (1934) 51 CLR 58, the owners of a fee simple in land, Mr and Mrs Lapin, transferred it to the wife of a lender as security for a loan they had taken out. When executing the transfer, Mr and Mrs Lapin had at no stage indicated that the transfer was as a security only, and their failure to do so enabled the lender's wife to take a legal title which appeared absolute and unencumbered. The Privy Council, reversing the decision of the High Court, held that Mr and Mrs Lapin had effectively represented to the world that title was absolute and thereby allowed for the possibility that another person may take an equitable interest in the property in good faith and for value. The court felt that it would be unfair to allow Mr and Mrs Lapin to enforce their priority in time as they were 'estopped' from doing so.[38]

The estoppel analysis is, however, often argued to be inappropriate to such priority disputes. Estoppel by representation requires proof of a clear and positive representation and, in many instances, it is difficult to infer this from the behaviour of a prior interest holder. The failure of a prior estate holder to adequately protect his interest does not necessarily constitute a direct representation that the estate is unencumbered; it is the party who receives the unencumbered estate and who fraudulently 'pretends' that he holds an absolute legal title to an unsuspecting third party who is responsible for the direct representation, not the prior estate holder (*Capell v Winter* [1907] 2 Ch 376).[39] Given the lack of clarity as to who is responsible for the representation made to the subsequent equity holder, some judges have preferred to adopt a 'reasonable foreseeability' test. Under this test, the court focuses upon only those situations where it can be established that it would have been

37 *Rimmer v Webster* [1902] 2 Ch 163, p 173.

38 See, also, the judgment of Gibbs CJ in *Heid v Reliance Finance Corp Pty Ltd* (1983) 154 CLR 326.

39 See, also, the critical examination of this application of estoppel principles by Meagher, RP, Gummow, WMC and Lehane, JRF, in *Equity Doctrines and Remedies*, 3rd edn, 1992, Butterworths, p 231.

'reasonably foreseeable' to the prior equity holder that a subsequent interest would be created (*per* Mason and Deane JJ, *Heid v Reliance Finance Corp Pty Ltd* (1983) 154 CLR 326).

Given the expansive developments in the application of the principles relating to equitable estoppel,[40] it would seem that courts are increasingly prepared to adopt a more flexible approach to the assessment of what acts or omissions can form the basis of a representation for the purpose of raising an estoppel. In *Walton Stores (Interstate) Pty Ltd v Maher*, for example, it was held that a failure of Walton Stores to contact the Mahers, after extensive contractual negotiations for a lease, and inform them of their decision not to go ahead with the lease amounted to a direct representation to the Mahers that the terms of the lease had been agreed to, and they were estopped from relying upon their strict legal rights. The failure of Walton Stores to contact the Mahers in light of the contractual negotiations entered into, their retention of the proposed counterpart lease agreement and the fact that Walton Stores had received actual knowledge that the Mahers mistakenly believed the contract to be going ahead was held to be sufficient to constitute a direct representation that the contract would be executed.

This analysis may be applied to disputes between competing equitable interests. For example, where an estate holder fails to hold on to the title deeds and hands them on to a third party, allowing the third party to represent to the world that he or she holds an unencumbered title, a promissory representation on the part of the prior estate holder that the title is not subject to any equitable claims may be referred. As the equitable jurisdiction is concerned with substance rather than form, it would seem unduly artificial to limit the form of representations that such an estoppel may uphold to those involving direct communication – it would be contrary to the newly liberated concept of equitable estoppel, founded upon the unconscionability associated with the denial of a representation which a person has, by her overall conduct, induced another to believe. The whole aim of the 'new' equitable jurisdiction in estoppel is to avoid unduly semantic and formalistic distinctions associated with the nature and form of the representation.[41]

Whilst estoppel is a common feature in priority disputes between equitable interests, the merit analysis incorporates a broad range of factors under its umbrella and should not be limited to estoppel arguments. Provided it can be established that the conduct would, with reasonable foreseeability, affect the interests of third parties, the conduct of a prior interest holder may range from mere carelessness to intentional disregard or actual negligence. It is contrary to the nature of the 'merit analysis' to impose specific rules or

40 See, eg, *Waltons Stores (Interstate) Ltd v Maher* (1988) 164 CLR 387; *Commonwealth v Verwayen* (1990) 170 CLR 394; *Commonwealth v Clark* [1994] 2 VR 333.

41 See, further, Lunney, M, '*Jorden v Money* – a time for reapppraisal?' (1994) 68 ALJ 559; and Finn, PD, 'Equitable estoppel', in *Essays in Equity*, 1985, LBC.

presumptions (*Jacobs v Platt Nominees Pty Ltd* [1990] VR 146). The most that can be said is that, in many cases, estoppel and estoppel related conduct may lead to a prior equitable interest being set aside. As noted by Mason and Deane JJ in *Heid v Reliance Finance Corp Pty Ltd* (1983) 154 CLR 326, p 341:

> For our part, we consider it preferable to avoid ... basing the postponement of the first to the second equity exclusively on the doctrine of estoppel and to accept the more general and flexible principle that preference should be given to what is the better equity in an examination of the relevant circumstances.

Consider the following examples.

(a) X has an equitable interest in a property pursuant to a deposit paid under a contract of sale for a large piece of land. Unbeknown to X, before this date, Y declared that he held the property on trust for Z. At the time of the declaration, Y told Z that he would put this declaration in writing, but Z told him not to bother about it and that he could draw up the declaration of trust when he was ready. Who has the better equity between X and Z?

(b) X acquires an equitable lien pursuant to an unpaid purchase price over property he is selling. X gives the title deeds to his solicitor prior to settlement. X's solicitor fraudulently represents to Y that he holds legal title to the property and Y subsequently acquires an interest in the property by way of an equitable mortgage. Who should have the better equity?

(c) X holds moneys received pursuant to a retirement fund under an express trust for the benefit of a small company. X, in breach of trust, uses the money to help Y, a struggling property developer, in obtaining the requisite capital to complete a highrise building development. Y is aware that the money which is being used is held by X as trustee under the retirement fund. X transfers money to Y and acquires an equitable charge over the property. The project subsequently collapses. Can the beneficiaries under the retirement trust bring an action against X or Y for the recovery of their moneys? This priority analysis is discussed in *Royal Brunei Airlines v Tan* [1995] 3 WLR 64.

9.5.1 *Equitable interests: merit analysis and the doctrine of notice*

The significance of a conducting a comprehensive equitable analysis for priority disputes between equitable interests was reinforced by Mason and Deane JJ in *Heid v Reliance Finance Corp Pty Ltd* (1983) 154 CLR 326, where their Honours noted that a consideration of all the relevant circumstances is necessary in order to uphold general questions of justice and fairness. The assumed primacy of this test has, however, been questioned by the majority of the Victorian Supreme Court in *Moffett v Dillon* [1999] 2 VR 480. The possibility of Australian courts introducing a narrower test, focusing more upon the issue of the notice of the subsequent equitable interest holder has been raised a number of times by earlier courts.[42] The majority, Brooking J and Buchanan JA, in *Moffett v Dillon* go one step further than previous decisions however and conclude that the existence of notice in a subsequent interest holder automatically negates any further priority analysis. This conclusion severely undermines the apparent breadth of the equitable 'merit analysis' test; notice of the existence of the prior equity by the subsequent interest holder is regarded by the majority as so fundamental that proof of its existence automatically negates any need to examine other pertinent considerations.

The facts of the *Moffett* case concerned a priority dispute between a prior equitable charge and a subsequent unregistered mortgage. The holder of the subsequent unregistered mortgage took with notice of the existence of the prior equitable charge. The question was whether existence of such notice automatically denied the subsequent interest holder any priority or, whether the existence of notice was merely one of the elements to consider in the overall merit analysis. Brooking J felt that the existence of notice was crucial. His Honour noted:

> ... there are two rules or principles at work in cases like the present, the rule that a person taking with notice of an equity takes subject to it and the rule where the equities are equal the first in time prevails. As regards the second rule, I have referred to the wide view taken by Mason and Deane JJ in *Heid v Reliance Finance Corp Pty Ltd* (1983) 154 CLR 326 that broad principles of right and justice will guide the court in determining whether the equities are equal ... I do not regard the question whether a person who acquired an equity did so with notice of a prior equity as no more than a consideration to which regard is to be had in determining whether one of the equities is better than the other. I regard the rule about notice as a distinct and fundamental one and I do not consider that Mason and Deane JJ intended to question its existence or to subsume this particular matter of notice under a broad question so as to make it no more than a consideration bearing upon which was the better equity.[43]

Brooking J concludes that where a subsequent interest holder is held to have taken with notice of the existence of a prior interest – the prior interest will automatically succeed and there is no need to examine the circumstances further. His Honour rationalises his introduction of this 'notice' test by referring to 'deeply rooted' equitable notions of conscience whereby a person taking with notice of an equity is bound by it and refers to the House of Lords in *Barclays Bank plc v O'Brien* [1994] 1 AC 180 where Lord Brown-Wilkinson notes that the 'doctrine of notice lies at the heart of equity' (at p 195).

42 See, eg, Knox CJ in *Lapin v Abigail* (1930) 44 CLR 166, at p 182, where his Honour notes 'If the holder of the subsequent equity acquired it with notice of the prior equity, his claim for priority necessarily fails'. See, also, *IAC (Finance) Pty Ltd v Courtenay* (1963) 110 CLR 550, *per* Taylor J at p 590.

43 See, also, *Platzer v Commonwealth Bank of Australia* [1997] 1 Qd R 266, *per* Davies JA, at p 273 – relied upon by Brooking J in *Moffett v Dillon*.

Nevertheless, whilst emphasising the fundamental importance of notice and incorporating it as a direct test in a priority dispute between equitable interests, Brooking J concluded that on the facts, the same result would have occurred under the broad 'merit analysis' test as there was nothing which would displace the priority in time of the registered equitable charge holder. The subsequent unregistered mortgagee argued that its interest was 'registrable', but Brooking J noted that registrability was an irrelevant consideration for merit analysis as it was primarily concerned with inequitable behaviour.

Buchanan JA agreed with Brooking J and noted that the application of the notice rule priority disputes between equitable interests was logical, and well grounded in authority. Buchanan JA noted that the prior in time rule would also reach the same result on the facts however the shorter route to the resolution was to be found under the 'notice' rule and that this was, therefore, the preferable approach. Neither Brooking J nor Buchanan JA indicated whether notice was restricted to 'actual notice' as existed on the facts or 'constructive notice' although it is to be presumed that in referring to the fundamental nature of the equitable doctrine of notice – their Honours are referring to the full scope of the doctrine and thereby intended to include constructive notice. Nevertheless, courts have been very reluctant to incorporate constructive notice into any aspect of the Torrens system. This reluctance is clearly apparent in *Macquarie Bank Ltd v Sixty-Fourth Throne Pty Ltd*(1998) 3 VR 133, where the Victorian Supreme Court expressly opposed the introduction of constructive notice into an examination of registered interests (the case dealt with a registered mortgage and not an unregistered interest), noting that if the doctrine of constructive notice were held to apply generally to the ordering of priorities under the Torrens system it would, in effect, introduce into the scheme of title by registration the notion of priority determinable by reference to the doctrine of the *bona fide* purchaser for value without notice, a doctrine at odds with the Torrens system.

The final judge in *Moffett v Dillon*, Ormiston JA, began his judgment with a consideration of the merits analysis approach and made the following comments:

> Merits in equity, are those matters which impinge, broadly speaking, on the conscience of those who seek its aid or are otherwise subject to its jurisdiction. So priority is to be resolved against the holder of the prior equity only if the other party can establish the first holder's want of 'merits' or comparative lack of 'merit'. That is essentially a negative enquiry into behaviour on the part of the holders of each of the equitable interests as to whether they can be shown to have been obtained or enforced in a manner which is so unconscionable or otherwise inequitable so as to deprive the holder of the earlier interest of the priority to which it is otherwise entitled, whether that behaviour be evidenced by fraud, unfairness, negligence, the wrongful creation of particular assumptions by representations or the like or in a number of other ways which reflect on the behaviour of the holders of each of the interests.

Ormiston JA did not concur with Brooking and Buchanan JJ on the issue of notice. His Honour felt that there was nothing to suggest that Mason and Deane JJ in *Heid's* case intended to confer any 'greater significance' upon notice than any of the other matters which may be taken into account to determine whether an interest should be postponed in 'fairness and justice' and that the 'better view' was that the *bona fide* purchaser for value without notice rule should not ordinarily apply between competing equitable interests.[44]

9.5.2 *Mere equities*

9.5.2.1 *Nature of a mere equity*

A mere equity is a personal right which is often accepted as containing, in a limited sense, equitable proprietary rights. Rights which tend to fall within this category are those which confer personal remedial rights upon an individual, enforceable against an ascertainable piece of property, usually land. Mere equities may, in fact, not constitute equitable interests at all because they are only enforceable against a particular defendant and are therefore not enforceable against the rest of the world. According to a strict definition of private property, where a right does not confer the ability to exclude the rest of the world, it cannot be truly defined as proprietary.[45] Nevertheless, in certain situations, the holder of a mere equity may enforce it against third parties, and this tends to elevate the interest into the proprietary sphere. The features of an equitable proprietary interest were broadly categorised by Lord Wilberforce in *National Provincial Bank v Ainsworth* [1965] AC 1175, pp 1247–48, who considered the distinction between personal and proprietary rights and noted:

> Before a right or an interest can be admitted into the category of property, or of a right affecting property, it must be definable, identifiable by third parties, capable in its nature of assumption by third parties and have some degree of permanence or stability.

Nevertheless, the equitable jurisdiction generally assumes a more flexible approach. As noted in *Story's Equity Jurisprudence*, 1881, Lt Eng Ed, Randall, AE (ed), 1920, London: Sweet & Maxwell, para 28, p 16:

> ... one of the most striking and distinctive features of courts of equity was that they could adapt their decrees to all the variety of circumstances which might arise and adjust them to all the peculiar rights of all the parties in interest.

In equity, a right may be recognised as holding quasi-proprietary characteristics because of the fact that it confers enforceable rights against property. For example, the right of a beneficiary under an unadministered

44 See, generally, Butt, P, *Land Law*, 3rd edn, 1996, LBC, para 1936; *Phillips v Phillips* [1861] 4 De GF & J 208, at pp 215–16.

45 See, eg, the judgment of Blackburn J in *Milirrpum v Nabalco Pty Ltd* (1971) 17 FLR 141.

estate is described in *Official Receiver in Bankruptcy v Schultx* (1990) 170 CLR 306, pp 314–15, as conferring an interest upon each beneficiary 'in seeing that the whole of the assets are treated in accordance with the executor's duties'. In this sense, the personal right of the beneficiaries to bring an action against the executor can, in some circumstances, have proprietary consequences, and in this respect can be described as an 'interest'. This relates back to the very foundation of the equitable jurisdiction: unlike common law estates, equitable interests are created where needed in order to accord justice to the circumstances. As Viscount Radcliffe noted in *Commr of Stamp Duties v Livingston* [1965] AC 694, p 712, 'Equity in fact calls into existence and protects equitable rights and interests in property only where their recognition has been found to be required in order to give effect to its doctrines'. In a broad sense, then, whenever a right to an equitable remedy exists, it may be described as an equity. To acquire a proprietary character, however, the right must be enforceable against identifiable property

Hence, it is often felt that a category of interests exists which represents a hybrid between equitable proprietary right and rights which are purely personal. This category of interests has come to be referred to as 'mere equities', or simply 'equities'.[46] The characteristics of such interests are that the holders have personal rights which are enforceable against the land and, in some circumstances, against third parties where they take with notice. The amorphous nature of such interests was summarised by Brooking J in *Swanston Mortgage v Trepan Investments* [1994] 1 VR 672, p 675, in the following way:

> ... a 'mere equity' is not a right of property and is accordingly contrasted with the equitable interest. It is difficult to define; Snell defines it as a right, usually of a procedural character, which is ancillary to some right of property, and which limits it or qualifies it in some way. Examples are a right to have a transaction set aside for fraud or undue influence, or to have a document rectified for mistake.

To understand best the character of the mere equity, it is necessary to consider a range of different examples. The first, and perhaps the most classic, example is the 'equity of acquiescence'. This is often described as a Lord Denning device because his Lordship was the first person to formulate it. In *Inwards v Baker* [1965] 2 QB 29, Lord Denning MR held that the right of a son to occupy a bungalow which he had erected on his father's land, with the acquiescence of his father, created an interest known as an 'equity of acquiescence'. His Lordship noted that this type of equity was well recognised in law. It arises from the expenditure of money by a person in actual occupation of land when he is led to believe that, as the result of that expenditure, he will be allowed to remain there. In substance, the equity of acquiescence is very similar to

46 See Skapinker, D, 'Equitable interests, mere equities, "personal" equities and "personal equities" – distinctions with a difference' (1994) 68 ALJ 593 and *op cit*, Meagher, Gummow and Lehane, fn 39, Chapter 4.

proprietary estoppel and constructive trust based upon unconscionable enforcement of strict legal rights. The only real difference is that each category of interest has developed along separate paths. In *Walton Stores (Interstate) Ltd v Maher* (1988) 164 CLR 387, Brennan J referred to the decision of *Inwards v Baker* in the context of a determination of proprietary estoppel and made the following comments:

> In cases of proprietary estoppel, the equity binds the owner of property who induces another to expect that an interest in the property will be conferred on him ... In all cases where an equity created by estoppel is raised, the party raising the equity has acted or abstained from acting on an assumption or expectation as to the legal relationship between himself and the party who induced him to adopt the assumption or expectation.

It is clear that this area may also overlap with the application of constructive trust based upon an unconscionable denial of a mutual intention. The interrelationship between estoppel, acquiescence and constructive trust was referred to by Coldrey J in *Rasmussen v Rasmussen* [1995] 1 VR 613, p 617, who noted that, in general terms, these actions extend 'to the enforcement of voluntary promises on the footing that a departure from the basic assumption underlying the transaction would be unconscionable'. However, his Honour explained that under an estoppel, the party estopped must have created or encouraged in the other party an assumption that the promise would be performed and the other party must, to the knowledge of the estopped party, have relied on that assumption to his detriment.

Where the facts involve the application of constructive trust, a full equitable beneficial interest will be conferred, whereas under acquiescence or estoppel, an applicant will acquire a personal right which is enforceable against the land but limited in scope.[47] The equity of acquiescence or proprietary estoppel right is only enforceable against the parties to the transaction, although it may attach to the property which is the subject of the transaction and would, in conscience, bind any purchaser who took the property with notice of the interest.

A further example of a mere equity is the equity of rectification. This interest will arise where the applicant can prove that he or she has a right to rectify a transaction because the transaction, as it stands, has been affected by fraud or does not reflect the 'true' agreement between the parties. The equitable right of the applicant to remedy the fraud actually constitutes an interest, particularly where the right impacts upon identifiable property. The nature of this interest has been well discussed in *Latec Investments Ltd v Hotel Terrigal Pty Ltd* (1965) 113 CLR 265.

47 See, generally, Neave, M, 'Three approaches to family property disputes – intention, belief, unjust enrichment and unconscionability', in Youdan, T (ed), *Equity, Fiduciaries and Trusts*, 1989, LBC.

In that case, the High Court held that the equitable interest by way of the charge acquired by MLC Nominees prevailed over the rights of the mortgagor to have a fraudulent exercise of the mortgagee's power of sale set aside.

Kitto J felt that the right of the mortgagor to have the sale set aside constituted a mere equity, or an equity of rectification. The interest of the mortgagor could not constitute a full equitable interest, according to Kitto J, unless and until the sale had been rectified and, if a third party acquires rights in the property in the interim, the prior equity will be unprovable against the third party. As stated by Kitto J (p 274):

> Where a claim to an earlier equitable interest is dependent for its success upon the setting aside or rectification of an instrument, and the court, notwithstanding that the fraud or mistake (or other cause) is established, leaves the instrument to take effect according to its terms in favour of a third party whose rights have intervened, the alleged earlier equitable interest is unprovable against the third party and, consequently, so far as the case against him discloses, there is no prior equitable interest to which his conveyance can be held to be subject.

Taylor J differed from Kitto J because he felt that the creation of an interest was not dependent upon the sale being set aside. His Honour concluded that, prior to the sale being set aside, the mortgagor held an interest which was recognisable in equity. His Honour made the following comments (p 289):

> I regard these authorities as establishing that where the owner of property has been induced by fraud to convey it, the grantor continues to have an equitable interest therein and that interest may be devised or assigned *inter vivos,* and that the grantor's interest in the property does not come into existence only if and when the conveyance is set aside.

The nature of the interest held by the mortgagor prior to the sale being set aside is to be distinguished from that of a full equitable interest. The equity to rectify a fraudulent transaction is a personal remedy, enforceable against the party who has committed the fraud. Nevertheless, where it has proprietary consequences, it can be properly described as an 'interest'.

Taylor J felt that a prior equity could be defeated where the holder has been estopped by his or her conduct from disputing the title of a subsequent person who takes in good faith for value without notice.

Menzies J agreed with Kitto J and noted that, once the right to rectify had been exercised, a full equitable interest would arise. His Honour felt, however, that where this had not occurred, a mere equity in the form of an equity to rectify existed and could be defeated by a *bona fide* purchaser for value without notice. (This case is discussed in detail in Chapter 5 at para 5.6.)

In *Breskvar v Wall* (1971) 126 CLR 376, the High Court concluded that the equitable right held by the Breskvars to have a fraudulent transaction set aside could constitute either a full equitable interest or a mere equity – the important point was that it was not paramount or superior to the subsequent equitable interest.

An interesting issue which has attracted a range of differing opinions is whether or not the 'equity' arising from a right to rectify a fraudulent exercise of a mortgagee's power of sale is a sufficient 'interest' in land to justify the application of a caveat (where the land is Torrens title) prohibiting the registration of the subsequent purchaser's transfer. This issue raises the whole question of whether the 'equity' constitutes a proprietary or personal right.

In *Sinclair v Hope Investments Pty Ltd* [1982] 2 NSWLR 870, the mortgagor alleged that the mortgagee had exercised the power of sale fraudulently, and the issue was whether the mortgagor was entitled to lodge a caveat prohibiting the registration of a transfer of the property to a subsequent purchaser from the mortgagee. Needham J held that while, prior to the transfer of the property, the mortgagor still holds the legal title to the property (under Torrens title), it was possible for the mortgagor to also retain an equitable interest in the land. In describing the character of this right, his Honour held that it is an equitable right to prevent the completion of a voidable sale, and it arose from the charge created by the mortgage and the action of the mortgagee in entering into the voidable contract.[48] His Honour noted:

> It is no less 'an equitable claim enforceable by reason of the principles of the Court of Chancery' than if the right existed shorn of the registered estate. Accordingly, in my opinion, the question whether the registered proprietor may lodge a caveat before the completion of the contract is not different from the question whether, after the contract has been completed and the transfer registered, the mortgagor may lodge a caveat to protect his right to have the sale set aside.[49]

In *Swanston Mortgage Pty Ltd v Trepan Investments Pty Ltd* [1994] 1 VR 672, the court directly discussed the *Latec Investments* decision in determining the nature of a right to have a fraudulent transaction set aside. The primary issue in the case was whether the mortgagor held an equitable interest in the right to have the sale set aside which was sufficient to be caveated.

The Victorian Supreme Court upheld an appeal from the court of first instance where it was held that the right of the mortgagor constituted a caveatable interest. Brooking J held that the mortgagor retained an 'equity' but not an 'interest' in the land, and based this conclusion on the reasoning of Kitto and Menzies JJ in the *Latec Investments* decision and rejected the judgment of Needham J in the *Sinclair* decision.

His Honour held that the equitable interest cannot arise until the sale has been set aside. Prior to this point, the mortgagor holds an equitable right to prevent the completion of a voidable sale and, according to Brooking J:

48 See, also, *Re Cross and National Australia Bank Ltd* [1992] Q Conv R 54-433 and *Re McKean's Caveat* [1988] 1 Qd R 524.

49 *Sinclair v Hope Investments Pty Ltd* [1982] 2 NSWLR 870, pp 874–75.

> ... this is not the definition of an equitable interest. It is not even a definition of a 'mere equity'. It is a definition of an 'equity' in the widest sense of that term, the right to seek an equitable remedy whether or not in aid of a property right.[50]

Hence, his Honour felt that the interest was not a caveatable interest but merely a right to seek equitable relief, and this was not an interest in land known to the law.[51] During the course of his judgment, Brooking J referred to the judgment of Richmond J in *Great West Permanent Loan Co v Friesen* [1925] AC 208, where it was noted (p 357):

> It is true that it [the mortgagor] is claiming the land adversely to the mortgagee, but it is doing so by virtue of its existing ownership and not by virtue of some new and distinct interest in the land brought into existence by the acts of the mortgagee.

The decision in *Swanston Mortgage* appears to be based upon the principle that a caveatable interest requires something more than a mere right to claim equitable relief against property. A caveat operates as a form of injunction, precluding all future dealings with the property, hence, Brooking J felt that it should only support a definable and more 'proprietary' form of interest, rather than a mere equitable right to rectify a fraudulent exercise of the power of sale. This seems an unusual qualification because there is very little else that the holder of such a right over Torrens title land can do in order to protect himself against the property being passed on to third parties. The very fact that the right is dependent upon a particular contingency before it ripens into a full equitable interest should not mean that its validity is completely denied. The importance of providing caveat protection to such 'contingent rights' was emphasised by Santow J in *Transfield Properties v Amox Aked Swift* (1994) 36 NSWLR 321, which dealt with the issue of whether a right of a grant of pre-emption in a lease constituted a caveatable interest. In that case, his Honour discussed the importance of caveat protection to both the holder of the right and to third parties taking the land, and noted that this protection was relevant, irrespective of whether the interest could be described as a proprietary interest or otherwise:

> ... it is certainly not unknown to the law for a lesser right which does not confer any interest in land to fructify into an estate in land. Thus, under a discretionary trust having land as its trust property, there could be a contingency in that trust which caused the interest of a beneficiary who, till then, had a mere expectancy in that land, to transmogrify into an equitable interest in the land. No one would suggest that this result should not follow merely because it involved some notion of contingency or the deferment of that interest until the fulfilment of that contingency ... There would be injustice if the holder of such a right, when triggered, would be unable to lodge a caveat

50 *Swanston Mortgage Pty Ltd v Trepan Investments Pty Ltd* [1994] 1 VR 672, p 681.

51 See, also, *Re An Application by Haupiri Courts Ltd (No 2)* [1969] NZLR 353; *Ex p Goodlet & Smith Investments Pty Ltd* [1983] 2 Qd R 792; and *Re Piles Caveats* [1981] Qd R 81.

to protect that interest by reason of the risk of a third party acquiring without notice.[52]

The exact proprietary character of mere or personal equities remains unclear. It has been suggested that an appropriate development may be to abandon the hierarchical division between equitable interests and to focus, instead, upon the nature and circumstances of the equitable right. Such an approach would concentrate upon the enforceability of an interest rather than the elaborate creation of labels.[53] This, in turn, would allow courts to examine issues of justice and fairness in the enforcement of the right, rather than becoming enmeshed in artificial and oblique divisions as to what form of interest exists. The mere equity discussions seem to 'smack of circularity' and, whilst it is appropriate properly to understand the differences between equitable rights, the focus of the equitable jurisdiction is more appropriately concerned with the substance of the dispute rather than the indistinct cogitations of form.[54]

9.5.2.2 Priority rules for mere equities

The priority rules which are applicable to competitions between mere equities were discussed by various judges in the *Latec Investments* decision. Where the competition is between a prior mere equity and a subsequent full equitable interest, the holder of the mere equity will lose priority to a *bona fide* purchaser of the subsequent equitable estate for value without notice.[55] This priority principle is applied rather than the *Rice v Rice* principle – prior in time where both equitable interests are equal – because it is felt that, as the prior equity holder does not have a full equitable interest, there can never be a balance between the interests. It would not be until a full equity is created that a court could undertake a consideration of whether the holder contributed in any way to the creation of the subsequent equity. Hence, following the *Latec Investments* decision, the *bona fide* purchaser principle is the appropriate priority rule. This accords with Lord Westbury, in *Phillips v Phillips* (1861) 4 De GF & J 208; 45 ER 1164, who felt that the legal estate will not be required for an application of the *bona fide* purchaser for value without notice defence where there are circumstances that give rise to an 'equity' rather than an 'equitable estate'.

It should, however, be noted that in *Breskvar v Wall*, the High Court preferred to apply the *Rice v Rice* priority principle, although it was not clear exactly what the status of the 'equity' was in that decision – and indeed the court appeared to refer to it as a full equitable interest. The application of the *Rice v Rice* priority principle was not categorically approved by the High

52 *Transfield Properties v Amox Aked Swift* (1994) 36 NSWLR 321, p 342.

53 See Wright, R, 'The continued relevance of divisions in equitable interests to real property' (1995) 3 APLJ 163.

54 See *op cit*, Meagher, Gummow and Lehane, fn 39, para 435.

55 See, also, *Forsyth v Blundell* (1973) 129 CLR 477.

Court and, due to a lack of clarity in this regard, courts have generally refused to regard the decision as binding authority.

The nature of the notice which would be applicable under this priority analysis will be the same as that which is generally applicable under the doctrine of notice and therefore includes both actual and constructive notice. This priority rule will apply to both general law and Torrens title land. Naturally, however, the character of the priority principle may be altered where the land involved is Torrens title and there has been some registration of the interests involved. Hence, where there is a competition between a prior mere equity and a subsequent legal estate, if the land is general law land then the legal estate holder will take priority if he or she is a *bona fide* purchaser for value without notice. Alternatively, if the purchaser holds a legal estate pursuant to a registered Torrens title, the purchaser will automatically hold an indefeasible title and will not be affected by notice. The only way in which the prior equity holder could protect his interest in such a situation would be to lodge a caveat although, as noted above, it is unclear whether a mere equity is a caveatable interest.

CHAPTER 10

DEEDS REGISTRATION SYSTEM

10.1 Introduction

In this chapter, we examine the nature and operation of the systems of land registration set up in Australia prior to the Torrens system, known generally as Deeds Registration Systems (DRS). Every state introduced a DRS; however, in some states, it has been eradicated because the aim is to eventually bring all old title land under the Torrens system of land registration. In most states, old title land is rare – most of it having already been transferred to the Torrens system. This process is complete in Queensland so there is no need for a DRS. In Victoria, the DRS still exists; however, with the introduction of the Transfer of Land (Single Register) Act 1998 (Vic), it is no longer possible to register deeds or documents under the DRS: s 22. If a person wishes to register a document or deed under the DRS in Victoria, it is necessary for the land to be brought under the application of the Torrens system. Section 9(2) of the Transfer of Land (Single Register) Act 1998 (Vic) gives the Registrar General the power to bring land under the operation of the Transfer of Land Act 1958 (Vic). The DRS still exists in Victoria as a record of deeds over old title land. However, for all practical purposes, it no longer has any use as a registration system, as the Torrens system provides a greater security to the registered title holder.

The conversion of all old title land to Torrens title land and the creation of a single system of registration is the ultimate goal for all Australian states and is near to being achieved in most states. Most land in Australia now comes under the application of the Torrens system and where it doesn't, legislative developments like the Transfer of Land (Single Register) Act 1998 have provided further impetus for the move to a single registration system. The DRS operated as a precursor to the Torrens system, and it is important to appreciate its effect because it still applies to all land interests not within the scope of the Torrens system and capable of being registered under the DRS – as well as providing a useful historical perspective of the early registration process and the different approaches assumed with the introduction of the Torrens system. The DRS was introduced with the specific aim of setting up a system for organising, structuring and prioritising interests in land through the implementation of a general register, prioritising registered interests according to their date of registration. Being the first system of land registration to be introduced, it pioneered the concept of 'registered' and 'unregistered' interests.

The DRS altered the traditional general law priority principles because it set out that priority depends upon the date when an interest is registered, not the jurisdictional character of that interest. In this respect, the DRS superimposed the statutory registration principles upon pre-existing common law and equitable principles (discussed in Chapter 9). The primary objective of the DRS was to introduce a system which provided a register where all interests affecting land – and executed by way of an instrument – could be noted. It was felt that such a register would enable subsequent purchasers of the land to search for interests relating to that land at a central location and, whilst registration is not compulsory, the priority conferred upon registered instruments provided an added incentive to contribute to the register.

Unfortunately, because the system retained the general law notion of a *bona fide* purchaser without notice, in reality the DRS did very little to amend the uncertainties associated with general law priority principles. One of the major problems with general law rules was that it was never absolutely clear whether a purchaser took a title free from defects and, in many situations, whether the doctrine of constructive notice applied. Whilst security measures could be taken in the form of specific covenants or extended searches back to the good root of title, nothing was ever guaranteed. Whilst the DRS attempted to alleviate these difficulties, its downfall was that it did not provide a direct guarantee of security. The best that can be said of the DRS is that, at the time, it introduced a much needed edifice for the categorisation of land interests. Beyond this, it never fully achieved its purported aims in establishing a greater and more absolute sense of security to purchasers of old title land.

10.2 History of the DRS

As the variety and type of interests in land expanded, it became increasingly important to provide a more structured method for recording such interests and notifying the general public of the true character of a particular piece of land. The methods which had evolved for conveying an interest in land were, essentially, private and secret in nature, making it difficult for future parties dealing with the land to discover the range of interests relating to land and their sphere of enforceability. Furthermore, the method of conveying by deed of release was unstructured and capable of being abused by fraud or forgeries and there was often very little indication of such defects in the title. In light of these problems, it was felt that a more systematic method of recording and structuring land conveyances and land interests should be created and that the most appropriate method of achieving this was through the introduction of specific statutory provisions.

Until the 19th century, many efforts to set up a general system of registration throughout England were unsuccessful. In 1825, New South Wales adopted a system known as the 'Deeds Registration System' pursuant to a

Deeds Registration Act 1825. A similar system was adopted in Victoria, Queensland and Tasmania.[1]

The DRS was set up as a system for the registration of all deeds and instruments affecting land; registration under this system was not compulsory. As set out under s 6 of the Property Law Act 1958 (Vic):

> All deeds conveyances and other instruments in writing (except leases for less than three years) of or relating to or in any manner affecting any lands tenements or hereditaments situated lying and being in Victoria may be entered and registered in the office of the Registrar General in the manner hereinafter directed; and all such deeds conveyances and other instruments in writing as aforesaid, if made and executed *bona fide* and for a valuable consideration and registered in conformity with the provisions of this Act, shall have and be allowed priority over every other deed conveyance or other instrument in writing ...

The instruments capable of being registered under the DRS did not *have* to be registered. However, if they *were* registered, they immediately gained priority over other instruments which were registered at a later date or which remained unregistered (subject to specific exceptions noted below).

The DRS is, therefore, a system whereby an interest or estate which is expressly created pursuant to an instrument is *capable* of being registered and gaining priority if the interest or estate holder desires. It is not necessary that the instrument actually notes a specific transaction; the instrument may effect a conveyance or it may simply note an interest. Importantly, registration under this system does not create the interest or alter the instrument in any way, but rather, provides notification of the effect of the instrument and confers priority upon the holder against other, specified holders.

The DRS only deals with expressly created interests which are either noted or created by way of a deed or pursuant to some other form of writing. Interests which do not require or depend upon written verification in order to exist are not capable of being registered under the system because there is no tangible reality to record, and therefore they are outside the scope of the system. Furthermore, the priority that the system accords can only apply to interests which are capable of being registered, which are *bona fide* and which, for whatever reason, are registered prior to the conflicting interest. This qualification to the application of priority principles is a severe impediment upon the general ability of the register to secure good title upon registration.

1 In New South Wales, the DRS is now set out in the Conveyancing Act 1919, Pt 23; Property Law Act 1958 (Vic), Pt 1; Registration of Deeds Act 1935 (Tas); Property Law Act 1974 (Qld), ss 241–49. In South Australia and Western Australia, legislative provisions do exist, although they differ from those applicable to the above states. See Registration of Deeds Act 1935 (SA) and Registration of Deeds Act 1856 (WA). All land in the Northern Territory and the Australian Capital Territory is now either leasehold or Torrens title land.

The DRS was introduced prior to the Torrens system. The statutory provisions applicable to the DRS only apply to instruments not coming within the scope of the registration system introduced by the Transfer of Land Act 1958 (Vic). This is clearly set out in s 4 of the Property Law Act, which expressly notes that no instrument affecting land, of which any person is registered as proprietor under the Transfer of Land Act 1958 (Vic), shall be registered under this Part.

10.3 Statutory operation of the DRS

10.3.1 Structure of the DRS

All of the statutory provisions relevant to the Victorian DRS are found in Part 1 of the Property Law Act 1958 (Vic). Part 1 of the legislation sets up a system of registration in the following manner. This chapter outlines the process and consequences of registration with reference to the Victorian legislation – a process which is similar in most states. It must be borne in mind, however, that following the introduction of the Transfer of Land (Single Register) Act 1998 (Vic), it is no longer possible to register a new dealing over old title land under the DRS without bringing that land under the Torrens system and thereby making Torrens system registration an imperative. Hence, the following references to registration under the Victorian legislation are intended purely as an historical illustration of the registration process as it used to apply in Victoria and as it still does apply in most other states:

(a) Section 7 of the Victorian statutory system requires the Registrar General to maintain a General Register of Deeds, which is open to the public to inspect. In order to register an instrument in the register, the instrument must be in writing, with the date clearly set out, the nature of the transaction, the consideration paid, and the names of all the parties involved. The original instrument and a sworn copy (memorial) must be deposited with the office of the Registrar General. Once received, the original copy will be allocated a reference number. Instruments are registered according to the order in which the references are allocated to them. The registration copy of the instrument is retained by the Registrar General and becomes part of the Register itself.

(b) Once the instrument is registered, it gains priority over all unregistered but registrable instruments and all later registered instruments relating to the land in issue and in conflict with the registered interest. According to s 6 of the Victorian system, priority can only be conferred where it is established that the instrument has been acquired *bona fides* for a valuable consideration. Apart from providing notification to all future dealers with the land, priority is one of the primary objects for registration. Priority is conferred by order of registration. Where it can be established that priority is warranted, the DRS can substantially alter the operation of the general law priority rules; an interest which is *bona fides* and received for valuable consideration, and which is registered, will receive priority over all later registered or unregistered but registrable interests, whether the character of the interest be legal or equitable in nature: the DRS draws no distinction between the status of legal and equitable interests.

(c) Apart from conferring priority, registration of the memorial has the effect of publicising the transaction relating to the land. Once registered, all future takers of the land will be able to view the instrument when actually searching the register or, alternatively, be deemed to have viewed it under the doctrine of constructive notice. Registration ensures public access and broadcasts the transaction in a manner which is contrary to the established history and traditional of privatising land transactions. The advantage of such a proclamation lies primarily in the fact that it provides a prominent statutory record for all future dealers with the land. Importantly, however, given the fact that it is a non-compulsory system and that some interests are unregistrable, it should be borne in mind that the DRS does not attempt to provide a complete and absolute record of *all* dealings.

10.3.2 Interests capable of being registered

Historically, any instrument in writing which relates to or in any way affects land, and which does not attract the operation of the Torrens system was capable of being registered. The only exception in Victoria was to leases under three years. The Transfer of Land (Single Register) Act 1998 now alters this, prohibiting registration under the DRS unless land is brought under the Torrens system: see s 22. The DRS does not apply to interests which are not embodied in or evidenced by deeds or instruments. An interest which has been recognised or created in land without any instrument being brought into existence is not capable of being registered under the DRS and therefore is not able to be defeated by other registered instruments affecting the same land. Interests not created or recognised by an instrument will be unaffected by the DRS and remain governed by the general law priority rules.

For example, the holder of an equitable beneficiary interest under a constructive trust cannot register their interest because the trust is imposed by the court, is not evidenced by a written instrument. Similarly, an equitable mortgage created by the deposit of title deeds without any actual writing, or an interest which may accrue by way of adverse possession, will not be capable of being registered and therefore will remain unaffected by the operation of the DRS. The registration of an interest over old title land will have no effect on interests which are not capable of being registered.

Importantly, the DRS does not exclude specific types of interests from registration: it merely differentiates between those interests which have been created in writing and those which have not. If the interest was not created in writing but, for evidential purposes, has subsequently been put into writing, then the interest will become registrable and, if unregistered, capable of being defeated. This does create a somewhat artificial situation in that, if an interest has arisen without reference to any instrument, it will not be affected by the DRS, whereas, if an interest has arisen without reference to any instrument, but happens to be subsequently written up, it may be. The system attempts to encourage the registration of all written records relating the land. The emphasis upon a written instrument or deed highlights the focus of the DRS: it is not concerned with the legal or equitable status of the instrument as much as the fact that the interest or dealing is expressly documented.

Instruments which are usually registered include deeds of conveyance, contracts for the sale of land, deeds of mortgage, lease instruments and instruments creating or evidencing easements or covenants. Despite being referred to as the 'Deeds Registration System', it is not necessary for the instrument to constitute a deed in order for it to be registered: any instrument may be registered provided that it is expressly created in writing in the form required. In Victoria, s 6 excludes from registration, whether in an instrument or otherwise, a lease operating for under three years. The justification for this appears to stem from the temporary nature of the transaction and the fact that future dealers of the land would generally take with notice of a lease anyway, because the tenants will usually be in possession. This provision also ties in with s 54(2) of the Property Law Act 1958 (Vic) which provides that a parol lease under three years, which takes effect in possession, for the best rent that can reasonably be obtained without taking a fine, may be legally enforceable despite not being executed by way of a deed.

Significantly, registration under the DRS is not a statutory formality requirement for the creation of an interest in old title land. Hence, registration will not improve the status of an interest – nor will it cure a defect. This is completely different to the operation of the Torrens system: see Chapter 11. Nevertheless, there are a number of company transactions which must be registered under the system in order for the transaction to be effective. These transactions include:

(a) a court order in pursuance of s 413 of the Corporations Law, which has the effect of transferring property coming within the operation of Part 1 of the Property Law Act 1958 (Vic) to a company pursuant to a reconstruction or amalgamation of any two or more companies;

(b) a court order in pursuance of s 1336 of the Corporations Law, vesting property coming within the operation of Part 1 of the Property Law Act 1958 (Vic) in the liquidator; and

(c) a court order in pursuance of s 568 of the Corporations Law, vesting property coming within the operation of Part 1 of the Property Law Act 1958 (Vic) disclaimed by the liquidator of a company in the persons entitled.

10.3.3 The method of registration

Registration of instruments is achieved by filing a memorial of the original copy in the office of the Registrar General for inclusion in the Registry. Pursuant to s 7(1) of the Property Law Act 1958 (Vic), a memorial must be written in ink, on parchment or durable paper, setting forth the date and nature of the instrument, the names and addresses of the parties, the witnesses (if any) and the land affected by the instrument. The memorial must be signed by one of the parties to the original instrument and certified by a 'competent' person (which includes a solicitor or barrister) to contain a just and true account of the particulars set out in the original instrument.

When a memorial is received by the office, it is endorsed with a reference number and the date and time of day when it was received. A receipt must be given to the person lodging the memorial, specifying the date and time of receipt by the office. Section 8 of the Property Law Act 1958 (Vic) sets out that memorials are numbered successively according to the order of time in which they are delivered into the office; this reference number is used to determine the order of priority where there are competing interests.

Once registered, all memorials are then bound in books which comprise the Register ,and this Register is required to be open for public inspection at convenient times. Where a purchaser is searching the title of a piece of old system land for the purposes of verifying an abstract of title given by the vendor, the primary point of reference will be the Register. A title searcher should copy all relevant entries in the memorials that make up the chain of title over the piece of land in issue. A purchaser will not be deemed to have constructive knowledge of interests not registered with the register unless, in the particular case, the circumstances would have alerted a reasonable person to the possibility of the existence of a further interest.

10.3.4 Priority upon registration

Unlike general law priority rules, priority under the DRS is allocated according to the time of registration; hence an earlier registered instrument will defeat a later registered instrument, whatever the character or status of the earlier registered interest. As noted above, however, priority can only apply against interests which are registered at a later time or which remain unregistered but capable of being registered. Where the interest is not created by an instrument or deed, the DRS will be inapplicable, and general law priority principles will continue to apply (*White v Neaylon* (1886) 11 App Cas 171).

There is a further, important qualification to the application of the DRS priority principles. As set out under s 6 of the Property Law Act 1958 (Vic), priority will only be conferred where the instrument is received *bona fide* and for a valuable consideration. The instrument must be *bona fide* in the sense that it must have been acquired in good faith, without being tainted in its creation or enforcement by any legal or equitable fraud. The relevant *bona fides* will be the *bona fides* of the person receiving the interest or benefit under the instrument. For example, where a purchaser is seeking to register a deed of conveyance, if it can be established that the purchaser has acted *bona fide*, priority may be conferred upon registration. An absence of *bona fides* on the part of the conveying party alone will not deprive the instrument of the priority it would otherwise gain by registration.

Any fraud or deceit by the receiving party will constitute a lack of *bona fides* (*Davidson v O'Halloran* [1913] VLR 367). Furthermore, and unlike the Torrens system, a person will not be *bona fides* for the purposes of registration if the person taking under the instrument had notice of the existence of an earlier interest over the land. Notice, for the purposes of *bona fides*, would seem to include both actual and constructive notice (*Sydney v Suburban Mutual Permanent Building & Land Investment Association v Lyons* [1894] AC 260). In order to constitute a lack of *bona fides*, however, the notice must be received or deemed to have been received prior to the execution of the instrument for which registration is sought – not prior to the actual registration. Notice received after the execution of the instrument, but before its registration, will not preclude priority. This principle has a special application with respect to the registration of interests arising under a sale of land.

For example, a purchaser enters into a contract for sale and, at the time of signing the contract and paying the deposit, the purchaser has no actual or constructive notice of the existence of any earlier interest affecting the property. In this situation, a purchaser may register the contract of sale and will acquire priority against any prior conflicting interest, because there is no lack of *bona fides*. The purchaser may then go on to settle under the contract and, upon executing the deed of conveyance, will acquire an unencumbered title because the registered contract of sale will take priority over the prior unregistered interest – provided the prior interest was capable of being registered. Alternatively, if the purchaser enters into a contract of sale without notice of any prior interest and does not register the contract of sale and subsequently, prior to settlement, acquires notice of the earlier interest, registration of the conveyance will not confer priority, because the purchaser could not be regarded as *bona fides*.[2] This qualification upon the conferral of priority under the DRS should be contrasted with the operation of the doctrine of notice under general law.

Furthermore, priority will only be conferred where it can be established that the purchaser or taker under the interest gave valuable consideration upon the making or execution of the instrument. In this context, valuable

2 See *Blackwood v London Chartered Bank of Australia* (1871) 10 SCR (NSW) Eq 56.

consideration will include money, money's worth or a future marriage, but not nominal consideration or simple love and affection (*Goodright v Moses* (1774) 2 Wm Bl 1019; 96 ER 599). Consideration may be valuable even if it is grossly inadequate, but not if it is so low as to effectively be illusory.

10.3.5 Consequences of registration

Registration may confer upon an interest a priority it would not otherwise have had under general law priority principles, but it cannot cure a defective title. Registration does not, in any way, alter the validity of the existing instrument – it merely imposes statutory priority principles upon that interest where it is registered. Registration will not confer any greater title upon an instrument than it would otherwise have had; hence, registration will not cure a instrument which is fraudulent, forged or illegal. This is a critical point. The focus of the DRS is upon the registration of the written instrument as a means of conferring greater coordination and prioritisation of land interests: it does not provide an absolute guarantee of the validity of the title registered.[3] Registration under the DRS can, however, substantially modify the operation of general law priority principles, and this is clearly evidenced in the decision of *Moonking Gee v Tahos* (1964) 80 WN (NSW) 1612.

On the facts of that case the vendor, Tahos, entered into a contract to sell property to the purchaser, Moonking Gee. Tahos then entered into a further contract for the sale of the same property to another party. The sale to Moonking Gee was never completed. However, settlement went ahead with the second purchaser. Moonking Gee subsequently registered her contract of sale prior to the registration of the second purchaser's deed of conveyance. The issue in the case was whether the registered equitable interest held by Moonking Gee could defeat the later registered legal interest of the second purchaser.

The court held that priority under the DRS was conferred according to the date of registration rather than the character of the interest, and consequently, the prior registered equitable interest of Moonking Gee defeated the later registered legal interest of the second purchaser. It was held that the *bona fide* purchaser for value without notice principle was inapplicable under the DRS, because the focus of the system was upon the first to register. As noted by Manning J, p 1615:

> For many years *Darbyshire v Darbyshire* (1905) 2 CLR 787 has been accepted in this State as authority for the proposition that, under s 12 of the Registration of Deeds Act 1897, the registration of an instrument conferring an equitable estate in land gives priority to the person entitled to that estate over a subsequent purchaser of the legal estate for value without notice ... I regard the decision in *Darbyshire's* case as having settled a rule which it is now much too late to reconsider.

3 Cf the purpose and function of the Torrens system, set out in Chapter 11.

Priority under general law principles could only have been conferred upon the prior equitable interest holder where it could be shown that the subsequent legal interest holder was not a *bona fide* purchaser for value without notice. In *Moonking Gee v Tahos*, the question of whether the later registered interest holder was a *bona fide* purchaser for value without notice was irrelevant, the primary focus being the date of registration. Nevertheless, the priority rules are the same as general law, where a legal interest is registered if the second purchaser (holding the deed of conveyance) registered prior in time, the second purchaser would only have acquired priority where it could be established that he took without notice of the existence of the prior equitable interest held by Moonking Gee. If actual or constructive notice could be proven, then the second purchaser would not gain priority because he would not be considered *bona fides*.

10.3.6 Conflicting instruments

Priority under the DRS will only apply where the later registered, or registrable but unregistered, instrument is in conflict with the prior registered interest. Where there is no conflict, no issue of priority will arise. It is important to distinguish between cases where no conflict exists and those where priority questions are relevant because of a conflict. If there is no conflict, priority principles are not relevant: *Boyce v Beckman* (1890) 11 LR (NSW) 139. It is important to note that the result in this case does not mean that registration under the DRS will not cure a title which is defective under the *nemo dat* principle. Where two instruments are in conflict, the first person to register his or her conveyance will acquire priority. This principle will, however, only apply where the instruments are actually in conflict. If the instruments are mutually consistent, because, as a matter of construction, the instrument creating the interest does not affect a pre-existing interest, or is held to be subject to it, then no priority dispute will arise.

A conflict may arise, as on the facts, where a later instrument purports to describe a conveyance in general terms and this is in conflict with a purported earlier conveyance in specific terms. This situation raises a classic conflict situation, because it is unclear what the intention of the grantor was. According to the decision in *Boyce v Beckman*, where the holder of the later interest registers that interest first, he will automatically be deemed to have priority, not because the DRS cures a *nemo dat* defect but, rather, because the DRS infers an intention on the part of the grantor to confer the full title to the person who first registers. Hence, in such a situation, the DRS is really making a determination as to who is the more deserving between two claimants. Nevertheless, where the later claimant, despite registering first, has notice of the existence of a prior interest, priority will not be conferred because it cannot be said that the claimant is a *bona fide* purchaser.

Where a later conveyance, which is registered, expressly notes that the taker is to take subject to all interests and encumbrances, the later taker will not defeat prior unregistered interests. In such a situation ,there is express notice and no conflict, and the mere fact that the instrument is registered will not improve its position (*Fraser v Clarke* (1872) 3 VR (E) 84).

10.4 Conclusions

The DRS was introduced as a forerunner to the Torrens system of land registration. Its aim of achieving greater structure and clarity for persons dealing with interests in land was, to a large extent, undermined by the fact that the priority that it conferred was not universal, and it retained the *bona fide* purchaser for value without notice rule. In effect, this meant that many of the difficulties and uncertainties associated with conveying land under general law principles were retained under the DRS. A purchaser of old title land who registers his interest is not guaranteed secure title: all that is truly conferred is a guarantee that where the purchaser is *bona fide* and not affected by notice, the purchaser will be given a better title than those interests registered at a later point or those interests which remain capable of being registered but, for whatever reason, are not registered.

As a result, following the inception of the DRS, purchasers are often in a similar position to that which they had been in prior to its introduction. This is an inevitable conclusion in a system which functions as a registration of title rather than 'title by registration'.[4] The registration system introduced by the DRS has achieved a greater structure and coordination of old title land interests through the establishment of a general registry; however, the real advantage of the system has been the notification it has provided for future dealers with the land of the existence of an interest in the land and, to a limited extent, the prioritisation of interests in land. No further security or certainty was conferred under the system and, indeed, its operation is increasingly becoming of historical significance only in most Australian states as the push towards a single system of registration advances.

4 See *Breskvar v Wall* (1971) 126 CLR 376; see, also, Hogg, H, *Deeds Registration in Australasia*, 1908, Sydney: Butterworths, for a detailed discussion on the issue of registration of instruments not coming within the ambit of the Transfer of Land Act 1958 (Vic).

CHAPTER 11

THE TORRENS SYSTEM

11.1 Introduction

The inherent difficulties associated with conveying old title land, particularly the uncertainties associated with general law priority rules, encouraged law reformers to introduce a new, more efficient and 'absolute' conveyancing system. What eventually emerged was the system known today as the 'Torrens' system of land registration. The founder of this system was Sir Robert Torrens, and it was first introduced in South Australia in 1858. The statutory system in Victoria was introduced in 1862 and its provisions are now codified in the Transfer of Land Act 1958; equivalent legislation exists in all states.[1]

Robert Torrens sought to rectify the problem of dependent titles under general law. He noted that the main difficulty with general law title was that the new grantor received a title which was dependent upon the title of a chain of predecessors. Proving the validity of such a chain was often expensive and never certain. Torrens felt that the remedy was to ensure that each grantor received a fresh title akin to an absolute grant from the Crown, so that retrospective investigation was no longer an imperative and *bona fide* purchasers could deal with the land on the faith of the dealings set out in the register. To effect this purpose, the legislation which was eventually introduced set out that registration conferred a new and independent title upon each grantor who would be subject only to those encumbrances already registered on the title. As Torrens himself noted, 'indefeasibility of title created by registration follows of necessity as a corollary to the principle of independent title'.[2]

Nevertheless, a range of exceptions to the notion of an 'indefeasible title' were introduced under the terms of the statute and developed by case law because of the injustices that an 'absolute' title inevitably caused. Hence, the title could be set aside where some fraud or error could be established unless

1 In Victoria, the Torrens system has been enacted in the Transfer of Land Act 1958; in New South Wales, the current Act is the Real Property Act 1900; in Tasmania, the Land Titles Act 1980; in Western Australia, the Transfer of Land Act 1893; in South Australia, the legislation exists in the amended Real Property Act 1886; in Queensland, the legislation is more recent and exists in the Land Title Act 1994; in the Northern Territory, the legislation is the Real Property Act (1886) – an amended version of the South Australian legislation; and in the Australian Capital Territory, the legislation is the Land Titles Act 1925 (which has been subsequently amended by the Land Titles (Amendment) Act 1995) (all hereinafter referred to as Torrens legislation)..

2 Torrens, R (Sir), *The South Australian System of Conveyancing by Registration of Title*, 1859, p 9, taken from Whalan, DJ, *The Torrens System in Australia*, 1982, LBC, p 15.

the new grantor took the title *bona fide* and for valuable consideration without notice of the fraud or error. Furthermore, registration of the title did not have the effect of destroying existing easements not noted upon the title. Finally, and of increasing relevance today, the registration of title did not destroy pre-existing personal obligations owed by the new grantor; the exceptions to indefeasibility are discussed in para 11.4.

The fundamental changes introduced by the Torrens system were enacted for the primary purpose of developing a safer and more absolute method of conveying land interests. The most innovative change which the system introduced was the idea that once registered, absolute security of title was guaranteed; there could be no worry of the title being either defective or subject to the existence of a previous interest because the very act of registration conferred a new valid title upon the grantor. In this way, the Torrens system abolished the inherent uncertainties associated with the old common law priority principles. Registration under the Torrens system transcended a mere regulatory or prioritisation objective as existed under the Deeds Registration System; registration under the Torrens system could actually cure a defective title and confer a secure title upon a new proprietor.

11.2 History of the Torrens system

As the inherent difficulties associated with conveying old title land became increasingly apparent, the desire to develop a new, more effective system gained impetus. The Torrens system has been attributed to the work of Sir Robert Torrens, but gained inspiration from a range of other sources.[3] The system did not eradicate all general law land, nor did it alter common law priority principles. The Torrens system was superimposed upon the pre-existing general law structure, and it only applies to land grants issued after the enactment of the first legislation and earlier land grants where there has been a successful application transferring the land under the Torrens system. Common law priority principles will still apply to all land grants issued prior to the introduction of the legislation, and therefore outside its ambit, or land interests which remain unregistered.

The first Torrens legislation was introduced in South Australia in 1858 and was rapidly followed by all other states and, by 1875, all Australian states had enacted Torrens legislation. The current Torrens system legislation in each state is as follows: Transfer of Land Act 1958 (Vic); Real Property Act 1900 (NSW); Land Title Act 1994 (Qld); Real Property Act 1886 (SA); Real Property Act 1886 (NT); Land Titles Act 1925 (ACT); Land Titles Act 1980 (Tas); and

3 Drafters noted the system of title registration set out under the Imperial Merchant Shipping Acts as well as the detailed proposals set out in the 1857 Report of the English Royal Commissioners. This material is dealt with in *op cit*, Whalan, fn 2, pp 5–6.

Transfer of Land Act 1893 (WA). Whilst these Acts retain the basic system as first introduced, substantial amendments have been added over the years.

The Torrens system is not uniform. Important differences exist in the functioning of the Torrens system within each state. It has been suggested that a uniform Torrens system would provide a more consistent and efficient conveyancing system for Australia and that the only thing standing in the way of uniformity is 'lethargy and parochialism'.[4] The lack of uniformity between the states increases the complexity and costs associated with conveyancing, and this seems to go against the basic aim of the Torrens system of introducing a more efficient and streamlined system. However, we are yet to see any major reform strategies in this area.[5]

11.2.1 The difference between the Torrens system and the Deeds Registration System

The vulnerability of the common law legal estate to defeat on the basis of the doctrine of notice, or through proof of a lack of *bona fides*, often resulted in many purchasers acquiring a legal title which, despite detailed and often complex title investigations, could never be absolutely guaranteed. The statutory procedure for registration under the Deeds Registration System did not remove these difficulties, because priority under this system was only conferred where the holder could prove that the title was acquired *bona fide* and for valuable consideration. By contrast, the Torrens system effectively provided 'title by registration'. Common law estates which came within the application of the Torrens system would, upon registration, acquire immediate protection and a guarantee of the security of title. Provided the person seeking registration had committed no fraud – mere notice of the existence of another interest does not constitute fraud – and no other statutory exceptions could be raised, the registered title is absolute and is only subject to those encumbrances expressly noted on the title.

The primary amendments introduced by the Torrens system can be summarised as follows:

(a) old system titles are comprised of what is referred to as a 'chain of title', comprising all of the relevant instruments and dealings and evidencing the history of the land. Such chains are often long and complex and require a great deal of effort and time on the part of the purchasers to

4 See Neave, M, 'Towards a uniform Torrens system' [1993] 1 Australian Property Law Journal 114, p 130.

5 See, also, the excellent article by Kirby, M, 'Uniform law reform: will we live to see it?' (1977) 8 Sydney Law Rev 1. See, also, the interesting papers by MacCallum, S, 'Uniformity of Torrens legislation' [1993] 1 Australian Property Law Journal 135 and Kerr, K, 'Property law – uniformity of laws: towards a national property practice' [1993] 1 Australian Property Law Journal 145.

search and verify. The Torrens system substituted a simple and more efficient methodology. The chain of title deeds was abolished and a central registry was established. Each 'parcel' of land coming under the legislation was to be recorded on a separate certificate, called a folio, which was kept at the central registry (known in Victoria as the Land Titles Office) of the capital city of each state. The folio of title would record the boundaries of the land, the name of the registered proprietor, and the nature and extent of all registered interests or encumbrances affecting it. For example, mortgages and easements affecting the land could be registered on the certificate of title rather than forming a chain of title documents. This simplified the 'investigation of title' process dramatically: instead of checking the entire chain of title, a purchaser of the land simply had to search the folio at the registry to see what interests were actually registered;

(b) the doctrine of notice, a central component of the common law priority principles, was abolished under the Torrens system. Subject to stated exceptions, any encumbrances not noted on the title have no effect upon the newly registered title of a purchaser, even if the purchaser took with notice of them. Furthermore, the legislation expressly states that mere notice does not constitute fraud.[6] In this way, the Torrens system provides an effective and secure guarantee to prospective purchasers as to the accuracy of the register;

(c) the method of conveying title under the Torrens system differs from that which occurs under general law. Under the Torrens system, the conveyance occurs through the registration of a properly executed transfer form rather than the execution of a deed of conveyance. Upon registration of the transfer, the new owner acquires a copy of the folio – known as the duplicate certificate of title – whilst the original remains with the central registry and forms a part of the register book. The duplicate certificate of title can be used, where needed, to effect further transactions over the land. Where a new interest is created over the land and is registrable, the document creating the interest should be lodged along with the duplicate certificate of title, so that the interest can be properly noted on both the original and duplicate certificates of title. All states are currently in the process of computerising the entire system of land folios so that, eventually, a certificate of title will be available upon computer disc. The first conversions to computer titles were made in 1983, and the conversion rate is moving rapidly along. All of the Torrens statutes entitle the register to be kept in a computerised form and clearly,

6 See Torrens legislation: NSW, s 43; Vic, s 43; SA, ss 186–87; WA, s 134; Tas, s 41; Qld, s 169(2); ACT, s 59; NT, ss 186–87.

once this conversion is fully executed, some of the difficulties associated with paper titles – such as loss, damage, theft, etc, – will be eradicated.[7]

11.2.2 The application of the Torrens system

In modern times, virtually all private land interests come within the ambit of the Torrens system. State legislation sets out that the Torrens system will apply to all land which has been alienated or granted by the Crown after the date of commencement of the Act – and the dates of the original legislation vary as noted above. In Victoria, it was 1862. The Torrens legislation also applies to land originally known as 'old title' land but subsequently converted to the Torrens system. Consequently, in Victoria, the only land which can be described as 'old title' or 'general law' land is that land which was issued by the Crown prior to 1862 and which remains unconverted. There is no general law land in the ACT or in the Northern Territory and very little remains in all states apart from Victoria and NSW.

Owners of general law land may voluntarily convert to Torrens title, and this is permitted under the legislation.[8] In Victoria, land interests which may be converted to Torrens title land include leasehold estates where a term of at least 10 years remains unexpired, life estates and the estate held by a mortgagor provided the mortgagee consents.[9] All conversion applications must be made in the appropriate form and must accurately describe the land and include the chain of title documents and a list of all known 'encumbrances over the land'. Before the title can be converted, the Registrar is required to provide full notification of the process in local newspapers in order to ensure that all persons claiming an interest in the land are aware of the impending conversion and can be properly included on the new folio.

Section 10(1) of the Transfer of Land Act 1958 confers a discretion upon the Registrar to determine whether or not the conversion to Torrens title should be accepted. In order to prevent any unfairness in this respect, investigation of an applicant's title when applying for conversion will be extremely thorough. However, as one of the primary aims of the Torrens system is to extend its application to as many private land interests as possible, undue or excessive criticism of such applications will only occur where clear doubts as to the accuracy of the applicant's title are apparent.

7 See Torrens legislation: Vic, s 27(2), (3); NSW, s 31B(2); SA, s 51b; Qld, s 8; Tas, s 33(3)(a); ACT, s 43(1); NT, s 47(1). In WA, the 'electronic dealing endorsing project' represents the first stage in the conversion process. See, also, Vic Law Reform Commission Report No 12 on the issue of computerised title.

8 Torrens legislation: Vic, s 9; NSW, s 14(2); WA, s 20; Tas, s 11; SA, ss 27–30.

9 Vic, s 9(1)(a)–(f), (2).

Any person claiming an interest in the land and objecting to the registration of the land under Torrens title may, pursuant to s 12 of the Victorian legislation, lodge a caveat to forbid conversion from going ahead. The caveator then has 30 days from lodgement in which to prove his interest and, during this period, the Registrar must suspend conversion proceedings. The conversion cannot go ahead until the caveat is removed.[10]

Compulsory conversion of title also exists in some jurisdictions. In all states except Western Australia, the Registrar has the general power to initiate and proceed with the process of conversion. Compulsory conversion also exists over specific land interests: land which is to be subdivided or used pursuant to a strata title scheme must be registered under the Torrens system.[11]

11.2.3 Registration

Once a folio has been created, the person described as the registered proprietor is entitled to deal with the estate or interest. Subsequent transactions over the land may be registered on the title where express provision is set out in the statute. In all jurisdictions, a subsequent transfer, mortgage or lease of the land may be registered and properly noted on the folio.

Once registered, the dealings will form a part of the register and the holder of the dealing or encumbrance will acquire the benefit of registration. The Registrar cannot refuse to register an instrument which is capable of being registered and which has been submitted in the proper form.[12] It should be stressed that registration is not compulsory; however, it is a usual process with most dealings because of the guarantee of security that registration confers. Unregistered interests will not obtain the guarantee of security associated with registration and, where a dispute arises, will remain subject to the common law priority principles.

The Torrens system draws a distinction between the 'registration' of an interest and the 'notification' of an interest. Registration confers the guarantee of a secure title, whereas notification merely announces to the world that the dealing exists: it does not guarantee its title. Hence, in some states, restrictive covenants – contractual promises which have become annexed to the land but which are not proprietary in nature (see Chapter 12) – may be *noted* on the title. This notification will ensure that a purchaser of land which is burdened

10 For provisions in other states, see Torrens legislation: NSW, s 74B–E; SA, ss 39–40; Tas, s 14; WA, ss 30–32.

11 Torrens legislation: NSW, ss 28C, 28EA; Tas, ss 17A, 18; Pt XIX AB and s 22(1)(e) of the Subdivision Act 1988 (Vic).

12 See *Registrar General (NSW) v Lee* (1990) 19 NSWLR 240.

or which acquired the benefit of a restrictive covenant is aware of its existence.[13]

Once registered, the interest will take effect as if it had been in the form of a deed – even if it had not.[14] A registered interest in this sense is similar to a common law legal interest. However, distinctions remain. Under common law, a legal interest is one which is enforceable pursuant to common law doctrines. A registered interest, on the other hand, is simply an interest which has been properly registered under the Torrens system and carries the statutory benefits of that registration.

Most unregistered interests will be equitable in nature, because most equitable interests are not capable of being registered on the folio. It is, however, possible that some unregistered interests will be legal in a common law sense whilst not being legal in a statutory sense. The mere fact that an interest is unregistered does not mean that it cannot satisfy the common law formality requirements. The Torrens legislation is only intended to supplement the fundamental common law doctrines, not to destroy them. Nevertheless, for clarity, interests in Torrens title land are generally referred to as either 'registered' or 'unregistered' in nature, whilst interests in general law land are either 'legal' or 'equitable' in nature.

The Torrens system does not purport to cover *all* interests existing in the relevant unit of land. Some interests exist outside of the system, because the system is not compulsory and some dealings may simply remain unregistered. Also, some interests are in fact incapable of being registered. The most prominent type of interest which is expressly excluded from registration or notification in all states is, as noted above, the equitable beneficial interest arising under the trust.[15]

The rationale for this exclusion lies in the desire to prevent the folio from becoming too 'clogged' with interests. If all equitable interests were registrable, the folio might be burdened with a huge number of interests, and this is contrary to the basic aim of introducing a simpler and more efficient system. Further, it is assumed that, as the equitable jurisdiction already provides beneficiaries with strong personal and proprietary protection, there is no need to confer additional statutory protections associated with registration.

Unregistered interests are not, however, completely ignored under the Torrens system. The statute provides for the protection of unregistered instruments through the lodgement of what are known as 'caveats'. Where the

13 Torrens legislation: Vic, s 42; Qld, s 169(1); Tas, s 40; NSW, s 42; SA, s 69; WA, s 68; NT, s 69; ACT, s 58.

14 Torrens legislation: Vic, s 40(2); Qld, s 161; WA, s 85; SA, s 57; NSW, s 36(11); Tas, s 48(7); ACT, s 48(8). There is no equivalent provision in the NT.

15 Torrens legislation: Vic, s 37; Qld, ss 109–10; Tas, s 132; SA, s 162; WA, s 55; NSW, s 82(1); ACT, s 124; NT, s 162.

holder of an unregistered interest lodges a caveat against dealings, it will operate as a kind of statutory injunction, freezing the registration of all future dealings for a 30 day period. This has the effect of giving notification to all future registered interest holders that an interest is claimed in the land and provides the unregistered interest holder with the opportunity of bringing court proceedings to enforce the interest.[16] Nevertheless, the caveat system does not override the primacy of the Registrar. If a *bona fide* purchaser does become registered before the caveat is lodged, then the purchaser will not be bound by the unregistered interest, even if he or she took with notice of it. See, further, para 11.6.

Registration under the Torrens system has three basic objectives:

(a) to provide a register from which persons who propose to deal with land can discover all the facts relevant to the title;

(b) to ensure that a person dealing with land which is registered is not adversely affected by any defects in the vendor's title which do not appear on the register; and

(c) to guarantee the conclusiveness of the register and to provide adequate compensation to any person who suffers loss as a result of this guarantee.[17]

11.3 Indefeasibility of title

The Torrens system operates upon the fundamental principle that registration confers an 'indefeasible title'. Indefeasibility is not a term which is actually used within the legislation. However, it is a term which has become a firm part of the Torrens language. The technical meaning of indefeasibility is indestructibility or an inability to be made invalid. This is true and untrue insofar as it applies to the provisions of the Torrens system. Upon registration under the Torrens system, an interest holder cannot have his or her interest defeated by an unregistered interest, even, as noted above, where the interest holder registers with notice of the existence of the unregistered interest. This does not, however, mean that the registered interest is completely indestructible. In the first place, the security that the Torrens system provides is not absolute: all registered interest holders will take subject to those encumbrances which have already been, or which may in the future be, registered on the title. Hence, the registered holder of the fee simple may be bound by a mortgage or a lease where those interests have also been registered. Secondly, a registered interest holder is fully capable of alienating his or her interest and, once a subsequent transfer of the interest is registered,

16 The operation of the caveat system is discussed in further detail later in this chapter.

17 The statutory mechanisms set up for the conferral of such compensation will be examined further in this chapter.

this subsequent registration will defeat the prior registration. In this sense, the indefeasible status of a registered title is only conferred upon the stated proprietor. Finally, and of increasing significance, the indefeasibility of title conferred upon a registered interest holder is subject to an extensive range of statutory and non-statutory exceptions in all states.

Hence, indefeasibility under the Torrens system is a relative concept: it refers to the fact that if a title is examined or attacked at a given point of time, it cannot be defeated or annulled. It does not mean that the title can *never* be defeated. The idea that indefeasible actually means 'indestructible' is not correct in the context of the Torrens system and, to this extent, the term may be criticised as an inappropriate description of the system.[18]

11.3.1 Paramountcy provisions

The statutory provisions which, in combination, have been held to confer the indefeasible status upon a registered interest holder are known as the 'paramountcy provisions'. The provisions exist in each state. In the Victorian legislation, the relevant provisions are as follows.

11.3.1.1 Section 40: effect of registration

Section 40 of the Victorian Transfer of Land Act sets out that the benefits of registration shall not be conferred upon an instrument creating, extinguishing or passing an estate or interest in land until that instrument is registered. Similar provisions exist in other states.[19] The section reads as follows:

> Subject to this Act no instrument shall be effectual to create vary extinguish or pass any estate or interest or encumbrance in on or over any land under the operation of this Act, but upon registration the estate or interest or encumbrance shall be created varied extinguished or pass in the manner and subject to the covenants and conditions specified in the instrument or by this Act prescribed or declared to be implied in instruments of a like manner.

A strict reading of this section may suggest that no interest at all can exist prior to registration, thereby implying that unregistered interests are not recognised under the system. This interpretation is, however, unlikely, given the other provisions in the legislation which specifically recognise the existence of unregistered interests. The commonly accepted view today is that the section does not preclude the existence of such interests but merely sets out that where capable of being registered, the benefits of registration will not be conferred until the instrument is actually registered.[20]

---

18 See *op cit*, Whalan, fn 2, p 296.

19 See Torrens legislation: SA, s 67; WA, s 58; Tas, s 49(1); NSW, s 41; ACT, s 57(1) and NT, s 67.

20 See *Barry v Heider* (1914) 19 CLR 197.

11.3.1.2 *Section 41: certificate of title is conclusive evidence of title*

Section 41 of the Victorian TLA is an evidentiary provision: it sets out that the certificate of title is to operate as conclusive evidence as to the proprietorship existing in a particular folio of land. This will be the case even where it is alleged that an informality or irregularity in an application, instrument or proceedings existed prior to the creation of the folio. Similar provisions exist in other states.[21]

11.3.1.3 *Section 42: conferral of indefeasible title upon registration*

The key indefeasibility provision in the Victorian system is s 42. Similar provisions exist in other states.[22] Section 42(1) reads as follows:

> Notwithstanding the existence in any other person of any estate or interest (whether derived by grant from Her Majesty or otherwise) which but for this Act might be held to be paramount or to have priority, the registered proprietor of land shall, except in the case of fraud, hold such land subject to such encumbrances as are recorded on the relevant folio of the Register but absolutely free from all other encumbrances whatsoever, except:
>
> (a) the estate or interest of a proprietor claiming the same land under a prior folio of the Register;
>
> (b) as regards any portion of the land that by wrong description of parcels of boundaries is included in the folio of the Register or instrument evidencing the title of such proprietor not being a purchaser from or through such a purchaser.

The effect of this section may be summarised as follows:

(a) that, once registered, the registered proprietor will have priority over the land despite the existence of other interests;

(b) that the registered proprietor will *only* be subject to those encumbrances actually noted on the register and the encumbrances set out in sub-ss (a) and (b); and

(c) that fraud will vitiate the priority of the registered proprietor. The exact nature of this fraud is not described or elaborated upon in this provision.

Section 42(2) goes on to set out:

> Notwithstanding anything in the foregoing the land which is included in any folio of the Register or registered instrument shall be subject to:
>
> (a) the reservations, exceptions, conditions and powers (if any) contained in the Crown grant of the land;
>
> (b) any rights subsisting under any adverse possession of the land;

21 See Torrens legislation: NSW, s 40(1A)–(1B); Tas, s 39; WA, s 63; SA, s 80; Qld, ss 36, 164; NT, s 80; ACT, s 52.

22 See Torrens legislation: WA, s 68; ACT, s 58; NT, s 69; NSW, s 42(1); Qld, s 38; Tas, s 40; SA, s 69.

(c) any public rights of way;

(d) any easements howsoever acquired and subsisting over or upon or affecting the land;

(e) the interest (but excluding any option to purchase) of a tenant in possession of the land;

(f) any unpaid land tax, and also any unpaid rates and other charges which can be discovered from a certificate issued under s 387 of the Local Government Act 1958, s 158 of the Water Act 1989 or any other enactment specified for the purposes of this paragraph by proclamation of the Governor in Council published in the *Government Gazette* – notwithstanding the same respectively are not specially recorded as encumbrances on the relevant folio of the Register.

Section 42(2) provides a further exception to the primacy of the registered proprietors title as established in s 42(1). Where an interest is classified under sub-ss (a)–(f), it is described as a 'paramount interest' and all registered interests must take subject to paramount interests. Paramount interests operate as an exception to the indefeasibility of registered title and will remain enforceable against all registered interest holders, despite the fact that they have not themselves been registered on the particular land folio. Similar provisions exist in other states.[23]

11.3.1.4 Section 43: abolition of the doctrine of notice

The primacy of registration, as set out in s 42(1), is reinforced in its effect by s 43 of the Victorian legislation. The aim of s 43 is to abolish the common law doctrine of notice. Similar provisions exist in other states.[24] The section reads as follows:

> Except in the case of fraud no person contracting or dealing with or taking or proposing to take a transfer from the registered proprietor of any land shall be required or in any manner concerned to inquire or ascertain the circumstances under or the consideration for which such proprietor or any previous proprietor thereof was registered, or to see to the application of any purchase or consideration money, or shall be affected by notice actual or constructive of any trust or unregistered interest, any rule of law or equity to the contrary notwithstanding; and the knowledge that any such trust or unregistered interest is in existence shall not of itself be imputed as fraud.

Section 43 operates to prevent a registered interest holder from being held accountable pursuant to the doctrine of notice. Hence, as soon as a purchaser is registered, he or she will take free from any outstanding unregistered

23 Torrens legislation: SA, s 69IV; WA, s 68; Tas, s 40(3); NSW, s 42(1); Qld, s 170(1); ACT, s 58; NT, s 69IV.

24 Torrens legislation: Qld, s 169(2); SA, ss 186–87; Tas, s 41; NSW, s 43; WA, s 134; ACT, s 59; NT, ss 186–87.

interest, even if he or she has notice of its existence prior to registration. Furthermore, whilst the nature of the fraud exception set out in s 42(1) is not positively defined, s 43 makes it clear that mere knowledge that a prior interest existed will be insufficient to constitute such fraud.

11.3.1.5 Section 44(1): the effect of fraud

Section 44(1) and (2) are unique to the Victorian TLA and their exact effect has been the subject of some debate. The purpose of s 44(1) is to set out expressly that any transaction which is procured or made by fraud shall be void as against the person defrauded. Section 44(2) qualifies the effect of s 44(1) by noting that nothing in the Act is to be read so as to deprive a *bona fide* purchaser for valuable consideration of an estate or interest. On the wording of s 44(2), it seems that, even where the proprietor from whom the *bona fide* purchaser received the estate is proven to have been registered through fraud, the title of the *bona fide* purchaser will not be invalidated.[25]

The combined effect of s 44(1) and (2) can be summarised as follows:

(a) any registration of title shall be void as against any person who has been defrauded, and no party who is a subject to the fraud shall receive the benefit of registration; and

(b) the court will uphold the registration, even if acquired by fraud, if voiding the registration has the effect of interfering with an interest acquired by a *bona fide* third party purchaser.

An important issue in the construction of these provisions is whether s 44(1) is qualified by s 44(2) so that a *bona fide* purchaser for value who becomes registered may obtain a good title even where the transaction is affected by fraud. Where such an interpretation is adopted, it is generally referred to as an 'immediate indefeasibility' construction, because the immediate rights of the registered proprietor take absolute priority. Alternatively, under a 'deferred indefeasibility' construction, a *bona fide* purchaser who becomes registered under a forged or a void title will not obtain a good title, although protection may be given to a subsequent registered *bona fide* purchaser.

Recent Victorian decisions have favoured the adoption of 'immediate indefeasibility' because it accords with the stated aim of the Torrens legislation in providing an absolute guarantee of title upon registration. For example, in *Vassos v State Bank of South Australia* [1993] 1 VR 318, Hayne J concluded that s 44(1) of the Victorian Torrens legislation referred only to such frauds in which the person seeking registration was actually physically involved.

25 The only other similar provision is that contained in s 47 of the Land Titles Act 1980 (Tas), which sets out that where a person fraudulently procures any certificate, title or recording in the register, the recording on the certificate or title shall be void as between all parties to the fraud.

Where the transaction has been tainted by fraud, however, and that fraud has not been committed by the person seeking registration, s 44(1) is inapplicable, and an immediate indefeasible title may be conferred as soon as registration occurs. His Honour interpreted the reference to 'fraud' in s 44(1) narrowly because he felt that to do otherwise would significantly interfere with the primary object of the Torrens system in conferring a secure and absolute title upon registration.[26]

11.3.2 Judicial development of immediate and deferred indefeasibility

The debate concerning the correct method of interpreting the indefeasibility provisions has resulted in the adoption of two distinctive approaches: that referred to as 'immediate indefeasibility', and that referred to as 'deferred indefeasibility'. As noted above, immediate indefeasibility favours the conferral of absolute title upon registration by a *bona fide* purchaser, whereas deferred indefeasibility would invalidate such a title where it could be proven that the transaction to which the *bona fide* purchaser became registered was obtained by fraud or otherwise invalid.

Until the 1967 Privy Council decision of *Frazer v Walker* [1967] AC 569, courts generally favoured the deferred indefeasibility approach (*Gibbs v Messer* [1891] AC 248). In *Frazer v Walker*, the Privy Council reversed its previous conclusions in *Gibbs v Messer*. On the facts of *Gibbs v Messer*, the registered proprietor of land, Mrs Messer, left the certificate of title with her solicitor for safekeeping, together with a power of attorney in favour of her husband, whilst she went off travelling. The family solicitor, Creswell, forged the signature of the husband (as his attorney) to a transfer of Mrs Messer's land to a fictitious person. Creswell then managed to secure the registration of this fictitious person. Subsequently, Creswell executed a mortgage, with the fictitious person as mortgagor, and then misappropriated the funds. The mortgagees acted in good faith and subsequently registered the mortgage. When Mrs Messer returned and discovered the fraud, she commenced proceedings, seeking cancellation of the certificate of title in the fictitious person's name and cancellation of the registered mortgage. The mortgagees claimed that they had an indefeasible title which could not be set aside by the fraud. The Privy Council ultimately held that the protection which the Torrens system gives to persons transacting on the faith of the register is limited to those who actually deal with, and derive a right from, an *actual* rather than a *fictitious* proprietor. A person who deals with somebody who is not the

26 See, also, *Eade v Zacharias Vogiosopoulos* [1993] V Conv R 54-458; *Coomber v Curry* [1993] V Conv R 54-464; *National Australia Bank Ltd v Maher* [1995] 1 VR 318; and *Grgic v Australia and New Zealand Banking Group Ltd* (1994) 33 NSWLR 722. See, also, Hepburn, S, 'Concepts of equity and indefeasibility in the Torrens system of land registration' [1995] 1 Australian Property Law Journal 41.

registered proprietor, and who turns out to be fictitious, does not transact on the faith of the register. Where the transaction by which such person acquires title is tainted by fraud, that person cannot acquire a valid and indefeasible title, although such a title may be passed on to a *bona fide* third party purchaser. On the facts, as the mortgagee had dealt with a fictitious person and had not passed on the title, Mrs Messer was successful in having the forged certificate and mortgage cancelled.

The decision in *Gibbs v Messer* is generally cited as authority for the adoption of a deferred indefeasibility construction of the Torrens legislation. It is possible, however, to rationalise the decision as an anomalous exception, restricted to its own peculiar facts.[27]

On the facts of *Frazer v Walker*, Frazer and his wife were the registered proprietors of a farm property in Auckland which was subject to a first mortgage. In 1961, Mrs Frazer, without the knowledge or consent of Mr Frazer, arranged to borrow £3,000 pursuant to a further mortgage secured over the property. This mortgage was subsequently registered. After no mortgage payments were made under the second mortgage, the mortgagees exercised their power of sale, and the property was sold to Walker in good faith. Mr Frazer responded by claiming that the second mortgage had been forged and that the sale by the mortgagees had occurred without his knowledge. Relying upon the decision in *Gibbs v Messer*, Mr Frazer claimed that his interest in the land was not affected by the purported mortgage, or by the sale to Walker, and sought an order that the mortgage be declared a nullity and that the land registrar cancel the entries in the registry and restore him and his wife as joint registered proprietors.

The Privy Council reversed its decision in *Gibbs v Messer* and effectively held that a forged mortgage became immediately indefeasible on registration. The court concluded that indefeasibility of title is central to the whole system of registration. No adverse claim, except as arises under established exceptions to indefeasibility, may be brought against a registered proprietor. The circumstances were held to be outside the 'fraud' exception – the mortgagees had passed the title on to a *bona fide* purchaser and the registration of his interest took priority to any purported unfairness committed against Mr Frazer. Consequently, the appeal was dismissed. No compensation was awarded to the Frazers because the loss did not occur through any fault of the registry or though any reliance upon the registry.

Immediate indefeasibility was subsequently endorsed by the Australian High Court in *Breskvar v Wall* (1971) 126 CLR 376. In that case, a fraudulent transfer was registered and title was passed on to a *bona fide* third party. Before the third party could register his interest, the Breskvars lodged a caveat to

27 The Privy Council in *Frazer v Walker* [1967] 1 AC 569 distinguishes *Gibbs v Messer* as a decision based upon its own particular facts.

prevent further dealings, and raised the issue of fraud. In considering the effect of the indefeasibility provisions in the Torrens legislation, Barwick CJ concluded that the certificate of title is conclusive evidence of the title of a registered proprietor. Once registered, unless an established exception can be raised, the title of the registered proprietor will be indefeasible. His Honour noted that the Torrens system is not a system of registration of title but a system of title by registration. That which the certificate of title describes is not the title which the registered proprietor formerly had, or which, but for registration, would have had. The title it certifies is not historical or derivative: it is the title which registration itself has vested in the proprietor. Hence, it matters not what the cause or reason for the invalidity of the instrument might be. Thus, on the facts, despite the fraud flowing from the void transfer, the Breskvars were unable to have the register amended. In *Leros Pty Ltd v Terara Pty Ltd* (1991) 106 ALR 595, the Australian High Court confirmed the authority of *Breskvar v Wall* and noted that the effect of the registration of an interest was to extinguish all prior unregistered estates or interests which, but for that registration would have conflicted with the proprietors estate – unless it fell within one of the recognised statutory exceptions. If an unregistered interest is not protected by caveat, a subsequent inconsistent dealing with land which is registered will extinguish the unregistered interest and it cannot be reasserted.

Despite this strong endorsement of immediate indefeasibility, there have been some persuasive arguments in favour of deferred indefeasibility, one of the strongest being the judgment of Gray J in the Victorian Supreme Court in *Chasfild Pty Ltd v Taranto* [1991] 1 VR 225. The facts of the case concerned the fraudulent registration of a mortgage over the defendants' land. The defendants claimed that they were unaware of the existence of the mortgage and that they had been tricked into handing over the duplicate certificate of title in the belief that they were making a $10,000 investment. The duplicate certificate of title was then fraudulently used to obtain mortgage moneys from a mortgagee who was unaware of the fraud. Ultimately, the question for the court was simple: with whom should the loss lie – the unsuspecting mortgagees or the duped defendants?

In a single judgment of the Supreme Court of Victoria, Gray J concluded that the certificate of title should be amended and the mortgage should be set aside. His Honour felt that the defendants had been unfairly deceived and that it would be both 'disappointing' and 'surprising' if the Victorian legal system allowed the defendants to be dispossessed of their own home through the enforcement of a forged mortgage.

Gray J concluded that the fraud referred to in s 44(1) of the Victorian legislation was fraud associated with the registration; a proprietor (the definition of which includes mortgagee) who becomes registered in such circumstances, even if innocent of the fraud, may be divested at the suit of a defrauded previous proprietor *unless* the proprietor (or mortgagee) has passed the title on to a *bona fide* purchaser who becomes registered. This construction of the legislation meant that any transaction tainted by fraud could be set aside, whether or not the proprietor who becomes registered is actually involved in the fraud.

Gray J justified this conclusion on the basis that the Victorian legislation has a different operation from the other states due to the inclusion of s 44(1). His Honour felt that the fraud referred to in s 44(1) could not have been intended to be the same fraud as that referred to in s 42, otherwise both sections would completely overlap. This prompted the conclusion that the fraud in s 44(1) was broader and would cover any fraud within the transaction rather than being confined to a fraud committed by the registered proprietor. On the facts, this meant that, even though the mortgagees had not actually committed the fraud, they could not obtain the benefit of registration when the transaction itself arose from a fraudulent dealing.

The decision in *Chasfild* has, however, been criticised, and subsequent decisions of the Victorian Supreme Court have refused to adopt Gray J's interpretation of the paramountcy provisions. In *Vassos v State Bank of South Australia* [1993] 2 VR 316, Haynes J concluded that s 44(1) was a provision which was unique to the Victorian legislation. Unlike Gray J in *Chasfild,* he found that the fraud alluded to in s 44(1) must be established by or on behalf of the person who seeks and obtains registration. His Honour felt that it was necessary to interpret the subsection in this way in order to sustain the basic aims of certainty and clarity under the Torrens legislation. Furthermore, his Honour felt that to create a broader fraud in s 44(1) would effectively render the fraud exception in s 42(1) superfluous. According to Haynes J, the proper construction of the paramountcy provisions is that s 42(1) provides a general rule to indefeasibility and an exception for cases of fraud, 'on the part of the person making the registration or that person's agent', whilst s 44(1) deals expressly with the consequences of such a fraud with respect to the register and the parties to the fraud. Section 44(2) then deals with the position of the *bona fide* purchaser for value. His Honour expressly favoured the immediate indefeasibility construction of the statutory provisions. This approach was approved in *Eade v Vogiosopoulos* [1993] V Conv R 54-458, where Smith J agreed that s 44(1) should be restricted to fraud which has actually been committed by the person seeking registration, noting that a person who presents for registration a forged or fraudulent document is not guilty of fraud if he honestly believes it to be genuine.

A great deal of academic debate exists concerning both the advantages and disadvantages of immediate and deferred indefeasibility and the intention of the drafters of s 44(1) of the Victorian legislation.[28] Currently, however, the

28 See Wikrama-Nayake, 'Immediate and deferred indefeasibility – continued' (1993) 67 LIJ 13; Schultz, J, 'Judicial acceptance of immediate indefeasibility in Victoria' (1993) 19 Mon ULR 326; *op cit*, Hepburn, fn 26.

courts appear to favour the immediate indefeasibility interpretation, and subsequent decisions of the Victorian Supreme Court have adopted the approach set out by Haynes J in the *Vassos* decision. In *Pyramid Building Society (In Liquidation) v Scorpion Hotels Pty Ltd* [1998] 1 VR 188, Nathan J in the Supreme Court of Victoria noted that he favoured judicial pronouncements which adopted immediate indefeasibility, and that it was only displaced by proof of a fraud on the part of the person seeking registration.[29]

11.4 Statutory exceptions to indefeasibility

Legislation in all states defines specific circumstances where the indefeasibility of a registered proprietor may be set aside. The primary categories of statutory exceptions are fraud and error. Where a statutory exception is established, the title of the registered proprietor will be automatically defeasibile. The range and scope of the statutory exceptions vary according to each state and the way in which the courts have interpreted them. The major statutory exceptions are detailed below.

11.4.1 Actual fraud

In all states, a person who acquires a registered interest by committing what is statutorily referred to as an 'actual fraud' will be liable to have his title rectified by the register. The 'fraud exception' is expressly set out in the Torrens legislation in all states, although it has not been positively defined in any statute. In the Victorian legislation the fraud exception is set out in s 42(1), and similar provisions exist in all other states.[30]

In South Australia and the Northern Territory, the legislation expressly sets out that the title of a registered proprietor is subject to forgery or disability, although such acts shall not affect the title of a *bona fide* purchaser for value without notice.[31] The scope of the provisions in South Australia and the Northern Territory have been the subject of some discussion, though it would seem clear that a title affected by a forgery or disability will not be impeached where it has been acquired by a *bona fide* registered proprietor.[32] This provision does not exist in any other state, so the issue of whether or not forgery or disability come within the ambit of statutory fraud remains

29 (1996) 136 ALR 166, p 192. See, also, *National Australia Bank v Maher* [1995] 1 VR 318, *per* Fullager J, p 333; *Coomber v Curry* [1993] V Conv R 54-464.

30 See Torrens legislation: NSW, s 42(1); WA, s 68; ACT, s 58; Qld, s 169.

31 See Torrens legislation: SA, s 69II; NT, s 69II. See, also, *Bank SA v Ferguson* (1998) 151 ALR 729.

32 See, in particular, the judgment of O'Loughlin J in *Wicklow Enterprises Pty Ltd v Doysat Pty Ltd* (1986) 45 SASR 247, p 260, and the discussion of this in Bradbrook, AJ, MacCallum SV and Moore, AP, *Australian Property Law*, 2nd edn, 1996, LBC, para 4.50.

debatable.[33] In other jurisdictions, the definition of statutory fraud has largely occurred through incremental judicial interpretation.

The current view is that actual fraud will only render a registered title defeasible where the registered proprietor or his or her agent has been privy to it.[34] Hence, fraud committed by another party where the registered proprietor is not involved will not render the title defeasible. The common law definition of fraud requires proof of some actual dishonesty. The equitable definition is broader in scope and covers a range of conduct which has 'unfair' consequences. Whilst the exact scope of statutory fraud remains unclear, the legislation clearly sets out that mere notification of the existence of another interest in the property prior to registration will not constitute fraud. Hence, in *Loke Yew v Port Swettenham Rubber Co Ltd* [1913] AC 491, knowledge of the existence of a prior interest in the property combined with fraudulent misrepresentations made by the registered proprietor were held to be sufficient to constitute actual fraud.

Examples of conduct which may constitute fraud by the registered proprietor include forgery, involvement in a fraudulent scheme designed unfairly to deprive another of his title, a breach of fiduciary duty, and, in some cases, breach of a contractual term to which the registered proprietor has expressly agreed. In *Bahr v Nicolay (No 2)* (1988) 164 CLR 604, Mason CJ and Dawson J in the High Court held that actual fraud may be committed by the registered proprietor *after* registration where he or she refuses to honour a contractual agreement entered into prior to registration. Their Honours felt that there was no reason why the fraud exception should not embrace fraudulent conduct arising from the dishonest repudiation of a prior interest which the registered proprietor has acknowledged or has agreed to recognise as a basis for obtaining title.

In contrast, Wilson and Toohey JJ preferred to recognise this conduct under the *in personam* exception, which is discussed below. The extension of the fraud exception by Mason CJ and Dawson J to include conduct committed by the registered proprietor after registration has been the subject of some criticism and, given the broad scope of the *in personam* exception, is yet to be subsequently endorsed.[35] In *Bank SA v Ferguson* (1998) 151 ALR 729, the High Court held that for a fraud to be made out 'it must operate on the mind of the person said to have been defrauded and to have induced detrimental action by the person' (at p 734). On the facts of the case, the bank was unaware of a

33 See *National Australia Bank Ltd v Maher* [1995] 1 VR 318; *Grgic v ANZ Banking Group Ltd* (1994) 33 NSWLR 202.

34 See the above discussion on deferred and immediate indefeasibility. See, also, *Pyramid v Scorpion Hotels* (1996) 136 ALR 166; Butt, P, *Land Law*, 1996, LBC, pp 735–38.

35 See Tooher, J, 'Muddying the Torrens waters with the chancellor's foot' [1993] 1 Australian Property Law Journal 1.

forged document, used by the bank in determining whether to approve a mortgage, and the mortgagor had not been affected. The forged document did not have the effect of harming, cheating or performing a dishonesty upon the mortgagor and, as such, the fraud exception could not be made out. Following this decision, it would seem that forged documents associated with a mortgage which do not cause actual detriment will not entitle a mortgagor to set aside a registered mortgage.

Another area where the fraud exception has been the subject of some debate is in the conduct of mortgagee banks. In many cases, it has been argued that banks should be imputed with fraud where they are either actually aware that a mortgage is forged or should have been so aware in the circumstances. This is particularly true where an agent of the mortgagee bank becomes aware that the mortgage documents have not been properly completed or that something is 'suspicious' about the transaction. The difficulty, however, is that, in all states, mere knowledge of the existence of another interest is expressly excluded from the definition of fraud, and only in South Australia and the Northern Territory is forgery expressly included as an exception to indefeasibility.

In *Australia Guarantee Corp Ltd v De Jager* [1984] VR 483, Tadgell J held that the knowledge of AGC, as a corporate financier, of an irregularity in the mortgage document and, in spite of this, their continuation with the registration of the mortgage, constituted actual fraud. His Honour noted that the Torrens system depends on the good faith of those presenting instruments for registration.[36] Similarly, the full court of the Victorian Supreme Court in *National Australia Bank Ltd v Maher* [1994] V Conv R 54-594 held that the insertion of title particulars by the bank manager to a mortgage document *after* the mortgage had been entered into by the mortgagors constituted fraud for which the appellant bank was responsible. In that case, Fullager noted that the sending on the path to registration of this forged instrument, which was uttering continuously its false representation that the mortgagor signed after the insertion of all the title particulars, was the cause of the registration and this sending on the path was done with 'fraudulent intent'. Furthermore, the fraud of the banks agent could be brought back to the bank as it occurred during the carrying on of the bank's official business. By way of contrast, in *Grgic v ANZ Ltd* (1994) 33 NSWLR 202, the court held that bank officers, who had witnessed a forged signature to a mortgage and certified the dealing to be correct for the purposes of the NSW legislation, had not committed a fraud. The court held that their conduct was not intentionally dishonest and did not amount to a reckless disregard because the bank officers were honestly misled by the person who had impersonated the true mortgagor. In *Pyramid v*

36 See, also, *Westpac Banking Corp v Sansom* [1995] ANZ Conv R 143 for a similar conclusion.

Scorpion Hotels [1998] 1 VR 188, Nathan J held that Pyramid Building Society had committed a fraud by reason of their lack of good faith in the transaction and the 'degree of blameworthiness' induced by a recklessness or indifference which resulted in the mortgage instruments being registered. On the facts, the solicitor acting for Pyramid did not believe that the corporate seal of the mortgagor had been properly affixed to the mortgage documents. Nathan J held that, in the circumstances, and in the light of the fact that Pyramid had carried out a company search over Scorpion and had ascertained the identity of the directors, they either knew or should have known that not all of the directors had authorised the mortgage and the 'lack of good faith' on the part of Pyramid disentitled them to rely upon the indefeasibility flowing from registration. His Honour noted that reckless indifference to truth, or falsity, can, in circumstances, constitute a fraud where suspicion is clearly brought home to the person seeking registration. Following this decision, it is clear that a failure to properly check documentation and corporate authorisation – in circumstances where a suspicion as to the *bona fides* of the transaction can reasonably be raised – will generally result in a lender having their indefeasibility set aside because their lack of good faith combined with their 'blameworthy' ineptitude will constitute an 'actual fraud'. In discussing the notion of fraud, Nathan J stated: 'I do not believe it is nutritious to define words like turpitude, baseness or wickedness too closely, but certainly "moral turpitude" goes beyond recklessness or indifference, and imports a departure from acceptable standards of moral behaviour as to be blameworthy.' It is clear from these cases that the title of the registered proprietor may be set aside if the agent of that registered proprietor or their authorised agent has committed a fraud which the registered proprietor was or should have been aware of.[37]

The significant issue for statutory fraud is proof of some dishonest intention or design. An administrative error or an error in the absence of design will generally fail to constitute statutory fraud. In *Macquarie Bank v Sixty-Fourth Throne Pty Ltd* [1998] 3 VR 153, the Victorian Supreme Court concluded that a mortgagee had not committed fraud because it failed to discover a forgery in circumstances where the attesting signatures were of two individuals who were not directors of the company. The court noted that in assessing the mortgagee's knowledge, it was not permissible to aggregate the knowledge of its officers and agents, each individually unaware of fraud to create a notional person with a dishonest intent. The court concluded that there was no wilful blindness here as this connotes some form of deliberate concealment or calculated ignorance which was not established on the facts.

In *Russo v Bendigo Bank* (1999), unreported, Victorian Supreme Court, 30 July, a 19 year old conveyancing clerk falsely attested that a witness was

37 See, also, *Assets Co Ltd v Mere Roihi* [1905] AC 176 on this point.

present when the plaintiff's son-in-law forged the plaintiff's signature on a mortgage which was later registered in favour of Bendigo Bank. Neither the bank nor its solicitor had any knowledge of this false attestation. The court held that this did not constitute fraud for the purposes of ss 42–44 of the Transfer of Land Act 1958 (Vic) because it requires a 'wilful and conscious seeking to defeat or disregard another's rights'. As there was no direct evidence of dishonesty on the part of the conveyancing clerk, the court found that there was nothing to suggest she was involved in the forgery by the son-in-law. Ormiston J noted that statutory fraud requires some conscious impropriety and should not be extended to include broader notions of equitable fraud as that might overwhelm the aims of indefeasibility. In this regard, his Honour noted that statutory fraud is founded on moral turpitude and this requires intentional, personal dishonesty rather than a falsity which carried no particular purpose or design.

11.4.2 Prior folio or certificate of title

The title of a registered proprietor will be not be valid against the interest or estate of a registered proprietor claiming the same land under a prior folio or certificate of title.[38] In the rare situation where two certificates of title are granted or issued against the same land, the title of the prior registered proprietor will prevail. This is the case even where the subsequent registered proprietor is a *bona fide* purchaser for value without notice, because the legislation expressly sets out that priority must lie with the holder of the certificate of title first granted.

11.4.3 Erroneous description of land

In all jurisdictions, the title of the registered proprietor will not be valid over any portion of land which may have been included in the certificate of title due to an incorrect description of the land or its boundaries.[39] Importantly, however, apart from Queensland and Tasmania, this exception will not apply to *bona fide* purchasers for value without notice. The purpose of this exception is, specifically, to invalidate erroneous descriptions of land in circumstances where the transferee knew of, or could be taken to have been aware of, the error. Where the transferee has innocently relied upon the incorrect description and purchased the property, the title will remain indefeasible. The rationale in this situation is that the innocent purchaser should not be made to suffer from the error of a third party.

---

38 This is clearly set out in the Torrens legislation in all states: Vic, s 42(1)(a); NSW, s 42(1)(a); SA, s 69V; WA, s 68; Tas, s 40(3)(b); NT, s 69V; ACT, s 58(a).

39 This is clearly set out in the Torrens legislation in all states: Vic, s 42(1)(b); NSW, s 42(1)(c); SA, s 69III; WA, s 68; Tas: s 40(3)(f); NT, s 69III; ACT, s 58(c).

11.4.4 *Paramount interests*

In all states, the Torrens legislation expressly excludes a category of interests from the effect of the indefeasibility provisions.[40] The scope of this category varies from state to state, but basically it includes interests which, due to their special character, can only properly survive where they remain unaffected by the registration process. The term 'paramount interest' refers to those interests which are unaffected by the statutory regime and which remain enforceable against a registered proprietor.

11.4.4.1 Easements

All jurisdictions expressly exempt easements from the application of the indefeasibility provisions.[41] The scope of protection varies from state to state. In Victoria, Tasmania and Western Australia, the legislation sets out that 'any easement howsoever acquired' will not be affected by the indefeasibility provisions. The breadth of this section appears to cover both legal and equitable easements whether arising expressly, impliedly or by way of prescription. In New South Wales, South Australia and Queensland, the wording is not as broad. In Queensland, South Australia, the Australian Capital Territory and the Northern Territory, the legislation applies in the case of 'any omission or misdescription of any right of way or other easement created in or existing upon land'. The exact meaning of 'omission or misdescription' is the subject of some debate. However, it has been held to mean 'left out' or 'not there' and to include 'implied easements'.[42]

In New South Wales, the wording is slightly different, and the exception applies 'in the case of any omission or misdescription of an easement subsisting immediately before the land was brought under the provisions of this Act or validly created at or after that time'.

11.4.4.2 Adverse possession

In all jurisdictions, interests acquired by way of adverse possession are expressly excluded from the application of the indefeasibility provisions, and whilst the statutory language varies from state to state, it would appear that where a possession can be proven to have been adverse to that of the true owner and to satisfy the requisite limitation period, the exception will arise.[43]

---

40 See Torrens legislation: Vic, s 42(2); NSW, s 42(1); SA, s 69IV; WA, s 68; Tas, s 40(3); NT, s 69IV; ACT, s 58.

41 The nature of easements is discussed in detail in Chapter 13.

42 See *Australian Hi-Fi Publications Pty Ltd v Gehl* [1979] 2 NSWLR 618 and *Stuy v BC Ronalds Pty Ltd* [1984] 2 Qd R 578.

43 See Chapter 4 for a more detailed discussion on the nature of adverse possession.

11.4.4.3 Leasehold interests

Protection is also given to unregistered leases in all states. In Victoria, the rights of all tenants in possession of land, excluding rights under an option to purchase the land, will constitute a paramount interest and remain unaffected by registration. In New South Wales, only tenancies for a term not exceeding three years are protected, and in South Australia and the Northern Territory, protection is only conferred upon one year tenancies. In all states, it must be established that the tenant remains in actual possession before the interest will come within the ambit of the statutory exception.

The breadth of the Victorian provision has been judicially considered in the decision of *Downie v Lockwood* [1965] VR 257. In this case, it was argued by the defendants that, whilst the lease was a paramount interest and therefore a statutory exception to indefeasibility, a right of rectification, which arose under an oral agreement concerning the actual terms of the lease, did not fit within the ambit of the exception. The court held that, whilst it is usually the case that a mere equity will not affect a subsequent purchaser for value, the right of rectification was a constituent of the whole leasehold transaction and consequently formed a part of the statutory exception. This decision effectively creates a different position between statutory paramount and common law interests in Victoria. The tenancy under the paramount interest provision includes all equitable incidents to the leasehold estate whilst, under general law, such equitable incidents would be defeated by a subsequent *bona fide* purchaser for value.

Other interests protected by the 'tenancy in possession' include:

(a) the equitable interest of a purchaser under a contract of sale (at law, this person is considered to be a tenant at will of the vendor);

(b) the equitable life estate of a devisee under a will (the devisee is at law a tenant at the will of the trustee); and

(c) the equitable leasehold interest of a person in possession under an agreement for a lease or informal lease.

Furthermore, if a person has notice of a sublease created under an existing leasehold interest before he obtains registration of his interest, and the sublease does not exceed three years, the purchaser will take subject to the lease because it comes within the ambit of a tenancy in possession.

Other miscellaneous paramount interests contained within the exception include: public rights of way; particular rates, taxes and charges relating to the land; rights reserved by the Crown grant; and rights relating to any portion of the land which has also been included in another, earlier certificate of title.

11.4.5 Registrar's power to correct the register

The Torrens legislation in all states confers a general, discretionary power upon the Registrar to correct the register.[44] In all jurisdictions, the Registrar has the power to correct errors contained upon the register and to include any entries mistakenly omitted, provided that, in so doing, the original entry is not erased or made illegible. This power is, however, limited to the extent that it cannot prejudice any rights which may have been acquired by a *bona fide* purchaser prior to the error or omission being corrected. In all states except Victoria and the ACT, the Registrar has a further power to cancel or correct any document which is believed to have been involved in some fraud.[45] Despite the potential ambit of this latter power, the Registrar is unlikely to exercise it so as to overwhelm the current immediate indefeasibility application of the Torrens legislation.

11.4.6 Section 71: South Australia and Northern Territory

In addition to the above statutory exceptions, the South Australian and Northern Territory legislation contain a further set of circumstances which are exempted from the effect of the indefeasibility provisions. Section 71 of the legislation in these states sets out that nothing in the Act shall be construed so as to affect the following rights or powers:

(a) the power of the Sheriff to sell the land of a judgment debtor under a writ of execution;

(b) the power of the court to order the sale of land;

(c) the right of an Official Receiver or of any trustee to the land in bankruptcy;

(d) the rights of a person with whom the registered proprietor has made a contract for the sale of land or any other dealing;

(e) the rights of a *cestui que trust* (beneficiary) where the registered proprietor is a trustee, whether the trust is express, implied or constructive; and

(f) the right of promoters of an undertaking to vest land in themselves by deedpoll pursuant to the Compulsory Acquisition of Land Act 1925 or any amending Act.

The section goes on to set out specifically that no unregistered estate, interest, power, right, contract or trust shall prevail against the title of a registered proprietor where that proprietor or any person taking through or under him takes *bona fide* and for valuable consideration.

---

44 Torrens legislation: Vic, s 103(2); NSW, s 12(3)(a); Qld, s 15; Tas, s 139; WA, s 188(ii); SA, s 220(4); ACT, s 14(1)(d).

45 Torrens legislation: NSW, ss 136–37; WA, ss 76–77; Tas, ss 163–64; SA, ss 60–63; ACT, ss 160–61; NT, ss 60–63; Qld, ss 15(1)(a) and 19.

11.5 Non-statutory exceptions to indefeasibility

In addition to the express statutory exceptions to registration, a range of non-statutory exceptions exist to impeach a registered title. The existence of these exceptions has been judicially endorsed and can be subject to a great deal of variation in scope and application.

11.5.1 The in personam *exception*

The *in personam* exception ensures that a registered interest holder, despite holding an indefeasible title, remains bound by legal rights arising out of his or her own conduct. A registered interest holder will continue to be responsible for contracts and legal obligations she enters into with respect to registered land: the registration will not invalidate such obligations. This principle is not so much an exception as a confirmation of the scope and effect of registration under the Torrens system. It was never intended that the Torrens system was to interfere with properly created personal obligations, and a registered interest holder should not be permitted to rely upon his or her registered title to escape the consequences of personal actions giving rise to legal or equitable rights in another person.[46]

The problem with the *in personam* exception is that the broader its scope, the greater the interference with the perceived objective of the Torrens system to provide a guarantee of secure title. Consequently, the courts have tended to confine the application of the *in personam* exception to clearly established legal or equitable rights. This was enunciated by Mason CJ and Dawson J in *Bahr v Nicolay (No 2)* (1988) 164 CLR 604, where their Honours held that the *in personam* exception was to be applied in such a way that it operated consistently with the aims of the Torrens system. Their Honours stated that personal obligations can only interfere with a registered title where they are properly and legally created, and to go any further than this would interfere with the security conferred upon a registered title holder.

Two of the most common types of *in personam* rights which are enforceable against a registered proprietor include:

(a) rights arising out of a contract entered into by the registered proprietor; and

(b) rights arising from a fiduciary relationship which the registered proprietor has either entered into or created.

For example, a registered proprietor will be bound by contracts for the sale of land into which he or she may have entered, mere equities arising out of his or her conduct, and other equitable rights arising in the particular circumstances.

46 The ambit of the exception was explored by the High Court in *Bahr v Nicolay (No 2)* (1988) 164 CLR 604. See, also, *op cit*, Tooher, fn 35.

Hence, a vendor who erroneously transfers more land than the vendor had contracted to sell is entitled to have the register amended so that the true contractual relationship between the parties can be reflected.

On the facts of *Bahr v Nicolay*, the High Court unanimously found that the exception was available in circumstances where a registered proprietor had expressly undertaken to respect the contractual right of the prior owners to exercise an option to repurchase the property. Mason CJ and Dawson J felt that the agreement gave rise to an express trust in favour of the persons holding the contractual right. Their Honours felt that upon transferring the land to the registered proprietor, the parties intended to create an express trust to protect the contractual right of the third party. Consequently, the registered proprietor held the contractual right as trustee for the benefit of the third party, and his personal obligations as trustee prevented him from asserting an indefeasible title. The remainder of the court found that the *in personam* obligations of the registered proprietor as trustee flowed from the imposition of a constructive trust, imposed in fairness in the circumstances. The rationale given was that there was no actual intention to create a trust relationship but that, in the circumstances, it was only fair that the court impose one.

In many situations, the *in personam* exception may overlap with the statutory fraud exception. The primary distinction lies in the fact that the *in personam* exception is much broader; under the *in personam* exception, there is no need to prove that a fraud has been committed: all that needs to be established is that the registered proprietor is subject to legally enforceable obligations which affect the enforceability of his or her title. Furthermore, statutory fraud will usually be confined to conduct entered into by the registered proprietor prior to registration . However, the *in personam* exception is subject to no such time restriction: *in personam* obligations entered into by a registered proprietor may be enforceable whenever those obligations accrue.[47]

Wherever a registered proprietor is a party to contractual or trust relationships, and the obligations flowing from those relationships affect the land, a registered title may be affected. The scope of this exception applies not only to expressly created contracts and trusts but also to resulting and constructive trusts.[48] Hence, where a registered proprietor has committed some unconscionable conduct or takes the property with notice that a fraud has been committed against another party, he or she may become a constructive trustee of the property and the *in personam* exception will prevent that proprietor from denying responsibility.[49]

47 Note, however, that Mason CJ and Dawson J in *Bahr v Nicolay* felt that statutory fraud could be committed after registration. See discussion at para 11.4.1.

48 For further discussion on the nature of trusts, see Chapter 5.

49 See, generally, *Pyramid Building Society v Scorpion Hotels Pty Ltd* [1998] 1 VR 188.

Care must, however, be taken when considering the nature and application of the notion of unconscionable. To expand the concept of unconscionability too greatly may undermine the indefeasibility goals of the legislation. As warned by Hansen J in *Koorootang Pty Ltd v ANZ Banking Group* [1998] 3 VR 16 (in *dicta* as the *in personam* exception was not actually raised on the facts), the danger of assuming that a person can defeat a registered title merely on the grounds of alleged unconscionable behaviour is that if it is not 'linked' to the recognised cause of action, 'the court may fall into the error of applying a subjective view of what the "fair result" ought to be'.[50]

In *Tanzone v Westpac* (1999) ATPR (Digest) 46-195, the New South Wales Supreme Court considered the nature of the fraud resulting from the *Bahr v Nicolay* decision. On the facts of *Tanzone*, the right to rectify was specified in the contract of purchase and Tanzone bought the land with notice of the existence of this right. Windeyer J considered the decision of *Bahr v Nicolay* and concluded that if applicable, a repudiation of the right to rectify would either amount to fraud or the registered proprietor would hold the property upon trust – thereby raising the *in personam* defence. Windeyer J noted that what *Bahr v Nicolay* establishes is that while notice itself cannot lead to a right *in personam*, notice together with an agreement to be bound by the interest can amount to unconscionable conduct justifying relief. The court, however, held that the contract in issue did not, upon a true construction, amount to an agreement to take subject to a right of rectification.

11.5.2 Inconsistent legislation

Legislation unconnected with the Torrens legislation, but enacted after the date it came into effect in each respective state, may override the Torrens legislation where it is established that it contains inconsistent provisions. Inconsistent legislation can have the effect of invalidating registered interests, creating unregistered interests, or completely removing the land from the operation of the Torrens system. Where such an inconsistency exists, the Registrar cannot provide conclusive evidence of the validity of title, and the title of the registered proprietor may be defeated. The major Australian authority on this is *Pratten v Warringah Shire Council* [1969] 2 NSWLR 161.

On the facts of that case, Pratten was the registered proprietor of a large area of land. After registration, the council lodged a planned subdivision of the whole area. The Local Government Act set out that, where land is needed to create a drainage reserve, the fee simple shall vest in the council. The local government legislation was passed after the date when the Torrens legislation in New South Wales was enacted and was inconsistent with the indefeasibility provisions it contained. The certificate of title did not identify this inconsistency and reveal to the new purchasers the overriding legislative

50 [1998] 3 VR 16, p 125.

rights of the local council, despite direct enquiries by the purchaser.[51] The purchaser argued that the indefeasible title should not be affected by the inconsistent legislation.

The court held that the council's statutory title should prevail over the title of the registered proprietor. It was felt that all Torrens legislation is inherently subject to rights created by overriding statutes. The absolute indefeasibility ordinarily flowing from registration will not arise where the fee simple has, pursuant to an overriding statute, been effectively removed from the registration system.[52] The fact that the subsequent legislation does not expressly mention the Torrens legislation does not prevent the provision from being interpreted as inconsistent and overriding the indefeasibility provisions.[53]

This exception can, however, only be raised where it is established that the subsequent statutory provision is directly inconsistent with the Torrens legislation. If it is possible to interpret the provisions consistently, it is unlikely that an indefeasible title will be struck down. For example, in *Breskvar v Wall* (1971) 126 CLR 376, the court held that s 53(2) of the Stamps Act 1894 (Qld), which set out that a transfer signed in blank was void at law, did not override the indefeasibility of a registered, *bona fide* third party purchaser acquiring title pursuant to a transaction involving a blank transfer. The High Court unanimously concluded that the Stamps Act was aimed at preventing invalidities occurring in the process of executing a transfer, whilst the Torrens legislation focused upon the effect of registration. Hence, once an interest was registered, the title of the interest holder became indefeasible, even where the instrument creating the interest contained a procedural invalidity.[54]

In *Lansen v Olney* (1999) 169 ALR 49, the Federal Court considered the validity of a pastoral lease granted to the Northern Territory Land Corporation under the Pastoral Land Act 1992 (NT), and the interaction between pastoral leases issued to the Crown under the Pastoral Land Act 1992 (NT) and indefeasibility provisions under the Real Property Act (NT). Sackville J confirmed the validity of the inconsistent legislation exception, noting that the principle of immediate indefeasibility does not necessarily result in the conclusion of indefeasibility because where a conflict between the title of the registered proprietor of land and an unregistered interest in the same land, created by a statute enacted later, the unregistered interest prevails. In considering whether there was anything in the language or structure of the

51 In Victoria, s 82(2) of the TLA allows rights acquired under state or federal legislation to be recorded on the certificate of title affected. However, this is not compulsory.

52 See, also, *Travinto Nominees v Vlattas* (1973) 129 CLR 1; *Attorney General (NT) v Minister for Aboriginal Affairs* (1990) 90 ALR 59.

53 *Travinto Nominees v Vlattas* (1973) 129 CLR 1.

54 See, also, O'Connor, P, 'Public rights and overriding statutes as exceptions to indefeasibility of title' (1994) 19 Mon ULR 649.

Pastoral Land Act 1992 (NT) which denied the Northern Territory the quality of indefeasibility ordinarily attached to a registered title under the Real Property Act (NT), Sackville J held that the drafters of the Pastoral Land Act assumed that, in the absence of express provision, the two acts would work together and that the drafters of the Pastoral Land Act assumed that leases granted under this legislation would be registered in accordance with the Real Property Act. His Honour noted that the position might be different if the Pastoral Land Act contained provisions prohibiting the Territory from obtaining registration of pastoral leases granted and in that situation, where express provisions existed, the 'inconsistent legislation' exception may be raised.

11.5.3 Volunteers

The issue of whether or not the Torrens system protects volunteers has been the subject of some debate. Early Victorian decisions felt that the Torrens system appeared to confer the protection of indefeasibility only upon purchasers for value, excluding volunteers from the ambit of this protection. In *King v Smail* [1958] VR 273, Adam J in the Victorian Supreme Court concluded that the express provisions of the Victorian legislation, in particular, the wording of s 43 of the Act, indicated that indefeasibility was only intended to be conferred upon purchasers for value and that registered volunteers would take title subject to any existing equities. His Honour noted:

> Are these mere volunteers, then, within the protection of s 43? In my opinion – clearly no. The protection given by s 43 to a registered proprietor, that is, a legal owner of land, against the consequences of notice, actual or constructive, of trusts or equities affecting his land has point where the legal owner is a purchaser for value. A purchaser of a value has, by virtue of this section, the immunity from prior equities of a *bona fide* purchaser of the legal estate without notice under the general law. On the other hand, to confer on a mere volunteer immunity from the consequences of notice would be illusory, for ... the volunteer was, on well settled rules of equity, subject to equities which affected his predecessor in title whether with or without notice of such equities.[55]

This decision was subsequently upheld by the court in *Rasmussen v Rasmussen* [1995] 1 VR 613. In that case, the Victorian Supreme Court concluded that the protection conferred under ss 42 and 43 of the Victorian legislation did not extend to volunteers. Coldrey J approved of the decision in *King v Smail*, noting that a distinction in the application of the indefeasibility provisions to a *bona fide* purchaser for value is both rational and principled, upholding what his Honour called an 'overriding principle of fairness' which 'on the one hand recognises the desirability of commercial certainty in property transactions and on the other allows full play to equitable precepts'.[56] In *Valoutin Pty Ltd v*

55 *King v Smail* [1958] VR 273, pp 277–78.

56 *Rasmussen v Rasmussen* [1995] 1 VR 613, p 634.

Furst (1998) 154 ALR 119, Finkelstein J also approved of the decision in *King v Smail*. His Honour stated:

> When it is accepted, as it must be, that section 43 does not relieve a volunteer from equities which affected his transferor it is difficult to see why section 42 should be held to give that protection. Such a view would be inconsistent with the structure and text of the Transfer of Land Act. It should also be noted that *King v Smail* was followed by Coldrey J in *Rasmussen v Rasmussen* [1995] 1 VR 613 in preference to *Bogdanovic*. In my view *King v Smail* correctly states the law.

The position in New South Wales is, however, quite different. Following the decision in *Bogdanovic v Koteff* (1988) 12 NSWLR 472, the New South Wales Court of Appeal held that the benefits of indefeasibility enure to both purchasers for value as well as volunteers. In that case, the court held that any argument suggesting that the Torrens legislation did not protect volunteers could not be upheld in light of the leading cases favouring the application of 'immediate indefeasibility'.[57]

In Queensland, s 165 of the Torrens legislation specifically sets out that a registered volunteer will acquire an indefeasible title. In the other states, the Torrens legislation is not worded so as to exclude the application of the indefeasibility provisions to volunteers and, in the absence of judicial opinion to the contrary, it is presumed that such protection would be conferred upon volunteers.

11.6 Unregistered interests and the caveat system

Unregistered interests are interests in land which have not been registered in accordance with the provisions in the Torrens system. The interest may be unregistered because it is registrable but not actually registered – registration under the Torrens system is not compulsory – or because the interest is incapable of being registered.

The Torrens system in all states recognises the existence of unregistered interests in a number of ways: it confers protection upon 'paramount interests'; it expressly prohibits the registration of particular types of interests; and it provides for the protection of unregistered interests through the creation of the caveat system.

Most unregistered interests are equitable interests, but unregistered interests cannot be described as 'equitable interests' in precisely the same way as they are described at general law. An unregistered interest does not have the same sort of equitable attributes, the main distinction being that an unregistered interest in land under the Torrens system is liable to be defeated

57 See the discussion on this by Butt, P, in 'The conveyancer' (1994) 68 ALJ 675. See, also, Raden, P, 'Volunteers and indefeasibility' (1999) 1 Australian Property Law Journal 8.

by the registration of an inconsistent dealing by a good faith purchaser, even if that purchaser has notice or knowledge of the interest.

11.6.1 The caveat system

11.6.1.1 Nature of the caveat

In all states, limited protection is given to unregistered interests in the Torrens system through the statutory protection regime known as the 'caveat system'. This is a system specifically designed for the protection of unregistered interests. The caveat system entitles the holder of an unregistered interest to lodge a 'caveat' over the title, informing all future dealers with the land of the existence of the unregistered interest and ensuring that the holder is notified of the lodgement for registration of any inconsistent dealings. Placing a caveat on the title to indicate the presence of an unregistered interest should be distinguished from registering an interest upon the title. A caveat is essentially a form of injunction, preventing the registration of any subsequent dealing over the land until the caveator has the chance to establish her or his claim. Caveats function as notification of an interest: once lodged they do not guarantee any title.

11.6.1.2 Caveat against dealings

A range of different type of caveats may be lodged under the caveat system. The most commonly used caveat is the caveat against dealings, lodged by a person claiming an estate or interest in the land. Under this form of caveat, the person claiming the interest lodges a caveat which prohibits the registration of all or particular dealings in the land which are inconsistent with the interest claimed by the caveator.[58] Where the caveat is properly lodged, a memorandum will be noted in the original folio and will remain there until an inconsistent dealing is lodged. Once an inconsistent dealing is lodged, a caveator will be notified and given a specified period of time (30 days in Victoria) in which to take court action and prove the enforceability of the interest. Once a caveat is lodged, and so long as it remains in force, the Registrar shall not give effect to a transfer or dealing or record in the register any change in proprietorship or register any interest in respect of the land over which the caveat is registered. However, no instrument lodged for registration before a caveat is lodged shall be in any way affected by the caveat.[59] Any person interested in the land may make an application to remove such a caveat, and upon receiving an application, the Registrar may give notice to the caveator that the caveat will lapse within a specified period.

58 Torrens statutes: Vic, s 89(1); SA, s 191; WA, s 137; NSW, s 74F; Qld, ss 122, 124; Tas, s 133; ACT, s 104(1), (1A); NT, s 191.

59 Torrens statutes: Vic, s 89(1); NSW, s 74F; SA, s 191; Qld, ss 122–24; WA, s 137; Tas, s 133; ACT, s 104(1), (1A); NT, s 191.

In Victoria, the period is 35 days unless, in the meantime, the caveator abandons the caveat or gives notice in writing of an intention to take proceedings to court.[60]

In Queensland, a caveat against dealings will not remain on the title indefinitely until an inconsistent instrument is lodged for registration. In that state, the caveator has three months from the date of lodgement to take proceedings in the Supreme Court to establish the claim, or 14 days where the caveatee serves a notice upon the caveator requiring such an action to be brought.[61] In South Australia and the Northern Territory, the registered proprietor may apply to have the caveat removed and, once this occurs, the caveator has 21 days in which to obtain a court order for an extension of the caveat, otherwise the caveat will lapse.[62] In all jurisdictions, a caveat may be withdrawn, an application may be made to the court seeking the removal of a caveat and, in all states except Tasmania, a caveat may be removed by the Registrar. If, upon the lodgement of an inconsistent dealing, the caveator decides to take no action, the caveat will automatically lapse at the expiration of the time period, and it cannot be renewed unless the dealing lodged is to pass to the caveator upon registration. If the caveator does take action and proves the interest, a priority dispute may arise between the caveator and the person who lodged the inconsistent dealing. If court proceedings find that the claim of the caveator is not substantiated, the court may make such order in relation to the caveat as the court thinks fit, and the Registrar shall give effect to it. If the proceedings are struck out, the caveat shall lapse.

11.6.1.3 The nature of a caveatable interest

An interest must be proprietary – whether legal or equitable in nature – in order to be protected by a caveat.[63] Most interests which are protected by caveat are equitable, but this is not a requirement. Courts are increasingly prepared to expand the range of caveatable interests in accordance with the emergence of new types of land interests. For example, the interest of a builder under a charging clause in a building agreement has been held to be caveatable.[64] Caveats are most commonly lodged to protect a purchaser after entering a contract of sale, especially after a terms contract. However, in practice, caveats are not usually lodged for contracts exceeding 60 days or where a mortgage is involved, because a mortgagee bank usually searches the title at least three times prior to settlement. Caveats are also commonly lodged

60 See Torrens legislation: Vic, s 89A(3), (4).

61 See Torrens legislation: Qld, s 126(2), (4).

62 See Torrens legislation: NT, s 191V, VI, VII; SA, s 191V, VI, VII.

63 *Swanston Mortgage Pty Ltd v Trepan Investment Pty Ltd* [1994] 1 VR 672.

64 *Henery Property Development Pty Ltd v James Dibben McLennan* ((1992) unreported, Victorian Supreme Court, 6 July, *per* Gobbo J); see the note by Butt, P, in 'Conveyancing' (1996) 70 ALJ 683.

to protect a lender under an unregistered mortgage or charge, or to protect an interest arising under a trust which is not able to be registered.

It has been suggested that an interest is only caveatable where it is proven to be capable of being registered. In *Classic Heights Pty Ltd v Black Hole Enterprises Pty Ltd* [1994] V Conv R 54-506, Batt J held that an interest in Torrens title land is not caveatable unless it is either evidenced by an existing registrable dealing or the caveator is able to require the registered proprietor to execute a registrable dealing. This decision takes a very narrow perspective of a caveatable interest and greatly reduces the efficacy of the caveat system in protecting a range of different forms of equitable interests. The decision was not followed in *Composite Buyers Ltd v Soong* (1995) 38 NSWLR 286, where Hodgson J held that a charge which was contained within an instrument which was unregistrable was a caveatable interest. His Honour noted that one of the aims of the caveat system is to protect the rights of equitable interests which are prohibited from registration; hence it is nonsensical to require a caveatable interest to be registrable.[65]

According to Hodgson J, the only requirement for a caveatable interest is that the interest be such that equity will give specific relief against the land itself, whether that be by way of requiring the provision of a registrable instrument, or in some other way.[66] This means that leases unable to be registered may nevertheless be caveated and protected in this way.[67] Furthermore, in *Re McKean's Caveat* [1988] 1 Qd R 525, Ryan J held that the registered proprietor of land had a caveatable interest where the mortgagee under a mortgage over the land improperly exercised its power of sale. This decision, however, does not cite and is contradictory to *Latec Investments Ltd v Hotel Terrigal Pty Ltd (In Liquidation)* (1965) 113 CLR 265 and was not followed by the Victorian Supreme Court in *Swanston Mortgage Pty Ltd v Trepan Investments Pty Ltd* [1994] 1 VR 672.

In that case, the Victorian Supreme Court concluded that a right to set aside an improper exercise of a mortgagee's power of sale was a mere equity and this was not a caveatable right. Brooking J notes that this right was, at best, an equitable right to prevent the completion of a voidable sale – 'an equitable claim enforceable by reason of the principles of the Court of Chancery'. His Honour felt that this was not the definition of an equitable interest – nor even a definition of a 'mere equity, but rather, a definition of an 'equity' in the widest sense of that term, the right to seek an equitable remedy, whether or not in aid of a property right.

65 See, also, *Hodges, Hall and Jovanovic v Markov* (1995) 19 Fam LR 241; Wikrama, W, 'Do caveats need supporting by registrable instruments' (1995) Victorian Law Institute Journal, February, at p 101.

66 *Composite Buyers Ltd v Soong* (1995) 38 NSWLR 286, p 288. See, also, the discussion on this in *op cit*, Butt, fn 57.

67 See problems outlined by Redfern, M in 'Case notes: courts and unregistered leases under the Victora Transfer of Land Act' (1995) 3 Australian Property Law Journal 11.

The nature of the interest claimed must be clearly and properly specified in the caveat in order for the interest to be properly protected. In *Leros Pty Ltd v Terara Pty Ltd* (1992) 106 ALR 595, the High Court held that a caveat which described a lease but failed to make reference to the option to renew did not provide any protection for the option to renew. In order to provide protection, the caveat must clearly specify the full nature of the interest. As noted by the court, 'specify' should be understood in the sense of 'mention definitely or explicitly'. If an unregistered interest is not properly specified in the caveat it may be defeated by the registration of a subsequent inconsistent dealing. Once an interest is defeated by registration of a subsequent inconsistent dealing, the unregistered interest will be completely extinguished; it does not become an inchoate interest capable of being.

11.6.1.4 Grounds for lodging a caveat

The Torrens legislation in all states provides a disincentive to the lodgement of a caveat without reasonable cause. Where a caveat is lodged without reasonable cause, the caveator may be required to compensate any person sustaining damage as a result of the wrongful lodgement. In such a claim, the onus is on the plaintiff to show that the caveator acted without reasonable cause rather than simply proving that the caveator had no caveatable interest.[68] It must be established that the caveator did not have an honest belief upon reasonable grounds that he had a caveatable interest.

11.6.2 Priority disputes between unregistered interests

Where several inconsistent unregistered interests affect land, it may be necessary for the court to determine which interest should take priority. Conflicts between unregistered Torrens law interests will generally arise where a registered proprietor provides a third party with the means to become registered as proprietor of the land and, in consequence, another person is led to purchase an interest in the land. Alternatively, a dispute may arise where the earlier of two purchasers of interests in land fails to lodge a caveat and, in consequence, a second purchaser acquires an interest in ignorance of the rights of the first purchaser. In such situations, the Torrens system draws heavily upon the general law priority principles. Despite the fundamentally different perspectives existing between the Torrens system and the general law, unregistered interests do not attract the indefeasibility provisions and are therefore subject to the general common law and equitable priority principles. General law priority principles are, as discussed in Chapter 9, centred around three primary considerations:

68 See *Commonwealth Bank of Australia v Baranyay* [1993] 1 VR 589.

(a) the date upon which the interest was created;

(b) the jurisdictional character of the interest; and

(c) the conduct of the parties involved.

One further consideration for unregistered interests under the Torrens system is whether or not the prior interest holder has lodged a caveat to protect that interest. In *Abigail v Lapin* [1934] AC 491, the Privy Council felt that the failure of the prior interest holder to lodge a caveat had the effect of reinforcing the 'apparent ownership' of the registered proprietor. This subsequently contributed to the creation of an equitable charge, and such an omission justified the postponement of that interest. Nevertheless, subsequent decisions have indicated that a failure to caveat will not automatically postpone the priority of an earlier interest where the interest holder has taken other steps to protect that interest. In *J & H Just Holdings Pty Ltd v Bank of NSW* (1971) 125 CLR 546, the court held that an equitable mortgagee who did not lodge a caveat but did obtain possession of the duplicate certificate of title should not lose priority in time. The High Court noted that the holder of an unregistered interest is not under a duty to lodge a caveat and that a failure to do so should not result in postponing conduct where the prior interest holder has already adequately protected the interest.

More recent cases have suggested that failure to lodge a caveat should not have a bearing on priority analysis because its purpose is to provide protection. In *Jacobs v Platt Nominees Pty Ltd* [1990] VR 146, the Full Court of the Victoria Supreme Court held that failure to lodge a caveat is not relevant to a priority dispute where other protective measures have been carried out or, in circumstances where it is not reasonably foreseeable, that failure to lodge a caveat would expose the interest holder to risk of a dispute. This will depend upon a proper assessment of the facts.[69]

In *Leros Pty Ltd v Terara Pty Ltd* (1992) 106 ALR 595, the High Court noted that failure to caveat should not have a direct impact upon priority disputes as it primarily concerns the enforceability of the claimed interest. The court recognised that the failure of a person entitled to an equitable estate or interest to lodge a caveat against dealings with the land does not necessarily involve any loss of priority which the time of the creation of that interest would otherwise give because the purpose of a caveat against dealings is to operate as an injunction to the Registrar General to prevent registration of dealings forbidden by the caveat until notice is given to the caveator so that he or she has an opportunity to oppose such registration. Hence, failure to lodge a caveat may not result in a loss of priority however it will result in the destruction of the unregistered interest upon the subsequent registration of an inconsistent dealing. Similarly, in *Avco Financial Services Ltd v Fishman* [1993] 1

69 See, also, *Person to Person Financial Services v Sharari* [1984] 1 NSWLR 745; *IAC (Finance) Pty Ltd v Courtenay* (1963) 110 CLR 550; cf *Osmanoski v Rose* [1974] VR 523.

VR 90, Tadgell J in the Victorian Supreme Court held that a prior unregistered mortgage held by a bank did not lose its priority in time, despite failing to caveat, because the purpose of lodging a caveat was primarily to provide 'protection' for the claimant rather than notification to the rest of the world. On the facts of *Avco Financial Services*, the mortgagee had retained the duplicate certificate of title and, approving of the principles enunciated in *Jacobs v Platt Nominees Pty Ltd* [1990] VR 146, Tadgell J noted that a registered first mortgagee who has possession of, or dominion over, the duplicate certificate of title would have no occasion to lodge a caveat to protect any subsequent mortgage he takes from the registered proprietor at a time before a further mortgage is granted to any other party. This is because the mortgagee would know that no other mortgage could be properly registered without his consent. Hence, holding the title documents is as good as or better than notice which a caveat could afford him of anyone's intention to register another mortgage.

11.7 State guarantee of title

Torrens legislation in most states enables persons suffering loss as a result of the operation of the Torrens system to seek compensation. The rationale underlying the introduction of a state guarantee of title is to ensure that any unfair or mistaken loss of title is properly compensated. In all states except the Northern Territory, a person who is deprived of all or a part of his or her interest in land and who suffers loss or damage may acquire a right to seek compensation from the state.[70] In all states except for Victoria and Queensland, the deprivation must be of an actual estate or interest in the land. In Victoria and Queensland, the deprivation is not expressly confined to an estate or interest in land and has been interpreted broadly. In all states, the loss will only be compensatable where it fits within one of the express statutory criteria, which vary according to the legislation in each state.

All states except Victoria provide compensation for the deprivation of an estate which has occurred as a consequence of fraud.[71] The fraud referred to in these provisions has been interpreted in a broader sense than that which is applicable under the paramountcy provisions. Fraud, in this context, refers to any situation where a person loses an interest in land to a registered proprietor due to 'fraudulent conduct' or 'fraudulent transaction' (*Northside Developments v Registrar General* (1990) 93 ALR 385).

All states provide compensation: (a) for loss incurred through the registration of any other person as proprietor; (b) for the deprivation of an interest as a consequence of bringing land under the Torrens system (except

70 Torrens legislation: Vic, ss 108–10; Qld, ss 173–75; Tas, ss 127–28; NSW, ss 126–33A; SA, ss 201–19; WA, ss 201–11; ACT, ss 143–51 and 154–55.

71 Torrens legislation: NSW, s 126; SA, s 203; Qld, s 173(a); WA, s 201; Tas, s 152.

where the interest holder had notice of the application of the Torrens system); and (c) where loss is suffered through any error, omission or misdescription contained in the Register.

In *Saade v Registrar General* (1993) 118 ALR 219, the High Court examined the meaning of 'erroneous registration' under s 126 of the Real Property Act (NSW) 1900. Section 126 operates in this context in the following way. Any person deprived of land, or of any estate, or interest in land in consequence of fraud or by the registration of any other person as proprietor of such land, estate or interest may bring an action for recovery of damages. Such an action is to be brought against the person upon whose application the erroneous registration was made; or who acquired title to the land, or to the estate or interest therein, through the fraud. In every case in which the fraud occurs upon a transfer for value, the transferor receiving the value is to be regarded as the person upon whose application the Certificate of Title was issued to the transferee. When such person liable for damages is dead, bankrupt or insolvent, or cannot be found within the jurisdiction, such damages with costs of action may be recovered out of the assurance fund by action against the Registrar General as nominal defendant. In interpreting the effects of this provision, the High Court noted that it did not apply to innocent third parties who have become registered from the fraudulent transfer. Indeed, to hold an innocent third party liable for an erroneous registration would be contrary to the aims and purposes of the Torrens system. This meant, however, that in such situations, on a technical reading of s 126, applicants could be refused relief. On the facts, however, the court interpreted s 126 liberally and held that Mrs Saade was entitled to compensation from the Assurance Fund because she had been defrauded out of her land 'in consequence of fraud' by Mr Saade and, at the date of commencing the action, the person who had perpetrated the fraud, Mr Saade, was out of the jurisdiction.[72]

Additional criteria for claiming against the Assurance Fund in Victoria include:

(a) the failure of a solicitor to disclose in a solicitor's certificate a defect in title or the existence of an interest or estate in the land (s 110(3)(a));[73]

(b) the loss or destruction of any document lodged at the office for inspection or safe custody or any error arising through an official title search (s 110(3)(e));

(c) the payment of any consideration to any other person on the faith of an entry in the register book (s 110(3)(d)); and

72 See Mendelow, P, 'Case notes: fraudulent deprivation and the Torrens Assurance Fund *Saade v Registrar General* (1993) 118 ALR 219' (1994) 3 Australian Property Law Journal 30.

73 This section refers to loss suffered as a result of a solicitor's certificate executed during the process of converting title.

(d) where the Registrar has exercised discretionary powers and the person suffering loss has not been privy to or a party to the exercise of power (s 110(3)(g)).

Compensation will not be payable in Victoria and Queensland in circumstances where the loss has been incurred as a result of the loss, fraud, neglect or wilful default of the claimant, his solicitor or agent, or of a claimant who derives title from a person whose solicitor or agent has been guilty of such fraud, neglect or wilful default.[74] This limitation imposes an onerous restriction upon compensation claims because it requires the claimant to prove that the loss did not occur as a result of his own conduct or that of the persons acting for him. This has proven to be a difficult task due to the breadth of the terms 'loss, neglect, fraud or wilful default'.

In all states except Queensland, compensation is not payable for loss incurred as a result of a breach of trust, or for loss incurred as a result of of the same land being included in two or more Crown grants or the same certificate of title unless the applicant can establish that the person liable is dead, has absconded or is unable to pay appropriate compensation.[75]

In Victoria, these exceptions are modified by the Legal Profession Practice Act 1958 (Vic) which establishes a guarantee fund to compensate clients who are defrauded by their solicitors and requires solicitors to maintain insurance policies to indemnify themselves against claims for professional negligence.

The process of bringing a claim is different according to each state. In all states except Victoria, a person who has suffered loss must bring an action against the individual responsible before bringing an action against the guarantee fund. An action may only be brought against the fund in circumstances where the first action does not provide full compensation or the action is not capable of being instigated. In Victoria and Queensland, an action may be brought against the fund directly.[76] Once an applicant has made a successful application against the fund, the aim is to place the person, as far as possible, in the position he or she was in prior to the mistake or fraud having occurred. In Victoria, the value of a deprived estate or interest is specifically stated to be assessed at the date of the loss, although no such restriction exists in other states.[77]

---

74 Torrens legislation: Vic, s 110(3)(a); Qld, s 174(1)(b).

75 Torrens legislation: Vic, s 109(2)(c); NSW, s 133; SA, s 212; Tas, s 151(1)(d); WA, s 196; ACT, s 147(b).

76 Torrens legislation: NSW, s 126(2)(c); SA, s 203; WA, s 201; Tas, s 152(2)(b)(iii); ACT, s 154(1)(a), (3); Vic, s 110(2); Qld, s 173.

77 Torrens legislation: Vic, s 110(4). See generally, Mendelow, P, 'Fraudulent deprivation and the Torrens Assurance Fund' (1994) 2 Australian Property Law Journal 279; Sherry, C, 'Torrens title compensation for loss – recommendations for reform' (1997) 4 APLR 1.

CHAPTER 12

COVENANTS OVER LAND

12.1 Introduction

This chapter considers the common law, equitable and statutory principles applicable to covenants over land. A covenant over land is, by general definition, a contractual agreement, set out in a deed, where two parties agree either to carry out or not to carry out specific obligations with respect to land.[1] The land covenant will generally provide a benefit to one piece of land and impose a burden over another.

For example, X owns a fee simple in land and decides to sell it to Y. As a part of the contract of sale, X requires Y to agree that Y will continue to repair the fencing using the same treated pine wood fencing as that currently existing around X's property which is located next to Y's property. In this situation, Y, as covenantor, and Y's land are subject to the burden of a covenant which is to benefit X's land: Y is burdened because he is unable to use any material other than treated pine to repair the fence. X is benefited because the overall character of the land is maintained through the construction of similar fencing.

Where the land contract imposes a burden over land, the covenant is referred to as a 'restrictive covenant', simply meaning that the agreement restricts the way in which the covenantor can use his property. One of the most important considerations respecting restrictive covenants over land is whether or not they are enforceable against third parties not privy to the original contractual arrangement. As we shall see, in certain circumstances, equity, but not common law, will enforce the burden of a restrictive covenant against a third party not privy to the original agreement.

In this respect, the focus of this chapter is upon how a covenant may be attached to land so that it is binding on subsequent takers of the land. This requires an analysis of the metamorphosis that can often take place between a simple contractual agreement between two parties concerning the usage of land, and a land covenant, which is so intrinsic to the character of the land, that it is effectively regarded as having become 'annexed' to the land, making subsequent takers of the land, who take with notice, bound by it.

1 Under common law, it was the practice to formalise important written documents by sealing them. A covenant originally simply referred to an agreement but, when the practice of sealing became commonplace, a covenant eventually came to be known as an agreement under seal. For greater detail, see Simpson, W, *A History of the Common Law of Contract: the Rise of Assumpsit*, 1975, OUP, Pt 1.

Annexation of a covenant to land will not be readily implied because of the serious consequences involved: the annexation effectively transforms a contractual right which is purely *in personam* in nature into a right which is enforceable against third party successors in title to the land not privy to the original agreement. The rules relating to such annexation are often perceived to be complex, technical and lacking in consistency, and, in the absence of statutory reform, remain bound up in established case law.[2]

Annexation is founded upon the notion that, where a contract relates innately to the constitution of a piece of land, it should be regarded as a part of the ownership spectrum of rights and duties rather than a separate personal agreement. This stems from the equitable origins of covenants – particularly covenants imposing a burden over the land. As noted by Cottenham LC in *Tulk v Moxhay* [1848] 2 Ph 774; 41 ER 1143, 'if an equity is attached to the property by the owner, no one purchasing with notice of that equity can stand in a different situation from the party from whom he purchased'.[3]

The Chancery jurisdiction recognised at a relatively early stage that equity would enforce the attachment of a land covenant to the land itself. This is not to say that the contract *becomes* the land but, rather, that it is considered to bind the land. A range of common law and equitable tests concerning the enforcement of the 'benefit' and 'burden' of a covenant exist. A detailed examination of the approach taken by the common law, the way in which the Chancery jurisdiction has embellished this approach and the codification of these tests under statute follows.

In modern times, the covenant plays a central role in the private use and development of land resources. It has the potential to allow landowners to plan and impose qualifications over land which can relate to anything from historical preservation to environmental protection. The modification of the doctrine of privity in land covenants has allowed landowners to assume greater control in the regulation, administration and preservation of land. Whilst some may regard such modification as heresy to traditional contractual principles, there is no doubt that, today, annexation of land covenants represents a popular and pervasive form of private land control.

12.2 Contractual basis of covenants

A covenant is fundamentally a contractual agreement. Whilst it may have proprietary implications where properly annexed to land, it remains in essence a contractual relationship between two parties. Hence, provided the agreement satisfies the basic contractual requirements, it will be automatically

2 See the discussion on possible reforms in New Zealand Property Law and Equity Reform Committee, *Report on Positive Covenants Affecting Land*, 1985, Wellington: Law Reform Commission.

3 *Tulk v Moxhay* [1848] 2 Ph 774, p 776; 41 ER 1143, p 1145.

enforceable between the parties privy to the original agreement. The person receiving the benefit of the covenant is known as 'the covenantee', and the person agreeing to be bound by the burden of the covenant is known as 'the covenantor'.

The covenant may be enforceable against third parties who are not privy to the original contract where the court deems either the benefit or the burden of the contract to have been annexed to the land. The justification for modifying the doctrine of privity is based upon the idea that the contract is so intrinsically related to the land that it effectively becomes a right associated with the land and is thereby capable of binding all subsequent takers.

In Australia, the ability to enforce land covenants against third parties has been statutorily codified. Section 56(1) of the Property Law Act 1958 sets out the following:

> A person may take an immediate or other interest in land or other property, or the benefit of any condition, right of entry, covenant or agreement over or respecting land of any other property, although he is not named as a party to the conveyance or other instrument.[4]

There has been much controversy over the exact effect of this legislation. On one hand, it appears to destroy completely the doctrine of privity as that doctrine applies to agreements relating to land because it categorically entitles all persons having a benefit in such an agreement to enforce that benefit despite not being a party to the original contract. The equivalent English provision was discussed in *Beswick v Beswick* [1966] Ch 538, p 557, where Lord Denning noted that the doctrine of privity was 'simply a rule of procedure which could be abrogated by statute'. However, the House of Lords in *Beswick v Beswick* [1968] AC 58 disagreed with this conclusion, stating that the legislation did not intend to undo 100 years of case law. The House of Lords felt that the Law of Property Act 1925 (UK) was simply a consolidation act, intended to codify the annexation principles as they had evolved under general law, but was never intended to make fundamental alterations to the law. Their Lordships concluded that it could not be that 'by a side wind ... Parliament ... slipped in a provision which ... revolutionised the law of contract'.[5]

The House of Lords in *Beswick v Beswick* concluded that s 56(1) of the 1925 Act simply intended to alter the common law to the extent that it enabled a covenantee or a taker from the covenantee, who had been named as such in an indenture under seal executed with the covenantee, to take the immediate benefit of the covenant, despite not actually being named a party to the indenture. It did not, contrary to Lord Denning's earlier conclusions, purport

4 This provision is also set out in property law statutes: NSW, s 36C; Tas, s 61; and SA, s 34. The legislation replicates s 56(1) of the Law of Property Act 1925 (UK), s 56(1).

5 *Beswick v Beswick* [1968] AC 58, p 79, *per* Lord Hodson.

to abrogate the common law doctrine of privity. Lord Reid made the following conclusions:

> Perhaps more important is the fact that the section does not say that a person may take the benefit of an agreement although he was not a party to it: it says that he may do so although he was not named as a party in the instrument which embodied the agreement.[6]

In *White v Bijou Mansions* [1937] Ch 610, Simonds J noted:

> ... under s 56 of this Act, only that person can call it in aid who, although not named as a party to the conveyance or other instrument, is yet a person to whom that conveyance or other instrument purports to grant some thing or with which some agreement or covenant is purported to be made.[7]

In *Stromdale and Ball Ltd v Burden* [1952] Ch 223, the court held that s 56(1) of the legislation enabled the plaintiff company to enforce the benefit of an option to purchase the unexpired residue of an underlease. On the facts, the plaintiff company was not a party to the deed of licence whereby the underlessee licensed sublessees to assign their lease to the plaintiff company, although the option to purchase (which was included in the deed of licence) was intended to be exercised by the plaintiff company. Danckwerts J held that the object of s 56(1) was to allow a person who is not privy to a contract, but nevertheless within the benefit of the covenant, to take advantage of the covenant, and he found in favour of the plaintiff company. In *Amsprop Trading Ltd v Harris Distribution Ltd* [1997] 2 All ER 990, the Court noted that s 56 did not operate to confer a benefit on a party not within the ambit of the expressly identified covenantee.

The legislation in Western Australia and Queensland is far broader than that contained in the states mentioned above, and the effect of the provisions is to categorically abrogate the doctrine of privity, although, in Western Australia, the third party must be in existence or identifiable at the date of entering into the covenant in order to gain an enforceable right.[8]

12.3 Annexation of covenants under common law

12.3.1 Nature of a benefit

The primary limitation upon the annexation of covenants under common law is that only the benefit of a covenant may be attached to the land – not the burden. A benefit will exist where it can be established that some advantage has been conferred upon the covenantee by the actual terms of the agreement. Generally, the party receiving the benefit will be the person who has actually

6 *Beswick v Beswick* [1968] AC 58, pp 66–68.

7 See, also, *Re Ecclesiastical Commrs for England's Conveyance* [1936] Ch 430.

8 Property law statutes: Qld, s 55(1); WA, s 11(2).

initiated the contractual arrangement, because it is this person who wants the restriction created. The common law will not enforce the burden of a covenant against a successor in title to the covenantor, even where the successor in title takes the land with actual knowledge of the existence of the covenant. The classic case establishing this principle is *Austerberry v Oldham Corp* (1885) 29 Ch D 750, CA. On the facts of that case, owners of land wanted to construct a new toll road between two villages. In pursuit of this, some of the owners of the adjoining land formed a joint stock company, which was represented by trustees, to acquire the necessary strips of land for the road. The trustees covenanted to maintain the road. In 1880, Oldham Corporation purchased the road from the trustees and subsequently declared it a public highway. The Corporation set out that the highway was repairable by the owners of land along the road at their own expense. The plaintiff was a successor in title to one of the owners of the land along the road who was not a member of the Corporation. The plaintiff claimed that the Corporation, as successor in title to the trustees and having purchased the land with notice of the express covenant entered into by the trustees to maintain the road, was liable for the costs of maintenance.

The Court of Appeal considered whether the burden of a covenant could pass to a successor in title at law. Lindley LJ noted that, under common law, a burden should not run with the land unless, upon a true construction, the covenant amounted to a grant of an easement or a rentcharge or some actual estate or interest in the land. His Honour felt that, on the facts, the covenant was a mere personal obligation, and such an obligation should not be held to run with the land because this would be contrary to the intention of the parties creating it. If the obligation was intended to attach to the land, then, the parties should have expressed it in the form of an actual estate or interest capable of forming a part of the land. His Honour made the following comments:

> I am not aware of any other case which either shows, or appears to show, that a burden such as this can be annexed to land by a mere covenant, such as we have here ... If the parties had intended to charge this land for ever into whosoever hands it came, with the burden of repairing the road, there are ways and means known to conveyancers by which it would be done with comparative ease ... They have not done anything of the sort, and, therefore, it seems to me to show that they did not intend to have a covenant which should run with the land.[9]

This case provides a classic example of the rigidity of the common law. The court was not prepared to enforce the burden of a covenant because a contractual obligation cannot be enforced against parties who are not privy to the agreement. The case represents firm authority for the proposition that,

9 *Austerberry v Oldham Corp* (1885) 29 Ch D 750, CA, p 759. See, also, *Forestview Nominees Pty Ltd v Perpetual Trustees* (1996) 141 ALR 687, where the Australian Federal Court approved *Austerberry*.

under common law, no successor in title to land will be bound by the burden of a covenant, whatever the circumstances. This decision has been categorically approved by the House of Lords in *Rhone v Stephens* [1994] 2 AC 310. In that case, Lord Templeman made the following comments:

> In these circumstances, your Lordships were invited to overrule the decision of the Court of Appeal in the *Austerberry* case. To do so would be to destroy the distinction between law and equity and to convert the rule of equity into a rule of notice. It is plain from the articles, reports and papers to which we were referred that judicial legislation to overrule the *Austerberry* case would create a number of difficulties, anomalies and uncertainties and affect the rights and liabilities of people who have for over 100 years bought and sold land in the knowledge, imparted at an elementary stage to every student of the law of real property, that positive covenants affecting freehold land are not directly enforceable except against the original covenator.[10]

12.3.2 Exceptions to the common law rule

Courts have, however, devised some methods for getting around the severity of the *Austerberry* principle. One of the classic principles which has developed in this context is the rule from *Halsall v Brizell* [1957] Ch 169. In that case, the court held that a successor in title to the covenantor cannot rely upon the *Austerberry* principle in circumstances where he has relied upon the same deed of covenant to enforce the benefit. This decision clearly requires courts to distinguish between covenants which blend a mutual benefit and a burden compared with those that impose a pure burden. The facts of *Halsall v Brizell* provide a classic example of this. The facts, as with the *Austerberry* case, concerned the passing of a covenant to contribute to the maintenance of roads and other amenities contained within a particular estate. The court held that the defendants, who were successors in title, were relying upon the same deed to enforce their right to use the roads and services as they were to deny the burden of their obligation to maintain those roads. In such a circumstance it was held that the *Austerberry* principle should not apply.[11]

The foundation of the rule in *Halsall v Brizell* is based upon the old principle enunciated by *Coke on Littleton* (230b), that 'a man who takes the benefit of a deed is bound by a condition contained in it though he does not execute it'. The rule will, however, only apply where it can be established that the benefit and burden were intended to pass under the same instrument.

---

10 *Rhone v Stephens* [1994] 2 AC 310, pp 321–22. See, also, *Thamesmead Town Ltd v Allotey* (1998) 30 HLR 1052.

11 In *ER Ives Investments Ltd v High* [1967] 2 QB 379, CA, it was held that, even where the benefit/burden was mutually contained in the same parol agreement, the *Austerberry* principle could not apply. See, also, *Thamesmead Town Ltd v Allotey* (1998) 30 HLR 1052, where the court noted that in circumstances where successors in title do not desire the benefit, they should not be bound by the burden: they have a choice.

The nature and application of the rule in *Halsall v Brizell* has subsequently been discussed in *Tito v Waddell (No 2)* [1977] Ch 106, where Megarry VC discussed the application of the benefit/burden principle under covenants. His Honour distinguished between instruments conferring pure covenant benefits or pure burdens against those conferring what he described as burdens arising pursuant to 'conditional benefits'. In the latter situation, a covenant would be drafted so that the conferral of a benefit was conditional upon the satisfaction of a specific burden, and in this way the instrument integrated both a benefit and a burden. According to Megarry VC, the rule in *Halsall v Brizell* can apply to a conditional benefit but, to apply to an instrument conferring a pure benefit and/or a pure burden, it must be proven that it was intended that the benefit and burden should, in fact, pass mutually and that the successor in title has acquired a sufficient benefit. It is not exactly clear what will constitute a 'sufficient benefit', although it would seem that where the burden is, in substance, an integral part of the benefit, the requirement may be satisfied (*Frater v Finlay* (1968) 91 WN (NSW) 730).[12]

Further methods of avoiding the stringent common law prohibition set out in *Austerberry* include making the successor in title to the covenantor enter into an indemnity covenant requiring the successor in title to indemnify the original covenantor for all damages owing from future breaches. It may also be possible to attach and enforce restrictive covenants to registrable encumbrances. In *Burke v Yurilla SA Pty Ltd* (1991) 56 SASR 383, the plaintiff sought to incorporate restrictive covenants into a rentcharge, which had the effect of preserving the residential character of each of the allotments referred to in the rentcharge. The court held that the rentcharge was registrable under the Torrens system, and the fact that it incorporated restrictive covenants did not make it unregistrable; consequently the restrictive covenants were enforceable.

12.3.3 *The 'touch and concern' test*

The benefit of a covenant will only bind a third party successor in title under common law where it can be established that it has become annexed to the covenantee's land. Annexation can only occur where it is proven that the covenant satisfies the classic test of 'touching and concerning' the land. This test focuses upon the character of the actual covenant. If it is clear that the covenant was primarily intended for the personal benefit of the covenantee rather than a usage which affects the mode of occupation of the land or the value of the land, then the covenant cannot be said to have satisfied the test. A determination of this issue will depend upon the individual facts. However,

12 Note, however, the judgment of Brooking J in *Government Insurance Office (NSW) v KA Reed Services Pty Ltd* [1988] VR 829, p 84, where his Honour noted that the 'pure principle' propounded in *Tito's* case is founded upon authority that will not sustain it and is at odds with settled and fundamental rules.

then it could have been annexed, but in the absence of an express intention, the benefit could not pass to such a large estate. Subsequent courts have consistently upheld this position, noting that a covenant can only pass where it fully benefits the land and, where the land is large or subdivided, this can only be properly achieved where the intention is specifically set out in the actual terms of the covenant (*Re Arcade Hotel Pty Ltd* [1962] VR 274).

In *Federated Homes Ltd v Mill Lodge Properties Ltd* [1980] 1 All ER 371, M Ltd owned land which was a development site comprising three separate areas of land, known as red, green and blue land. In 1971, M Ltd conveyed the blue land to the defendants. To satisfy preliminary planning permission, M Ltd was required to enter into a covenant restricting the number of dwellings which could be erected on the blue land. The covenant did not expressly apply to the red and green land. Federated Homes ultimately came to be the owners of the red and green land. A chain of assignments for the benefit of the covenant existed with respect to the red land. However, the transfer of the red land contained no express assignment of the benefit of the covenant to the plaintiff, and the issue was whether or not it passed so that the plaintiff could restrain the defendant from building at a greater density than was permitted by the terms of the covenant. The defendant argued that, in the absence of an express intention, the covenant ought to be read as passing only for the benefit of the land it actually affected and not for the benefit of every part of that land, so that, in effect, the benefit of the covenant did not pass to the holders of the red land. The trial judge found in favour of the plaintiff and held that the benefit of the covenant had passed despite the red land not being expressly referred to in the original covenant. The Court of Appeal agreed and dismissed the defendants' appeal.[14] Brightman LJ made the following comments:

> I find the idea of the annexation of a covenant to the whole of the land but not to a part of it a difficult conception fully to grasp. I can understand that a covenantee may expressly or by necessary implication retain the benefit of a covenant wholly under his control, so that the benefit will not pass unless the covenantee chooses to assign; but I would have thought, if the benefit of a covenant is, on a proper construction of a document, annexed to the land, *prima facie* it is annexed to every part thereof, unless the contrary clearly appears.[15]

The decision in *Federated Homes* has not been fully accepted by Australian courts. However, statutory provisions in both Victoria and Western Australia now specifically deal with these difficulties. Section 79A of the Property Law Act 1958 (Vic)[16] reads as follows:

---

14 See, also, *Roake v Chadha* [1983] 3 All ER 503.

15 *Federated Homes v Mill Lodge Properties Ltd* [1980] 1 All ER 371, p 378.

16 See, also, Property Law Act 1969 (WA), s 49.

> It is hereby declared that when the benefit of a restriction as to the user of or the building on any land is or has been annexed or purports to be annexed by an instrument to the other land the benefit shall, unless it is expressly provided to the contrary, be deemed to be and always to have been annexed to the whole and to each and every part of such other land capable of benefiting from such restriction.

Section 79A has been interpreted as a deeming provision, applying the benefit of a covenant to the whole or each and every part of the land in the absence of any contrary intention expressly noted by the terms of the covenant (*Re Miscamble's Application* [1966] VR 596).

Section 78(1) of the Property Law Act 1958 (Vic) sets out the statutory equivalent to the annexation principles existing under general law.[17] The section reads as follows:

> A covenant relating to any land of the covenantee shall be deemed to be made with the covenantee and his successors in title and the persons deriving title under him or them, and shall have effect as if such successors and other persons were expressed. For the purposes of this subsection in connection with covenants restrictive of the user of land 'successors in title' shall be deemed to include the owners and occupiers for the time being of the land of the covenantee intended to be benefited.

Whether this legislation alters the existing general law principles relating to annexation of the benefit is unclear. The traditional interpretation of the provision is that it codifies the requirements existing under general law, although it takes away the need to set out an express intention to bind successors in title, as such intention is deemed by the terms of the provision. A more controversial interpretation of the identical United Kingdom provision, noted by the court in *Federated Homes Ltd v Mill Lodge Properties Ltd* [1980] 1 All ER 371 (and discussed above) is that the section takes away the need to prove an intention to bind successors in title at all, so that, once it is established that the benefit of the covenant touches and concerns the land, it is automatically deemed to have been intended to pass to successors in title.[18] This view has not yet been accepted by Australian courts, as s 78(1) does not appear to have been given such a broad application, and, even if this argument is raised, to imply such a significant alteration to the general law would require a clear and cogent statutory intention which Australian courts, to date, have not been prepared to do.[19]

---

17 Provisions in other states are as follows: property law statutes: WA, s 47; Qld, s 53; Tas, s 71; ACT, s 109; NSW, s 70. There is no equivalent provision in South Australia.

18 See the discussion on this issue in Wade, 'Covenants – a broad and reasonable view' (1972) 31 CLJ 157; Hayton, D, 'Revolution in restrictive covenants law?' (1980) 43 MLR 443; and Todd, 'Annexation after *Federated Homes*' [1985] Conv R 177.

19 See the discussion on this issue in Bradbrook, A, MacCallum, S and Moore, A, *Australian Real Property Law,* 2nd edn, 1996, LBC, pp 18–21. This issue was not raised by the High Court in *Forestview Nominees Pty Ltd v Perpetual Trustees WA Pty Ltd* (1998) 152 ALR 149.

More recent English authority appears to go against the conclusions of *Federated Homes Ltd v Mill Lodge Properties Ltd*. In *Morrells of Oxford Ltd v Oxford United FC* [2001] 2 WLR 128, the English Court of Appeal considered the impact of the similarly worded English equivalent of s 79 of the Property Law Act 1958 (Vic). In that case, the court clearly concluded that the statute cannot operate to alter the intention of the original contracting parties and indeed, its purpose is not to presume an intention to pass to successors in title but, rather, to operate as an interpretive tool.

On the facts of that case, the local authority conveyed land to the claimant's predecessor in title in 1962 to form the site of a public house. The conveyance included under cl 2 a purchaser's covenant that 'the [purchaser] and its successors in title will at all times hereafter observe and perform the restrictions following in relation to the property', including a covenant that it would use it only as a public house, and by cl 3(a), a vendor's covenant by the local authority that for the benefit of the land conveyed 'the vendors will not at any time hereafter permit any land or building erected thereon within half a mile radius of the land hereby conveyed which is in the ownership of the vendors at the date of this conveyance' to be used as a brewery or club or licensed premises. In 1996, the local authority agreed to sell adjacent land, some or all of which lay within half a mile of the claimant's public house, to land developers for the construction of a new football stadium as well as a hotel and leisure centre. The claimant argued that the development would breach the restrictive covenant injunction.

The trial judge held that cl 3(a) was intended to bind the vendor in the original transactions, but not any successors in title and that it could not be deemed to bind the successors in title under s 79 of the Law of Property Act 1925. The Court of Appeal dismissed the appeal by the claimant finding that the proper construction of cl 3(a) was that it did not intend to bind successors in title and that s 79 of the Law of Property Act 1925 was to be used in circumstances where the words provisionally read in by the statute could in the particular commercial context usefully supplement the words of the particular document. Where, however, the meaning inferred under the statute would be inconsistent with the purpose or intention of the creators of the covenant then s 79 would be excluded. Hence, the purport of s 79 is to extend the application of the covenant to successors in title in circumstances where such an extension is consistent with the wording and intent of the original covenant.

Where the successor in title acquires an equitable estate, the benefit of the covenant may only be enforced by the successor in title where the annexation has satisfied the tests set out in the equitable jurisdiction. See discussion on equitable annexation below.

It is not necessary to prove that the successor in title to the covenantee has a legal estate which is identical to the original covenantee – as long as it can be established that the estate is recognised and enforceable under common law, this will be sufficient for the 'common law' jurisdiction to apply; this approach is consistent with s 78(1) of the Property Law Act 1958 (Vic) and equivalent statutory provisions in other states.[20]

One final possibility with respect to statutory annexation is that s 62 of the Property Law Act 1958 (Vic)[21] automatically passes the benefit of covenants to successors in title to the benefited land. Section 62(1) reads as follows:

> A conveyance of land shall be deemed to include and shall by virtue of this Act operate to convey, with the land, all buildings, erections, fixtures, commons, hedges, ditches, fences, ways, waters, watercourses, liberties, privileges, easements, rights and advantages whatsoever, appertaining or reputed to appertain to the land, or any part thereof, or at the time of conveyance, demised, occupied or enjoyed with, or reputed or known as part of or appurtenant to the land or any part thereof.

The argument is that the reference to 'rights and advantages whatsoever' includes a reference to the benefit of a covenant. The question as to whether or not this broad reference would include the benefit of a covenant has not been fully determined, although if 'rights and advantages' are given a natural interpretation, there seems to be no reason why the provision could not include the benefit of covenants.[22]

If the successor in title acquires an equitable interest, the benefit of the covenant can only run under the equitable jurisdiction. This principle was established in the old decision of *Rogers v Hosegood* [1900] 2 Ch 388, CA. On the facts of that case, Rogers and his associated partners owned a fee simple which had been divided into a number of blocks. The entire land was subjected to an old title mortgage with the effect that Rogers and his partners retained an equity of redemption in the land. One block of the land owned by Rogers and his partners was transferred to the Duke of Bedford and, as a part of the conveyance, the Duke covenanted with Rogers and his partners and their heirs and assigns that neither he, nor his heirs or assigns, would build more than one house on the block, and it would be used only as a private dwelling. Sir John Millais then purchased a different block from Rogers and his partners, without knowledge of the existence of the benefit of the covenant and without any express assignment of it. Hosegood was the successor in title to the block of land held by the Duke of Bedford and they took with notice of the existence of the covenant entered into by the Duke. Hosegood wanted to erect buildings in contravention of the covenant and the plaintiffs, and the devisees of the block of land held by Sir John Millais sought to restrain him. One of the issues for the court to determine was whether or not the benefit of

20 In other states' property statutes: Qld, s 53(1); WA, s 47; Tas, s 71; NSW, s 70.

21 Property law statutes: Qld, s 239; WA, s 41; Tas, s 6; NSW, s 67; SA, s 36.

22 For a discussion on this issue, see Wade, 'Covenants – a broad and reasonable view' (1972) 31 CLJ 157 and *Sutton v Shoppee* (1963) 63 SR (NSW) 853.

the covenant was annexed to the land. Collins LJ held that one of the difficulties involved with the case was that the covenant was made with the mortgagors of the land rather than with the absolute owners, so that the only interest which the covenantees held was the equity of redemption. Whilst this precluded the benefit of the covenant from being annexed at law, his Honour noted that a court of equity would not regard such an objection as defeating the intention of the parties and:

> ... therefore, when the covenant was clearly made for the benefit of certain land with a person who, in the contemplation of such a court, was the true owner of it, it would be regarded as annexed to and running with that land, just as it would have been at law but for the technical difficulty.[23]

Hence, where the estate of the covenantee and the successor in title to the covenantee is equitable, the benefit can only be annexed according to the principles which have evolved in the equitable jurisdiction. The annexation process in equity is very similar to that existing under the common law. It must be established that the covenant was intended to be passed and that it binds the land. Once the issue of annexation has been determined, a court of equity may then go on to consider whether the conscience of the successor in title to the covenantor is bound by the burden of the covenant. On the facts of the case, the court ultimately concluded that the assigns of Sir John Millais were entitled to enforce the restrictive covenant against the defendant and that the defendant's appeal should be dismissed. The application of the equitable jurisdiction to the annexation of the benefit of a covenant is discussed below.

12.4 Enforceability of covenants in equity

The rigidity of the common law in consistently refusing to enforce the burden of a covenant against a successor in title became problematic in England with the rapid expansion of private dwellings and urban development. In such an environment, the need for a more comprehensive approach to the promotion of private land organisation and usage became increasingly acute. Eventually, the Chancery jurisdiction, performing its role of rectifying the deficiencies of the common law, intervened to allow successors in title to the covenantor to enforce the burden of a covenant in specific circumstances.

The classic equitable decision which introduced this method of enforcement was *Tulk v Moxhay* [1848] 2 Ph 774; 41 ER 1143. On the facts of that case, Moxhay was the successor in title to the covenantor. Tulk was the original covenantee, and he wanted to enforce the burden of the covenant against Moxhay. In essence, the covenant set out that the covenantor and his heirs and assigns should 'keep and maintain the garden and the iron railing around it in its original form and in proper repair as a square garden and pleasure ground in an open state, uncovered with any buildings, in a neat and

23 *Rogers v Hosegood* [1900] 2 Ch 388, CA, p 394.

ornamental order'. Moxhay wanted to build on the land and Tulk filed for an injunction to restrain Moxhay from using the land for any purpose other than a garden. One of the issues on appeal was whether or not the burden of a covenant could run with the land.

Lord Cottenham LC felt that the Court of Chancery had jurisdiction to enforce the particular covenant. He went on to consider the issue of whether or not a purchaser from the covenantor could violate the terms of the original contract of sale without the court having any power to interfere. His Lordship felt that the question was not whether the covenant runs with the land but whether a purchaser shall be permitted to use the land in a manner inconsistent with the contract entered into the by vendor/covenantor when the purchaser had specific knowledge of the existence of the covenant. His Lordship felt that, ultimately, this was inequitable and contrary to the conscience of the equitable jurisdiction. It would effectively enable the covenantor to sell the land the next day for a greater price than that which he had purchased it for in consideration of the purchaser being able to escape from the liability of the covenant. His Lordship felt that the question is not whether the covenant runs with the land, but rather, if an equity is attached to the property by the original owner, no one purchasing with notice of that equity can stand in a different situation from the party from whom he purchased. The rule set out in *Tulk v Moxhay* has been subsequently affirmed by Australian courts (*Burke v Yurilla SA Pty Ltd* (1991) 56 SASR 382).[24]

In *Forestview v Perpetual Trustees* (1998) 152 ALR 149, the High Court considered the application of the *Tulk v Moxhay* principle to the contemporary Australian jurisdiction.

In *Forestview Nominees Pty Ltd v Perpetual Trustees WA Ltd* (1998) 152 ALR 149, the High Court (Gaudron, McHugh, Gummow, Kirby and Hayne JJ), after considering the principles on which the doctrine in *Tulk v Moxhay* is founded, unanimously held that it would not be repugnant to the doctrine for the tenants of a shopping centre on the benefited land to be excluded from the terms of a restrictive covenant. The court emphasised that the intention of the parties to the covenant is paramount, particularly when considering whether the terms of the covenant supported 'the doctrine in *Tulk v Moxhay* with respect to the passing of the benefit of restrictive covenants'. Excluding the tenants from the benefit of the covenant was simply an 'expression' of the *Tulk v Moxhay* principles.

On the facts of the case, Perpetual Trustees WA Ltd purchased from National Mutual Life Association of Australasia Ltd (NML) a shopping centre, and one hectare of the surrounding 4.9 hectares which had not been subdivided. The parties entered into a restrictive covenant which prohibited the vendor 'and all subsequent registered proprietors of the balance of Lot 738

24 See, also, the excellent discussion of the decision in Bell, T, '*Tulk v Moxhay* revisited' [1981] Conv R 55 and Griffith, W, '*Tulk v Moxhay* reclarified' [1983] Conv R 29.

from selling goods, having market stalls or showrooms on the remainder of Lot 738. There was an exception that allowed for the selling of minor convenience items. Perpetual lodged two caveats over Lot 738 giving notice that it possessed an unregistered restrictive covenant over the land. At about this time, NML entered into negotiations to sell the remainder of Lot 738 to Forestview Nominees Pty Ltd (Forestview). Forestview discussed with Perpetual the restrictive covenant and it was registered with the modification that it did 'not enure for the benefit of any tenant for the time being of the benefited land'. It was further stated in cl 1.1 of the restrictive covenant that 'the restrictive covenant is not entered into for the benefit of any tenant for time being of the benefited land'.

Forestview became the registered proprietor of the burdened land (that is, the remaining 3.9 hectares of Lot 738 after subdivision). Forestview wanted to develop the burdened land as a retail shopping centre and therefore sought declarations that the restrictive covenant did not create a binding interest on the burdened land, did not bind successors in title of NML, and did not prevent the burdened land from being leased to others who may sell goods or construct a shopping centre. An injunction restraining Perpetual from enforcing the covenant was also sought. Forestview then sold the land to an associated company, Silkchime Pty Ltd.

At first instance, Carr J, held in favour of Perpetual finding that Perpetual, as covenantee, could enforce the restrictive covenant against Silkchime regardless of whether the covenant 'is annexed to and thus runs with the amalgamated shopping centre land because both Forestview and Silkchime had notice of the restrictive covenant'.

Forestview and Silkchime appealed to the Full Federal Court and subsequently, to the High Court. The Full Court of the Federal Court (French, Einfeld and Nicholson JJ) dismissed the appeal. French J considered that whether there is a passing of the covenant is a matter of construction. It was argued for Forestview and Silkchime that the *Tulk v Moxhay* doctrine had not been complied with because the tenants of the shopping centre did not obtain the benefit of the covenant. This was not accepted by French J. After considering the criteria required for the doctrine to apply it was held that the doctrine is *sui generis* and the covenant can 'attach to some but not all of the interests in a piece of land'.

The High Court of Australia held, in a joint judgment (Gaudron, McHugh, Gummow, Kirby and Hayne JJ), that the restrictive covenant is effective and enforceable, notwithstanding the exclusion of the shopping centre tenants from it. The High Court examined the founding principles of the *Tulk v Moxhay* doctrine. Historically, the doctrine was based on the 'equitable doctrine of notice; thus a defence of *bona fide* purchaser for value who took without notice may protect against the imposition of a restrictive covenant. The High Court, however, concluded that the correct rationale for imposing the burden of the restrictive covenant on parties other than the covenantor was that equity imposes upon the successor to the covenantor 'a constructive duty' which is 'co-extensive' with the express duty of the covenantor to the covenantee. Hence, successors in title to the burdened land are bound by the covenant not because of privity of estate, but rather, the equitable principle of 'privity of conscience'. The court rejected the traditional view that the burden of a restrictive covenants passes with the land in a manner akin to an equitable easement – preferring to describe the relationship as more akin to a trust relationship – binding not the land as such, but the individual conscience of the successor in title to the burdened land.

In determining whether the benefit of a restrictive covenant will pass, the High Court emphasised the importance of determining the intention of the original parties to the covenant as this goes to the very heart of the matter. The reason for the importance of intention is that, 'the requirement is an expression, rather than a denial, of the preference of equity for intention over form and to the giving effect to the intention evinced in the terms of the restrictive covenant in question'. Their Honours noted:

> It follows that the basis upon which equity deals with the attachment to the benefited land and the transmission of the benefit of restrictive covenants is that which was identified by Ames nearly a century ago. He said that the right of third persons to the benefit of restrictive covenants is the result of the just and simple principle: that equity will compel the promisor to perform his agreement according to its tenor. If the restrictive agreement, fairly interpreted, was intended for the sole benefit of the promisee, only he can enforce it. If on the other hand it was intended for the benefit of the occupant or occupants of adjoining lands, then such occupant or occupants may compel its specific performance.

The High Court did not examine relevant statutory provisions in any significant detail. On the facts, it was clear that the intention of the covenant was to exclude enforcement of the tenants. In considering whether this intention was repugnant with the *Tulk v Moxhay* principle, the court noted that the essential criterion was whether the value of the land was affected and that in the circumstances, the covenant affected the value of the land and limitations on the enforcement of the covenant were only one factor to consider in the process of valuation. In conclusion, the court felt that the exclusion of the tenants was within the scope of the *Tulk v Moxhay* principle.

Following *Forestview* and the High Court's re-examination of the *Tulk v Moxhay* doctrine, it is important to emphasise that the passing of the burden of a covenant is based upon entirely different principles from the annexation principles applicable under common law. A successor in title to the covenantor will be bound by the burden of a covenant where it would be inequitable and against the conscience of the court to allow him to deny it.[25] This issue

25 Spry, F, 'Restrictive covenants: the High Court on the *Tulk v Moxhay* doctrine' (1999) 6 APIJ 2.

primarily depends upon a determination that the purchaser took with notice of the existence of the covenant. There are two further qualifications to the *Tulk v Moxhay* principle. The first is that equity will only enforce the burden of a covenant against a successor in title to the covenantor where it can be established that the covenant is, in substance, negative or restrictive in nature. The second is that the covenant must benefit identifiable land.

12.4.1 *Covenant must be restrictive or negative in nature*

Equity will not enforce the burden of a positive covenant, because such a covenant requires the performance of positive acts, which often involve further expenditure and effort on the part of the successor in title. According to the courts of equity, it would be unfair to bind a successor in title to such acts, even where they take with notice of the existence of the positive covenant. By binding a successor in title to the burden of a positive covenant, it is felt that the equitable jurisdiction would be overwhelming rather than supplementing the contractual principles under common law. It is one thing to bind a third party, not privy to the original covenant, to the burden of a restrictive covenant – the argument being that the successor in title bought the property knowing that particular rights would not be passed on – but quite another to hold a successor in title, not privy to the original covenant, to the performance of positive acts over the burdened land. Positive covenants require a successor in title to actually perform a particular act which she has not agreed to in the first place, and can result in the third party having to pay out additional amounts. The imposition of such onerous duties upon successors in title is a serious incursion on the doctrine of privity. Hence, the equitable jurisdiction will not uphold such covenants, whatever the circumstance. As noted by Brett LH in *Haywood v Brunswick Permanent Benefit Building Society* (1881) 8 QBD 403, CA, p 408:

> ... a covenant to repair is not restrictive and could not be enforced against the land ... the reason for no court having gone farther is that a mandatory injunction was not in former times grantable, whereas it is now; but I cannot help thinking, in spite of this, that if we enlarge the rule ... we should be making a new equity, which we cannot do.

The determination of whether a covenant is restrictive rather than positive in nature will depend upon the substance of the agreement, that is, what the covenantor is actually required to do by the terms of the covenant. Simply because the wording appears to be restrictive does not automatically mean that it *is* restrictive. Where positive acts of expenditure and performance are to be carried out by the terms of the covenant, the covenant will generally be considered positive (*Haywood v Brunswick Permanent Benefit Building Society* (1881) 8 QBD 403, CA). A covenant to keep premises in proper repair will generally constitute a positive covenant, whereas a covenant preventing a person from erecting particular buildings or from using the land in a way other than that specified, will generally be restrictive. Of course, there are situations where covenants are drafted in restrictive terms but which, in substance, are positive. For example, a covenant not to build any building other than that which is specified in the covenant would be positive in nature because it requires actual expenditure, despite the fact that in form it appears to be restrictive. The focus upon the actual effect of the covenant rather than its wording stems from the old equity maxim, 'equity looks to substance rather than form' (*Shepherd Homes Ltd v Sandham (No 2)* [1971] 2 All ER 1267).

12.4.2 Covenant must benefit identifiable land

The second qualification to the *Tulk v Moxhay* principle is that the burden will only be enforced against a successor in title to the covenantor where it can be established that the covenant actually benefits identifiable land. If there is no identifiable land, or the terms of the covenant do not sufficiently identify the benefited land, the burden of the covenant will be unenforceable (*London County Council v Allen* [1914] 3 KB 642, CA). This requirement is also a part of the common law 'annexation' test. In order for the benefit of a covenant to be annexed to the land, the land to be benefited must be sufficiently identifiable and proximate. The focus of the equitable jurisdiction is not upon a strict assessment of annexation but, rather, upon general considerations of fairness. The rationale underlying the *Tulk v Moxhay* decision is that a successor in title to the covenantor should be bound by the burden of a restrictive covenant where he or she has notice of it, because, otherwise, there would be no point in the original covenantee entering into the covenant in the first place, as it would not effectively preserve the value of the covenantee's land. This rationale cannot, however, apply where the covenant does not sufficiently relate to, identify and benefit the covenantee's land.

As discussed above, a covenant will benefit the covenantee's land where it can be proven that it relates to the land itself rather than the covenantee personally (*Tooth & Co Ltd v Barker* (1960) 77 WN (NSW) 231). Furthermore, it must be established that, at the date of actually entering into the covenant, the covenantee owned the land which was to be benefited. Where the covenantee does not actually own any benefited land at the date of entering into the covenant, it cannot be argued that the benefit is annexed to the land, as there is no land in existence for it to become annexed to (*London County Council v Allen* [1914] 3 KB 642, CA).

The need to prove an intention to pass the burden of a covenant by setting out an express intention in the wording of the agreement has, as with the requirements for annexing the benefit under common law, been abolished by statute.[26] Section 79(1) of the Property Law Act 1958 (Vic)[27] reads as follows:

26 Note the discussion in *Morrells of Oxford Ltd v Oxford United FC* [2001] 2 WLR 128 on the English s 79(1) in para 12.3.3.

27 Property law statutes: NSW, s 70A; Tas, s 71A; WA, s 48; Qld, s 53(2). There is no equivalent provision in South Australia.

> A covenant relating to any land of a covenantor or capable of being bound by him, shall, unless a contrary intention is expressed, be deemed to be made by the covenantor on behalf of himself, his successors in title and the persons deriving title under him or them, and subject as aforesaid, shall have effect as if such successors and other persons were expressed.

12.4.3 *Annexing the benefit in equity*

Where the benefit of a covenant has passed to a successor in title who has acquired a legal estate in the land, and the issue is whether the successor in title to the covenantee can enforce against the original covenantor, the common law principles relating to annexation (with statutory modifications) are applicable. On the other hand, in a situation where a successor in title to the covenantee is wanting to enforce the benefit of a covenant against a successor in title to the covenantor, the whole question must be determined by the equitable jurisdiction. The reason for this is because only the equitable jurisdiction recognises the ability to pass both the benefit and the burden of a covenant. Following the *Austerberry* decision, the common law has steadfastly refused to enforce the burden of a covenant against a successor in title. What this means is that where both the benefited and burdened lands have passed to successors in title, equity will decide whether the covenant is enforceable.

The equitable jurisdiction follows the same principles as exist under the common law for annexation of the benefit of a covenant, although two primary differences exist, both stemming from the different perspective of the equitable jurisdiction. First, the equitable jurisdiction is inherently discretionary and, consequently, may assume a more flexible approach, taking into account factors such as laches, the conduct of both the parties and the consequences of the decision. Secondly, where annexation of the benefit of a covenant has occurred in equity, only equitable remedies will be applicable for the enforcement of the covenant.

Annexation of the benefit of a covenant will occur in the equitable jurisdiction where it is established that the covenant 'touches and concerns' the land (the same principles applying as under common law annexation); that the covenant was intended to bind successors in title (statutory modifications applying as under common law annexation); and that the benefit sufficiently relates to and identifies benefited land. The equitable jurisdiction follows the same basic principles for annexation as the common law. The effect of passing the benefit in equity has been noted by Collins LJ in *Rogers v Hosegood* [1900] 2 Ch 388:

> These authorities establish the proposition that, when the benefit has been once clearly annexed to one piece of land, it passes by assignment of that land, and may be said to run with it, in completion as well of equity as of law, without proof of a special bargain or representation on the assignment.[28]

28 *Rogers v Hosegood* [1900] 2 Ch 388, p 393. See, also, *Renals v Cowlishaw* (1878) 9 Ch 125.

12.5 Assignment of covenants

Where the benefit of a covenant has not been expressly annexed to the land, whether under common law or pursuant to the equitable jurisdiction, it is possible for the benefit of the covenant to be expressly assigned to a successor in title. The difference between assignment and annexation is that, under annexation, once the covenant can be said to relate to the intrinsic character of identifiable benefited land, it automatically runs with the land. Alternatively, an assignment requires positive acts by the assignor towards the assignee. To be valid under law, an assignment must comply with the requirements set out in s 134 of the Property Law Act 1958 (Vic),[29] which reads as follows:

> An absolute assignment by writing under the hand of the assignor (not purporting to be by way of charge only) of any debt, or other legal thing in action, of which express notice in writing has been given to the debtor, trustee or other person from whom the assignor would have been entitled to claim such debt or thing in action, shall be and shall be deemed to have been effectual in law (subject to equities having priority over the right of the assignee) to pass and transfer from the date of such notice ...

The statutory requirements can be listed as follows:

(a) the assignment must be made in writing by the assignor;

(b) the assignment must, in substance, constitute a transfer of the right; and

(c) express notice in writing to the debtor or trustee (or, in this case, covenantor) must be given.

The legal requirements for the assignment of choses in action will apply where the benefit of the covenant is capable of passing under common law. Hence, where a successor in title taking a legal estate from the original covenantee wishes to enforce the benefit of a covenant against the original covenantor, and annexation under common law principles has not been satisfied, the benefit of the covenant may be expressly assigned in accordance with the above statutory requirements. On the other hand, where the successor in title to a covenantee wishes to enforce the benefit of a covenant against a successor in title to the covenantor, the equitable jurisdiction must be resorted to. If annexation of the benefit has not occurred according to the equitable principles, then the benefit of the covenant may be expressly assigned, provided the assignment satisfies the equitable criteria.

The requirements necessary to prove an express assignment of the benefit of a covenant in equity may be summarised as follows:

(a) the covenant itself, or the context in which the covenant was granted, must establish that the covenant was intended to benefit the land rather than the covenantee personally;

29 Property law statutes: WA, s 34; Qld, s 11; SA, s 29; Tas, s 60(2); NSW, s 23C.

(b) the assignment of the covenant must occur contemporaneously with the assignment of the benefited land, because the covenant can only be enforced over the benefited land and therefore they must be mutually conferred (*Re Union of London and Smith's Bank Ltd's Conveyance* [1933] Ch 611); and

(c) there must be adequate proof of an intention to assign the benefit of the covenant. Equity does not require any particular form. This requirement is generally satisfied where the assignment is set out in writing. Unlike the statutory position, however, proof of intention does not mean the assignor must give the covenantor express notice.

Once the benefit of a covenant has been assigned, the assignee may enforce it against the covenantor. It has been suggested that an express assignment of the benefit of a covenant, whether at law or in equity, will automatically result in the covenant being annexed to the land, so that it will pass with all future conveyances of the land (*Rogers v Hosegood* [1900] 2 Ch 388). This argument is based upon the notion that, once it is proven that the covenant is intended to pass with the land, annexation should be automatic. The concept has not been fully accepted in Australia although, if the statutory provisions are given a broader interpretation, it is possible that, once the requirements for an express assignment have been satisfied, the statute will automatically deem annexation to have occurred.[30]

12.6 Restrictive covenants and the Torrens system

The Torrens system of land registration operates to guarantee the security of the title for all persons dealing with registered interests. Covenants have, traditionally, created problems for the Torrens system because of the fact that the burden of a restrictive covenant may, in equity, be binding upon a piece of land without being set out in the title. The difficulty with allowing restrictive covenants to be registered is that, in essence, the covenant is a purely contractual obligation which simply attaches to the land. The Torrens system has attempted to alleviate the difficulties associated with covenants over Torrens title land by incorporating provisions like s 88 of the Transfer of Land Act 1958 (Vic),[31] which allows restrictive covenants to be notified upon the certificate of title of the burdened land. Section 88(1) reads as follows:

> The Registrar shall have power and shall be deemed always to have had power on the folio of the register for land subject to the burden of a restrictive

30 Note the discussion by Butt, P, in *Land Law*, 3rd edn, 1996, LBC, para 1748, where he notes that the 'judicial *dicta* supporting the "deferred annexation" argument are inferential only'.

31 See, also, Transfer of Land Act 1893 (WA), s 129A; Land Titles Act 1980 (Tas), ss 102–04; and Conveyancing Act 1919 (NSW), s 88(3)(a). No specific provisions are detailed in the applicable legislation in Qld, SA, ACT or NT. In these states, restrictive covenants may be protected through the application of a caveat.

> covenant to make a recording of such covenant and of any instrument purporting to create or affect the operation of such covenant, and when such covenant is released, varied or modified by agreement of all interested parties or by order of a competent court to delete or amend that recording.

Section 88(3) sets out that a recording in the register of any restrictive covenant shall give it no greater rights than it has under the instrument creating it. The combined effect of these provisions is to allow a restrictive covenant to be noted on the title of burdened land, but not to confer any registered, indefeasible status upon it. The covenant will simply operate as notification, so that all persons dealing with the burdened land will be aware of the existence of the covenant when searching the title. In order to be properly notified upon the title of the burdened land, a restrictive covenant should be created in writing – either on the actual transfer or through a separate deed – as the Registrar General will require a written document to attach to the title. Unlike easements, however, as the covenant is merely contractual, there is no requirement that the covenant be executed by deed to be legally enforceable.

There have been some difficulties concerning the enforcement of restrictive covenants where they have not been noted expressly on the title. As the Torrens system guarantees the conclusiveness of the register, it would be somewhat anomalous to subsequently hold that an unregistered restrictive covenant will be binding upon the new registered proprietor. In some cases, even where the restrictive covenant has been noted on the title, the full character of the restriction and the land it is purported to benefit is often not included. The matter has been raised in the Victorian Supreme Court in *Re Dennerstein* [1963] VR 688. On the facts of that decision, Dennerstein's land had previously constituted a part of the Como Estate, which, in 1911, vested in the trustees of the will of A. The estate was subdivided, and the majority of the lots were sold at auction. Each lot was sold subject to express building restrictions. On registration of the transfers to the purchasers, the restrictive covenant was noted on the appropriate certificate of title as an encumbrance. However, the title did not indicate the character of the restriction – in particular, the fact that it arose pursuant to provisions contained within a building scheme – and it did not indicate the character of the land which was to be benefited.

The issue in the case was whether the restriction bound successors in title to the burdened land. Whilst the covenant was noted on the title, it was argued that the register guarantees conclusive title, and purchasers should not be obliged to investigate beyond the register in order to appreciate the full character of the title. The court agreed with this. Hudson J concluded that notification of a restrictive covenant was not necessarily sufficient to bind a successor in title to the burdened land, because it often constituted insufficient notice. His Honour felt that a purchaser was not bound to carry out such inquiries and searches and make further deductions beyond the scope of the register. Even where further materials are available, they are often difficult to determine.

Hudson J made the following comments:

> In my view, a purchaser of land under the Transfer of Land Act is not bound to prosecute inquiries and searches and make deductions such as would be involved if Mr Searby's contentions were accepted. Even when all the materials and evidence in relation to the circumstances under which an estate has been subdivided and sold are available it is not by any means easy to determine whether the sale of allotments in the estate has been made under or pursuant to a common building scheme. To require a person interested in purchasing one of those allotments to make this determination after obtaining the necessary evidence perhaps years after the original sale if it is available would render conveyancing a hazardous and cumbersome operation, and, in the case of dealings in land under the operation of the Transfer of Land Act, would defeat the object of the Act and destroy in large measure the efficacy of the system sought to be established thereby.

On the facts, it was difficult to determine from the covenant noted on the title whether the sale of allotments in the estate had been made pursuant to a building scheme; to require a person interested in purchasing an allotment to make this determination, perhaps years after the original sale, would render conveyancing a hazardous and cumbersome operation and would defeat the purpose of the Torrens system. Hence, on the facts, a successor in title to the burdened land could only be bound by the restrictive covenant where the existence of the building scheme, the nature of the restrictions imposed thereunder, and the benefited and burdened lands affected by the scheme were clearly outlined. Other states have not expressly rejected this decision, although, in New South Wales, the statutory provisions entitling the notification of a restrictive covenant appear to have been given greater credence.[32]

Finally, it is possible that restrictive covenants could be registered over land where they are incorporated into other registrable proprietary rights (*Burke v Yurilla SA Pty Ltd* (1991) 56 SASR 382). Where registered as a part of a proprietary right, the registration will operate as notice to all persons dealing with the burdened land of the existence of a restrictive covenant.

12.7 Extinguishment and modification of covenants

12.7.1 Mutual ownership

One of the essential requirements for the enforceability of covenants is the separate ownership of the benefited and burdened land. Where each of these pieces of land become owned and possessed by the same person, a restrictive

32 See Conveyancing Act 1919 (NSW), s 88(3) and *Re Mack and the Conveyancing Act* [1975] 2 NSWLR 623.

covenant will automatically be extinguished.[33] It is important to note that a restrictive covenant will not be extinguished where one person owns both lands but does not occupy both lands (*Post Investments Pty Ltd v Wilson* (1990) 26 NSWLR 598).

For example, A owns two blocks of land and leases one block out to B. Consequently, A owns and possesses one block of land and owns but does not possess the other, because B is in possession. At the time of entering the lease, B covenants with A not to use the land for any other purpose than a private dwelling. The restrictive covenant between A and B is enforceable because, even though A *owns* both blocks of land, A does not *possess* both pieces of land, and therefore is still reliant upon the covenant to enforce the restriction. When the lease has expired and possession of the second block of land reverts to A, there will no longer be any need for the covenant, as A does not have to enforce a restriction over himself. Hence, when the lease expires, the restrictive covenant will be automatically extinguished.

Similarly, if only a part of the burdened land, but not the whole of it, is acquired by the holder of the benefited land, the covenant will only be extinguished to the extent of the ownership. If the restrictive covenant does not affect the part of the land which has been acquired it will not be extinguished at all, whereas, if the restrictive covenant affects the whole of the burdened land, it will not apply to the land acquired but will remain binding upon the rest of the land (*Gyarfas v Bray* (1989) 4 BPR 9736).

12.7.2 Agreement

A covenant may be modified or discharged where both parties expressly or impliedly agree to it, provided they are fully entitled to the land and are of full age and capacity. The agreement may be expressly executed by both parties in writing and subsequently placed within the chain of title or lodged with the DRS for registration or, under Torrens title land, lodged with the Registrar so that any restrictive covenant noted on the title may be properly discharged. See s 88(1B) of the Transfer of Land Act (Vic) 1958 and equivalent provisions in other states.[34]

A covenant may be impliedly modified or discharged where it can be proven that the parties, through a course of conduct, intended to do so. For example, where the owner of benefited land has submitted to a continual course of usage which is completely inconsistent with the nature of the

33 Although, note that in New South Wales and Tasmania, this common law principle has been abrogated by statute – Conveyancing Act 1919 (NSW), s 88B(3)(c) and Land Titles Act 1980 (Tas), s 103.

34 See, especially, Conveyancing Act 1919 (NSW), s 88(1)(c), which sets out that no restrictive covenant will be enforceable against a successor in title unless it clearly sets out the persons having the right to release, vary or modify the restriction, other than those having a right by law to do so.

restrictive covenant, or the owner has consistently ignored breaches of the covenant, it may be argued that the owner has impliedly consented or acquiesced to a variation or discharge of the covenant. Mere inactivity will not necessarily amount to a discharge, as it must be proven that some positive inconsistency exists, sufficient to constitute an understanding or belief on the part of the burdened land owner that the covenant has been modified or discharged (*Bohn v Miller Brothers Pty Ltd* [1953] VLR 354). The equitable principles relating to laches or acquiescence will also be applicable in this context.

12.7.3 Bona fide *purchaser for value without notice*

A restrictive covenant will not be enforceable against a successor in title who is a *bona fide* purchaser for value without notice. As discussed in para 12.4, the foundation of the *Tulk v Moxhay* principle, which results in the enforceability of the burden of a covenant against a successor in title, is that the successor in title takes with notice of the existence of the burden. Where no notice exists, equity will not enforce the burden. In order to ensure that a purchaser acquires proper notice of the burdened land, the restriction should be either registered with the DRS or a copy of it included in the chain of title where the land is old title land or properly noted upon the register where the land is Torrens title land. Notice in this regard includes both actual and constructive notice: see para 9.4.3.

12.7.4 Relevant statutory provisions

A number of statutory provision deal with the issue of extinguishing restrictive covenants. In Victoria, s 84(1) of the Property Law Act 1958 sets out:

> The court shall have power from time to time on the application of any person interested in any land affected by any restriction arising under covenant ... by order wholly or partially to discharge or modify any such restriction (subject or not to the payment by the applicant of compensation to any person suffering loss in consequence of the order) upon being satisfied:
>
> (a) that by reason of changes in the character of the property or the neighbourhood or other circumstances of the case which the court deems material the restriction ought to be deemed obsolete or that the continued existence thereof would impede the reasonable user of the land without securing practical benefits to other persons or (as the case may be) would unless modified so impede such user; or
>
> (b) that the persons of full age and capacity for the time being or from time to time entitled to the benefit of the restriction whether in respect of estates in fee simple or any lesser estates or interests in the property to which the benefit of the restriction is annexed have agreed either expressly or by implication by their acts or omissions to the same being discharged or modified; or

(c) that the proposed discharge or modification will not substantially injure the persons entitled to the benefit of the restriction.[35]

The legislation confers a fairly broad discretion to discharge a covenant where it is claimed to be obsolete. However, an applicant should clearly establish that the covenant is either outdated or no longer beneficial or advantageous to the benefited land before it may come within the ambit of s 84(1)(a).

The onus of establishing the appropriate ground is upon the applicant and, if the case is ambiguous, a court is unlikely to modify or extinguish the covenant. Even where a ground is established, the court retains a general discretion to refuse an application (*Post Investments Pty Ltd v Wilson* (1990) 26 NSWLR 598). Generally speaking, a court will exercise discretion with respect to successors in title to the burdened land. However, where an original covenantor makes an application, a court may be more reluctant to allow the statutory provisions to overturn a valid and enforceable contractual arrangement (*Re Makin* [1966] VR 494). Courts are not obliged to take into account external factors in exercising their discretion, provided one of the established grounds has been made out. Hence, further considerations such as hardship, the effect on the value of the land, environmental factors and town planning considerations do not have to be taken into account, although a court may, in its residual discretion, have regard for such issues. Where a ground for discharge or modification is upheld, the court may award appropriate compensation to be paid by the applicant to the person entitled to the benefit of the restriction where it can be proven that the order would cause that person loss.

12.8 Remedies

Usual contractual remedies apply to covenants; hence, where a breach of covenant can be established, a damages award may be issued. The original covenantee may claim damages for a breach, as may a successor in title where the benefit of the covenant is held to have run with the land (*Smith and Snipes Hall Farm Ltd v River Douglas Catchment Board* [1949] KB 500, CA). The measure of damages will depend upon the nature of the breach, but generally damages will include all loss flowing from the breach of covenant so that the covenantee is restored to the position he was in prior to the breach. Damages may include loss actually incurred as a result of the breach as well as relevant loss of bargain damages, although this will depend upon the individual circumstances. Where it cannot be proven that the land of the covenantee has

35 Relevant statutory provisions in other states are as follows: Conveyancing Act 1919 (NSW), s 89(1); Transfer of Land Act 1893 (WA), s 129(c); Property Law Act 1974 (Qld), s 181; Conveyancing and Law of Property Act 1884 (Tas), s 84c(1). The Qld and Tas legislation add grounds concerning public policy and where the covenant no longer secures any substantial value or benefit to the land, and the power appears to allow courts to impose conditions upon orders made, where it is proven that it would be reasonable to do so.

been reduced in value, it may be that under common law, the only damages available will be those relating to the direct financial expenses incurred – and nothing further (*Surrey County Council v Bredero Homes Ltd* [1993] 1 WLR 1361).

Where the covenant is enforceable in equity, only equitable remedies will be available. Hence, an applicant may seek to have the covenant specifically enforced where damages prove inadequate and all of the discretionary requirements for the issuing of such a decree have been satisfied. Alternatively, an applicant may seek injunctive relief in the equitable jurisdiction in the form of a mandatory injunction where the breach has already occurred or a *quia timet* injunction where an applicant has firm grounds for believing that a breach may occur in the future. Pecuniary relief in the form of Lord Cairns Act damages[36] may also be awarded in addition to, or substitution of, injunctive relief or a decree of specific performance. Of course, as with all equitable remedies, usual equitable discretions will apply, so that hardship, laches, conduct of the applicant and the form of relief applied for will be relevant considerations.

12.9 Schemes of development

Modern society has witnessed the inception of large scale development projects which often include what may be described as 'building schemes'. These schemes routinely include restrictive covenants over each portion of land, aimed at sustaining the value, character and amenity of the land. The purpose of these restrictions is to provide reciprocal benefits and burdens to each owner of the block in order to create a systemised land development scheme. Due to the difficulties associated with the application of common law and equitable rules of annexation and assignment of restrictive covenants, special rules have been introduced to deal with these schemes. The problem with the application of the 'usual' rules to subdivided land is best highlighted through an example:

X, the owner of a large block of land, subdivides the land in order to create a number of blocks, and wants to create a 'scheme of development'. X wants to impose restrictive covenants over each block relating to the usage of the land, in order to preserve its character and amenity. The benefit of the covenant is for X, as owner of all the blocks, and all of the subsequent owners of each block. X sells block 1 to Y, who enters into the covenant. X sells block 2 to W, who enters into the covenant. The benefit of the covenant with respect to block 2 is said to be annexed to block 1. However, the difficulty is that, at that point, X does not own block 1 – Y does. Therefore, under general law principles, the benefit cannot be annexed and Y cannot enforce the covenant against W and so forth.

36 Based upon the Chancery Amendment Act 1858 (UK), s 2.

The 'building scheme' rules will only apply where it can be firmly established that a 'scheme of development' exists. The four primary characteristics of schemes of development were set out by Parker J in *Elliston v Reacher* [1908] 2 Ch 374 (p 384):

(a) both the plaintiffs and the defendants must derive title from a common vendor;

(b) prior to selling the lands held by the plaintiffs and defendants, the vendor laid out his estate, or a defined portion, for sale in lots subject to restrictions intended to be imposed on all the lots;

(c) that these restrictions were intended by the common vendor to be and were for the benefit of all the lots intended to be sold;

(d) that both the plaintiffs and defendants, or their predecessors in title, purchased their lots from the common vendor upon the footing that the restrictions subject to which the purchasers were made were to enure for the benefit of the other lots included in the general scheme whether or not they were also to enure for the benefit of other lands retained by the vendors. This requirement will generally be implied where the other three elements have been satisfied.[37]

Where these four requirements can be proven and a scheme of development is established, the equitable jurisdiction will allow the restrictive covenants to be enforced against successors in title, whatever the date of the actual purchase of land may have been. Hence, even where the covenantee does not hold any interest in land, the benefit of the covenant may still accrue. Where the lots are sold over a period of time, equity may still enforce restrictive covenants – it is not necessary to prove that, at the date of entering into the covenant, the owner of the blocks owns the particular block to which the benefit of the covenant is attached. The important element is intention: it must be established that the common vendor intended each of the lots to acquire the benefit of the restriction and, conversely, to be bound by the restriction. The key issue in proving a scheme is establishing an intention to create a 'mutual reciprocity' and, once this can be proven, a court will generally uphold the enforceability of the covenants despite the inherent difficulties under 'usual' restrictive covenant principles (*Baxter v Four Oaks Properties Ltd* [1965] Ch 816).

Where the scheme of development applies to Torrens title land, the purchaser must be able to discover the nature of the scheme from the document lodged for notification with the Register (*Re Dennerstein* [1963] VR 688).

Finally, whilst the general law principles set out that a restrictive covenant will be extinguished where one person acquires mutual ownership of both the burdened and the benefited land, this principle is inapplicable to schemes of development because they are enforceable on the basis of an intention to

37 These elements have now been accepted in Australia. See *Cousin v Grant* (1991) 103 FLR 236.

confer 'reciprocal rights'; this intention should not be thwarted merely because at some stage each block of land was held by a common owner: to do so would be to undermine the whole basis of the scheme (*Texaco Antilles Ltd v Kernochan* [1973] AC 609).

CHAPTER 13

EASEMENTS

13.1 Introduction

An easement is an intangible right over land, traditionally classified as a form of real property. Easements are also known as 'incorporeal hereditaments'. Incorporeal hereditament is an old Roman term, used to describe rights which do not have any substantial existence but which are nevertheless proprietary because they relate to and are enforceable over real property and are capable of being inherited. Easements are enforceable through real actions; hence, despite their incorporeal nature, they are considered to constitute a form of real property, because the owner of land which is subject to the benefit of an easement is entitled to enforce the right which is the subject matter of the easement against the owner of the burdened land and this right is enforceable against the rest of the world. Easements come in a variety of forms and cover an increasing range of rights. One of the primary and defining characteristics of the easement is that it does not constitute a possessory right; the holder of an easement may exercise certain rights over the land, but those rights are not possessory. Where the right to take possession of land is conferred, the right is properly described as a lease rather than an easement.

Easements have been recognised since medieval times, as the terminology in this area of law suggests. However, much of the legal development did not occur until necessitated by the major social developments and upheavals of the 18th and 19th centuries.[1] With increasing population, higher density living and an emerging diversity of land usage, it became necessary to introduce specific legal principles for the creation and enforcement of additional rights over land. The proper elaboration of such principles was vitally important in order to cater for the new economic needs of society; easements helped sustain and encourage a systemised and progressive development of residential and industrial land usage. Easements were an important part of the industrial revolution because of the diversity of rights they could represent and because of the status of the right. Unlike its close relative, the restrictive covenant, the easement is a proprietary creature; once created, it will confer an enduring and enforceable right upon the holder against the rest of the world.

Basically, an easement constitutes an additional right which attaches to one piece of land in order to confer a specific privilege or additional benefit over another piece of land. This privilege is suffered by the 'servient tenement'

1 See, generally, Holdsworth, W, *An Historical Introduction to Land Law*, 1972, OUP.

holder and enjoyed by the 'dominant tenement' holder. The main function of the easement is to provide the dominant tenement holder with a right which is exercisable over the servient tenement which is important and necessary for the proper enjoyment of the dominant tenement, but which does not amount to an automatic, natural right enjoyed by all land owners. Two classic forms of easement are the right of way and the right of support. The right of way entitles the holder to access her land via a pathway or entrance on the servient tenement. The right of support entitles the holder to prevent the owner of the servient tenement from removing a supporting wall or fence. There are many other rights which may form the subject matter of an easement, although some rights are so vague, indistinct and obtuse that they are incapable of doing so. In order to constitute an easement, the right has not only to provide some additional privilege to the dominant tenement holder, it must confer a benefit which is properly identifiable and able to be enforced against the servient tenement. The type of rights which easements represent inevitably vary with the changing social milieu. As noted by Lord St Leonards in 1852, in *Dyce v Hay* 1 Macq HL, p 312: 'The category of servitudes and easements must alter and expand with the changes that take place in the circumstances of mankind.'

13.2 Proprietary nature of easements

13.2.1 Easements distinguished from other similar rights

A 'natural' right is a right which naturally flows with, or is incidental to, the ownership of an estate or interest in the land; it is a right which is an automatic extension of an estate in land and therefore does not need to be additionally created. Classic examples of natural rights include the right to the natural flow of water from an established source (*Swindon Waterworks Co Ltd v Wilts and Berks Canal Navigation Co* (1875) LR 7 HL 697) and the right to use and enjoy the land, the right to shade under a tree on the land and the right to produce grown on the land. There is no need to create additional easement rights in circumstances where such rights are already naturally conferred.

Whilst, conceptually, easements are similar to restrictive covenants, there is a pivotal difference between the two. Restrictive covenants are contractual, and therefore are primarily only enforceable *in personam*, whereas an easement confers an *in rem* right which is enforceable against the rest of the world. Being proprietary in nature, easements do not need to be annexed to the land or to satisfy particular equitable tests in order to run with the land: all that needs to be established is that the requirements for a valid easement exist and that the easement has been properly created.

Furthermore, easements generally confer different types of rights from those applicable to restrictive covenants. In order to be enforceable in equity, a covenant must be restrictive, whereas an easement may be positive or negative in nature, the primary requirement being that it must accommodate the dominant tenement and be properly defined. Easements tend to confer rights specifically related to the usage of the dominant tenement, whereas restrictive covenants tend to impose prohibitions restricting the usage of the burdened land but leaving the usage of the benefited land unaffected.

An easement also differs from a *profit à prendre*. A *profit à prendre* is similar to an easement in that it confers a right, but the right is to take some part of the soil, minerals or natural produce upon the land (*Manning v Wasdale* (1836) 5 Ad & E 758). A *profit* is essentially a right to take tangible produce from the land itself rather than a right of usage. Unlike easements, a *profit à prendre* may exist privately or be mutually shared amongst a range of holders. Furthermore, a *profit à prendre* may be imposed over specific land for the benefit of a dominant tenement and, in such case, is referred to as an 'appurtenant *profit*' or, alternatively, it may exist as a '*profit* in gross' where it provides no identifiable benefit for a dominant tenement. *Profits* may be expressly or impliedly created under common law or equity, as is the case with easements. However, the principles relating to implied easements of necessity would not apply to the *profits* because the *profit* is regarded as an extraneous right and not one of exigency.

A *profit à prendre* cannot exist unless it directly relates to the character of the land itself or the flora, fauna or produce of the land, the *profit* will be invalid unless it refers to this 'produce' of the land. Classic examples of *profits* include the right to chop down firewood and the right to gather fruit or vegetables from the land. The right must involve the taking of specific produce from the land rather than a right to produce upon the land because the *profit* is essentially a right to take from the land, not a right to occupy and use the land (*Permanent Trustee Australia Ltd v Shand* (1992) 27 NSWLR 426).

Easements differ from licences because a licence is non-proprietary and merely confers permission to enter land; a licence is not a proprietary right to actually use the land. Furthermore, licences may be revoked, where the circumstances require it, whereas, as an easement constitutes a proprietary interest, once properly created, it cannot be unilaterally revoked.

Finally, an easement differs from a lease because, as noted above, the defining feature of an incorporeal hereditament is that it does not confer any right to possession. A lease constitutes a non-freehold estate which will exist for a specified duration and which confers exclusive possession upon the lessee for that period of time. An easement constitutes a right of usage over the land, which may exist indefinitely but which cannot amount to a right to confer exclusive possession. An easement is an 'additional' right over land – the right to possess land is a component of the freehold estate. Any easement which attempted to confer a right to exclusive possession may either be struck down or, in substance, it may be read as creating a lease.

13.2.2 *Positive and negative easements*

Easement rights may be positive or negative in nature. Positive easements entitle the dominant tenement holder to carry out certain activities or to conduct a particular usage over the servient tenement. Examples of positive easements include rights of way, a right to use and enjoy parklands, and a right to enter the servient land to install and maintain sewerage pipes. On the other hand, negative easements are easements which, in substance, have the effect of circumscribing the behaviour of the servient tenement holder. A negative easement constitutes a restriction on the proprietary rights of the servient tenement holder. A classic example is the right of support, others include a right to the flow of air through a defined aperture, and the right of the dominant tenement holder to receive light. Whilst, in form, a negative easement may appear to confer positive rights upon the dominant tenement holder, in substance the right is actually negative as it restricts the activities of the servient tenement holder. For example, a right to support from a building effectively precludes the servient tenement holder from demolishing the building or in any way reconstructing the building so as to leave the adjoining building unsupported.

One of the criticisms that is often levelled at negative easements is that they interfere with the fundamental proprietary right of the servient tenement holder to use and enjoy the land. Where this interference is too extensive, courts have held, for policy reasons, that the easement should not be enforced. The classic decision on this is *Phipps v Pears* [1965] 1 QB 76. On the facts of that case, the owner of two adjoining houses decided to demolish one of them and build a new house which directly supported the adjoining house and prevented one side of the wall from having to be weatherproofed. Subsequently, the properties were conveyed to different purchasers. The purchaser of one of the properties proceeded to demolish his property in accordance with a directive from the local council. The effect of this demolition was to leave the adjoining wall, which was not weatherproofed, unsupported and vulnerable to the elements. The plaintiff was the purchaser of the adjoining house, and as the wall suffered damage due to exposure, he argued that he held an implied easement entitling him to protection from the weather and the neighbouring defendant had breached this easement.

The Court of Appeal concluded that no such easement existed. Lord Denning felt that a right to protection from the weather was not an easement which was known by the law and, furthermore, was not one which the courts were prepared to protect. His Lordship felt that such a right would, in substance, amount to a negative easement, severely restricting the right of the servient tenement holder to use and enjoy the land as he or she saw fit. According to his Lordship, it would be unfair to enforce such rights because of the negative effect they would have upon residential development, in particular, the right to redevelop and redesign property. Furthermore, on the facts, it would have been unfair to hold the defendant liable to a breach of an implied covenant when the demolition itself was a result of a governmental directive. Hence, it would seem that the enforceability of any new right which amounts to a negative easement will be approached with caution by the courts.

The judgment of Lord Denning in *Phipps* may be criticised on the ground that it overlooks the fact that restrictions can be imposed upon landowners in the form of restrictive covenants. Whilst this may be true, it is important to remember that the prohibitions imposed by restrictive covenants are quite different in form and scope to negative easements. A restrictive covenant is a contractual prohibition, and may only be enforceable against a successor in title to the covenantor where the successor in title takes with notice of its existence and the restriction identifies and benefits particular land. Further, unlike easements, restrictive covenants cannot be implied, they must be expressly created. A negative easement, on the other hand, where upheld, creates a proprietary right which may endure, despite the fact that the servient tenement holder has no notice of its existence. Whilst the negative easement must identify and benefit the dominant tenement, it is enforceable as an incorporeal hereditament, not as a contractual right. Hence, it may be argued that courts are right to be circumspect when examining the enforceability of new forms of negative easements, because the consequences can be quite deleterious upon the servient tenement holder. This issue may take on an increasing significance with the acceleration of high density, inner city living where basic rights such as plants, trees, garden and airspace are becoming a rarity.

13.3 Requirements for a valid easement

13.3.1 Dominant and servient tenement

Before a valid easement can be recognised, it must be established that it attaches to a servient tenement for the benefit of a dominant tenement. The servient tenement is the land which is burdened by the easement. The dominant tenement is the land which is benefited by the easement. The dominant tenement does not, however, have to be land. it is possible for an easement to exist which benefits another easement. Hence the rule is not restricted to tangible forms of property (*Hanbury v Jenkins* [1901] 2 Ch 401).

If it is established that there is no dominant tenement, the easement is known as an 'easement in gross'. The common law will not enforce an easement in gross because the courts have held that, where there is no benefited land, the right is no different from a personal licence. An easement is an intangible right which exists for the benefit of land and, if the land does not exist, the right cannot be properly described as proprietary. As noted by Cresswell J in *Ackroyd v Smith* (1850) 10 CB 164, pp 187–88:

> ... a right unconnected with the enjoyment or occupation of the land cannot be annexed as an incident to it; nor can a way appendant to a house or land be granted away, or made in gross; for, no one can have such a way but he who has the land to which it is appendant. If a way be granted in gross, it is personal only, and cannot be assigned ... It is not in the power of a vendor to create rights not connected with the use or enjoyment of the land, and annex them to it.

There has, however, been some debate concerning the validity of easements in gross. It has been argued that if it is possible to create a *profit à prendre* in gross and for certain statutory bodies to create easements in gross, the common law should not adopt such a prohibitive stance.[2] Certainly, in some circumstances, it may be unfair to refuse the enforcement of a right which provides a clear 'land benefit' to a person simply because the benefit does not seem to attach to any particular land. For example, it may be unjust and too pedantic to refuse to recognise that a right to land an aircraft over suitable land may constitute an easement simply because it is the aircraft and the safety of the passengers that will benefit rather than any identifiable dominant tenement. On the other hand, if the right is, in substance, personal in nature, it may be better to create and enforce it as a personal licence rather than artificially extend the category of easements. Many new easements confer mutual personal and proprietary benefits but are classified as 'easements' because of the greater advantages such a classification confers (*Evanel Pty Ltd v Nelson* [1995] NSW Conv R 55-759).

There are a number of statutes entitling governmental bodies to enforce easements in gross. In Victoria, s 187A of the Local Government Act 1989 entitles a council to enforce an easement in gross.[3] The section reads as follows:

> If any right in the nature of an easement or purporting to be an easement or an irrevocable licence is or has been acquired by a council whether before or after the commencement of the Local Government Act 1958, the right is deemed for all purposes to be and to have been an easement even if there is no land vested in the council which is benefited by the right.

Whilst a dominant tenement must exist before an easement will be enforceable under common law, it does not need to be expressly defined in the easement, provided it can be properly inferred from all of the circumstances.[4] As noted by Upjohn LJ in *Johnstone v Holdway* [1963] 1 QB 601 (p 612):

---

2 See, further, Sturley, S, 'Easements in gross' (1980) LQR 557 and McLean, D, 'The nature of an easement' (1966) 5 University of Western Ontario Law Rev 32. Note, also, that easements in gross are enforced in the United States – but not in any other common law country.

3 See, also, Conveyancing and Law of Property Act 1884 (Tas), s 90A(1); Law of Property Act 1936 (SA), s 41a; Conveyancing Act 1919 (NSW), s 88A(1) on the issue of the enforceability of easements in gross by the Crown or local councils

4 See, also, *Re Maiorana and the Conveyancing Act* (1970) 92 WN (NSW) 365.

> In our judgment, it is a question of construction of the deed creating a right of way as to what is the dominant tenement for the benefit of which the right of way is granted and to which the right of way is appurtenant. In construing the deed, the court is entitled to have evidence of all material facts at the time of the execution of the deed, so as to place the court in the situation of the parties.

This principle has now been endorsed by statute with respect to the creation of rights of way.[5] Section 197 of the Property Law Act 1958 (Vic) sets out:

> Whenever in any conveyance of land or in any deed of grant a right to use any road or way has been granted to the purchaser or to the grantee his heirs and assigns, such right, although it be not granted into, out of and from the land conveyed to the purchaser, or described in the deed as owned by the grantee, shall nevertheless be deemed to be a right appurtenant to the land conveyed, or owned, as the case may be, and every part thereof and not a right in gross.

13.3.2 The easement must accommodate the dominant tenement

An easement will only be enforceable at law where it can be proven that the easement operates to provide a benefit to the dominant tenement. Where the benefit that is provided is personal in nature or does not sufficiently attach to the dominant tenement, the right will be unenforceable as an easement, because the connection to the land will be insufficient. As the basis of the easement is an incorporeal right over land, it is not within the power of a grantee to create an easement conferring rights not related to the land. In such a situation, the right cannot be truly described as an easement. This has been clearly established in the classic authority, *Ackroyd v Smith* (1850) 10 CB 164. In that case, it was held that an attempt to confer rights upon a party which are unconnected with the use and enjoyment of the land will merely operate as a licence or a covenant on the part of the grantors and will create no proprietary right in the form of an easement.

An easement can only accommodate the dominant tenement where there is a sufficient degree of proximity between the dominant and servient tenement. If the tenements are a long distance apart, it will be difficult to establish that the dominant tenement has received a benefit from land. This does not mean that the dominant and servient tenements must be physically contiguous; they must, however, be sufficiently proximate so that the right attaching to the burdened land provides an active ascertainable benefit to the dominant tenement (*Todrick v Western National Omnibus Co Ltd* [1934] Ch 561).

An easement can only accommodate the dominant tenement where the right relates to the use and enjoyment of the land and not the personal enjoyment of the owner. This is clearly revealed in the decision of *Hill v Tupper* (1863) 2 H & C 121; 159 ER 51. On the facts of that case, the right conferred was a right to use and enjoy boats on a canal which abutted the dominant

---

5 Cf the New South Wales position in the Conveyancing Act 1919, s 88.

tenement. The court held that such a right was primarily associated with personal pleasure and, as such, was unconnected with the physical enjoyment of the land itself.

It is not necessary for the owner of the dominant tenement to acquire a benefit from the easement alone; where a right benefits the dominant tenement as well as persons unconnected with the ownership of the land, the right may still constitute an easement (*Re Ellenborough Park* [1956] 1 Ch 131). Furthermore, it will be sufficient for the right to accommodate a business conducted on the land, as this is perceived to be a right which actually provides a benefit to the dominant tenement (*Copeland v Greenhalf* [1952] 1 Ch 488).

A right may accommodate the dominant tenement despite the fact that it only provides a benefit to a small portion of the land. Hence, for example, a right of way which benefits only a small portion of the overall dominant tenement can still constitute an easement. As noted by Hood J in *Registrar of Titles ex p Waddington* [1917] VLR 603 (p 606): 'It is difficult to see what benefit can be derived in the enjoyment of a bit of land one link square from a right of carriageway over an adjacent street. But such a benefit is not impossible.'

This has been logically extended to apply to subdivided land. In *Gallagher v Rainbow* (1994) 68 ALJR 512, the court held that there will be a presumption that an easement which benefits the whole dominant tenement will also benefit each of its subdivided parts unless the easement, upon a proper construction, was only intended to benefit the dominant tenement in its original entirety.

13.3.3 Separate ownership of the dominant and servient tenements

Where one person owns and possesses both the dominant and servient tenements, there can be no easement; there is no need to confer additional proprietary rights over land already owned; an owner can, for example, exercise a right of way over land which she herself owns. It is nonsensical to create an easement over your own land – it is a superfluous right. As noted by Lord Esher MR in *Metropolitan Railway Co v Fowler* [1892] 1 QB 165, 'You cannot have an easement over your own land'.

Where one person owns both tenements but does not possess both, an easement may arise. Hence, where the owner of the servient tenement leases out the dominant tenement, the dominant tenement holder may acquire easement rights over the servient tenement for the duration of the lease. Upon the expiration of the lease, these rights will expire. There are some statutory provisions dealing with subdivision and strata title ownership in this respect. In New South Wales, an easement may be created where a plan of subdivision is registered, despite the fact that ownership to both tenements is vested in one person (s 88B(3) of the Conveyancing Act 1919 (NSW)).[6] In Tasmania, implied or statutory easements created over strata title flats will not be destroyed where ownership to both tenements is vested in one person; such easements shall be suspended for the duration of mutual ownership and may be revived once mutual ownership is extinguished (s 75ZB of the Conveyancing and Law of Property Act 1884 (Tas)).

13.3.4 The easement must be capable of forming the subject matter of a grant

A right which is vague, obscure and indistinct may not constitute a valid easement because such rights do not, in substance, confer a definitive benefit upon the dominant tenement. Particular types of rights have been held to offend this requirement. Rights of *ius spatiandi*, that is, rights conferring the privilege of wandering over land, have traditionally been held to be incapable of forming the subject matter of an easement. Such rights are usually distinguished from rights to use and enjoy garden land and facilities. In *Re Ellenborough Park* [1956] 1 Ch 131, it was held that the right to enjoy the garden in the square known as Ellenborough Park, which was granted to all the tenants in common owning land around the park, constituted a valid easement because a right to use and enjoy the garden was a valid form of recreation over land and should be contrasted from a mere right to roam and wonder over the land. This decision was subsequently confirmed in *Riley v Pentilla* [1957] VR 547.

In *Evanel Pty Ltd v Nelson* [1995] NSW Conv R 55–759, the court held that a right, described as a 'right of footway' over the garden, was capable of forming the subject matter of an easement. This was so despite the fact that the right was limited to a specific land and was described in restrictive terms as a right of footway.

As with rights of *ius spatiandi*, rights of pure recreation had traditionally been held to be incapable of forming the subject matter of an easement (*Mounsey v Ismay* (1865) 3 H & C 486; 159 ER 621). The rationale seems to be that such rights are flimsy and insubstantial and provide little definable benefit to the dominant tenement. Nevertheless, as society changes and greater emphasis and importance are placed upon recreational facilities, the basis of this rule is being reassessed. Certainly, in *Evanel Pty Ltd v Nelson* [1995] NSW Conv R 55–759, the court emphasised the fact that a right to access garden facilities, whether by way of a footway or otherwise, is very closely linked to general rights of recreation; such rights can confer an important benefit upon land, particularly in high density areas and housing development estates where shared recreational facilities are regarded as an essential component of land ownership.

6 A similar provision exists under the Land Title Act 1994 (Qld), s 86.

In *City Developments Pty Ltd v Registrar General of Northern Territory* [2000] 135 NTR, sections of land adjoining a natural lake and foreshore land received grants of easement, which were registered. Conditions of the grants of easement included that covenantee was authorised by the grantee to enter upon and use the land burdened by the easement for private recreational purposes and, *inter alia*, have free and uninterrupted passage across and use of the grantor's land, and the right to leave boats on the lake. The claimants argued the easement did not benefit the land, but individuals; and that the term 'private recreational purposes' was too vague to form the subject matter of a grant of easement. The Supreme Court of the Northern Territory upheld the validity of the right as an easement and held that there is no reason in law why an easement cannot be granted for recreational purposes – which means the action of recreating (oneself or another) or fact of being recreated, by some pleasant occupation, pastime or amusement. The term 'recreational purpose' is to be construed sensibly and reasonably in the context of rural lakeside recreation and can therefore include walking across and around the lands surrounding the lake, swimming and boating and recreational activities such as photography, birdwatching and other passive, recreational pursuits. The court noted that *jus spatiandi* – or wandering at large – is simply one method of exercising a right of enjoyment over a lakeside garden and the existence of this method should not automatically mean that a recreational easement is incapable of forming the subject matter of a grant.

13.4 Creating easements

13.4.1 Legal and equitable easements

An easement may be expressly created at law or in equity. For a legal easement to exist, s 52(1) of the Property Law Act 1958 (Vic) requires the easement to be set out in the form of a deed.[7] Where the easement relates to Torrens title land, s 40(2) of the Transfer of Land Act 1958 (Vic) sets out that the registration of the easement will deem the instrument to take effect as if it were a deed, even if it has not been created pursuant to a deed.[8]

Where an easement is not created pursuant to a deed, or remains unregistered, it may be enforceable in the equity jurisdiction in a number of situations. Where a valid and enforceable agreement to create an easement is entered into by two parties, equity may enforce the easement where common law would not because of a failure to comply with the statutory formalities. Hence, if a vendor of land agrees as a term under a contract of sale to confer a right of way over his land to the purchaser of adjoining land, and the contract

7 For other states, see property law statutes: WA, s 33; Tas, s 60(1); SA, s 28; NSW, s 23B.

8 For other states, see Torrens legislation: WA, s 85; SA, s 57; Qld, s 161; Tas, s 48(7); ACT, s 48(4); NT, s 57; NSW, s 23(11).

is valid and enforceable, the purchaser may enforce the easement in equity (*Walsh v Lonsdale* (1882) 21 Ch D 9). It would need to be established that the contract was in writing in order to satisfy s 126 of the Instruments Act 1958 (Vic) which sets out that all contracts for the sale or other disposition of interests in land must be in writing, signed by the person to be charged, or a lawfully authorised person.[9]

Alternatively, easements may be enforceable in equity on the basis of proprietary estoppel or part performance. In a situation where the owner of a servient tenement has agreed with the owner of a dominant tenement to grant an easement and, in accordance with that agreement, the dominant tenement holder has exercised rights over the servient land with the approval of the servient tenement owner, the easement may be enforceable in equity despite the fact that it does not constitute a deed or, if Torrens title, has not been registered, so as to confer legal title. Similarly, if the owner of the servient tenement has encouraged the owner of the dominant tenement holder to believe that an easement has been granted, the dominant tenement holder may bring an action claiming the servient tenement is estopped from denying the existence of the easement on the basis of the principles set out in *Walton Stores (Interstate) Ltd v Maher* (1988) 164 CLR 387.

The creation of an easement by estoppel was evidenced in *Dabbs v Seaman* (1925) 36 CLR 538. On the facts of that case, Seaman purchased land which he subsequently subdivided into two one acre lots and sold the eastern block to Smith, and, in the conveyance, described the land as bounded on one side by a 20 foot lane which formed another part of Seaman's land. The certificate of title received by Smith showed that his land abutted the lane. Seaman subsequently purchased a strip of land along another road which provided alternative access to the northern portion of his land, so that the land reserve in the 20 foot lane was no longer necessary. Nevertheless, the land was too narrow to sell; therefore, Seaman purchased a larger block of land to the west of the strip with the intention of consolidating both blocks to create a larger block for sale. Meanwhile, Smith died and devised the land to D, and the certificate of title referred to a 20 foot lane without any mention of an easement over the lane. D tried to purchase the lane from Seaman but was unsuccessful. Seaman then applied to consolidate the two titles and for the deletion of the reference to the lane on D's title. D would not agree to this. Seaman sought a declaration that no right of way over the land existed in favour of D, and therefore that he should be able to consolidate both titles. D appealed to the High Court, and the appeal was upheld. One of the grounds for upholding the appeal was that Seaman was estopped from denying the existence of the easement which he had helped to construct when selling the land to Smith. The court noted that where a person holds good title pursuant

9 See property law statutes: Qld, s 59; SA, s 26 and NSW, s 54A. In WA, see Statute of Frauds 1667, as amended by the Law Reform (Statute of Frauds) Act 1962.

to an estoppel claim, he or she can give good title to a subsequent purchaser even where the purchaser takes with knowledge of the circumstances raising the estoppel (*Sarat Chunder Dey v Chunder Laha* (1892) LR 19). See, also, 13.4.4 and 13.6 on *Dabbs v Seaman*.

13.4.2 *Express grants*

Apart from the jurisdictional enforceability of an easement, consideration needs to be given to the way in which the easement is created. An easement which is expressly conferred to a purchaser of land at the time of purchase is commonly referred to as an 'express grant'. A grant will arise in any circumstance where the holder of the servient tenement confers a right to the holder of the dominant tenement. The grant will be express in circumstances where the grant has been directly referred to. Hence, a vendor may expressly confer a right upon a purchaser in order to ensure that the purchaser is able to enjoy the same rights as he did whilst owner.

For example, X owns two blocks of land adjoining each other; the right to access block 1 can only be achieved by following a pathway across block 2. X decides to sell block 1 and, as a part of the contract of sale, agrees to confer a right of way over block 2 – in the same form that X, as owner, had used – to the new purchaser. In order to confer this right, X enters into an express agreement to confer the right, and the deed is properly executed expressly conferring a grant of easement to the purchaser. This type of easement is known as an express grant because X (the servient tenement holder) intended to grant the right to the purchaser (the dominant tenement holder) as a part of the purchase agreement.

An express grant will be legal where all of the formality requirements for the creation of legal estates have been complied with. Alternatively, an express grant will be equitable in circumstances where the legal requirements have not been complied with; however, a clear intention to grant such a right can be established, and it would be unfair or unconscionable to deny the existence of the right.

13.4.3 *Express reservations*

An express reservation will arise where the holder of the dominant tenement expressly reserves an easement right over the servient tenement which is being transferred to a third party. Unlike a grant which refers to a right which is transferred, a reservation refers to a right which is retained.

For example, X owns two blocks of land adjoining each other. Block 1 can only be accessed via a path crossing over block 2. X enters into a contract of sale to sell block 2 to Y. The contract specifically sets out that the right of way over block 2 is to be reserved in favour of X, and the reservation is executed by way of a deed. This type of arrangement is commonly referred to as an express reservation of an easement: the vendor expressly reserves the right to utilise the land being sold in the same way it was utilised when the purchaser owned both blocks of land. The reservation is made expressly to ensure that the land retained by the vendor retains the benefit of this right.

As with an express grant, an express reservation will constitute a legal interest where all of the legal requirements for the creation of such interests have been complied with, or equitable where held to be enforceable by the equitable jurisdiction. It is, however, difficult to establish an express reservation which is equitable in nature. Doctrines such as part performance and proprietary estoppel are more appropriate in circumstances where the dominant tenement holder acts in accordance with an alleged agreement to issue a grant and the servient tenement holder acquiesces. An agreement to reserve a right is more difficult to establish because the dominant tenement holder is acting in accordance with her own alleged actions rather than those of the servient tenement holder.

13.4.4 Implied grants and reservations

Some easements may arise impliedly where the circumstances indicate that the easement was intended to pass, where the right has been previously and consistently enjoyed over the land, or where the easement is one of necessity. These situations are particularly relevant where the dominant and servient tenements have, at some stage, been owned by the same person who has consistently enjoyed the use of land which has now passed to a third party. In such cases, where the owner transfers either or both the dominant or servient tenement, it may be possible to imply a concurrent grant or reservation of an easement. Implied easements of grant to the purchaser of the dominant tenement and easements of reservation, where the dominant tenement is retained and the servient tenement is sold, may arise; however, the test for implying a grant is different from that applicable when implying a reservation. The basic principle has been set out in the classic decision of *Wheeldon v Burrows* (1879) 12 Ch D 47.

The facts of that case concerned several transfers of land by Tetley. Tetley owned a number of pieces of land including vacant land and a silk factory with workshops abutting onto the rear of the vacant land. The vacant land was sold to the plaintiff, who then devised it to his wife. The land was conveyed to the plaintiff together with all 'easements and appurtenances' attaching to the land. Tetley did not expressly reserve any right over the vacant land upon executing this conveyance. Tetley subsequently sold the silk factory and workshops to the defendant. The windows to the workshop abutted the vacant land. The plaintiff boarded up these windows, preventing light from entering the workshops. The defendant wanted to prevent her from blocking this light and alleged that his transfer contained an implied grant of an easement to light. The court rejected the claim of the defendant and upheld the right of the plaintiff to board up the windows. During the course of his judgment, Thesiger LJ set out the classic rule concerning the application of implied easements:

> I think that two propositions may be stated as what I may call the general rules governing cases of this kind. The first of these rules is that, on the grant by the owner of a tenement of part of that tenement as it is then used and enjoyed, there will pass to the grantee all those continuous and apparent easements (by which, of course, I mean quasi-easements) or, in other words, all those easements which are necessary to the reasonable enjoyment of the property granted and which have been, and are at the time of the grant, used by the owners of the entirety for the benefit of the part granted. The second proposition is that, if the grantor intends to reserve any right over the tenement granted, it is his duty to reserve it expressly in the grant. Those are the general rules governing cases of this kind, but the second of those rules is subject to certain exceptions. One of those exceptions is the well known exception which attaches to cases of what are called ways of necessity.[10]

On the facts of the case, the court held that, as Tetley had not expressly reserved the right to access light when transferring the vacant land to the plaintiff, and the right did not constitute an easement of necessity, the benefit of the right could not impliedly pass on to the defendant.

The basis of the *Wheeldon v Burrows* rule may be summarised as follows:

(a) courts will imply a grant to the transferee of the dominant tenement of all continuous and apparent rights which are necessary to the reasonable enjoyment of the property and which have in fact been used by the transferors over that property so that they constitute quasi-easements or where such a grant was commonly intended by both parties; and

(b) courts will only imply a reservation to the transferor where it can be established that the easement is one of necessity or where it was commonly intended to have been reserved. All other rights should be expressly reserved in order to remain enforceable. The rationale for this restrictive test is based upon the 'non-derogation of grant' principle. A transferor should not be entitled to claim rights in derogation of the grant unless he or she has expressly reserved those rights or the right is vital and necessary for the proper use of the property retained by the transferor.

The test for implied grant is quite different from the test for implied reservation. The implied grant test is positive in nature: it allows all easements which are already in use and are therefore continuous and apparent to impliedly pass to the transferee. On the other hand, the test for an implied reservation is negative: it precludes the implication of any reserved rights unless such rights are of necessity or were commonly intended to pass. The test for implied grants is more flexible and not as strict as that pertaining to implied reservations (*Goldberg v Edwards* [1950] 1 Ch 247). The reason for this

10 See para 13.4.4.1.

lies in what has been referred to as the 'non-derogation' principle. A person selling servient land who wishes to retain rights over that land should set those rights out expressly: a court will not readily imply such rights because they detract from the ability of the new owner fully and freely to enjoy the land. On the other hand, a person purchasing dominant land should receive all those rights which were previously exercised by the owner over that land because they impliedly attach to the land. The only requirement is that these rights be 'continuous and apparent'.

The words 'continuous and apparent' have been the subject of much interpretation. In *Ward v Kirkland* [1967] Ch 194, p 255, Ungoed-Thomas J concluded that the words 'continuous and apparent' should be read together and must indicate a right which is obvious and is recogniseable by a 'permanent mark on the land itself, or at least by some mark which will be disclosed by a careful inspection of the property'. Where it can be established that the right is one which was used regularly by the previous owner, and is important for the overall enjoyment of the land, the right is likely to satisfy the test. Importantly, the 'continuous' requirement does not mean that the grantee must prove that the right was in perpetual use: a reasonably regular usage will suffice (*Suffield v Brown* (1864) 4 De GJ & S 185).

It is also necessary to prove that the right is reasonably necessary for the enjoyment of the land. All that has to be established here is that the right is generally connected with the use or enjoyment of the land. Where the right is personal in nature or unconnected with the proprietary character of the land, it will not satisfy this requirement. However, the test is to be distinguished from the 'easements of necessity' test as it is not as strict (*Stevens & Evans v Allan & Armanasco* [1955] WALR 1).

The rule in *Wheeldon v Burrows* is subject, and may yield to, the intention of the parties: *Selby District Council v Samuel Smith* [2001] 01 EG 82.

13.4.4.1 Easements of necessity

An implied reservation of an easement can only occur where the right is one of necessity. A necessity easement can only arise where it can be proven that the easement is vital for the use of the land in issue. The classic and most common example of this arises with landlocked land. Where an owner of land cannot access their property without utilising a right of way over adjoining property, the right will generally be classified as an easement of necessity. The traditional rationale underlying this approach lies in public policy concerns, land should not remain landlocked so that it effectively becomes useless and unoccupied (*Dutton v Tayler* (1701) 2 Lut 1487; 125 ER 819).

Increasingly, courts are beginning to recognise easements of necessity on the basis of an actual or presumed intention by the parties. Hence, the focus of the analysis lies in the determination of mutual intention rather than the application of public policy. As noted by Ross J in *Bolton v Clutterbuck* [1955] SASR 253, p 268:

> In my view, no reservation of an easement, whether of necessity or otherwise, should be implied unless upon the evidence the court can reasonably infer an intention common to both parties that the property conveyed should be subject to the easement claimed.

This was approved by Hope J in *North Sydney Printing Pty Ltd v Sabemo Investment Corp Pty Ltd* [1971] 2 NSWLR 150, who noted:

> It seems to me that the balance of authority establishes that a way of necessity arises in order to give effect to an actual or presumed intention. No doubt difficulties could arise in some cases because of differing actual intentions on the part of the parties, but it seems to me that at least one must be able to presume an intention on the part of the grantor ... that he intended to have access to the land retained by him.[11]

On the facts of *North Sydney*, it was argued that an implied easement of necessity arose with respect to a lot retained by a vendor following a subdivision for the purposes of commercial development. Following this subdivision, the lot was landlocked and could only be accessed via a laneway to a public street. No intention to retain any right to the laneway was apparent, but the plaintiff argued that, as a matter of policy, a court will always enforce such an easement where the land is effectively landlocked. The court held that easements of necessity would not be implied simply on the basis of public policy. Some presumed or actual intention had to be established. Such intention did not exist on the facts because, initially, the vendor had intended access to occur only upon a consolidation of the lots. The court would not enforce an easement of necessity in the absence of such intention. Nevertheless, the plaintiff was not left without any relief because he retained the power to compel such a consolidation which would effectively produce access.[12] This difficulty is unlikely to arise again following legislative developments controlling subdivisions. In Victoria, s 98 of the Transfer of Land Act 1958 sets out that the proprietor of an allotment of land set out on an approved plan of subdivision shall:

> ... be entitled to all such easements of way, drainage and for the supply of specified essential services as may be necessary for the reasonable enjoyment of the allotment or any building thereon, as if such easements had been expressly granted.[13]

---

11 *North Sydney Printing Pty Ltd v Sabemo Investment Corp Pty Ltd* [1971] 2 NSWLR 150, p 155.

12 Compare this decision with the English decision in *Nickerson v Baraclough* [1980] Ch 325, where Megarry VC concluded that the *North Sydney* decision did not negate the existence of the public policy rationale, although this was overturned by the Court of Appeal ([1981] 2 WLR 773; 2 All ER 369), where it was held that easements of necessity should be based upon intention derived from all of the circumstances rather than public policy. See also Coldham C, 'Easements of necessity: *Nickerson v Barraclough*' (1982) 132 NLJ 224.

13 See the equivalent provision in Conveyancing and Law of Property Act 1884 (Tas), s 90B.

For an easement of necessity to exist, it must be established that the easement is necessary rather than merely convenient. If a right of way claimed under an easement merely constitutes a more appropriate method of access than one already in existence, the right will not generally be one of necessity (*Union Lighterage Co v London Graving Dock Co* [1902] 2 Ch 557). For example, if the right of way provides a quicker, easier method of access than that currently existing, the right may not be one of necessity. The issue will depend upon a construction of the individual circumstances, although the test is strict and it would seem that the easement must be proven to be absolutely essential before it will be enforceable.

Most easements of necessity arise with respect to rights of way; however, other forms of rights may also be held to be 'necessary', depending upon the circumstances. For example, a right to ventilation may be vital for both health and hygiene in circumstances where a business on the dominant tenement cannot function without proper access to fresh air and circulation (*Wong v Beaumont Property Trust Ltd* [1965] 1 QB 173). Where the right is claimed to be absolutely necessary to the proper use of the dominant tenement, but imposes severe restrictions over the servient tenement, the easement may be unenforceable. This was clearly emphasised by Lord Denning in *Phipps v Pears* [1965] 1 QB 76, where he noted that a right to support from a neighbouring wall, whilst being an important right for a dominant tenement holder would, if enforceable, severely limit the rights of the servient tenement holder. His Lordship noted:

> ... if such an easement were to be permitted, it would unduly restrict your neighbour in his enjoyment of his own land. It would hamper legitimate development ... if we were to stop a man pulling down his house, we would put a brake on desirable improvement. Every man is entitled to pull down his house if he likes.

Easements of necessity can pass under the Torrens system in most states because the wording of the legislation covers this. Section 42(2)(d) of the Transfer of Land Act (Vic) sets out that 'easements, howsoever acquired over or upon or affecting land, will remain unaffected by the indefeasibility provisions'.[14] Easements can pass under general law land pursuant to the general provision set out in s 62 of the Property Law Act 1958 (Vic), which sets out that all conveyances of land shall be deemed to include all rights, privileges, easements appertaining or reputed to appertain to the land at the time of the conveyance.[15]

13.4.4.2 *Intended easements*

Where the easement cannot be classified as one of necessity, it may be reserved or granted where a clear mutual intention between the parties can be

14 See, also, Torrens legislation: Tas, s 40(3); WA, s 68.

15 See, also, property law statutes: Tas, s 6; WA, s 41; SA, s 36; Qld s 239; and NSW, s 67.

determined. The intention must, however, be direct and defined (*Pwllbach Colliery Co Ltd v Woodman* [1915] AC 634). Intention may either be express or derived from the circumstances surrounding the acquisition or transferral of the property. It must be established that both the dominant and servient tenement holders have the same common intention. As summarised by Griffith CJ in *Horsfall v Braye* (1908) 7 CLR 629, p 645: 'The foundation of the doctrine of implied contract or grant is that the stipulation set up must necessarily have been intended by the parties, so that without the implication, their manifest intention would be defeated.'

Intentional easements are not restricted to easements of necessity: they may include any right which both parties particularly intended to pass. Where the property is being transferred for a specifically definable purpose, a court will generally presume that, in the absence of a contrary intention, the parties intended to confer all rights which are naturally associated with that purpose. A good example of an intended easement is the right to utilise mutual drainage and sewerage pipes upon the construction of a detached or semi-detached property and the right to the continual flow of water through such pipes (*Pyer v Carter* (1857) 1 H & N 916; 156 ER 1472; *Watts v Kelson* (1871) 6 Ch App 166).

13.4.4.3 Legislative provisions

Where the land which is the subject of the conveyance is described in words which indicate that it is adjacent to, abutting on, or bounded by a road, street or other public laneway, a court will generally presume that the conveyance was intended to include a right of way over that road or street (*Dabbs v Seaman* (1925) 36 CLR 538). The rationale here is that the descriptive character of these words specifically implies that the owner was intended to be able to utilise the public laneway to access the property. This type of implication is specifically covered by the general application of s 62 of the Property Law Act 1958 (Vic), which sets out that a conveyance of land shall be deemed to include all 'buildings, erections, fixtures, commons, hedges ... easements ... appertaining or reputed to appertain to the land ...'.[16]

Furthermore, where the land is affected by an approved plan of subdivision, each owner will be statutorily entitled to all easements necessary for the reasonable enjoyment of the subdivision as if they had been expressly created. In Victoria, this is set out in ss 97 and 98 of the Transfer of Land Act 1958. According to s 97, where any proprietor subdivides land into two or more parts and is required to lodge a plan of subdivision with the Registrar, the plan shall clearly indicate, *inter alia*, all easements which are to be set aside for the use of the proprietors of the land being subdivided. Section 569A of the Local Government Act 1958 sets out what must be included within plans of

16 See, also, property law statutes: NSW, s 67; Qld, s 239; Tas, s 6; WA, s 41; SA, s 36.

subdivision, and requires all existing easements and proposed reservations of easements to be clearly stated and, if not, the municipal authority can refuse to approve the plan.

Section 98 of the Transfer of Land Act 1958 (Vic) implies certain easements to the owners of each lot:[17]

> The proprietor of an allotment of land shown on an approved plan of subdivision or a lot shown on a registered plan shall be entitled to the benefit of the following easements which shall be deemed at all times to have been appurtenant to the allotment or the lot, namely:
>
> (a) all such easements of way and drainage and for party wall purposes and for the supply of water gas electricity sewerage and telephone and other services ... as may be necessary for the reasonable enjoyment of the allotment or lot and of any building or part of a building ...; and
>
> (b) in the case of the subdivision of a building, all such additional easements of way drainage support and protection and for the supply of water gas electricity sewerage and telephone and other services to the allotment ... as may be necessary for the reasonable enjoyment of the allotment or the lot ...

13.4.5 Easements by prescription

Easements may be recognised by the courts in circumstances where an acquiescence by the owner of the servient tenement can be presumed. Easements by prescription arise where a general acquisition can be proven from the combined factors of possession, usage and expiration of time. Importantly, however, easements arising by prescription should be distinguished from adverse possession rights. Limitation rights differ in substance from prescriptive rights; a right acquired through adverse possession will completely extinguish all rights held by the land owner over the area covered by the possession, whereas an easement by prescription will not extinguish the rights of the servient tenement holder but, rather, will confer an additional right upon the holder of the dominant tenement. Limitation rights are destructive, whereas prescriptive rights are acquisitive. The principles relating to adverse possession are discussed in detail in Chapter 4.

The only way in which an easement by prescription can arise in Victoria is pursuant to the common law doctrine of 'lost modern grant'.[18] This doctrine has a long history and was developed by the judiciary in order to overcome the original requirement, set out in the Statute of Westminster 1189, to prove enjoyment of a right over land which had been exercised 'from time

17 Similar provisions exist in Tasmania: Conveyancing and Law of Property Act 1884 (Tas), s 90B.

18 Statutory provisions setting out the methods of acquiring an easement by prescription are set out in Prescription Act 1832 (UK) and Prescription Act 1934 (Tas). The common law doctrine of 'lost modern grant' applies throughout Australia.

immemorial'. Under the doctrine of lost modern grant, a court would presume that an easement existed in circumstances where 20 years of continuous use of the right could be established. The essence of the doctrine of lost modern grant is the judicial presumption that, following the expiration of a 20 year period, an easement right which was assumed to have originally been expressly granted and lost, is revived. The underlying rationale of the doctrine is that a servient tenement holder must have intended to permit the right if he or she did not exercise legal rights of interference for a 20 year period. Naturally, this assumption of a 'revived' right is a fiction. However, the doctrine has been expressly approved by the House of Lords in *Dalton v Angus* (1881) 6 App Cas 740 and by the High Court of Australia in *Delohery v Permanent Trustee Co of New South Wales* (1904) 1 CLR 283. Prescriptive rights are not, however, enforceable against Crown lands (*Thwaites v Braye* (1895) 21 VLR 192).

The five principle elements of the doctrine were set out by the House of Lords in *Dalton v Angus* and can be summarised as follows:

(a) One person must openly and without consent or force exercise rights against the land of another.

The right which is exercised must be against land which is owned by another person and the right should be constant, peaceful and open. Where the right is forcefully exercised or has been consented to by the true owner, no prescription can arise. Furthermore, it must be clear that the dominant tenement holder is actually asserting a right in the nature of an easement (*Eaton v Swansea Waterworks Co* (1851) 17 QB 267).

(b) The servient tenement holder must have knowledge that the right is being enforced.

The owner of the servient tenement must be proven to have knowledge that the right is being exercised – whether that knowledge be actual or constructive – in order to establish prescription. Knowledge and acquiescence are the important elements for prescription, rather than consent, because prescriptive rights differ from licences. The mere fact that the exercise of the right is public, and therefore not secret, does not necessarily mean that the servient tenement owner has knowledge of it – this is particularly the case where the servient tenement is occupied by a tenant. Without proving that the knowledge has been brought home to the actual owner of the servient tenement, no prescription can arise (*Union Lighterage Co v London Graving Dock Co* [1902] 2 Ch 557).

(c) The servient tenement holder must have the legal ability to interfere with and prevent the exercise of the rights and fail to do so.

As the basis of prescription is an implied permission, it must be established that the servient tenement holder has the legal ability to interfere with and prevent the continued exercise of the right. Proof that the servient tenement holder has this ability and has not actually exercised it provides a further basis for the implication of acquiescence and the recognition of a prescriptive right.

(d) The right must be continually used for the entire prescriptive period of 20 years.

It must be clearly established that the dominant tenement holder regularly exercised the right against the servient tenement in a permanent rather than a temporary fashion for the entire 20 year period (*Hollins v Verney* (1884) 13 QBD 304). It is possible for rights accrued by a predecessor in title to be added to the period provided the exercise of the right is substantially the same and there is no interruption. Prescriptive rights will not, however, apply against rights to light and air which require no positive act (ss 195 and 196) of the Property Law Act 1958 (Vic).

(e) The right should be exercised against the fee simple owner of the land.

The right must be continually exercised against the fee simple owner of the servient tenement. In circumstances where the right is exercised against a tenant in occupation of the dominant tenement, it may be possible to acquire prescription against both the fee simple owner and the tenant (*Purgh v Savage* [1970] 2 QB 373). Prescriptive rights will not, however, arise between a landlord and tenant.

The whole foundation of easements by prescription was rationalised by Fry J (advising the House of Lords) in *Dalton v Angus* (1881) 6 App Cas 740, 773 as follows:

> ... the whole law of prescription and the whole law which governs the presumption or inference of a grant or covenant rest upon acquiescence. The courts and the judges have had recourse to various expedients for quieting the possession of persons in the exercise of rights which have not been resisted by the persons against whom they are exercised, but in all cases it appears to me that acquiescence and nothing else is the principle upon which these expedients rest.

Provided the requirements outlined by *Dalton v Angus* are satisfied, there is no need to prove that the right was exercised 'as of right' – in the belief that it was exercised by the holder to the exclusion of all others. This is not a requirement of the easement by prescription: *R v Oxfordshire County Council ex p Sunningwell Parish* [2001] 1 AC 335.

Where a prescriptive right can be established, the holder will acquire an enforceable easement, with the same rights as those which have been assumed by the dominant tenement holder for the duration of the period. Prescriptive easements may arise and are enforceable against general law land and Torrens system land. See para 13.6 below.

13.5 Alteration, extinguishment and remedies

13.5.1 *Alteration and extinguishment*

Easements may be varied or destroyed where circumstances arise which reveal that the rights are no longer enforceable or satisfactory. This may occur as a result of an express agreement between the dominant and servient tenement holder or impliedly through a change in material circumstances making the easement outdated, unnecessary or unfairly cumbersome upon the servient tenement holder. The circumstances are considered below.

13.5.1.1 *Changes in the dominant and servient tenement*

Where alterations have been carried out upon the dominant tenement, resulting in the easement right becoming superfluous, an intention on the part of both parties to abandon the right may be inferred. Naturally, the type of changes which would raise such a presumption will vary according to the individual circumstances. Some relevant considerations include:

(a) character and form of the dominant and servient tenements;

(b) the necessity of the right and its overall significance to the altered dominant tenement;

(c) the effect that particular obstacles may have upon the proper enforcement of the right; and

(d) the expectations of the dominant and servient tenement holders.

For example, if a dominant tenement holder has constructed a large, established access to property, which was previously only accessible pursuant to a right of way, this right may be impliedly abandoned. Furthermore, where it can be proven that the dominant tenement has been materially altered to such an extent that further enforcement of the easement would prejudice the rights of enjoyment and use held by the servient tenement holder, it may be implied that the easement has been abandoned (*Colls v Home & Colonial Stores Ltd* [1904] AC 179). Generally, however, the usual remedy for a servient tenement holder would be to seek injunctive relief to prevent an alteration significantly increasing the existing burden on the servient tenement; an implied abandonment of the easement will only occur where the alterations to the dominant tenement have been carried out and, as a result, the new rights cannot be properly separated from the existing easement rights. See *Ankerson v Connelly* [1906] 2 Ch 544.

Alterations to the servient tenement will not as readily imply an abandonment of the easement. This is because the changes have not been made by the holder of the right, and unless it can be clearly established that the changes were mutually agreed upon and both parties intended to abandon the easement, the right may still be enforceable (*Treweek v 36 Wolseley Road Pty Ltd* (1973) 128 CLR 274).

13.5.1.2 *Express agreement to release*

An easement may be abandoned where the dominant and servient tenement holders have expressly or impliedly agreed that this should occur. The enforceability of the agreement will depend upon the type of land involved and particular jurisdictional requirements. First, all such agreements must be in writing in order to be enforceable.[19] Torrens title land may be released from an easement where the prescribed form for surrender of an easement is properly executed and registered over the title.[20] Old title land may be released from an easement at common law where the agreement is executed by way of a deed. Where the agreement does not constitute a deed, it may nevertheless be enforceable in the equity jurisdiction if there is a sufficient written memorandum to evidence the agreement or if part performance or proprietary estoppel can be established (*Davies v Marshall* (1861) 10 CB (NS) 697).

Generally, only the servient and dominant tenement holders need be parties to the agreement, although, where other parties will be affected, their consent should also be obtained.

13.5.1.3 *Abandonment*

An easement may be extinguished where the dominant tenement holder is proven to have abandoned the easement. Whether such an abandonment has occurred will always be a question of fact for a court to determine; focus is given to conduct or inactivity which directly suggests that the dominant tenement holder no longer intends to assert the right. Mere non-use of the easement right will not automatically result in a presumption of abandonment. A court will generally consider a range of factors pointing towards an overall intention to abandon (*James v Stevenson* [1893] AC 162). Important considerations in assessing whether or not an abandonment has occurred include:

(a) the length of time of non-use by the dominant tenement holder;

(b) the failure of the dominant tenement holder to assert legal rights where the easement rights are interfered with;

---

19 In Victoria, see Instruments Act 1958 (Vic), s 126 and Property Law Act 1958 (Vic), ss 53–54. In other states, see property law statutes: NSW, s 54A; Qld, s 59; SA, s 26; Tas, s 36; ACT, s 54A. The original Statute of Frauds 1667 (Imp) remains in force in Western Australia and Northern Territory.

20 In Victoria, Tasmania and New South Wales, the Torrens legislation entitles the Registrar to cancel all easement rights as soon as a proper form to surrender, release, or vary the easement is registered. See Torrens legislation:Vic, s 73(2); Tas, s 108(1); NSW, s 47(6)(6A). On the other hand, in Queensland, Western Australia, South Australia, ACT and the Northern Territory, the Registrar only has the power to remove an easement where the agreement is backed by a court order: Qld, s 181; WA, s 129C(1)(b); SA, s 64; ACT, s 103E; NT, s 64.

(c) the character and development of the dominant tenement and the continuing suitability of the easement; and

(d) the acquiescence of the dominant tenement holder to the creation of impediments to the effective exercise of the easement.

For example, in *McIntyre v Porter* (1983) 2 VR 439, an easement in the form of a right of way was held to have been abandoned because of the non-use by the dominant tenement holder combined with the availability of an alternative means of access. Furthermore, and importantly on the facts, the planting of a hedge along the original access point, with the acquiescence of the dominant tenement holder, creating a significant impediment in the ongoing use of the easement was held to be a significant factor in the courts determination that the right of way had been abandoned.

Whilst the common law does not presume that easements are automatically abandoned after a designated period of time – although, obviously, the greater the length of time, the more likely that an abandonment may be implied – there are statutory provisions to this effect. Under s 73(3) of the Transfer of Land Act 1958 (Vic), where it can be proven that an easement has not been utilised for a period of not less than 30 years, this shall constitute sufficient evidence that the easement has been abandoned.[21] In New South Wales, s 49(1) of the Real Property Act 1900 gives the Registrar General a broad power to cancel the recording of an easement where it has been abandoned; evidence of abandonment may include proof of non-use for a 20 year period. However, the provision does not make this an automatic presumption, and gives the Registrar General the power to consider the overall circumstances and evidence relating to abandonment.

Under the Victorian Torrens system, an easement shall continue to be enforceable until it has actually been removed from the register. Section 73(1) of the Transfer of Land Act 1958 (Vic) states that a registered proprietor may make an application in an approved form to the Registrar for the deletion from the register of any easement, in whole or in part, where it has been extinguished or abandoned. If the easement is not expressly removed from the register, it will continue to be enforceable despite the fact that the 30 year period of non-use under s 73(3) has been satisfied or where it has been proven that the easement has been abandoned under common law. The rationale for this lies in the fact that, in Victoria, the register is intended to provide a conclusive summary of the title; hence, where an interest is still noted on the title, it will remain enforceable.[22]

21 See, also, Transfer of Land Act 1893 (WA), s 229A; Real Property Act 1900 (NSW), s 49(2); and the Land Titles Act 1980 (Tas), s 108(3) for equivalent provisions where a period of 20 years of non-use can be established.

22 Compare this approach to that in New South Wales, where s 89(1) of the Conveyancing Act 1919 (NSW) specifically gives the courts the power to extinguish or modify easements despite the fact that they remain recorded on the register. See, also, Torrens statutes in Western Australia, Queensland and Tasmania for equivalent provisions.

13.5.1.4 *Unity of title*

An easement will automatically be extinguished where it can be established that the dominant and servient tenement holders are the same person. Obviously, in such a situation, there is no need for the easement right to continue because the owner is entitled to exercise rights over the servient land where he or she is the owner. Furthermore, the easement will not be automatically revived where the servient tenement is subsequently sold: in such a situation, a new easement should be created.

Where, however, the servient tenement is owned but not possessed by the dominant tenement holder, an easement may still exist. This will occur where the servient tenement is leased out. In such a situation, the easement will continue for the duration of the lease and, once the reversion expectant vests in the landlord at the expiration of the lease, the easement will automatically be extinguished (*Richardson v Graham* [1908] 1 KB 39). On the other hand, in a situation where one person has joint possession, but not ownership, of the dominant and servient tenements, the easement will not be automatically extinguished but will remain suspended for the duration of the joint possession (*Thomas v Thomas* (1835) 2 CM & R 34; 150 ER 15).

13.5.1.5 *Statutory provisions*

There are a number of miscellaneous statutory provisions entitling particular bodies to extinguish, alter or modify existing easements. In Victoria, the power of the Supreme Court pursuant to s 84 of the Property Law Act 1958 (Vic) is restricted to modification or variation of restrictive covenants, and does not include easements. By comparison, in Western Australia, Queensland, New South Wales and Tasmania, statutory power is conferred upon the Supreme Courts to extinguish easements where specific grounds can be established.[23]

In New South Wales, s 88k of the Property Legislation Amendment (Easements) Act 1995 (which has now been inserted into the Conveyancing Act 1919 (NSW)) allows the Supreme Court to impose an easement over land against the wishes of the servient tenement holder where it is reasonably necessary for the effective use or development of other land that will have the benefit of the easement. The court will only impose the easement if use of the land receiving the benefit of the easement is consistent with the public interest, if the owner of the servient tenement may be adequately compensated and if the applicant has made all reasonable attempts to obtain the easement in issue.[24]

---

23 See Transfer of Land Act 1893 (WA), s 129c; Conveyancing and Law of Property Act 1884 (Tas), Pt XVA; Property Law Act 1974 (Qld), s 181; and Conveyancing Act 1919 (NSW), s 89(1).

24 See similar provision in Property Law Act 1974 (Qld), s 180.

In Victoria, however, municipal councils have specific statutory rights to alter, modify or extinguish easements in particular circumstances. Under s 36(1) of the Subdivision Act 1988 (Vic), a municipal council has the power to acquire or remove an easement over any land which is subject to a subdivision to which the Act applies where it is felt necessary in order to effect an economical and efficient subdivision.

13.5.2 Remedies for infringement

13.5.2.1 Construction of rights

The scope of the rights contained within an easement will depend upon its natural construction. Under a basic right of way, the dominant tenement holder will receive all rights which ordinarily flow from the words of the easement. Where the easement limits a particular height, width and method of use, the dominant tenement holder will be bound by this. For example, a right of way may be restricted to pedestrian rather than vehicular use, or it may be restricted to particular types of vehicles – for example, cars may be permitted whereas large trucks and buses may be outside the scope of the right. Generally, in the absence of any express words to the contrary, the holder of the easement will be under a duty to repair the right of way and will have rights of access to effect this purpose (*Byrne v Steele* [1932] VLR 143).

Where the easement is impliedly created, the scope of the rights will depend upon the type of implied easement. For example, an easement of necessity which has been impliedly reserved for a land owner will generally only confer the most basic rights, whereas an easement which is continuous and apparent, and which has impliedly passed to a purchaser, will contain the same rights as those previously exercised by the vendor.

The basic rules of construction for an express easement are that the court must give the words their ordinary and natural construction and, whilst consideration may be given to the circumstances in existence at the date of creating the easement, parol evidence is inadmissible. Circumstances which may be relevant to such an assessment include: the nature of the servient tenement; the purpose for which the right was intended; and the burden which was intended to be imposed upon the servient tenement. In the absence of any express provisions to the contrary, a right of way will be construed in a manner which is in accord with the nature of the servient tenement (*Elliott v Renner* [1923] St R Qd 172 (FC)).

The importance of construing a grant of easement in light of the circumstances existing at the date of creating the grant has been reinforced by the courts. In *SS & M Ceramics Pty Ltd v Kin* ((1995) unreported, 3 October), a right of way was granted which entitled the existing and all successive owners of the dominant tenement to 'pass and repass along the servient tenement'. The right was expressed to have been conferred 'at all times ... with or without motor cars, trucks or other vehicles … for all purposes connected with the use and enjoyment of the dominant tenement'. The owner of the dominant tenement conducted a fruit shop business on it, and the right of way was used consistently for the delivery of supplies to the shop. The question was whether the easement entitled the people making the deliveries to park their vehicles while in the process of packing and unpacking the goods. The majority of the Court of Appeal held that this activity was not permitted by the terms of the easement. An important consideration in this determination was that, at the time when the easement had been created in 1955, the dominant tenement had not been built upon to the extent it had at the date of the court hearing; vehicles could enter the dominant tenement and make their deliveries and, as such, there was no need to utilise the right of way for this purpose. Later expansion of the dominant tenement prevented such access, although this development did not mean that the rights originally intended to be conferred under the right of way could, correspondingly, be expanded. As the right to stop, park and make deliveries on the right of way had not been contemplated in 1955, such rights could not be enforceable today. The court held that the words of the grant of easement had to be construed in light of the events at the time when the easement was created.

This is not, however, to suggest that rights to stop and park could never be contemplated under a right of way. In *Butler v Muddle* [1995] NSW Conv R 55–745, it was held that a right of way contained only such rights as were reasonably necessary for the enjoyment of that right of way. Hence, a right to park where it was necessary for the enjoyment of the right could be included, but not where it was, in substance, an additional privilege.

The scope of the right of way has been statutorily codified. Pursuant to s 72(3) of the Transfer of Land Act 1958 (Vic), any registered easement which uses the words 'right of carriageway over' shall be construed in accordance with the rights set out in Sched 12 to that Act, which reads as follows:

> Together with full and free right and liberty to and for the registered proprietor for the time being of the land herein described … to go pass and repass at all times hereafter and for all purposes and either with or without horses or other animals carts of carriages into and out of and from the said land or any part thereof through over and along the road or way or several roads or ways delineated ...[25]

Rights conferred under other types of easements will depend upon the particular circumstances. Rights associated with more ethereal easements, such as the right to light, can often be difficult to interpret. Nevertheless, it has been held that the right to uninterrupted access and enjoyment of light and air in the doors and windows of a building is a valid and enforceable easement (*Commonwealth v Registrar of Titles (Vic)* (1918) 24 CLR 348) and that the

25 See, also, Torrens legislation: WA, s 65 and Sched 9; NSW, s 181A(1) and Sched 8; Tas, s 34A(1) and Sched 8; ACT, s 81 and Sched 7.

quantum of light conferred under such a right will be that which is necessary for the usual occupation of the tenement, whether it be residential or business in nature, and which is in accordance with ordinary notions of mankind (*Colls v Home & Colonial Stores Ltd* [1904] AC 179).

Most easements fit within well established categories, although it is possible, as noted by the High Court in *Commonwealth v Registrar of Titles (Vic)* (1918) 24 CLR 348, to create new forms of easements. The rights associated with new easements will, naturally, depend upon their character and scope. Whilst courts will take care in the recognition and enforcement of new forms of negative easements, the rapid expansion of technology, the creation of differing forms of energy sources and the need to sustain land in accordance with developing environmental concerns have meant that new forms of easements will carry updated and differing rights. Ascertaining the purpose and scope of these new 'easement rights' may become increasingly difficult, and references to 'ordinary notions of mankind' are fraught with conceptual difficulties. The problem is not only in properly defining such a broad, generalised and vague rule, but also in determining whether any 'ordinary' community notions exist in areas which are developing, which were previously unknown and sometimes highly controversial.[26]

13.5.2.2 Remedies for infringement of easement rights

Where it is established that rights conferred under an easement have been infringed, the holder will have a range of remedies available. Where the infringement is continuing and the holder of the dominant tenement wants to stop it from occurring, he may seek injunctive relief to prevent the infringement from continuing as well as common law damages (or equitable damages where the easement is enforceable in equity) to compensate the holder for any damage incurred as a result of the infringement.

Injunctive relief is the most commonly sought remedy, and it may be mandatory, prohibitive, interim or *quia timet* in nature. Generally, in order for a court to grant injunctive relief, it must be established that the infringement is serious and continual and that the holder of the easement has not acquiesced in the breach.

Common law damages may be claimed where it can be proven that a person has infringed an easement. Proof of actual damage or loss to the land is not necessary; where it is established that an easement right has actually been breached, damage will be assumed. The measure of damages will generally be calculated in accordance with the depreciation of the property as a result of the infringement, and all the usual principles associated with the availability of common law and equitable damages will apply.

26 See, further, eg, Mosketwitz, A, 'Legal access to light: solar energy imperative' (1976) 9 Natural Resources Law 177 and Bradbrook, A, *Solar Energy and the Law*, 1984, LBC.

The self-help remedy of abatement is also available to the holder of an easement right, entitling him or her to access to the servient tenement in order to stop an infringement or obstruction. A person exercising the abatement remedy should act reasonably when entering the servient tenement, and the holder will only have the right to carry out such acts that will result in a cessation of the infringement or obstruction – nothing further. Courts are generally disinclined to endorse the remedy of abatement because of the danger that it will result in further conflict and a breach of the peace (*Hill v Cock* (1872) 26 LT 185).

13.6 Easements and the Torrens system

Easements over Torrens title land may be expressly created in accordance with the prescribed forms set out under the Torrens legislation. The Transfer of Land (General) Regulations 1994 set out specific forms for the creation, surrender and registration of easements over Torrens title land, and reg 14 makes the use of these forms compulsory.

Once registered, an easement will be noted on the certificate of title of both the dominant and servient tenement holders. It is not, however, compulsory to register easements, because an unregistered easement will stand outside the indefeasibility provisions. All easements properly created over Torrens title land come within the category of interests known as paramount interests. These interests are specifically set out in s 42(2)(a)–(f) of the Transfer of Land Act 1958 (Vic).[27] A paramount interest will be enforceable against the existing registered proprietor and all subsequent registered proprietors, even where it remains unregistered, as it is not defeated by a subsequent registration (*James v Stevenson* [1893] AC 162). Section 42(2)(d) of the Victorian Act sets out:

> Notwithstanding anything in the foregoing the land which is included in any folio of the register or registered instrument shall be subject to ...
>
> (d) any easements howsoever acquired subsisting over or upon or affecting the land.

On the wording of this section, it seems that, in order for the exception to apply, the easement must already be in existence and must affect the land in issue, by providing either a benefit or a burden. The requirement that the easement must be 'subsisting' applies to both expressly and impliedly created easements. It has been held that an easement created as a result of the doctrine of *Wheeldon v Burrows* could apply and be enforceable against Torrens title land (*Taylor v Browning* (1885) 11 VLR 158). This approach has, however, been the subject of some discussion, as it is often claimed that it undermines the security objective of the Torrens system because it requires prospective

27 See, also, Torrens legislation: WA, s 68; Tas, s 40(3); NSW, s 42(1)(A1); Qld, s 170(1)(c); SA, s 69IV; NT, s 69IV; ACT, s 58b.

purchasers to search for additional evidence beyond the actual register, and this is inimical to the whole philosophy of a system based upon the absolute guarantee of the register. A similar approach is taken by the legislation in Tasmania and Western Australia.[28]

The discussion by the High Court in *Parramore v Duggan* (1995) 70 ALJR 1 on the operation of Tasmania's Land Titles Act 1980 provides an interesting example of a more restrictive approach to the indefeasibility exception. Section 40(3)(e) of the Act sets out that a purchaser of the servient tenement will acquire an indefeasible title except with respect to:

> (i) an easement arising by implication or under a statute which would have given rise to a legal interest if the servient land had not been ... under Torrens title ...

On the facts of the case, an easement existed over old title land. Subsequently, the dominant tenement was brought under the Torrens system, and the benefit of the easement was expressly noted on the title. When the servient tenement was brought under the Torrens system, however, there was no mention of the burden of the easement. The subsequent purchaser of the servient tenement argued, therefore, that he was not bound by the burden of the easement. At issue was the scope of s 40(3)(e). Significantly, the section did not appear to provide an exception to easements which had been expressly created but not noted on the title: it referred only to implied or statutorily created easements. The Tasmanian Supreme Court found in favour of the dominant tenement holder and concluded that s 40(3)(e) did intend to cover express easements.

The High Court unanimously disagreed with this interpretation. In the leading judgment, Toohey J concluded that express easements could be registered under the Deeds Registration System and therefore could be easily brought to the attention of the Registrar when the servient tenement was brought under the Torrens system. The aim of s 40(3)(e) was to cover easements which were not so easily detected – namely implied and statutory easements – and so the section should not be extended to cover express easements. The decision provides a rather perverse limitation for the Tasmanian legislation and, as the following discussion reveals, is clearly inconsistent with the broader approach taken by other states to the exception.

In New South Wales, s 42(1)(A1) of the Real Property Act 1900 sets out that a registered proprietor will take indefeasible title except where it can be established that there has been an:

28 See Torrens legislation: Tas, s 40(3); WA, s 68.

> ... omission or misdescription of any easement subsisting immediately before the land was brought under the provisions of this Act or validly created at or after that time under this or any other Act or a Commonwealth Act.[29]

The meaning of 'omission' has been given a broad interpretation by the New South Wales Court of Appeal in *Dobbie v Davidson* (1991) 23 NWLR 625 to include 'left out' or 'something which is not there – for whatever reason'.[30] The easement does not, however, have to be registered to come within the ambit of the provision. Nevertheless, in New South Wales, the definition of omission will not include implied easements arising under the *Wheeldon v Burrows* principle, because to extend the term in such a way would undermine the conclusiveness of the register.[31]

Furthermore, under the NSW section, as in Victoria, it must be established that the easement which was omitted or misdescribed was either existing immediately before the land was registered or validly created at, or after, that time by legislation. It would seem that 'subsisting' means validly and properly created, and in New South Wales, this only applies to express easements; in this sense, the NSW provision is narrower than the Victorian provision. The NSW legislation will, however, include easements which are already in existence but not registered, as well as those which are actually created at the date of the transfer but omitted or misdescribed by the register provided that the owners of the dominant and servient tenements have done all that is required to be done by them to comply with the statutory formalities associated with the creation of easements (*James v Registrar General* [1968] 1 NSWLR 310).[32] It is not clear what the new reference in s 42(1)(A1) to 'validly created under this Act' actually means. Technically, an easement will not be validly created under the Act until the transfer or plan of subdivision which creates it is actually registered: the mere execution of the appropriate documents would not, under this interpretation, be satisfactory.[33]

It would seem that the exception to indefeasibility will also include easements arising by way of equitable estoppel. In *Dabbs v Seaman* (1925) 36

29 This provision was added in 1995. The forerunner to this provision in NSW was s 42(1)(b), which set out that the registered proprietor will take an indefeasible title except 'in the case of the omission or misdescription of any right of way or other easement created in or existing upon any land'. A provision similar to s 42(1)(b) also exists in South Australia, Australian Capital Territory and Queensland. See Torrens legislation: SA, s 69(IV); ACT, s 58b; Qld, s 170(1)(c).

30 In this sense, the court disapproved the earlier decision in *Australian Hi-Fi Publications Pty Ltd v Gehl* [1979] 2 NSWLR 618, which adopted a narrower interpretation of 'omission' and confined it to its particular facts. The *Australian Hi-Fi* decision was, however, approved by the Supreme Court of Queensland in *Stuy v BC Ronalds Pty Ltd* [1984] ACLD 98.

31 It has, however, been held that easements created under the *Wheeldon v Burrows* principle will constitute an exception to indefeasibility in Victoria (see discussion above), Tasmania, Western Australia, South Australia and probably Queensland: see discussion in *Pryce and Irving v McGuinness* [1966] Qd R 591.

32 See McMorland, 'Omitted easements' [1976] New Zealand Law Journal 51.

33 See Butt, P, 'Conveyancing' (1996) 70 ALJ 348 on the new NSW provision and Butt, P, *Land Law*, 3rd edn, 1996, LBC, paras 2067–71.

CLR 538, the High Court held that a registered proprietor was estopped from denying the existence of an easement which he had, upon a true construction of the facts, helped to create.[34]

In conclusion, validly created easements which exist or are intended to exist prior to the registration of a title will, in most states, come within the indefeasibility exception. In Victoria, Western Australia and Tasmania, the breadth of the provision results in an inevitable incursion upon the principles of indefeasibility. In order to read the provision consistently with the indefeasibility provisions, it is probably best to consider the rights contained within s 42(2)(a)–(f) of the Victorian Act as existing outside the indefeasibility structure.

In other states, particularly NSW, the aim of the provision is narrower in focus: it is not to exclude easements from the operation of the indefeasibility provisions altogether but, rather, to provide an exception to indefeasibility and the conclusiveness of the register where it can be established that a validly created easement existed and was either omitted, whether through failure to discharge an obligation or, in the broader sense, through sheer neglect, or through an actual misdescription on the title. In these provisions, the exception to indefeasibility is more limited than the Victorian counterpart because of the need to prove the existence of a valid easement and to satisfy the definition of 'omission' or 'misdescription'. Nevertheless, problems still exist; the broader the interpretation given to 'omission', the greater the difficulty in reconciling the provision with the fundamental aims of the Registrar to provide an absolute and conclusive title.

34 Note, however, that in *Torrisi v Magame Pty Ltd* [1984] 1 NSWLR 15, Powell J held that an easement which was enforceable under the principles of proprietary estoppel did not come within the indefeasibility exception against a registered successor in title. See, also, Baalman, J 'Easements by estoppel' (1958) 31 Australian Law Journal 800.

CHAPTER 14

MORTGAGES

14.1 Security interests

A mortgage is a form of security interest, commonly arising over real property. In essence, a mortgage is simply a secured loan contract. It is relevant to property law because the security interest actually confers a proprietary right upon the lender (the 'mortgagee') in the secured property which is enforceable against the borrower (the 'mortgagor') where the terms of the loan contract are breached and the lender must enforce his security interest. Mortgages are one of the most common forms of security interests in existence. Most people contemplating the purchase of a piece of property will do so with the assistance of a loan, which is secured by a mortgage. It is important to appreciate exactly what type of interest is transferred to the mortgagee upon executing the mortgage so that the difference between an absolute title and a 'security' title is understood.

Security is generally understood to refer to any transaction whereby a lender, apart from holding personal rights which are enforceable against the borrower, is given additional 'security' in the form of a right which is exercisable against definable property. Security transactions are extremely popular because they provide a lender with an additional sense of protection against the possibility of a borrower being unable to repay the borrowed amount. A lender holding nothing but an enforceable personal obligation against the borrower can be in a precarious situation because of the possibility that, where a default occurs, the borrower may become bankrupt or simply be unable to repay the amount borrowed. The advantage of a security interest is that it places the lender in a much stronger position; the lender holds an actual interest in the secured property, which is capable of being realised in circumstances where the borrower is in default and the debt is incapable of being discharged by the borrower personally.

A security interest will be proprietary in nature where it confers upon the mortgagee *in rem* rights which are enforceable against a specific and identifiable piece of property. The mortgagee actually holds a proprietary interest in the property which is capable of being alienated; however, this right cannot be realised until it is clear that the mortgagor is in default of the primary obligation; the interest is only a 'security'. The rights of a security holder are not as absolute as those held by ordinary common law and equitable estates and interests. This disparity has been well summarised by Sykes:[1]

1 Sykes, E and Walker, S, *The Law of Securities*, 5th edn, 1993, LBC, p 10.

> The security interest is therefore an aggregation or bundle of proprietary rights, though not necessarily of ownership rights; that is, rights which habitually form part of the ownership bundle. It differs from other interests of a proprietary character in that the person entitled always holds subject to the potentiality of the debtor either getting back her or his property, or, as the case may be, coming to hold it free from the burden constituted by the interest of a creditor ... Even in those rare cases where the concept was that full dominion passed to the creditor, as in the case of the Roman mortgage, the debtor still had at least a contractual right to redeem.

The holder of a security interest, whilst retaining a proprietary right which is enforceable against the whole world, holds this interest subject to the defined purpose of the transaction. A security interest holder can only enforce the right in circumstances where the borrower fails to discharge the debt; this stems from the fact that the security interest is only conferred upon the lender as a form of protection for the repayment of the loan. Where the loan is properly repaid, there will be no further need for the security to exist, and the interest may be discharged. Hence, the primary purpose of the security interest is to operate for a limited period of time as a protective device; where the terms of the primary debt are satisfied, there will no longer be any need for the security interest and the mortgagor may 'redeem' the secured property.

14.1.1 Classification of security interests

Securities have traditionally been classified into three primary categories based upon the old Roman division of transactions. These categories are *fiducia, pignus* and *hypotheca*.[2] *Fiducia* refers to security transactions where the actual proprietary interest is transferred over to the lender for the duration of the loan. *Pignus* refers to security transactions where possession of the property, but not actual ownership in that property, is transferred over to the lender. *Hypotheca* refers to security transactions where the lender is not given ownership or possession but, rather, enforceable rights against the property which may be pursued where the debt is not repaid.

This classification may be conveniently summarised today as the mortgage *stricto sensu*, the possessory security and the charge. These three types of security interests reflect the different forms of mortgages existing with respect to old title land, Torrens title land and personal property.

14.1.1.1 Mortgage stricto sensu

This type of security represents the classic form of mortgage. Under such a mortgage, the mortgagee receives full legal ownership in the secured property for the duration of the debt. Legal title to the secured property is transferred into the name of the mortgagee whilst the mortgagor retains a

2 See *op cit*, Sykes and Walker, fn 1, p 14.

purely equitable interest in the property entitling him to redeem the secured property once the debt has been fully satisfied. The interest retained by the mortgagor is commonly referred to as an 'equity of redemption'.

In order for a mortgage *stricto sensu* to arise, the legal title to the secured property must be properly vested in the mortgagee; where the legal conveyance is ineffective, but it is clear that the parties intended to create a mortgage, the transaction may be enforceable in equity (see Chapter 5 generally).

Once legal title to the secured property is properly vested in the mortgagee, he or she will hold that title as security for the full and proper satisfaction of the debt. The mortgage *stricto sensu* is the usual form of mortgage associated with general law land. Under the Torrens system, however, a registered mortgagee will acquire a statutory charge in the secured property, legal title remaining with the mortgagor.

The ownership rights conferred upon a mortgagee under a mortgage *stricto sensu* are similar to, but not as absolute as, full ownership. A mortgagee can only exercise ownership rights in the event of a default in the loan contract and, once the loan has been properly discharged, the mortgagor will have both a contractual and an equitable right to redeem the secured property by transferring legal title to the mortgagor. Furthermore, where a default in the loan contract entitles the mortgagee to exercise rights against the secured property, the mortgagee cannot simply assume full control over the property: in exercising security rights, the mortgagee is obliged to consider not only his or her own interests in discharging the debt, but also the interests of the mortgagor in the remainder or surplus of the property. This is discussed in more detail at para 14.3.5.2.

14.1.1.2 Possessory security

A possessory security confers upon the lender the right to retain possession of property in circumstances where a debt has not been repaid. This type of interest can only exist where the lender holds actual possession or an enforceable right to possession, and is commonly associated with chattels rather than real property. A possessory security may only arise where the transaction relates to specifically identifiable property which has been actually or constructively delivered into the hands of the lender.

One of the classic forms of possessory securities is the lien. The holder of a legal lien will have the right to retain possession of the property until the debt has been discharged, but no right to exercise a power of sale is conferred. A lien may be expressly created, but will usually arise automatically in the particular circumstances of the transaction. A lien may be enforceable under common law or it may be recognised by the equitable jurisdiction in circumstances where it would be unfair to deny the security interest of a party within a particular transaction.

One of the classic forms of particular lien is the vendor's lien for the unpaid purchase price of the property. Where a purchaser has entered into a contract for sale and paid a deposit, the vendor will hold the legal title to the property as constructive trustee until settlement occurs and legal title is properly transferred. Until the balance of the purchase price is paid, the vendor will also retain an equitable lien in the property, which will entitle the vendor to retain the property until the full purchase moneys are transferred (*Bloxam v Sanders* (1825) 4 B & C 941; 107 ER 1309).[3] The unpaid vendor's lien has, however, been abolished in Queensland by virtue of s 176 of the Land Titles Act 1994, which specifically states that a vendor of registered land will not hold any equitable lien on the land by reason on non-payment of a part or any of the purchase moneys. This abolition has not unduly affected the position of vendors in Queensland because, as a matter of conveyancing practice, most unpaid purchase moneys would be secured by a bill of mortgage.

14.1.1.3 Charge

A charge will confer upon the holder rights which are enforceable against the property if the debt is not discharged, but it does not confer full ownership and a right to use, enjoy and possess the property. As it is intangible in nature, a charge will subsist over property despite the fact that the property may change hands although, as with other proprietary interests, it is capable of being defeated by a *bona fide* purchaser for value without notice. The holder of a charge may enforce his rights against the property in circumstances where the borrower under the loan contract is in default, and the manner of such an enforcement will be similar to other forms of security interest; a charge holder is obliged to take into account the interests of the borrower when enforcing rights against the secured property.

The holder of an equitable charge holds a similar interest to that held by an equitable mortgagee, in the sense that both hold intangible rights which are enforceable against the secured property. The difference between the two lies in the fact that a charge holder does not have as extensive a range of remedies as the mortgagee because no right of foreclosure exists. Traditionally, the remedy of foreclosure will only apply where a transaction is, in substance, considered to constitute a mortgage rather than a pure charge. Under old title land, a transaction is regarded as a mortgage 'in substance' where the parties execute a transfer of the legal title for the primary purpose of securing a debt. Under Torrens title land, where a mortgage is executed in the appropriate form and registered on the title, the parties will receive all of the rights and obligations associated with mortgages. In summary then, a charge is a lesser form of security interest because the range of remedies available for its enforcement are not as comprehensive as those applicable to mortgages.

3 See, also, *Heid v Reliance Finance Corp Pty Ltd* (1984) 154 CLR 326.

14.1.2 General law mortgage

A legal mortgage over general law land will generally take the form of a mortgage *stricto sensu*. This means that the mortgagee receives a conveyance of the legal title to the secured land for the duration of the debt. One of the terms of the mortgage agreement, which is also enforceable in equity, is the promise by the mortgagee to reconvey the land to the mortgagor once the mortgagor has fully discharged the debt. See further discussion on the right to redeem at para 14.3.1.

The equitable right of redemption held by the mortgagor, and the right of the mortgagee to apply for an order of foreclosure, have, traditionally, been associated with general law mortgages because of their particular relevance to mortgages involving a conveyance of legal title.

Historically, one of the great difficulties associated with general law mortgages was that, where the contractual provisions were inoperative, the security purpose of the contract could be overwhelmed. Hence, where, for example, a mortgagor failed to discharge the mortgage debt on the date specified in the contract, the mortgagor had no contractual right to redeem the property despite the fact that the debt had been repaid. Consequently, there was a need for greater recognition of the rights of the mortgagor to redeem secured property which had been transferred to the mortgagee. This was where the Court of Chancery stepped in. The equity jurisdiction focuses upon the security character of the conveyance; where the mortgagee is fully and properly reimbursed of all the principal and interest moneys owing under the loan, equity takes the view that, in fairness, and in light of the fact that the conveyance is only intended to operate as a security, the mortgagee should have no further claim to the property. Hence, equity upholds the right of the mortgagor to redeem the secured land upon proof that the debt is fully discharged. Redemption in equity constitutes a proprietary right in favour of the mortgagor entitling her to have the property reconveyed into her own name, even though the debt is discharged at a later date to that specified in the contract (*Salt v Marquess of Northampton* [1892] AC 1). See further discussion on the equity of redemption at para 14.3.1.

A further difficulty historically associated with general law mortgages lay in the fact that it was difficult for mortgagees to foreclose over land in substitution for the repayment of the debt. Due to the extensive nature of the right to redeem – and its enforceability under the Courts of Chancery – it was hard for a mortgagee actually to 'foreclose' over the secured land and retain the land in full substitution for moneys owing under the mortgage. Eventually, however, the Courts of Chancery upheld the right of the mortgagees to apply for foreclosure over secured land once the contractual right to redeem had expired, and, where granted, it effectively extinguished the equitable right of redemption (*Carter v Wake* (1877) 4 Ch D 605). (See further discussion on the right of foreclosure at para 14.3.6.)

As the general law mortgage takes the form of a transfer of legal title to the mortgagee, specific formality requirements for the execution of a proper conveyance must be complied with. The formality requirements for the conveyance of a piece of general law land have been discussed in Chapter 9. In Victoria, a mortgage is actually defined as a conveyance pursuant to s 18(1) of the Property Law Act 1958 and will therefore attract the relevant statutory formalities for the creation of legal interests in land. Basically, all that is required is that the conveyance be executed by way of a deed as set out under s 52(1) of the Property Law Act 1958.[4]

Due to the serious nature of the transaction, the actual mortgage contract will also, generally, take the form of a deed, as set out in the statutory schedules. Nevertheless, a mortgage is not required to be executed by deed; a mortgage contract need only comply with the formality requirements for creating a valid and enforceable contract. The primary requirement for a mortgage contract is that the agreement reveals an intention to create a mortgage. This means that the agreement should indicate that the mortgagor is conveying his or her land to the mortgagee subject to the contractual right of the mortgagor to redeem the secured land once the loan has been discharged in full compliance with the terms of the agreement. Proving a mortgage is not always easy, particularly where the transaction appears to represent a straightforward conveyance. Nevertheless, a court will focus upon the substance rather than the strict form of the agreement and consider the full circumstances and context of the agreement. Often, this type of determination will depend upon the underlying commercial purpose of the agreement. This is well illustrated in *Westfield Holdings Ltd v Australian Capital Television Pty Ltd* (1992) 32 NSWLR 194. On the facts of the case, the plaintiffs were granted an option to purchase land by the defendants who had borrowed money from a related company in order to effect the purchase of that land. The loan agreement was structured in a form which was similar to a mortgage arrangement. Repayments of principal and interest under the agreement were calculated over a 10 year period, with provision for the full repayment of the loan in circumstances where the plaintiff exercised the option to purchase and paid the defendants the purchase price. At issue was whether or not the loan agreement actually constituted a mortgage. The court held that, despite the fact that the form of the agreement resembled a mortgage, the commercial purpose of the arrangement meant that, in substance, the parties had not intended to create a mortgage. Young J held that, on the facts, the mortgagee was not a traditional bank or lending institution and the mortgagor defendants intended to exchange their title for a leasehold interest and distribute rental payments amongst particular company loans for business and taxation purposes. Given this underlying

4 See Chapter 9 for interstate provisions.

commercial objective, it was inappropriate to classify the arrangement as a traditional mortgage giving rise to the usual rights and obligations.

In Victoria, many practitioners setting up mortgages over old title land utilise the statutory mortgage form set out in the Scheds 7 and 8 to the Property Law Act 1958.[5] One of the important statutory requirements for an old title mortgage is that the conveyance be specifically subject to a contractual provision for redemption. Other contractual provisions generally contained in the mortgage agreement include the terms of repayment, the date for repayment and the respective rights of the mortgagee and mortgagor concerning the property during the term of the mortgage.

14.1.3 Torrens title mortgage

Most land in Australia either comes under, or has been specifically brought within, the application of the Torrens system. Hence, most mortgages entered into today are Torrens title mortgages. The Torrens mortgage is significantly different in form from the general law mortgage. The most substantial difference lies in that fact that there is no conveyance of the legal title to the mortgagee. Where registered, the Torrens mortgage confers a statutory charge upon the mortgagee, whilst the mortgagor retains legal title to the property as registered proprietor. Where unregistered, the Torrens mortgagee cannot acquire the benefit of registration. However, where equity is prepared to recognise and enforce the agreement, the mortgagee will acquire an equitable charge in the property. The right to mortgage Torrens land and the effect of such a mortgage is specifically set out in s 74(1)(a) and (b) of the Transfer of Land Act 1958 (Vic), which reads as follows:[6]

> (1) The registered proprietor of any land:
>
> (a) may mortgage the land with the payment of an annuity by instrument of charge in an appropriate approved form;
>
> (b) may charge the land with the payment of an annuity by instrument of charge in an appropriate approved form.
>
> (2) Any such mortgage or charge shall when registered have effect as a security and be an interest in land, but shall not operate as a transfer of the land thereby mortgaged or charged.

One of the primary benefits of the Torrens title mortgage lies in the fact that the mortgagor retains legal title and therefore may still exercise ownership rights against the property, provided those rights are in accordance with the terms of the mortgage agreement. Hence, it is not necessary to confer specific rights of possession upon the mortgagor as is the case with general law

5 Schedule 7 incorporates the covenants set out in the Property Law Act 1958, s 117 and Sched 8 applies to s 206. See similar schedules in interstate property statutes.

6 See Torrens legislation: SA, s 132; WA, s 106; Tas, s 73; NSW, s 57(1); Qld, s 74; ACT, s 93; NT, s 132.

mortgages. (See further discussion on this at para 14.3.2.) Furthermore, the mortgagor may enter into a transaction which deals with or relates to the legal title of the land provided it is in accordance with the terms of the mortgage agreement, which generally requires the consent of the mortgagee. Hence, a Torrens title mortgagor may create a lease, enter into a subsequent mortgage transaction, or even sell the property.

Registration of a Torrens title mortgage will ensure that the interest of the mortgagee is binding upon all future persons dealing with the land. Registration provides effective notice to the rest of the world that the particular title is encumbered by a statutory charge and, until discharged, this charge will remain attached to the land. Upon registration, any mortgage agreement will take effect as a deed even if not executed as such. Section 40(2) of the Transfer of Land Act 1958 (Vic) sets out that, upon registration, every instrument shall have the same effect as if it were properly executed as a deed.[7] This means that when a mortgage instrument is registered, all the rights and privileges usually applicable to deeds executed under the common law will also apply to the registered mortgage. Where a Torrens title mortgage agreement remains unregistered, the mortgage may be enforceable in the equitable jurisdiction. (See further discussion on equitable mortgages at para 14.1.4.)

A mortgagee holding an unregistered mortgage will not, however, acquire the benefits of registration, namely, an indefeasible title: all unregistered mortgages are capable of being defeated according to the usual priority principles discussed in Chapter 9. The only method of protecting unregistered mortgages under the Torrens system is to lodge a caveat on the title which will effectively operate to provide a mortgagee with notification of all future dealings lodged for registration over the land. (See Chapter 11 on the Torrens system.)

As Torrens title mortgages do not result in a conveyance of the legal estate to the mortgagee, rights traditionally associated with mortgages under general law – such as the equitable right of redemption and the right to seek foreclosure – are not as appropriate. Statutory provisions do, however, specifically confer such rights upon Torrens title mortgagees. Section 81 of the Transfer of Land Act 1958 (Vic) sets out that, apart from other rights specifically conferred by the Act, a first mortgagee has 'the same rights and remedies at law and in equity as he would have had if the legal estate in the mortgaged land had been vested in him as mortgagee'. Furthermore, s 79 of that Act specifically confers a right on the part of the mortgagee to make an application in an approved form to the Registrar for an order for foreclosure.[8]

7 See Torrens legislation: WA, s 85; SA, s 57; NSW, s 36(11); Qld, s 161.

8 See Torrens legislation: WA, s 121; NSW, s 62(1); SA, ss 141–42; Tas, s 86; Qld, s 78(2)(c)(ii).

The suitability of the equitable right of redemption to Torrens mortgages remains unclear. Whilst there is no 'legal title' to redeem, the mortgagor will still want to have the statutory charge discharged and courts have held that this right is akin to the equity of redemption existing under general law mortgages. Hence, the right of Torrens title mortgagors to hold the property free from all encumbrances may, for the purposes of the Torrens legislation, be described as a right of redemption (*Re CL Forrest Trust* [1953] VLR 246). As noted by Lord Wright in *Abigail v Lapin* [1934] AC 491, p 501:

> Provision is made by the Act for mortgages in statutory form, and for their registration; in such a case, the legal estate remains in the registered proprietor of the fee simple, and the mortgage constitutes a charge of debt on the land; hence it may not be technically correct, though it is common, to speak of the mortgagor as having the equity of redemption, though legal title remains in him.

Courts have consistently applied the traditional law and practices of general law mortgages to the Torrens system despite the significant changes that the Torrens system of registration introduced. One reason for this transmutation may lie in the fact that these rights are equitable in origin, and the principles of fairness they enshrine are, in substance, applicable to all land mortgages, despite their variation in form.

The distinction between general law mortgages and torrens title mortgages was highlighted by the High Court in *Figgins Holdings Pty Ltd v SEAA Enterprises Pty Ltd* (1999) 162 ALR 382. On the facts of that case, a mortgagor, Lamina, granted a lease to a lessor, Figgins. Lamina defaulted on a mortgage it owed to the Bank and the Bank purported to exercise its power of sale and sell the property to SEAA. Before this occurred, Lamina entered into a Deed of Variation over the lease agreement with Figgins. Under the terms of this variation, Figgins removed its stock but left certain shop fittings and similar items. Figgins paid to Lamina the agreed 'new rent' which was a reduced amount. No notice was given by the bank to Figgins requiring it to pay any rent directly to the Bank. The bank knew that Figgins was paying rent at the new rate and took no steps either to demand that rent be paid to itself or that it be paid at a higher or different rate. The issue in the case is whether Figgins is liable to SEAA in respect of the difference between the amounts in fact paid under the lease as varied and the amounts payable under the lease as it stood before the Deed of Variation. The case made by SEAA turns upon two propositions: the first is that the Bank was not 'bound' by the Deed of Variation in the sense that the rights which the Bank otherwise enjoyed to receive payments by Figgins under the Lease in its original form were not curtailed by the Deed of Variation. The second proposition is that, as 'successor in title' to the Bank, SEAA is in the same position as the Bank and that Figgins is liable to SEAA for arrears under the Lease. The case deals with the operation of the Torrens system and privity between the lessor and the lessee.

In particular, the court examined the nature and effect of s 81 of the Transfer of Land Act 1958 (Vic). Gaudron, Gummow and Callinan JJ made the following comments at p 396:

> A mortgage of land under the Torrens system is the creature of statute and its incidents depend upon the provisions of the statute and so much of the general law as is availed of by or under those provisions. Under the Torrens system, a mortgage of land does not convey the legal estate to the mortgagee but operates as a charge on the land. Unlike a mortgage of land under old system title, the legal estate under the Torrens system remains in the mortgagor. Section 74(2) of the Act expressly declares that a mortgage 'shall when registered have effect as a security and be an interest in land, but shall not operate as a transfer of the land thereby mortgaged'. Furthermore, a Torrens system mortgage, unlike a common law mortgage does not itself confer upon the mortgagee the right to possession of the land. However, s 81 of the Act gives the mortgagee the same rights and remedies as he or she would have a mortgagee, if the land had been mortgaged at common law, that is, under 'old system' title. But that does not mean that the effect of s 81 is to transfer the mortgagor's estate to the mortgagee during the term of the mortgage. Such a conclusion is not sanctioned by the language of s 81 and would sit oddly with the terms of s 74(2) of the Act ... While s 81 confers rights and consequential remedies on the mortgagee, it does not affect the content or quantum of the mortgagor's estate in the land after the execution of the mortgage. That this is so is clear from s 81(3) which provides that, without the consent in writing of the mortgagee, the mortgagor shall not commence an action in respect of any cause of action 'for which a first mortgagee may sue under the foregoing provisions of this section'. Furthermore, once consent is given, the mortgagee 'shall not be entitled to bring in his name any action in respect of such cause of action'. Sub-section (3) makes it clear that s 81(1) does not transform the Torrens system mortgage into an old system mortgage and that it leaves the legal estate vested in the mortgagor who, with the consent of the mortgagee, can pursue the same causes of action which the mortgagee has been given.
>
> Given the nature of the Torrens system mortgage, it hardly seems possible to confer the mortgagee all the rights and remedies of a common law mortgagee and, at the same time, to maintain that the mortgagor retains all the rights that are incidental to the ownership of the land under the Torrens system. Furthermore, given the terms of s 81(1), it seems difficult to conclude that the common law rights of a mortgagee apply only to the extent that they consistent with the fundamental nature of the statutory mortgage. Plainly, the operation of s 81 must make considerable inroads into the legal rights attaching to the mortgagor's ownership of land under the Torrens system. It may be that the common law rights of a mortgagee by s 81(1) extend so far as to apply even general law rights which the Property Law Act makes inapplicable to a Torrens system mortgage.

The court went on to consider the impact of s 77(4) of the Transfer of Land Act 1958 which, on the facts, resulted in the estate or interest of Lamina as registered proprietor vesting in SEAA 'as proprietor by transfer' and with SEAA being 'freed and discharged from all liability on account of such mortgage'. Hence, contrary to the submissions by SEAA, it is not privy with nor does it claim under the bank. In this way, s 77(4) is consistent with the scheme of title by registration and the nature of the statutory mortgage provided for in s 74(2), as well as with the conferral by s 81(1) of rights and remedies 'as if' the reversion were vested in the mortgagee and until the happening of certain events. The result is that the rights of SEAA against Figgins do not include the arrears claimed in the Notice.

14.1.4 Equitable mortgages

Equitable mortgages may arise in circumstances where the formality requirements for the creation of a legal mortgage – whether under general law or Torrens title – are not complied with or where the estate which is being mortgaged is an equitable estate. The equitable jurisdiction will only enforce a mortgage where it can be established that the parties clearly intended to create a security interest and the circumstances are such that it would be against the conscience of the court to deny the existence of a mortgage.

If it would be inequitable in the circumstances to uphold the finding of a mortgage – then the court may refuse to recognise it. In *Maguire v Makaronis* (1997) 144 ALR 729, the High Court held that an equitable mortgage did not exist in circumstances where, despite a clear intention to provide loan moneys on the security of property, the transaction amounted to a breach of fiduciary duty. The mortgage was, therefore, set aside on the condition that the loan moneys were repaid by the borrower. The High Court referred to 'the considerations of general public policy which found the long standing principle that those in a fiduciary position who enter into transactions with those to whom they owe fiduciary duties labour under a heavy duty to show the righteousness of the transactions'.[9]

An equitable mortgage of a legal estate will arise where it can be established that the parties intended to create a legal mortgage but, because the formalities for the creation of a deed have not been complied with, the mortgage is only enforceable in the equity jurisdiction. In this situation, equity relies upon two primary maxims: 'equity deems that to be done which ought to be done' and, 'equity looks to intent rather than form'. As noted by the court in *Walsh v Lonsdale* (1882) 21 Ch D 9, an agreement to create an interest which would have been enforceable under common law may be enforceable in equity where it can be established that a court would issue a decree of specific performance.

It must be established that the agreement to create the mortgage complies with all of the usual contractual requirements under common law. Hence, the mortgagee must have actually lent the mortgagor loan moneys so that the requirement of valuable consideration is satisfied. Furthermore, it must be

9 See, also, *CIBC Mortgages v Pitt* [1994] 1 AC 200.

proven that the mortgage transfer, whilst not in the form of a deed, is, nevertheless, evidenced in writing (in order to satisfy the requirements of s 126 of the Instruments Act 1958 (Vic)) or supported by sufficient acts of part performance to render the agreement enforceable in equity. Where the alleged mortgage is purely based upon part performance, and no express mortgage contract exists, the parties must rely upon statutory provisions for the implication of specific rights. In this context, it should be noted that, if the land is general law land, s 101(1) of the Property Law Act 1958 (Vic), which operates to confer a power of sale upon mortgagees, will not apply, as the section is only applicable to mortgages which have been created by way of a deed.

The level of intention required to prove a mortgage in equity will vary according to the circumstances. As equity is concerned with substance rather than form, there is no need to describe or refer to the agreement as a mortgage in order for it to be recognised as a mortgage (*Avco Financial Services v White* [1977] VR 561). Courts do, however, focus upon the true commercial objective of the transaction and if, upon a realistic assessment of the circumstances, no security purpose can be established, then equity will not enforce the agreement as a mortgage. For example, in *Re Wardle* (1990) 22 FCR 290, it was held that an oral agreement to create a mortgage could not be established purely on the basis that the purported mortgagee made a bill facility available to the purported mortgagor, because such acts of performance did not unequivocally point towards a mortgage agreement.

The High Court has clearly indicated that, whilst some transactions may have similar features to a mortgage, this does not necessarily mean that the transaction *is* a mortgage. In *Stern v McArthur* (1988) 165 CLR 489, Deane and Dawson JJ, in the majority, drew an analogy between an instalment contract and a purchase with the aid of a mortgage, noting that the forfeiture provision in the instalment contract could be likened to a security interest held by a mortgagee. Nevertheless, the distinction between the two transactions remained: the loan contract was a purely personal right, whereas the mortgage transaction conferred a security interest upon the mortgagee and a right of redemption upon the mortgagor.[10]

It will only be where the terms of the agreement or the surrounding circumstances clearly indicate that the borrower intended to confer upon the lender a security interest in identifiable property that a court of equity will be prepared to enforce a transaction as a mortgage. Hence, in *Eyre v McDowell* (1861) 11 ER 871, it was held that a loan contract which entitled the lender to obtain any default or deficiency in repayments by means of 'entry, foreclosure, sale or mortgage' of the borrower's lands was, in substance, a mortgage transaction.

10 *Stern v McArthur* (1988) 165 CLR 489, p 529.

An equitable mortgage may also arise where mortgaged estate is equitable in nature. Equitable mortgages over the interest of a beneficiary under a trust or a second mortgage over the equity of redemption held by a mortgagor are quite common. Where a mortgagor under a general law legal mortgage decides to mortgage his or her equity of redemption, the mortgage will take effect as a mortgage by way of conveyance. However, as the interest being conveyed is purely equitable in nature, there is no need to execute a deed of conveyance: a written conveyance will be sufficient.

Mortgage agreements over equitable interests are legislatively required to be in writing because of the need to ensure that all equitable transactions are properly evidenced. The formality provisions for transactions dealing with equitable interests are set out in s 53(1)(a)–(c) of the Property Law Act 1958 (Vic).[11] The creation of an equitable mortgage is likely to constitute a creation and a disposition under sub-s (a) or (c) and, therefore, in order to be enforceable, the mortgage must actually be created in writing.

Finally, one of the most common ways in which equitable mortgages over land may arise is where the borrower has deposited the title deeds to land that he owns with the lender. In this situation, an equitable mortgage is usually implied (*Mathews v Goodday* (1861) 31 LJ Ch 282). The court presumes that the conduct of the mortgagor in handing over title documents amounts to an intention to confer upon the mortgagee a security interest in the property. In the context of Torrens title land, this is particularly true, because, where a mortgagee holds the certificate of title, no future dealings can be registered over the land without the knowledge of the mortgagee, because registration cannot occur without the production of the certificate of title (*J & H Just (Holdings) Pty Ltd v Bank of New South Wales* (1971) 125 CLR 546). Holding the title documents will usually be adequate protection for an unregistered Torrens title mortgagee; nevertheless, some mortgagees may require the additional security of a caveat lodged over the title, especially as this may have an impact on priority disputes between unregistered interests (*J & H Just (Holdings) Pty Ltd v Bank of New South Wales*).[12]

As the mortgage arises impliedly from the conduct of the mortgagor in depositing the title document, there is no need for a written memorandum of mortgage to be executed (*Re Wallis & Simmonds (Builders) Ltd* [1974] 1 WLR 391). Nevertheless, written instruments are often included in the deposit, and where this occurs, a court will generally construe the document to determine whether the parties truly intended to create a mortgage. Whilst, in most cases, an equitable mortgage is presumed from a deposit of title deeds, there are some circumstances where the deposit of title documents

11 See property law statutes: WA, s 34; Tas, s 60(2)(a); SA, s 29(1)(a); NSW, s 23C; Qld, s 11(1)(a).

12 In Qld, however, an equitable mortgagee cannot lodge a caveat without the consent of the registered proprietor (Land Titles Act 1994, s 122(2)).

with a lender will not create a mortgage or a charge over the land but, rather, a possessory lien. This will be a matter of construction and will depend upon the individual facts of each case, but commonly occurs where the deposit is accompanied by a document, the terms of which clearly indicate that a mortgage was not intended (*Re Wallis & Simmonds (Builders) Ltd* [1974] 1 WLR 391).

14.2 Sources of mortgage rights

Once it is established that a mortgage exists, the range and scope of each parties' rights need to be considered. This process cannot be properly carried out without a determination of the type of mortgage involved, because some mortgages are not created pursuant to an express mortgage contract or are created in such a way that specific statutory provisions are inapplicable.

The statutory rights set out in the Property Law Act 1958 (Vic) (PLA) and its state equivalents will only apply where the mortgage instrument has been executed by way of a deed. Furthermore, s 4 of the PLA sets out that no instrument registered under the Torrens system is to be registered under the deeds registration system as set up under the PLA. Section 3(2) of the Transfer of Land Act 1958 (Vic) (TLA) reinforces this by prohibiting any such registration. Section 86 of the PLA sets out that, apart from a few miscellaneous provisions, including the right to appoint receivers, the provisions set out in Pt II, Div 3 will not apply to Torrens title mortgages. Hence, equitable general law mortgages will not receive the benefit of the statutory provisions set out in Pt II, Div 3 of the PLA where they are not executed by way of a deed. Torrens title mortgages cannot be registered under Pt 1 of the PLA and cannot seek to rely upon the primary mortgage provisions set out in Pt II, Div 3 of the PLA.

The provisions of the TLA and its state equivalents do not expressly confine their application to registered Torrens title mortgages, although the provisions may be interpreted to apply purely to registered mortgages. In Victoria, it may be argued that the reference in s 74(2) to mortgages taking effect as statutory charges upon registration means that all of the following provisions are confined in their application to registered mortgages. In *Ryan v O'Sullivan* [1956] VLR 99, the court held that the provision for foreclosure in the Victorian TLA did not apply to an unregistered equitable mortgage, but the mortgagee was entitled to make an application to the court for such an order in its inherent equitable jurisdiction. It has been suggested that the whole tenor of the Torrens legislation is that the statutory powers should only be exercised by the holder of a registered mortgage.[13] This is not a strictly accurate interpretation of the Victorian Torrens legislation, as it does clearly recognise and protect unregistered interests in Pt V; further, if the legislature

13 See, especially, *op cit*, Sykes and Walker, fn 1, p 317, where this view is expressly noted.

had intended to exclude unregistered mortgages from the provisions of Pt IV, Div 9 of the Transfer of Land Act 1958 (Vic), it certainly makes no express mention of such a prohibition and, surely, such a dramatic exclusion warrants a specific reference.

The matter is made easier in some states as the Torrens legislation contains express restrictions. In NSW and the ACT, the Torrens legislation contains powers which are expressly restricted to registered mortgagees, whilst in SA and the NT, the Torrens legislation expressly defines mortgagee and mortgagor as 'registered mortgagee and mortgagor'. The relevant provisions will be discussed in para 14.3.

Where it is clear that the statutory provisions do not apply, the parties will generally have to rely upon either the specific terms set out in the mortgage contract or, in the absence of such terms, curial intervention by the court.

14.3 Rights and duties of the parties

14.3.1 The equitable right of redemption

14.3.1.1 Historical development in the Chancery jurisdiction

Under a general law mortgage, the mortgagor retains what is called an 'equity of redemption' in the property, whilst the mortgagee acquires the legal estate. The equity of redemption is a proprietary right which has been held to exist as soon as it is determined that the transaction constitutes a mortgage (*Kreglinger v New Patagonia Meat & Cold Storage Co Ltd* [1914] AC 25). The history of the equity of redemption dates back to the early 17th century period of the Court of Chancery.[14] During this time, the Chancellor began to recognise the inherent unfairness in situations where loan contracts had been repaid but, because repayment did not strictly comply with the terms of the contract, the mortgagor had no legal right to enforce a reconveyance of the secured property. The Court of Chancery felt that, where a lender refused to reconvey property which he or she had impliedly agreed to do once the debt had been settled, it amounted to bad faith, and it would be against the conscience of the court to condone such behaviour. In this fashion, equity first began to interest itself in mortgage transactions. As noted by Maitland:

> In consequence of its doctrine that a mortgage is merely a security for money, a security which can be redeemed although, according to the plain wording of the mortgage deed, the mortgagee has become the absolute owner of the land, [the Courts of Chancery] drew almost every dispute about mortgages into the sphere of its jurisdiction and had the last word to say about them.[15]

14 See *op cit*, Sykes and Walker, fn 1, pp 50–51.

15 Maitland, FW, *Equity*, 1910, CUP, p 266.

Hence, during the early stages, the reason underlying intervention by the Chancery jurisdiction stemmed from the belief that, in conscience, relief against the forfeiture of the mortgagor's interest should be granted.[16] Eventually, Courts of Chancery began to enforce, as a matter of course, the mortgagor's right to redeem secured property where the loan had been discharged, rather than simply doing so in exceptional circumstances. This represented a major development in the evolution of the equity of redemption. In equity, the interest came to be accepted as a proprietary rather than a contractual or a personal right. The foundation underlying the enforcement of the equitable right of redemption moved from a desire to provide relief against forfeiture to a recognition of the underlying 'security purpose' of the transaction. This evolution occurred over a number of centuries, culminating in the acceptance by Lord Hardwicke of the equity of redemption as a valid equitable estate, existing to ensure that the security purpose of the transaction is complied with (*Casborne v Scarfe* (1737) 1 Atk 603; 26 ER 377).

14.3.1.2 Distinction between the contractual and proprietary rights of redemption

Once it had been accepted that the equity of redemption was proprietary in nature, it was clear that such an interest arose as soon as a mortgage transaction was created and would not be extinguished upon the passing of the contractual date for redemption. It is important to distinguish between the equitable estate and the contractual right. In most mortgage contracts, an express term will exist conferring upon the mortgagor the right to redeem the mortgaged property, provided the mortgagor repays the outstanding debt upon the contractual date specified. This 'right to redeem' is purely contractual in nature and cannot be enforced once the contractual date for repayment has passed.

By contrast, the equitable right of redemption will arise as soon as the mortgage transaction is entered into and, as it is not dependent upon the mortgage contract, will remain enforceable until properly discharged by a court of equity. One of the classic situations where a court of equity will discharge a mortgagor's equity of redemption is where it has approved an application by the mortgagee for a foreclosure order (see para 14.3.6 for further discussion on this). Finally, as the equity of redemption is a proprietary right, it may be alienated by the mortgagor and will be subject to the usual priority principles, and therefore capable of being defeated under the *bona fide* purchaser for value without notice rule.

16 See, especially, Meagher, RP, Gummow, WMC and Lehane, JRF, *Equity Doctrines and Remedies*, 3rd edn, 1992, London: Butterworths, para 4006.

14.3.1.3 Clogs on the right of redemption

Equity will not permit the mortgage transaction to impose any impediments or 'clogs' upon the proper enforcement of the mortgagor's right of redemption (*Samuel v Jarrah Timber Co* [1904] AC 323). This prohibition is deeply ingrained in the equitable jurisdiction, the rationale being that impediments which, in substance, prevent the full and proper reconveyance of the secured property to the mortgagor are against the conscience of the court. The equitable jurisdiction has long been ready to interfere with any usurious stipulation in a mortgage which prevents the mortgagor from properly exercising his or her right of redemption. As noted by Viscount Haldane LC in *Kreglinger v New Patagonia Meat and Cold Storage Co Ltd* [1914] AC 25 at p 34:

> ... it is the essence of a mortgage that in the eye of a court of equity it should be a mere security for money, and that no bargain can be validly made which will prevent the mortgagor from redeeming on payment of what is due, including principal, interest, and costs ... whenever a right to redeem arises out of the doctrine of equity, he is precluded from fettering it. This principle has become an integral part of our system of jurisprudence and must be faithfully adhered to.

There are a number of different ways in which an impediment may be imposed upon the equitable right of redemption. These include:

(a) specific contractual provisions which completely extinguish the right of redemption;

(b) specific contractual provisions which limit the enforceability of the right of redemption;

(c) specific contractual provisions which make the enforceability of the right of redemption conditional; and

(d) specific contractual provisions which entitle the mortgagor to exercise his or her right of redemption but which alter the method in which it may be exercised.

Each of these categories are considered in turn:

(a) Contractual provisions extinguishing the right of redemption

The classic example of this type of impediment is the conferral upon the mortgagee of an option to purchase the mortgaged property. Equity has always taken a very strict approach to such clauses and, where contained within the mortgage agreement, they will generally be struck down (*Vernon v Bethel* (1762) 2 Eden 110; 28 ER 838). The rationale for this approach is that the inclusion of such a term cannot be truly considered to be the result of a free and voluntary choice because, in the words of Lord Henley, 'necessitous men are not, truly speaking, free men, but, to answer a present exigency, will submit to any terms that the crafty may impose on them'.[17]

(b) Contractual provisions limiting the exercise of the right of redemption

Where a clause has the effect of limiting the mortgagor's right to redeem, a court of equity will generally only intervene if the limitation qualifies the enforceability of the equitable right of redemption and is proven to be unconscionable. The most common clauses in this category are those imposing limitations upon the period of time in which a mortgagor can validly exercise the right of redemption. Where the mortgagor tenders the appropriate payment on the exact day for repayment named in the mortgage document, the mortgagor may enforce her contractual right of redemption. Usually, a mortgagor cannot tender payment before the named contractual date although, in New South Wales, statute allows a mortgagor to redeem the mortgaged property even though the contractual date has not yet been reached. Redemption in such circumstances will be allowable provided that the mortgagor pays to the mortgagee interest on a principal sum secured for the unexpired portion of the term of the mortgage in addition to that already owing under the mortgage at that date (s 93(1) of the Conveyancing Act 1919 (NSW)).

Clauses which have the effect of limiting the time frame in which a mortgagor may exercise a contractual right of redemption will only be invalid if the restriction proves unconscionable in the circumstances. Hence, if a clause entitles a mortgagor to redeem after having paid a set amount of mortgage instalments – and not beforehand – a court will only strike it down if it proves to be unconscionable and oppressive in the circumstances. On the other hand, a clause which actually obstructs the proper exercise of the equitable right of redemption will be automatically struck down because the right is regarded as fundamental to the mortgage transaction. This issue was directly raised in the decision of *Knightsbridge Estates Trust Ltd v Byrne* [1939] Ch 441. On the facts of that case, a mortgage was granted which contained a covenant stating that the mortgage was repayable through instalments over a period of 40 years. The mortgagors claimed to be entitled to redeem the secured property upon repaying the loan prior to the expiration of 40 years.

The English Court of Appeal held that, where the contractual right to redeem has been postponed to such an extent that it is effectively illusory, equity will grant relief by allowing for redemption. A court of equity will only interfere, however, where it can be established that the limitation is unconscionable, oppressive and against the conscience of the court. On the facts, the court held that there was nothing oppressive or unconscionable in the mortgage transaction, and hence there was no basis for equitable

17 See *Vernon v Bethel* (1762) 2 Eden 110; 28 ER 838, p 839.

intervention; the term preventing the mortgagor from redeeming the property for 40 years was a valid and justifiable term of the mortgage transaction and should not be struck down purely because it required the mortgagor to pay the loan debt over a 40 year period. According to the Court of Appeal, a clause will not be unconscionable and oppressive just because it defers redemption for a long period. See, also, *Fairclough v Swan Brewery Co Ltd* [1912] AC 562; *Davis v Symons* [1934] Ch 442.

(c) Contractual provisions which impose a condition upon the right to redeem

Where a mortgage transaction imposes a 'collateral stipulation upon a right of redemption' by creating a contractual condition in the mortgage, additional to the usual mortgage covenants, the condition may be struck down where, after the mortgagor has tendered full and proper payment, it continues to fetter the secured property.

The most common forms of collateral stipulations are those relating to restraint of trade. Where a stipulation continues after redemption (it will not be in issue where it does not) and places the mortgagor in a different position from that which he or she was in prior to entering the mortgage, the restraint will usually be struck down. In *Noakes v Rice* [1902] AC 24, p 30, Lord Macnaghten set out the general test in this regard:

> ... equity will not permit any device or contrivance designed or calculated to prevent or impede redemption. It follows as a necessary consequence that, when the money secured by a mortgage of land is paid off, the land itself and the owner of the land in the use and enjoyment of it must be as free and unfettered to all intents and purposes as if the land had never been made the subject of the security.

This principle is to be applied very broadly, and will cover both direct and indirect stipulations, even those appearing to be personal in nature. For example, in *Bradley v Carritt* [1903] AC 253, it was held by the House of Lords that an agreement by the mortgagor to 'use his best endeavours to ensure that they would always thereafter sell the tea produced by the mortgagee or, if the tea was sold through another broker, give to the mortgagee the commission the mortgagor would have earned had it been sold through him' was an impermissible fetter. This was an interesting decision, because the stipulation did not directly burden the secured property, namely, the shares in the tea company. Despite the overly personal character of the covenant a majority of the court felt that it indirectly affected the mortgaged property because it obliged the mortgagor to keep the mortgagee as a tea broker and, in effect, retain a controlling share in the tea company.

In some circumstances where it can be established that the collateral stipulation, whilst contained within the mortgage transaction, is, in effect, a separate and independent agreement, the stipulation may be upheld. This was set out in *Kreglinger v New Patagonia Meat Co* [1914] AC 25. On the facts of that case, the lenders, a firm of woolbrokers, acquired a floating charge over the assets of the borrowing company, in exchange for a £10,000 loan. The woolbrokers also acquired a pre-emptive right to purchase all sheepskins sold by the company so long as the lender was willing to purchase. This latter right extended for a duration of five years, and the loan was repaid after two and a half years. The issue in question was whether the restraint of trade covenant constituted an impermissible fetter upon the right of redemption. The House of Lords held that the restraint of trade covenant did not constitute an impermissible fetter because it was, in substance, a separate transaction from the mortgage contract. The court felt that, even though the covenant was contained within the mortgage contract and was a condition precedent to the mortgage moneys being made available, it should still be regarded as a separate and independent agreement. On the facts, the court found that the mortgagor had agreed to the trade restriction in order to obtain the mortgage moneys; this type of reciprocal arrangement was, in fact, to separate agreements placed in the single contract for convenience. (See, also, *De Beers v British South Africa Co* [1912] AC 52.)

The exception noted in *Kreglinger* can only be applied where the stipulation represents a true and genuine attempt to create a separate transaction. Where, in substance, the stipulation constitutes a part of the mortgage transaction and impedes the right of redemption, it will be struck down, even in circumstances where the stipulation is physically set out in a separate transaction (*Toohey v Gunther* (1928) 41 CLR 181).[18]

A contractual fetter will only be struck down where it can be established that it does actually 'impede' the right to redeem. Hence, if the stipulation results in the mortgagor acquiring a different property, or property which is subject to a confining limitation, the stipulation will be invalid. On the other hand, if the stipulation effectively amounts to a condition to the performance of the right of redemption, it may constitute a valid term of the mortgage and, as such, be enforceable. For example, the requirement that a mortgagor agree to sell some products manufactured by the mortgagee as a condition to the granting of the loan would probably constitute a valid condition precedent: see the decision in *Santley v Wilde* [1899] 2 Ch 474.

Mortgages involving restraint of trade clauses are not as common today as most mortgages are residential in nature and banks have developed streamlined procedures for the application, form and process of domestic mortgages. Litigation in this area tends to arise from business transactions where, in most cases, the parties are commercially competent and the covenants are entered into with specific business objectives in mind. In such cases, the restrictive approach taken by the equitable jurisdiction to collateral

18 Note that, in SA, legislation imposes a general prohibition: s 55a(2) of the Law of Property Act 1936 sets out that any collateral covenant to the mortgage will be invalid once the mortgage debt has been extinguished.

stipulations may conflict with the intentions of the parties. Recent cases have tended to avoid the difficulties associated with the imposition of collateral stipulations by characterising the transaction as something other than a mortgage agreement. Where a commercial transaction is entered into with specific objectives in mind and, as is often the case, involves a complex hierarchy of parties (as opposed to a traditional lender and borrower) a court may interpret the transaction as a basic commercial sale or loan contract rather than a mortgage, even where the form of the agreement resembles a mortgage. This ensures that the purpose of the agreement is sustained and that specific terms are not struck down as restrictions upon the right of redemption. In modern commercial transactions, the practice of the court is to intervene only where the particular provision is clearly unconscientious or oppressive. See *Westfield Holdings Ltd v Australian Capital Television Pty Ltd* (1992) 32 NSWLR 194 and *Commercial Bank of Australia Ltd v Amadio* (1983) 151 CLR 447.

Hence, the mere fact that a mortgage contract imposes a collateral advantage will not, in itself, automatically result in the advantage being struck down in the absence of unconscionable conduct. Nevertheless, the context in which a mortgage provision is enforced may be sufficient to prove it inequitable. In *Thomas v Silvia* (1994) 14 ACSR 446, Santow J in the Supreme Court of New South Wales considered the question of where a stipulation literally capable of permitting accretion of past unsecured debt of the assign to the assigned charge would constitute a clog on the equity of redemption either directly or by way of impeding the equitable right to redeem. In the process of considering this matter, his Honour considered the modern approach of courts to clogs on the equity of redemption:

> It has been authoritatively held that a clog on the equity of redemption does exist where the effect is merely to 'impede' its exercise ... However, in contemporary jurisprudence the doctrine of clogging has been interpreted in a less formalistic, more substantive manner. This has been consonant with Equity's wider modern remedial jurisdiction, based on unconscionability. Thus Equity will not intervene merely by reason of the mortgagee obtaining a collateral advantage. But it will intervene if there is unconscionable conduct, the more readily found in the case of a necessitous borrower ... In my view in 1992, the rule only applies where the mortgagee obtains a collateral advantage which in all the circumstances is either unfair or unconscionable. It may be that the court presumes from the mere fact of a collateral advantage that the transaction is unconscionable unless there is evidence to the contrary, but the principle does not extend to invalidate automatically ... I conclude that in the present circumstances to permit the charge, without the chargor's consent, to cover the assignee's pre-assignment indebtedness, or for that matter, indebtedness arising post-assignment from a pre-assignment contingent liability on the assignee's part, merely by reason of an extended definition of bank and a generally drawn 'all obligations' clause, is to impede the mortgagor in exercising its equity of redemption and thus to constitute a clog. It is also unfair or unconscionable for the assignee, as mortgagee.

(d) Contractual provisions which affect the method of exercising the right of redemption

A contractual condition which impedes the way in which the right of redemption is exercised by requiring the future activities of the mortgagor to be conducted in a specific way may also constitute an impermissible fetter.[19] One of the classic cases in this regard is that of *Santley v Wilde* [1899] 2 Ch 474. On the facts of that case, a mortgage over a leasehold estate contained a collateral stipulation which set out that the mortgagor was only entitled to repay the outstanding amount and redeem the secured property once the mortgagee had been paid one-third of the total rents she received from underletting the property. The Court of Appeal held that this stipulation did not constitute an impermissible fetter upon the right to redeem because it did not actually prevent the mortgagor from exercising the right and was, in fact, a separate agreement. According to the court, the clause could only be invalid if it was unconscionable, procured by fraud or undue influence, or made the right to redeem illusory. This is a somewhat unusual decision, as it seems to uphold the imposition of additional charges on the land, whereas other similar limitations have been automatically struck down. Nevertheless, the decision may be rationalised on the basis that the provision actually confers a valid 'conditional term' to the exercise of the mortgage contract.[20] If the stipulation is a vital condition of the mortgage agreement, then it will not be struck down unless it can be proven to be unconscionable, oppressive and against the conscience of the court. Other forms of contractual stipulations which have been struck down because of the limitations they have placed upon the way in which the right to redeem may be exercised include a provision requiring the right to redeem to be exercised only where a restraint of trade requirement has expired,[21] and a provision attempting to restrict the right to redeem to a particular person.[22]

14.3.2 Right to possession

A mortgagor in a mortgage over general land has no immediate right to possess the secured property, because legal ownership in the property passes to the mortgagee. Under such a mortgage, the right to immediate possession lay with the mortgagee as the mortgagee holds legal title. The only way that

19 This category of contractual restraints is discussed in *op cit*, Sykes and Walker, fn 1, pp 77–78, where the authors have noted that the relative 'passivity of equity in the absence of factors of actual oppression or characteristics rendering the right of redemption illusory'.

20 See *op cit*, Sykes and Walker, fn 1, p 78. Note also that the decision was criticised by Lord Macnaghten in *Bradley v Carritt* [1903] AC 253. Also, *Santley v Wilde* was not cited by the Privy Council in *Fairclough v Swan Brewery Co Ltd* [1912] AC 565, where a postponing clause was struck down in similar circumstances.

21 See *Esso Petroleum Co Ltd v Harper's Garage (Stourport) Ltd* [1968] AC 269.

22 *Salt v Marquess of Northampton* [1892] AC 1.

the mortgagor can remain in possession of the property is where a form of lease is granted to the mortgagor. Most old system mortgages contain what is known as an 'attornment clause', whereby the mortgagor 'attorns' the secured property and becomes a tenant to the mortgagee. The rent payable under such leases usually equates with the payment of the mortgage instalments. A lease created pursuant to an 'attornment clause' does not actually confer a legal, non-freehold estate upon the mortgagor but, rather, is enforceable in equity on the basis of estoppel (*Partridge v McIntosh & Sons Ltd* (1933) 49 CLR 453). Nevertheless, the relationship sufficiently resembles a lease, so as to entitle a mortgagee the right to summary recovery of possession where the mortgagor is in default, or in accordance with the terms of the attornment clause. The lease does not, however, come within the scope of most protective statutes, including the residential tenancies legislation. Where no attornment clause exists, the mortgage may expressly or impliedly allow a mortgagor to remain in possession of the mortgaged premises for a specific duration of time, thereby creating a fixed term tenancy.

Under a Torrens title mortgage, the mortgagee retains a charge over the secured land, and the actual legal estate is vested in the mortgagor. Hence, there is no need for the mortgagor to have a right of possession conferred, because the immediate right to possession lies with the mortgagor. In Victoria and Western Australia, this position has been somewhat qualified by the effect of s 81(1) of the Transfer of Land Act 1958, which sets out that a first mortgagee shall, until discharge of the mortgage, sale or foreclosure, 'have the same rights and remedies at law and in equity ... as he would have had if the legal estate in the mortgaged land had been vested in him as mortgagee with a right in the mortgagor of quiet enjoyment until default in payment ...'.[23]

The exact effect of s 81(1) is not clear. However, on the face of it, it would seem to confer the same rights to possession upon a mortgagor under a Torrens title mortgage as held by a mortgagee under a general law mortgage who has the legal estate vested in him. It has been suggested that the provision creates a statutory tenancy by deeming the mortgagee to hold the legal estate, with no right to possession accruing until the mortgagor commits a default, upon which, a statutory redemise of the reversionary estate occurs (*Tarrington v Smith* (1894) 20 VLR 90).[24] The difficulty with this interpretation of s 81 is that it appears to directly contradict s 74(2) of the Act, which expressly sets out that the legal estate is vested in the mortgagor. Furthermore, there would be no reason to incorporate an express provision entitling the mortgagee to take possession of the property upon default – as is set out in s 78(1) of the Victorian Act – if a statutory tenancy existed.

23 See WA Torrens legislation: WA, s 116.

24 This is the view accepted by Sykes. See *op cit*, Sykes and Walker, fn 1, pp 248–49.

Nevertheless, the prevailing authority would seem to favour the 'statutory tenancy' approach despite the fact that most standard form mortgage deeds do not rely upon this provision alone and generally include a term expressly conferring landlord rights upon the mortgagee.[25] See *City Mutual Life Assurance Society Ltd v Lance Creek Meat Works Pty Ltd* [1976] VR 1.

14.3.3 Right to lease

Under general law, as the mortgagor does not hold the lease estate, he or she will not hold the right to possession and therefore cannot lease out the property. If the mortgagor holds as a tenant pursuant to an attornment clause, the mortgagor cannot confer a lease upon a third party because the attornment is only enforceable upon the basis of estoppel: it is a personal right against the mortgagee, and does not confer an actual estate upon the mortgagor. If, however, the mortgage deed expressly or impliedly creates a fixed interest lease in favour of the mortgagor, it will be possible for the mortgagor to sublet, although this will usually only be acceptable with the consent of the mortgagee. Furthermore, the Property Law Statutes in some states confer an express power to lease upon the mortgagor, provided there is nothing to the contrary in the mortgage deed.

In Victoria, s 99 of the Property Law Act 1958 sets out that a 'mortgagor of land while in possession shall have power to make from time to time any such lease of the mortgaged land ... as is authorised by this section'. Section 99(3) sets out that the lease cannot exceed a term of seven years. Furthermore, the lease should be at the best rent that can reasonably be obtained, and all leases will contain a right of re-entry upon rent not being paid within a period not exceeding 30 days.[26]

A mortgagee under a general law mortgage may grant a lease because the legal estate has been transferred to him or her. If, however, the lease continues after the mortgagor has exercised his or her right of redemption, the lease may be invalidated as an impermissible fetter.

A mortgagor under a Torrens title mortgage retains the legal estate and may, therefore, grant a lease. However, this is subject to a statutory requirement that the mortgagee give consent to the lease.[27] In Victoria, s 66(2) of the Transfer of Land Act 1958 expressly states that consent of a mortgagee is only required with respect to registered leases. Hence, it may be assumed that consent is not required where the lease is to remain unregistered or need not be registered (that is, leases which are for three years or less). It is not,

25 Note that the Torrens statutes in every state specifically confer a right to possession upon a mortgagee where the mortgagor is proven to be in default: Vic, ss 78, 86; Qld, s 78(2); WA, ss 111, 116; SA, s 137; Tas, s 82; NSW, s 60; ACT, s 96; NT, s 137.

26 See property law statutes: NSW, s 106; Tas, ss 19–20.

27 See Torrens legislation: Vic, s 66(2); Qld, s 66; WA, s 91, NSW, s 53(4); SA, s 118; Tas, s 64; NT, s 118; ACT, s 84.

however, clear from this provision whether unregistered leases executed without the consent of the mortgagee will be binding upon the mortgagee. The mortgage contract will usually require the mortgagee's consent for all leases anyway, whether they be registered or otherwise.

Where the mortgagor has executed a valid lease, he or she will be entitled to all rents and profits from the lease. Where the mortgagor is in default, however, the mortgagee will be entitled to retain the rents and profits by exercising rights pursuant to the reversionary estate.

Prior to default, a Torrens title mortgagee only holds a statutory charge in the property which carries no immediate right to possession, and hence no lease could be conferred. Section 81(1) of the Transfer of Land Act (Vic) has been interpreted to deem a statutory tenancy until default, and might, theoretically, entitle a mortgagee to lease out the 'implied reversionary estate', but nothing more. After default, the Torrens title mortgagee is, following the above interpretation of s 81(1), in the same position as a general law mortgagee, and can grant a lease provided it does not interfere with the right of redemption. The Property Law Act provisions will not apply to the granting of a lease by a mortgagee over Torrens title land, although specific provisions may be expressly incorporated into the mortgage contract.

14.3.4 Power to appoint a receiver

A general law mortgagee has the power to appoint a receiver to manage the secured property pursuant to s 101(1)(c) of the Property Law Act 1958 (Vic). This section will not apply to equitable mortgages, because it is only applicable where the mortgage has been made by deed.[28] The section is qualified by the application of s 109 of the Property Law Act 1958 (Vic), which sets out that a receiver cannot be appointed until it is established that the mortgagee is entitled to exercise the power of sale. Once this is established, a receiver may be appointed by the mortgagee. There is no particular form required, and any clear expression of an intention to appoint a receiver will be sufficient. Sections 86 and 102 of the Property Law Act 1958 (Vic) expressly make the statutory power to appoint a receiver under s 101(1)(c) applicable to Torrens title mortgages.

Once a receiver is appointed, he or she will be deemed to act as the mortgagor's agent, making the mortgagor solely responsible for the acts of the receiver (s 109(2) of the Property Law Act 1958 (Vic)). This provision makes the appointment of a receiver an attractive remedy to a mortgagee, because it ensures that all moneys are properly paid into court and yet prevents the mortgagee being liable for any damage or loss suffered as a result of the appointment. The primary object of the receiver is to receive all rents and

28 See property law statutes: Qld, s 83(1)(c); SA, s 47(1)(c); Tas, s 21(1)(c); NSW, s 109(1)(c); WA, s 57(1)(c); ACT, s 109(1)(c).

profits relating to the land and pay them into court; the mortgagor should not interfere with this task. Some of the duties of a receiver, as listed in s 109(3) of the Act, are the right to demand, recover or litigate to recover all income relating to the land and to exercise any powers which have been expressly delegated by the mortgagee, including the right to sell or lease the mortgaged property. As the mortgaged property does not actually vest in the receiver, the receiver may only bring an action in the name of the mortgagor or mortgagee, and both the mortgagor and the mortgagee will be entitled to bring proceedings against a receiver for a failure to properly exercise statutory obligations (*Leicester Permanent Building Society v Butt* [1943] Ch 308).

A court of equity has an inherent jurisdiction to appoint a receiver. This is now codified in s 37(1) and (2) of the Supreme Court Act 1986 (Vic), which empowers the court to appoint a receiver whenever the court feels it to be 'just and convenient'. Either the mortgagee or the mortgagor may apply to the court in the exercise of its jurisdiction, and the court has jurisdiction over both general law and Torrens title mortgages. Generally, a court will only appoint a receiver where there is some default by the mortgagor and litigation is pending between the parties. Applications under the court's inherent jurisdiction are not as common as those made under the statutory power because the powers of the receiver are limited, and most transactions must obtain the sanction of the court before they can proceed.

14.3.5 *Power of sale*

One of the most common methods by which a mortgagee may enforce his or her rights over the secured property upon a default by the mortgagor is through the power of sale. Under this power, a mortgagee may sell the secured property to a *bona fide* purchaser, in good faith, in order to satisfy the mortgage debt. The definition of sale is very broad and will include public auction as well as a private contract. A properly exercised power of sale will automatically extinguish the mortgagor's equity of redemption, although the personal covenant will remain until it is clear that the proceeds from the sale fully satisfy the mortgage debt and associated expenses incurred in selling the secured property.

A power of sale will generally be included in the mortgage agreement, but it may also arise through the application of statutory provisions. Mortgagees under general law mortgages may have the power expressly conferred upon them through the mortgage contract or, where the mortgage is in the form of a deed, may exercise the statutory right set out in s 101(1)(a) of the Property Law Act 1958 (Vic).[29] Mortgagees under equitable mortgages over general law land may not exercise the statutory power to sell the mortgaged property. This

29 Property law statutes: Qld, s 83(1)(a); NSW, s 109(1)(a); SA, s 47(1)(a); WA, s 57(1)(a); Tas, s 21(1)(a).

is because, as noted above, such mortgages are not generally executed in the form of a deed, and therefore do not attract the statutory provision if there is no express mortgage contract; the proper remedy in such circumstances is foreclosure: a court has an inherent power to order a judicial sale in lieu of a foreclosure application (see para 14.3.6 for a more detailed discussion on this).

Mortgagees under Torrens title mortgages may have the power incorporated pursuant to the mortgage agreement or by application of the Torrens legislation. Section 77(1) of the Transfer of Land Act 1958 confers a power on a mortgagee, upon default by the mortgagor and once all of the notice requirements have been satisfied, to sell the secured property.[30] It is generally felt that the statutory remedies for a Torrens title mortgagee will not apply to unregistered equitable mortgagees, although, as with general law equitable mortgagees, they are entitled to seek a curial decree of foreclosure (*Ryan v O'Sullivan* [1956] VLR 99).[31] The rationale for this exclusion is based upon the general scheme of the Torrens legislation: most of the rights and privileges under the legislation are conferred upon registered interest holders in order to promote and safeguard *bona fide* purchasers who are dealing with the register. Nevertheless, s 77(1) does not expressly exclude unregistered mortgages – hence, there is scope for debate about the rights of unregistered mortgagees – although applying the power to an equitable mortgage would be difficult because the mortgagee does not hold any legal right to possession.[32]

The statutory power under the Property Law Act differs in substance from that contained under the Torrens legislation. Section 101(1)(a) sets out that the mortgagee shall have the right to exercise a power of sale where there has been a default in the payment of the mortgage instalments and it is established that the default has continued for one month following the proper delivery of a notice of demand, or interest under the mortgage is in arrear and unpaid for one month, or there has been a breach of some other provision contained within the mortgage deed or in the Act entitling the mortgagee to exercise a power of sale.

Section 77(1) of the Torrens legislation sets out that the Torrens mortgagee is entitled to exercise a power of sale where there has been a default in either the payment of the mortgage instalment or in any other term of the mortgage for a period of one month, notice is properly served upon the mortgagor, and the default continues for a *further* one month. Under the Torrens system, an initial one month period of default, plus a further one month period of default following notice, must be established. This additional default period does not

30 Torrens legislation: Qld, s 84; NSW, s 111; SA, ss 132–33; WA, ss 106–08; Tas, s 77.

31 See, also, *op cit*, Sykes and Walker, fn 1, p 317.

32 See *op cit*, Sykes and Walker, fn 1, pp 317–18.

appear in the Property Law Act and emphasises the significance of the notice requirement when exercising a power of sale under a Torrens title mortgage.

In England, unlike Australia, the courts have a greater discretion to interfere in the payment of arrears and may refuse to allow a mortgagee possession of the property if it believes that the mortgagor is likely to be able, within a reasonable time, to pay any sums due under the mortgage. Section 36 of the Administration of Justice Act 1970 (UK) allows a court to adjourn proceedings for possession, make a possession order and suspend it, or postpone the date for delivery of possession for such period as the court thinks fit. The definition of 'reasonable time' will depend upon the individual circumstances and, whilst there is no burden on a court to issue such an extension, it has been held that a court may postpone possession for a period of as long as 13 years (*Cheltenham & Gloucester Building Society v Norgan* [1996] 1 All ER 449).

14.3.5.1 Notice requirements

The notice requirements that must be complied with before a mortgagee may exercise a power of sale are more detailed under the Torrens legislation than their property law counterparts. Proper and valid notice of an intention by the mortgagee to exercise a power of sale where a default is not remedied has come to be regarded as a vital element in the exercise of the power. It is important that the mortgagor be clearly aware of the nature of the default entitling the mortgagee to exercise the power of sale and, where a mortgage contract exists, notification requirements should be carefully detailed in the power of sale provision.

Where a default has occurred, the mortgagee must provide the mortgagor with a full and accurate description of the nature of the default, the manner in which the default may be remedied, and the time frame for doing so. Where the default relates to the non-payment of a mortgage instalment, the notice should indicate whether the terms of the mortgage require the default to be remedied through the payment of the single instalment or whether the entire balance of the mortgage becomes payable. Unclear, ambiguous notices will be invalid, as they do not serve the purpose of informing the mortgagor of the full details concerning the default.

Under the Property Law Act 1958 (Vic), notice should be served on the mortgagor, or on one of two or more mortgagors, stating the nature of the default, the way in which it may be remedied, and that the power of sale will be exercisable if the default is not remedied one month after the service of the notice (s 103(a)).

The Transfer of Land Act 1958 (Vic) requires the notice to be in writing, to state the nature of the default, to require the mortgagor to remedy the default, and to point out that if the default is not remedied within one month of service, the mortgagee may exercise a power of sale. The notice may be properly served upon the mortgagor by delivering it personally, leaving it at the usual last known place of abode or business, posting it by registered mail as a letter addressed to the person at the usual or last known place of abode or business, or, if a corporation, leaving it at or posting it to its registered office or principal place of business in the state (ss 76(1) and 113). If one of these statutory modes of service has been utilised, the fact that the mortgagor has not actually received the notice, for whatever reason, will be irrelevant.

Where the notice does not provide a full and accurate summary of the breach and the requirements for remedying the breach, it may be invalid. Not all erroneous notices will be invalid. Where the notice has a simple arithmetic error, it will not necessarily be invalid. In *Campbell v Commercial Banking Co (Sydney)* [1881] 2 NSWLR 375, the court held that a notice of demand which requested more from the mortgagor than was actually due was not invalid: it still informed the mortgagor of the situation and of his rights in the circumstances, and it was clear that if the mortgagor had tendered the correct amount owing, it would not have been refused by the bank. (See also *Barnes v Queensland National Bank Ltd* (1906) 3 CLR 925.) Nevertheless, if the notice makes it clear that the mortgagee will not accept anything other than the incorrect amount as stated, it may well be held to be invalid, as it is misleading to the mortgagor.[33]

14.3.5.2 Manner in which the sale must be exercised

A mortgagee may enter into a contract to sell the secured property at any time after the notice period has elapsed. Prior to the sale being entered into, the mortgagor will retain his or her equity of redemption; once the sale actually occurs, the right of redemption will be extinguished.

When exercising a power of sale, the mortgagee is primarily acting for his or her own interests by ensuring that the secured debt is discharged. The mortgagee is also obliged to consider the interests of the mortgagor and must act in good faith when exercising the power, because any surplus in the proceeds of the sale, after the debt has been fully discharged, must be returned to the mortgagor. Hence, a mortgagee cannot simply sell the property with complete disregard to its market value to obtain the price necessary to discharge the mortgage debt. Under the Property Law Act 1958 (Vic), proceeds of the sale are to be applied, first, to costs, charges and expenses properly incurred in the sale; secondly, in discharging the mortgage debt; and thirdly, to the mortgagor (s 105).[34] Under the Torrens legislation, proceeds of the sale are to be applied, first, to costs, charges and expenses properly incurred in the

33 See *Stephenson Developments Pty Ltd v Finance Corp of Australia Ltd* [1976] Qd R 326 and *Clarke v Japan Machines (Australia) Pty Ltd* [1984] 1 Qd R 404.

34 See property law statutes: Qld, s 88; NSW, s 112(4); SA, s 50; WA, s 61; Tas, 23(3).

sale; secondly, in discharging the mortgage debt; thirdly, in discharging any subsequent mortgages; and fourthly, to the mortgagor (s 77(3)).[35]

The exact nature of the mortgagee's duty in exercising the power of sale is not clear. In Queensland, s 85(1) of the Property Law Act 1974 expressly sets out that the mortgagee is under a duty 'to take reasonable care to ensure that the property is sold at the market value'. No equivalent statutory duty exists in Victoria. Section 77(1) of the Transfer of Land Act 1958 requires the mortgagee to act in good faith and have regard to the interests of the mortgagor.

It would seem that the duty is not quite as high as a tortious duty of care, and the equitable principle of good faith, rather than the more onerous common law duty of care, has generally been accepted as the required standard for mortgagees by Australian courts.[36] By contrast, the English Court of Appeal has adopted basic negligence principles in holding that mortgagees owe a duty of care towards the mortgagor when exercising a power of sale (*Cuckmere Brick Co Ltd v Mutual Finance Ltd* [1971] Ch 949). This has meant that, in England, mortgagees must make a far more comprehensive analysis of mortgagor interests when exercising a power of sale than currently exists in Australia. It would seem that, despite the English duty being formulated in terms of a tortious duty of care, its foundation is based in equity. In *Medforth v Blake* [2000] Ch 86, Sir Richard Scott VC noted:

> I do not accept that there is any difference between the answer that would be given by the common law to the question what duties are owed by a receiver managing a mortgaged property to those interested in the equity of redemption and the answer that would be given by equity to that question. I do not, for my part, think it matters one jot whether the duty is expressed as a common law duty or as a duty in equity. The result is the same. The origin of the receiver's duty, like the mortgagee's duty, lies, however, in equity and we might as well continue to refer to it as a duty in equity.

This was confirmed in *Yorkshire Bank Plc v Hall* [1999] 1 WLR 1713, where Lord Justice Robert Walker noted that a mortgagee's duty to the mortgagor or to a surety depend partly on the express terms on which the transaction was agreed and partly on duties (some general and some particular) which equity imposes for the protection of the mortgagor and the surety. The mortgagee's duty is not a duty imposed under the tort of negligence, nor are contractual duties to be implied.[37]

In *Raja v Lloyds TSB Bank* [2001] EWCA Civ 210, Judge LJ in the English Court of Appeal approved of the equitable foundation of the mortgagee's

35 Torrens legislation: Qld, s 88; NSW, s 58(3); SA, ss 135 and 135a; WA, s 109.

36 The existence of a duty was established in *Pendlebury v Colonial Mutual Life Assurance Society Ltd* (1912) 13 CLR 676 and reaffirmed in *Henry Roach (Petroleum) Pty Ltd v Credit House (Vic) Pty Ltd* [1976] VR 309.

37 See, also, *Parker-Tweedale v Dunbar Bank plc* [1991] 1 Ch 12; [1990] 2 All ER 577; *Downsview Nominees Ltd v First City Corp Ltd* [1993] AC 295; 3 All ER 626.

'duty of care' noting that it is a modern manifestation of the principle that, whatever the entitlement of the mortgagee in possession at common law as the legal owner, it would be unconscionable for him to sell the property at a culpable valuation.

The good faith obligation in Australia requires the mortgagee to give a fair and reasonable consideration to the interests of the mortgagor, although this does not mean that they must act reasonably in compliance with a specific standard of care.

In *Commercial and General Acceptance Ltd v Nixon* (1981) 152 CLR 491, Aickin J held that the duty of a mortgagee exercising his or her power of sale of the mortgaged property extends to taking reasonable care to obtain a proper price, and a mortgagee will be liable to the mortgagor for the consequences of negligent conduct of any agent they may have appointed. However, this case was determined on s 85(1) of the Property Law Act (Qld), which specifically imposes a higher duty of care.

The obligations owed by a mortgagee in exercising the power of sale were further considered by the High Court in *Forsyth v Blundell* (1973) 129 CLR 477. On the facts of that case, a mortgagee over Torrens title land arranged for a public auction to be held, with the reserve price of $120,000, being the amount owing under the mortgage debt. Before the auction, a prospective purchaser expressed an interest in the property to the mortgagee by proposing to pay out the mortgage debt or bid up to $150,000 at the auction. The mortgagee refused and subsequently sold the property privately to a second purchaser for $120,000 without informing the second purchaser of the earlier offer and without attempting to obtain an increased price; it seemed probable on the facts that, if the second purchaser had been informed, he would have been prepared to purchase the land at a higher price. After the contract, but prior to completion of the sale, the mortgagor sought a declaration that the sale by the mortgagee had not been exercised in good faith. The majority of the court held that the mortgagee had exercised the power of sale improperly. Walsh J held that a mortgagee does not have to act negligently in order for the sale to be exercised improperly. His Honour felt that impropriety of various kinds may breach a 'good faith' obligation and conduct will not be restricted to actual fraud (p 496):

> What has sometimes been described as fraud on the power, and sometimes as wilful or reckless disregard of the interests of the mortgagor, and sometimes as a sacrificing of the interests of the mortgagor, does not necessarily involve, in my opinion, commission of an actual fraud.

According to his Honour, conduct amounting to a reckless indifference to the interests of the mortgagor, whilst not fitting within the ambit of actual fraud, could form a sufficient basis for injunctive relief. This decision seems to require the 'good faith' obligations of the mortgagee to constitute something more than the simple avoidance of negligence or actual fraud. According to

Walsh J (with whom Mason J concurred), the obligation is a positive one: it requires a mortgagee actively to consider the interests of the mortgagee.[38]

In *Latec Investments Ltd v Hotel Terrigal Pty Ltd* (1965) 113 CLR 265, the court held that the mortgagee had exercised the power of sale improperly by selling to a subsidiary company and, in this way, had exercised 'pretence and collusion in the conscious misuse of the power'.[39] Whilst the mortgagee had not actively refused to consider the interests of the mortgagor, as in *Forsyth*, it was clear that the mortgagee had exercised the sale in bad faith because the transaction was not at arm's length

In considering whether the obligation of good faith has been satisfied, the whole conduct of the mortgagee must be examined; the mortgagee should take all reasonable steps in the particular circumstances to obtain the best price available for the secured property and should proceed with due caution in executing the sale.[40]

Where a mortgagor establishes that a power of sale has been improperly exercised, the relief which she may seek will depend upon how far the contract has been executed. If the contract has been entered into but not completed, as was the case in *Forsyth v Blundell*, a mortgagor may seek injunctive relief to prevent a sale from going ahead; proof of an improper exercise of the power of sale would generally constitute a sufficient ground for injunctive relief to be awarded. Where the contract has been completed, the only option for a mortgagor under Torrens title land will be to lodge a caveat over the property. It has been held in *Sinclair v Hope Investments Pty Ltd* [1982] 2 NSWLR 870 that a mortgagor in such a situation does have a caveatable interest. The caveat will operate like a statutory injunction, freezing all future transactions until the mortgagor applies to have the sale set aside.

Needham J made the following comments:

> The question is whether the mortgagor, maintaining his registered title, has, nevertheless, in his proprietary right to enjoin the completion of his mortgagee's contract for the sale of his land, a caveatable interest in the land. I do not think that the fact that the mortgagor remains the registered legal owner makes it impossible for him to hold, at the same time, an equitable interest in the land. The right, which is an equitable right, to prevent the completion of a voidable sale, is not one which arises solely from his position as registered proprietor. It arises from: (1) the charge created by him by entering into the mortgage; (2) the action of the mortgagee in entering into the voidable contract. It is no less 'an equitable claim enforceable by reason of the principles of the Court of Chancery' than if the right existed shorn of the registered estate.

38 It should be noted that Menzies J dissented and found that the obligation to act in good faith had been satisfied on the facts, because the mortgagee had acted 'reasonably' in the circumstances.

39 *Latec Investments Ltd v Hotel Terrigal Pty Ltd* (1965) 113 CLR 265, p 274.

40 See *Gattuso v Geelong Building Society* [1989] Aust Torts Reports 69-281, for a summary of the general 'good faith' obligations owed by a mortgagee.

> Accordingly, in my opinion, the question whether the registered proprietor may lodge a caveat before the completion of the contract is not different from the question whether, after the contract has been completed and the transfer registered, the mortgagor may lodge a caveat to protect his right to have the sale set aside.

By contrast in *Swanston Mortgage Pty Ltd v Trepan Investments Pty Ltd* [1994] 1 VR 672, Brooking J in the Victorian Supreme Court concluded that a mortgagors right to rectify an improper exercise of a mortgagee's power of sale was, following the decision in *Latec Investments Ltd v Hotel Terrigal Pty Ltd* (1965) 113 CLR 265, not an interest 'known to law' – and therefore not caveatable.

It should be noted that, where the purchaser is registered and is *bona fide* for value without notice, the Torrens legislation will provide full protection. (See Chapter 11 on the Torrens system.)

Where the contract has been completed under a general law mortgage, the legal estate will pass to the purchaser. The purchaser will retain priority and defeat any interest held by the mortgagor where he or she is a *bona fide* purchaser for value without notice.

14.3.6 Foreclosure

Where a mortgagor is in default and no longer holds a contractual right of redemption, the mortgagee has the option to exercise a power of sale or to institute proceedings whereby the mortgagee forecloses over the secured property. Foreclosure is an old, litigious remedy which a court of equity would issue in order to discharge the equity of redemption held by the mortgagor. Once the equity of redemption had evolved, it was necessary for the Courts of Chancery to establish a remedy which would effectively discharge this equitable estate. Once a foreclosure order is issued, the secured property will vest absolutely in the mortgagee, extinguishing completely the mortgage debt. Foreclosure is an order generally associated with old title mortgages because, in such transactions, legal title to the secured property is already vested in the mortgagee, making it easier to award foreclosure and extinguish the mortgagor's right of redemption. Nevertheless, mortgagees under Torrens title mortgages have been given express statutory authority to seek an order of foreclosure (s 79(1) of the Transfer of Land Act 1958 (Vic)).[41]

Where foreclosure is granted by way of a curial order, the process is commenced by the granting of a decree *nisi*, whereby the nature of the default and an account of the exact amount owing under the mortgage debt is set out. The court will then make an interim order stating that the mortgagor has a specified period of time (usually about six months) within which to remedy the default, otherwise the foreclosure application will go ahead. If the

41 Torrens legislation: SA, s 140; Tas, s 85; NT, s 140, NSW, s 61; ACT, s 97.

mortgagor does not remedy the default within this period, the mortgagee may seek to make the order *nisi* absolute. Once this occurs, the secured property will vest absolutely in the mortgagee and, pursuant to s 87 of the Property Law Act 1958 (Vic), will have the effect of extinguishing all existing personal covenants between the mortgagee and the mortgagor.[42]

The procedure for a foreclosure action under s 79 of the Transfer of Land Act 1958 (Vic) and its interstate equivalents is very similar; however, it is limited in scope to circumstances where the mortgagee has attempted to exercise the power of sale by way of an auction and the highest bid obtained is insufficient to satisfy the moneys owing under the mortgage debt. Furthermore, the procedure is purely administrative in nature, the foreclosure order being issued by the Registrar. Where the power of sale does not raise the requisite funds and this can be proven by way of an auctioneer's certificate, the mortgagee must then execute a statutory declaration setting out:

(a) that the mortgagor has continued to be in default of the principal or interest for a period of six months;

(b) that a valid and proper notice requiring the default to be remedied has been served on the mortgagor; and

(c) a statement setting out the mortgagee's intention to make an application for foreclosure, which is also served upon the mortgagor and every person noted upon the register.

Once these requirements have been received in the proper form, the Registrar will then advertise the land for sale in a newspaper once a week for three weeks, and then appoint a time, at least once month later, when the foreclosure order will proceed. The mortgagor will be entitled to redeem the property at any time prior to the final foreclosure order being issued. Upon the foreclosure order being issued, all existing personal covenants between the mortgagee and the mortgagor will be extinguished pursuant to s 87 of the Property Law Act 1958 (Vic).[43] The statutory procedure for seeking a foreclosure order is inapplicable in Queensland, where a foreclosure order can only be issued by a court.[44]

Unregistered equitable mortgagees will not be entitled to avail themselves of the administrative process of foreclosure as set out in s 79(1), because, as noted when considering the availability of the statutory power of sale, the general scheme of the Act appears to preclude the application of such rights to interests which remain unregistered. Nevertheless, equitable mortgagees may avail themselves of a curial foreclosure order.

42 Property law statutes: WA, s 53; NSW, s 100.

43 This section applies by virtue of s 86 of the Property Law Act 1958 (Vic), which sets out that s 87 specifically applies to mortgages under the Transfer of Land Act 1958 (Vic).

44 RSC (Qld) Ord 6 r 12.

In most circumstances, a mortgagee would not seek a foreclosure order where the value of the property is significantly below the amount owing under the mortgage debt, because, as the foreclosure order has the effect of extinguishing all debts, the mortgagee may lose money. Most mortgagees tend to prefer the power of sale, because it is quicker, more efficient and generally better able to provide an exact measure of the mortgage debt – and even where it does not, the personal covenants existing between the mortgagor and mortgagee are not extinguished. A Torrens mortgagee is statutorily obliged to try the power of sale and prove its adequacy before seeking a foreclosure order.

Where a court has issued a foreclosure order, there is some discretion for the court to re-open the order, but seldom will a foreclosure order be overturned. The circumstances generally warranting a re-opening of the order include: a mistake or error in the proceedings prior to the order being made absolute; a genuine mistake by the mortgagor as to the nature of the process or the date of payment; and a misunderstanding of the effect of the order being made absolute in circumstances where the value of the land greatly exceeds the amount outstanding on the mortgage debt. Even where a re-opening of the order is accepted, a court will only overturn it in circumstances where the mortgagee is able to confer possession of the land over to the mortgagor; if the mortgagee has sold the land in the interim, this will not be possible, and the foreclosure order will usually remain in force (*Campbell v Holyland* (1877) 7 Ch D 166).

14.4 Discharge of the mortgage

A general law mortgage may be discharged where it can be established that the mortgagor has completely satisfied the mortgage debt. Discharge may be achieved under general law through enforcement of the right of redemption, whereby the mortgagor seeks a reconveyance of the legal estate into his or her name. The redemption action may be sought in contract (where the payment has been tendered prior to or on the date specified in the contract) or in equity (where payment has not been tendered until after the contractual date). See para 14.3.1.2. In Victoria, the right of redemption will become enforceable when the mortgagee executes an endorsed receipt under seal. Where this occurs, a reconveyance of the legal estate will be deemed (s 115 of the Property Law Act 1958 (Vic)).[45] The memorandum of discharge may then be lodged for registration under the deeds registration system.

Where a mortgagor seeks to redeem prior to the contractual date, all that will be owing, following the introduction of uniform credit legislation, is the total balance owing.[46] Where a mortgagor seeks to redeem in equity after the

45 See, also, Conveyancing Act 1919 (NSW), s 91(1) and (3). The memorandum should be registered.

46 See Consumer Credit Code, s 77.

contractual date, the established rule is that the mortgagor must give the mortgagee at least six months' notice. The justification for this time period is to give the mortgagee time to discover a new investment. If the mortgagor does not wish to wait six months, he or she may offer six months' interest to the mortgagee.[47] The 'six months' rule will not apply in circumstances where the mortgagee agrees to redeem and executes a memorandum of discharge at an earlier date.

Under a Torrens title mortgage, a discharge of the mortgage will be effected where a memorandum of discharge has been properly lodged for registration. In Victoria, this is required pursuant to s 84(1) of the Transfer of Land Act 1958 (Vic).[48] Once the discharge has been registered, the statutory charge over the secured land will be released, although the personal covenant between the mortgagee and mortgagor may still exist. (See *Perpetual Trustees Estate & Agency Co (NZ) Ltd v Morrison* [1986] 2 NZLR 140.)

The usual procedure for discharging a mortgage debt is, first, to tender the full amount of principal and interest owing. A mortgagor will generally require a payout figure from the mortgagee in order to ensure that the proper amount owing is tendered. Notice should be given by the mortgagor to the mortgagee that he or she intends to execute a full discharge, so that the mortgagee has sufficient time to execute the appropriate documents. In the absence of any provision to the contrary, the amount should be paid over to the mortgagee.

Where a vendor is selling land which is subject to a mortgage, and the sale is to be executed 'free from all encumbrances', the usual procedure is for a vendor to execute a release of mortgage and, once the funds have been made available upon settlement, to have these funds paid over to the mortgagee, who will then organise to have the memorandum of discharge registered on the title, prior to registration of the transfer into the name of the new purchaser.

14.5 Priorities and tacking

14.5.1 General law priority principles for mortgages

The priority principles relevant to general law mortgages are identical to those discussed in Chapter 9. It is important to understand the priority principles in the context of mortgages, because it is often necessary to determine the order of priority amongst several mortgagees. As noted in Chapter 9, the relevant priority principle will depend upon whether the mortgage interest is legal or

47 See discussion on this in *op cit*, Sykes and Walker, fn 1, p 82.

48 See Torrens legislation: Qld, s 81; WA, s 123; ACT, s 101; NSW, s 65(1); SA, ss 143–44; NT, ss 143–44; Tas, s 59.

equitable in nature. A brief overview of the principles discussed in Chapter 9, as relevant to mortgages, follows.

Where a legal mortgage over general law land has been executed, the land will automatically pass to the mortgagee. Any further attempt to create a legal mortgage will be ineffective because, under the *nemo dat* principle, once a legal mortgage has been properly executed, the mortgagor no longer holds the legal title and therefore has no title with which to create a second mortgage. The second mortgage must, at best, be regarded as equitable in nature – the secured property being the equity of redemption.

In a competition between a prior legal mortgage and a subsequent equitable mortgage, the legal mortgage will take priority, provided it can be established that the legal mortgagee has not acted with fraud or negligence and assisted in the creation of the mortgage (*Northern Counties of England Fire Insurance Company v Whipp* (1884) 26 Ch D 482). Generally speaking, if it can be established that the legal mortgagee is guilty of actual fraud, or of wilful or gross negligence, or is estopped from denying the validity of the equitable mortgagee's title, or the agent of the legal mortgagee has exceeded his or her authority, the priority of the legal mortgagee will be postponed.

In a competition between a prior equitable mortgagee and a subsequent legal mortgagee, the legal mortgagee will take priority if the mortgagee is a *bona fide* purchaser (this reference includes mortgagee) taking the property without any notice of the equitable mortgagees interest (*Pilcher v Rawlins* (1872) 7 Ch 259). The doctrine of notice in this context will include both actual and constructive notice, and it must be established that the mortgagee is *bona fide* and has given good value (see s 199(1)(a) of the Property Law Act 1958 (Vic), which incorporates both actual and constructive notice in this context). Once a *bona fide* purchaser (mortgagee) takes the property without notice of the prior equity, all successors in title to the legal mortgagee will take free from the prior equitable mortgage, even if he or she had notice of it (*Wilkes v Spooner* [1911] 2 KB 473).

In a competition between two equitable mortgagees, the prior in time will take priority, provided both are equal (*Rice v Rice* (1853) 2 Drew 73). The equality of each mortgage will depend upon a general assessment of the circumstances, but will include fraud, negligence and estoppel. A prior equitable mortgagee, for example, may be less meritorious because the mortgagee has in some way contributed to the belief in the second mortgagee that no prior, competing interest was in existence. This could occur if the first equitable mortgagee failed to safeguard their security by holding on to the title documents.

In a competition between a prior mere equity, such as an equity of rectification – assuming that this type of interest actually constitutes an estate – and a full equitable or legal interest, the subsequent equitable or legal mortgagee will have priority where it can be established that he is *bona fide* and took for value without notice (*Latec Investments Ltd v Hotel Terrigal Pty Ltd*

(1965) 113 CLR 265). It should be noted that, following the opinion of Kitto J (supported by Lord Upjohn in *National Provincial Bank v Ainsworth* [1965] AC 1175), a mere equity, unconnected with a legal or equitable estate, is a purely personal, rather than *in rem*, right.

The priority principles are slightly altered where a deed of mortgage has been registered with the Registrar General's office pursuant to s 6 of the Property Law Act 1958 (Vic). Registration is not compulsory, and can only be achieved where the mortgage is set out in an instrument. All registered mortgage instruments will take priority over unregistered and later registered instruments, even where the registered mortgage is equitable and the unregistered or later registered mortgage is legal (*Moonking Gee v Tahos* (1963) 63 SR (NSW) 935). Priority will only be conferred, however, where it can be established that the instrument was executed *bona fide*, without notice of a prior estate at the date of the instrument being executed, and for valuable consideration.

14.5.2 Tacking under general law

Subsequent advances under mortgages may be 'tacked' on to a mortgage instrument under general law in a number of circumstances. The first is generally known as *tabula in naufragio*. Under this principle, a subsequent mortgagee may gain priority for a mortgage interest where he or she joins it with an earlier, prior in time mortgage. Hence, where a mortgagee obtains a third mortgage over the land, not knowing that a legal and an equitable mortgage already exist, the mortgagee may acquire the first legal mortgage and therefore gain priority over the second equitable mortgage. If, however, the first legal mortgagee transfers the mortgage interest in breach of trust, no such priority will be conferred (*Bates v Johnson* (1859) 70 ER 439).

Where a first mortgagee makes further advance on a mortgage, that mortgagee may 'tack' those advances onto the first mortgage, ensuring that those advances will gain priority as against any subsequent mortgage over the land, provided that, at the time of making the further advance, the first mortgagee had no knowledge of the existence of the second mortgage (*Wyllie v Pollen* (1863) 3 De GJ & Sm 596; 32 LJ Ch 782). Similarly, where a first mortgage contains a covenant entitling the mortgagee to make further advances, such advances may be 'tacked' on to the first mortgage and will acquire priority against any subsequent mortgage, provided the advance is issued without the mortgagee having notice of the existence of the subsequent mortgage (*Hopkinson v Rolt* (1861) 9 HL Cas 514).

In Victoria, the general principles of tacking have now been replaced by s 94 of the Property Law Act 1958 (Vic), which sets out that tacking will be abolished except in three situations:

(a) where an arrangement to that effect has been made with the subsequent mortgagees;

(b) where the first mortgagee had no notice of the subsequent mortgage at the time of making the further advance; and

(c) where the mortgagee is under a contractual obligation to make a further advance – whether the mortgagee has notice of a subsequent mortgage or not.[49]

14.5.3 Priority principles under Torrens title mortgages

As discussed in Chapter 11, under the Torrens system, a registered mortgage will acquire an indefeasible status. This effectively means that the registered mortgagee will only be affected by those interests actually noted on the title, and will take free of all prior, unregistered mortgages, subject to proof that the registered mortgagee has committed no fraud. The range of statutory and non-statutory exceptions to the indefeasibility principle are well summarised in Chapter 11.

In summation, the priority principles applicable to Torrens title mortgagees are as follows:

(a) a prior registered mortgagee will take priority against a subsequent registered mortgagee;

(b) a registered mortgagee will take priority against a prior equitable mortgagee, even if the registered mortgagee took with notice of the equitable mortgagee, provided the registered mortgagee has not acted fraudulently in obtaining the mortgage;

(c) a registered mortgagee will take priority against a subsequent, equitable, unregistered mortgagee, provided (as under general law) that the mortgagee has not committed statutory fraud or any conduct which may raise the *in personam* exception: see discussion in Chapter 11; and

(d) in a competition between two unregistered, equitable mortgages, the prior in time will prevail, provided both interests are equal (as in a competition between competing equitable general law mortgages). Consideration will be given to the conduct of the prior equitable mortgagee, in particular to whether his or her actions have contributed to the creation of the subsequent equitable mortgage. Strong consideration in this context is given to the failure of the prior equitable mortgagee to caveat his or her interest and thereby provide notification to the rest of the world of the existence of the interest. See *Abigail v Lapin* (1930) 44 CLR 166; *Butler v Fairclough* (1917) 23 CLR 78 and *J & H Just (Holdings) Pty Ltd v Bank of New South Wales* (1971) 125 CLR 546.

49 See, also, property law statutes: Qld, s 82 (which also purports to apply to Torrens title land); Tas, s 38.

14.5.4 *Tacking principles for Torrens title mortgages*

Whilst s 94 of the Property Law Act 1958 (Vic) covers the tacking principles for general law mortgages, there is no equivalent Torrens title provision. It would seem, however, that the general law rules will cover tacking situations under Torrens title mortgage.[50] As noted by Sykes, the tacking principles may still be relevant under the Torrens system, despite the indefeasibility principles and the abolition of the doctrine of notice, because unregistered equitable mortgages may still be created, and general prior priority and tacking principles will be relevant where there is a dispute.[51]

50 Section 94 of the Property Law Act (Vic) 1958 will not apply to Torrens title mortgages because it is not expressly referred to in s 86 of the Property Law Act (Vic) 1958.

51 See *op cit*, Sykes and Walker, fn 1, pp 462–63. See, also, *Mercantile Credits Ltd v Australian & New Zealand Banking Group* (1988) 46 SASR 407.

CHAPTER 15

LEASES

15.1 Introduction

A lease is a personal, contractual agreement between an owner of land and a tenant, whereby the owner agrees to transfer the right to exclusive possession in the land to the tenant for a specific and definable period of time – which must be less than the duration of time for which the owner holds the interest – usually in return for the payment of a nominated rental. The primary characteristics of a lease contract are: the intention to confer exclusive possession of land upon another person; the term of exclusive possession being less than the term for which the lessor holds the land; and the regulation of this exclusive possession by specific contractual provisions. The vital characteristic of the lease is exclusive possession. It is this feature which transforms the lease from a personal, contractual right into a form of real property, existing for the duration of time that the tenant is entitled to possession. Where the possession conferred is not exclusive, the arrangement cannot constitute a lease.

The leasehold interest is classified as a 'non-freehold' interest because of the fact that, unlike freehold estates, it exists for a defined period of time, and it has not traditionally been included in the feudal confines of freehold estates.

Where a lease is legally created, it will vest a leasehold interest in the tenant. The owner of the land will become known as the 'landlord' or 'lessor', whilst the person holding the leasehold interest is the 'lessee' or 'tenant'. The landlord will retain a reversionary estate for the duration of the lease, which will vest in possession once the lease is extinguished.

Unlike other interests in land, the leasehold interest is primarily a contractual arrangement which, because of its application to land and its conferral of exclusive possession, has come to be recognised and classified as an interest in land. This has not, however, always been the case. Historically, leases were regarded as personal rather than real property. The primary implication of this was that leases were not supported by real actions and therefore a dispossessed tenant did not hold a proprietary or real right to seek recovery of the land when dispossessed. Today, even though the lease is commonly regarded as a form of real property and referred to as a leasehold 'estate', it is still, predominantly, a contractual creature. Most standard form lease contracts today contain not only the primary leasing agreement but also the rights and duties of the tenant whilst in possession.

15.2 Nature of the leasehold interest

15.2.1 Historical development

The lease agreement evolved during the period spanning the 12th to the 16th centuries. In the 12th century, a 'villeinage' represented what is known today as the modern lease; where a villeinage existed, the 'villein' (tenant) was allotted land by the lord of the manor (lessor) for an indefinite period of time. The status of the villein could loosely be described as a tenant at will, although the 'tenancy' was not capable of being legally enforced.

The first form of legal protection for the villeinage did not emerge until the 13th century, when the common law began to recognise the contractual foundation of the villeinage. This meant that a villein could sue his landlord for damages for a breach of lease, but it did not entitle a dispossessed tenant to regain possession. At this point, the lease was not regarded as a form of real property, although its contractual foundation meant that a lease contract could properly be regarded as a legally enforceable, personal right.[1]

Due to the inappropriate nature of contractual remedies for tenants unfairly dispossessed, the common law courts eventually developed an action entitling a 'villein' to recover possession of land over which he or she held a 'villeinage'. This action was known as the *quare ejecit infra terminum*. This action was, however, of limited use, as it was only available against the landlord or successors in title to the landlord, and not against any third party. Where the villein was dispossessed by a third party unconnected to the agreement, it was not possible to claim possession of the land.

Eventually, by the late 15th century, villeins acquired a more complete right to claim possession of the land which came to be referred to as the writ of ejectment or *de ejectione firmae*. Under this writ, a tenant who was disseised of land could actually reclaim the land itself. This writ was so popular that it became a common remedy sought by dispossessed freeholders. (See a full discussion of this in Chapter 2.)

The evolution of the writ of ejection meant that leasehold interests acquired rights akin to real property, thereby increasing the similarities between leases and real property. Nevertheless, the distinction between freehold and non-freehold estates remained. Leases could not actually be classified as real property because the old 'real actions' for recovery of the land were still inapplicable to lessees, and the tenant did not therefore acquire seisin. Furthermore, leases were still legally recognised as personal property; for example, the old principles of intestate succession did not apply to leases

1 See, generally, Plucknett, W, *A Concise History of the Common Law*, 5th edn, 1956, OUP, pp 570–74.

because they were not regarded as real property.[2] The close relationship between leases and real property eventually resulted in leases being placed in the hybrid category referred to as 'chattels real', thereby acknowledging the 'dual character' of the newly evolved leasehold estate.

In modern times, the differences between real property and leases are minimal. The most important ones may be summarised as follows:

(a) the holder of a freehold estate retains seisin of the land, whilst the holder of a leasehold interest does not have seisin. Where a lease is granted, seisin will remain with the lessor, who acquires a 'freehold reversion'; and

(b) the holder of a leasehold interest cannot fragment it into a life estate. This is a consequence of the fact that the lease exists for a specific duration of time. Hence, a lessee who holds an estate for a period of 10 years cannot transfer that lease to a third party for the duration of that person's life; the lease will automatically extinguish at the expiration of 10 years. Furthermore, the holder of a leasehold estate cannot confer a future interest upon a third party. It is, however, possible for a lessee to confer a sublease upon a third party provided it exists for a shorter duration than the head lease (see para 15.2.5).

15.2.2 Contractual nature of the lease

The essence of the lease is the lease contract entered into by the lessor and lessee. The lease contract is governed by usual contractual principles. The substance of the contract is the transfer of exclusive possession of the premises for a specific duration. The terms and conditions of this possession will generally be clearly set out within the lease contract. Usual contractual provisions include obligations of the lessee with respect to the upkeep of the rental premises; the maintenance obligations of the lessor and the nature and consequences of a default by the lessor. Lease covenants are discussed in more detail at para 15.4.1. Consideration for the transfer of exclusive possession will generally be the payment of a periodical sum of money, generally referred to as 'rent'.

Once a valid and enforceable lease contract is entered into, and the relevant formality requirements for the creation of legal leases are complied with, or the agreement is such that it is enforceable in equity, the lessee will acquire a leasehold interest. The paramount purpose of the lease contract is to confer an interest upon the lessee. Once this is achieved, title will vest with the lessee and may divest where the terms and conditions of the lease contract are

2 Note that, today, legislation in NSW has intervened to apply the same rules concerning intestate succession over real property as to personal property, so that, in this regard, there is little difference between the two: Real Estates of Intestates Distribution Act 1862 (NSW); Probate Act 1890 (NSW).

not complied with. Hence, if, for example, the lessee failed to pay the agreed rent over a period of time, the lease contract would generally entitle the lessor to terminate the lease and evict the lessee, thereby extinguishing the lessee's title.

Some principles relevant to ordinary contractual relationships are inappropriate when applied to leases because they interfere with or impede the title of the lessee. For example, the doctrine of frustration is often felt to be inapplicable to lease contracts.[3] The reason for this is that the primary purpose of the lease contract is to transfer exclusive possession to the lessee, which thereby confers non-freehold title; once this is achieved, the agreement cannot be frustrated even if the lessee is unable to use the premises. This general principle is supported by the Victorian decision of *Lobb v Vasey Housing Auxiliary (War Widows' Guild)* [1963] VR 239, where Hudson J noted (p 247) that where a lease contract has been properly effected and a lease estate transferred, 'it can no longer be said that what was agreed or contemplated by the parties has been rendered impossible or frustrated'.[4]

The House of Lords has, however, suggested that the transfer of a leasehold interest may not, in some cases, be the primary purpose of the lease agreement. For example, where all that is desired is the use and possession of the land, the acquisition of an estate is simply a consequence, not an aim or purpose, and, in such circumstances, it is possible to suggest that the primary purpose might be frustrated (*National Carriers Ltd v Panalpina (Northern) Ltd* [1981] 1 All ER 161).

15.2.3 Different forms of leases

Variation in the form of leases will purely depend upon their duration. Some leases will exist for an extensive period of time, whilst others are far shorter, their continuation being periodic in nature.

15.2.3.1 Fixed term lease

A fixed term lease is a lease expressly created to exist for a defined period of time. The actual length of time for which the lease is to continue is not important, hence a fixed term lease may exist for one month or 99 years. However, the duration must be defined, certain and express. Hence, at the time when the parties are entering into the lease contract, the length of time that the lease is to exist for must be clear; the exact date of termination must be unambiguously set out. Where the duration is dependent upon an event, the date of which is unclear at the time when the lease agreement is entered into,

---

3 See, generally, *Lobb v Vasey Housing Auxiliary (War Widows' Guild)* [1963] VLR 239.

4 See, also, *Re Equity Trustee and Considine's Contract* [1932] VLR 137.

no fixed term lease can exist. For example, a lease which is to exist until a building is competed will be invalid. It is, however, possible to create a valid fixed term lease which is to exist for the duration of the lessee's or a third person's life. A fixed term lease for life is different from a life estate: the lease is a non-freehold estate creating contractual relations between the lessor and lessee, whilst a life estate is a freehold estate, and a contract between the transferor and transferee is not usually in existence.

Very rarely, a long term fixed lease may be transformed into a fee simple. Where a fixed term lease has existed for a term in excess of 300 years, with more than 200 years remaining and little or no rent payable, there is statutory provision entitling the lease to be enlarged into a fee simple.[5]

15.2.3.2 Periodic lease

Unlike a fixed term lease, a periodic tenancy can be created by either an express agreement or implied from the circumstances. A periodic lease is a lease which exists for a succession of periods. It may arise expressly wherever a lessee agrees to pay periodic rental, whether it be weekly, fortnightly or monthly, in return for exclusive possession. More frequently, however, periodical tenancies are actually implied from the nature of the period for which rent is paid. Hence, where a lessor agrees to allow a lessee to remain in possession periodically upon the expiration of a fixed term lease a periodic lease may be implied.

Like the fixed term lease, a periodic tenancy will confer a leasehold interest upon the lessee. It is not necessary, as with fixed term leases, that the exact date of termination be specified at the date of commencement, because periodic leases may continue for a succession of periods. This does not mean that the periodic lease exists indefinitely and therefore offends the basic premise of the non-freehold estate. The periodic lease is regarded as existing for a defined time because it must exist for at least as long as the initial period. Periodic leases do not operate as an expiration and re-lease at the end of each period but, rather, the successive periods are treated as one continuous period, with the expiration of one period acting as a springboard for the continuation into the next period. The successive nature of the periodic lease does not prevent it from being accepted as a valid form of leasehold interest which will continue until it has been properly terminated by notice from either party.

In implying a periodic lease, the courts will first examine the intention of the parties; where there is no direct evidence available, the most usual method is a consideration of the period for which rent is paid. Hence, a monthly periodic lease may be inferred where rent is paid monthly and a fortnightly

5 Property Law Act 1958 (Vic), s 153; Conveyancing Act 1919 (NSW), s 134; Conveyancing and Law of Property Act 1884 (Tas), s 83.

periodic lease may be inferred where rent is paid every second week. Where a periodic lease is inferred following the expiration of a fixed term lease that exceeded one year in duration, it is generally presumed that the periodic lease will be yearly. In *Moore v Dimond* (1929) 43 CLR 105, the High Court held that there is a strong presumption of a yearly overholding periodic lease in cases where the fixed term lease exceeds one year. The rationale for this is that shorter periods would not adequately represent the true intentions of the parties in such circumstances. This position has been statutorily modified in some states, where legislation provides that yearly tenancies shall not be implied by the payment of rent and that any tenancy which does not set out its duration will be presumed to be a monthly tenancy at will.[6]

15.2.3.3 *Tenancy at will*

A tenancy at will confers an exclusive right to possession for an indefinite period of time which may be terminated at any time at the will of either party. A tenancy at will may be expressly or impliedly created. The distinctive feature of a tenancy at will is that it is based upon a personal relationship between the parties and will determine upon any alienation of the property by the lessee, whether that alienation be voluntary or involuntary in nature.[7]

Examples of circumstances where a tenancy at will may arise include:

(a) where an agreement expressly sets out that a lessee shall occupy premises as tenant at will only;

(b) where a prospective purchaser is permitted to enter into occupation during negotiations for sale or prior to final settlement; and

(c) where a prospective tenant is permitted to occupy premises during the negotiations for a lease.

A tenancy at will and a short term periodic lease are virtually identical. The only real difference lies in the fact that the focus of the tenancy at will is upon the intention to confer exclusive possession and the duration is assessed retrospectively. By contrast, it is clear that a periodic tenancy will exist for at least as long as the first period. The tenancy at will has been described as 'an apt legal mechanism to protect the occupier during such a period of transition; he is there and can keep out trespassers'.[8]

6 Property law statutes: WA, s 71; NSW, s 127(1); Qld, s 129(1).

7 For example, where either party dies – *Commonwealth Life (Amalgamated) Assurance Ltd v Anderson* [1945] SR (NSW) 47.

8 *Heslop v Burns* [1974] 3 All ER 406, p 416.

15.2.3.4 *Tenancy at sufferance*

Unlike a periodic tenancy or a tenancy at will, a tenancy at sufferance can only arise by implication of law. The conditions for the creation of a tenancy at sufferance are that the tenant has entered the land under a lawful title and has continued in possession after that title has come to an end *without* the actual consent or disapproval of the landlord.

The most common situation where a tenancy at sufferance occurs is when a lease for a fixed term expires and does not contain any provision for holding over. If the parties are in the process of negotiating for a fresh lease and the lessor does not actually object or consent to the lessee remaining in possession whilst rent is not being paid or accepted, the continuing possession may constitute a tenancy at sufferance.

This form of tenancy cannot be assigned, devised or sublet. Furthermore, it may come to an end without either party to the lease issuing any formal notification. For example, if the lessor actually enters into occupation of the premises, or indicates that he objects to the continued occupation by the lessee, the tenancy will be extinguished and the lessee will become a trespasser.[9] The fragile nature of the tenancy at sufferance indicates the personal character of the interest, and it is questionable whether it should be truly classified as a non-freehold estate.[10]

15.2.4 Distinction between a lease and a licence

Leases and licences are closely related but quite different. It is common for a lease to be confused with a licence, particularly in residential, domestic situations. For example, where a residential lease is held by two occupants who subsequently take on a boarder, unless the boarder is placed upon the lease, the rights of the boarder will constitute a mere licence.

A licence is essentially authority to enter land which prevents the person to whom it is granted from being regarded as a trespasser but which does not actually confer an exclusive right to possession; hence, a licence is merely legal permission for entry and it does not constitute an *in rem* interest.[11] A bare licence is a personal licence to occupy which is not coupled with a contract. A contractual licence is a personal licence which is conferred by a binding contract. The nature of such a licence will be determined by the terms and conditions of the licence contract.[12]

---

9 *Fry v Metzelaar* [1945] VLR 65.

10 Note that Bradbrook, A and Croft, C, *Commercial Tenancy Law In Australia*, 2nd edn, 1997, Sydney: Butterworths, para 2.20, describe the tenancy at sufferance as a 'mere fiction'.

11 See *King v David Allen & Sons Billposting Ltd* [1916] 2 AC 54.

12 See, for eg, *Cowell v Rosehill Racecourse Co Ltd* (1936) 56 CLR 605; *Hounslow London Borough Council v Twickenham Garden Developments Ltd* [1971] 1 Ch 233.

A boarder or lodger will generally hold a contractual licence, although the exact nature of the relationship will depend upon the circumstances. In cases where no express agreement exists, courts will generally rely upon the oral agreement between the parties. In determining what the parties intended, consideration will generally be given to the nature of the occupation: does the lodger have exclusive possession? – does the landlord re-enter the premises without bothering to seek permission from the occupant? – and is the occupation intended for profitable purposes or is it purely a domestic and 'social' occupancy where a person has been permitted to reside as a guest?[13]

Builders contracted to renovate, repair or build on the property of another usually enter the premises pursuant to a contractual licence. In most situations, the terms of such a licence include a provision entitling the licensor to revoke the licence where any dispute arises. In England, the court in *Hounslow London Borough Council v Twickenham Garden Developments Ltd* [1971] 1 Ch 233 held that where a licence was revoked in breach of contract, equity could provide relief to restrain the negative stipulation. This effectively meant that the licence became irrevocable insofar as it offended the terms of the contract. This decision has not been followed in Australia (*Graham H Roberts Pty Ltd v Maurbeth Investments Pty Ltd* [1974] 1 NSWLR 93). In *Corporate Affairs Commission v Australian Softwood Forest Pty Ltd* (1978) 3 ACLR 502, Helsham CJ noted that a licence was *prima facie* revocable unless granted in aid of an enforceable property right.

In some instances, the circumstances do not clearly delineate whether the arrangement was intended to operate as a lease or a licence. In such cases, the court must consider what the parties properly intended. A lease will only be inferred where a clear intention to confer full title and exclusive possession can be established. This is clearly inappropriate in circumstances where permission to occupy land is given purely for limited employment purposes. Builders and other temporary workers will rarely be able to establish that a lease was intended, but it is possible in circumstances where the exclusive occupation of the land is essential for the proper performance of the obligations. For example, it has been held that the manager of a nursery held a lease over premises he occupied at the nursery because it was necessary in order for him to maintain and safeguard the plants (*E & W Hackett Ltd v Oliver* [1953] SASR 19).[14]

The primary differences between a lease and a licence can be summarised as follows:

(a) a lease confers exclusive possession to the land upon the lessee, thereby conferring a title in the form of a chattel real. A licence does not confer such possession and does not confer any title;

13 See, eg, *Varella v Marscovetere* [1954] VLR 550; *Murphy v Simpson* [1957] VR 598.

14 Cf *Warder v Cooper* [1970] Ch 495.

(b) as a chattel real, a lease constitutes an interest in land (an *in rem* right), whilst a licence constitutes a personal right (an *in personam* right);

(c) a lease under Torrens title land is a registrable interest whereas a licence is not and may not be so registered;

(d) a lease interest is capable of being assigned or alienated (subject to any terms contained within the lease contract) whilst a licence, as a personal right, cannot be assigned or alienated unless provision to do so is expressly created;

(e) as the lessee acquires exclusive possession, the lessor cannot enter the lease premises without the prior permission of the lessee without it constituting trespass. By contrast, a licensee does not acquire exclusive possession and the licensor will be able to enter the premises without committing a trespass – although it may breach one of the express terms of the licence; and

(f) particular statutory provisions are only available to leases and not licences. For example, the Residential Tenancies Act 1980 (Vic) does not apply to licences as it only applies to tenancy agreements (s 6(1)).

15.2.5 Sublease and assignment

A lessee holding a leasehold interest will, as the holder of an *in rem* interest, be entitled to alienate it as he or she thinks fit, provided it is in accordance with the terms of the lease contract. Where a lessee transfers the entire estate over to a third party, there will be an assignment of the lease and, given that there is only privity of contract between the primary lessor and lessee, it may be necessary for the assignee to enter into a new contract with the lessor. By contrast, where a lessee disposes of only a portion of the lease, the transaction may well create a sublease whereby the third party effectively becomes a tenant under the sublease, whilst the original lessee retains the benefit of the head lease. It is important to appreciate the difference between these two transactions in order to understand when they arise.

15.2.5.1 Sublease

A subtenancy can only arise where the tenant disposes of a part of the possession conferred in the 'primary' or 'head' lease rather than the entire duration. Where a sublease is created, there will be no privity of contract between the original landlord and the subtenant, and so, generally, consent of the landlord is a pre-condition. Where a sublease is created, it will have the same characteristics as other forms of leases. A sublease is simply a lease granted by a lessee already holding a leasehold estate. Hence, a sublease may be fixed, periodic or at will, as is the case with all leasehold estates.

The subtenants will be governed by the sublease agreement and not the head lease. Each lessee will be responsible to his owner/lessor, as each lease confers not only privity of estate but also creates privity of contract. A usual term of most sublease contracts is the requirement that the sublessees observe the lease covenants under the head lease. This is required in order to ensure that the actions of the sublessees do not result in a breach of contract by the head lessee. As compliance with the terms of the head lease is vital for the continuance of both lease interests, the incorporation of a term ensuring the grant of the sublease does not constitute a breach of the head lease is both necessary and judicious.

Where a lessee grants a sublease in breach of the terms of the head lease, the sublease will remain, but the sublessor will be in breach of contract. Such a breach will generally entitle the head lessor to recover possession of the premises from all parties – including the sublessees.[15] Where a lessee under a tenancy at will or a tenancy at sufferance attempts to assign or sublet the lease, it will automatically expire without conferring any sublease.[16]

A lessor cannot unreasonably withhold consent. It has recently been held in Australia that a lessor is entitled to withhold consent and will be acting reasonably where motivated by the predicted damage that granting the sublease would cause to the future prospects of leasing surrounding land; it would seem that a lessor will be acting reasonably wherever it can be established that the sublease will cause immediate financial damage.[17] Where the refusal is not financially motivated, courts will need to consider the circumstances carefully. When deciding whether or not consent has been unreasonably withheld, the inherent right of the lessee, as holder of an interest in land, to alienate that right must be borne in mind. Where a sublease has been granted without the consent of the landlord, under common law it is not voidable; the landlord holds the right to forfeit the lease but it is not void *ab initio*.

The lessor is not obliged to give a lessee any express reasons for refusing consent, and the burden is upon the lessee to establish that the refusal is unreasonable.[18] Where consent is given conditionally, in all states except South Australia and Tasmania, no fine or sum of money shall be payable in exchange for such consent.[19] In Victoria, s 144(1) of the Property Law Act 1958 sets out that, where the right to sublease or assign is limited (rather than

15 *Massart v Blight* (1951) 82 CLR 423.

16 *Martin v Elsasser* [1878] 4 VLR (L) 481. This exception does not apply to such tenancies arising under legislation in Western Australia, New South Wales and Queensland: Property Law Act 1974 (Qld), s 129(1); Property Law Act 1969 (WA), s 71; Conveyancing Act 1919 (NSW), 127(1).

17 *JA McBeath Nominees Pty Ltd v Jenkins Development Corp Pty Ltd* [1992] 2 Qd R 121.

18 *International Drilling Fluids Ltd v Louisville Investments (Uxbridge) Ltd* [1986] 1 Ch 513, CA.

19 Property law statutes: Vic, s 44(1); NSW, s 132; WA, s 80(1); Qld, s 121(1).

prohibited), and this limitation is subject to the landlords consent, the landlord cannot require a fine or sum of money in return for granting consent unless it is a payment of a reasonable sum for legal or other expenses, and such consent cannot be unreasonably withheld.

A sublease must be granted for a term which is less than the head lease. Where a sublease is granted for a term equal to or greater than the duration of the head lease, it will constitute an assignment.[20] It is possible for successive subleases to be executed, provided the duration of the head lease is not completely extinguished.

Whilst common law regards the rights of sublessees as having been extinguished where the head lease is terminated, statute now provides some protection to subtenants in such circumstances. The legislation is similar in all states and sets out that where a landlord is seeking to forfeit a head lease and re-enter the premises for a breach of any lease covenant, a court may, upon the application of a subtenant, make an order vesting the entire leasehold estate in the subtenant.[21] Such an order can only be effected where it can be established that the subtenant has acted properly and reasonably and has not participated in the breach of covenant.

Furthermore, where a merger between a head lease and a reversionary estate occurs, statutory provisions expressly preserve the continuance of any sublease in existence. The legislative provisions are similar in most other states.[22] Section 139(1) of the Property Law Act 1958 reads as follows:

> Where a reversion expectant on a lease of land is surrendered or merged, the estate or interest which as against the lessee for the time being confers the next vested right to the land shall be deemed the reversion for the purpose of preserving the same incidents and obligations as would have affected the original reversion had there been no surrender or merger thereof.

15.2.5.2 Assignment

Where a lessee disposes of the entire lease to a third party, the disposal will constitute an assignment. Where an assignment is executed, the assignor will remain liable to the lessor for all breaches of the lease contract which were committed prior to the execution of the assignment. Furthermore, the assignor will retain privity of contract with the landlord and, for the remainder of the term of the lease, will be liable for any breach of covenant.

20 *Beardman v Wilson* (1868) LR 4 CP 57.

21 Property law statutes: Vic, s 146(4); NSW, s 130; Landlord and Tenant Act 1936: SA, s 12; Tas, s 15(3); WA, s 125.

22 Property law statutes: NSW, s 122; WA, s 75(1); Qld, s 115(1); Tas, s 82.

The new third party assignee to the lease will not be liable under the original lease contract. Any liability incurred by the assignee/lessee will be a consequence either of a new contractual arrangement or the title conferred upon the assignee/lessee. If no new contractual arrangement is entered into, the assignee/lessee can only be liable for breaches of the lease covenant where it is established that the covenant is annexed to the land. This requires proof that the covenant 'touches and concerns' the land – the relevant tests are discussed in Chapter 12, para 12.3.3.

The test for determining whether or not a lease covenant touches and concerns the lease premises has been summarised in *P & A Swift Investments v Combined English Stores Group plc* [1989] AC 632, *per* Lord Oliver of Aylmerton (p 642):

> (1) the covenant benefits only the reversioner for time being, and if separated from the reversion, ceases to be of benefit to the covenantee; (2) the covenant affects the nature, quality, mode of user or value of the land of the reversioner; (3) the covenant is not expressed to be personal (that is to say, neither being given only to a specific reversioner nor in respect of the obligations only of a specific tenant).

The primary consideration in this test is that the covenant relates to the use of the land rather than the personal use of the parties to the lease. If the covenant is better regarded as a personal' contract, then it will not be annexed to the land and cannot be enforced by assignees. Covenants which touch and concern leased premises will generally be those which concern the character of the property itself; for example, the maintenance, repair or structural obligations of the lessee with respect to the land or the financial upkeep of the property including obligations relating to the rent, rates, insurance, advertisement fees.[23]

The position is highlighted in the following example. A executes a 10 year, fixed term lease with B, who later assigns the entire 10 year interest to C. C then sublets the premises for two years to D, who then assigns this two year interest to E. A then sells the property to F. Privity of contract here will exist between A and B, B and C, C and D, and D and E. In each of these independent relationships, both parties can enforce their respective contractual obligations. The landlord/tenant relationship, however, only exists between F and C and C and E. The original lease agreement was between A and B, but B has assigned the entire lease interest to C and A has assigned the reversionary estate in the land to F. In this situation, there is no privity of contract between F and C, and unless a new contract is entered into, the lease covenants may only be enforced where they are proven to touch and concern the land. Similarly, there is no privity of contract between F and E; no

23 See, generally, for examples of touch and concern covenants, *Martyn v Clue* [1852] 18 QB 661; 118 ER 249; *Vernon v Smith* (1821) 5 B & Ald 1; 106 ER 1094 (KB).

enforceable legal, contractual relationship exists between the primary landlord and the subtenant, and E will only be bound by covenants which attach to the reversionary estate held by F.

Where a tenant assigns the leasehold estate to an assignee, the assignee will be able to sue the landlord for a breach of covenant where it can be established that the particular covenant satisfies the touches and concerns test discussed above. Similarly, the landlord will also be able to sue the assignee for any breach of covenant, provided the covenant touches and concerns the land. An assignee will only be liable for those breaches of covenant which occur after the assignment has taken effect and the assignee is vested in possession. If the assignee assigns the lease to a third party without making good the breaches, the assignee will remain liable for all those breaches she has committed.[24]

Where the lessor assigns the reversionary estate, each state has introduced legislation dealing with the passing of the benefit of all covenants attached to the land. The provisions are identical in each state. Section 141(1) of the Property Law Act 1958 (Vic) reads as follows:[25]

> Rents reserved by a lease, and the benefit of every covenant or provision therein contained, having reference to the subject matter thereof, and on the lessee's part to be observed or performed, and every condition of re-entry and other condition therein contained, shall be annexed and incident to and shall go with the reversional estate in the land ...

Where a landlord assigns the reversionary estate to an assignee, the benefit of any covenant annexed to the land will pass with the estate. The section makes no mention of the need for the covenant to touch and concern the land; however, it has been interpreted to follow the common law requirements.[26] Once the estate is assigned, the right to sue for past or present breaches will vest in the assignee. Courts have reached this conclusion on the basis of the express inclusion in the statutory provisions of the words 'shall be annexed and incident to and shall go with the reversionary estate in the land'.[27]

Legislation has also been introduced in each state dealing with the passing of the burden of a covenant.[28] Section 142(1) of the Property Law Act 1958 (Vic) reads as follows:

> The obligation under a condition or of a covenant entered into by a lessor with reference to the subject matter of the lease shall, if and as far as the lessor has power to bind the reversionary estate immediately expectant on the term granted by the lease, be annexed and incident to and shall go with that reversionary estate, or the several parts thereof, notwithstanding severance of

24 The classic authority on this is *Spencer's Case* (1583) 5 Co Rep 16a; 77 ER 72 (KB).

25 Property law statutes: NSW, s 117; Qld, s 117; WA, s 77; Tas, s 10.

26 *Davis v Town Properties Investment Corporation Ltd* [1903] 1 Ch 797.

27 *Ashmore Developments Pty Ltd v Eaton* [1992] 2 Qd R 1 (FC).

28 Property law statutes: Vic, s 142; NSW, s 118; WA, s 78; Qld, s 118; Tas, s 11.

consequently, a leasehold interest existed. His Honour therefore found that, in substance, a lease was intended, and the relationship could therefore be subject to a determination by the Fair Rents Board.

Windeyer J also concluded that a lease existed, yet he applied a slightly different test because he focused more upon the 'intention of the parties' than the quality of the possession. He noted that whether the transaction creates a lease or a licence depends upon the actual intention of the parties involved; it will require a consideration of the nature of the right which the parties intended the persons entering the land to have. If the intention was to give exclusive possession, then the interest will be a leasehold interest and will be proprietary in nature. In considering the intention of the parties, attention should be given to the overall purpose of the transaction. The grant of a limited right of re-entry for specific purposes – such as the carrying out of repairs – is not inconsistent with an intention to confer a lease, because the definition of 'exclusive possession' is relative: it refers to the granting of control over the premises rather than absolute and uninterrupted occupation. The 'intention' test was not accepted by the majority of the court but it has been used in a number of subsequent decisions.

Whilst the nature of the possession conferred remains the foremost test for the determination of the existence of a lease in Australia, courts will sometimes consider the general circumstances of the agreement. In this respect, the character of the leased premises can be significant. For example, if the lessor does not hold a freehold estate or a leasehold interest in the premises, he or she will not be able to confer exclusive possession. Furthermore, where the transaction is for advertising purposes it is often suggested that the agreement should constitute a licence, because the transaction does not really contemplate an 'exclusive possession'. In *Claude Neon Ltd v Melbourne and Metropolitan Board of Works* (1969) 43 ALJR 69, the High Court held that an agreement to confer exclusive advertising space over parts of a roof and exterior wall did constitute a lease because the lessee held 'general control' over those areas, and this was enough to establish a form of exclusive possession. Similarly, in *Addiscombe Garden Estates Ltd v Crabbe* [1958] QB 513, an agreement conferring the right to use and enjoy a clubhouse and tennis courts for two years in consideration of the payment of 'court fees' was held to constitute a leasehold agreement because the nature of the premises required exclusive possession if the right was to be properly enjoyed. Furthermore, the court held that the inclusion of an express clause conferring a right upon the owner to enter the premises for the purposes of repairs indicated an intention to grant a leasehold interest, because such a clause would have been unnecessary if all that had been given was a licence.

Under the 'intention test' enunciated by Windeyer J in *Radaich v Smith*, an intention to confer a leasehold interest may be derived from the express terms, the nature and the circumstances of the transaction involved.[32] It must, however, at least be proven that the parties intended to enter into legal relations before a lease agreement can exist.[33] The intention test has not been generally accepted within the Australian jurisdiction, although, in England, it has been held by Lord Denning that:

> ... the intention of the parties is the paramount consideration and, while the fact of exclusive possession, together with the payment of rent, is of the first importance, the circumstances in which exclusive possession has been given and the character in which money paid as rent has been received are also matters to be considered.[34]

The Australian position has been well summarised by Brennan CJ in *Wik Peoples v State of Queensland and Others/Thayorre People v State of Queensland and Others* (1996) 141 ALR 129, p 145:

> ... it is the substance of the rights conferred and not the description of the instrument conferring them which is the ultimate touchstone for determining whether a lease has been granted ...

It is sometimes the case that the express intentions of the parties conflict with the character of the agreement involved. For example, where exclusive possession is conferred upon a person, but the agreement specifically states that the transaction is to operate as a 'licence', a potential conflict exists. It is clear, following the majority decision in *Radaich v Smith*, that the defining quality will be the character of the possession rather than the intention of the parties. Hence, where exclusive possession exists, the agreement will constitute a lease, even if it is not described as one.[35]

The concept of exclusive possession has been increasingly utilised by courts in determinations involving pastoral leases and native title – with much consideration being given to the impact of exclusive possession upon native title rights. Courts are increasingly aware of the problems associated with the incorporation of concepts like exclusive possession into the native title arena and the need to remember that exclusive possession is itself, under general law, a relative concept. As noted by Black CJ and Sackville J in *Anderson v Wilson* [2000] 171 ALR 705:

> Under the general law, a legal right of exclusive possession connotes a tenancy and is secured by the lessee's right to maintain ejectment and, after entry, trespass: *Radaich v Smith* (1959) 101 CLR 209 at 222 *per* Windeyer J. But it is not necessarily easy or appropriate to apply a concept developed for one purpose

32 See *Errington v Errington and Woods* [1952] 1 KB 290 (CA).

33 See, eg, *Heslop v Burns* [1974] 3 All ER 406.

34 *Isaac v Hotel de Paris Ltd* [1960] 1 WLR 239, p 245.

35 The position in Australia can be contrasted with the English and New Zealand jurisdictions where it has been held that the express intention of the parties will override the existence of exclusive possession. See *Isaac v Hotel De Paris Ltd* [1960] 1 WLR 239; *Daalman v Oosterdijk* [1973] 1 NZLR 717.

(that is, distinguishing between a lease and a licence, usually in the context of commercial disputes) for quite a different purpose (determining whether the rights conferred on the holder of a statutory lease are inconsistent with the continued entitlement of Aboriginal people to native title rights). Particularly is this so when it is remembered that the common law accepts the idea of relative claims to possession, or relativity of titles. Under the general law, a person in possession of land can maintain an action against third parties, other than a person having a superior title. In short, exclusive possession of land does not necessarily connote rights good against all the world. It follows that to say a person has rights to exclusive possession does not necessarily demonstrate that that person is able to exclude all third parties from access to his or her land.

15.3.2 *Duration of the lease*

One of the requirements of a fixed term lease is that the duration of time for which the lease is to exist be specific and identifiable. The expressed period of time for which the lease is to operate must be clearly set out, and the events must be bound to happen. This requirement does not apply to periodic leases because they are not fixed in time.

Leases may commence from the date when the lease agreement is executed, they may be backdated or specified to take effect in the future. It must be clear, when entering into the lease agreement, when the lease is to commence and when it is to expire; if the commencement of the lease is dependent upon the happening of an event, that event must be ascertainable with certainty. For example, a fixed term lease which is specified to commence 'when the parties are ready' would be invalid. Where a lease is specified to operate retrospectively, the parties may be liable under the lease covenants, although the lease will not take effect legally until it is properly executed.[36]

A lease which is specified to take effect in the future is known as a 'reversionary lease' because the conferral of exclusive possession is deferred until a future date. The date cannot, however, be more than 21 years after the date when the instrument purporting to create the lease has been executed or it will be void; this does not apply to options to renew due to come into effect more than 21 years after the creation of the lease.[37]

Where no commencement date is set out, courts will generally assume that the lease is to commence upon the date on which it is either executed or orally agreed to.[38] If the period of the lease is not fixed by reference to an exact time or event, the lease may be presumed to be periodic in nature.

36 *Bradshaw v Pawley* [1979] 3 All ER 273.

37 See property law statutes: Vic, s 145(3); NSW, s 120A(3); WA, s 74(3); Qld, s 102(3).

38 *Sandill v Franklin* (1875) LR 10 CP 377. See discussion in *op cit*, Bradbrook, MacCallum and Moore, fn 30, para 12.19.

15.3.3 *Formal requirements for the creation of a legal lease*

Where the parties have reached an express agreement to confer a lease interest, the nature of the lease will depend upon the statutory formalities complied with and the nature of the land involved. A lease of general law land will be legal in nature where the lease agreement complies with the relevant provisions in the property law statutes. In Victoria, s 52(1) of the Property Law Act 1958 sets out that an interest in land needs to be executed by deed in order to be legal. The requirements for a valid deed are discussed in Chapter 9.

Section 52(2)(d) goes on to state that this provision will not apply to leases or tenancies or other assurances not required by law to be made in writing. Section 54(2) sets out that nothing in the foregoing provisions will affect the creation by parol of leases taking effect in possession for a term not exceeding three years (whether or not the lessee is given a power to extend the term) at the best rent which can be reasonable obtained without taking a fine.[39]

Section 54(2) has three primary requirements. A written lease does not need to be made by deed if:

(a) the lease is at the *best rent* which can *reasonably* be obtained *without taking a fine*;

(b) the lease takes effect in possession; and

(c) the duration of the lease (together with the duration of any option for the renewal or extension of the lease) does not exceed three years.

The meaning of 'best rent' must be determined having regard to all the circumstances, including the duration and the conditions of the lease. Oral tenancies which are to commence at a future date will not constitute tenancies 'in possession' and are therefore not privy to this statutory exception. Furthermore, a strict application of the section assumes that any oral tenancy arrangement commencing after the execution of the lease document (as is the case with most lease transactions) will be ineffective. In *Haselhurst v Elliot* (1945) VLR 153, Herring CJ held that an oral tenancy which was due to commence a few days after the execution of the lease agreement was not a tenancy 'taking effect in possession'. This decision has produced some uncertainties as to the meaning of the legislation, making it advisable for all leases to be executed by way of a deed.

Leases of old title land may be registered under the Deeds Registration System. Registration of a lease under this system can only occur where the lease is expressly created, because only those interests evidenced by an instrument are capable of being registered. Registration under the Deeds Registration System does not cure any inherent defect in the lease nor change its character, but it is important because of the benefits with respect to priority

39 See property law statutes: NSW, s 23D(2); WA, s 35(2); SA, s 30(2); Qld, s 10(2); Tas, s 60(4).

disputes. A *bona fide* lease registered under the Deeds Registration System will defeat all later registered interests or all interests capable of registration but not actually registered to the extent that they are inconsistent with the lease. Hence, where a lessee holds a lease for a significant duration of time, or where it is valuable or commercially profitable, registration may be appropriate in order to secure its status.

Provision exists in all Torrens legislation deeming the provisions of the property law statutes to apply unless expressly or impliedly excluded. Consequently, the above provisions will also apply to all unregistered leases over Torrens title land. Where a lease is registered, it will be deemed to take effect as if it were executed by way of a deed. A lease for any period exceeding three years (including subleases) may be registered as an encumbrance on a title under the Torrens system, provided it is in the correct form (*Crowley v Templeton* (1914) 17 CLR 457). The Registrar will be entitled to refuse registration of any lease not in the proper form.

It is not, however, necessary for a lease over Torrens title land to be registered, because leases constitute 'paramount interests' and therefore remain unaffected by the 'indefeasibility' provisions. In Victoria, s 42(2)(e) of the Transfer of Land Act 1958 sets out that the interests of any tenant in possession will remain unaffected by the indefeasibility provisions. The scope of this exception is very broad in Victoria and includes all equitable rights attached to or arising from the lease.[40] In New South Wales, the legislation only applies to leases of a term exceeding three years.[41] The provisions in other states vary in scope:

(a) (WA) 'any prior unregistered lease or agreement for lease or for letting for a term not exceeding five years to a tenant in actual possession' (s 68 of the Transfer of Land Act 1893);
(b) (SA and NT) any lease 'where at the time when the purchaser becomes registered a tenant shall be in actual possession of the land under an unregistered lease or an agreement for a lease or for letting for a term not exceeding a year' (s 69 III of the Real Property Act 1986 (SA); s 69 VIII of the Real Property Act 1986 (NT));
(c) (Qld) all 'short leases' – defined to mean leases for a term of three years or less (s 170(1)(b) of the Land Title Act 1994);
(d) (Tas) a periodic tenancy; a lease taking effect in possession for a term not exceeding three years at the best rent that can be reasonably obtained without taking a fine; a lease capable of taking effect in equity alone (s 40(3) of the Land Titles Act 1980); and

40 *Downie v Lockwood* (1965) VR 257.

41 See Real Property Act 1900, s 42(1)(d).

(e) (ACT) 'any prior tenancy for a term not exceeding three years' (s 58(d) of the Real Property Act 1925).

15.3.4 *Equitable leases*

A lease which is unenforceable at law may be enforceable in equity if it can be established that the parties intended to confer a lease and it would be inequitable to refuse to uphold the agreement. There are a number of circumstances where equity may apply:

(a) where the parties entered into a valid lease agreement, intending to create a lease interest, but the legal formality requirements for the creation of the lease have not been complied with;

(b) where the parties enter into a valid agreement to grant a lease which is held to be enforceable in equity;

(c) where the parties have entered into a valid agreement to grant a lease and the terms have been partly performed; and

(d) where the equitable jurisdiction holds that a lessor is estopped from denying the existence of a valid lease.

Equity will enforce a lease agreement which is unenforceable or invalid at law on the basis of the maxim 'equity deems that to be done which ought to be done'. The classic authority for this is *Walsh v Lonsdale* (1882) 21 Ch D 9. On the facts of that case, the parties entered into an agreement to grant a future seven year lease over a shed and certain other buildings and machinery. The agreement stated that the formal lease, when drafted, would contain a covenant that, on any given day, the landlord could demand that the tenant pay one year's rent in advance. No formal lease was ever drafted. The tenant went into possession, paying rent quarterly in arrears. Eighteen months later, the landlord demanded a year's rent in advance, and when it was not paid, purported to exercise the common law right of distress. The tenant sued for damages for illegal distress and for an injunction to restrain the distress. The tenant argued that, as the seven year agreement was unenforceable at law, he was a yearly periodic tenant holding the property on such terms as were consistent with a yearly tenancy, and that payment of a year's rent in advance was therefore not required. The English Court of Appeal rejected this argument, holding that, as the parties had entered into a binding contract to grant a lease for which a decree of specific performance was available, the contract and its terms were enforceable in the equitable jurisdiction to the same extent as they would have been had a formal legal lease been executed. Thus, as the remedy of distress would have applied at law if the lease had been executed, the remedy was also available in equity.[42]

42 See, also, *Tottenham Hotspur Football & Athletic Co Ltd v Princegrove Publishers Ltd* [1974] 1 WLR 113.

The *Walsh v Lonsdale* principle will not apply unless the agreement is specifically enforceable in equity and constitutes a binding contract under normal common law principles. Furthermore, the parties must have reached final agreement on the essential details of the lease, that is, the property to be leased, the amount of rent, and the commencement and duration of the lease. Other, more detailed terms regulating the possession do not need to be specified. If this is not the case, and certain terms are open to negotiation, the contract will be unenforceable, both in law and in equity. An agreement for a lease which is still under negotiation, or which contains a clause noting that provisions may be discussed or amended as the parties see fit, will not be enforceable in equity. In *Chan v Cresdon* (1989) 64 ALJR 111, the High Court held that a guarantor's liability could only arise under a lease were the rental liability had been incurred through a legally executed interest.[43]

All agreements for lease must comply with the original requirements of the Statute of Frauds 1677, re-enacted in Victoria in s 126 of the Instruments Act 1926, which states that no action can be brought upon any contract over land unless it has been made in writing and signed by the party to be charged.[44] This provision is applicable to lease agreements over both general and Torrens law land.

Where the *Walsh v Lonsdale* principle applies, a court of equity will enforce the agreement, upholding an equitable lease which is akin to, but distinctive to a legal lease. A tenant under an equitable lease does not actually hold a legal estate in the land but, rather, an enforceable right which is liable to be defeated by a subsequent *bona fide* purchaser for value without notice.

The nature and effect of the *Walsh v Lonsdale* equitable lease was summarised by Carnwath J in *R v Tower Hamlets London Borough Council* [1999] QB 1019:

> The doctrine of *Walsh v Lonsdale*, which is based on the equitable maxim that 'equity looks on that as done which ought to be done' is that a specifically enforceable lease is as good as a lease. There may be circumstances in which an equitable interest is overreached, but in most cases a person with an equitable lease is in the same position as a person who has had a legal estate vested in him by a deed.

A lease may also be enforceable in equity under the equitable doctrine of part performance. The equitable doctrine of part performance is an exception to the rule requiring a written memorandum or note of the contract for a lease. This doctrine will arise wherever an unenforceable agreement at law is susceptible to a decree of specific performance and the terms of the agreement have been

43 See, also, *S & E Promotions Pty Ltd v Tobin Brothers* (1994) 122 ALR 637; *Elmslie v FCT* (1993) 118 ALR 357.

44 Conveyancing Act 1919 (NSW), s 54A; Law of Property Act 1936 (SA), s 26; Property Law Act 1974 (Qld), s 59; Conveyancing and Law of Property Act 1884 (Tas), s 36. In WA, s 4 of the old Statute of Frauds 1677 remains applicable in this respect.

partly performed by one of the parties. To constitute a sufficient act of part performance, the act must unequivocally, and of its own nature, refer to the alleged lease agreement. An act will be sufficient to establish part performance of a lease where it indicates a clear intention to confer exclusive possession; for example, a tenant entering into possession of the premises, paying rent and the rent being accepted by the landlord.[45] Alternatively, the handing over of keys by the landlord or the payment of a security deposit by a tenant will also constitute acts which are 'sufficiently referable' to a lease agreement. It has been held that acts of part performance must directly relate to the particular lease in issue; in *O'Rourke v Hoeven* [1974] 1 NSWLR 622, it was held that alterations to lease premises related to a first lease but could not constitute acts of part performance for a second lease over the property because they were not 'sufficiently referable'.

An equitable lease may also be created under equitable estoppel principles. Where a landlord is precluded from denying that he or she represented to a tenant that a lease exists, a landlord may be estopped from denying that a valid lease exists.[46] The estoppel prevents either party from raising breach of covenant claims or lack of title claims as a defence to the claim of a valid and enforceable lease. For example, in *Industrial Properties (Barton Hill) Ltd v Associated Electrical Industries Ltd* [1977] 2 All ER 293, Roskill LJ stated (p 311):

> ... a lessee or tenant who has had possession for the whole of the term is thereafter estopped from denying his lessor's or landlord's title in respect of the period for which he has had possession ...

Where the estoppel is based in equity, the foundation of the action is the unconscionable denial of a representation that has led either party to believe that a valid lease is in existence.[47] An estoppel may be claimed in equity despite the fact that the lease agreement is not in writing, because estoppel operates irrespective of the statutory requirements.[48]

Different priority principles apply to the enforceability of equitable interests. Equitable leases will always be defeated by a *bona fide* purchaser for value of a legal estate without notice. Finally, equitable leasehold interests may be dependent upon statutory provisions for the conferral of specific rights and obligations in the absence of any expressly concluded contract; in such cases, the contractual rights and obligations expressly conferred under a

45 See, eg, *Tornatora v Palatinus* [1966] WAR 14, where the acts of a lessee in continuing to remain in possession after the expiry of the lease term, paying a higher rental and the water rates, were held to constitute 'sufficiently referable' acts of part performance.

46 See, generally, Prichard, C, 'Tenancy by estoppel' (1964) 80 LQR 370 and, for an example of the application of estoppel principles, *Walton Stores (Interstate) Ltd v Maher* (1988) 62 ALJR 110.

47 *Commonwealth v Newcrest Mining (WA) Ltd* (1995) 130 ALR 193.

48 See *Walton Stores (Interstate) Ltd v Maher* (1988) 62 ALJR 110.

legal lease agreement may differ from the statutory obligations applicable to the equitable lease.

15.4 Lease covenants

The lease is essentially a private contractual arrangement and the parties are capable of incorporating as many terms into the agreement as they mutually decide upon. These terms may be fundamental or non-fundamental in nature. The remedy for a breach of the covenant will differ depending upon how each covenant is phrased. If the covenant is fundamental, a right of recision exists at common law and in equity in favour of the injured party, whereas if the covenant is not fundamental, the remedy may be damages and/or injunctive relief.

If a particular term is structured as a non-fundamental covenant, there will generally be a provision in the lease document enabling the landlord to terminate the lease upon its breach. This right is generally conferred by a provision known as the 'forfeiture provision'. In effect, the forfeiture provision gives the landlord or the tenant the right to forfeit the lease whenever a breach of any covenant occurs. The forfeiture provision must be expressly incorporated and will not be readily implied.

The courts will resolve any dispute concerning the meaning of any of the terms of a lease in accordance with usual common law rules relating to the construction of documents. The first and primary rule is that, where a potential breach will result in the forfeiture of a leasehold interest held by the tenant, any ambiguity in determining the breach will be resolved in favour of the tenant.

Secondly, any term of the lease should be interpreted in light of the contents of the entire lease as well as the surrounding circumstances. In the event of an ambiguity, a covenant should be construed against the covenantor in favour of the covenantee. Unless the lease actually states that a particular covenant is conditional upon the performance of another, the covenants will be enforced separately. What this means is that the breach of one covenant by one party will not necessarily entitle the other party to breach another covenant within the lease. For example, if the landlord breaches the obligation to repair, the tenant is not automatically entitled to withhold rent.

15.4.1 Usual express covenants

The following covenants are said to be 'usual' covenants and generally form a part of the leasehold agreement:

(a) a covenant by the landlord ensuring that the tenant has quiet enjoyment;

(b) a covenant by the tenant to pay the rent;

(c) a covenant by the tenant to pay the rates and taxes, except for those expressly set out as being payable by the landlord;

(d) a covenant to keep and deliver up the premises in good and tenantable repair; and

(e) a covenant permitting the landlord to enter the rented premises to inspect its condition.

These are covenants which are usually included within a standard form lease agreement. Furthermore, as the definition of 'land' within the property law statutes has been held to include leases – whether they be over general law or Torrens title land – all of the benefits and rights connected with ownership of the land will be conferred upon the lessee for the duration of the lease.[49]

Usual covenants included within leases may vary according to the circumstances involved, the nature of the agreement and the social climate of the lease. As noted by Sir George Jessel MR in *Hampshire v Wickens* (1878) 7 Ch D 555 (pp 561–62):

> Usual covenants may vary in different generations. The law declares what are usual covenants according to the then knowledge of mankind. Now what is well known at one time may not be well known at another time, so that you cannot say that usual covenants never change.

If covenants are not expressly included within a lease, they may be implied (over and above the usual terms). Many fundamental covenants will be implied at common law in order for the agreement to function as a basic lease; others may be implied where necessary to give 'business efficacy' to the contract.

15.4.2 *Implied covenants in law*

Covenants may be implied in a number of circumstances. First, covenants may be implied through a natural construction of the express terms of the lease; secondly, covenants may be implied by statute; and thirdly, covenants may be implied from the nature of the lease. This final category of covenants is often referred to as 'covenants in law'. Covenants in law and implied statutory covenants are discussed below.

15.4.2.1 Covenants in law

Implied covenants in law refer to those covenants which are legally assumed to arise from the nature of the lease transaction itself. Each covenant will only apply where there is no express provision to the contrary.[50] Implied covenants in law are as follows:

49 Property law statutes: Vic, s 18(1); NSW, s 7(1); SA, s 7; WA, s 7; Tas, s 2; Qld, s 4.

50 *Malsy v Eichholz* [1916] 2 KB 308; *Miller v Emcer Products Ltd* [1956] 1 Ch 304.

(a) Implied covenant that a furnished dwelling is fit for habitation

The principle of *caveat emptor* applies to leased premises, and there is no general obligation under common law for a landlord to make repairs or improvements to the leased premises. Furthermore, a lessor is not obliged, under the common law, to disclose to the lessee the defective state of repair of the premises before entering into a lease. In the absence of an express provision, there is no implied warranty that the premises are habitable or are physically or legally fit for the purpose for which they are leased, or that they will continue to be habitable or useable. There are, however, a number of exceptions to this principle which can be summarised as follows:

- where the landlord has remained in occupation of common parts of a building, in which case, he or she will have an obligation to keep it in substantial repair;
- where the disrepair of the landlord's adjacent property interferes with the enjoyment or some other right of the tenant, in which case, the landlord may be obliged to have it repaired;
- where the defective building of the lease premises by the builder/landlord renders the premises unfit or dangerous;
- where the tenant enters into a lease of a dwelling house or building whilst it is still in the course of being built; and
- where the premises are let furnished.

In *Karaggianis v Malltown Pty Ltd* (1979) 21 SASR 381, it was held that, where the lessor remains in occupation of parts of the building essential to the lessee's enjoyment of the tenancy, then, unless the obligation to maintain and repair has been placed entirely upon the tenants, the landlord is under an implied covenant to take reasonable care to keep the parts of the building still under his or her control in reasonable repair. This obligation is very important for commercial leases, because it effectively requires the landlord of a shopping complex or highrise building to repair essential facilities, such as drainage or toilet blocks, which are in common usage. The principle does not require the lessor to repair *all* common areas but, rather, only those areas *essential* to the lessee's enjoyment and use of the premises. This duty is qualified by the obligation of the tenant to do what is reasonably necessary for themselves. There are a range of cases examining the implied obligations concerning fitness for habitation and repair.

The landlord will be under an implied duty to keep the premises fit for habitation where the premises are leased furnished. In *Smith v Marrable* (1843) 11 M&W 5; 152 ER 693, it was held that the tenant of premises which had been leased furnished was entitled to quit the lease upon discovering that the place was infested with bugs, because the landlord was under an implied duty to provide a dwelling which was fit for habitation. This principle does not apply where the leased premises are unfurnished (*Cruse v Mount* [1933] Ch 278). Furthermore, the covenant will only apply to the condition of furnished premises at the start of the lease.[51] A furnished property has been held to be unfit for habitation where it has defective drainage or infectious diseases, such as measles or tuberculosis, but not where the electrical appliances are in a dangerous condition.[52]

(b) *Implied covenant to use the premises in a tenant-like manner*

All tenants to a lease should use the leased premises in a proper manner, taking care to ensure that it is properly maintained and not allowed to fall into disrepair. The requirement has been well summarised by Lord Denning in *Warren v Keen* [1954] 1 QB 15, CA, who noted that the tenant should take proper care of the place and do all the little tasks around the property which are reasonably required. His Lordship provided some examples (see p 21), noting that the tenant:

> ... must, if he is going away for the winter, turn off the water and empty the boiler; he must clean the chimneys and windows when necessary; he must mend the electric light when it fuses; he must unstop the sink when it is blocked by waste. In short, he must do the little jobs about the place which a reasonable tenant would do. In addition, the tenant must not damage the property wilfully or negligently nor allow third parties to do so.

Undoubtedly the character of housing has changed since this judgment was made – certainly cleaning chimneys and emptying boilers is not as common with the advent of electric heating and gas hot water; nevertheless, the principle underlying the judgment is important. A tenant should look after the leased premises whilst he is in possession in substantially the same manner as the owner.

If the property falls into disrepair through fair wear and tear or lapse of time, or for any reason not directly connected with the possession of the tenant, the tenant will not be liable to repair it.

(c) *Implied covenant that the lessee will have quiet enjoyment of the premises*

A covenant entitling the lessee to quiet enjoyment of the leased premises will be implied into all leases in the absence of an express covenant to the contrary. This covenant entitles the tenant to a right of quiet and peaceful possession without interruption, and imposes an obligation upon the landlord to allow

51 See *Pampris v Thanos* [1968] 1 NSWR 56, where the court held that there is no implied warranty that the furnished house will continue to be fit for habitation during the term of the lease.

52 See *ibid*.

the tenant to remain peacefully in possession during the term of the lease, free from interruption. The tenant's right to quiet, uninterrupted possession is regarded as an imputed right of all lease agreements, being a natural consequence of the conferral of exclusive possession.

This covenant will be breached where the landlord has personally interrupted the lessee's quiet enjoyment. Examples where this has been found to have occurred include removal of the doors and windows of leased premises by the landlord and cutting off the gas and electricity supplies in order to force the tenant to vacate the premises. The scope of the covenant will depend upon the nature and circumstances of the alleged breach. For example, in *Miller v Emcer Products Ltd* [1956] 1 Ch 304, the court found that the landlord's refusal to allow a tenant use of the adjacent toilet block did not amount to a breach of an express term conferring quiet enjoyment upon the tenant. By contrast, in *Martin's Camera Corner Pty Ltd v Hotel Mayfair Ltd* [1976] NSWLR 15, the failure of the landlord to keep drainage clear, resulting in a flooding of the leased premises, was held to constitute a breach of the covenant for quiet enjoyment.

Not all harassment suffered by the lessee will come within the scope of the covenant. In order to breach the 'quiet enjoyment' covenant, it must be established that the landlord has personally committed the disturbance. Where the landlord is not directly responsible, or the direct causal link flows from the actions of third parties, the covenant will not be breached.[53]

The covenant for quiet enjoyment can be overridden by the enforcement of rights under a head lease. Hence, if a lessee breaches a covenant and the head lessor exercises a right to terminate the lease, the sublessee cannot claim that this amounts to a disruption of his or her quiet enjoyment of the lease.

(d) Implied covenant not to derogate from the grant

There is an implied covenant that where a lease is granted to a tenant for a particular purpose, a landlord must not derogate from the grant actually given to the tenant. The rationale is that, where a lease is given for a specific purpose, the landlord must not to use the land retained by him in such a manner that it renders the leased premises unfit for the purpose.[54]

Hence, if a landlord gives away a part of land for a commercial lease, he will be prevented from doing anything on the remaining portion of land which might result in the premises being unfit to carry on the business. This covenant partially overlaps with the covenant for quiet enjoyment, although the covenants apply to different land: non-derogation refers to the way in

53 See *Gordon v Lidcombe Developments Pty Ltd* [1966] 2 NSWR 9; *Kenny v Preen* [1962] 3 All ER 814.

54 *Browne v Flower* [1911] 1 Ch 219.

which the land retained by the landlord is used, whilst quiet enjoyment refers to the way in which the leased land is interfered with. In *Karaggiannis v Malltown Pty Ltd* (1979) 21 SASR 381, the court held that a landlord who substantially interfered with common areas to the extent that rights of access to potential customers for the business being conducted on the leased premises were reduced had derogated from the grant and was in breach of the implied covenant.

The full ambit of this covenant remains unclear; however, a landlord will generally be in breach in circumstances where the lease is granted for a particular purpose and the activities on the landlord's land substantially interfere with the ability of the tenant to carry out that purpose. The most common circumstances where this type of situation may arises is where the lease is granted for the purpose of conducting a business.[55]

(e) Implied duty of the tenant not to commit waste

Waste is a tortious doctrine preventing a life tenant from damaging the property or letting it fall into a state of dilapidation which would be detrimental to the interests of the remainderman. The same principle is applicable to leasehold interests. If a tenant permits the property to fall into an unsatisfactory state of repair detrimental to the interests of the landlord, he may be tortiously liable under the doctrine of waste. This covenant is very similar in form to the obligation to use the premises in a tenant-like manner.

(f) Implied duty to yield up possession

The common law implies a covenant requiring the tenant not only to vacate the premises at the conclusion of the lease, but also to make sure that the landlord is able to retake possession with a minimum of difficulty. Hence, to satisfy this covenant, the tenant must make sure that all of the furniture has been removed, the keys handed over, and any subtenant in occupation has been removed.[56]

(g) Landlord's duty to inspect and keep the premises in reasonable repair

A landlord owes a duty of care to the tenant. The standard was described by McCardie J in *Maclenan v Segar* [1917] 2 KB 325 as follows:

> Where the occupier of premises agrees for reward that a person shall have the right to enter and use them for a mutually contemplated purpose, the contract between the parties (unless it provides to the contrary) contains an implied warranty that the premises are as safe for that purpose as reasonable care and

55 See *Harmer v Jumbil (Nigeria) Tin Areas Ltd* [1921] 1 Ch 200.

56 See *Henderson v Squire* (1869) LR 4 QB 170.

> skill on the part of anyone can make them. The rule is subject to the limitation that the defendant is not to be held responsible for defects which could not have been discovered by reasonable care or skill on the part of any person concerned with the construction, alteration, repair or maintenance of the premises.

In *Northern Sandblasting Pty Ltd v Harris* (1997) 188 CLR 313; 146 ALR 572, the High Court confirmed that a landlord owes a duty of care to a tenant to make leased premises as safe for the purpose as reasonable care on the part of the landlord can make them. On the facts of that case, a landlord was liable to the daughter of its tenants when she suffered injury as the result of defective electrical wiring in the leased premises in which she lived. It thus follows from that case that, under the general law, a landlord of residential premises owes a duty of care to the members of his or her tenant's household. What is unclear from the reasons for decision in that case is the precise content of that duty. The injuries sustained by the tenants' daughter in Northern Sandblasting were the result of the combination of two electrical defects. One, a defective connection of the earth wire at the power box, which was apparent at the commencement of the tenancy and would have been discovered if a properly qualified electrician have inspected the property prior to the commencement of the tenancy. The other was defective wiring associated with the stove. Whilst the landlord had arranged for the stove to be repaired by an apparently competent electrician, the repairs were done negligently. Dawson, Gummow and Kirby JJ each held that the landlord did not owe the tenants' daughter a duty of care with respect to either one of the electrical defects which combined to cause her injuries. Dawson J ((1997) 188 CLR 313, p 344) rejected that there was any general obligation to inspect, considering that the duties of a landlord to a tenant were not analogous to that of the occupier to an invitee. Toohey and McHugh JJ held that the landlord had a non-delegable duty with respect to the stove repairs which it had undertaken to have carried out. Toohey J (at CLR 349) considered that there were evidentiary and general difficulties in finding a breach of duty as a result of a failure to inspect. Likewise, Kirby J also rejected the requirements for inspection, stating at (p 394):

> The imposition of a duty of regular and repeated inspections of domestic electricity systems was sustained neither by evidence of common practice nor by common sense.

Brennan CJ and Gleeson J each held that there was a more general duty of care. Brennan CJ (p 340) considered that the standard of care was the same as is required of occupiers towards those who enter occupied premises by consent and for reward and it requires an inspection of the premises.

Gaudron J (p 360) made the following comments:

> Having regard to the control which, at the beginning of a lease, a landlord exercises over the state of the premises and, also, the extent to which members of the household are then dependent upon the landlord for their safety, a

> landlord's duty at that point cannot, in my view, be limited to defects of which he or she is aware.

Kirby J noted that such a duty may be extended to include inspections against all number of perils that could arise and the potential was too vast. On the facts, his Honour noted that the electrical fault would not have been obvious to an untrained observer such as the landlord.

The decision in *Northern Sandblasting* was confirmed in *New South Wales v Watton* [1999] NSW Conv Rep 55-885. In that case, the tenant had been injured some five months after the commencement of his tenancy due to an electrical fault in the wiring of the premises which the trial judge found would have been discovered on a proper inspection of the premises prior to the commencement of the lease that the inspection in fact carried out by the landlord at that time had been inadequate.

The trial judge applied the High Court decision in *Northern Sandblasting* and held that the landlord was under a duty to properly inspect the premises before the commencement of the lease, that it had not done so and was therefore liable to the tenant for the damages. On appeal, the landlord argued that the High Court in *Northern Sandblasting* did not impose a duty to inspect the premises prior to the commencement of the lease and the Court of Appeal agreed noting that once the lease commences, the landlord owes a duty of care to the tenant to make leases premises as safe for the purpose as reasonable care and skill on the part of the landlord can make them.

The exact nature of the duty of care owed by the landlord was further explicated by the High Court in *Jones v Bartlett* [2000] 176 ALR 137 where Gleeson CJ noted that the content of the landlord's duty to the tenant will be conterminous with a requirement that the premises be reasonably fit for the purposes for which they are let, namely habitation as a domestic residence. In discussed the scope and content of this duty, Gleeson CJ made the following comments at (p 144):

> Premises will not be reasonably fit for the purposes for which they are let where the ordinary use of the premises for that purpose would, as a matter of reasonable foreseeability, cause injury. The duty requires a landlord not to let premises that suffer defects which the landlord knows or ought to know make the premises unsafe for the use to which they are to be put. The duty with respect to dangerous defects will be discharged if the landlord takes reasonable steps to ascertain the existence of any such defects and, once the landlord knows of any, if the landlord takes reasonable steps to remove them or to make the premises safe. This does not amount to a proposition that the ordinary use of the premises for the purpose for which they are let must not cause injury; it is that the landlord has acted in a manner reasonably to remove the risks. … What constitutes the taking of reasonable steps will, as Dawson J noted in *Northern Sandblasting*, depend on all the circumstances of the case. What is reasonable for premises let for the purpose of residential housing may be less demanding than for premises let for such purposes as the running of a school,

> or the conduct of a hotel or club serving liquor. Moreover, the reasonableness of steps to be taken will be affected by the terms of the lease, including the level at which the rental is pitched, the obligations the parties allocated inter se and any specification of limited purposes to which the premises be put. It will also be affected by the terms of any applicable statutes, such as residential tenancy statutes. In some jurisdictions there may be statutory requirements which supplant any common law duty or which impose a higher duty than the common law.

Following these decisions it would seem that there will be a general duty of care not capable of exclusion by the terms of the lease[57] which requires the landlord to positively place the premises in a safe condition at the time of the commencement of the lease.

Further, it would appear to follow quite properly from these decisions that landlords will also be under a continuing obligation to their tenants to inspect and keep the premises in reasonable repair whether positively required of the landlord by the terms of the lease or statute or not. These obligations apply in addition to those already existing under statute – and whilst residential tenancy legislation already imposes equivalent obligations, most retail tenancies legislation is deficient in this area and therefore these developments will inevitably have a significant impact for tenants under such leases.[58]

15.4.4.2 *Implied statutory covenants*

The covenants existing under common law have been added to by specific statutory provisions. These provisions are pretty much uniform throughout the states. In Victoria, they are set out under s 67 of the Transfer of Land Act 1958, which applies to leases over Torrens title land.[59]

(a) Implied covenant to pay rent and taxes

First, s 67(1)(a) of the Transfer of Land Act 1958 (Vic) implies a covenant that the tenant will pay the rent reserved by the lease at the times mentioned and all rates and taxes payable in respect of the rented premises except for those exclusively payable by the landlord under any state or local government legislation.[60] The aim of this provision is to ensure that the tenant pays the agreed rental for the leased premises. It does not alter any of the pre-existing common law rules concerning the payment of rent. It is the primary obligation

57 *Assaf v Kostrevski* (1998) unreported, 30 September, CA (NSW).

58 See, generally, Redfern, M, 'Case notes: *Northern Sandblasting* once again' (1999) 7 Australian Property Law Journal 16.

59 Note that, in New South Wales and Queensland, the implied covenants in the Torrens legislation also apply to leases over general law land.

60 Torrens legislation: NSW, s 84(1)(a); SA, s 124(1); WA, s 92(i); Qld, s 105(a); Tas, s 66; ACT, s 119(a); NT, s 124(1).

of the tenant to pay the rent to the landlord and, where this does not occur, the landlord may forfeit the lease even if a third party has paid the arrears.[61] Further, the statutory provision does not alter the rule that the rent is only payable in arrears and that, where payment is not made, the landlord is not under a duty to mitigate his losses.[62]

The statutory provision will apply to all leases of Torrens title land, whether registered or unregistered, because the definition of a lease in this context is not confined to registered encumbrances. The statutory provision can only apply where a rental amount is expressly prescribed in the lease and the time period for payment is scheduled. Where the lease contains no requirement for rent, and thereby confers a rent free tenancy, the statutory provision will be inapplicable.

(b) Implied covenant by the tenant to keep the premises in good repair

Section 67(1)(b) of the Transfer of Land Act 1958 (Vic) requires the tenant to keep and yield up the lease premises in good and tenantable repair, with accidents and damage from storm, tempest and reasonable wear and tear excepted.[63] Good, tenantable repair is defined broadly to include such repair as, having regard to the age, character and locality of the property, would make it fit for the occupation of a reasonably minded tenant of the class who would be likely to take it (*Proudfoot v Hart* (1890) 25 QBD 42).

The tenant will only be in breach if the damage is of a substantial nature. In some circumstances, the tenant may be obliged to make repairs *before* the damage actually occurs, although this does not mean that the tenant must actually renew or improve the premises. Usually, the tenant will not be obliged to carry out structural repairs or to rectify defects in the premises existing at the commencement of the lease. If, however, the lessee covenants to keep the premises in good repair, that may, depending upon the age and character of the property, impose an immediate obligation upon the lessee. In such circumstances, the tenant may be obliged to repair immediate problems, such as floors that are unsafe or rotting, broken windows, missing locks, and dirty or damaged walls and ceilings.

What constitutes good and tenantable repair is always a question of degree, but what must be considered is whether that which the tenant is being asked to do can properly be described as repair, or, more accurately, a renovation resulting in the landlord acquiring a wholly different premises to that which was initially transferred.

---

61 *Harrison v Petkovic* [1975] VR 79.

62 *Maridakis v Kouvaris* (1975) 5 ALR 197.

63 Conveyancing Act 1919 (NSW), s 84(1)(b); Real Property Act 1886 (SA), s 124(2); Transfer of Land Act 1893 (WA), s 92(ii); Property Law Act 1974 (Qld), s 105(b); Land Titles Act 1980 (Tas), s 22.

(c) *Implied covenant entitling the landlord to re-enter the premises for inspection and failure to pay rent*

In Victoria, pursuant to s 67(1)(c) of the Transfer of Land Act 1958 (Vic), the landlord has an implied right to enter the leased premises once a year at a reasonable time of the day.[64] Different notification periods apply in each state. In Victoria and Western Australia, however, there is no requirement to give notice for this inspection. The only qualification is that the entry must be 'at a reasonable time of day'. In Queensland, the landlord is entitled to enter at any time provided 'two days' notice is given'. In South Australia, Tasmania and the Northern Territory, the landlord may enter at any 'reasonable time'; and in New South Wales and the ACT, the landlord is entitled to enter 'twice a year on two days' notice'.

Section 67(1)(d) of the Transfer of Land Act 1958 (Vic) gives the landlord a right of re-entry where the rent is one month in arrears, despite the fact that no legal or formal demand for payment of the rent has been made.[65] The statutory right effectively replaces the common law rule that the landlord has no right of re-entry in the absence of an express term. Section 67(1)(d) also gives the landlord the right to re-enter for a breach or non-observance of any other covenant, either implied by law or expressed in the lease, which has continued for the period of one month. This is also the position in Western Australia. In New South Wales, Queensland and the ACT, the breach must have continued for two months; in South Australia, Tasmania and the Northern Territory, it must have continued for three months.

15.5 Remedies

A range of different types of legal and equitable remedies are available for the enforcement of leasehold estates.

15.5.1 Forfeiture

Where a tenant breaches one of the express or implied terms of the lease contract, the landlord will be entitled to forfeit the lease. Forfeiture is a right of the landlord, but it only becomes operative where a breach of the lease agreement can be established. The right of forfeiture is not, however, an automatic right in all circumstances. There is no right to forfeiture for covenants implied under common law, although, the implied statutory provisions have reinforced this situation by entitling a landlord to re-enter the

64 See Torrens legislation: NSW, s 85(1)(a); WA, s 93(i); SA, s 125(2); Qld, s 107(a); Tas, s 67(a); NT, s 125(2); ACT, s 120(a).

65 See Torrens legislation: NSW, s 85(1)(d); WA, s 93(ii); SA, s 125(3); Qld, s 107(d); Tas, s 67(b); ACT, s 120(d); NT, s 125(3).

premises. In many situations, a forfeiture clause will be contained within the lease agreement. Where a right to forfeit exists in the contract, the lease will be voidable, and the landlord may elect whether to continue with the lease and obtain damages or exercise a right of re-entry.

A tenant may claim relief against forfeiture in equity where all rental arrears and costs have been paid prior to a court order being executed. The rationale underlying this is that the forfeiture provisions are purely intended to operate as security provisions and should not unfairly deprive the lessee of an estate where the moneys have in fact been paid.[66] This position is now codified in legislation in all states which sets out that, where a tenant has paid all of the arrears of rent and costs into court or to the landlord at any time before the hearing for the recovery of possession, all further proceedings shall cease. If this does not occur, the court has a discretion to grant relief against forfeiture within a six month period after the court order for recovery has been made.[67]

15.5.2 Damages

The High Court has held that a lease contract may be repudiated and damages for the prospective loss of profit will be available despite the fact that, previously, such relief was not available. Traditionally, repudiation and damages were unavailable for a breach of a lease covenant because the lease contract was regarded as a conveyance of an interest in land rather than an ordinary contractual relationship. In *Shevill v Builders' Licensing Board* (1982) 149 CLR 620, the full High Court noted in *dicta* that a landlord was entitled to repudiate a lease contract and sue not only for the arrears in rent due, but also for prospective damages flowing from the loss of bargain where the payment of rent was expressed to constitute an essential term and the term is breached.[68] On the facts of the case, the court held that the lease contract in issue did not specify that payment of rent was an essential term and, as such, its breach did not confer a right to repudiatory damages on the landlord. It is clear from this decision the court felt that in cases where payment of rent is specified to constitute an essential term, failure to pay rent will entitle a landlord to a claim for repudiatory damages.

66 The equitable jurisdiction has now been reinforced by the High Court in *Legione v Hateley* (1983) 152 CLR 406.

67 Supreme Court Act 1986 (Vic), ss 79, 80 and 85; Landlord and Tenant Act 1899 (NSW), ss 8–10; Landlord and Tenant Act 1936 (SA), ss 4, 5, 7 and 9; Property Law Act (Qld), ss 123–28; Common Law Procedure Act 1854 (Tas), ss 183–85; and Supreme Court Civil Procedure Act 1932 (Tas), s 11(14).

68 The decision was followed in *Progressive Mailing House Pty Ltd v Tabali Pty Ltd* (1985) 57 ALR 609 and by the majority in *AMEV-UDC Finance Ltd v Austin* (1986) 162 CLR 171, although the dissenting judgments in *AMEV* were highly critical of the decision.

The *dicta* of the *Shevill* decision was applied in the subsequent decision of *Progressive Mailing House Pty Ltd v Tabali Pty Ltd* (1985) 157 CLR 17, in which the High Court concluded that a tenant who had breached the lease contract by failing to keep the leased property in proper repair, subletting without consent, and being four months overdue with rent had effectively repudiated the lease agreement and that, consequently, the landlord was entitled to terminate the lease and seek loss of bargain damages. In *Shevill*, Wilson J noted that 'repudiation of a contract is a serious matter and is not to be lightly found' and, further, that 'no principle of law requires me to hold that consistently late payment of rent without more is sufficient to establish repudiation of a lease'.[69] By contrast, the breach was regarded as 'repudiatory' in *Progressive Mailing* because the facts involved successive breaches of covenant; the lessee was not only late in paying the rent but had also committed other significant breaches of the lease contract.[70]

In *Progressive Mailing*, Mason J specifically stated that the ordinary principles of property law apply to lease contracts in the same way as they apply to other forms of contract, thereby rejecting the traditional common law position that lease contracts are in a different category to other types of contracts.[71] The traditional approach has been summarised by Lord Denning in *Total Oil Great Britain Ltd v Thompson Garages (Biggin Hill) Ltd* [1972] 1 QB 318 (p 324): 'A lease is a demise. It conveys an interest in land. It does not come to an end like an ordinary contract on repudiation and acceptance.' Following the decision in *Progressive Mailing*, the distinctive character of the lease contract has been rejected in the determination of repudiation principles.[72]

The nature and meaning of a repudiation within a lease contract was further expounded in the subsequent High Court decision of *Laurinda Pty Ltd v Capalaba Park Shopping Centre Pty Ltd* (1989) 63 ALJR 372. On the facts of that case, the court held that a failure to register the lease, as required in the original lease contract, did amount to a repudiation on the part of the landlord, entitling the tenant to terminate the lease. The court upheld the decision in *Progressive Mailing* and specifically noted that, in a lease contract, the process of determining whether a breach of covenant constitutes a repudiation occurs by assessing the conduct of the defaulting party and determining whether or not it is a consequence of that person's inability to perform the terms of the lease contract, or of his intention either not to perform the terms agreed upon or to perform them in a manner substantially

69 *Progressive Mailing House Pty Ltd v Tabali Pty Ltd* (1985) 157 CLR 17.

70 Note that Wilson and Deane JJ regarded the case as one of 'fundamental breach'.

71 This proposition was subsequently supported in *Wood Factory Pty Ltd v Kiritos Pty Ltd* (1985) 2 NSWLR 105 and *Hawkett & Anor v Tailgate Taxi Trucks Pty Ltd* [1991] V Conv R 54-400.

72 A lease was terminated on the basis of a tenant's repudiation in *Rikpa Pty Ltd v Maggiore Bakeries Pty Ltd* [1984] V Conv R 54-155.

inconsistent with the original terms of the agreement.[73] In *Laurinda*, the court concluded from the facts that the lessor repudiated the agreement for the lease because it suited the commercial interests of the lessor to delay registration whilst it negotiated for new finance. The deliberate acts of the lessor in delaying the execution, stamping and obtaining the mortgagee's consent and the registration of the lease, amounted to repudiatory conduct, particularly as the lessor was aware of the lessee's need to register the lease in order to effect a proper sale of the business.

Whether a lessor is required to mitigate her loss remains unclear. The current position appears to be, if the lessee breaches lease covenants or abandons the premises, the lessor is not required to terminate the lease, may continue to sue for rent for the duration of the lease, and is not obliged to mitigate the loss.[74] If, however, a landlord accepts a repudiation by a tenant, the landlord has a duty to mitigate damages according to ordinary contractual principles.[75] Nevertheless, given the uncertainty surrounding the obligation to mitigate, it is generally advisable to include an express term in the lease contract, clarifying the duties of a lessor in this regard.

15.5.3 *Merger and surrender*

Under the old common law principles, a lease would be automatically extinguished where the leasehold estate and the reversionary interest became vested in one person absolutely. This process became known as a 'merger'. Under the equitable jurisdiction, the merger was not automatic, and its occurrence depended upon the overall intention of the parties. The position has now been adopted in legislation, and each state has similar provisions.[76] In Victoria, s 185 of the Property Law Act sets out:

> There shall be no merger by operation of law only of any estate the beneficial interest in which would not be deemed to be merged or extinguished in equity.

Hence, merger is no longer an automatic occurrence unless there has been a surrender of the lease; where the lease is surrendered, the leasehold simply ceases to exist. Subject to the intention of the parties, merger may occur where a lease is assigned to the holder of the reversion or where the reversion is acquired by the lessee. Following the introduction of the legislation, these instances will depend upon proof that a merger was intended by the parties.

A lease will be surrendered where a lessee gives over the leasehold interest to a lessor who agrees to accept it. Where the lease exceeds three years, the

---

73 See, in particular, the judgment of Deane and Dawson JJ, (1985) 157 CLR 17, p 382, on this issue.

74 *Maridakis v Kouvaris* (1975) 5 ALR 197.

75 *Nangus Pty Ltd v Charles Donovan and Others* [1988] V Conv R 54-319.

76 Property law statutes: NSW, s 10; SA, s 13; WA, s 18; Qld, s 17 – no equivalent provisions exist in Tasmania, ACT or NT.

surrender must be expressly executed by deed. Where the lease is under three years, the surrender must be in written form because of the statutory requirements relating to the disposition of interests in land.

In summary, a lessee must comply with the following formalities when surrendering a lease:

(a) to surrender a lease in excess of three years, the surrender must be executed by way of a deed;

(b) to surrender a lease for three years or less, the surrender must be in writing, signed by the lessee or his agent; and

(c) where the lease is a registered lease over Torrens title land, it is prudent – although not compulsory – to have the surrender noted on the folio; whilst the schedule to the Torrens legislation does not include a form for surrender, it will probably be accepted by the Land Titles Office if it is in the form of a transfer of lease as contained in Sched 6 to the Transfer of Land Act 1958 (Vic).

A surrender may also occur by operation of law where an act is committed by one of the parties to the lease, with the consent of the other party, which is inconsistent with the continued operation of the lease. A surrender by operation of law will generally arise where the lessee vacates the premises and the lessor resumes possession following a specific agreement to terminate the tenancy.[77]

15.6 The Retail Tenancies Reform Act 1998 (Vic)

The Retail Tenancies Reform Act 1998 (Vic) (RTRA) was passed on the 28th April 1998. Section 50 of the new Act repeals the old Retail Tenancies Act 1986 (Vic). Section 51(1) of the new Act sets out that the old Retail Tenancies legislation continues to apply to retail leases to which it applied immediately before its repeal, and to disputes arising under retail leases to which it applied immediately prior to its repeal.

15.6.1 Disclosure requirements

The RTRA strengthens the disclosure requirements of landlords with respect to retail premises. The purpose of these provisions is to enhance the protection of prospective retail tenants through the provision of detailed estimates of costs they must incur – the purpose being to ensure that prospective tenants are better informed and therefore better able to determine whether or not to go ahead and enter into a particular retail lease.

Section 8 requires a landlord of retail premises to give a prospective tenant a detailed disclosure statement, at least seven days prior to the tenant entering

77 *Buchanan v Byrnes* (1906) 3 CLR 704.

into a retail premises lease, in the form set out in the Schedule to the Act. Information which needs to be included within this statement includes: the rent payable, the period for which it is payable, the date on which a rent review will occur and the adjustment method; an estimate of the outgoings payable by the tenant for air conditioning, ventilation, building intelligence and emergency systems, security, fire protection, insurance, electricity, water, telephones, gas and oil, lifts and elevators, public address and music, signs, uniforms, child minding, car parking, gardening, cleaning, disposals, land tax, local government rates and charges, repairs and maintenance, contribution to sinking fund, sewerage and drainage rates and charges, management costs, pest control, audit fees and any other charges to be borne by the tenant.

Section 17 requires a landlord to give to the tenant a similar disclosure statement where the tenant holds an option to renew a lease for a further term or the landlord proposes to renew the lease

If a proper disclosure statement is not furnished to the tenant, the tenant is entitled to withhold payment of rent until the expiration of seven days after such a statement is disclosed, and the tenant will not be liable to pay rent for this period: s 8(2).

15.6.2 Tenant's business plan

The RTRA improves the position of a retail landlord by ensuring that prospective tenants provide an outline of the business they propose to enter into in the leased premises. Section 9 requires a prospective tenant of a retail premises to give the landlord a plan relating to the business that the prospective tenant proposes to carry on at the retail premises. The business plan must be prepared or endorsed by a financial adviser of the prospective tenant.

15.6.3 Rent review

The RTRA provides detailed rental review provisions for leases coming within its jurisdiction. Section 12(1) sets out that the retail lease must state the time when rent reviews are to take place and the basis or formula on which the reviews are to be made. Section 12(2) sets out that rental review formulas *must* be based upon one of the following methods:

(a) a fixed percentage of the base rent;

(b) an independently published index of prices, costs or wages;

(c) a fixed actual amount;

(d) the current market rent of the retail premises;

(e) another basis or formula prescribed by the regulations.

Section 12(3) sets out that any rental review clause which is not based upon one of the above listed methods will be void to the extent that it prevents the rental from being appropriately reduced. If the review clause does not specify how the rent is reviewed, the provision will be void: s 12(4). If the current market rent is used as the formula, the current market rent is to be taken as the rent obtainable at the time of the review in a free and open market, between a willing landlord and a willing tenant in an arm's length transaction, where the parties have acted knowledgeably, prudently and without compulsion and the retail premises were vacant and to be let on similar terms contained in the current retail lease and all other relevant land valuation factors have been taken into account: s 12(5).

Rental provisions which set out that the rent is to be determined by reference to the turnover of the business will be void unless the lease specifies how the rent is to be determined: s 13(1). Section 14(1) sets out that a tenant will only be obliged to furnish details concerning the turnover of the business to the landlord for the purpose of determining rent and the landlord must not communicate this information to any other person without the consent of the tenant.

15.6.4 *Urgent repairs*

The RTRA sets out that the landlord to a retail premises lease is responsible for ensuring that the structure of fixtures, appliances, gas, electricity, water, drainage and other service are maintained in good repair: s 25(1). Where urgent repairs need to be carried out and the tenant has taken reasonable steps to notify and arrange for the repairs to be carried out by the landlord and is without success, the tenant may personally arrange for the repairs to be carried out, giving the landlord 14 days written notice of the repairs which have been made and the cost and the landlord will be liable to reimburse the tenant for the reasonable cost of the repairs or $5,000, whichever is less: s 25(3). Urgent repairs are defined as work necessary to repair or remedy a fault or damage in the structure of fixtures in the retail premises or appliances or services to the retail premises which either have, or will cause substantial effect to the tenant's business: s 25(4).

15.6.5 *Dispute resolution*

The dispute resolution process under the RTRA sets out that a dispute must undergo compulsory conciliation and then, if it is unable to be resolved, referred to arbitration. The arbitration is to be conducted in accordance with the provisions of the Commercial Arbitration Act 1984, although arbitrators are given the additional power to make declarations as to the rights of the parties to the dispute and to grant injunctive relief in any case in which the Supreme Court would have such power: ss 33–43.

15.7 Residential tenancies legislation

Statutory protection exists in each state of Australia for residential tenancies. In Victoria, the relevant act is the Residential Tenancies Act 1997.[78] The residential tenancies legislation is one of the most comprehensive statutes regulating tenancy law. Whilst there are significant variations to the legislation in each state, the basic purpose of the legislation is to regulate and provide greater protection to tenants of leases coming within the definition of a residential tenancy, which will generally include leases where the predominant use of the premises is residential rather than commercial or some other purpose. The legislation in each state has established specialised tribunals to deal with residential tenancy disputes, and has conferred broad discretion upon members of the 'tribunal' to resolve such disputes. Another important purpose of the Residential Tenancies legislation in each state is to uphold and reinforce the public interest associated in the improvement in the quality and availability of the rental housing and the social advantages associated with improved living conditions.

The exact terms of the legislation existing in each state varies but, generally, the legislation has introduced reform in the areas of: the formalities associated in the creation of leases; the payment of rent and additional monetary sums; rent increases; excessive rents; security deposits; as assignments and subleases; anti-discriminatory provisions; tenant protection clauses; repairs; termination of tenancies; and penalties for breaches of the terms of the legislation; provisions governing the obligation of tenants making applications for residential leases to provide holding deposits: see, for example, s 50 of the Residential Tenancies Act 1997 (Vic), which requires a tenant to provide what is known as an application deposit as a sign of good faith, which will be refunded within 14 days if the lease agreement goes ahead; the implementation of general obligations upon the landlord to keep the leased premises in good repair, to provide funds for urgent repairs and to ensure that the premises are clean and functioning properly. These duties complement the recently recognised common law obligation upon the landlord to exercise reasonable care; the introduction of new rules concerning the relevant period of notice required to be given prior to a termination and the introduction of 'special rights' upon tenants to remove fixtures during the currency of the tenancy.

One of the important changes for Australian residential law was the abolition of the common law notion that all leases had to confer exclusive

78 For the residential tenancies legislation, see Residential Tenancies Act 1987 (NSW); Residential Tenancies Act 1980 (Vic); Residential Tenancies Act 1994 (Qld); Residential Tenancies Act 1995 (SA); Residential Tenancies Act 1987 (WA). Less comprehensive legislation affecting residential tenancies is also to be found in the Tenancy Act 1979 (NT) and the Landlord and Tenant Act 1949 (ACT). For reform considerations in Tasmania, see Bradbrook, AJ, 'Residential landlord-tenant law reform in Tasmania' (1988) 6 U Tasmania L Rev 83 and see also Bradbrook, AJ, 'Residential Tenancies law – lessons from France' (1997) 5 Australian Property Law Journal 8.

possession in order to function as a lease and confer proprietary benefits. Under the legislation in most states, a residential tenancy agreement is defined as an agreement under which a person grants another person, for valuable consideration, a right (which may, but need not, be an exclusive right) to occupy premises for the purpose of residence – and the legislation will apply to all such rights. The main exemptions to this are: premises situated in a hotel, motel or educational institution; premises ordinarily used for holiday purposes; premises situated in a hospital, nursing home or like institution; premises created or arising under the terms of a contract of employment; premises forming part of a building in which other premises are let by the landlord to the tenant for the purposes of a trade, profession or business carried on by the tenant; and premises that are included in or on other premises let to the tenant for the purpose of a farm or orchard.

Furthermore, the Australian legislation introduces reform to common law duties of landlords concerning the maintenance and repairs to the leased premises. The basic division recognised in all the state enactments is that the landlord is under a duty to put the premises into good condition at the commencement of the lease and to ensure that they remain in good condition for the duration of the lease.[79] The duty of tenants is restricted to repairing damage caused by themselves or their invitees, and to notifying the landlord of any need for repair.

Finally, the Australian legislation allows a tenant to assign or sub-let the lease and whilst the landlord is entitled to refuse consent, in his or her discretion, the legislation requires the landlord to justify any refusal to grant such consent.[80]

Apart from a few very minor amendments, the residential legislation in each state remains largely unchanged.

The above discussion represents a brief overview of the Residential Tenancies legislation; a full examination of the residential tenancies legislation is beyond the scope of this text.

79 See State acts above at: NSW, s 25; Vic, s 97; Qld, s 103; SA, s 68; WA, s 42.

80 See State acts above at: NSW, s 33(b); Vic, s 108(2); Qld, s 145(2); SA, s 74(2)(b); WA, s 49(2).

CHAPTER 16

CO-OWNERSHIP

16.1 Introduction

Interests in land may be fragmented under the doctrine of estates. Where this occurs, different types of estates and interests are created over a single piece of land. For example, the owner of land may hold a fee simple reversion in the land whilst a third party retains a leasehold interest. Fragmentation under the doctrine of estates is based upon time: freehold estates exist indefinitely, whilst non-freehold estates must exist for a specified period of time. Interests in land may also be fragmented according to the jurisdiction in which they are enforced. Hence, an estate in land may be legal in nature or, where it is not recognised by the common law, it may be equitable in nature.

Fragmentation of estates and interests must be distinguished from co-ownership. Co-ownership is not concerned with different types of estates and interests but rather with ownership of a single estate or interest by two or more persons. The focus of co-ownership is upon mutual ownership. Land cannot be regarded as co-owned just because a range of people claim different interests over the same land. A co-ownership relationship will only arise where two or more people claim ownership to the *same* interest in land. Each co-owner may hold an identical share in the estate or an aliquot part of the estate representing the amount of money they have individually contributed to the property.

The fact that two or more persons own a single piece of land does not mean that the interest is no longer defined by the right to exclude. The interest is still property in the sense that the rest of the world can be excluded: each co-owner is not considered to be 'the rest of the world' but, rather, individual owners. Private property is defined by the right to exclude, and the power to exclude is conferred upon the owner, whether the owner be one, two or more persons. Hence, each co-owner acquires an individual *in rem* right in the land which is enforceable against all persons except other co-owners.

The law concerning the rights and obligations of co-owners has become an increasingly important issue in a society where mutual ownership is thriving. Obviously, where the ownership of an interest in land is vested in a number of people, conflicts can arise concerning the proper management of the property. The principles existing under co-ownership law concern the status of the co-owner relationship and the character of the rights and duties owed by all co-owners of land. The determination of what form of co-ownership exists and whether it remains in existence is extremely important, because this can greatly affect the outcome of a co-owner dispute.

16.2 Types of co-ownership

The fundamental feature of all co-owner relationships is the joint right of each co-owner to possess the land. Where this right does not exist, the relationship cannot be truly defined as a co-ownership. Hence, the rights of several beneficiaries under a trust to the ownership of land cannot be described in terms of a co-owner relationship, because the beneficiaries are not entitled to an immediate right of possession. Once it is established that a mutual right of possession exists in a number of persons, the important issue to determine will be what form of co-owner relationship exists. There are two fundamental types of co-ownership: the joint tenancy and the tenancy in common. A joint tenancy can only exist where the rights and interests held by each co-owner are identical and satisfy what are known as the 'four unities'. Where the four unities cannot be proven, but a joint right to possession exists, the co-ownership will generally constitute a tenancy in common.

16.2.1 Joint tenancy

A joint tenancy is a form of co-ownership where each co-owner holds a part of the entire estate but not a separate, proportionate share. Each joint tenant is seised of the whole of the land, but cannot be regarded as holding an independent share. Hence, one joint tenant holds the whole estate jointly with the remaining joint tenants, but individually holds nothing except the right to jointly use, possess and enjoy the land subject to the like rights of the other joint tenant(s). The position has been aptly summarised by Latham CJ in the High Court decision of *Wright v Gibbons* (1949) 78 CLR 313 (pp 320–35):

> The interests of each joint tenant in the land held are always the same in respect of possession, interest, title and time. No distinction can be drawn between the interest of any one tenant and that of any other tenant ... Logical as may seem the deduction that joint tenants have not interests which in contemplation of law are sufficiently distinct to assure mutually to one another, there are many considerations which show that, to say the least, the consequence cannot be called an unqualified truth ... For purposes of alienation each is conceived as entitled to dispose of an aliquot share.

As a general rule, a joint tenant cannot deal with the land in a manner binding upon the other joint tenants. For example, one joint tenant cannot, without the consent of the others, enter into a binding agreement to sell the whole of the land or mortgage the entire estate which will be binding upon the remaining joint tenants.

A joint tenancy will not simply arise where two or more persons purchase land together. In order to establish a joint tenancy, two vital characteristics must be proven: it must be established that the four unities exist and the right of survivorship must apply.

16.2.2 *The four unities*

The essence of a joint tenancy is similarity and unity between all interest holders. Hence, where a joint tenancy exists, the interest of each joint tenant should be indistinguishable. Where each interest is in accordance with the four unities, the similarity in ownership is absolute. If the interest of a co-owner does not display an accordance with one or more of the unity requirements, the relationship cannot be properly described as a joint tenancy because each interest is not absolutely identical. The four unities are unity of possession, interest, title and time.

(a) Unity of possession

Unity of possession is a feature common to both a joint tenancy and a tenancy in common, as it is a basic requirement for all co-owner relationships. Unity of possession exists where each and every co-owner is entitled to possess the land. Possession in this sense does not refer to exclusive possession of a particular part of the land but, rather, a general right along with all other co-owners to occupy, use and enjoy the entirety of the land. Unity of possession confers an entitlement upon all co-owners to mutually use and possess the land.

For example, if A, B and C hold a joint tenancy over land and A purports to lease her interest in the land over to X, there can be no co-ownership relationship between A, B and C. A retains a reversion interest in the land, for the duration of the lease and during this time she does not have any right to possess the land, as this has been conferred to X. Hence, no unity of possession exists between A, B and C.

(b) Unity of interest

The interest of each of the joint tenants must be identical in nature, extent and duration before a co-owner relationship can be properly characterised as a joint tenancy. Unity of interest requires each co-owner to be jointly seised of exactly the same estate, acquired at exactly the same time.

For example, if X, the fee simple owner of land, transfers an estate to A for the duration of his life and to B for 10 years, A and B do not take the land as joint tenants. This is because separate estates have been individually conferred upon A and B: A holds a life estate *autre vie* and B holds a leasehold estate. In this situation, no valid co-ownership will exist because it is not a case where two people hold an interest in the same land but, rather, where two separate estates have been conferred upon different parties. Furthermore, X could not pass a valid lease to B where she has already passed a life estate to A; X has no possession to confer to B.

In order to satisfy unity of interest, it must also be proven that the interests of each joint tenant are identical in quantity. If one co-owner is given a two thirds interest in land whilst the remaining co-owner is given a one third interest, no joint tenancy can exist, even if the type of estate given is the same.

However, the fact that one co-owner holds an additional future estate as well as the interest under the co-ownership does not mean that unity of interest does not exist. The interest which is relevant is that which is the subject of the actual co-ownership. Hence, if X and Y both hold an interest in land for the life of Z, the relationship may be a joint tenancy, even if X also retains the fee simple remainder.

(c) Unity of title

All parties must derive their interests from the same title, the same document, or the same act in order for a joint tenancy to exist. Where one co-owner acquired his interest by way of a different instrument or document, no joint tenancy can exist, because there is no unity of title and the co-owner relationship must constitute a tenancy in common. The rationale for this requirement is that interests acquired by different acts are not truly identical in nature.

For example, if X conveys her fee simple estate to A and B jointly, a co-ownership relationship between A and B exists. If A then conveys her interest over to C, so that B and C own the property jointly, the co-ownership relationship between B and C cannot constitute a joint tenancy, because B acquired her interest pursuant to a different instrument: hence, there is no unity of title.

Furthermore, the act of one co-owner in transferring her interest in the land over to a third party may constitute a severance of the joint tenancy. The methods by which a joint tenancy may be severed will be further examined in para 16.5.

(d) Unity of time

Finally, a co-owner relationship can only constitute a joint tenancy where the interests of each joint tenant have vested at exactly the same time and by virtue of the same event. This requirement often overlaps with unity of title because, where interests have not been conferred pursuant to the same act, they will generally not have been conferred at the same time. Unity of time requires interests to have been granted and to vest at the same time; if one co-owner receives the same interest from the same document as the other co-owners, but the vesting of that interest is conditional upon the happening of an event, then no joint tenancy can exist, because there is no unity of time between the interests.

For example, X conveys fee simple remainder interests in land to A and B upon the occasion of them graduating in law. A and B graduate in law in 1996 and 1997 respectively. X dies in 1998 and the interests of A and B are vested in possession. A and B co-own the land but not as joint tenants because there is no unity of time. The condition imposed upon the remainder estates held by A and B was inherently variable and, consequently, made it extremely unlikely that the interests of A and B would vest simultaneously. A joint tenancy could only have arisen if A and B graduated at the same time.

One exception to this rule are limitations contained in a conveyance to uses in order to give effect to the grantor. For example, X conveys a fee simple to Y upon trust for A and B for life and after their deaths upon trust to such of their children who attain the age of 21 years, in fee simple. Although the interests of the children of A and B may vest at different times, they will not infringe the unity of time requirement.[1]

16.2.3 The right of survivorship: jus accrescendi

The other fundamental feature of all joint tenancies is the right of survivorship or the *jus accrescendi*. The right of survivorship is a natural characteristic of all joint tenancies, and any co-owner relationship where it is excluded or otherwise exempted cannot constitute a joint tenancy. The right of survivorship is essentially a principle of inheritance and, stated simply, entitles the interests of the remaining joint tenants to expand equally where one joint tenant dies. When one joint tenant dies, his interest is extinguished completely and will not pass on to his estate. Upon the extinguishment of the joint tenant's interest, the corresponding interests of the surviving joint tenants are enlarged. The fact that the deceased joint tenant has devised her estate is irrelevant; the interest of a joint tenant is no more capable of devolution by will than it is capable of devolving upon an intestacy. Furthermore, as a will cannot take effect until the death of a joint tenant, it will be too late to sever the joint tenancy. The right of survivorship will automatically apply to all joint tenancies unless it can be established that the joint tenancy has been severed prior to the death of a joint tenant (see discussion on severance at para 16.5).

The operation of the right of survivorship stems from the inherent character of the joint tenancy. Each joint tenant is seised of the entire estate, and consequently, each is subject to the like seisin of the other.

For example, A, B and C are joint tenants of a fee simple estate and A subsequently dies. By her will, A devises her portion in the land to X. As the co-owner relationship remained a joint tenancy up until the death of A, the right of survivorship means that B and C will become seised of the entire

1 This limitation includes conditions contained within a will (*Kenworthy v Ward* (1853) 11 Hare 196; 68 ER 1245).

estate and X will receive no interest. A, B and C were seised of the entire estate together and, upon A's death, B and C remain seised of the entire estate. Upon B's subsequent death, C will be seised of the entire estate and, as no mutual ownership continues, the joint tenancy will cease. If A had legally alienated her aliquot share in the land to X prior to her death, the joint tenancy between A, B and C would have been severed and the co-ownership relationship between X, B and C would constitute a tenancy in common as unity of title does not exist.

Where the deaths of two joint tenants occur in circumstances which render the order of death uncertain, legislation in Victoria resolves this difficulty by presuming the deaths to have occurred in the order of seniority, and accordingly, the younger shall be deemed to have survived the elder.[2]

Due to the general uncertainty surrounding death, the right of survivorship confers no special privilege on any particular co-owner. Each joint tenant owes reciprocal obligations and is entitled to reciprocal benefits, where they happen to accrue. This dual benefit/burden can only be assumed by a living person. Hence, as a corporation cannot die in a natural sense, under common law a corporation is incapable of being a joint tenant, either with another corporation or with a natural person. Nevertheless, given the difficulty of such a prohibition in an increasingly corporatised world, statutory provisions now ensure the right of a corporation to acquire and hold any real or personal property in a joint tenancy in the same manner as it were an individual.[3]

16.2.4 Joint tenancy and Torrens legislation

Where the land subject to the co-ownership is Torrens title land, the Torrens legislation further regulates the functioning of the joint tenancy. In Victoria, New South Wales, Western Australia, South Australia and the ACT, the Torrens legislation sets out that where two or more persons are registered on the title as joint proprietors, they are deemed to be entitled to the land as joint tenants.[4] The wording of s 30(2) of the Victorian legislation is:

> Two or more persons who are registered as joint proprietors of land shall be deemed to be entitled thereto as joint tenants ...

---

2 Property Law Act 1958 (Vic), s 184. See also Conveyancing Act 1919 (NSW), s 35; Presumption of Survivorship Act 1921 (Tas), s 2; Succession Act 1981 (Qld), s 65; Property Law Act 1969 (WA), s 120(e), where it is set out that in the event of an uncertain death, the court is to treat the corresponding disposition to the co-owners as one occurring pursuant to a tenancy in common.

3 Property law statutes: Vic, s 28; NSW, s 25; SA, s 24C; WA, s 29; Tas, s 62; Qld, s 34.

4 Torrens legislation: Vic, s 30(2); NSW, s 100(1); WA, s 60; SA, s 74; ACT, s 54(2); NT, s 74. A similar provision exists in Tasmania, where the Land Titles Act 1980, s 44 sets out that two or more persons named as transferees or proprietors of an interest or estate in land shall, in the absence of words of severence, be entitled as joint tenants.

In New South Wales and Queensland, the common law presumption in favour of joint tenancies has been reversed: Conveyancing Act 1919 (NSW), s 26(1); Property Law Act 1974 (Qld), s 35. This reversal in inapplicable to transfers to trustees, executors, administrators and mortgagees – obviously the right of survivorship is appropriate to such commercial situations.

The functioning of these deeming provisions is somewhat unclear because of the words 'persons who are registered as joint proprietors'. It is not clear whether this refers to persons already registered expressly as joint tenants, or to persons who are entitled to be registered as joint tenants because of compliance with the four unities and the right of survivorship principles, or whether it simply deems all co-ownership relationships which are registered to constitute joint tenancies. In order to resolve this uncertainty, the land titles office in most states requires co-owners to specifically state the character of their co-ownership upon the land transfer documents.

The Torrens legislation in most states also endorses application of the right of survivorship to joint tenancies. In Victoria, s 50 of the Transfer of Land Act 1958 provides that, upon the death of any person registered with any other person as joint proprietor of any land, the Registrar, on the application of the survivor and proof to the satisfaction of the Registrar of the death, shall register the applicant as the proprietor thereof and, thereupon, such survivor shall become the transferee of such land and be the registered proprietor.[5]

16.2.5 Tenancy in common

If a co-owner relationship does not satisfy the requirements for the creation of a joint tenancy, then it will constitute what is known as a 'tenancy in common'. A tenancy in common is a form of co-ownership which confers a proportionate share of the estate upon each co-owner and, unlike the joint tenancy, does not require unity and conformity between each co-owner's interest, although unity of interest or title may fortuitously exist. As a co-owner, each tenant is entitled to possession of the whole of the land as well as holding a share in the undivided land. Entitlement to an undivided share of the land is the foundation of the tenancy in common. Legislation in New South Wales, Queensland and the Australian Capital Territory sets out that any disposition of a beneficial interest in property, whether with or without the legal estate, to two or more persons will be deemed to operate as a tenancy in common.[6]

A tenancy in common usually arises because the co-owner relationship does not constitute a joint tenancy because one or more of the four unities are not present:

5 Torrens legislation: NSW, ss 100–01; SA, ss 74 and 188; WA, ss 60 and 227; Tas, ss 44 and 100; ACT, s 54(1); NT, ss 74 and 188 – but cf Qld, s 56(1).

6 Property law statutes: NSW, s 26(1); Qld, s 35; ACT, s 3.

(a) Example 1 – A conveys land to B and C jointly, setting out that B is to take one-third and C is to take the remaining two-thirds. A co-owner relationship exists because B and C jointly own the land and are jointly entitled to possess the land. The relationship is a tenancy in common because there is no unity of interest.

(b) Example 2 – A conveys a fee simple in land to B and C jointly, making the interest of C conditional upon him attaining the age of 25. The relationship is a tenancy in common because there is no unity of interest.

(c) Example 3 – A conveys land to B for life, remainder to C and D when they turn 21. In 1996, B attains the age of 21; in 1997 C attains the age of 21; and, in 1998, B dies. The relationship is a tenancy in common because the contingent remainder interests of C and D vested at different times. The interest of B vested in title in 1996 and the interest of C vested in 1997 and, consequently, there is no unity of time.

(d) Example 4 – B and C are joint tenants. B conveys his interest to D, severing the joint tenancy with C. The new owners of the land are C and D. The relationship between C and D is a tenancy in common because there is no unity of title or time.

As each tenant in common holds a distinct, undivided share of the land, they are able to deal with their undivided shares as they wish. Hence, a tenant in common may alienate his undivided share *inter vivos* or bequest it or encumber it in any way provided it does not interfere with the rights of the remaining tenants in common. Importantly, the right of survivorship does not apply to a tenancy in common, so that upon the death of one tenant in common, the interests of the remaining tenant(s) will not be enlarged.

16.2.6 Other forms of co-ownership: coparcenary

Whilst the two dominant forms of co-owner relationships are the joint tenancy and the tenancy in common, other miscellaneous forms of mutual ownership have existed. An historical example is coparcenary. Coparcenary is a form of mutual ownership stemming from the common law inheritance rules. Where there was no male heir but numerous female heirs, the female heirs would inherent the land as coparceners, that is, as co-owners. Coparcenary resembled both the the tenancy in common and the joint tenancy relationships because, on the one hand, the interests of each coparcener could vary in shape and form, but on the other, where one coparcener released an interest, the interests of the remaining coparceners could be correspondingly enlarged. The existence of coparcenary diminished significantly with the abolition of the old common law 'descent to the heir' rules.[7]

7 See Statute of Wills 1540.

16.3 Methods of creating a co-owner relationship

It is a bit of a misnomer to talk of the creation of co-owner relationships when a relationship of some sort must automatically arise wherever land has been transferred to two joint owners. The real concern underlying the so called 'creation' of co-owner relationships is the differing presumptions which exist under law and in equity where there is no express or implied intention set out in the transfer documentation. Where no express intention exists and it is possible for the co-owner relationship to assume either form, it is necessary to resort to jurisdictional presumptions. Different principles exist under common law and in equity.

16.3.1 Common law approach

In the absence of any evidence to the contrary, the common law favours the presumption of a joint tenancy. The rationale for this is steeped in history. The old common law courts generally felt that a joint tenancy would be easier to manage because, under such a relationship, title eventually and usually passed on to a single owner. This made conveyancing and the investigation of title by purchasers easier and, importantly, it enabled a swifter and more efficient collection of feudal dues. Whilst the basis for this rationale has long since passed, the common law has retained the presumption – although the significant ramifications of a joint tenancy have encouraged the common law to modify the application of this presumption through a stringent approach to the interpretation of 'words of severance'. Where the wording of a transfer indicates, even to the slightest extent, an intention to confer an undivided share to each joint owner, the common law presumption will be rebutted. Furthermore, in some rare instances, the courts have been prepared to recognise the creation of a tenancy in common, despite an absence of words of severance, where it is deemed expedient and therefore appropriate.[8]

16.3.1.1 Words of severance

Words of severance are words that are used by the creator of a co-owner relationship which imply an intention to confer a distinct share in the land to each co-owner and therefore create a tenancy in common. The words do not have to state this intention expressly; any words indicating an intention to confer proportionate interests upon joint owners will be sufficient. Hence, words including: 'in equal shares', 'share and share alike' and 'amongst or respectively' would all constitute words of severance. The position has been well stated by Hatherley LC in *Robertson v Fraser* (1871) 6 Ch A 696:

8 See, in particular, the decision of *Re Barbour* [1967] Qd R 10.

> Anything which in the slightest degree indicates an intention to divide the property must be held to abrogate the idea of a joint tenancy, and to create a tenancy in common.

On the facts of *Robertson v Fraser*, a codicil to a will set out that a third party was to be appointed as a further beneficiary to a residuary estate so that the third party 'may participate' in the bequest with the other two beneficiaries. The question for the court was whether or not the word 'participate' constituted a word of severance, rebutting the common law presumption of a joint tenancy. If it did, the relationship could constitute a tenancy in common, entitling the next of kin to gain a one-third share of the estate.

The Court of Appeal held that anything in the codicil indicating in the slightest degree an intention to divide the property would sever the joint tenancy. Hatherley LC felt that the word 'participate' was just as strong as 'amongst' or 'respectively' because it revealed an intention to divide the estate between the joint owners making the tenancy in common a more suitable creation.

In other instances, provisions contained in either inter vivos dispositions or wills which indicate that moneys are to be advanced to a child beneficiary for the purposes of maintenance or education will automatically create a tenancy in common. This is because any such advance must be extracted from the distinct 'share' held by the child, and the child can only hold such a share under a tenancy in common.[9]

Sometimes, a deed will contain contradictory or conflicting expressions and it is not clear which intention is to be followed. In such a situation, the basic principle is that the first words in a deed prevail, whilst in a will, it is the last words.[10]

16.3.2 *The approach of equity*

As the notion of ownership in equity differs substantially from that under common law, the approach of equity to co-ownership must naturally reflect equitable ownership principles. The equitable jurisdiction will always presume a tenancy in common rather than a joint tenancy. Like the common law, the rationale for this approach in equity is historical. Traditionally, courts of chancery felt that the tenancy in common reflected a fairer and more accurate form of co-owner relationship. The modern equitable jurisdiction has adopted this approach in three primary situations:

(a) where the property is purchased in unequal shares, making it unfair to assume that all owners are equally seised of the entire estate. In such a

9 See *Re Ward* [1920] 1 Ch 334.

10 *Forbes v Git* [1922] 1 AC 256.

situation, equity will presume that a tenancy in common was intended so that each co-owner holds according to the amount she actually paid (unless this presumption is itself rebutted by a presumption of advancement). Obviously this presumption is founded upon the premise that a person should only be entitled to a share in property which is proportionate to his or her respective contribution to the purchase price (*Calverley v Green* (1984) 59 ALJR 111). If the property is purchased in equal shares, or if there is a clear intention that one owner wished to confer a benefit upon the other owner, then equity may uphold the creation of a joint tenancy (*Carmody v Delehunt* [1984] 1 NSWLR 667);

(b) where money is advanced for the purposes of a mortgage, equity presumes that each mortgagee shall hold a share proportionate to the amount of money actually advanced. The rationale for this presumption is that, generally, where money is advanced pursuant to a mortgage, it is the intention of each lender to retain an interest in the security equivalent to the amount he has given over.[11] This presumption may be rebutted where it can be established that the lenders intended to acquire the mortgage jointly and mutually. Usually, mortgages will contain what is called a joint account clause, so that the mortgagor may repay the mortgage loan to one of the mortgagees and be able to have the entire mortgage discharged.[12] Without such a clause, the mortgagor may have to obtain a separate receipt from each individual 'tenant in common' mortgagee, making the discharge of the mortgage difficult and time consuming;

(c) where partners jointly acquire land during the usual course of a partnership business, equity presumes that each partner holds the land as a tenant in common. The rationale for such a presumption is that such acquisitions usually have an investment purpose and it would be unfair for the 'right of survivorship' principle to operate (*Lake v Gibson* (1729) 1 Eq Ca Abr 290; 21 ER 1052).

The above three circumstances represent the primary categories of equitable presumption. It seems, however, that these categories are not exhaustive. Wherever it can be established that the purchasers of land acquired it for independent business purposes or mutually exclusive investment purposes, equity will presume that the purchasers hold the land as tenants in common, even if they are legally regarded as joint tenants. For example, in *Malayan Credit Ltd v Jack Chia MPH Ltd* [1986] All ER 711, the Privy Council held that a five year lease over the seventh floor of an office block in Singapore was held by the grantees as tenants in common. Their Lordships did not feel that the cases in which the equitable jurisdiction presumed a tenancy in common were rigidly confined to unequal purchase money, mortgagees and partners,

11 This rationale is set out in *Morley v Bid* (1798) 3 Ves 628, p 631; 30 ER 1192, p 1193, *per* Arden MR.

12 The 'joint account clause' is now implied by statute in the property law statutes: Vic, ss 112–13; NSW, ss 96A and 99; SA, ss 54–55; WA, ss 67–68; Qld, s 93; Tas, s 30.

because the equitable jurisdiction is inherently discretionary and flexible. Equity may infer a tenancy in common in any circumstance where it can be established from the facts that the beneficial interest was intended to be held by the grantees for their joint, individual business purposes.[13]

Lord Brightman summarised the three alternative positions which could arise:

(a) the lessees at the inception of the lease may hold the beneficial interest therein as joint tenants in equity so that equity follows the law: this will be the case only if the circumstances are clearly not within the three primary presumptive categories or there are no circumstances dictating to the contrary;

(b) the lessees at the inception of the lease may hold the beneficial interest as tenants in common in equity in equal shares; or

(c) the lessees at the inception of the lease hold the beneficial interest as tenants in common in unequal shares.

The Privy Council concluded that the third option was most appropriate on the facts, because the lease had clearly been taken to serve separate commercial interests and the parties had settled their occupations prior to the lease being granted, individually measured the areas, and were invoiced for their respective shares relating to the deposit and rent separately.

Where the equitable jurisdiction presumes a tenancy in common, the confusing situation can arise whereby the co-owners may be joint tenants at law whilst being simultaneously regarded as tenants in common in equity. This dual characterisation of the co-owner relationship is a difficult concept to grasp, but is simply a reflection of the way in which legal and equitable interests are fragmented. A joint tenancy at law may arise over a jointly owned legal estate; if, however, the joint tenancy attracts one of the circumstances raising the equitable presumption, each legal joint tenant will hold the excess amount he or she has been conferred under the joint tenancy upon trust for the benefit of the tenant in common who made the contribution.

For example, A and B purchase land together as joint tenants. A contributes 70% of the purchase price whilst B contributes 30%. As legal joint tenants, both A and B are treated as owning 50% of the land. Nevertheless, this situation would raise the 'unequal purchase price' presumption in the equity jurisdiction, so that A and B would be regarded as tenants in common holding interests proportionate to the amount of money each contributed to the purchase price. To ensure a fair representation of individual contributions, equity would enforce a trust against the additional 20% interest held by B, so

---

13 *Malayan Credit* was approved by the Australian High Court in *Delehunt v Carmody* (1986) 68 ALR 253.

that B would hold this amount for the benefit of A as trustee under a purchase money resulting trust: see the discussion on resulting trusts in Chapter 5.

16.4 Rights and duties of co-owners

The rights and duties of each co-owner reflect her status as owner and occupier of the land. Specific rights and duties have been established to co-ordinate co-owner relationships because of the problems that invariably arise with multiple ownership of the same land. Common disputes arising within co-owner relationships concern the use and occupation of the property, the obligation to keep the property in good repair and upkeep, and the right to receive rents and encumber the land. The exclusive rights and obligations naturally associated with ownership of land are shared amongst each co-owner so that no single co-owner has the right to exclude or overwhelm the proprietary rights of the other co-owner; the aim is to distribute fundamental proprietary rights and duties evenly amongst each of the co-owners.

16.4.1 Duty to pay occupation rent

Once a co-owner relationship is properly created, each co-owner – whether joint tenant or tenant in common – has the right to use and possess the property. Unity of possession is a feature of all co-owner relationships.

Unity of possession means that each co-owner has the right to possess the property; hence, when one co-owner occupies the property, there will be no need for that co-owner to pay rent to the non-occupying co-owners because he is simply exercising ownership rights (*Moisley v Mahony* [1950] VLR 318). Nevertheless, there are three situations where a co-owner will be obliged to pay occupation rent.

16.4.1.1 Wrongful exclusion

Where one co-owner wrongfully excludes the remaining co-owner(s), the occupying co-owner can be made to pay rent known as occupation rent. The definition of 'wrongful' in this context includes illegal, violent or threatening behaviour. The position is well evidenced in the decision of *Dennis v McDonald* [1982] 2 WLR 275, where a wife was forced to leave property she co-owned with her husband due to the violent behaviour of the husband. In this situation, the court held that the wife had been wrongfully excluded and, consequently, the husband was obliged to pay occupation rent. Where, however, one co-owner who was in occupation of the land voluntarily leaves the land, this cannot be regarded as a wrongful exclusion by the remaining co-owner(s), and in such a situation, no occupation rent will be payable (*Forgeard v Shanahan* (1994) 35 NSWLR 206).

16.4.1.2 *Express agreement*

Where an express agreement between all of the co-owners exists, stating that rent should be paid by an occupying co-owner, and the agreement is signed by each of the co-owners, the co-owner may be obliged to pay occupation rent; the agreement will overwhelm the natural exemption of the co-owner.

16.4.1.3 *Claim for improvement/repairs*

Where a co-owner who is in sole occupation claims money from the remaining co-owners for improvement or repair to the property, he or she will be obliged to pay occupation rent for the period of time that the improvements were being carried out. The occupation rent may be offset against the claimed benefits for improvement or repair. Importantly, occupation rent in this category purely represents a set-off from the claimed 'improvement' costs rather than a positive amount owing, hence no rent is actually payable. Occupation rent will not be available where the circumstances reveal that the remaining co-owners had either expressly agreed or intended to waive the improvement liability; the amount claimed for improvements or repairs can only be obtained where the remaining co-owners have properly consented to the cost and it represents actual repairs or improvements rather than periodical expense for ordinary maintenance.

The amount of occupation rent payable is based upon the current market rental and the proportionate interest which is occupied. This figure may, however, be varied to accord with market forces and the differences in the amount normally payable by an unknown tenant; an actual co-owner of the land may be more likely to look after the property and therefore the rent may be reduced. The basic calculation for occupation rent can be illustrated in the following example. A, B and C are joint tenants in land. It is agreed that A will occupy the land to the exclusion of others in return for the payment of occupation rent. The amount payable by A will represent two-thirds (that is, the interests of B and C) of a current market rental. Hence, if the current market rental is $210 per week, then A will be obliged to pay $140 per week.

16.4.2 *Repairs and improvements*

The fundamental premise for repairs and improvements over co-owned land is consent: where one co-owner seeks to recover an amount for repairs or improvements that he or she may have paid for with respect to the co-owned land, under common law the remaining co-owners will not be obliged to pay their portion unless they have previously agreed to incur the expense (*Leigh v Dickeson* (1884) 15 QBD 60). This will be the case even where the remaining co-owners benefit from the repairs or improvements carried out. The rigidity of this principle has inevitably caused unfairness in a number of circumstances, eventually attracting the application of the equitable jurisdiction.

In the equitable jurisdiction, where one co-owner carries out lasting improvements or repairs, that co-owner will acquire an equity in the land to the value of those repairs where a failure by the remaining co-owners to contribute to the cost would confer an unfair benefit upon those co-owners (*Squire v Rogers* (1979) 39 FLR 106). Hence, the making of permanent improvements by one tenant in common in sole occupation gives rise to an equity over the land, analogous to an equitable charge, enforceable in the event of partition or a distribution of the value of the land amongst the tenants in common (*Brickwood v Young* (1905) 2 CLR 387). The co-owner carrying out the work cannot obtain more than his or her outlay, even if the outlay dramatically increases the value of the land.

In *Squire v Rogers* (1979) 27 ALR 330, the Federal Court of Australia, on appeal from the Supreme Court of the Northern Territory, discussed this issue. On the facts of the case, the joint lessee of a lease in perpetuity of land in the Darwin area had lived on the leasehold land for about 16 years. During this time, the defendant had made improvements to the land to provide accommodation for visitors and to establish a caravan park. There was evidence that the defendant's expenditure on improvements amounted to approximately $100,000 but, because of the devastation caused by Cyclone Tracey in 1974, the actual increase in the value of the land was only about $15,000. The court agreed that in no case can the co-owner who has improved the property obtain more than his outlay, although such outlay may have trebled the value of the property. Furthermore, the increase in the value of the land represents the limit of what a co-owner can actually receive, even though his actual outlay may be far larger. On the facts, this meant that the defendant could only recover about $15,000 from the co-owners of the lease.

The equitable right is analagous to an equitable charge, and will run with the land to benefit all successors in title to the co-owner effecting the repairs and improvements. The equitable jurisdiction will only recognise improvements and repairs which are of a lasting nature; hence, ordinary maintenance repairs will not generally be included within the definition of 'repairs'.[14] The actual definition of 'improvements' is very broad and includes not only physical and structural improvements but also financial improvements, such as an increased payment of the mortgage which has the effect of reducing the overall loan over the property.[15]

14 Eg, in *Forgeard v Shanahan* (1994) 35 NSWLR 225, it was held by Meagher J in the New South Wales Court of Appeal that payments for insurance premiums and pest control were not within the definition of 'improvements and repairs'.

15 *Leigh v Dickeson* (1884) 15 QBD 60; *Henderson v Eason* (1851) 17 QB 701.

16.4.3 *Rents and profits*

Where one co-owner has received rents for the occupation of property in excess of the other co-owner(s), there is no common law principle entitling the remaining co-owner(s) to obtain the portion representing their interests, and it is left to the equitable jurisdiction to remedy any unfairness arising in such circumstances. Under the equitable jurisdiction, the remaining co-owners are entitled to claim an account from the receiving co-owner where the receipt of income or profit represents more than that co-owner's fair share.[16] If the income or profit was acquired purely as a consequence of the work of the receiving co-owner, the remaining co-owner(s) cannot claim an account, but where the amount is received due to use or occupation of the land alone, an account will be available.[17]

Assuming that an equitable jurisdiction to grant an account exists, the usual situation where an account may be claimed is where one co-owner receives rents or profits for the occupation of the entire land from a third party and does not distribute these rents and profits to the remaining co-owners. An account for excess rents and profits from a co-owner in occupation is only recoverable over rents received by virtue of the property itself. Hence, co-owners can only receive an account for rents and profits where they have actually been received from third parties who have used the land. The co-owner in receipt is, however, entitled to set off the liability to pay over a portion of the rents and profits against any expenses he or she may have properly incurred in the process of obtaining the rents or profits.

There are a number of further qualifications respecting the right of co-owner(s) to seek an account against excess rents and profits received by another co-owner. First, where the rents and profits have been acquired as a result of use by a third party of improvements carried out at the expense of the receiving co-owner, the full cost of the improvements may be set off against the liability to account – provided the co-owners consented to the improvements being carried out (*Squire v Rogers* (1979) 39 FLR 106). Secondly, the right to an account will not exist where the receiving co-owner has obtained the consent or acquiescence of the remaining co-owners to spend the rent or profits on improvements to the property (*Squire v Rogers* (1979)).

---

16 An account is available under the inherent equitable jurisdiction. See: Meagher, RP, Gummow, WMC and Lehane, JRF, *Equity Doctrines and Remedies*, 3rd edn, 1992, Sydney: Butterworths, para 2512. See, also, *Re Tolman's Estate* (1928) 23 Tas LR 29. Note that it is possible that with the removal of the 1705 Statutes 4 & 5 Anne c 3, s 27 by the Imperial Acts Application Act 1969 (NSW), and Imperial Acts Application Act 1980 (Vic), the statutory source of the jurisdiction to grant an account was removed in those states. This interpretation assumes, however, that no independent equitable jurisdiction exists, and there is early authority to suggest that such an assumption is incorrect (*Strelly v Winson* (1685) Vern 297; 23 ER 480).

17 See, generally, *Henderson v Eason* (1851) 17 QB 701; 117 ER 1451.

Finally, a co-owner cannot be paid occupation rent *and* claim an account for rents and profits, because this would result in double compensation.

A right to an account constitutes an equitable charge and will run with the land for the benefit of successors in title to the claimants, but it may be defeated by a *bona fide* purchaser for value without notice.

16.4.4 Encumbrances over the property

A co-owner, whether a tenant in common or a joint tenant, is entitled to encumber his or her interest in the land provided it does not unduly interfere with the seisin of the remaining co-owners (*Hedley v Roberts* [1977] VR 282). Hence, leases, mortgages and easements may be created by one co-owner to apply over the share of the land held by that co-owner and, provided the interest does not interfere with the rights enjoyed by the remaining co-owners, the remaining co-owners must submit to it.

It is possible, although quite rare, for a lease to be granted by one co-owner over his share in the land. The granting of the lease would not interfere with the rights of the remaining co-owners because the right to shared possession would still exist although, for the duration of the lease, it would exist between the tenant and the remaining co-owner; however, the practical inconvenience of such an arrangement may make it difficult to find a suitable lessee.

The effect of an encumbrance upon the co-owner relationship will vary according to its nature. In the case of a tenancy in common, the encumbrance will only bind the undivided share held by the co-owner entering into the encumbrance. In the case of a joint tenancy, one joint tenant may enter into an encumbrance that binds his or her overall interest, but if it results in a separation of the interest held by that co-owner, one or more of the four unities may be destroyed and the joint tenancy severed.

16.5 Termination of a co-owner relationship

Co-owner relationships may be terminated in a number of ways depending upon whether it is a tenancy in common or a joint tenancy. Where a tenancy in common is terminated, no co-owner relationship will exist at all, so that title to the property is no longer vested in two or more persons. Alternatively, where a joint tenancy is terminated, it may be either extinguished completely or severed, whereby it reverts into a tenancy in common.

16.5.1 Terminating a tenancy in common

A tenancy in common will be terminated where title to the land vests in possession of one person so that there are, literally, no longer any co-owners of the land. A vesting of this nature may occur where title is transferred or devised to a single tenant.

16.5.2 *Severance of a joint tenancy*

Severence is the word used to describe the conversion of a joint tenancy co-owner relationship into a tenancy in common. A joint tenancy will cease to be a joint tenancy and will become a tenancy in common wherever one of the four unities is destroyed so that it can no longer be said that each co-owner holds exactly the same interest, acquired at the same time, by virtue of the same act. It is not possible to sever unity of interest because it defines the very character of the estate or interest conferred. If different interests are conferred upon co-owners, no joint tenancy will exist in the first place. Similarly, unity of possession cannot be severed because it represents the foundation of all co-owner relationships. However, unity of time and title may be severed, and it is the destruction of either of these two unities that commonly results in the conversion of a joint tenancy into a tenancy in common. For example, where one joint tenant acquires a greater or different interest at a later time, or acquires the same interest pursuant to a different document or instrument, a joint tenancy will be severed.

Importantly, severance of a joint tenancy can only occur during the lifetime of a joint tenant, because, once a joint tenant dies, the right of survivorship will operate to enlarge the interests of the remaining joint tenants. Hence, most cases alleging a severance of the joint tenancy claim that it has occurred prior to any death of a joint tenant, in order to avoid the operation of the right of survivorship.

16.5.3 *Severance by alienation*

The most common method of severance is by way of alienation. In this case, one joint tenant alienates his or her interest in the land to a third party. The third party receives the interest and shares with the remaining joint tenant(s). The co-owner relationship between the third party and the remaining joint tenants cannot be a joint tenancy because the four unities do not exist; the new co-owner does not have unity of title or time because she acquired the interest at a later date, pursuant to a different document to the remaining joint tenants. There will also be no unity of interest where the interest transferred to the new co-owner differs from that retained by the remaining joint tenants.

In *Wright v Gibbons* (1949) 78 CLR 313, a legal severance was effected through the mutual transfer of interests by each joint tenant. On the facts, Olinda, Ethel and Bessie were registered as joint tenants. Olinda and Ethel wished to sever the joint tenancy. They attempted to do so by executing a document setting out that Olinda transferred her one-third share to Ethel and Ethel transferred her one-third share to Olinda. This document was then registered. The issue in the case was whether or not the document was effective to sever the joint tenancy because, if not, Bessie, the last survivor, would acquire the entire property by right of survivorship. It is clear that an alienation to a third party would have effected a severance of the joint tenancy; the question for the court was whether an alienation between co-tenants would have the same effect. The court held that the execution and registration of the document did constitute a legal severance of the joint tenancy, despite the fact that the interests conveyed by each co-tenant were identical. Latham CJ made the following comments (p 323):

> If there are three joint tenants, A, B and C, and one joint tenant, A, transfers his interest to another joint tenant, B, the result is that A then has no interest in the land, B becomes a tenant in common as to one-third interest in the land, and remains a joint tenant with C as to a two-thirds interest. If, subsequently, B transfers to A the interest which he still has as joint tenant (A having become a stranger to the title, his interest having passed to B), there is a further and complete severance. A becomes a tenant in common as to one-third interest with B and C, the transfer working a severance of the joint tenancy between B and C in the two-thirds interest in the land. The final result is that A, B and C become tenants in common each having a one-third interest.

Where there are three or more co-owners in the joint tenancy and one co-owner has alienated his or her interest to a third party, the relationship between the third party and the remaining co-owners will be a tenancy in common, but there will be no severance between the remaining joint tenants.

For example, A, B and C own Torrens title land pursuant to a joint tenancy. A purports to sell her interest in the joint tenancy to X. Upon registration, X becomes the new legal owner of A's interest in the joint tenancy. The co-owner relationship between X, B and C is a tenancy in common, because there is no unity of title or time. Nevertheless, the co-owner relationship between B and C will remain a joint tenancy, because the transfer to X did not effect a severance between these two co-owners.

A severance of the joint tenancy by alienation can occur despite the fact that the remaining joint tenants have no knowledge of it and have not consented to it. Hence, severance by alienation can be voluntary or involuntary: *Sistron v URH* (1992) 117 ALR 528.

16.5.3.1 Severance by alienation in equity

A legal severance of the joint tenancy will occur where one joint tenant has legally alienated his or her interest to a third party. Severance can, however, also occur prior to the legal estate passing. Severance in equity may result where the equitable jurisdiction is prepared to recognise and enforce the alienation despite the fact that it has not complied with all of the legal requirements. Where a specifically enforceable contract to transfer the interest is entered into by a joint tenant with a third party, equity may enforce the alienation and effect the severance.

For example, A and B own land as joint tenants. A enters into a specifically enforceable contract to sell her interest in the land to C who pays a deposit.

The contract of sale is enforceable in equity. Prior to the legal estate passing, C will acquire an equitable interest in the land as a beneficiary under a constructive trust with the vendor, A, as trustee. The creation of this interest will effect a severance of the joint tenancy in equity. At law, pending the legal transfer of the estate to C, A and B remain joint tenants. However, equity will compel A and B to hold the legal title on trust for B and C as tenants in common in equal shares.[18]

A severance in equity may also occur where one joint tenant purports to make a gift to a third party, and the gift, whilst not legally valid, complies with the equitable requirements in that the co-owner/donor has done everything which he alone can do to pass the gift. For general law land, the equitable requirements will be complied with where the co-owner/donor has executed a deed of transfer and, for Torrens title land, where the co-owner/donor has signed and handed over a transfer of his interest in registrable form and either given over the duplicate certificate of title or carried out all that is necessary to make it available for registration. In such a case, equity will enforce the alienation and the remaining joint tenants will hold their legal title as constructive trustees of the land for the benefit of the donor and the remaining co-owner(s).[19]

In *Corin v Patton* (1990) 64 ALJR 256, Patton and his deceased wife were joint registered proprietors of land in NSW. Mrs Patton, who was terminally ill, attempted to sever the joint tenancy between herself and her husband by executing a transfer of her interest in the land to her brother, Mr Corin. Under a deed of trust executed at the same time, Corin agreed to hold the property on trust with Mrs Patton as sole beneficiary. The transfer of Mrs Patton's interest was not registered before her death, and she had not organised for the duplicate certificate of title to be made available in order for the title to be registered. It was argued that Mrs Patton had intended to effect a severance of the joint tenancy, and that this intention was evidenced through the construction of the trust. The High Court concluded that a mere statement of intention, without anything more, should not affect the unity of title. According to the court, if statements of intention were sufficient to sever an interest, it would produce an atmosphere of uncertainty, making it difficult to determine the precise ownership of the interests which had been the subject of the statement. Furthermore, there would be no point in maintaining, as a separate means of severance, the making of a mutual agreement between the joint tenants.

McHugh J and Mason CJ went on to consider the different ways in which a joint tenancy could be severed. Their Honours noted that a severance could occur where the legal or equitable estate of one joint tenant was transferred to

18 See the discussion of severance in equity in *Corin v Patton* (1990) 64 ALJR 256, *per* Deane J, pp 270–71.

19 *Ibid.*

a third party and the transfer was enforceable either at law or in equity. On the facts, it was ultimately held that there was no effective alienation, either at law or in equity, because the donor, Mrs Patton, had not done everything which she alone could do to effect the transfer; she had not arranged for the production of the duplicate certificate of title, and this meant that the equitable requirements had not been properly satisfied.

In his judgment, Deane J first examined the nature of a joint tenancy, and then went on to consider the basis for severance. His Honour held that the substance of a joint tenancy, whilst it subsists, lies in the equality and the personal character of the interests of the joint tenants in the undivided rights which constitute ownership of the whole. When one joint tenant dies during the subsistence of the joint tenancy, his or her interest ceases, and the interests of the remaining joint tenants expand by accretion. When there is only one survivor, then the joint tenancy will have run its course.

Deane J went on to examine the foundation of severance in equity. His Honour noted that, where equity imposes a trust to give effect to an actual or presumed intention of the joint tenants, or to do equity between them, there is no difficulty in understanding how all joint tenants come to be bound by a trust of the whole property. The conceptual difficulty, however, lies with the case where the equitable interest operates between only one joint tenant and a third party. The explanation of why the assignee's equitable rights *in personam* against the assignor should bring about a conversion in equity of the overall joint tenancy into a tenancy in common would seem to be that equity, disregarding the imperfection of the analogy between the equitable rights of a beneficiary and actual ownership of the trust property, has treated the transfer of those rights of a beneficiary as equivalent in equity to an *in rem* assignment of the actual property. On that basis, the court will then superimpose equitable rights and interests to mirror what would have been the legal position if the assignment had been effective at law.[20]

16.5.3.2 Severance by a single joint tenant

Severance by the actions of a single joint tenant may be achieved where a single joint tenant re-transfers his or her interest or sets up a trust. It must be clearly established that the joint tenant intended to confer an interest upon a beneficiary and there must be more than a unilateral manifestation of intention: *Burgess v Rainsley* [1975] Ch 429. Where one joint tenant declares that he holds his aliquot interest as trustee for the benefit of a named third party, the joint tenancy will be severed. In such a case, whilst there is no legal alienation of the interest, the creation of the trust is sufficient to destroy unity of interest and sever the joint tenancy,[21] the joint tenant has transferred her

20 *Corin v Patton* (1990) 64 ALJR 256, pp 275–76. See, also, *Sistron v URH* (1992) 117 ALR 528.

21 See, generally, Sherry, B, 'Unilateral severance of joint tenancies' [1995] 3 Australian Property Law Journal 1.

absolute ownership of title to a trustee title. Alternatively, a joint tenant may sever a joint tenancy through the alienation of an interest to himself. Section 72(3) of the Property Law Act 1958 (Vic) entitles a person to transfer land to himself.[22] This action will sever a joint tenancy because there is no longer any unity of title; one joint tenant has acquired his interest through a different instrument. An alienation by a joint tenant to himself can only sever the joint tenancy if the alienation complies with all of the legal requirements for transfer.[23]

16.5.4 Severance by mortgage

16.5.4.1 Mortgage over general law land

Where a joint tenant enters into a mortgage over old system land, a severance of the joint tenancy will occur because old system mortgages require an deed of conveyance to be executed as security for the repayment of the mortgage loan.[24] The execution of a deed of conveyance to the mortgagee will result in the mortgagee acquiring the title of the co-tenant ,and there will be no unity of title between the mortgagee and the remaining co-tenants. Once the mortgage is discharged, the joint tenancy cannot be revived. An equitable mortgage over old system land has also been held to sever a joint tenancy, because the co-tenants no longer hold unity of interest or title, although this has been the subject of some debate because, generally, the conferral of an equitable charge upon a mortgage will not sever a joint tenancy.[25]

16.5.4.2 Mortgage over Torrens title land

Where a joint tenant enters into a mortgage over Torrens title land, the mortgage will not have the effect of severing a joint tenancy. A Torrens title mortgage will simply confer a statutory charge upon the mortgagee once registration, and this will not interfere with the unity of title, time, interest and possession held by the co-tenants. The granting of a mortgage charge – or any charge for that matter – will not affect a severance, as it does not involve an actual alienation of any interest.[26]

---

22 See general law statutes: NSW, ss 24 and 44(2); SA, s 40(3); WA, s 39; Tas, s 62(2) and Law of Property (Miscellaneous Provisions) Act 1958, s 3.

23 Where a co-owner of chattels deals with them in a manner inconsistent with the rights of the true owner excluding them from possession, he/she may be guilty of conversion: *Re Gillie ex p Cornell* (1996) 150 ALR 110.

24 *Re Pollard's Estate* (1863) 3 De GJ & S 541; 46 ER 746.

25 See the discussion on this by Butt, P, in *Land Law*, 3rd edn, 1996, LBC, para 1446. Note, also, the contrary authority of *Guthrie v Australia & New Zealand Banking Group Ltd* (1991) 23 NSWLR 672.

26 *Patriche v Powlett* (1740) 2 Atk 54; 26 ER 430.

If the mortgagor/co-tenant predeceases the other joint tenants, the mortgagee's charge will be extinguished, as the interest over which it applied is no longer in existence as it has passed on to the remaining joint tenants. If, however, the mortgagor survives the other co-tenants, the charge will expand to apply to the entire land, because that is the interest to which the mortgage relates.

16.5.5 Severance by lease

Where one joint tenant grants a lease over land, there are differing views as to whether it will effect a severance of the joint tenancy. English cases support the view that a lease will sever a joint tenancy even if the lease is to one of the joint tenants, because the lease gives a lessee a right to possess the land to the exclusion of the lessor/co-tenant granting it. In such a situation, there is no unity of possession between the co-tenants and, hence, no joint tenancy.[27]

By contrast, Australian cases argue that a lease will not extinguish a joint tenancy but merely suspend it for the duration of the lease, because, once the lease expires, the lessor/co-tenant will be vested in possession again.[28] Whilst the position is not entirely clear, it would seem that if the lessor/co-tenant dies prior to the expiration of the lease, his estate will receive the rental payments; however, the right of survivorship may still apply to the reversionary estate held by the lessor/co-tenant during the term of the lease.[29]

16.5.6 Severance by merger

If, following the creation of a joint tenancy, one joint tenant acquires a further estate in the land, different from that already held, the joint tenancy will be severed, because the two interests will merge, effectively destroying unity of interest.

For example, if A and B are joint tenants over a fee simple remainder and the life estate in the same land is subsequently transferred to A, the joint tenancy will be severed because there is no longer a unity of interest between A and B. In such a situation, the life estate will merge with the fee simple remainder to give A an absolute fee simple estate in the land. By contrast, if it is set out from the start that A and B are to hold for life as joint tenants, with the remainder in fee simple to A, then a joint tenancy may exist over the life estate alone. Once the life estate is extinguished, the joint tenancy will

27 See *Cowper v Fletcher* (1865) 6 B & S 464; 122 ER 1267. See, also, the discussion by Buttery, 'Leases by joint tenants' (1944) 17 ALJ 292.

28 See *Frieze v Unger* [1960] VR 230; *Wright v Gibbons* (1949) 78 CLR 313.

29 *Fulton v 523 Nominees Pty Ltd* [1984] VR 200, esp the judgment of Tadgell J, and *Guthrie v ANZ Banking Group Ltd* (1991) 23 NSWLR 672.

automatically terminate because it was only the life estate that was subject to the joint tenancy.

16.5.7 *Severance by agreement*

The equitable jurisdiction may enforce an agreement between all of the joint tenants that henceforth they will all hold as tenants in common. Where such an agreement is enforceable, it will effect a severance of the joint tenancy.[30] The consideration for such an agreement will generally consist in the agreement by each co-tenant to relinquish joint tenancy rights in return for proportionate, undivided shares as tenants in common.

Where such an agreement is entered into, it will be immediately enforceable in equity, despite the fact that the the co-tenants are legally recognised as joint tenants. In this situation, as with alienation in equity, if one of the co-tenants dies, the remaining co-tenants will hold any interest they receive pursuant to the right of survivorship on trust in proportionate shares for the remaining co-tenants.

The agreement must be express, but it does not need to be put into a written document; it is possible to imply an agreement from the conduct of the joint tenants or from an oral discussion. An intention to transform a joint tenancy into a tenancy in common may occur where the parties exhibit clear preferences to treat their interests as distinct and separate shares, as where each co-tenant executes a will.[31]

A court will usually treat an agreement to sever the joint tenancy as immediately effective, even though it contemplates the occurrence of future events. Hence, an agreement between the joint tenants to sell the property and divide the proceeds between them normally severs the joint tenancy in advance of the sale or division, even where the anticipated events never occur.[32]

16.5.8 *Involuntary severance*

Severance of a joint tenancy may occur involuntarily where a court order is issued to transfer shares to individual co-tenants. A court may order the property to be sold and the proceeds to be distributed between the co-owners, or it may order one joint tenant to transfer his or her interest to the other joint tenant(s). This often occurs under family law, and, pursuant to s 79 of the

30 See *Williams v Hensman* (1861) 1 J & H 546; 70 ER 862; see, also, *McIntyre v Gye* (1994) 122 ALR 289.

31 *Re Wilford's Estate; Taylor v Taylor* [1934] VLR 129. Importantly, the execution by one co-tenant of a will is insufficient evidence of an agreement to sever a joint tenancy: it must be established that all of the co-tenants have executed wills.

32 See discussion in *op cit*, Butt, fn 25, para 1456.

Family Law Act 1975 (Cth), a court may order a settlement of jointly owned property and, under s 87, the court may approve a maintenance agreement between the parties.

Involuntary severance can also occur in bankruptcy proceedings. Section 58 of the Bankruptcy Act 1966 (Cth) provides that, upon sequestration, the property of the bankrupt will vest in the trustee in bankruptcy. Where the bankrupt is a joint tenant, this will have the effect of severing the joint tenancy and creating a tenancy in common between the trustee in bankruptcy and the remaining joint tenants.[33]

16.5.9 Severance following homicide

Under public policy principles, a person may not benefit from his or her own crime; hence, a joint tenant who murders a fellow joint tenant cannot claim the victim's interest in the land pursuant to the right of survivorship. The courts will prevent this unfair result through the application of equity: a constructive trust will be imposed so that the joint tenant who has committed the crime will hold the deceased joint tenant's interest on trust for the benefit of the deceased joint tenant's estate. The constructive trust will effectively produce a severance of the joint tenancy in equity.[34]

For example, if A and B are joint tenants and A murders B, the legal estate vests in A by right of survivorship. Equity, however, will force A to hold the beneficial interest on a constructive trust for himself and for B's estate as tenants in common in equal shares. A's legal position alters because A is transformed into a constructive trustee, thereby effecting a severance of the joint tenancy as unity of title no longer exists.

A court will not usually examine the circumstances of the killing to see whether or not it was justifiable or excusable, because civil courts are reluctant to consider in any detail issues of intent, guilt and motive.

16.5.10 Severance by partition

A joint tenancy may be severed where the land is partitioned, so that each co-owner becomes the sole, independent owner of a separate, smaller division of the land. A voluntary partition may occur where a conveyance or transfer from all of the co-owners to each of them respectively of an equal portion of the land is executed.

Compulsory partition is impossible under common law without the mutual consent of all the co-tenants. Statute now allows compulsory partition. Essentially, upon the application by any one or more of the co-owners, the

33 See, generally, *Re Francis ex p Official Trustee in Bankruptcy* (1988) 82 ALR 333.

34 See *Rasmanis v Jurewitsch* (1969) 70 SR (NSW) 407.

court may appoint trustees and vest the co-owned property in them and order a 'statutory trust for sale'. The statutory trust for sale requires the trustees to sell the property and hold the proceeds in a way that gives effect to the rights of each co-tenant. As an alternative, courts may order a sale in place of a partition. Once this occurs, the co-tenants will lose their interests in the land itself and lose their right to occupy the land; all that remains is the right to have trustees perform the sale properly and to receive their respective shares in the sale proceeds. A court will not order a partition in breach of laws prohibiting the subdivision of land but may frame its decree so that physical division is subject to any necessary subdivision approval. If a mortgage exists over the entire land or share of land, no partition can be ordered unless the mortgagee has given prior consent.[35]

35 See, eg, the Victorian provisions in the Property Law Act 1958, ss 222–23, and the NSW provisions in Conveyancing Act 1919, Div 6, s 66G(1).

INDEX